Jean Moorcroft Wilson is a lecturer in English at the University of London. She has written, among other things, biographies of Virginia Woolf, Isaac Rosenberg, Charles Hamilton Sorley and William Watson. She is married to Virginia Woolf's nephew, with whom she runs a publishing house. They have five children.

What the critics said:

'Her mastery of detail is impressive, but what distinguishes her approach is the way in which she analyses the war poetry, placing it in its biographical context, and revealing Sassoon's progress from Brooke-like enthusiasm in 1914 ... through the angry satires, to the striking of a more prophetic note in the poetry written towards the end of the war.'

Mark Bostridge, *Independent on Sunday*

'A compelling tale'

Ian Hamilton, *Sunday Telegraph*

'Moorcroft Wilson's book will be invaluable to historians of the period.'

Andrew Motion, *The Times*

'Based on years of .research and well-fuelled by Sassoon's family and friends who granted Wilson access to a mass of private papers, this is the first volume of what promises to be the definitive biography of an important and neglected poet. If the next volume is as careful and as compassionate, as well as equally critical, then a long-delayed job will have been worth the waiting for.'

Robert Nye, *The Scotsman*

'Praise the Lord and pass the ammunition and the rhyming dictionary. The canon of works on the Great War poets has finally been augmented by a biography of the most influential of them all. ... provocative and perceptive ... Skilfully and unobtrusively, [Wilson] pieces together Sassoon's journey from unquestioning patriot to outspoken dissident. ... Wilson has done much to ... paint the features of a great poet who deserves much more than a faceless obscurity.'

Hugh MacDonald, *The Herald (Glasgow)*

'With care and courtesy, Moorcroft Wilson traces Sassoon's poetic development … a solid and substantial foundation for further exploration.'

Times Educational Supplement

'Jean Moorcroft Wilson's account of all this is thorough and perceptive. Unlike so many biographers, she takes trouble to build up subordinate characters; she seems at home on the Western Front, in literary salons and on the hunting field; her comments on Sassoon's poetry are both expert and common-sensical. You long to see what she will make of the rest of Sassoon's long and, presumably, anti-climactic career.'

Jeremy Lewis, *Observer*

'… a competent and meticulous work, sympathetic to the man and well-informed about his milieu.'

Robert O'Byme, *The Irish Times (Dublin)*

'It is satisfyingly meaty in its detail … but the story moves forward briskly … As Sassoon's poetry is now read rather less than Owen's or Rosenberg's it is good to have Dr Wilson's sensitive account of his transformation into one of the great poets of protest.'

Michael Hall, *Country Life*

'… fair and reasonable; and, when it comes to talking about - Siegrfried's idealised passions for handsome young men, [Wilson] is sympathetic and engaged.'

Sebastian Faulks, *Literary Review*

'Jean Moorcroft Wilson has produced a biography many authors would have liked to have written … discovering new material, pursuing hints from the Diaries and tracing relations and friends or their descendants. The result is a meticulous and enormously interesting book. … her exhaustive research has enabled us to see a more rounded character and has explained much that previously was only hinted. … In all this is a fascinating first volume.'

Richard Emeny, *Despatches*

Siegfried Sassoon

Siegfried Sassoon

The Making of a War Poet

A Biography
(1886-1918)

Jean Moorcroft Wilson

Routledge

New York

Paperback edition published in the
United States of America in 2005 by
Routledge
270 Madison Avenue
New York, NY 10016
www.routledge-ny.com

Routledge is an imprint of the Taylor and Francis Group

First published in 1998 by
Gerald Duckworth & Co. Ltd.
90-93 Cowcross Street
London EC1M 6BF

Cataloging-in-Publication-Data is available
from the Library of Congress

ISBN 0-415-97383-X

Printed in Great Britain

Contents

For dearest Cecil
and
in memory of Martin Taylor

Plates

29. Staff of Marlborough College, 1903.
30. Staff of Henley House, early 1900s.
31. Sassoon in the grounds of Henley House.
32. Sassoon and his prizewinning horse, 'Cockbird'.
33. Sassoon on 'Rubicon'.
34. Norman Loder, Master of the Atherstone Hunt, in March 1914.
35. Edmund Gosse, Sassoon's first patron.
36. Edward Marsh, 1912, another important patron.
37. Sassoon at the Army School, Flixécourt, May 1916.
38. David Cuthbert Thomas ('Dick Tiltwood' of the *Memoirs*), *c*. July 1915.
39. Theresa Sassoon and Hamo in the garden at Weirleigh on his embarkation leave for Gallipoli.
40. Theresa Sassoon alone in the garden at Weirleigh.
41. 'Dame' Nellie Burton with 'Siegfried'.
42. Robert Ross, 'friend of friends', 1916.
43. Lady Ottoline Morrell, Julian Morrell and Sassoon at Garsington in November 1916.
44. Lady Ottoline Morrell.
45. Sydney Carlyle Cockerell, Sassoon's 'bearded and spectacled magician'.
46. Robert von Ranke Graves, taken near the time he met Sassoon in November 1915.
47. Officer Cadet Wilfred Owen, 1916.
48. Captain W.H.R. Rivers, R.A.M.C.
49. Foot inspection.
50. Vivian de Sola Pinto, on sick leave, Hampstead Heath, 1917.
51. Lena Ashwell Concert Party, Y.M.C.A., Egypt.
52. John Masefield.
53. Lennel House, Coldstream, as it was when Sassoon was there.

Introduction

'But surely there is one? There *must* be!' Such has been the almost invariable response when people learn that I am engaged on the first full-scale life of Siegfried Sassoon. But it is an extraordinary fact that Sassoon, one of the greatest and best-known of the First World War poets, has until now lacked a biography.[1] Eighty years have elapsed since that War ended and thirty years since his death, yet the reading public still waits, its curiosity excited rather than satisfied by his own partial accounts of his life. Most of the other pieces of the jigsaw are in place, the minor poets as well as the major, but the conspicuous gap at the centre has remained. And until it is filled, the picture is incomplete.

The importance of this cannot be exaggerated, for of all the First World War poets Sassoon is the most pivotal, his relationships shedding light over a wide area of modern literature. Not only was he a close friend of well-known patrons of the day, such as Edmund Gosse, Edward Marsh, Robert Ross and Ottoline Morrell, but he also had links with almost every poet of the period. He knew Robert Graves, Robert Nichols and Wilfred Owen intimately, exercising a significant effect on all three of them. Though Charles Hamilton Sorley died before he had a chance to meet him, Sassoon recognized his fellow-Marlburian's power and after the War helped to promote the work of another outstanding but neglected poet, Isaac Rosenberg. He also became a lifelong friend of Edmund Blunden. All these poets' stories have been told, but not Sassoon's.

One positive result of this long wait, however, is that it is now possible to tell Sassoon's story more frankly than it would have been even twenty years ago. This is particularly true of his struggles to come to terms with his sexuality, a conflict he wanted to describe himself, but which the law made difficult during his lifetime. It was, ironically, not until the year of his death, 1967, that homosexual acts between consenting males over twenty-one were made legal, a context which largely explains his own failure to write the book he envisaged in 1921:

It is to be one of the stepping-stones across the raging (or lethargic) river of intolerance which divides creatures of my temperament from a free and unsecretive existence among their fellow men. A mere self-revelation, however spontaneous and clearly-expressed, can never achieve as much as –

1

well, imagine another Madame Bovary dealing with sexual inversion, a book
that the world must recognize and learn to understand.[2]

Even in the 1990s it has not been easy to write about Sassoon's
homosexuality, not because we suffer from the same taboos Sassoon did,
but because in our less restrictive times it is hard to convey the difficulties
he faced. When I asked a homosexual writer friend how I should deal with
the 'problem' of Sassoon's sexuality, he replied, 'What problem? If he had
been a heterosexual, you would not have considered it a "problem".' But as
I pointed out to him, it was Sassoon himself who found it one.

Sassoon's was a particularly complex character, more contradictory
than most. Perhaps because he came from two very different backgrounds
he seemed to be pulling in opposite directions most of his life. On the one
hand there was the hearty extrovert, 'Mad Jack', physically daring, even
bloodthirsty at times; on the other a timid, hypersensitive introvert with
strong spiritual needs. Known as a great warrior, he nevertheless spent
less than a month at the Front. He could write an almost completely
autobiographical account of just one side of his personality, *Sherston's
Progress*, and fill three books, yet leave his more private, creative side out
altogether.

Rather than a 'contradictory' character, however, he preferred to think
of himself as a 'multiple personality'.[3] It seemed to him in 1918 that he was
a different person with each new poet he met, and in the 1920s he felt
positively 'kaleidoscopic'.[4] Richard Church's theory was that Sassoon had
a 'fissure' in his personality.[5] However it is expressed, the fact remains
that there is no one label, or set of labels, which will cover Sassoon. Just
as he felt himself to be a different person with each poet he met, so each
person who met him saw him differently.

The one quality no one questioned was his generosity which became
legendary, especially after he inherited money. His 'spiritual' biographer,
Dame Felicitas Corrigan, also claims that no one has ever doubted that he
was a gentleman.[6] But there are many who would challenge what that
term implies. Sassoon was certainly gentle, kind, honourable and extremely altruistic at times, but there is no doubt that he could also be
snobbish, arrogant, even unkind too. Ottoline Morrell, who detected a
streak of cruelty in him, nevertheless went on to describe him as 'very
sympathetic'.[7] Likewise she follows charges of self-centredness and aloofness with praise of his perceptiveness of all things around him. Geoffrey
Keynes rejoiced in his 'patent egocentricity' yet thought him a 'wonderful
friend'.[8] And Osbert Sitwell found him timid as a writer, but far from timid
in other directions. The dichotomy between the contemplative aesthete
and man of action, implicit in Sitwell's comment, is perhaps the least
controversial description of Sassoon's personality.

Sassoon said that he became a 'ruminant onlooker' after the War was
over,[9] but even before it began that side of his personality was well

developed. At the same time, when the opportunity arose he stepped into the role of literary lion and successful socialite as though to the manner born. For someone who was almost pathologically shy – so much so that when he gave his first public reading in 1917 he was practically inaudible – it is puzzling to witness the ease with which he took to his meteoric social rise in the 1920s. It is likewise difficult to reconcile his undoubtedly exhibitionist streak with his later craving for anonymity and his hermit-like existence in the country.

He claimed to be non-intellectual, even simple-minded, suggesting that *Sherston's Progress* should really have been called *Simpleton's Progress*, yet he was clearly an astute judge of characters and situations. His deep pessimism was balanced by an unusually optimistic belief in life; no one but Sassoon, for example, would seriously have believed that his public protest against the conduct of the War could have had any real effect on the War Cabinet and High Command.

Though Stephen Tennant, one of his most intimate friends, found him extremely 'moody' at times – he could be silent for long spells – Tennant informed a researcher that 'in a good mood he told funny stories, and then he roared with laughter and charmed every one'.[10] Tennant was not the only one to appreciate the pronounced sense of fun this sometimes very earnest man displayed. As a child Hamo Sassoon remembers some wonderful jokes played on him by his uncle. And George Byam Shaw, Sassoon's godson, remembers the vivid picture his father painted of Sassoon driving along with both feet out of the car window.

The contradictions seem endless: the basically conservative countryman contemplating life as a Socialist Member of Parliament in a London constituency, the dandyish youth being mistaken for a tramp at a friend's wedding in later life, the physically adroit sportsman being so clumsy that he dropped his meal from a restaurant balcony on to the diners below, the ultra-conformist who became an arch-rebel, the quintessential Englishman of the middle-class, public school, horsey variety who stemmed from an exotic Middle Eastern background, the practising homosexual who married and had a child, the Jew who became a Roman Catholic.

No biography of such a complex character can be entirely straightforward. Sassoon himself claimed: 'My real biography is my poetry'.[11] And, writing his biography of George Meredith he added:

> In imagination I am confronted by [Meredith's] protesting presence as he was in his prime. He reminds me that though I have been thinking about him for many months with concentrated industry while exploring a mass of printed material concerning his career, I am still far from justified in generalizing about what he was like. He asks me to consider the impossibility of unshrouding an author who preferred his personality to be private. He goes on to say, in most kindly and forbearing tones, that a man cannot be re-created from a few printed letters which happened to be preserved, and

3

were never intended to be used for the purpose of propping him up like a ventriloquist's dummy.

What I was in my forties (he concludes) can never be known to you or anyone else. You can see *through* me, but you will never see *into* me. The best of me is in my books, such as they are. Make what you can of them, particularly the poems ...[12]

Fortunately, making what *I* can of Sassoon's work has proved a particularly exciting task, since his development is far from predictable. Few people reading his juvenile imitations of the Romantics and Pre-Raphaelites, would have guessed at his emergence as one of the finest satirists of the First World War. His is a dramatic journey from his lutes and nightingales to his 'scarlet majors at the base'. When I started this biography seven years ago, though Sassoon had been included in Bernard Bergonzi's, Paul Fussell's, John H. Johnston's and Jon Silkin's authoritative surveys of First World War literature,[13] there was only one major assessment of his work, written by Michael Thorpe.[14] Since then there have been at least three more books of criticism in which Sassoon has either played an important part, or taken centre stage.[15] Another is about to be published.[16] By coming at his work from a different angle, that of the biographer, I hope to contribute to this continuing critical debate.

There is one significant way in which this biography differs from Sassoon's on Meredith (and many other literary figures): far from a 'few printed letters', I have discovered a mass of unpublished material in addition to the large amount already in print. It is one reason I have decided to divide the work into two separate parts. Sassoon was a prolific letter-writer and, perhaps because he has remained in the public consciousness since 1917, very few letters have been lost. Similarly, he himself rarely threw letters away, though he may occasionally have destroyed some. Working with the permission of his son, Mr George Sassoon, I have read the majority of these letters, including such gems as both sides of the correspondence between Sassoon and T.E. Lawrence, now in the hands of a private collector. Even more importantly, I have also located part of a fourth volume of autobiography which has never been published.

My main problem has, therefore, been quite different from those I faced in writing about two other war poets, Isaac Rosenberg and Charles Hamilton Sorley: I have had to select from a very large body of material. I may have erred on the side of inclusion rather than exclusion, but this is because often details can help build up a clearer overall picture. To learn that Sassoon's favourite colour was peacock-blue, for example, or that he was fond of onions, does help bring him to life. In many cases such details also illuminate the poetry: the fact that his greatest fear in the War was of being blinded, for instance, seems highly relevant when reading 'To Victory', with its opening line, 'Return to me, colours that were my joy'.

Just as there is a plethora of unpublished biographical material, so there is a great deal of early unpublished or privately printed work. And while much of it is of no real distinction, it has seemed to me important to give the flavour of it. Only then can the reader fully appreciate the distance Sassoon travelled between his juvenilia and his maturity.

Finally, there is the sheer pleasure of telling Sassoon's story in detail. Unlike the many writers who lead sedentary lives, he was a man of action caught up in the bloodiest conflict in history. Much has been written about a war in which ten million men were killed, thirty-six million wounded and countless others profoundly affected, but I hope that telling it from Sassoon's singular viewpoint will illuminate new areas. No one who participated in that War wrote about it more frankly than he did. Essentially he was two people. One was an excitable young man caught up in the exhileration of things such as patrolling at night in No Man's Land. The other was the one who, back at home, had the time to think about the War and never hesitated to say that, in the light of the German peace overtures, what was happening to his friends and to his men was wrong. We are in an age of protest and his conversion from unquestioning support of the Allies to fierce denunciation of their conduct has rightly become a *cause célèbre* and Sassoon himself an icon for our age.

1

Heredities

'Our heredities are, I think, of all things the most fascinating notion.'
Letter from Siegfried Sassoon to H.M. Tomlinson,
15 March 1956

A tall, athletic figure in army service dress stood at the mouth of the River Mersey, watching a scrap of purple and white material bobbing lightly on the waves. It was the ribbon of his Military Cross awarded to him for conspicuous courage on the Western Front. Looking back on the scene with the detachment of thirteen years, Siegfried Sassoon was deeply aware of both the irony and futility of his gesture:

> Wandering along the sand dunes I felt outlawed, bitter, and baited. I wanted something to smash and trample on, and in a paroxysm of exasperation I performed the time-honoured gesture of shaking my clenched fists at the sky. Feeling no better for that, I ripped the M.C. ribbon off my tunic and threw it into the mouth of the Mersey. Weighted with significance though this action was, it would have felt more conclusive had the ribbon been heavier. As it was, the poor little thing fell weakly on to the water and floated away as though aware of its own futility. One of my point-to-point cups would have served my purpose more satisfyingly, and they'd meant much the same to me as my Military Cross.
> Watching a big boat which was steaming along the horizon, I realized that protesting against the prolongation of the War was about as much use as shouting at the people on board that ship. [1]

In many ways Sassoon's was a highly individual response to a deeply emotional conflict. But it was also one which was determined by many extreme influences, not least of them those resulting from his family background.

Siegfried Sassoon was the product of two very different cultures. His father's family, the Sassoons, often referred to as the Rothschilds of the East, were almost completely Oriental in outlook, manners and dress until the arrival of Siegfried's grandfather in England in 1858.[2] This made their rapid acclimatization to Europe within one generation all the more remarkable. They claimed to trace their ancestry back to King David himself, but it is not until the birth of Sason ben Saleh in 1750 that any real

7

documentary evidence exists. By this time the family had settled in Baghdad, in Mesopotamia (modern day Iraq), among the first Jews to do so.

The Sassoons were Sephardic Jews, whose name means 'joy'. Unlike the Ashkenazy Rothschilds, who rose dramatically from the Frankfurt ghettoes, the Sassoons were reputed to have been courtiers and merchant princes from their earliest days. Sason ben Saleh was the last in a line to serve as 'Nasi' (prince of the captivity) to the Caliph's court in Baghdad. Appointed to this post (which included the job of Chief Treasurer) in 1778, Sheik Sason, as he was known, officiated for thirty-eight years, collecting the heavy military and other taxes imposed on his fellow Jews and at the same time building up a trading empire.

As Baghdad decayed under the Ottoman Empire and governors came and went at an alarming speed, Sheik Sason's own position grew increasingly precarious. By the time he retired from public life in 1817, it was clear that his eldest surviving son David, born in 1792, would not be chosen to succeed him at court. A tyrannical ruler hostile to the Sassoons had succeeded as Pasha and David was eventually thrown into prison in 1828 for his resistance to the new regime. Though ransomed, at huge cost to his father, David quite rightly feared for his future and escaped first to Basra at the head of the Persian Gulf, then to the emerging commercial centre of Bushire on its northern shore.

Left virtually a beggar, David is said to have spent his first nights at Bushire in a warehouse keeping rats at bay with his pistol. However, his quick wits and business acumen helped him to re-establish himself quickly as a merchant and very soon his family was able to join him there. By 1830 David had started a small export trade from Basra to India, where prospects seemed to him promising, following the breach in the East India Company's monopoly. So hopeful that in 1832, borrowing money from a fellow Jewish trader, he set out for Bombay with the four children of his first marriage and his second wife Fahra. Here the trading venture really mushroomed, refounding the Sassoon dynasty. And to his great-grandson Siegfried Sassoon the story of 'old David's starting the enormous merchant business' from scratch was the main interest of his father's family.[3]

David Sassoon established his business mainly by opening up trade in China and eventually Japan. He exported opium and cotton in exchange for Chinese tea and silk and the two eldest of his eight sons set up branches of his firm in the East. At the same time David consolidated his Persian connections, sending another of his sons there to open further branches. By the time of the Indian Mutiny in 1857, 'David Sassoon and Sons' was one of the most powerful firms in the Orient. Still not satisfied, however, David continued to expand his business, finally sending his third son, Sassoon David ('S.D.') Sassoon, the first child of his second marriage, to open a small branch in London at the end of 1858.

David had chosen S.D. partly because he felt that England's less extreme climate would be better for his uncertain health and partly because he was already more Western in outlook than his two older brothers. He had, for example, already adopted Western dress before leaving India, the first of his family to do so. A carefully posed photograph taken shortly before S.D. left for England shows his tall, thin figure in dress-suit and bow-tie contrasting oddly with his father and two older brothers, whose flowing Eastern robes seem more appropriate to their Oriental looks. Whilst S.D. avoids the camera, the patriarch looks firmly at it. S.D.'s grandson Siegfried inherited his height and his shyness from S.D. rather than from his father, Alfred Ezra, a small man full of social confidence. S.D. set out for England in 1858, leaving his young wife Fahra (anglicized to Flora) to follow a few months later with their three-year-old son, Joseph, and baby daughter, Rachel.

S.D. imagined that his small office in Leadenhall Street would represent an unimportant branch of 'David Sassoon & Sons'. It must, therefore, have come as a shock both to S.D. and the family when, with the outbreak of the American Civil War in 1861 and the blockade of Alabama's rebel ports, Indian cotton was suddenly in frantic demand by desperate Lancashire cotton mills. The strain apparently was too much, for S.D. died of a heart attack not many years later aged thirty-five in 1867, only three years after his father's death. His younger brother Reuben was sent immediately to replace him, and another brother, Arthur, followed five years later.

S.D.'s next to youngest child, Alfred – Siegfried's father, who was only six when S.D. died – was the first Sassoon to be born in England, in 1861. Together with the death of David, the family's Oriental founder, and the arrival of two more Sassoon brothers in London, these events, all in just over a decade, mark a turning-point in the Sassoons' history. From the 1860s onwards their fate is increasingly bound up with England. The patriarch had left his sons very wealthy indeed – they had at least £500,000 each – and, with their father's encouragement, they had also acquired property of their own. They were now free to travel and did so in style. Abdullah (Albert) followed his three brothers to England in 1873 and set himself up lavishly.

Stories told of the brothers' palatial houses and extravagant entertainments abound;[4] they were at this point fabulously rich. Siegfried's father's generation of the family no longer needed to earn its own living, though many of them continued to work for the family business. When Alfred grew up, he turned to the arts, which his immediate ancestors had had little time for. Admittedly his father, S.D., had as a young man dabbled in journalism, helping to edit a new Hebrew-Arabic periodical in Bombay and later, in England, had translated and written papers for Indian journals. But his desire to write had sprung from a mainly scholarly interest; what exactly drove his children is unclear. Alfred became first a gifted violinist, and then a student in sculpture at the Royal Academy,[5] and his daughter, Rachel, took up writing professionally if a little erratically.[6]

By strong contrast Siegfried's mother's family, the Thornycrofts, had been dedicated to art, for three generations in some cases, by the time he was born.[7] His mother's maternal grandfather, John Francis (1780-1861) had begun life as a farmer at Thornham on the Norfolk coast. Having met and married a relative of Nelson's, he had gone to London for the great man's funeral.[8] On his return, he carved a model of the funeral car in pieces of jet found on the sea-shore.

Backed by local patronage from the Vernon family and the famous agriculturist Coke of Holkham, Francis made repeated attempts to earn his living at various types of sculpture in London. Three times he was forced to return to his Norfolk farm, but after eighteen years he finally established himself as a sculptor of portrait busts (family legend has it that his exasperated wife threw his first commissioned work out of the window). Among Francis's best-known busts are Lord Nelson's daughter, Horatia, Princess Charlotte, King William IV, Queen Victoria and, through his patron the Duke of Sussex, most of the Whig Statesmen concerned with the passing of the 1832 Reform Bill.[9]

A similar spontaneous impulse to sculpt in almost identical circumstances possessed Siegfried's maternal grandfather – and Francis's future son-in-law – Thomas Thornycroft. Intended, like Francis, for farming, Thomas had from his earliest years shown far more interest in drawing and carving. He displayed great ingenuity and energy in making sculpting tools for himself out of old cart wheels and broken files, but none whatever in the practical work of farming. His mother, Ann, who had been left a widow with three sons after only seven years of marriage, soon realized this. So she sent him, together with her youngest, Isaac, to the local Grammar School, keeping the middle son William at home to carry on the farm.

Thomas continued to resist all attempts to interest him in anything but sculpture, proving this rather pointedly by ruining the scalpels of the surgeon to whom he was temporarily apprenticed in his efforts to carve marble with them. Another local surgeon, Mr Dickinson, found Thomas's work so promising that he recommended him to an influential patron, Davenport of Calverley, who in turn brought Thomas's case up with the Duke of Sussex.

The result of this extended affair was that in 1835, supported by an unusually understanding mother, Thomas set out from his home in Cheshire for London to become apprenticed to the Duke's other protégé, John Francis at his house at 56 Albany Street near Regent's Park. He almost immediately fell in love with Francis's sculptor daughter, Mary, whom he married in 1840. *The Dictionary of National Biography* remembers Thomas for his group of Commerce on the Albert Memorial, but posterity will probably remain aware of him through his statue of Boadicea and her

Daughters, which he worked at for most of his life, but which was not erected at Westminster Bridge until after his death. His equestrian statues, particularly of Queen Victoria and Prince Albert, are scattered over a number of northern towns.

It was, however, not only a strong dedication to art which distinguished the Thornycrofts from the Sassoons. In sharp contrast to the Eastern family of merchants who gravitated naturally towards the city to carry on their trading, the thoroughly English Thornycrofts had farmed lands in Cheshire for generations. Their roots were deep in English soil. Thomas's father, John Thornycroft (1791 – 1822), had farmed at Great Tidnock, Gawsworth, near Macclesfield, which had been in the family for three generations. They claimed descent from the ancient Gawsworth family of de Thornicroft which had lived at Thornycroft Hall since the thirteenth century. But whatever their former social position, by the nineteenth century they were of solid yeoman stock, unlike the Sassoons at the Baghdad Court.

Neither as rich as the first and last Sassoons, nor as poor as David in flight from Baghdad, the Thornycrofts were comfortably established. Their farm was said to produce the finest cheese in Cheshire and they survived the various problems which affected farming during their tenancy of it. Theirs was a middle course without the exoticism, drama and glamour of the Sassoons, but with its own strong appeal. They had a deep love of the countryside around them, which Thomas's children came to share when they returned, as they frequently did, to visit their relatives. One of the younger generations of Thornycrofts, who knew Siegfried and his mother's family well, said that the two families failed to understand each other at all. A gift of flowers from the Thornycrofts, she said, must be something you had grown yourself, whereas Sassoon flowers had to be bought.[10]

Another salient feature which distinguished the Thornycrofts from the Sassoons was the dominance of strong women in the shaping of its family history. It seems ironic that the Jewish Sassoons, with their matriarchal bias, produced no significant example of female influence, though there were a number of gifted women among them and some memorable hostesses.[11] Yet, from the patriarch David, down through sons such as Albert, Reuben and Arthur and great-grandsons such as Philip, Victor and Siegfried Sassoon, it is the men who dominate the family.

The Thornycroft history, on the other hand, begins with Ann Cheetham (1785-1875), who married Siegfried's great-grandfather, John Thornycroft, the Saturday before the Battle of Waterloo. When she was left widowed only seven years later with three young sons, she took up the running of the farm with great success at a time when a female farmer was far from usual. For the next twenty years she managed to keep going through a difficult period, becoming well known for her independence and hard work. On one occasion, during the riots provoked by the Corn Laws, a mob surrounded the local market-place and threatened to stone the first farmer who tried to leave. No one but Ann dared to do so, clearing a way for her male colleagues. Her fierceness was well-known to trespassers who, when they attempted to steal her cranberries, would not only be ordered off her land but have their rakes and baskets confiscated too. Yet she was generous, always keeping a large egg-custard ready for anyone who came to beg for food at her farm.

In the next generation Ann's daughter-in-law, Siegfried's grandmother, Mary Thornycroft, also proved an exceptionally distinguished sculptor, one of the few women sculptors of the Victorian age to receive public recognition. She was – almost certainly to her own embarrassment – more successful than her husband, Thomas, whom she revered. Siegfried remembered her as a gracious and beautiful old lady, but history recognizes her as the creator of royal portraits. She was commissioned to make marble busts of Queen Victoria's numerous children, more or less as they were born, as well as many other members of the Royal Family. In addition she created some 'ideal' statues, of which 'Skipping Girl' is probably the best.

All Mary's daughters began by sculpting or painting. Though none achieved their mother's fame, Helen Thornycroft became a well-known watercolourist and Vice-President of the Society of Women Artists. Siegfried's mother, Theresa, though she did not pursue her early promise as an oil-painter, remained highly independent and survived circumstances which would have daunted a less determined woman. Blanche Thornycroft, Mary's granddaughter and Siegfried's cousin, helped her father John with many of his famous engineering achievements as well as becoming a woman engineer in her own right. Like her great-grandmother, Ann, and grandmother Mary, she was a pioneer in a largely male domain. None of these Thornycroft women had set out deliberately to challenge the male-dominated areas in which they found themselves, but by comparison with the Sassoon women or any other women of their time, their achievements are remarkable.

Siegfried Sassoon made similar generalizations about the two families and their probable influence on his own temperament. In early and middle life he felt he was more of a Thornycroft.[12] Growing up in the country like his Thornycroft ancestors, when his life was peopled almost exclusively with Thornycroft relatives, he identified closely with them. His mother, moreover, was antagonistic to the Sassoons who had, with one exception, rejected her, and for many years they hardly entered his consciousness.

Siegfried's first real awareness of his father's side of the family came abruptly when, at the age of eight, he met his Sassoon grandmother at his father's death-bed. Having never seen her before, he was fascinated by her foreignness and aura of wealth. It was on the same occasion that he was first shown the Sassoon family tree, starting with his great-grandfather David. Though very miserable about his father's hopeless condition and particularly unhappy about his mother's exclusion from the scene, he clearly remembered wondering what 'all those other Sassoons' were like.[13]

A few months later, just after his father's death and Siegfried's subsequent illness, he thought again of his ancestors, whom he was already beginning to romanticize. He had borrowed a filigreed scent-bottle from his mother which had been given to her by his father and had once contained attar of roses. As he lay recuperating in a little tent on the lawn, the faint smell of the scent, which he imagined to have come from his father's ancestral home of Persia, seemed to him 'a sort of essence of my father's Oriental extraction'.[14]

In his day-dreaming Siegfried always placed his ancestors in Persia, though some of them had lived in India for two generations by the time his father was born. Presumably Persia seemed to him more romantic. It also fitted in neatly with another momento of his father which he treasured, Alfred's copy of Fitzgerald's *Rubáiyát of Omar Khayyam*. Siegfried's description of this privately printed quarto edition of 1883 reveals a similar impulse to romanticize his father:

> The boards of its binding were covered by a damask of faded rose-colour figured with old gold, and the queer coarse-woven paper on which it was printed contributed further to its esoteric attractiveness.[15]

Siegfried immediately identified both with the *Rubáiyát*'s Persian background and its melancholy outlook. Like Fitzgerald, who remained a life-long favourite, he felt that he was all his life 'apprentice to the business of idleness'[16], but it was initially the Persian connection which drew him to the past. For, though he had been constantly reminded of the wealth of his father's family, it was clearly their exoticism and esoteric beliefs which appealed to him as a child. Even as a young man he continued to equate Persia with mystery and romance and to identify himself proudly with both. When he came to write poetry he began with heavily romantic lyrics, choosing a quotation from another writer on the East, Charles Doughty, with which to preface one of his earliest volumes, *Sonnets and Verses* (1909):

> In the first evening hour there is some merrymake of drum-beating and soft fluting, and Arcadian sweetness of the Persians singing in the tents about us; in others they chant together some piece of their devotion.

As Siegfried himself pointed out, his own Persian ancestry qualified him to claim that he was singing in his tent and that some of his pieces were devotional. He admitted that he may also have been remembering his tent on the lawn during childhood where he sniffed the attar of roses.[17] His somewhat clichéd view of the Sassoons at this time is best summed up in an early poem, 'Ancestors', written some time between 1908 and 1915 (one of his few poems on the subject):

> Behold these jewelled, merchant Ancestors,
> Foregathered in some chancellery of death;
> Calm, provident, discreet, they stroke their beards
> And move their faces slowly in the gloom,
> And barter monstrous wealth with speech subdued,
> Lustreless eyes and acquiescent lids.
>   And oft in pauses of their conference,
>   They listen to the measured breath of night's
>   Hushed sweep of wind aloft the swaying trees
>   In dimly gesturing gardens; then a voice
>   Climbs with clear mortal song half-sad for heaven.
>
> A silent-footed message flits and brings
> The ghostly Sultan from his glimmering halls;
> A shadow at the window, turbaned, vast,
> He leans; and, pondering the sweet influence
> That steals around him in remembered flowers,
> Hears the frail music wind along the slopes,
> Put forth, and fade across the whispering sea.
>
> (C.P. pp. 46-7)

In 1914, when Siegfried eventually got to know David Sassoon's youngest daughter, his great-aunt Mozelle, he was delighted by the detailed account she could give him of his father's family.[18] He had so often felt himself placed in a false position when people assumed that he knew what he called 'the conspicuous Sassoons'.[19] Though his mother had taught him vaguely to venerate his great-grandfather, his great-aunt's more factual descriptions made David seem much less mythical to Siegfried, then aged twenty-seven. She was also able to make the other members of the Sassoon family seem less remote and fabulous.

Siegfried saw himself as a 'poor relation', and relatively speaking he was, but it was never primarily their money which fascinated him. His attitude towards Sassoon money was both disdainful and apologetic. Sending Robert Graves £23 for his twenty-third birthday in 1918, he refers to his 'Semitic sovereigns none of which I have the least right to call my own'.[20] And on another occasion, when he himself was about to inherit Sassoon money, he writes, again to Graves in 1927:

> they made it in the East by dirty trading, millions and millions of coins. They spent it all in draper's shops and jewellers and pastry cooks and brothels. They hire large mausoleums and get cremated at Golders Green. They smoke Coronas and worship German royalties and dissolute peers.[21]

Nonetheless, as Sassoon grew older, his attitude towards his father's family mellowed until by his seventies he felt that his eastern ancestry was stronger in him than the Thornycrofts.

There is little doubt that Siegfried did inherit something from the Sassoons, if only physically. Like his grandfather and great-grandfather, he was tall, spare and muscular, unlike the Thornycroft men who tended to be short. His friends attributed other characteristics to his Oriental ancestry, not all of them entirely convincing. One warned him that his hands 'were somewhat over-illustrative', for example, and another detected in him 'a very definite Oriental streak' of cruelty.[22] A third suggested that his early 'deals' in books showed his Sassoon blood coming out, and a fourth, more fancifully, that 'in the Hebrew fashion of the Bible, Jew in this as in so much else, Sassoon always wrote with his heart as well as his head, the heart being the seat of understanding ...'[23] One of his closest friends felt that Sassoon, 'like *all Oriental men* was *very secretive* – Reticent, and very eccentric'.[24] And in Sassoon's own later choice of pseudonyms there were many oblique but none too subtle references to his Jewishness, as well as some bad puns – 'Elim Urge', 'Solly Sizzum', 'Sigma Sâshun'.

Sassoon himself stated that an obviously inherited Sassoon feature was his tendency to adopt a mystic role in his poetry. 'As a poetic spirit', he wrote, 'I have always felt myself – or wanted to be – a kind of minor prophet' and he refers in his autobiography to 'some angry prophet in my remote ancestry'.[25] Michael Thorpe spells this out in his comments on Siegfried's 1933 volume of poems, *The Road to Ruin*: 'His is the irascible voice of the Old Testament prophet'.[26]

As with Siegfried's opinion of the Sassoons, not all his comments take such a positive view of Jewishness. In his 1917 diary, exasperated by the evident profit some people were gaining from the War, he wrote:

> Lieutenant X is a nasty, cheap thing. A cheap-gilt Jew. Why are such Jews born, when the soul of Jesus was so beautiful? *He* saw the flowers and the stars; but they see only greasy bank-notes and the dung in the highway where they hawk their tawdry wares.[27]

Perhaps he felt personally ashamed of what he elsewhere called 'Jew profiteers'.[28] Nonetheless, being far less conscious of his Jewishness than others, it may have come as something of a surprise to find himself and his brother included in 'The Hebrew War List' at Cambridge University. (The fact that Sassoon makes no mention of discrimination against him as a Jew does not mean that he did not experience it – given the historical context, it would be odd if he had not. But it does suggest that it was not a serious problem for him. He seems to have been far more conscious of his position as a poor relation of an affluent family.)

It is far easier and more tempting to speculate about the traits Sassoon inherited from the Thornycrofts, partly because he himself was more articulate on this subject. While he entirely omitted his Jewish side from his thinly-veiled autobiographical novel, *Memoirs of a Fox-Hunting Man* in 1928, he made much of his hero's love of the country, something he firmly believed he had inherited from his mother's yeoman stock. In the straight autobiography which followed his fictionalized trilogy in the late thirties and early forties, he states categorically that being a 'poor relation' of the Sassoons was compensated 'by being half a Thornycroft in blood and more than that in hereditary characteristics'.[29] Welcoming Stanley Jackson's plan to write a history of the Sassoons in 1965, Siegfried nevertheless felt that a book about the Thornycrofts would be much more worthwhile. He believed that he had inherited from his mother what he called the 'Thornycroft sanity', which enabled him, introspective as he was, to 'stand aside and look at myself – and laugh'.[30] Be this as it may, it was a trait shared by both his mother and father. And if he meant that he had a balanced approach to life, it can only possibly be true of his later years.

Less controversial is his claim that his artistic talent derived from the Thornycrofts. Their complete dedication to art from his great-grandfather's generation onwards must have had a profound influence on Siegfried, who not only wrote poetry and prose, but also loved and performed music and drew and painted throughout his life. Though the visual arts were his immediate ancestors' main concern, music was an important feature of their family life. Most of Thomas and Mary Thornycroft's children either sang or played a musical instrument and musical evenings and 'glees' were one of their greatest pleasures. This musical side was undoubtedly reinforced by Sassoon's father, who was musically gifted, but it also owed a great deal to his mother's family.

Siegfried himself made a direct link between the Thornycrofts' tradition in sculpture and his own chosen art form, poetry. Writing to a young friend in 1948 he claimed that he was:

> essentially, *sculptural* in my conceptions of verse, (probably because my mother's family were sculptors – she herself was a *designer* rather than a painter) ... I want verse to be strongly shaped.[31]

Another trait Siegfried attributed to his mother's family was his frugality: 'Like a true Thornycroft I detest waste and luxury and excess in anything' he wrote to a friend in 1942, rejoicing in the fact that he was saving money through the wartime shortage of servants.[32] Though extravagant as a young man, particularly where horses were concerned, he grew more careful until, by the time he inherited money in 1927, he hardly knew what to do with it. 'The idea of being "much better off" has brought me no particular sense of pleasure', he wrote in his diary. 'I can't see what good it will do me in my everyday life; and it certainly won't help me to write better poetry. I can be generous to my friends, and give a lot of it to my mother. That seems to be about all there is in it'.[33]

Surprisingly enough, Sassoon never theorized about qualities he may have inherited in common from both sides of his family – industriousness, honesty and ingenuity. He did, however, become convinced that it was not so much what he drew separately from each race which formed his character but the particular way in which these combined. 'You have got it *right* about my Jewish blood', he wrote to a friendly critic in 1965. 'My artistic talent derives from the Thornycroft side. But what made me different from the gracious serenity of Uncle Hamo [Thornycroft]'s work was the mixture of west and east. The daemon in me is Jewish'.[34] More jocularly he referred elsewhere to being a mixture of 'Cheshire Cheese farmers and Oriental aristocrats'.

Sassoon's most direct link with his family's past came through his maternal grandmother, Mary Thornycroft, who died just after his eighth birthday. When she came to live with his family in the spring of 1894, she seemed to him the epitome of angelic old ladyhood 'dignified in the serene consolations of old age'.[35] On one occasion only – a visit from her eldest son – did he glimpse the 'glorious vitality' she must have had in her prime.[36] He had been told of her distinction as a sculptor and her beautiful long hands symbolized for him the Thornycroft tradition in sculpture. He was sad when she died at the age of eighty-five, after a brief illness in the hard winter of 1894 to 1895, but anxious to know when his mother's mourning would decently allow her to take him ice-skating again.[37]

Mary Thornycroft's outstanding characteristics seem to have been those attributed to her work – gaiety, elasticity and youthful vigour.[38] Oscar Wilde is said to have referred to Mary's *'jeunesse éternelle'*, an unintentional irony, for from the time she met her future husband, at least, she lied about her age, being seven years his senior. Born in 1809, she was nearly thirty-one when they married on the unusual date of 29 February 1840. (Had *she* proposed to *him*? Or was she just very sensitive to the passing of the years?) Nonetheless, in spite of her seniority in age and her greater talent in art she not only revered but looked up to Thomas and touchingly wrote in reply to a letter from Thomas's earliest patron, Mr Dickinson: 'I have been devoted to his profession with one object in view: the pride of seeing Thorny [her nickname for Thomas] a great sculptor'.[39]

I suspect that their marriage worked both not only because they loved and respected each other, but also because Mary was very long-suffering. When Thomas, who was mechanically-minded, started his own iron-foundry in the not over-large house they had moved to at 39 Stanhope Street near Regent's Park, four years after their marriage, she endured the soot and smoke. When, with growing interest in engineering, he built a model railway and steam locomotive which occupied a substantial part of their studio and later made a model steamboat using the cylinders from the train, she allowed that too. But her patience must have been sorely tried when he then went on to build a twenty-seven foot steamboat, admittedly in two halves. With only her husband's cousin, Elizabeth Thornycroft, to help in the house, she had a great deal on her hands.

Throughout it all and through the birth of seven children in quick succession, Mary went on sculpting with great mental energy and physical stamina. She had started working at an early age, showing her first piece at the Royal Academy at twenty-one, and was still working at the age of seventy-six.[40] As both she and Queen Victoria produced their respective babies, Mary sculpted them, undeterred by her own pregnancies. She would often work to within two days of her delivery. As early as 1842 she sailed with her husband to Rome, already seven months pregnant with their second child, and Thomas himself delivered their elder son. To her sixth child, Hamo, who also became a sculptor, she wrote at the age of seventy-one: 'Stick to the clay, my boy ...' She was never happy unless she had 'a piece of clay to play with'.[41] Work dominated even her death as she chose to be buried next to her eldest son's busy shipyard at Chiswick, her husband agreeing with her that they must 'lie within the sound of the hammers'.[42]

In spite of her robustness Mary was highly sensitive and particularly responsive to children, as many of her finest sculptures show. Though she agreed with Thomas when straitened circumstances in the early 1850s made it sensible to send their younger son, Hamo, away at the age of four to live on his childless uncle's farm, she was deeply unhappy about the decision; it was the only occasion on which he remembered seeing his mother cry. In spite of his banishment to Cheshire he adored her and grew very close to her after his return to the family at the age of thirteen. He described her glowingly to his fiancée in 1883 as 'a trusty jewel in an emergency ... inspired more than most with good judgement'.[43] Mary's children, in recognition of her strong maternal qualities, referred to her among themselves simply as 'the mother'.

Allowing for normal family tensions, particularly with her eldest surviving daughter, Alyce, Mary seems to have been an unusually understanding mother. In spite of what her youngest son identified as the family's strong High Church and Tory principles, she took his engagement to an avowed agnostic and Radical more calmly than did her daughters. She was strictly principled but never as self-righteous as the Thornycrofts tended to be. When the son-in-law who had abandoned her youngest daughter lay dying she asked, in a spirit of genuine forgiveness, to be remembered to him.

Ultimately, Mary was much more than a gifted, determined woman and a devoted mother. Though she is unlikely to have had much formal education, she was well-read and kept up with all the 'heavies', as the monthly reviews were known. Siegfried recalled proudly that her favourite reading was *Hudibras* and *Tristram Shandy*, at the time not at all the type of literature women ordinarily read. Always bright and gay she relished attractive clothes and parties equally. True to her emancipated state she never wore the crinoline then in fashion but enjoyed long, flowing silk dresses in rich colours. Striking to look at, even in old age she was considered beautiful and her close neighbour, the painter G.F. Watts was often heard to say of her face 'The bony structure is so fine'.[44]

If Mary had faults they stemmed from an inability to understand anyone weaker than herself, particularly if they sinned against her own dedication to aesthetic ideals and self-discipline. When one of her granddaughters grew a little too plump for her classical tastes, she reproved her. Mary's response to the unfortunate girl's protest that she could not help it was 'You *must* help it!'[45]

Thomas Thornycroft, Siegfried's grandfather had some very obvious faults; though both Mary and his children forgave him for these. His great-granddaughter claimed that he was the most extraordinary of the Thornycrofts. Certainly he was the most extreme. Full of warmth and charm, a man with many close friends, he could also appear egotistical, querulous and insatiable. The same stubbornness which enabled him to become a sculptor against high odds could make him seem aggressive at times.

During a not wholly successful career he often found himself blocked by conservative committees of civic dignitaries. In these circumstances his fighting instinct and outspokenness, combined with a quick wit, could make him both argumentative and impatient. He did not suffer fools gladly, and often chose to sacrifice a potential commission rather than concede to those he considered his inferiors. In a scathing letter in which he refuses to compete for a memorial statue of Sir Robert Peel he writes:

> I have had no time to spare for Peel hunting. Although solicited to compete I have refused to do so unless under agreement to be paid for my sketch [i.e. model]. The committee know nothing of art, votes are always pledged to particular candidates before the competing sketches are assembled ...
>
> It is not the most agreeable job to meet the enlightened taste of Mr Public for big-bodied, small-legged Peels in coats and smalls. I do hope to spend my days in the relation of forms more akin to those which stood in hall or temple responsive to the Greeks' keen sense of beauty.[46]

In spite of Thomas's reference to classical sculpture, part of the reason he failed to succeed may be his innovativeness. At a time when sculpture stuck closely to a tradition of heavily draped and stylized forms, Thomas created a statue of Queen Victoria in a close-fitting riding-habit with features more accurately detailed than was usual. The *Times*' critic promptly complained that the Queen's body was 'too anatomical ... Nudity is not exactly consistent with the idea of a Sovereign, who is not to be considered as a fine specimen of human beauty, but, if the term may be used, of superhuman dignity'.[47] Thomas, however, continued resolutely to reject the convention of immortalizing contemporaries in Athenian costume, and his commissions dwindled noticeably after the untimely death of his patron, Prince Albert, in 1861.

When sculpting began to fail him, he turned with equal enthusiasm to his other great interest, engineering. As an apprentice with John Francis in the mid-1830s he had become friends with Thomas Page, Brunel's assistant engineer in the building of the Thames tunnel and the architect of the Lambeth and Battersea Embankments. And by 1838 Thomas was already talking to his future father-in-law about 'railways, steam-navigation and suchlike topics'.[48]

Even before his patron's death he had busied himself with engineering projects when commissions were scarce. First he designed and built a threshing-machine for his farmer brother, Will. One of the first to be worked by steam, it was in use for the next fifty years. Thomas's next project was the iron-foundry at Stanhope Street. This was followed by a steady stream of inventions, from a six-foot telescope and model railway to a series of progressively larger steam-boats. When his elder son, John, began to develop his father's interests, Thomas sent John off to Jarrow to learn boat-building, then to Glasgow University to study design. He bought a piece of land at Chiswick, where he helped John set up a small shipyard and here they built the steam-launch John had designed for his father, *The Waterlily*.[49] Thomas spent many hours cruising up and down the Thames in her and, but for Mary's absence, would happily have lived on board the little boat.

This fascination with engineering is perhaps not so surprising as it first seems. Sculptors and engineers must both be able to visualize in three dimensions, as well as have a good grasp of the mathematics of weight and balance. Siegfried's mother told him that her brother John had 'the calculating faculty'. Another feature Thomas passed on to both his sons (but not to his grandson Siegfried) was his practical ingenuity. When the little flat he and Mary rented in Rome in 1843 had no stove, he built one himself, as well as delivering his elder son there. When the house he moved to in Wilton Place in 1861 proved unsatisfactory, possibly because the studio became too crowded, he bought a cabbage field opposite Holland Park in the mid-seventies and had his own home built there with *three* studios, calling it Moreton House.[50]

As a husband and father Thomas was very affectionate. He could be explosive, particularly with his son Hamo, but he genuinely cared for his family. Though his wife was more successful, he showed no signs of jealousy and when his younger son, in turn, began to outstrip him, he was similarly generous-minded. It was his willingness to step down from the Royal Academy's list of nominees which enabled Hamo to become an

Academician at the unusually early age of twenty-nine. All things considered he was an endearing as well as a remarkable man.

Both Thomas and Mary epitomize Victorian virtues in their prodigious industriousness, resourcefulness and multiplicity of interests. Many of these virtues they passed on to their children, together with their outstanding abilities. With the exception of Frances, whose energies were concentrated on her large family, each of the Thornycroft children was preoccupied with design. This entered as strongly into John's engineering inventions as it did into Hamo's sculpting or Alyce, Helen and Theresa's painting.

Alyce (1844-1906), the eldest surviving daughter, began as a sculptor and at the age of twenty exhibited at the Royal Academy. Later she turned to painting, mainly portraits of her family in the style of their friend and neighbour, Watts. Her bronze bust of her mother is in the National Portrait Gallery, and a bust of Siegfried's brother was among fourteen works she exhibited at the Royal Academy between 1864 and 1892. As the eldest unmarried daughter, Alyce was expected to stay at home to look after her parents, but she made her resentment painfully clear. She became unbalanced to the point of madness after her parents' deaths and died relatively young at the age of sixty-three. Siegfried, who shared a disastrous family holiday with her in 1897, summed up family opinion when he recalled her magnificent looks and voice, her charm and her uncontrollable temper, all of which reminded him of the tragedienne, Mrs Siddons.[51] His most vivid memory of Aunt ' Lula', as she was called, was of her in his mother's studio, smashing one of the busts she had just sculpted, with a hammer. He dedicated a manuscript collection of *Poems* 'To Aunt Lula' in 1898, when he was twelve, a sign perhaps of his closeness to her.

Helen (1848-1912), nicknamed 'Nello', was also a sculptor turned painter. In 1862, at the age of fourteen, she was one of the first women to apply for a Royal Academy studentship. Accepted on the basis of her work, she was then rejected when Landseer discovered her age: 'Send her back to the nursery!' he is reported to have said.[52] Two years later she was accepted and in the same year exhibited her bust of her sister Frances. Even more prolific than Alyce, she had twenty-six works accepted by the Royal Academy during the next forty years. She established her reputation as a painter with watercolours of flowers and Scottish and Greek landscapes. For many years she was Vice-President of the Society of Women Artists.

Helen's independence showed itself in a number of ways. She was one of the first women to have her hair bobbed, ostensibly because she had once caught it in John's machinery while helping him, as she often did, with one of his inventions. She also wore waistcoats, ties and suits, stopping short only at trousers. Yet the family insisted that she was in no way masculine, pointing out that her waistcoats were *flowered silk* ones.[53] As the younger of the two unmarried daughters, she was able to leave home and had her own cottage in Monmouthshire, keeping a flat in London at Moreton House. Like Alyce she died relatively young at sixty-four. Siegfried must have met her when she came to her mother's deathbed and also when he visited Moreton House during the 1890s. He owned at least seven pictures by his aunt and photographs and copies of many others.

Siegfried's mother Theresa, known as 'Trees' (from the abbreviation 'Threesa') and later, by extension, 'Ash', was the youngest of the family. Born in 1853, she learnt to carve and model as a child, but quickly turned to painting. She attended Queen's College, Harley Street, where her close friends were the future painters Nellie Epps (later Gosse) and Catherine Brown Hueffer, before being admitted to the Royal Academy Schools in 1890. (She was the only one of the three sisters to enter as a painting student.) Very close to her brother Hamo, whom she nicknamed 'Gull', she made several cultural trips abroad with him, including one to the Paris Salon of 1877. She also modelled for him occasionally. By the age of twenty-two she had exhibited the first of seven paintings at the Royal Academy. Other works were exhibited at the Royal Society of Painters in Watercolours, the Grosvenor Gallery and the Society of Women Painters.

Siegfried insisted that she was primarily a designer and it was her composition which attracted attention. Her most successful picture was one which apparently made a sensation at the Academy Exhibition of 1889; called 'The Hours', it had twenty-four figures floating across the sky from darkness to light. Siegfried knew the picture well and, recalling it on his twenty-first birthday, he wondered if he could ever write as good a poem as 'The Hours' was a picture:

> For in that noble design I had always felt something of the poetry which I could never put into words; and in it I could recognize my kinship with the strength and simplicity of my mother's imagination.[54]

Theresa carried on painting after her marriage, sometimes using Siegfried and his brothers as models in her largely religious pictures, Siegfried posing on one occasion as the infant Jesus for her 'Nativity'. As the boys grew older and more unmanageable, however, Theresa was forced to give up serious painting, although she did carry on drawing. There was always a drawing-board in her sitting-room and as late as 1930 she produced illustrations for a special edition of her son's *Memoirs of a Fox-Hunting Man*, with Siegfried as her model for Sherston.

Theresa, Helen and Alyce all sat at various times to each other and to the sculptors of the family, Thomas, Mary and Hamo. Frances (1846-1929), nicknamed 'Fanny', though not a professional artist, spent many hours in the studio modelling her head or limbs for various works in progress. Her own ambitions were musical. Possessed of a fine contralto voice, she wanted to become an opera singer, but gave up the idea when she met and married her brother John's manager at the Chiswick ship-building works, John Donaldson.[55] Siegfried grew very fond of Uncle 'Don', as he was called, and sent him some of his poems, a sign of great trust. He also went to visit the ten 'little Dons', as his cousins were known. Before her marriage, Fanny may well have been the organizing force behind the family's frequent musical evenings held in the studio at Wilton Place. (Later on at Moreton House there was a music-room which housed a lovely old rosewood piano.) She and Hamo certainly took a leading part in the singing parties, or 'glees', which were also held there. The Thornycroft children formed a Glee Club, as well as the more predictable sketching club set up by the girls, called 'The Critics'. Together they went to operas and 'Pop' concerts.[56] It was Theresa's passion for Wagner which led her eventually to call her second son Siegfried in honour of the great musician's work.

Another shared enthusiasm in the Thornycroft family, and related to their love of literature as well as painting, was their admiration of the Pre-Raphaelites. In the late 1860s Hamo had met Burne-Jones, who had introduced him to the William Morris style of decoration, and this had made a deep impression on him. Not long afterwards Theresa went as an RA student to another Pre-Raphaelite's studio, that of Ford Madox Brown. A fellow-student there, as at school, was Edmund Gosse's future wife Nellie, who not only became Theresa's best friend but was also the means of introducing her brother Hamo to Gosse. This started a life-long friendship which undoubtedly encouraged the family's literary interests. (Theresa, for example, found it hard to resist reading Scott's Waverley novels when she was supposed to be completing a picture for the family's sketching club.) However it started, the Pre-Raphaelite phase showed itself in some amusing ways. Great emphasis was henceforth laid on the fact that most of the Thornycroft children had reddish hair. (True to form, Siegfried described his mother's as 'Venetian' red.) Alice changed her name to the more mediaeval 'Alyce', Ellen became 'Helen', William chose 'Hamo' in imitation of a remote thirteenth-century ancestor and Georgiana, christened after her aunt, abandoned family loyalty and adopted her middle name, 'Theresa'. The Pre-Raphaelite influence may also have had something to do with the daughters' increasingly High Church leanings, though this may also have been due to the advent of a particularly handsome young curate at their local church. Theresa remained a devout Christian all her life and brought Siegfried up accordingly.

The Thornycrofts were not, however, all piety and culture. They were also united by a love of things physical. There were family walks on Sundays in Hyde Park; in summer they swam in and rowed on the Thames; in winter they visited the Davis Street Baths and ice-skated if the weather allowed. Hamo fenced with his friend, Blake Wirgman, and in 1872, when England was threatened with invasion, joined the Artists' Rifles and taught his enlightened sisters musketry drill. Theresa was also an excellent horsewoman, a skill she passed on to Siegfried, though she could never persuade him to share her love of swimming.

When Theresa got to know her future husband, Alfred Sassoon, in 1883, she was at the height of her physical and artistic powers. She was also blessed with a very good sense of humour, which he shared. Their relationship developed from a family acquaintance started in the early 1860s, when Theresa's mother sculpted Alfred's parents, and was reinforced by her brother Hamo's commission to make a half-size statue of Alfred's sister, Rachel, in 1882.[57] Theresa, who became friends with Rachel, started visiting the Sassoons' splendid Elizabethan mansion, Ashley Park, near Walton-on-Thames.[58] Family legend has it that she was recovering from her rejection by a Cheshire farmer, Jack Walker, in favour of a barmaid.[59] Whether or not this is true, she showed no sign of it as she and Alfred played jokes on each other with a merriment common to both. Despite the fact that she was eight years older than he, they were clearly becoming emotionally involved, even intimate, when she wrote to Hamo in 1883, ostensibly about a quiz book:

> Young Sassoon brought your letter which you had directed to Ashley [Park]. I am going there on Thursday next. Have just discovered a copy of Mangnall's Questions which he has put among my books as a joke at my not knowing a date which he did not know himself. I cannot think how to revenge the insult.
> The best plan will be to ask him questions out of it on the whole I think.[60]

Alfred Sassoon was only six when his father had dropped dead at the Langham Hotel in 1867. His mother, Flora, partly to compensate for this loss, spoilt him and his younger brother Frederick outrageously. When Alfred showed a talent for the violin she bought him not one but two Stradivariuses and sent him for a long, expensive series of lessons with the maestro, Sarasate. Gifted as Alfred undoubtedly was, his mother's reaction must seem to us now excessive, but she herself was not at all realistic about money. Her husband had left her a substantial fortune, which she went through rapidly. Unaware of how much it took to maintain her glorious but crumbling mansion, its large staff and her children's privileged private education, she spent so lavishly that by the 1880s she had already exhausted a great deal of the money.

Whether from temperament or example, Alfred followed in his mother's footsteps. After a few frivolous undergraduate terms at Exeter College, Oxford,[61] he used his liberal allowance to finance the Grand Tour still expected by some rich young men. Alfred's stopped short in Paris, however, where he took an elegant house and entertained royally. Sarah Bernhardt, attracted no doubt by his prodigality as well as his dark good looks, referred to him as the 'rich nabob' and compared his wealth to that of Croesus.[62] Slim and handsome, with an attractive cleft in his chin, Alfred sported a thick moustache and, even in his thirties when he was dying of tuberculosis, looked worthy of the description given him of 'a ladies' man'. Whether another charge of 'caddish insouciance' was also inappropriate is impossible to say. Certainly he had great personal charm, but then so had Theresa. Alfred also much admired her skill as an artist and, presumably as a result of her influence, enrolled himself as a student in sculpture at the Royal Academy in the autumn of 1883.

Apart from their love of art and well-developed sense of humour, Alfred and Theresa shared a physical adroitness which in Alfred's case showed itself in cricket as well as riding and dancing. Years after his death Siegfried, who also loved cricket, recalled a remark about his father by the old one-legged shoemaker who umpired their local matches: 'A rare good one he was at getting his bat down to a shooter'.[63] Siegfried inherited not only Alfred's aptitude at cricket and riding but also his love of music and his distinctive good looks, even down to the cleft in his chin.

It is not difficult to imagine Alfred and Theresa, two rather spoilt children, fun-loving, generous, physically attractive and attracted to the physical, falling deeply in love. Nor is it hard to understand Alfred's mother's horrified reaction when they started to talk of marriage in 1883. Brought up in strict Jewish orthodoxy herself, surrounded by unquestioning orthodoxy within the Sassoon family, excessively proud of its lineage, Flora simply could not understand her son's desire to marry the eminently English and Christian Theresa. She instantly made her objections very clear – and expected to be obeyed.

Flora, who came from a devout and wealthy Baghdad family, the Reubens, was used to having her own way. Her quiet, scholarly, undemonstrative husband had offered very little resistance to his elegant young wife and she was not ready to accept any from her second son. Renowned within the Sassoon family for her indomitability, Flora also had an unpredictable temper which most people feared. No one could be more generous, as Brighton Council discovered when she presented a large piece of land to them as a public park, after finding two urchins trespassing in private grounds for lack of a place to play. But there was a quixotic element even in her generosity, as the Brighton Police Force discovered when she ordered six dozen of the best melons to be delivered to their station one very hot day. 'Formidable' was the family's word for Flora but not, it seems, to Alfred.

Perhaps because she had indulged him so, Alfred ignored her warnings about marrying out of the Jewish faith. When she threatened to stop his liberal allowance, he went straight to Somerset House to consult his father's will.[64] Having established that his income was independent of his mother's approval, he renewed his offer of marriage to Theresa. Theresa was so deeply in love that she had been quite prepared to marry him without his money, though her brother had warned Alfred that their parents were unlikely to agree. She found no difficulty, therefore, in accepting him with his money and in November 1883 they became secretly engaged. Their first intention was to marry the following April, but such was their impatience that by January 1884 Hamo was called in to help them organize a wedding by special licence. The licence may also have been needed because of Alfred's Jewishness, as well as their eagerness to marry. The secrecy is less puzzling; neither Mrs Sassoon nor Theresa's parents were to know, in case they managed to stop the ceremony.

Meantime Theresa, who had been deeply upset at Mrs Sassoon's opposition and a certain amount of wavering on Alfred's part, continued painting at her friends', the Wallaces', house in Glassinghall near Glasgow, where she had escaped in despair. (It is perhaps no coincidence that she painted a picture of the demented Ophelia during this time.)

Once Hamo had arranged for the wedding to take place at their local church, St Mary Abbott's, Kensington, Theresa returned to London with a friend, Eliza Perks. She and Alfred were married on 30 January 1884, with Eliza Perks, Hamo and his friend Edmund Gosse as witnesses – an auspicious literary sponsorship for the future poet.

Theresa's parents were then informed and their reaction was positive: 'Theresa's wedding is still a great excitement here: Alyce and the parents are very happy,' Hamo wrote to his fiancée two days after the event.[65] Mary Thornycroft immediately organized an 'At Home' afternoon, when all her women friends came to congratulate her – all, that is, except Mrs Sassoon.

It is clear from Hamo's remark that 'Mrs Sassoon has *not yet* been' [my italics], that everyone expected her finally to capitulate, but they had reckoned without her stubbornness and genuine distress. Much as she doted on Alfred, she could not condone his marriage out of the faith. For one thing, by marrying a Gentile woman, he ensured that any children of the marriage would be Gentile, since Jewishness is deemed to pass through the female line. With her eldest son, Joseph, already appearing a confirmed bachelor and Frederick, her youngest, offering little prospect of marriage, Mrs Sassoon must have been bitterly disappointed by Alfred's depriving her of acceptable grandchildren and heirs. In her rage, she rushed straight to the synagogue to curse any children born of what she saw as an unholy union. She also declared her son officially dead, saying funeral prayers and even sitting the ritual period of mourning for him. Until his last illness she would have nothing to do with him and ordered Joseph, Rachel and Frederick to act similarly. Most significantly of all from her grandson Siegfried's point of view, she cut Alfred out of her will. Though she had spent a great deal of her fortune by the time she died in 1919, even a small part of her money would have made some difference to Siegfried's life at that time.

One unexpected result of Alfred's rebellion was the marriage of his brother, Joseph, shortly afterwards. As withdrawn and scholarly as his father, with a love of first editions, antique furniture and esoteric languages, Joseph had been content to spend most of his time in the Ashley Park library. Like Alfred he showed no interest in the family business and the rest of the Sassoons began to think the Ashley Park branch either too proud or too inadequate for commerce. In any case, money stopped flowing in from the family business. Unlike Alfred and Frederick, Joseph had completed his degree at Oxford, where he had led a quiet and studious life at Christ Church. Also unlike Alfred, he was ill at ease with women. Flora, undaunted and still implacable, stepped in to arrange a marriage for him and Joseph set out dutifully in an Astrakhan coat and hat for Russia to meet his arranged bride, Louise de Gunzbourg. Young, rich, beautiful and above all strictly orthodox, Louise had everything that Theresa lacked in Flora's eyes. Out of gratitude perhaps, for it was not what anyone expected, Flora allowed Louise to take over at Ashley Park, leaving to join her many kinsmen in Brighton. She must have been even more grateful when Louise proceeded with great efficiency to bear Joseph five sons and two daughters.

Joseph obeyed his mother's commands and saw virtually nothing of Alfred or his family after his marriage. His sister Rachel, however, was not prepared to give up her friendship with Theresa, let alone her brother. Slight and delicate as she looked, with her pale skin and large, dark eyes, she had her mother's determination. Frustrated herself by the narrow world of Jewish orthodoxy, she may even have applauded Alfred's action. More than that, she genuinely valued Theresa's friendship and continued to visit her even after Alfred was no longer with her. Artistic herself, but thwarted in her ambition to write seriously or to achieve anything she thought worthwhile, she undoubtedly admired Theresa's gifts and dedication. For a time Rachel consoled herself with unpaid hospital nursing, which her mother grudgingly allowed, but eventually she, too, married 'out'. Though her mother raged, her reaction was not nearly so violent, possibly because Rachel married money and, in any case, would as a female carry on the Jewish line. Flora may also have been badly shaken by the loss of one child and unwilling to risk that of a second.

All these repercussions would probably have seemed both extraordinary and irrelevant to Alfred and Theresa as they set out on their honeymoon, destination unknown. 'We had a festive happy letter from the happy pair this morning', Hamo reported to his fiancée on 1 February 1884. It was a happiness that lasted just long enough to produce Siegfried and his two brothers.

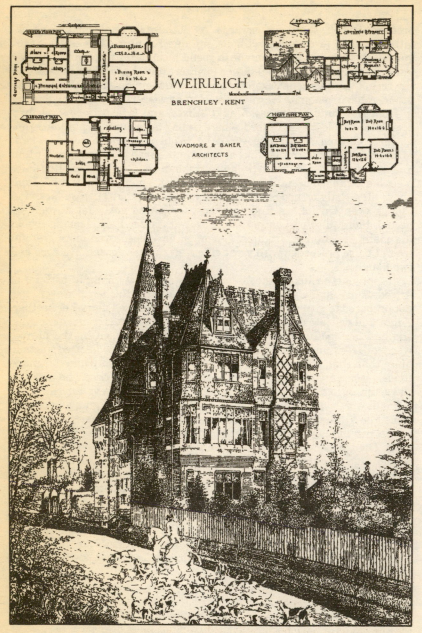

"WEIRLEIGH"

BRENCHLEY, KENT

WADMORE & BAKER
ARCHITECTS

Weirleigh, Sassoon's childhood home.

Childhood in the Garden
(1886-1895)

Siegfried Loraine Sassoon was the second of three sons born to Alfred and Theresa in the four years following their marriage. The first, Michael Thornycroft Sassoon, arrived only eight and a half months after the ceremony, on 14 October 1884. The slight prematurity was probably due to his being one of twins, since it is unlikely that Theresa's strict religious principles would have allowed her to anticipate marriage.[1] Pride in the Thornycroft family clearly decided his second name, but the choice of first name is more puzzling. 'Michael' appeared in neither the Sassoon nor the Thornycroft family trees at that time. Religious though she was, Theresa is unlikely to have called her first-born after the archangel, as one Thornycroft descendant suggested.[2] The choice of godfather, however, is more understandable, since the nominee, John Belcher, a distinguished architect and friend of the Thornycrofts, was designing a studio for Theresa and Alfred at the time of Michael's birth.

With Siegfried Loraine, born two years later on 8 September 1886, the situation is reversed. The choice of names is clear, whereas the godfather is not. Theresa chose to call her second son Siegfried mainly because of her admiration for Wagner's operas, but also because at eleven pounds he was an exceptionally large baby. 'Loraine' was chosen as a tribute to the clergyman who had advised Hamo and Theresa when they were organizing her clandestine marriage in January 1884 and who was presumably Siegfried's godfather.[3] Like Michael he was christened at St Stephen's, a High Anglican church in Tunbridge Wells.[4]

With Hamo Watts, born less than a year after Siegfried on 4 August 1887, the choice of names and godfather is entirely understandable. By choosing 'Hamo' his parents were expressing their affection for Theresa's brother, who had been so helpful in arranging their marriage. The second name is a reference to the painter G.F. Watts, the illustrious Thornycroft family friend who also agreed to be their third son's godfather. Siegfried grew up admiring the Watts paintings which surrounded him and was envious of his younger brother's sponsor. Ironically, Hamo took no interest in either Watts or his work. He treated his second name as a joke, saying that he ought to have been called 'Hamo What Sassoon'.

No more children followed after 1887 and, though by today's standards this would not be surprising, in the late-Victorian period it was a small family. One explanation may lie in Theresa's age. When her last child was born she was thirty-four, an age at which some women's fertility starts to decline rapidly. Like her mother, who had also married a man appreciably younger than herself, Theresa was very sensitive about her age and had already started to lie about it. In order to make the eight-year gap between herself and Alfred seem less, she had given her age as twenty-nine, not thirty, on their marriage certificate. Later she was to deduct at least four years from her age, emulating her mother who had subtracted five from hers.

Another possible reason for the absence of more children is that Alfred and Theresa, both of whom loved freedom and independence, deliberately limited their family by some form of birth control, though Theresa's religious principles make this unlikely.[5] The most probable explanation is that by 1887 to 1888 their passionate relationship, which was to end tragically for all concerned, was already in crisis.

In 1884, however, Alfred and Theresa were still extremely happy. As soon as they returned from their honeymoon, they started looking for a house. They had decided to live in the country. Alfred had grown up in what was a distinctly rural area in the 1860s and 1870s and Theresa had greatly enjoyed visits to her Thornycroft farming relatives in Cheshire. In addition, though Alfred's income was generous, it was not princely and they may have felt that it was better to have a large house outside London than a more modest one in it.[6]

Together they decided on the Weald of Kent, which was then quite unspoilt by modern developments. The agricultural problems which were affecting many country areas towards the end of the nineteenth century had left Kent relatively untouched. Another important consideration was its proximity to London and its excellent rail network. And since it had not yet become commuter country, house prices were still quite reasonable.

The strongest motive for choosing Kent, however, may have been personal recommendation. In 1883 Hamo Thornycroft had become engaged to Agatha Cox and had grown to love the countryside around her home near Tonbridge. He had also found the train journey from Charing Cross very convenient on the many visits he paid Agatha. It was almost certainly on his recommendation that Alfred and Theresa started house-hunting in that area. From the Thornycroft family house in Melbury Road, where they were staying meantime, Alfred set out on 22 April 1884 with his father-in-law to inspect a large, rambling edifice near Paddock Wood, called Weirleigh. Alfred had already rejected a house at Penshurst, a village five miles to the south-west of Tonbridge famous for its Sir Philip Sidney connexions. He had found it 'too low and damp'.[7]

Weirleigh, which was on a hill just outside the village of Matfield, was a few miles further from Tonbridge but only a mile and a half from the railway station at Paddock Wood. Hamo and Agatha had walked over to see it from Tonbridge and obviously thought it worth recommending. (The upright Hamo would have liked the Latin inscription over the door: *Vero nihil verius*, or, Nothing is truer than truth.) Theresa had a chance to see the area again for herself when she and Alfred accompanied the rest of her family down to Tonbridge on 17 May for Hamo's wedding, though by that time Alfred had already bought Weirleigh. His only objection to the house had been the price, but this was evidently overcome. Perhaps the bidding at the auction on 14 May had been less keen than anticipated. Whatever the explanation, by the time Michael was born in October, the Sassoons were comfortably established there. It was to remain Theresa's home for the rest of her very long life.

Messrs. WALKER and RUNTZ at the Mart, London, on Wednesday, May 14, at 2, in one lot, the artistic and conveniently arranged FREEHOLD RESIDENCE, built in a most substantial manner from the designs of a well-known firm of architects, and known as Weirleigh, Brenchley, Kent, containing nine bedrooms, well-proportioned drawing and dining rooms, breakfast room, library, study, serving lobby, domestic offices, store rooms, cellarage &c. The grounds are very beautiful and attractive, they are tastefully laid out with lawns, shrubberies, ferneries, &c., and are filled with choice blooming shrubs, fruit and other trees, and herbaceous plants, and contain two vineries and picturesque buildings for potting and tool houses, fruit room &c.; a productive orchard with stable, cow shed, poultry houses, fowl runs, duck pond, &c. The whole containing about seven acres, and forms one of the choicest residential properties in Kent. May be viewed by cards and particulars, plans and views of the house obtained of Messrs. Billinghurst and Wood, Solicitors, 7 Bucklesbury, London E.C.; of E. Hillman, Esq., Solicitor, Lewes, Sussex; at the Rose and Crown Hotel, Tonbridge; Royal Kentish Hotel, Tunbridge Wells; Mitre Hotel, Maidstone; Saracen's Head Hotel, Ashford; and of the Auctioneers, 22 Moorgate Street, London.

The Times, 23 April 1884

Weirleigh was sold as a 'gentleman's residence' and Alfred was determined to appoint it as such. His will refers to 'all my furniture, plate, plated goods, linen, glass, china, books, manuscripts, pictures, portraits, prints, statuary, musical instruments ... Also my wines, liquors and consumable stores and provisions and all my horses, carriages, harness, saddlery and stable furniture and all my plants and garden and farm utensils, tools and implements.' Not content with that, Alfred also decided to have a studio and stable-block added to the property and commissioned the Thornycrofts' friend, John Belcher, to design these. Theresa intended to carry on painting and Alfred clearly wanted to encourage her, as well as continuing to work at sculpting himself.

It is impossible to exaggerate the importance of Weirleigh to Siegfried, both as a child and as a young man. Though critical of its rather eccentric architecture, particularly its tiled central tower which rose sixty feet from the road to which it was too close, and while he agreed with his mother's criticism that it was 'full of waste space and designed without decorum'[8], he loved Weirleigh deeply. His lyrical account of boyhood in *The Old Century* centres firmly around the rambling Victorian house and lovingly describes its many distinctive features.

Built in the 1860s it had been added to, probably in the 1870s, by its previous owner, Harrison Weir, from whom it also derived its odd name. Weir, a well-known artist in his day, was so proud of his tower that he had a large lamp lit in it every evening so that it could be seen for miles around.[9] Theresa's reaction to the tower was one of dislike, which turned to apprehension once she found herself with three mischievous boys on her hands. She had the entrance to it altered in an unsuccessful attempt to hide it from her sons.

Siegfried's earliest memories centred round the day and night nurseries at the southern end of the first floor, overlooking the front gate and well away from his parents' and visitors' bedrooms. Alfred and Theresa's world revolved around the spacious, low-windowed drawing-room on the ground floor which led straight out into the garden with its dramatic view of the Weald. An equally large dining-room also looked out over the Weald to the north. The solid stone basement was given over to a servants' hall and kitchen, as well as various store-rooms. The attic floor too was taken up mainly by servants' bedrooms. For a town-dweller from the late twentieth century, to whom every inch of living-space is precious, Weirleigh today seems full not so much of Theresa's dismissive 'waste space' but of elbow-room; it seems an ideal home in which to bring up three energetic boys.

When the adult Siegfried, as his mother's executor, arranged in 1947 to sell Weirleigh, he described it to a friend as 'badly designed, short of bedrooms and on a main road' but added 'the garden is lovely'.[10] However critical he became of the house, he always remembered its gardens with deep affection. It was not so much the 'lawns and shrubberies' of *The Times*' advertisement, as its size, diversity and secret corners where he and his brothers could hide and act out exciting fantasies. It consisted, since it sloped considerably, of 'upper', 'lower' and 'bottom' lawns with a large kitchen garden and orchard even further down the hill. Apart from a host of herbaceous borders and old-fashioned shrubberies, it boasted a working vinery, a Peony Walk, an alcove draped in Virginia creeper, a tennis court, a pond, pigeon bath, mounting block and several potting sheds. Added to these were Theresa's newly-built studio and an old cottage which the previous owner had used as his studio. John Richardson, the son of Siegfried's beloved groom Tom, worked for two years as a gardener's boy at Weirleigh in the twenties and said the timetable never varied. As the seasons came and went, so various rituals of lifting, sowing, thinning and planting out would be repeated.

The same varieties of flowers would appear year after year, to be gathered in generous armfuls by the impetuous Theresa to give to departing friends. In one passage of his autobiography alone Siegfried mentions tea-roses, lilies, tree-peonies, lavender, grapes, plums, blackcurrant bushes, melon and cucumber frames, asparagus-beds, raspberry-canes, rhododendrons, a bird cherry and an old leaning may tree. Trees figured largely in his memories of Weirleigh's garden – the magnolia near the front gate, the fig in the pump-yard, the Wellingtonia and large cedar tree on the upper lawn, the red may trees below his bedroom window, the crab-apple, the Irish yews, the quince which grew beside the little pond and the sweet-briar hedge in which cricket-balls got lodged. He could never think of the garden afterwards without a sense of heartache, as if it contained something which he had never quite been able to discover. Its elusive promise continued to haunt his sleep long after he had left it:

> With a sense of abiding strangeness [he wrote in his first prose recreation of childhood] I see myself looking down from an upper window on a confusion of green branches shaken by the summer breeze. In an endless variety of dream-distorted versions the garden persists as the background of my unconscious existence.[11]

Weirleigh garden was an Aladdin's cave to a small boy, but the view from it was, if possible, even more magical to Siegfried. The horizon seemed always blue to him as a child, with a mystical haze that encouraged his already pronounced day-dreaming. He fell into that category of children who are genuinely appreciative of their surroundings and maintained, well into adulthood, that Weirleigh had as good a view as anyone could wish to live with.[12] He was able to run his eyes along more than twenty miles of a low-hilled horizon never more than twelve miles away. With his toy telescope he could identify to the north-east a group of pine-trees on the skyline towards Maidstone and, nearer at hand, the twenty or more distinctive cowls of Beltring hop-kilns. The foreground formed a gentler view of meadows, orchards and the less dramatic oast-houses of smaller hop-farms. Several rivers threaded their way through this peaceful landscape, the most familiar being the tiny Beult and Teise which eventually joined the much larger Medway. Toy-trains made their leisurely way up the valley to London and down to the coast, whistling derisively, or so it seemed to the small boy, as they bustled through his local station of Paddock Wood without stopping.

It was a magnificent view in all weathers which made a deep impression on an acutely sensitive child, leaving Siegfried with a lasting love of nature. This comes through repeatedly in his work, all but his harshest satires. As late as 1910, when he had been writing poetry for at least thirteen years, he realized that he had only two real subjects, one of which was 'early morning'.[13] Two poems written almost certainly while he was still living at Weirleigh between 1907 and 1914 suggest that dawn had a special significance for him. In 'Before Day', which Edmund Blunden praised as a 'beautiful natural song of personality and England's meaning',[14] Siegfried implies that he finds a particular kind of freedom and inspiration in the moment before the day begins. The setting is obviously Weirleigh and the view from its garden:

> Come in this hour to set my spirit free
> When earth is no more mine though night goes out,
> And stretching forth these arms I cannot be
> Lord of winged sunrise and dim Arcady:
> When fieldward boys far off with clack and shout
> From orchards scare the birds in sudden rout,
> Come, ere my heart grows cold and full of doubt,
> In the still summer dawns that waken me.
>
> When the first lark goes up to look for day
> And morning glimmers out of dreams, come then
> Out of the songless valleys, over grey
> Wide misty lands to bring me on my way:
> For I am lone, a dweller among men
> Hungered for what my heart shall never say.
>
> (*CP*, p. 64)

The quiet mysticism of this sonnet remains a recognizable feature of Sassoon's poetry throughout his career. So too does his love of nature, which was both stimulated and fed by his childhood in the glorious Weald of Kent. The second poem, 'Daybreak in the Garden', based on his habit of stealing downstairs at dawn as a child, lovingly dwells on the sounds and sights he experienced in the garden, as well as features of the actual garden – its multiple lawns, may trees and Peony Walk:

> I heard the farm cocks crowing, loud, and faint, and thin,
> When hooded night was going and one clear planet winked:
> I heard shrill notes begin down the spired wood distinct,
> When cloudy shoals were chinked and gilt with fires of day.
> White-misted was the weald; the lawns were silver-grey;
> The lark his lonely field for heaven had forsaken;
> And the wind upon its way whispered the boughs of may,
> And touched the nodding peony-flowers to bid them waken.
>
> (*CP*, p. 59)

Siegfried's prose reminiscences of Weirleigh's garden include more mundane details, such as the fact that it was tended by a full-time staff of three – a head-gardener, Mr Reeves, and two under-gardeners, Mabb and Ely. The Sassoon boys appreciated Mr Reeves in particular, since they could always guarantee to provoke his uncertain temper. Their favourite trick was to throw his own seed-potatoes at him from the tangled undergrowth at the garden's extremities. Another was to jeer at him from an upstairs window as he took his turn unwillingly with Mabb and Ely at the pump for an hour daily, the time it took to supply the house with water. Mr Reeves, who was short, bearded and brown-bowlered, lived with his wife in rooms above the newly-built stable block just down the hill from Weirleigh. Mabb and Ely, who tolerated the potato-throwing with a better humour, were local men and came in daily. So was the odd-job man, who also helped in the garden when he was not too busy trimming and filling oil-lamps, carrying wood and coal for the fires, cleaning shoes or doing other work considered unsuitable for the maids.

Like most middle-class Victorian households, the Sassoons had at least three maids and a cook, whose names changed from time to time but whose functions remained constant. Mrs Battersen, the cook in Siegfried's childhood, reigned 'below stairs' so that life should run smoothly above. John Richardson, the groom's son, who frequently visited her kitchen as a child and young man, remembers it as a place of ceaseless activity. He was particularly fascinated, as Siegfried no doubt was, by the turnspit in front of the fireplace. He also vividly recalled the iron coal-range, the large table on which Mrs Battersen worked, the primitive earthenware sink with its one cold tap and the numerous cupboards and shelves filled with crockery and copper saucepans of all sizes. Just outside the kitchen door, in the days before refrigerators, was a larder dug out of a deep bank. As a small boy John would be given a glass of milk and a large slice of cake. He might even be allowed to play with the spit, while his mother collected or delivered household sewing.

Siegfried's recollection of the same kitchen in *The Memoirs of a Fox-Hunting Man* is less sympathetic and displays what he admits was 'a well-developed bump of snobbishness as regards flunkeydom and carriage-and-pair ostentation as a whole'.[15] It also reveals an early aversion to women in general. As the protagonist, George, returns from his first ride alone, humiliated because his pony has cantered home without him, he passes the 'fat, red-faced cook' in the basement and is immediately surrounded by the 'gaping' kitchen-maid and parlour-maid.[16] He feels himself 'inundated by exasperating female curiosity and concern' and resents the 'feminine fussiness'.

The kitchen-maid to whom he refers so dismissively was the lowliest servant in the household. Sometimes known as the scullery-maid, she would have had to do all the menial tasks below stairs. Her namelessness in Siegfried's autobiography is probably an indication of how low she ranked in the hierarchy. The housemaid, on the other hand, *is* named – Lizzie. She was responsible for most of the cleaning above stairs. It would be her job to clean the bedrooms, make the beds, beeswax the broad oak staircase and the parquet floor in the drawing-room and polish the Spanish leather-screen behind the piano, similarly the Sheraton sideboard in the dining-room and the rest of the furniture.

Emily Eyles, the parlourmaid, was ostensibly in charge of lighter duties in the drawing- and dining-rooms. While Theresa herself arranged the bowls of flowers which filled each room, Emily would set out the blue and yellow eggshell china and 'polite little cakes and sandwiches' which Siegfried remembered as part of the ritual welcome for 'dear old ladies' visiting from their summer retreat at Tunbridge Wells:

> An open barouche from the livery stables would bring them, in their best bonnets, along the dozing afternoon road – just a comfortable hour's drive if you told the coachman to take the hills at a walk.[17]

Besides waiting on such guests, Emily's duties were, in theory, to serve the family at meals, answer the front door and to do a little light dusting. In reality, as the boys grew more boisterous and Theresa more harassed, Emily devoted most of her time to them. She was much tougher than her innocent blue eyes and fair hair led people to think, possibly because, as Siegfried suggests, she had inherited her blacksmith father's fortitude. She joined in the boys' roughest games and then, when they finally felt like sitting still in the evenings, would read them their favourite books – *Coral Island*, *Tom Sawyer*, *Around the World in Eighty Days*, *Black Beauty*, *Treasure Island* and, rather unexpectedly, *The Diary of a Nobody*.[18]

The boys' official minder was Mrs Mitchell, who had been their nurse ever since Siegfried could remember. Just as Mrs Battersen ruled in the kitchen, so Mrs Mitchell conducted her reign of terror in the nursery. Devoted as Michael, Siegfried and Hamo were to their mother, they took far more notice of Mrs Mitchell. She represented the Old Testament for Siegfried, while his more indulgent 'Mamsy', as he called Theresa, represented the New. Mrs Mitchell was what is commonly called a 'tartar', though Siegfried's 'nursery Jehovah' is perhaps more accurate. With her hard gipsy face, her relish for the lugubrious and a mind as dark as the 'glory-hole' where she kept her prized possessions next to the nursery, Mrs Mitchell tried to frighten her charges into submission. Those who disobeyed were locked into the same 'glory-hole' until they repented. Yet for all her harshness, bad temper and old-fashioned ideas, Siegfried seems to have felt some affection for her, even if only that bred of familiarity. Her monthly trips by carrier's van to visit her daughter in Tunbridge Wells and her weekly perusal of her only reading matter, *The Kent and Sussex Courier*, became part of his life. Over the years he and his brothers shared a number of jokes and treats with her. Siegfried particularly liked the way she exclaimed 'Oh my stars and garters and Betty Martins!' when surprised.[19]

Mrs Mitchell was very conscious of her superiority to the other servants and Siegfried remembered her dominating proceedings at the 'Servants' Hall Party', held annually in Theresa's large studio, just as she held sway in the nursery. Theresa was a devoted mother but she had less influence than Mrs Mitchell, mainly because of the prevailing system of the day. Siegfried has left no personal memories of his first three years, but it is safe to say that they were dominated by Mrs Mitchell and the nursery routine. As each baby arrived it would be fed and cared for by her and, as each grew old enough, he would eat his meals at the nursery table with her, not with 'Mamsy' and 'Pappy' in the large north-facing dining-room. Since Theresa believed in the virtues of fresh air, there would be daily walks with Mrs Mitchell, rides in the dog-cart[20] and plenty of playing in the garden under nanny's stern eye.

Mrs Mitchell's strict discipline was, however, softened for Siegfried by the presence of his two brothers. As small children Michael, Hamo and he were very close indeed, and not only in age. They had their own private mental territory, as most children do, 'and a very independent one it was', according to Siegfried.[21] The fact that there were three of them enabled them to manage very well without other children and their mother's attempts to introduce 'little friends' were all fruitless.

This small self-contained world ran smoothly for Siegfried until at least his fourth year when his parents' relationship began to crumble. Before he was five his father had left home and one of Siegfried's first clear memories of childhood is of his conflict of feelings when Alfred returns on one of his weekly visits to his sons. The visit itself is eagerly awaited and thrilling: Alfred brings original presents, such as guava jelly, pomegranates and funny unbreakable toys, romps with them on the nursery floor and tells them wonderful jokes. In spite of his joy Siegfried is conscious, even at four, of his mother's extreme unhappiness. This is brought home to him sharply when Theresa, contrary to her usual custom of locking herself in the drawing-room, and perhaps with a forlorn hope of reconciliation, bumps into Alfred and the boys in the garden. All the merriment of a noisy wheelbarrow ride evaporates as Alfred remains stubbornly silent and Theresa looks deeply hurt. As a small, helpless child all Siegfried wants is for them to be reunited – 'for I wanted to enjoy my parents simultaneously – not alternately'.[22]

Alfred and Theresa seem to have been happy together at Weirleigh for at least the first four years of their married life and it is sad that Siegfried was too young to remember or appreciate it. Whilst bearing in quick succession three children whom she adored, Theresa launched herself enthusiastically into the role of Victorian country hostess with Alfred at her side. They gave and received lunches, dinners, teas, even weekends with a prodigality that would overwhelm most late twentieth century mortals. On the 22 January 1887, for example, only three and a half months after Theresa had had Siegfried and was already pregnant with Hamo, she and Alfred went to dinner with Hamo and Agatha Thornycroft, who were living nearby. The latter returned the visit on 26 April.[23] And so life went on, filled with the ritual of 'calling' on neighbours and setting in train a host of social engagements, all serviced by at least eight full-time staff.

One of the Sassoons' favourite forms of entertainment, which Theresa had enjoyed before marriage and which gave full reign to Alfred's talents, were musical evenings. Theresa's older brother John sometimes attended these with his daughter Mary. Her recollection, corroborated by Siegfried, was of Alfred playing wild gipsy music. He had a collection of old musical instruments – a viola da gamba, some 'dim-gilt' lutes and guitars – but his favourite remained the violin, which he played with what Mary felt was an almost diabolical abandon and skill.[24] Theresa's piano playing was sedate and amateurish by comparison but she enjoyed music enormously and made sure it was part of her sons' lives even after her husband had left.

Another interest Theresa shared with Alfred, riding, was indulged freely at Weirleigh. It is significant that one of their first additions to the property had been to have a large stable-block built. Here they kept several thoroughbreds and at least two ponies, one to pull the lawn-mower and one for the dog-cart. (There is a charming photograph of Theresa driving her sons in a smart two-wheeled trap with brass lamps.) The groom, who slept in the tack-room in those early years, would not only look after the horses but also drive Theresa out in the trap when she travelled locally. Though Alfred shared Theresa's love of horses, he disliked what he called 'horsey-society' and almost certainly did not hunt. Theresa, who was a fearless rider, frequently did. When Hamo visited her in 1893 he commented on his 'lovely ride on a thoroughbred mare with Theresa on her Swift' and Siegfried himself referred to his mother hunting, which he claimed had influenced his own love of the sport.[25]

Apart from horses, Alfred and Theresa also shared an interest in their newly-built studio where they worked together, at least to begin with. Not surprisingly, and unlike most modern mothers, Theresa found it easier to carry on painting when her children were little. When Siegfried was only three, for example, she exhibited his favourite picture, 'The Hours', at the Royal Academy. Once the boys were capable of sitting still, she used them as models and took Siegfried on at least one of her painting expeditions.[26] Siegfried did not remember his father painting but describes a picture executed by Alfred at this time from the window of the big upstairs room over the studio itself:

a panoramic and amateurish watercolour of the view across the Weald; very green and uninhabited he had made it look, though perhaps he had left out some of the distant details on purpose.

Almost as an afterthought, he underlines the difference between his parents: 'My mother would have made it look much more what it really was ...'[27] There is no mention of Alfred continuing to sculpt, in spite of having enrolled himself as a sculpture student at the Royal Academy and given 'sculptor' as his profession on his marriage certificate in 1884. Siegfried does, however, refer to a large statue of 'The Dying Gladiator' in the studio and we know that his Aunt Alyce was sculpting there in the mid-1890s.

One activity Theresa could not join in with Alfred was cricket, though she may have gone to watch him play on the local village-greens at Matfield and Brenchley. It was not only Alfred's skill which made him popular with the villagers on these occasions, but his sharp sense of humour which they remembered nostalgically long after he had left.

As late as March 1888 Alfred and Theresa were holidaying alone together in Venice and clearly enjoying it. Hamo reported to his wife on 19 March that Theresa had written enthusiastically of Venice, not then at its warmest: however, their 'enthusiasm seems to keep them warm'.[28]

Was this holiday an attempt to revive a flagging interest on Alfred's part? It is impossible to say, but by May 1889 Theresa appears to be on her own at Weirleigh when Hamo visits her there. She also makes frequent trips to London on her own between the end of 1889 and March 1890, when Hamo finally confirms that her marriage is in pieces. Writing to his wife on 11 March 1890 he also reveals a deep-rooted anti-Semitism which may explain Alfred's lack of closeness to Theresa's family:

Theresa were it not for her three bairns would be very lonely at Weirleigh as her husband is behaving like a madman. He is a caution to us Westerns. Don't be tempted to marry where there [is] Eastern blood and a Sematic [*sic*] nostril. Poor Theresa. She is a plucky one indeed, and a treasure of a woman and one of the brightest of companions possible. For justice sake there should have been a purgatory for such as he.[29]

By 1891 Alfred has left Weirleigh for good, having run away, according to the family, with Theresa's best friend. One version is that the lady in question was Jewish, and the 'match' set up by Alfred's family to lure him back to the faith. It is more likely, however, that Siegfried was nearer the truth when he wrote that his father had run away with the novelist Constance Fletcher, who wrote under the pseudonym George Fleming and who had been a close friend of Oscar Wilde. The relationship does not seem to have lasted long. By 1892 Alfred Sassoon is established to all appearances on his own at 8 Pembroke Studios, Pembroke Gardens in London. He probably moved there when the studios were built in 1891. What is certain is that he is still describing himself, in *Kelly's Post Office Directory*, as a 'sculptor'. His neighbours are all aspiring artists and he is once more back in the bohemian world from which Weirleigh had temporarily separated him.

Years later, when Siegfried searched for his father's studio, he went mistakenly to Pembroke Square and failed to find it, but the search in itself is significant. He was 'intensely interested' to discover that his friend Sydney Cockerell had met a Sassoon in the early nineties in the company of an artist named Randall:

> This must have been my father, who was then in his early 30s, pale and delicate looking, with a dark moustache. Anything you can recollect of your impression of him would be of the deepest interest to me – favourable or otherwise. My own memory of him is that he was moody, rather quiet, but extremely good company when in good spirits – (very fond of making jokes). He had the artistic temperament, but no talent, except in his violin-playing, which is described by those who heard him, as really remarkable. At that time, however, he was unhappy and declining into consumption, and his married life had ended in failure through incompatibility of temperament.[30]

Just as Siegfried had got his father's address slightly wrong, so is it likely that Alfred's artist friend was not 'Randall' but Henry Ryland, who moved into the newly-built Pembroke Studios from Bolton Studios in 1891 and was living at no. 2 while Alfred was at no. 8. (Ryland painted a great deal between 1890 and 1893.)

Siegfried's low opinion of his father's abilities as a sculptor almost certainly derived from his mother, since he never saw anything executed by him in this discipline. It may also have been Theresa who blamed the failure of their marriage on incompatibility of temperament, a theory which Siegfried would no doubt have found comforting.

Added to an undeniable difference of temperament between the religious, hard-working Theresa and her more light-hearted husband were a number of other factors. Living in the country, while it delighted Theresa, particularly in her new maternal role, almost certainly frustrated Alfred's highly-developed need for a rich social life. Unlike Theresa he missed the stimulus of London which allowed for a much wider circle of friends. Alfred's reputation as a 'womanizer' was probably well-founded and, though he seems to have been in love with Theresa when they married, he probably came to miss the variety of women he had enjoyed in Paris, for example, as a precocious teenager.

There was also a huge cultural gap between Alfred, the first member of a distinguished, orthodox Jewish family to be born in England, and Theresa, an extremely devout Christian whose family was totally dedicated to art. Though Alfred had renounced his faith for Theresa, he could not have entirely rid himself of his orthodox upbringing and it is unlikely that he would have sympathized deeply with her strong High Anglican beliefs.

Another factor which must have become more important as time passed was the difference in age between the two. When Alfred began to tire of Theresa in 1889, he was still only twenty-eight. Whereas she, in her late thirties, was beginning to settle down in the country with their three children, he was obviously far from ready for the role of dutiful husband and family man. The almost immediate arrival of children after their hasty courtship and marriage did not allow either of them much freedom together, but Theresa may have felt that she did not have all the time in the world. Whether Alfred left because he was in love with Theresa's best friend is probably irrelevant, since that affair came to a rapid end and he could have returned to his wife afterwards had he wished. Taking into consideration his increasingly bad health in the early nineties he must have felt very hostile indeed, both to his wife and to Weirleigh, not to have done so. Even his love for his sons could not bring about the reconciliation for which Siegfried longed. It is possible that Alfred's own early loss of his father had damaged his ability to carry out the role satisfactorily himself. Siegfried never doubted his affection, but he did mourn his father's stubborn refusal to talk to or even see his mother following the break.

Though Theresa was very unhappy after Alfred left, she was resilient and even while Hamo is accusing her husband of behaving 'like a madman' in March 1890, he praises her as 'a plucky one ... one of the brightest'. By December 1893 he tells his wife that Theresa is 'as merry as ever'.[31] In later life Siegfried wrote of his mother that:

> Time teaches one to admire such people, who refuse to pull a long face however deeply life may have hurt them, and whose cheerfulness is born of courage as well as being the outcome of their abundant aliveness.[32]

Alfred himself was not particularly happy in his new situation, but he clearly found it preferable to living with Theresa. It was their children who suffered the most, Siegfried possibly most of all. Though he thought that his father was such an incalculable character that it was useless trying to imagine what effect he would have had on his upbringing, he nevertheless remembered Alfred's repeated promise that he would take him to see foreign countries. He cherished all the relics left behind by his father – his musical instruments, his amateurish painting and, in particular, the copy of Fitzgerald's *Rubáiyát* – because they brought back sharp memories of a father he had enjoyed, interruptedly, for too short a time. He was to spend most of his childhood and quite a lot of his adulthood setting up substitute father-figures and reacting to the predominantly female world to which his father had abandoned him.

The most immediate effect of Alfred's departure, however, was to make Siegfried emotionally more dependent on his mother, to whom he felt unusually close. When a friend asked in later life about his relations with Theresa, he replied: 'Yes, in a way I suppose I *was* my mother's favourite. She always said I was her "second self" '.[33] He also told a relative that he and Theresa were 'like one person'.[34] His mother, who identified with his imaginative nature more closely than with her two other sons' rather practical outlook, decided early on that Siegfried would become a poet, although she wisely never urged him to write poetry. For his third birthday she had inscribed a copy of Coleridge's lectures on Shakespeare to him, almost as though hoping to influence events.

When Siegfried did finally start writing poetry it was initially for his mother. In the quarrel between his parents, though he continued to love his father, his sympathies inclined more to his mother, whose unhappiness he witnessed at first hand. This close identification with her from an early age made it very difficult for him to separate himself from her when he grew older. However much they disagreed he found it virtually impossible to oppose her in case he increased her sufferings. His awareness of the sacrifices she had made is evident in a poem he wrote 'To My Mother' in 1928, when he was in his early forties and still unmarried:

> I watch you on your constant way,
> In selfless duty long grown grey;
> And to myself I say
> That I have lived my life to learn
> How lives like your unasking earn
> Aureoles that guide, and burn
>> In heart's remembrance when the proud
>> Who snared the suffrage of the crowd
>> Are dumb and dusty browed ...
> For you live onward in my thought
> Because you have not sought
> Rewards that can be bought.
>> And so when I remember you
>> I think of all things rich and true
>> That I have reaped and wrought.
>> (*CP*, pp. 268-9)

As a small child the closeness of family relations, even without a father, made for a security which Siegfried constantly looked back on with longing. But his view of the past was not quite so 'golden' as Michael Thorpe has suggested in his introduction to *The Old Century*.[35] His first attempt to write about his life, at the age of six or seven, was, on the contrary, entertainingly realistic:

Once upon a time there was three brothers. The eldest Michael a the second Siegfried a lazy cowerdly boy Hamo a savadge but beautiful boy and they sometimes quarreld, a quarrelsome family and thats all I know about that family.

'A Story about Weirleigh Brenchley Kent'[36]

2. Childhood in the Garden (1886-1895)

Siegfried's appreciation of male beauty, it seems, began at an early age.

Until at least 1895, when Siegfried was nine, Michael eleven and Hamo eight, the brothers were, in spite of their quarrels, very united in their tastes and treated in a very similar manner. Theresa kept their hair long and dressed them in smocks for longer than usual. (In a photograph taken in 1894 Hamo still has his hair in ringlets at the age of eight and all three boys are wearing smocks, albeit over knee-length white shorts.) When they were finally promoted to 'boys' ' clothes, they all wore identical brown jerseys and corduroy shorts.

Their mother's deep suspicion of boarding-schools, particularly the catering arrangements, led her to keep them at home until long past the usual age for boys of their class. She firmly believed that all her sons were delicate and that it would be a mistake for their 'brains to be overtaxed by a conventional education'.[37] In the context of Alfred's worsening tuberculosis in the early nineties, her fears are understandable and, in Siegfried's case at least, justified.

As a result of Theresa's distrust of schools Siegfried's education up to the age of eight and a half was, in his own words, 'elementary and irregular'.[38] It was left entirely to his nanny, Mrs Mitchell, and his mother to teach him to read and write. Judging from the first example we have of his work – an exercise book entitled *Celebrated Storeys*, begun in 1893 and inscribed to his mother sometime in 1894 or 1895 – they were neither of them outstanding teachers and he was not a natural scholar. The hand is slightly immature for a child of eight or nine and the spelling, punctuation and grammar are erratic. The coloured illustrations to the book and its lovingly illustrated borders, however, indicate someone of lively imagination. This is confirmed by the numerous stories, which range from those based on giants, kings, princesses, lucky rings and golden apples to more realistic ones, such as the 'Story About Weirleigh' already quoted. Another tale, with the tantalizing title 'I will dance thank you mam', describes a 'stout young man' who promises Mrs Mitchell that 'the young gentlemen could go to the mills in the spring'. The reference here is to a genial traction-engine driver, whom the brothers had met in real life and insisted should be invited to the Annual Servants' Hall Party. His offer to take them to the mills in the spring was clearly his way of saying thank you. With painful honesty and some poetry Siegfried records the outcome:

But we have not gone yet. all though the spring is long past. THE END.

The sequel, neatly titled 'I dont dance thank you mam', reveals that Siegfried's sense of humour as well as his ability to write vividly developed very early:

the man with the violin ... played very badly. so reeves said. go and get the

43

organ for nobody can dance to all this squeaking. So they got the organ. and the violin man said, Oh it goes through my Head like a bullet through cheese But he had to put up with it and so I believe he was very glad when supper time came. and Mrs Mitchell ask the stout young man to dance but he said. I dont dance thank you mam ...

In *Celebrated Storeys* the picture of the three Sassoon boys is particularly interesting: while Siegfried and Michael wear caps, Hamo – 'the savadge but beautiful boy' – has long hair and looks extremely feminine. There are at least five drawings of churches, which played a regular part in the boys' lives, some horses, a number of ships, accurately detailed by the nephew of the naval architect John Thornycroft, and some cartoons, one of Weirleigh's nursery. An illustration of the naval battle between China and Japan suggests that Siegfried was also being taught a little history. His preface – placed with some originality in the middle of the volume – claims not only that 'This book con[t]ains seventeen stories six pictures at the end it is the largest book I have written', but that he has also produced 'nine small books'. His scholarly 'Index' lists among these 'The Black Fairy Book', 'The Coulerd Fairy Book' and 'Little Storys'. (He freely admitted later that Andrew Lang's *Blue Fairy Book* was his model, for his 'undistracted imagination had been decently nourished' as a child 'on poetry, fairy-tales and fanciful illustrations'.[39])

Clearly Theresa believed that the combination of stimulating reading, imaginative writing and copious illustrating were the most important aspects of Siegfried's primary education, and he always retained his early habit of illustrating his work, often very beautifully. His main interest and ability was, however, in words and his mother recognized this. She read aloud to him her favourite poets, primarily the Romantics and the Pre-Raphaelites, which became his earliest poetic influences.

Another notebook surviving from Siegfried's childhood contains descriptions and illustrations of various butterflies, which suggests that he was also being introduced to some basic natural history in a fairly unsystematic fashion.[40] The only overtly academic subject Theresa attempted to teach him was Latin, when he was eight, but since her own knowledge of it was woefully limited and he had no natural gift for languages this was not a success and he remained stuck at *mensa*.[41] There must also have been some basic arithmetic, since the adult Sassoon remembers his delight as a child at missing some lessons in the subject. Unlike words or images, it failed to rouse his interest, so he tried to avoid it.

Of far greater interest to Siegfried and his brothers was their own world of games and outdoor activities. They had the usual assortment of pets – cats, tortoises, a series of canaries – and, less usually, a grey parrot. One of their favourite games was putting a cat in the dumb-waiter outside the dining-room and sending it down to the kitchen. Mischievous boys, full of physical energy, they preferred sliding down the banisters to walking downstairs, and needed a vent for their high spirits. The garden was much less rule-ridden than the house and in reasonable weather they spent the greater part of the day outdoors. For, as Siegfried himself asked: 'How could anything interesting happen ... indoors?'[42] Apart from throwing seed-potatoes at the irascible Mr Reeves, another favourite sport was to crawl in through the vinery window and borrow his 'squirt' which never failed to enrage him. Just as interesting, because it was also forbidden, was their attempt at trampolining on the net Theresa had ordered to be put over the garden pond in case they fell in. It eventually sagged so badly that it gave Siegfried the illusion of walking on water, a sensation he dreamt about many years later.[43]

Siegfried was particularly keen on butterfly-hunting, which they all pursued for a time, but their greatest shared interest was in a ramshackle hut they had made for themselves out of a hundred 'real red bricks' their mother had bought for the purpose.[44] Known as 'The Build', it enabled them to escape from the nursery even in wet weather. Siegfried, fed on Romantic literature, wanted it to have a second storey, which he dreamily imagined as a long loft containing sacks of malt. As it was, the boys enjoyed the seclusion of their single storey, sowing nasturtiums and tomatoes, which never came up, and on special occasions inviting their mother and Mrs Mitchell to tea there.

It was largely up to the boys to entertain themselves and this they managed to do in a way that would daunt a town child of the late twentieth century. In spite of the three years' gap between oldest and youngest, they all behaved as if they were the same age. When Theresa bought them a black pony, they all learnt to ride at the same time, though eventually Michael and Hamo lost interest. When she decided it was time for them to learn to swim, they were all taken down to the Medway at Wateringbury for lessons from Ted Avery. When, in the harsh winter of 1894 to 1895, she introduced them to ice-skating, they shared the one pair of boots available and tottered round the frozen pond in them in turn. Though Siegfried enjoyed these sports, except for swimming, he was extremely timid to begin with. No one watching him on his little pony would ever have anticipated that he would one day become a hard rider to hounds and winner of several point-to-points.

Theresa did attempt something of a social life for her sons, but her efforts at polite teas and dancing classes in the studio failed dismally. The boys, in their self-contained world, neither needed nor wanted them. More successful were the trips she organized beyond Weirleigh and its immediate surroundings. Because these were rare, they seemed very exciting to Siegfried. By the age of eleven, he claimed, he had been to no more than a dozen public entertainments in his life, and those included the circus, pantomimes, a Paderewski Recital in Tunbridge Wells and Maskelyne's Mysteries at the Egyptian Hall.[45] It is doubtful whether any of these took place before he was six, although he did pay a memorable visit to his uncle John Thornycroft's works at Chiswick before that age. It was not until 1893, his seventh year, that Siegfried started to make a systematic record of events, though the only 'event' as such was the boys' second visit to the Thornycroft works to see the launching of Uncle John's torpedo-gunboat, HMS *Speedy*.

After setting up the Thornycroft ship-building works at Chiswick with the help of his father in 1866, John had made rapid progress. Leaving the business side in the extremely efficient hands of his brother-in-law, John Donaldson ('Don') in 1872, he carried on with his inventions and soon established his name with his high-speed launches and his torpedo-boats. His first torpedo-boat built at Chiswick, the *Lightning*, was bought by the Royal Navy and named No. 1 Torpedo Boat. He then went on to design faster boats to carry the newly invented Whitehead torpedo. By 1885, the year before Siegfried was born, he had built twenty-five torpedo-boats for the Royal Navy, with a guaranteed speed of 19 knots. He also sold torpedo-boats abroad, including the *Ariete* with a speed of 25 knots to the Spanish navy. This caused some alarm to the British Government, which immediately ordered twenty-five boats of the same size and speed but with a superior fire-power, the forerunner of the destroyer. In the early 1890s three '27-knotters' were built and launched at Chiswick, almost certainly the occasion which Siegfried refers to as his first visit to his uncle's works. His second visit would have been on 18 May 1893, when the 3-funnel torpedo-boat, HMS *Speedy*, was launched by Lady Hamilton, wife of the First Lord of the Admiralty.[46] In 1902 Thornycroft's became a public company and in the same year its founder was knighted.[47]

When Siegfried went to see HMS *Speedy* launched in 1893, however, he knew little about his uncle's genius. 'Uncle John invented the tubular boiler' was the rather comic description he had learnt to attach to him as a child.[48] Nor did he have a very intimate knowledge of John's large family. He got to know them much better when he and his brothers were taken by Theresa to spend a month with them at their house on the Isle of Wight two years later. He was never to feel as close to his uncle John as he did to John's younger brother Hamo, but he greatly admired him. His first vivid impression of him, when John paid a brief visit to Weirleigh in 1894, was of a 'remarkable looking man, with his ruddy face, absent-minded eyes, and greying red-gold hair and beard'.[49] His main impression of him when he went to stay at John's family home the following year was of a 'pink-faced and fluffy-bearded man', 'smiling seraphically' as he busied himself in the garden. John's grand-daughter said that he looked 'exactly like Father Christmas', which is certainly the impression Siegfried gives.[50]

John, who was ten years older than his youngest sister Theresa, had married fourteen years before her in 1870. His seven children, by Blanche Coules, were, therefore, considerably older than the Sassoon boys. When they went to stay in 1895 the eldest son and five daughters were all grown-ups in their eyes and even the younger son, Tom, was a full-blown schoolboy. Siegfried was impressed by his highly practical, confident, handsome cousins. He admired Tom's real sailing-boat, his hideout at the top of a lime-tree and his knowledge of birds' eggs. While describing the month's holiday as 'glorious', he seems to have been rather overwhelmed by his cousins' physical prowess. Even their photographs came out 'splendidly'. When he went butterfly-hunting with his cousin Mary, he was 'dumb with admiration at the way she chased about with her large green net'.[51] The effortless skill with which she set her specimens made him feel rather depressed about his own untidy little collection at home. Even the house, Steyne, which was large and beautiful, overawed him.[52]

In such an uneventful childhood as Siegfried's, it is not surprising that this visit made a deep impression. So regular was the Sassoon boys' existence that, in winter particularly, even softened by hindsight, it seemed monotonous. Sitting day after day on the 'window-shelf' in the nursery passage, watching the rain trickle down the pane, they welcomed diversions, however unfortunate. When their apple-store was robbed in 1894 it provided a certain thrill and when Mrs Mitchell thought she heard burglars a short time later there was even more excitement. Theresa, who was very courageous, marched out of the pump-yard with an air-gun, attended by a shivering maid. But the burglars, if they existed, were unwilling to respond to her determined challenge.

This monotony was broken in 1894, a year dominated by grandmothers: Grandmama Thornycroft came to live at Weirleigh in the spring and the boys met their Sassoon grandmother for the first time in the autumn. Mary Thornycroft had become increasingly frail since the death of her husband Thomas, who had died at Weirleigh in 1885, the year before Siegfried was born there (though she had been well enough to spend the Christmas of 1893 with Theresa). By the spring of 1894 Mary, then nearly eighty-five, was installed permanently at Weirleigh, perhaps because her eldest, unmarried daughter, Alyce, lacked her youngest daughter's calm competence as a nurse.

Mary lived peacefully at Weirleigh through the summer and autumn of 1894, her presence probably preventing Theresa from taking the boys away on holiday that year. Siegfried remembered her in a black silk gown with white ruffles, sitting by the drawing room fireside window which had been double-glazed to protect her from draughts. The only sign of agitation he recalled was when she saw her grandsons climbing the Wellingtonia tree in the garden. Whilst Siegfried was aware that his grandmother was someone to be looked up to as well as loved, he did not realize then her true distinction as a sculptress. Her powers of empathy, even with a small child, had shown themselves when she had patched his old toy cow and he was grateful. He was not, however, particularly close to her, and when she died of pneumonia brought on by the severe winter of 1894-5, he could not honestly say that he missed her deeply.

Her last illness at the end of January 1895 had been exciting in a macabre way. The boys were forced to lead a subdued life in the nursery while John, Helen and Hamo, who were staying at the Camden Arms in Pembury, and Alyce, who had been put up in nearby Matfield, came daily to their mother's bedside. Several medical men, among them Theresa's own local physician, Dr Neild, were in attendance and Siegfried had dim memories of their carriages, with lamps like golden eyes, waiting outside the house in the middle of the night. Theresa seems to have been as anxious about her brothers' and sisters' well-being as her mother's and kept them all supplied in their respective inns with such luxuries as turtle soup and champagne, while they waited for the end. When it came, on 1 February, it was as peaceful and happy as death ever can be. Mary, who had lasted longer than anyone had expected, recovered from her delirium shortly before she died and sang 'Cradle-Song' to her assembled children, a bitter-sweet ending.[53]

Siegfried recovered rapidly from his grandmother's death. But his father's, less than three months later, left him utterly desolate. By the beginning of 1894 it had become clear that Alfred was seriously ill with what Mrs Mitchell called, with lugubrious relish, 'a galloping consumption'. Giving up all pretences of a carefree bohemian life, he had left his studio in Pembroke Gardens and moved to 50 Grand Parade, Eastbourne, probably for its sea air, milder climate and proximity to his mother.

Early in 1894 Mrs Mitchell, whom Siegfried suspected of being in collusion with his father against his mother, had taken the boys to stay at Eastbourne for several weeks. Though Alfred talked quite gaily of being well again and taking them abroad, Siegfried found him dreadfully thin and coughing badly. Alfred continued to lose weight and Siegfried began to realize that, however hard he prayed for 'Pappy's' recovery, death was becoming as inevitable as the incoming tide on Eastbourne beach. An awareness of it appears plainly on Alfred's face in the last photograph he arranged to have taken with his sons. As Siegfried points out, the boys look 'much too tidy and smirksome to be real. The only reality was in my father's face'.[54]

After the depressingly wet summer of 1894, it was quite clear to everyone, even the eight-year-old Siegfried, that his father had not much longer to live, however hard he prayed and consulted his toy cow. Alfred made his last will on 14 November and Mrs Mitchell took Siegfried and his brothers to Eastbourne again the same month. It was to say goodbye. This time it was not the shrimp teas Siegfried remembered but his father's relentless cough and his first meeting with his Sassoon grandmother, Flora.

The contrast with Mary Thornycroft, whom he was seeing daily at Weirleigh at this time, must have been striking. Unlike Mary, Flora was small and, as Siegfried tactfully put it, 'had rather a brown face'. She was very lively and, though equally as kind and delighted to see her grandsons as Mary, was not at all what they expected a grandmother to be. She looked, as indeed she was, much younger than Mary and dressed smartly rather than artistically. She had a disconcerting way of laughing at them when they were not trying to be funny. Though she looked as though she could be dignified, Siegfried found her flaunting of the Sassoon family tree rather vulgar.[55] In contrast Grandmama Thornycroft, sitting in her corner seat at Weirleigh, sipping her port wine and asking magnanimously to be remembered to her erring son-in-law, seemed restrained and more truly dignified.

The few days Siegfried spent forlornly in his father's sick-room at Eastbourne, depressed rather than cheered by the profusion of exotic flowers Flora had brought with her from Brighton, were engraved indelibly on his mind:

> From across the years it comes back to me, that picture of the sick-room, with dusk falling and 'Pappy's' face propped up on the pillows, and Grandmama Sassoon bending over us while her other son Joseph stood with his hands in his pockets, staring moodily out at the sunless seaside winter afternoon. And it comes back to me, that sense of being among strangers, with 'Pappy' being killed by that terrible cough, and the queer feeling that although this new grandmama was making such a fuss of us, it would make no difference if we never saw her again ... And I remember my miserable feeling that the only thing which mattered was that my mother ought to be there, and that these people were unfriendly to her who loved my father as they had never done and would have come to him with unquestioning forgiveness.[56]

Alfred lingered on until 18 April, 1895.[57] Although Siegfried was told that his death was a 'happy release' his grief was such that he was not allowed to go to the funeral with his brothers. His desolation stemmed from the feeling that 'so much happiness ... could never happen, now that he was dead, for he had made everything seem so promising when we were with him before he was ill'.[58]

His brothers' account of the funeral on 22 April 1895 gave Siegfried fresh cause for misery. Flora's last-minute reconciliation with her son had resulted in a Jewish burial at the New (Novo) Sephardic Cemetery in London's Mile End Road, where he was buried in one of a number of graves reserved for the Sassoon family. The foreignness of the occasion had frightened Michael and Hamo. To their childish eyes there was something queer and gruesome in the Jewish ceremony, held in Hebrew, particularly since they knew that their father had given up the Jewish faith when he married their mother. It also horrified Siegfried to think of his father being buried in a strange, squalid-sounding place rather than in their local Brenchley churchyard with its large yew trees and friendly bells.[59] 'The thought of Heaven', he remembered, 'was no help to me when those imagined sounds of outlandish lamentations were in my ears. I felt death in a new way now, and it seemed as though our father had been taken away from us by strangers'.[60]

Siegfried's grief for his father was complicated by the fact that Alfred, whom he adored, had sent no farewell message to Theresa, whom he also loved deeply. The division of loyalties that inevitably followed made him even more unhappy. He could see how brave and unselfish were his mother's attempts to comfort him and his brothers, but he was powerless to help her in return.

Alfred's will, though giving his address as Weirleigh, spelled out his antagonism towards Theresa. Even Mrs Mitchell, whom Siegfried believed had plotted against Theresa, seems to have been treated more kindly, with an annuity of £100. Theresa received only a legacy of £200. It is true that she inherited the personal possessions Alfred had left behind him at Weirleigh, except his Stradivarius. Some of his jewelry was valuable, enabling her to buy the family an occasional luxury, such as a new horse for Siegfried when he outgrew the little black pony. Most of what she was left, however, belonged to Weirleigh, which was held in trust for Alfred's sons.

Another significant aspect of the 1894 will is the change in trustees. In 1885, when Alfred had drawn up a 'post-nuptial' settlement, he had included Theresa's brother, Hamo, and her brother-in-law. John Donaldson, as his trustees. By November 1894 he had dropped Hamo and the third 1885 trustee, Russell Barrington, retaining John Donaldson as trustee and adding the Thornycroft family solicitor, Herbert Lousada. Both Donaldson and Lousada are left as much money as his wife, £200. Alfred's abandonment of Hamo suggests that the latter's strong reaction to his brother-in-law's infidelities had reached his ears. Perhaps Hamo had even tried to talk to him about the situation. On the other hand, John Donaldson was known in the family as a good businessman with a sound sense of money. It was he alone, according to John Thornycroft's granddaughter, who had brought about the financial success of the Chiswick ship-building works.

Alfred's will instructs Donaldson and Lousada to invest his money in such stocks as they think fit and to hold it in trust for his children until they reach the age of twenty-one. It is the trustees, rather than Theresa, who are to pay out money for the children's education and make them an allowance if they think it justifiable. Alfred's estate is valued at £5,410 1s. 1d., a great deal of money in 1895 but hardly the kind of sum one would expect from the wealthy Sassoons. Thomas Thornycroft, for example, when he died ten years earlier had left £11,046 3s. 3d. By defying his mother, Alfred had cut himself off from her money, even though he received money from his father's will. He had also increased his expenditure considerably by running two households from about 1890 onwards, and he was not in the habit of stinting himself. It is not surprising that Siegfried later saw himself as a 'poor relation' of the almost uniformly rich

Sassoons. His own allowance, when he started to receive one, was sufficient for him not to have to work but not enough for him to live as he would have liked.

In April 1895, money was far from Siegfried's mind. It had, however, probably caused Mrs Mitchell to leave, an event which was to change his life considerably. Whether it was Alfred's generous annuity or Theresa's deep suspicion of her which prompted the break is not clear, but shortly after the funeral she emptied out her 'glory-hole', packed her bags and left. It was the end of an era. Far from ideal in Siegfried's eyes, Mrs Mitchell nonetheless represented stability and continuity in his already disturbed life. Her departure increased his strong sense of loss and consequent insecurity. On the evening she had gone he remembered how curious it was to be left out in the chilly garden until dusk without anyone coming, as she usually did, to call him in.

The combination of the cold, his own low state and possibly weak lungs (at least so his mother thought) brought on an attack of pneumonia that same evening which took Siegfried into a very different world for the next two months. To begin with, his temperature rose to 105° and he became delirious. In his own words, he inhabited a strange but fascinating region which was like being outside the world altogether. It seemed to him afterwards that he had had a supernatural revelation: 'Those vague multitudes under enormous flame-lit arches – what could they have been if they were not something to do with death'.[61]

His attempt to follow his father, if that is what it was, failed, mercifully for Theresa. Her feelings as she watched the third person she loved struggling for life that year can only be guessed at. Her joy at his recovery was correspondingly great and her subsequent fussing over him wholly understandable. When her favourite son began to feel better and the May days grew warmer, she had a little tent erected for him on the lawn. Every day he was carried down to spend the day there. Theresa thought him far too weak to walk and Siegfried, who enjoyed being spoilt and still felt fragile, kept up this ritual for as long as he could.

Siegfried dated his first real desire to be a poet from his convalescence in the early summer garden. His senses, already sharpened almost unbearably by the recent experience of his father's death and his own brush with it, responded quiveringly to the beauty of his surroundings and the unaccustomed solitude. He lay there, revelling in the blue visions of the Weald beyond the green treetops, as he listened to the sounds of the garden and the daily household rituals – his brothers playing in the 'Build' or practising their music in the drawing-room, the gruff voices of gardeners, jays squawking, scythes being sharpened in the orchard, or his mother's voice as she set out on her leisurely afternoon ride.

Except for the unavoidable interruptions of the mid-morning egg-nog prescribed by Dr Neild and various meals, he was left almost entirely alone and he loved it: 'I was beginning to discover that solitude could quicken my awareness of aspects within me and around me. My pneumonia had revealed that I had a mind with which I liked to be alone'.[62] It was the beginning of poetic consciousness, if not yet of actual poetry; the poetry was to come only a year later.

3

Lutes and Nightingales
(1895-1900)

The last five years of the nineteenth century are crucial to Siegfried's development. He begins this period with his father's death uppermost in his mind. His subsequent illness and isolated convalescence strengthen his vague ambitions to become a poet and the next four years show him trying to make that dream a reality. His education, which had been entrusted initially to the amateurish hands of his mother and Mrs Mitchell, took a more resolute turn with Theresa's appointment in September 1895 of a professional tutor, the first of several; though he remained far removed from the world of conventional schooling. Still living largely in his own world, the only time he seems to become aware of outside events is when Queen Victoria's Diamond Jubilee is celebrated in 1897 with numerous bonfires across the Kentish Weald and the planting of a Jubilee Oak on Matfield Green. More importantly, from his point of view, he is granted a whole day off from schooling.

By 1895 both Siegfried and Michael might reasonably have been expected to be sent away to school but Theresa, now left entirely on her own, could not bring herself to part with them. As Siegfried later realized, she kept her children at home from a growing distrust of the outside world. Having acted recklessly once by rushing into marriage with Alfred, she was not ready to put her faith again in anyone but herself. She did, however, recognize the need for more professional teaching than either she or Mrs Mitchell had been able to provide.

Siegfried's introduction to more formal education was a very gentle one. Though Theresa had already planned the change by March 1895, she softened the impact by inviting an old friend of hers, Miss Ellen Batty, to 'do lessons' with her sons in the spring of that year.[1] Siegfried's pneumonia in April left him so weak that he was excused work whilst recuperating in June. Therefore, instead of introducing him to the harsh world of mathematics, Latin and other traditional school subjects, Miss Batty helped nurse him through his convalescence, becoming his 'devoted slave' in the process.[2] She kept him amused with an endless fund of stories about India, where many of her relatives had gone to rule the Empire.

Though not a professional governess, Miss Batty had looked after nephews and nieces in the school holidays and had invented an 'interminable improvisation about a *punkah-wallah*' which had kept them, and was to keep Siegfried, amused.³ She also entertained Siegfried with numerous stories from the Old Testament. He was familiar with most of them, since Theresa made sure that her sons received an adequate Christian upbringing. But Miss Batty made the stories seem new and exciting, in spite of the special voice she reserved for the Bible. Siegfried, perhaps with vague notions of his Jewish heritage in mind, had always found the twelve tribes of Israel interesting and his mother's old friend enabled him to imagine it all without reference to his Bible illustrations. This tribute to her narrative powers should not be underestimated, since he was, and was to remain, heavily dependent on the visual element in art. His response to its aural impact also emerged in his relish for the names in these Biblical stories, Pharaoh and Solomon in particular. He was later to argue that poetry must have both a visual and aural appeal.

Miss Batty's ramblings through English history were less uniformly successful. Her pupil's response to it was highly subjective and she herself was hardly less so, being inclined to gloss over the wicked characters, and make the best of the doubtful ones. Siegfried became inattentive when the Roman conquest of Kent was reached, but very interested by the Danes because they were said to have had red hair like his Thornycroft relatives. He took a special interest in Queen Elizabeth because there was a clock in Weirleigh's dining-room reputed to date from her reign. This early reaction to knowledge is characteristic of his future response, which continued to be both intensely imaginative and almost entirely subjective.

His new teacher's contribution to his education would probably not have resulted in spectacular examination marks, but she clearly stimulated his already active imagination in a way that Mrs Mitchell had failed to do. She also gave Siegfried an entirely different idea of the world from Mrs Mitchell's cramped, suspicious and cynical view of it. This idealism caused Siegfried some misery during his convalescence, since he had led her to imagine that Mrs Mitchell had in some way been responsible for his catching pneumonia. It was a great relief to him when he finally blurted out the truth, that he had invented the story of Mrs Mitchell deliberately dampening his sheets before she left. This lie had given him a very real fear of going to Hell, which he felt had been averted by his confession, though he was not yet sure of Heaven despite gentle reassurances from his teacher.

Miss Batty's physical appearance presented an equally striking contrast to Mrs Mitchell's hard gipsy face and forthright manners. Ellen Batty, 'with her wide mouth and rather sallow face which wrinkled and puckered like a tomato under her black hair that was streaked with white', was vague both in dress and habits.⁴ She also allowed the boys freedoms which Mrs Mitchell would not have countenanced, such as putting her Indian beads in the pigeon-bath to see what they looked like in water.

3. Lutes and Nightingales (1895-1900)

One thing Mrs Mitchell and Miss Batty undeniably had in common, was their gender. As women they perpetuated the almost exclusively female world which Siegfried had inhabited since his father's abrupt departure. It was perhaps in an effort to change this that Theresa hired a male tutor for her sons in September 1895, though it is more likely that this was her only option. In any case the person who came to take the job was by no means aggressively masculine, a point which the adult Siegfried emphasizes in his autobiography. Conveniently named Mr Moon, he was affectionately dubbed 'Moonie', a name which aptly reflected his gentle character. Describing him as 'one of the mildest of men', Siegfried claimed that 'nobody could have been more like an indulgent tutor and less like a stern taskmaster'.[5] In his fictionalized account of childhood Siegfried, with his love of puns, neatly transforms Mr Moon into Mr Star, but his character remains the same – 'a gentle, semi-clerical old person', who rules with meek authority.[6]

An elementary schoolmaster who had conveniently come to live in the nearby village of Matfield on retirement, Mr Moon was a tall, stooping man with silver hair, dressed always in the same shabby black tail-coat and wide-awake hat. He spoke in measured sentences with a mild, almost apologetic manner. His teaching methods, though not exciting, were moderately successful. He introduced the Sassoon boys to grammar, simple arithmetic, Latin, a little geography, some natural history and the predictable outline of English history. But he also read to them from Lamb's *Tales From Shakespeare* and *Robinson Crusoe*, and started them on some amateur woodwork. Siegfried preferred the reading, his brothers the carpentry. Whatever the response Mr Moon remained patient, methodical and unhurrying. With Siegfried, at least, he had need of all these qualities, particularly when it came to Latin. Looking back, the poet realized that in a curious way his difficulty in learning languages was linked with his intense response to words, already pronounced by the 1890s. As he explained in *The Old Century*:

> My brain absorbs facts singly, and the process of relating them to one another has always been difficult. From my earliest years I was interested in words, but their effect on my mind was mainly visual. In a muddled way I knew that they had derivations, but my spontaneous assumption was that a mouse was called a mouse because it was mouse-like.

Elsewhere he emphasizes that he was distracted from the meaning of words not only by their appearance but by their sound. So that when, in the autumn of 1897, Theresa decided that her sons needed a language teacher to supplement Mr Moon's almost exhausted stock of knowledge, Siegfried found himself in trouble.

Fräulein Stoy, unlike Mr Moon, lived in and added yet further to the female presence at Weirleigh. She was, nevertheless, as far away from the feminine fussiness Siegfried dreaded as it is possible to be. Her inevitable nickname, 'Frowsy', seemed to Siegfried, who appreciated her, inappropriate. Small and oldish with shrewd but kind grey eyes and the complexion of a weathered apple, she was 'unchivvying' but determined.[7] She always achieved her end except, ironically, in the vital matter of teaching Siegfried French and German. He vividly remembered his afternoon lessons with her in the old nursery, which Mr Moon had vacated in favour of the large room above Theresa's studio. Staring out of the window at the rock-garden, Siegfried desperately tried to learn the German word for window. In retrospect he realised the Fräulein's limitations. Had she thought to point out the connection between the German 'Fenster' and the French 'fenêtre', he believed it might have helped. Putting it as kindly as he could, for he had been fond of her, Siegfried concluded that her teaching, like Mr Moon's, 'lacked illumination'.[8]

Miss Stoy was no more successful at teaching Siegfried music. The explanation seemed to stem from her inability to stimulate his strongest feature, his imagination. Though music later became one of the central interests of his life, with Miss Stoy he showed very little ability. In spite of a genuine desire to play the piano, inspired partly by a growing love of Beethoven's piano sonatas, his progress was so poor that by the end of two years with Miss Stoy they had both lost all confidence in him performing even tolerably well. His brothers fiddled competently through their Corelli and Handel violin sonatas before guests, but Siegfried's painful fumblings at a little Reinecke piece were disastrous. (He was the only one not to have taken up the violin in emulation of their father.)

At the same time as Siegfried's artistic ambitions were suffering setbacks, however, his physical endeavours were unexpectedly flourishing. Though he continued to dislike swimming and was less than enthusiastic about the boxing, fencing and club-swinging that a Sergeant Ryan introduced into the curriculum in 1898, by the summer of that year he suddenly conceived a life-long passion for two activities – riding and cricket. It is unlikely that he would have become addicted to these most English of sports had it not been for the presence of one person, Tom Richardson.

George Thomas Richardson had come to Weirleigh as the Sassoons' coachman in 1890. Then aged about twenty, he had started his working life at fourteen in stables. His career is accurately detailed by Siegfried in *Memoirs of a Fox-Hunting Man*, where Tom Dixon is closely modelled on Richardson; a period as 'odd man' to a sporting farmer in the Vale of Aylesbury and a subsequent three years as under-groom to a hard-riding squire who subscribed handsomely to Lord Henry Nevill's Hounds at Eridge Park only twelve miles from Weirleigh. Richardson came to the Sassoons from his native Lamberhurst well recommended, not only as an excellent coachman but also, to quote his son, 'a good keen rider in the saddle'.[9] Though Weirleigh was two miles outside Lady Nevill's calling circle, Tom was anxious to maintain contact with Eridge Park and to have a 'young gentleman' who hunted would be one way of satisfying his own passion for the sport. For at least the first eight years of his service with the Sassoons, however, he had to be content with a rather tamer routine. He ran his stable of three saddle-horses, one carriage-horse and a pony, accompanied Theresa, at a respectful distance, on her afternoon rides and drove her in the trap or carriage whenever necessary. Though Theresa hunted occasionally with the Eridge Hounds it was not an important part of her life nor, consequently, of her groom's.

By the time Siegfried got to know Tom well in 1898, he and his wife were established above the stables and already had two children. On his arrival at Weirleigh in 1890 as a single young man, Tom had been given a tip-up bed in the harness room. Five years later, when he married old Mrs Thornycroft's pretty maid, Emma Wheatley Oakins, who had stayed on at Weirleigh after her employer's death, he was promoted to the two-floor apartment over the coach-house. The previous occupant, the bad-tempered Mr Reeves, had been skilfully disposed of by Theresa and the replacement head gardener, Ned Farris, was in no need of quarters since he had his own house in Matfield village.

Tom was the first of Siegfried's many father-figures, or perhaps more accurately, father-substitutes. There might be more famous ones, such as Thomas Hardy, Edmund Gosse, Robert Ross and the eminent psychologist Dr Rivers, but there would never be anyone who inspired quite the same hero-worship. In what Siegfried himself called his 'fictionized reality'[10], *Memoirs of a Fox-Hunting Man*, a thinly-disguised Tom is introduced in the first paragraph and the even more transparently disguised Siegfried, as the protagonist George, tells us on the second page: 'My admiration for him was unqualified'. Tom's son, John Richardson, maintains that Siegfried 'idolized' his father; he certainly *idealized* him in his fiction. He also seems to have turned to Tom as an antidote to the almost overwhelming female presence at Weirleigh. After his humiliating failure to control his pony has exposed George in *Memoirs of a Fox-Hunting Man* to the hen-like clucking of the female staff, Tom's 'tactful silence' on the subject convinces him of the groom's 'infinite superiority to those chattering females in the kitchen'.[11]

Tom Richardson seemed, even to his son, a rather awesome figure. With his composed features and reserved manner he was 'the embodiment of the efficient groom and the superior private servant'.[12] Tall and handsome, he was always immaculately turned out, either in the Sassoons' livery of blue thigh-length coat with silver buttons, white breeches, high black leg-boots with a tan band round the top, white stock and black top hat or, when following Theresa and later Siegfried to the hunt, in a dark grey suit cut with riding breeches, fawn-coloured gaiters and bowler hat. Siegfried never saw Tom drive even a pony-cart without looking as though it were a carriage and pair.

In spite of a certain aloofness, Tom was persuasive, even artful, in his dealings with Theresa, luring her on to new purchases for the stables in which he took so much pride. Theresa needed little encouragement, and over the years sold many pieces of the jewelry left to her by Alfred to finance the deals. Siegfried, whilst beginning to share her passion for horses, could not help regretting the sale of his father's striking brown diamond.

Together with Tom's persuasiveness went an infinite tact which helps to explain his success in teaching Siegfried not only to ride but to ride extremely well. There was, to use Siegfried's own words, an 'unmanly' element in the nature of this 'dreaming and unpractical' boy, which Tom handled with great delicacy.[13] Whether or not Theresa, who lisped, actually said, as John Richardson claims: 'I have the highest wegard for Wichardson. I would twust him with my vewwy life' is impossible to prove.[14] And by 1898 he had gained Siegfried's entire confidence. After a timid and shaky start on the little black pony shared by all three Sassoon boys, Siegfried even felt sufficiently secure to tackle jumping. Terrified as he was at this new stage, Tom persuaded him to persevere and Siegfried eventually graduated to a full-sized hunter, Sportsman, in 1898.

Sportsman had cost Theresa nothing. A present from someone who wanted him to have a good home, he had done a lot of work and was very much over at the knees. Nevertheless Siegfried adored the handsome chestnut with his three white stockings and Roman nose. Every morning he would run down to the stables to give Sportsman his lump of sugar and discuss his next ride with Tom. Dressed in his brown velveteen riding-suit and matching cap, he would go out for long excursions with Tom, immaculate in his uniform. Their favourite route was through some hilly, remote country which they reached by way of Kipping's Cross on the Tunbridge Wells road. They always stopped on the bridge over the brook by Dundale Farm, because this was the point at which Kent ended and Sussex began. Siegfried could never detect any difference between the two but liked the idea of having a foot in each county. He enjoyed the gentle explorations of the Weald, being 'one of those people on whose minds riding produces a profoundly serenifying effect'.[15] Less gently, Tom would sometimes take him into a neighbouring field for a gallop, in preparation no doubt for the hunting he hoped lay ahead.

When Siegfried eventually tackled his first meet it was with even more trepidation than he had felt at his first jump. However, with an impetuosity and daring which contrasted oddly with his timidity, and which was to characterize him throughout the First World War as 'Mad Jack', he found himself following one of the hardest riders to hounds over a difficult fence. 'Quite a young thruster', the Master of Hounds concluded, but with typical self-effacement Siegfried implies that the truth was very different. The incident shows nevertheless that Tom's training had been a rigorous and successful one.

Before any serious hunting started, however, Tom was also encouraging Siegfried to enjoy cricket. (If we are to believe *Memoirs of a Fox-Hunting Man*, he took the ten-year-old Siegfried to Canterbury Cricket Week in 1897 to see Prince Ranjitsinhji play.) An exceptionally good player himself, he initiated Siegfried, Michael and Hamo into the rudiments of the game on Weirleigh's lower lawn on summer afternoons. He complemented Mr Moon's accurate but gentle lobs with more intimidating overarm bowling and his stylish left-handed batting increased Siegfried's hero-worship, giving him something to emulate. Tom had quickly become captain of the local cricket team, which played its home fixtures a few hundred yards from Weirleigh on Matfield Green and Siegfried, who had possibly seen his father performing well on the same pitch, became an ardent supporter of the club. He hardly dared hope that one day he, too, would play for them but practised assiduously nevertheless.

So great was Siegfried's passion for the game that in 1896 when pains in his hip-joint, diagnosed as 'outgrowing his strength', led to another poetic interlude of lying out on the lawn, he sacrificed it to indulge his 'craving for cricket'.[16] This is one of relatively few references to cricket in his first volume of autobiography, because he had already described it so lovingly and in such detail in *Memoirs of a Fox-Hunting Man*. His 'Flower Show Match' chapter in that book has deservedly become a minor classic of cricket literature.

Siegfried's passion for cricket is in an honourable tradition and may be explained in various ways. It seems to have been the only team sport at which he excelled, an aspect he appreciated even more when the time came for him to attend school. Perhaps also it was the only team sport which allowed a self-confessedly dreamy child time to dream. In addition cricket took him into an exclusively male society, offering another opportunity of escape from the largely female world of Weirleigh. It was certainly to become a solid bond between him and a number of his closest male friends, Edmund Blunden and Dennis Silk in particular. Blunden, in his *Cricket Country*, devoted a whole chapter to describing Sassoon the cricketer and imagining him as the captain of a team of living poets who loved cricket.[17] It was Blunden, too, whose match against Siegfried's local village team at Merton College, Oxford, gave rise to one of Siegfried's most revealing remarks about cricket. 'In these times', he was to write in the shadow of War in June 1939, 'one values the humanity of such an occasion greatly. It is like the good old England holding its own against the modern pandemonium'.[18]

In the same way he loved horses 'because they were so completely unmodernizable, so independent of fashion' and, like himself, 'refused to move with the times'.[19] He had begun both sports in the beautiful setting of the Weald of Kent and they were linked inextricably for him with a noble tradition he saw endangered by subsequent events. He clung to both not only because he found them physically exhilarating, but because they represented a way of life that was being threatened, particularly with the advent of the First World War. Whilst fighting in that War he was sustained partly by memories of leisurely cricket matches on village greens and all that they symbolized for him.

What cricket epitomized for him was not entirely solemn, however. His quirky sense of humour and appreciation of eccentricity, well-developed even as a child, led him to create such cricketing characters in *Memoirs of a Fox-Hunting Man* as the prosperous saddler, William Dodd, the one-legged umpire Bill Sutler, Crump, Peckham and Parson Yalden, who bring back in all their variety the days before mass communication and media personalities, days for which Siegfried frankly confesses a partiality:

> The players all looked so unlike one another then; and there was an air of alfresco intimacy about their exploits which lent them a fuller flavour than seems perceptible now.[20]

There is a photograph of Siegfried with the Matfield Cricket Club in about 1897 which captures this flavour, as well as the young boy's excitement at participating – he holds the scorebook – and the bucolic nature of the team. The names and occupations of the members are equally evocative of a vanished era. Tom Richardson, as captain, stands in the centre with Siegfried crouching in front of him. The thin, bearded figure to Tom's left is the Sassoons' tutor, Mr Moon, the man with a moustache to Tom's right is the Squire's son, Richard Marchant (a Kent player), their central position suggesting their superior social standing. The tall dark youth next to Marchant is Will Larkin, one of several cricketing Larkins in Matfield, and next to him is Will Butler, the wooden-legged umpire, also ironically the village cobbler, immortalized by Sassoon in *Memoirs of a Fox-Hunting Man*. The stout figure to Mr Moon's left has not been identified, but on the far left is another village character, Alec Read. Kneeling in the centre front row to Sassoon's left is the village carrier, Tom Homewood, who made his leisurely journey to Maidstone three times a week and who featured in *Memoirs of a Fox-Hunting Man* as 'John Homeward'. (Sassoon was to preserve a series of photographs of Homewood, who died in 1939 aged seventy-five. On the back of one photograph someone, possibly Theresa, has noted: 'Homewood is a fair man. Blue eyes?') On the extreme right, also kneeling, is Weirleigh's head gardener, Ned Farris, and second from the right is 'Curly' (Harry) Fuller. 'Scunger' Austin kneels on the far left. A similar photograph of Matfield Cricket Club in 1898 shows Siegfried, again as scorer, sitting in front of the team in cap and Norfolk jacket, on a very rough-looking pitch.

Neither Michael nor Hamo Sassoon appears in these two photographs of Matfield Cricket Club. And it was 1897, almost certainly the date of the first photograph, that Siegfried pinpoints as the beginning of a divergence between himself and his brothers. By the summer of that year, he relates in *The Old Century*, 'it had become obvious that my brothers preferred their workshop to anything else'. They were very 'important' about it and only played cricket when they could 'spare the time'.

Clearly both Michael and Hamo took after their grandfather, Thomas Thornycroft, and his eldest son, John. They set up a workshop together on the top floor of the old cottage beyond Theresa's studio and with their lathe and carpenter's bench started to be serious engineers. Siegfried's vague description of their activities comically underlines the difference in temperament between himself and his more scientific brothers: 'They soldered things together, made bits of iron red-hot and then hit them with a hammer ...'[21] (He is unlikely to have been quite as ignorant as this suggests.) Michael and Hamo loved not only making things but finding out how they had been made. On one occasion they dismantled their mother's Queen Elizabeth clock, which never worked again. And whilst they worked they sang a comic song which Siegfried grew sick of hearing: 'Our lodger's such a nice young man ...' The only time their activities seem to have stimulated his imagination was when they converted bulbous gun-metal handles from the studio windows into shiny brass cannons and made ammunition for them from a clock-weight to fire at the vinery. In spite of gunpowder stolen from the potting-shed, the shot did not reach its mark – to Siegfried's intense disappointment. Normally, however, he kept well clear of his brothers' activities and their paths continued to diverge for the rest of their lives, except for a brief truce over cricket. While he devoted himself almost entirely to the arts, both Michael and Hamo became professional engineers.

In a collection of 'poems, drawing and a story' produced in 1898, Siegfried vents his scorn for engineers in 'A Modern Lunatic', subtitled none too subtly, 'a warning to all who have an inclination that way'.[22] In the story itself he imagines lunatic engineers ascending in a large balloon, 'worked by some oil motor, which is usually a great deal more oily and odourous [*sic*] than useful'. The inevitable crash occurs, followed by 'a long paragraph in the papers on "Lunatics at Large", otherwise, "Engineers" '. His greatest scorn, however, is reserved for aspiring engineers who dare to trespass into the field of art and attempt to paint an enormous picture 'not unlike a large and hideous production of a piece of painted crazy patchwork'. That this is a reference to Michael is obvious from a large 'Rot' scrawled across the story in another hand and Siegfried's response: 'This foolish and characteristic note was made by a beastly ass called M------ Sassoon, who thinks he knows all about engineering – His immediate future is a lunatic asylum'. Clearly Siegfried felt threatened when the budding engineers tried to invade his territory. This incident was more than the usual childish squabble; it highlighted Siegfried's deep suspicion of all things mechanical, which remained with him for the rest of his life.

He would open his article, 'Rambling Thoughts on Horses and Hunting' in the 1950s, for instance, with the words: 'I must begin by warning my readers that I am a man of confirmed pre-Machine Age mentality; animals mean a great deal to me; engines do not interest me at all'.[23]

Michael, who was born two years before Siegfried and died two years after him, did not continue to trespass into the art world but devoted his life to engineering. His childhood coincided with the emergence of the motor car and his adolescence with that of the aeroplane, both of which fascinated him. After an undistinguished academic career at Malvern and Cambridge, he came down without a degree, marrying young and serving an engineering apprenticeship with his uncle's firm, Thornycrofts, at Basingstoke. Shortly afterwards he emigrated to Canada, where he started his own car-repair workshop and supervized the mechanical equipment at a nearby salmon fishery-cum-canning factory.[24]

When he returned to England in 1920, shortly after the birth of his third and last child, he helped found a small engineering company, William Godfrey and Partners. His passion for cars led him to collect a number of 'classics', including a steam-driven car, a Riley tri-car, an 8 horsepower de Dion Bouton and a Humberette, which he drove for several years in the London to Brighton Veteran Car run. In the 1930s he also joined the newly opened West Malling Flying Club and in middle age learnt to fly in Amy Johnson's De Havilland Moth which he bought. His mother-in-law, Mrs Stroud aged eighty, and his youngest son, Hamo, aged twelve, learnt with him. Physically daring, like Siegfried, he went in for aerial acrobatics and continued to fly until the end of his long life.[25] His energy and ingenuity also led him in the 1930s to start a loganberry and himalaya-berry (i.e. giant blackberry) farm. He used part of the ten acres at the back of the house he moved to in Matfield (Hatherleigh) for their cultivation and sent his produce to Covent Garden Market.

Nicknamed 'Billy' in childhood, Michael was quite different from Siegfried. Not so acutely sensitive and far more outgoing, he became known locally as 'Jack-the-lad', a reputation which his middle brother could never have acquired, even though it may have been completely unfounded. Certainly he liked women and when his first wife, Violet, died, he quickly remarried.[26] He was, to quote John Richardson, both 'loveable' and 'popular' in Matfield. His violin-playing perhaps best sums up the difference between himself and Siegfried; while he learnt the mechanics of music rapidly, his playing was not sufficiently sensitive to interest Elgar, who had been asked to consider teaching him in 1900. Siegfried, on the other hand, found music-making difficult, as his early fumblings at the piano show, but his response to music itself was both passionate and sensitive. Michael's youngest son, Hamo, does not remember his father sharing Siegfried's interest in family history – 'only in a facetious kind of way'.[27]

In spite of being the eldest, Michael seems to have been generally less responsible, or more easy-going, than his younger brother, at least in the latter's eyes. When Siegfried lent Michael money, for example, he did not expect to be repaid.[28] After their mother's death Siegfried told a friend that she had made him the executor, since 'my brother is rather casual about seeing to things'.[29] Theresa may also have felt closer to Siegfried, whom she certainly favoured above Michael as a child. Nevertheless Michael remained fond of 'Onion', as he affectionately called Siegfried, and was always delighted to see him, a sentiment that was sometimes not reciprocated.

The bond between Siegfried and his younger brother Hamo seems to have been stronger, perhaps because they were closer in temperament. They were even closer in age, with less than a year between them. Both seem to have reacted more violently to the loss of their father than Michael. Both were self-confessed homosexuals by the age of twenty-four and Siegfried found comfort in his younger brother's calm acceptance of something which had caused him, in his own words, 'great perplexity and unhappiness'.[30] Hamo's 'intensely humorous way of looking at things', as Siegfried saw it, was another feature they had in common.[31] Hamo is portrayed in his mother's delicate Pre-Raphaelite painting of him as a young man of great sensitivity and is said to have shown promise as a sculptor. Until the brothers' divergence in 1897 Hamo had shared more of Siegfried's interests than Michael. When Siegfried was ill in 1895 he was anxious to do anything he could for him and even lent him a stag beetle he had caught in the pump-yard. And he and Siegfried hunted moths and butterflies together until engineering intervened.

Though like Siegfried in some ways, Hamo was very different from him in others. In spite of his poetic good looks, he did not share Siegfried's intense response to poetry. When Theresa praised her second son's early poem about a mermaid, Hamo's matter-of-fact mind rebelled. He accused Siegfried of having 'mermaids on the brain'. Since everyone knew there weren't any, he argued, Siegfried 'must be going barmy'.[32] He remained unmoved by Siegfried's taunt that only people with imagination could understand what mermaids meant. The incident signalled a parting of the ways, all the more painful to Siegfried because he had initially felt closer to Hamo. He should perhaps have realized earlier, when Hamo had shown so little interest in his painter godfather, Watts, or his pictures, that his younger brother lacked his own reverence for art. Hamo's practical mind seems to have had no time for dreams or nostalgia and, unlike Siegfried's, dwelt little on the past. He loved strenuous occupations, such as chopping or digging and, once the brothers' childhood closeness had passed, planned a grand destruction of the fort which had replaced their 'Build' in the garden.

Though younger than Siegfried, when the two of them finally reached public school, within a term of each other, it became clear that Hamo was the more self-possessed and wise of the two. When they left, it would be Siegfried who was advised 'Try to be more sensible'.[33] Hamo, though not academically brilliant, was methodical and diligent and clearly had no need of such advice. At Cambridge it was the same: Hamo got his degree with no fuss even though it did take him an extra year to do so. He was working as an engineer in Argentina when War broke out in 1914 and, again with no fuss, came home at once to join the army. His early death in the First World War would be partly responsible for the savage turn Siegfried's poetry took in 1916.

In *Memoirs of a Fox-Hunting Man* not only does the protagonist-narrator lack both father and mother, he also has no siblings. Clearly Siegfried had a strong sense of isolation in childhood which must have increased significantly after his brothers' interests began to take them in a different direction from his own. Even before the rift he had felt it necessary to invent an idealized companion in whom he could confide, as though in preparation. This revolved around his toy, Moocow, which became something of a fetish to him and he used to:

> converse with her when I was alone, and around her I created a dream existence. She ceased to be a toy cow, and became a companionable character with whom I shared interesting adventures, in regions of escape from my surroundings. (I called her 'she', but I thought of her as neither one thing nor the other – my idea about men and women being that they dressed differently so as to show the difference ...)[34]

It is interesting to note that in the fictional *Memoirs of a Fox-Hunting Man*, this 'ideal companion' is masculine – 'that "other boy" ' – whereas in his factual accounts of life his 'dream friend' has no sex.

Siegfried had begun to savour solitude in 1895 when convalescing from pneumonia. By 1897 he was able not only to cope with but even to relish it. Apart from riding and sometimes playing cricket without his brothers, he continued his butterfly-collecting without Hamo and took to fishing in the orchard pond or roaming the neighbouring Gedges Wood alone. Looking back on childhood in the poem 'It was the Love of Life' he concluded: 'That loneliness it was which made me wise.' (*CP*, p. 212) He had already started to write poetry just before the rift came, but its advent speeded up the process. Between 1896 and 1899 he produced at least nine notebooks of poetry, most of them illustrated and with stories included.[35]

Siegfried started writing poetry in earnest during his second period of lying out alone on the lawn in the spring of 1896. The opening poem in the first notebook anticipates many others on his favourite season:

> ... List! the larks are gaily singing.
> Swallows nestle in the eves.

3. Lutes and Nightingales (1895-1900)

> Hush! Springs silver bells are ringing.
> Green are growing all the leaves.

Whilst not strikingly original, this first effort shows that the nine-year-old had a reasonable grasp of metre, rhyme and stanza form and could invent his own metaphor and personification, as well as emulate the poetic diction and other trappings of the Romantic poetry he so loved. With a few exceptions, it was poetry about nature which occupied him throughout these childhood volumes. Larks and swallows were joined by thrushes and nightingales, spring and winter were complemented by summer and autumn, the countryside of Kent supplemented by the seascape of the Isle of Wight, which he visited for a month in August 1896, and that of Norfolk, where Theresa took her sons for two months in the summer of 1897.

Having read the Pre-Raphaelites avidly and devoured Longfellow, Tennyson and Shelley, as well as other Romantics, Siegfried was also anxious to make the connection between autumn and decay, winter and death, the sea and life itself, night and outcast souls. A poem which claims to have been written even earlier than 1896 – 'Autumn 1895' – shows a predilection for melancholy themes, not surprising in view of the deaths of both his father and his grandmother earlier that year. After describing the passing of autumn, which is haunted by a 'sad spirit', the poet turns to winter:

> For the cold of winter it had come at last.
> Perchance it now would toss that spirit back.
> Into the grave, with a cold and chilling blast
> Over the awful pillar of black death.

Siegfried claimed that his fascination with death in his earliest poems was a result of reading Shelley, particularly the opening lines of *Queen Mab*:

> How wonderful is Death,
> Death and his brother Sleep!

which had led him to believe that all the best poetry was gloomy, or at any rate solemn. Shelley's poetry made him feel the same way as Tintoretto's *Last Judgement*, a copy of which hung in his mother's studio. Describing his favourite themes at that time as Eternity and the Tomb, he explained his fascination with death as a desire not to disappoint his 'audience', that is his mother, by being 'insipid and unimaginative'.

Apart from fuelling her son's imagination with Romantic poetry, Theresa also fed it with pictures. Not only did she fill the house with the works of her favourite painter, Watts, but she also took Siegfried to see a big Exhibition of his work in London when he was eleven. There he found in Watts's loftiness and grandeur another model for his aims in poetry. When he returned home he tried to put into words the feelings roused in him by one of the painter's most lofty and symbolic works, 'The Court of Death'. This piece duly appeared in *More Poems*, 1897, under the same portentous title:

> *The Court of Death*
> There lay the lake of sleep: eternal sleep
>   That looked so still.
> And far beyond, the palace of King Death
>   Who hidden lay:
>   ...
> The nobleman came up with bowèd head
> The loyal knight came there to lay his sword
> There at the foot of death, who robed in black
> Looked on the people who came up to him
> To throw themselfs, into the sea of gloom.
>   ...
> And he spake thus: 'I hold the lives of men
>   From the beginning to the end.'
>   And, yea, behind him angels stood
>   Guarding the things unknown, beyond the Tomb.

By the time Siegfried visited the Watts Exhibition in the winter of 1897, he had completed two volumes of poetry, one started in 1896 and the second finished by March 1897 to mark his mother's birthday. He had almost collected a third for her Christmas present. The two 1897 volumes have become separated from their companions, probably because Siegfried used one for reference when writing his autobiography in the mid-1930s and lent a researcher another in the 1960s. They are now at Cambridge University Library, donated by Sir Rupert Hart-Davis. Siegfried himself has quoted from the earlier of them to demonstrate his preoccupation with death. His fascination with Medievalism, caught from the Pre-Raphaelites, also emerges:

> So evening fell and everything seemed sad
> And overcome by weariness and gloom.
> Slowly a knight in snowy samite clad
> Was borne away to the darkness of the tomb.[36]

The formula in these second and third volumes is very similar to that of Siegfried's first, but in his fourth volume, dated 1898 and undedicated, some of his own personality begins to emerge in a series of humorous poems which anticipate, very faintly, his satiric War poetry. Portentous poems, on such topics as autumn, winter, twilight and the 'ocean' (rather than the plain old 'sea') are now combined with spirited satires on selected topics. His prose attack on engineers, makes its first appearance in this fourth volume and there is also an equally scornful piece 'To a Motor-Car'

(Siegfried shared his mother's extreme distrust of cars and his own experience with them later on suggests that he would have been wise to avoid them.):

> If Motor-cars did not stink so
> Perhaps they would not be so bad
> When they go by the folks say, Oh!
> Use their hankerchiefs and look sad.
>
> They seem to have St Vitus dance.
> When they stand still they shake like fun.
> I've heard they use them much in France.
> I fear the folks from France will run.[37]

'To a Pig', 'To a Wasp' and 'The Stork', all humorous, are followed by a ten-stanza poem on 'Natural History', later expanded. Though this attempt at satiric compression fails, it is interesting to see Siegfried experimenting with it so early in his career:

> The Lion is an animal, very unkind
> For he eats Indian babies with toe-nails and rind.

A number of poems in this fourth volume are repeated in the following three volumes, also produced in 1898: *Poems*, dedicated to his unfortunate Aunty Lula who had accompanied the Sassoons on their Norfolk holiday the previous year, *The Blue Poetry Book*, dedicated to his mother's friend Helen Wirgman, and *The Red Poetry Book*, dedicated to his Uncle Hamo. Apart from three rather rambling pieces, Aunty Lula's *Poems* is essentially the same collection as that presented to Helen Wirgman for Christmas 1898. Uncle Hamo's *Red Poetry Book*, also presented as a Christmas present, contains only about half the poems, possibly because his nephew ran out of time, or patience, when transcribing them. (It is interesting to note that his 'Mamsy' does not receive an inscribed collection of poems for her birthday this year, but Robert Louis Stevenson's *The Master of Ballantrae*.)

In 1899 he wrote two new volumes. Though again there is a great deal of overlap between them. Indeed some of the poems have already appeared in the 1898 volumes. The most interesting addition to the January 1899 notebook is an ambitious poem on 'The Year', in which Siegfried quotes lines from his current favourites, Shakespeare, Shelley and Tennyson, on a left-hand page and gives his own poem on each month on a right-hand page. This tiny, leather-bound, gold-tooled notebook is sparsely illustrated, in contrast to most of the earlier volumes where the pictures sometimes outnumber the poems. Romantic tendencies continue to express themselves in such pieces as 'To a Skylark' and 'To a Nightingale', with their obvious debt to Shelley and Keats. The last production this year

– and for some time to come – is 'The Poems by S. L. Sassoon', which largely repeats the contents of the January volume. It is executed in coloured inks, but the illustrations, promised on the title page, are meagre. The childish exuberance of the earlier volumes is giving way to a more self-conscious approach.

There is not a great deal in these nine volumes to indicate the poet Siegfried was to become. He himself dismissed them in later life as 'scribblings …. Automatic poetising – not an idea in it – only a delight in the noise of polysyllables'.[38] Some characteristic interests and concerns, however, are already beginning to emerge. He is plainly attempting to emulate one of his models, Tennyson, who made him 'see everything he wrote quite distinctly' and enchanted him 'with his words and cadences'.[39] Siegfried is drunk on words in the 1890s – it comes as no surprise to learn that Swinburne was one of his heroes – and his love of their sound together with their visual impact dominates his poetic technique from the start. The tone is predominantly melancholic:

> I
> Weary and gray, dawn and day
> And the mists of morning rose.
> Damp and dark, and weary lark
> As the shades of evening close.
> II
> Wind and cold, and snowy wold
> As the dark of twilight fell.
> Withered flowers and dying hours
> And many a funeral bell.

Here and throughout the nine volumes Siegfried's attachment to traditional verse forms and his unwillingness to venture far outside them also emerges, his favourite stanza remaining the simple rhymed quatrain. There are moments when a genuine poetic impulse, truly inspired by the natural beauty around him, escapes the heavy weight of nineteenth-century tradition and Siegfried's own voice is heard. An early favourite which reappears in several later volumes describes one of the great loves of his life, horses:

> To Sylvia: a Horse
> So gentle and so mild is she
> As she gallops o'er the grass.
> The grasses bend
> The wind makes way
> As though to let her pass.

Another equally simple poem, 'To the Wild Rose', anticipates the limpidity of much of his later nature poetry:

3. Lutes and Nightingales (1895-1900)

> In glory grows
> The sweet wild rose.
> In every place
> Of sweet repose
> In kingly grace
> It hangs its petals down
> As though it wore a crown.

Theresa admired this poem so much that she had it set to music and Siegfried had to suffer the excruciating embarrassment of hearing his cousin Mary perform it before guests.

The majority of the poems composed between 1896 and 1899 are, however, largely exercises. The few prose pieces written during the same period tend to be more original and far less romantic. Two stories about cats, 'The Story of Peter' and 'Something About Myself', though somewhat rambling, are full of lively details, much of it drawn from life. At one point Peter, a large tabby of dubious morals, is 'caught on the table with his head in the milkjug', at another he holds a friendly conversation with a rat whom he is 'too fat and too lazy [sic]' to chase. 'Something About Myself', which was written nearly a year after 'The Story of Peter', shows more skill in the handling of narrative. The autobiography of a 'common' garden cat, it describes in lurid detail his fight with 'three great vulgar cats' and the subsequent death of his mother:

> 'That finishes the ole gal' I remarked gaily, for I never did like her piticularly. But here I must end my story, for my uncle is going to give me a snarling lesson. Though, I might tell you, I am a kitchen cat now, and catch lots of mice.[40]

The liveliness of the narrative, its humour and use of the first-person narrator in 'Something About Myself' anticipate by more than thirty years Siegfried's first novel, *Memoirs of a Fox-Hunting Man*. As Dame Felicitas Corrigan has suggested, the dramatic monologue was to become his favourite medium of expression in both prose and poetry, whether in the early *Joan of Arc*, *The Daffodil Murderer*, 'The Old Huntsmen' and individual poems, or in his fictional and straight autobiographical trilogies. His temperament inclined, even at an early age, to subjective rather than objective expression. He chooses a first-person narrator again for another piece of prose in 1898, 'A Little About Me', the story of a hound called Atalanta. This piece, later jokily renamed 'Atalanta in Kenneldom' with reference to Swinburne's 'Atalanta in Calydon', also allows him to show off his knowledge of hunting terms, learned largely from another favourite writer, the novelist Surtees.

Siegfried's prose and verse at this time have little in common, except for their response to his physical surroundings at Weirleigh. One of his first poems, 'Old Mayfield', for example, is almost certainly a thinly-disguised reference to the local village 'with its houses broad and low'. As Siegfried became more independent and was given more freedom to roam, he became correspondingly more familiar with his own village and its inhabitants. By the age of nine he had been allowed to walk the few hundred yards to the little sweet shop in Matfield to buy three-penny-worth of percussion caps for his toy pistol, 'bull's eye' sweets or a bar of chocolate cream.

Based around a large village green and pond, Matfield is still almost as self-contained and picturesque as it was when Siegfried visited its sweet shop a hundred years ago. Because the railway had been expected to go through the village, Matfield had expanded rapidly during the late nine-teenth century to overtake its neighbouring 'mother' parish of Brenchley. By Siegfried's day it already boasted, besides three general stores, two bakeries, a butcher's, a Post Office, a cobbler's, a forge, a laundry, a coachbuilding and wheelwright's shop and three public houses, as well as St Luke's Church (built 1876), Ebenezer Chapel and, by 1890, a Parish Hall. Modern supermarkets and machines have put paid to the forge, the laundry, the wheelwright's and one of the general stores, but the pubs still flourish and of the two general stores, the Post Office and the butcher's have also survived. Similarly, Squire Marchant's fine Georgian house still dominates the village green, though it is no longer inhabited by Marchants. Its gilded clock no longer strikes in the cobbled courtyard as it did for Siegfried a century ago when he accompanied the Squire's pretty daughters, May and Bessie, home from Weirleigh along his favourite footpath.[41]

Tom Richardson's son, John, also recreated Matfield as he experienced it not so long after Siegfried; its shops, its rituals and its families – the Homewoods, the Larkins, the Farrises, the Fletchers, the Johnsons, the Fullers, the Seymours. He has also reminded the modern reader, however, that conditions were far from ideal for many of the local inhabitants:

Farming was the livelihood of most of the population of our part of Kent, and the carters, ploughmen, stockmen and labourers worked long and hard in all weathers for very low pay and holidays were non-existent. Most of them lived in cottages which were not much more than hovels, with no sanitation other than a nasty little building situated at the extreme end of the garden; as far as possible in fact from the cottage; the reason for this became evident if one went near it. Water supply was often from a shared well and had to be hauled up on a windlass and carried in buckets. Most such cottages had a useful piece of garden which would always be used for growing vegetables; this would be a necessity of existence for the man and his wife and family and not just a means of beating old 'so and so' at the annual Brenchley Horticultural Show ...

But somehow or other the 'Cottagers' as they were known to the Gentry managed to rear large families under these conditions. I have often thought though, what a life of everlasting drudgery and hardship it must have been for the wives. Daughters, on reaching the school leaving age, fourteen, would be employed as housemaids or kitchen maids in the houses of the gentry where they would live-in, thus making more room in their homes for burly brothers who were growing up. These girls, although they worked hard for long hours and were rigorously disciplined by senior servants, at least lived in clean conditions and learned cleanly ways, and had three good meals a day ...

So this is what lurked beneath the charm of rural beauty in our part of Kent, with its wooded hills, its apple, cherry and plum orchards, the neat regimented hop fields, raspberry and currant plantations. The charm of red tiled villages with ancient grey stone churches; the outlying farms with their oasthouses and barns. Cricket being played on village greens on long lazy Saturday afternoons, when rustic wives, ostensibly there to watch the game, sat gossiping and knitting, enjoying a few hours rest. This was the only relaxation for the wives after a week of hard toil.[42]

Siegfried paints a very different picture of his childhood surroundings, presenting us with an unashamedly nostalgic vision which omits the harsh realities he must have glimpsed, or at least guessed at, as a child. *His* Matfield is a 'dawdling homespun' world, full of sunshine and local characters. It is background rather than foreground. Whilst John Richardson builds up a vivid picture of Matfield's shops and people, Siegfried sketches in only a few romantic details – the weatherbeaten village carrier, 'geese going single file across the green', the lame blacksmith and the more colourful members of the cricket-team.

Siegfried's response to Matfield and Brenchley was not just a matter of literary choice; it was also a result of his social position in the district, which separated him from most of its inhabitants. Like George, in *The Memoirs of a Fox-Hunting Man*, he would not have been allowed to 'associate' with the village boys. Even the sons of neighbouring farmers were considered 'unsuitable'. For his mother, and by extension for himself, the world was divided into people on whom one could, and must, 'call' and those who were 'socially impossible'.[43] It is not surprising, therefore, to find his descriptions of childhood dominated by what he himself dubbed 'the local gentry'.

Theresa's social round extended to a radius of about ten miles – the distance she could conveniently travel by carriage or pony-trap. Her friends would, of course, include the vicar, the doctor and any other of the professions, their wives and their children. In reality this translated into a fairly circumscribed world of the vicars of Matfield and Brenchley and their families, the local doctor, Neild, Squires Marchant and Morland and their families, two ex-Army officers, Major Horrocks and Captain Ruxton, and their wives, and several assorted spinsters of genteel background, such as Miss Woodgate and Miss Martin.

Siegfried's favourites, whom he described in both his autobiographical and fictional accounts of childhood were Major Edgeworth Horrocks, white-bearded and rubicund, and his ancient, very deaf sister, Clara, Captain Hay Ruxton who farmed at Broad Oak and had been the first Chief Constable of Kent, and Squire Marchant's children, three of whom were either painted or sculpted by his mother.[44] The girls, Bessie and May, presented a striking contrast to his childish eyes, May 'fair, like a corn-field' and Bessie dark as 'a damask rose'.[45] Though he admired the practical and accomplished May greatly, he identified more closely with Bessie's tolerant, impulsive nature. (He kept a photograph of Bessie at about the age she must have been when he described her in *The Old Century* and corresponded with her after her marriage.) He also liked their brother, Richard, whom he partially transformed into Jack Barchard in *The Memoirs of a Fox-Hunting Man*[46] and enjoyed trespassing on the land of another brother, Stephen, in nearby Gedges Wood.

Theresa also liked her neighbours, but she found them rather limited. They never went away, she complained, and some of the ladies were rather 'hen-like'. A positive and imaginative person herself, she devised several answers to this problem, some of which livened up Siegfried's childhood considerably. On occasion, when she felt herself 'becoming an absolute cabbage' as she put it, she would ride twenty miles to spend a night with one of her oldest friends, Florence Bramwell, a brilliant talker of cosmopolitan views. Another of her solutions was to liven things up herself, as she had vowed to do when she first arrived at Matfield. One such attempt was the founding of a Poetry Society in the winter of 1896.

Siegfried, who evidently relished the memory, has left us an entertaining account of this society, though it is highly unlikely that he remembered it in such detail as he provides. Shelley had been chosen by Theresa for the first meeting but the members, gathered mainly from the unmarried ladies of the district, were understandably intimidated by the need to produce an essay on the subject. Instead Bessie Marchant gave a bashful but pleasing performance of 'Ode to the West Wind', aided no doubt by her youth and prettiness.[47] Her successor, Miss Martin, who was reputed to be 'a great reader of solid literature' but singularly lacked Bessie's charms, almost sent her audience to sleep with her rendition of 'Adonais'.[48] Meantime the Sassoon boys, bored by a wet afternoon which had limited numbers to ten ladies, crouched hidden in a dusty loft formed by ornate canopies on either side of the drawing-room fireplace. When a long-repressed sneeze exploded from one of them, all three were banished indignantly from the room, though Siegfried suspected that the ladies had laughed about it afterwards. At least he and his brothers had managed to put an end to Miss Martin's dirge-like rendering of 'Adonais'.

The incident shows Siegfried in an engaging light as a normal, mischievous little boy. Clearly his poetic ambitions did not prevent him enjoying a childish prank which, in the event, ruined the reading of a beautiful poem. There was certainly nothing solemn or priggish about him then and he was never to lose his robust sense of humour. On the contrary he remained capable of enjoying similar jokes all his life.

There is very little detail about Theresa's second meeting, on Coleridge, which was presumably as uninspiring as the first. At any rate, the Poetry

Society was allowed to lapse and she turned her formidable energy to other diversions. The most successful of these, as far as Siegfried was concerned, was a series of *tableaux vivants*, then very much in fashion. Both the designing of the costumes and the painting of the scenery provided an outlet for Theresa's somewhat thwarted artistic impulses. Though the actual sewing of the clothes was left to the long-suffering Emily Eyles, Theresa was kept very busy organizing the cast. Not content with commandeering the Marchant sisters and other young locals, she sent for the Gosse children and some of her sister Fanny Donaldson's ten children, and a number of Donaldson nieces accordingly arrived from Chiswick. In addition 'sedate gentlemen' – sedate at least in the eyes of the young Siegfried – were roped in to play other roles.

Siegfried's own part in proceedings was limited to a scene called 'Queen Margaret and the Robbers', in which he played the young Henry VI, and another from *A Midsummer Night's Dream*, where he was cast as Mustard Seed. Other *tableaux*, acted out on a small stage in the dining-room with the aid of red velvet curtains, included 'Two's Company, Three's None', 'She Stoops To Conquer', 'Bluebeard's Wives' and 'Drink To Me Only With Thine Eyes'. Siegfried was particularly thrilled by Bessie's appearance in the last, and the goriness of Bluebeard's murdered wives. Steeped as he was in Romantic literature and art, and acutely sensitive to every type of beauty, he drank it all in. He was no less excited by a second production, staged this time in his mother's studio and based largely on Royal Academy picture subjects.

In the age before cinema or television such simple visual pleasures as *tableaux vivants* created great excitement, particularly in a quiet rural district of Kent, but they could not last, nor be endlessly repeated. Theresa, however, had other distractions which Siegfried registered as welcome diversions in his largely uneventful routine. His mother had a constant stream of visitors to Weirleigh, especially in the summer when the garden was at its loveliest. The ones her son remembered most vividly were her London friends, who came from that mysterious world beyond the Medway.

One of Theresa's oldest London friends was Nellie Gosse, but her visits were not as frequent nor as long as either of them would have liked. Nellie's marriage to the great Edmund Gosse, though it was to prove useful to Siegfried, kept her very busy in London. She had married shortly after her student days at the Royal Academy with Theresa and like Theresa had three children.[49] The eldest, Tessa (named after Theresa), spent the summer of 1897 with the Sassoons in Norfolk and the son, Philip, became friendly with Siegfried later. On the few occasions when their mother managed to visit Weirleigh, far from bringing her London literary world to Kent, she was quite content to sit and gossip with 'Trees', as she affectionately called Theresa, in the garden with an air of 'lulled contentment'.[50] Able to forget her famous guests and busy social life for a moment, she seemed to Siegfried relieved to be part of the apparent simplicity of Theresa's existence.

When Siegfried was only ten he had already reaped the benefit of her connexions. Theresa had shown Nellie one of his first works, dramatically entitled 'George the Berglerear' (presumably 'burglar'); Nellie must have realized the strength of his literary ambition, for one of his most treasured birthday presents in 1896 was a copy of Edmund Gosse's *The Naturalist of the Sea Shore*, inscribed with great tact to 'Mr Siegfried Sassoon'. The budding poet particularly admired two lines of poetry at the end of the book and could not resist inserting them into one of his own early efforts, wondering if his mother would notice the difference:

> Now came still evening on, and twilight grey
> Had in her sober livery all things clad.[51]

Much as Siegfried admired Nellie Gosse, she was not his favourite guest. There was no doubt in his mind that Helen Wirgman was the most exciting person who came to visit his mother at Weirleigh in the 1890s. 'Wirgie', as she was called by adults and children alike, was an old friend of all Theresa's family. She had become acquainted with the Thornycrofts through the relationship of her brother, Theodore Blake Wirgman, with Theresa's brother, Hamo. Theodore, an artist like Hamo, had painted portraits of Hamo and Hamo's other close friend, Gosse, as well as Gosse's wife Nellie. Wirgie herself had no profession. She lived on a small income and had travelled widely abroad. As a result her French and German were excellent. A highly cultured person, who endured living in London, which she disliked, only for its pictures, music and French and German plays.

Theresa believed that she had had the talent to become a successful actress but Siegfried thought that her real forté was music. Though not of professional standard, she played the piano with such intense imagination, emotional warmth and vitality that she inspired Siegfried to persist in his own woeful fumblings. She was, to use his own words, 'quite the most wonderful musician' he had heard as a child.[52] (His friend Bessie Marchant remembered her music as 'soul-stirring'.) Wirgie's rendition of the Beethoven piano sonatas seemed to him better even than that of Paderewski, whom he had heard at Tunbridge Wells. Among her favourite composers were Schumann and Beethoven. When she was playing the last movement of the *Moonlight Sonata* or the first page of the *Pathétique*, Siegfried felt 'that she was expressing all the stormy and tremendous things which she couldn't say in any other way' and he longed to be able to emulate her.[53]

Wirgie's was altogether a stormy personality. As Siegfried discovered, she was difficult and easily offended. When he had dared to joke about his Uncle Don's undeniable bulk, she had been quite 'huffy' with him for several hours, though she knew he loved his uncle and his large family almost as much as she did. They had once walked all the way home from Siegfried's favourite 'Watercress Well', at least half an hour from Weirleigh, in complete silence because Wirgie had been so angry with him for prodding a toad rather hard to see how fast it could go. Far from being thrown by Wirgie's bad tempers, Siegfried withstood them very well. He himself often suffered similar irrational outbursts and identified closely with her highly emotional response to life. She was unlike any other adult he had met, particularly in her willingness to join in his activities. Whether this meant trampling wildly across the wire-netting Theresa had placed cautiously on the garden pond, in pursuit of butterflies, or acting absurd parts in the miming game of Dumb Crambo with him, she entered into everything with a wholeheartedness and abandonment Siegfried shared.

Unlike most grown-ups too, Wirgie understood nonsense and when Siegfried came out with muddled sentences in his over-excitement, she never said 'Don't be silly', merely that she thought such sentences as 'The studio was playing Ludo with a poodle in a puddle' only occurred in the game of Consequences. Her own sense of humour was highly developed, ranging from the verbal – '10,000 times have [I] seized a pen, preparatory to penning you a plump piece of prose, puffing forth my praise of your perfect appreciation of G. Meredith as a pastmaster in penmanship,' she wrote to him on one occasion – to the visual – 'Dear Siegfried, / Well ? ? ? ? ?' – she started another letter, leaving the rest of the page completely blank in a manner worthy of the novelist Sterne. She told good stories, often against herself, such as the time she tripped on a highly polished floor and only saved herself from falling by grabbing a rather apprehensive and extremely stout vicar. 'The Honourable Mrs Caboodle' as she sometimes called herself, told Siegfried that she believed laughter was 'almost a greater bond of union than seriousness', though there was undeniably a serious side to their relationship. In some ways Wirgie filled the gap left, not only by his highly emotional and very playful father, but also by his brothers' defection to engineering. She may also have unwittingly encouraged his growing independence from Michael and Hamo.

Over fifty when Siegfried first met her in 1896, Wirgie had lost her early good looks. To the young boy she seemed 'rugged-looking', especially when she was feeling cross,[54] and referred to herself on one occasion as 'a very old wreck'. She also struck him, however, as 'very distinguished', particularly when she wore her 'old, old mulberry silk garment', as she described her only garden-party dress.[55] (This had been on the occasion of Queen Victoria's Diamond Jubilee, which they had celebrated together in the garden at Weirleigh in 1897.) She spoke slowly and her 'low, mouth-closed laugh' seemed to him to suit her name exactly (was he half-rhyming 'Wirgie' with 'gurgle'?). Her deeply humorous glance remained in his mind, long after he had, to his regret, lost touch with her. Thinking back on his relationship with her sixty-five years after it began, he felt that she had been 'a sort of genius … imaginative and impulsive', which helped explain her strong appeal for him and other children.[56]

It was no chance, therefore, that Siegfried had dedicated one of his first volumes of poetry to Wirgie. She had very strong views on poetry, as on most subjects, and could be relied on to tell the truth. Her hero was Meredith, whom she had known personally, and she encouraged Siegfried, wisely, to become less vague and more physical in his work, like him. Siegfried thought her a very 'percipient' judge of poetry and continued to seek her advice for more than a decade.

Helen Wirgman fitted completely into the daily routine at Weirleigh, but Aunt Rachel was quite a different matter. After her support of her brother's marriage to Theresa and defiance of her mother's ban on relations with them, she had remained a close friend of Theresa's, even after Alfred's desertion. She visited Weirleigh throughout the nineties, her visits tending to be both dramatic and brief. If, as often happened, she missed the scheduled train, she would hire a special private one at considerable cost for the journey from Charing Cross to Paddock Wood. After crawling up Gedges Hill in the station fly she would spend several hours closeted with Theresa. then leave just as suddenly. However impulsively undertaken, such visits always included lavish boxes of fruit and sweets for the household and parcels of books for the boys.

Rachel's abrupt arrivals and departures and her long conversations with Theresa at Weirleigh were partly caused by her temperament, which was volatile in the extreme. They were also a result of an increasingly desperate personal problem she needed to share with one of her closest friends – a reversal of their roles in 1883 when Theresa had turned to her for support. In 1887, three years after her brother's marriage, Rachel Sassoon had herself married out of the Jewish faith.

Unlike Alfred, she was not banished from the family, perhaps because, as I have suggested, her mother could not stand the loss of a second child, possibly because Flora shared the Orthodox view that the Jewish line passes through the female. Another explanation is simply that Rachel's husband, Frederick Beer, was exceedingly wealthy. The son of a financier from Frankfurt, who had made a fortune on the Stock Exchange, Frederick was himself a gentle man, too sensitive and unassertive for his father's tastes but well suited to Rachel's artistic temperament. Small and dark, he also resembled Rachel physically and they were, to begin with, ideally matched. With Frederick's £20,000 a year to add to her own comfortable income, they bought a splendid house at Seven Chesterfield Gardens, which boasted one of the most imposing staircases in Mayfair. Liveried servants, luxurious carriages and priceless works of art completed the scene. Before long, however, it became apparent that Frederick was far from well. Mysterious headaches, bewildering changes of mood and creeping paralysis eventually led doctors to diagnose the tragic cause of his deteriorating health – inherited syphilis. Theresa's evasive explanation to her puzzled sons was that 'poor Mr Beer has a bad heredity'. Either his mother, purportedly an opera-singer, had plied other trades, or his father had caught the disease from a previous mistress and passed it on to her and thus his son. It was not surprising that Frederick and Rachel had no children, for he in turn had passed the disease on to his wife, though this was not immediately apparent. When Siegfried came to describe his uncle and aunt's sad life, he consulted a doctor friend who advised him to drop the words 'raving' and 'dementia', possibly the most tell-tale indications of syphilis, if he wished to gloss over the true situation.[57]

When Siegfried first recalled Aunt Rachel in the Nineties, however, there was little sign of her future fate. She was no vaguer than she had always been and was still capable of becoming animated after a short time with her favourite nephews and sister-in-law. She showed her affection lavishly, insisting on visits to London, when her brown-liveried coachman and footman would meet Siegfried and his family in a magnificent brougham at Charing Cross and drive them to an exotic lunch at Seven Chesterfield Gardens, Mayfair. The boys were fascinated by the glass bridge and mirrored passageway that led to the dining-room and the novelty of brilliant electric lights. Even as a child, however, Siegfried felt vaguely oppressed by the hot-house, sickroom atmosphere and his aunt's increasingly distracted manner. Nevertheless, he managed to enjoy her afternoon entertainments, which ranged from a visit to Maskelyne's Mysteries at the Egyptian Hall to a private performance of an act of Gluck's *Orpheus*, sung by Rachel's friend Julia Rivoli, or a visit to the theatre. After seeing *As You Like It* on one such occasion, Siegfried could not help wishing that Aunt Rachel could be whisked away to the Forest of Arden and happiness. It was his first visit to a proper theatre and it seemed to him a 'lovely dream'.[58]

Rachel was undeniably eccentric. Her vagueness was not an affectation and her lavish spending, which earned her the nickname 'Madame Midas', was carried out in an impulsive and odd manner. Having taken over *The Observer*, which her husband had inherited from his father, she suddenly decided to buy *The Sunday Times* for herself in 1893. (It cost £11,000.) Whilst personally nursing a gravely ill husband through the nineties, she edited both papers simultaneously and also wrote leaders, book reviews and occasional feature articles. Though both papers declined in circulation during her editorship, neither folded and she did make some impressive decisions. The most memorable of these was her printing of the 'confessions' of Major Esterhazy, the man whose evidence had convicted the Jewish officer, Captain Dreyfus, of treason. Though Esterhazy subsequently retracted the confession and *The Observer* was forced to pay him £500 to settle a libel suit, Rachel had made her mark. Later evidence vindicated her decision, which had been prompted not only by a natural reaction to anti-Semitism but also by a consistent horror of any cruelty or social injustice. She also insisted in her journalism on an objective approach to politics, an almost unheard-of attitude for the day.

It should be said that, in spite of the emphasis history has placed on Rachel's erratic behaviour and nightmarish dilatoriness – her leaders were usually delivered in her indecipherable hand by a footman at the eleventh hour – she must have been both shrewd and competent to have edited both papers for over a decade in difficult circumstances. It was also an age when women editors of national papers were even rarer than they are today. Only after her husband's death in 1902 did she begin to lose her grip, sending in strange leaders on anything that took her fancy, including cannibalism, leaving articles half-finished and entirely neglecting to open review copies which had, in any case, been piling up in her library, dining-room and drawing-room for years.[59]

Siegfried, who noted the growing mountains of unopened review copies, preferred to remember his aunt in her prime, when, for example, she had organized an *Observer* stand at the Hotel Cecil for the Press Bazaar in 1896. He and his brothers had on that occasion been invited to act as pages of *The Observer* in silk breeches and frilly white shirts (the pun was intentional). When the Princess of Wales and the Duke of Cambridge arrived at their stand, the boys were supposed to sweep off their plumed hats and bow. Siegfried, who was dreaming as usual, failed to interpret Michael's nudge in the ribs and suffered the humiliation of having his hat knocked off for him by one of his brothers. Aunt Rachel's only reaction was to console him with a signed copy of H.G. Wells's *The Time Machine*, little knowing that her nephew would one day become good friends with the author. She also bought him a cricket bat at Wisden's on his next visit to London. At the same time she ordered a complete cricket set for her husband, whose increasing debilitation she refused to accept.

When Frederick Beer did eventually die in 1902 she reacted with complete disbelief, first refusing to have him buried, then locking herself in her room and rejecting all food. In desperation her doctors sent for her closest friend, Theresa, who finally persuaded her to eat. She gave up her editorship of *The Observer* and *The Sunday Times* not long afterwards in 1904 and went to live in a big house outside Tunbridge Wells. Attended by a large staff she spent the years until her death in 1927 there, gradually succumbing to the disease which had killed her husband.

Rachel was still relatively happy when Siegfried became conscious of her presence at Weirleigh in the nineties. She was his favourite aunt, and not just because she was so generous. Consciously or not, he was deeply attached to the one member of Alfred's family who had stood by his mother, himself and his brothers. This 'queer, brilliant woman', as he called her, also shared many of his father's qualities and, incidentally, his own. All three were witty, charming and volatile. (Siegfried referred later to her 'emotional, poetic nature'.) They all loved books and music – Rachel had composed and even published pieces for the piano and other instruments. They were also physically attractive, the same intense expression in their dark eyes compelling attention. Where they differed was in their reaction to town and country. Both Alfred and Rachel flourished in London and seemed rather out of place in the English countryside. In Siegfried his Thornycroft rural ancestry seems to have predominated and ultimately he came to prefer the country, though there were times when he felt drawn to the more immediate stimulus of the town.

As a child, however, his norm was the country and visits to Aunt Rachel were no more than brief interludes in the usual round of events. By the summer of 1899 this routine had changed somewhat with the departure of Michael for prep school and the advent of a new tutor for Siegfried and Hamo, Mr Hamilton. Fresh from Rugby and Cambridge, Clarence Hamilton presented a sharp contrast with Mr Moon in almost every way imaginable. Brought in by Theresa in an attempt to drag her younger sons up to standard before they joined Michael at prep school, he was young, sporty and handsome and greatly admired by Siegfried. His clean-shaven good looks, muscular figure and stylish clothes contrasted strikingly with Mr Moon's shabby, stooping appearance. Though planning to become a clergyman after his year with the Sassoons, he had none of Mr Moon's clerical airs.[60] His was, rather, a 'muscular Christianity'.

Unsophisticated as Siegfried was at the age of twelve, he recognized that Mr Hamilton completely eclipsed poor old Mr Moon. Even the determined Fraulein Stoy, who continued to teach him French, German and music, became altogether subsidiary to the new tutor and his fresh approach. 'The Beet', as his two charges nicknamed the ruddy-complexioned graduate, was clearly a welcome masculine presence at Weirleigh. A photograph of Siegfried and Hamo taken by Hamilton in the garden suggests that he was also a very understanding tutor who did not terrorize his pupils. Holding an inside-out umbrella above their heads, though the sun is clearly shining, they are both grinning mischievously at the camera, almost certainly held by Mr Hamilton himself. It is interesting to note too that, in spite of being the elder of the two, Siegfried is half hiding behind Hamo who is the taller and more confident looking. They are in a quasi-uniform of Norfolk jackets with knickerbockers, knee-length woollen socks and stout lace-up shoes. They look very happy.

While Siegfried recognized his tutor's tact, good-nature and modesty and appreciated his more energetic teaching methods, it was Mr Hamilton's sporting abilities he most admired. A member of the Cricket Eleven at Rugby and Captain of his college cricket team at Cambridge, 'the Beet' was an exciting addition to Siegfried's cricketing ambitions in 1899. In his first match at Brenchley, Mr Hamilton lived up to his reputation, knocking up a stylish thirty in an important game. On the highly irregular pitch of Matfield Green, however, he suffered the fate of what locals called 'the toffs' and failed to score at all. Siegfried was mortified by his hero's fate, but Mr Hamilton seemed highly relieved to have escaped from the dangerously bumpy pitch unscathed. He wisely decided to limit his cricketing to Brenchley's more conventional pitch, where he played a consistently excellent game. His lustre was increased still further in Siegfried's eyes when he learnt that Mr Hamilton had been a friend of the famous cricketer G.L. Jessop at Cambridge.

One marked effect of Mr Hamilton's presence on Siegfried was to make him feel that writing poetry was somehow priggish or unmanly. In 1898 Siegfried had produced four volumes of poetry and in January 1899, only four months before the new tutor's arrival, he had produced two more volumes. Yet during Mr Hamilton's year with the family he wrote no poetry at all. It was not that Mr Hamilton actively discouraged him, in fact he included poetry in the curriculum. But it was not the kind of poetry to inspire Siegfried to further efforts of his own. Learning by heart such 'public' poems as Tennyson's 'Revenge' and 'Defence of Lucknow' and reading aloud Canto I of Spenser's *Faerie Queene* was not calculated to stir the creativity of a boy whose favourite poems included Keats' 'Ode to a Nightingale'.

Siegfried maintained that he was, in any case, beginning to lose his early ecstasies and inspirations, but it may well have been that he could not sustain them in the no-nonsense masculine world of Mr Hamilton, which was not conducive to poetry. His literary tastes, such as they were, ran more to prose and he presented Siegfried with at least one prose work during his stay, Charles Kingsley's *The Heroes, or Greek Fairy Tales for My Children* (1899). He may also have encouraged him to read Scott's stirring adventure stories, which Siegfried was enjoying by the late 1890s. Another possible explanation is that, whilst desperately trying to catch up on all the conventional schooling that he lacked – he was between four and five years behind boys of his age in the system – Siegfried had no energy left for poetry. These were conflicts he was to experience repeatedly in his career, tensions between the outer and inner worlds, between his sporty, physical side and his introverted, dreamy self. His work is often at its best when he is trying to reconcile the two worlds, as in his war poetry, or *The Memoirs of a Fox-Hunting Man*.

Whatever Mr Hamilton's negative effects on Siegfried's poetry, Theresa regarded him as her saviour. Her sons began to look as though they would be ready to go to prep school at last and their behaviour also improved under their new tutor's firmer hand. (They had had a reputation for being very naughty in Church, for example.)

Even if Mr Hamilton had not been there, 1899, the last year of the old century, was by its very nature an exciting one. To add to the excitement, the Boer War broke out and everybody began to scan the newspapers anxiously. On a more personal level, their beloved Uncle Don died after a long illness. This time Siegfried attended the funeral, with Mr Hamilton and Hamo. (It may have been at this funeral that Hamilton first met Siegfried's cousin, Nellie Donaldson, whom he later married.) As Siegfried watched his uncle's coffin drawn along by four of his favourite Clydesdales and saw the miserable faces of his ten Donaldson cousins, he felt that his own poems about death had been very shallow indeed. The outside world was beginning to break in on him and for a time poetry seemed both inadequate and inappropriate.

The century ended, however, on a more positive note. Hamo insisted that they celebrate the advent of the new by the destruction of the old. Though Siegfried resisted the idea of burning down their childhood Fort, he was bought off by his more determined brother and felt a certain exhilaration as he watched the past go up in flames. It was the beginning of the end of childhood. In only four more months he would leave Weirleigh for his first sustained visit to the outside world.

4

'Harum-Scarum Schoolboy'
(1900-1904)

The first four years of the twentieth century find Siegfried facing wholly new situations as he attempts to join the system from which his mother deliberately excluded him, that of boarding school. Still living largely in his own world, he is only dimly conscious of the Boer War because he is given a day off school to celebrate the Relief of Mafeking in 1900. And he seems wholly unaware of the significance of Victoria's death the following year.[1] Yet, he struggles to conform and to catch up on his neglected education, learning to deal with the outside world and with people other than those in his close family circle.

Siegfried's first prolonged sortie into the outside world was to the New Beacon Preparatory School. Situated about a mile and a half from Sevenoaks in the district of Cross Keys, it was only fourteen miles from Weirleigh, a comfort no doubt to his over-protective mother. The New Beacon had been recommended by the boys' governess, Fraulein Stoy, whose previous charge and brightest pupil, Nevill Forbes, had attended it in its former incarnation as The Beacon in Sevenoaks itself. Though Forbes had only been there for three terms in 1896 before leaving for public school, he had achieved outstanding results, being first in Latin, French and English, second in Greek and fifth in Maths, all in the top set. Siegfried was to become a friend of Nevill after both had left school. For the time being he was only a rather irritating example of the perfect pupil, referred to constantly by Fraulein Stoy who had taught him the two subjects at which he excelled and Siegfried did not – languages and music.

Nevill's father was a close friend of the New Beacon's founder, John Stewart Norman. Norman had come to Sevenoaks in 1882 to take over The Beacon, 'a school for the sons of gentlemen preparatory to the great Public Schools of this country'. Founded in 1863 in St John's Road, the school had gradually declined until by 1882 it had no pupils at all. With the help of his dynamic wife, Alice Mary (née Square)[2] and two fellow-masters from his previous school, Plymouth Grammar, Norman had set about the revival of The Beacon. Then in his twenty-eighth year, a classical scholar of St Paul's and Corpus Christi, Cambridge, Norman was determined, energetic and imaginative. He was also a perfectionist, who planned his school's curriculum down to the last detail, to include not only all the predictable disciplines of the day – Latin, Greek and Maths – but also less established subjects such as English, French, German, History, Geography, Music and Art. Each of six sets, which were dictated by ability rather than age, had detailed schedules for each subject, carefully defining and limiting the syllabus.

Norman's enlightened approach to education also prompted him to broaden extra-curricular activities to include, besides the usual games of cricket, football, hockey and rugger, such things as carpentry, boxing, fencing, swimming, club-swinging and golf. From Monday to Saturday the mornings were spent in the classroom after an 'early school' of poetry and New Testament readings. Wednesday and Saturday afternoons were half-holidays and the rest were divided between more lessons and games. Sunday was devoted mainly to religion Norman himself, as a lay-reader, usually took the evening service.

The Beacon had flourished under Norman's rule and by 1887 had fifty-eight pupils, many from well-known Sevenoaks families. Before its previous decline it had been well-known for preparing boys mainly for Eton and had had a large clientele among the landed gentry of the county and Southern England. Norman widened its appeal and by the time the first Sassoon arrived at The Beacon in September 1899, the school was also known for its naval, military and Scottish connections, its four chief outlets to public school being Wellington, Charterhouse, Marlborough and the local Tonbridge; it also sent a number of boys to Dartmouth.

September 1899 had been the last term of The Beacon. By January 1900 The New Beacon had opened in the larger premises which Norman had been planning since at least 1897. Short of space for both lessons and games, and anxious to move to a more attractive area, Norman had bought about twenty acres of land in the Cross Keys area for £2,600. Having already arranged a sizeable loan, Norman was ready to start building a completely new school on the site in 1898 and by January 1900 was ready to move in, despite problems with drains, flues and rats. (The site had originally housed a Pest House.) Including architects' fees and the price of the land, the venture had cost him just over £10,000, a huge investment for the time. Several extras, such as a separate masters' house cum sanatorium and a gardener's cottage had had to be abandoned on the way, suggesting that Norman had borrowed as much as he dared.

The result was an attractive red-brick building set in spacious grounds, reassuring no doubt to a mother like Theresa Sassoon, who worried constantly about her sons; at 600 feet above sea level the New Beacon seemed particularly healthy. The main body of the school, which formed three sides of a square, contained classrooms down the centre and a large dining-room and schoolroom running off at right-angles at either end. Above both wings were two large dormitories called 'Big' and 'Little Big' by the boys, the 'Little' indicating the age of the boys rather than the size of the rooms. When Siegfried and Hamo joined Michael at the New Beacon in its second term on the new premises, Siegfried was in 'Big' and his younger brother in 'Little Big'. Apart from the classrooms, which seem by today's standards rather cramped, all the public rooms were light and airy.

Theresa's main concern, the food, was well looked after, if we are to trust the glowing account of vast roasts and satisfyingly filling puddings given by the founder's son.[3] There was also a matron, Miss Mills, devoted to the boys' welfare even if this meant, as it did in Siegfried's case, finding them shirts that their unworldly mothers had failed to supply. Theresa had dutifully packed knickerbocker suits, Eton collars, 'dickeys' and bowlers for her sons' weekend wear, but had not realized that shirts were necessary. And Siegfried's worst moment as a new boy occurred when a kind master encouraged him to remove his jacket during cricket practice and he was forced to confess to his shirtless state.

When Siegfried and Hamo arrived at the New Beacon in April 1900, Michael was in his third term with Mr Norman. He had started at The Beacon in September 1899, moved to the new premises in January 1900 and was therefore something of an old hand. The impact of leaving home must consequently have been softened somewhat for Siegfried, particularly as he also had his younger brother with him. Nevertheless, he suffered acutely to begin with. It was not only home-sickness. The fact that, at nearly fourteen, he was much older and larger than most of the other boys, instead of increasing his confidence, made him feel even more inexperienced and helpless. It seemed to him as he gazed at his 'play-box', which had been dumped down unceremoniously in the tin hut serving as a temporary gym, that he had left his private life at Weirleigh and that all he could call his own was contained in that box. His insecurity was further increased by his lack of shirts, though that was soon remedied by Miss Martha Mills, who treated each boy as though he were her own special charge. With only forty-six boys, all boarders, the New Beacon was not a large school, but it was large enough and confusing enough for Siegfried to long to be back at Weirleigh with his tutor Mr Hamilton.

One great consolation to Siegfried in his early days was the sympathy of the Chief Assistant Master, Mr Jackson. Of all his experiences at the New Beacon, he most clearly remembered the moment on his first day when Mr Jackson, sensing his misery, encouraged him to go and console himself with a hearty tea. Siegfried found the second-in-command less intimidating than Mr Norman, though he came to like the latter just as much, albeit in a different way. E. M. Jackson's appeal for a young boy probably lay in his excellence as both a teacher and a sportsman. He not only taught the next to top set in Classics but also coached the first team in one of Siegfried's favourite sports, cricket. (In fact, it was what he was 'keenest on' altogether at the New Beacon.[4]) In addition, Jackson excelled at golf, an activity Siegfried took to enthusiastically under his guidance. He started by caddying for Mr Jackson at Lord Hillingdon's nine-hole course on the nearby Wildernesse Estate and had derived some amusement from the frustrations of his headmaster, a decidedly inferior golfer to Mr Jackson. He also had fond memories of the time Mr Jackson took a group of boys holidaying on the Norfolk Broads:

> My mind would contain a spontaneous renewal of the smell of soles frying in the cabin of our boat, and perhaps a memory of the spacious solitude of Hickling Broad on some quiet September evening with a yellow sunset flaming beyond the reedy margins.[5]

Mr Jackson's love of Norfolk and his outstanding ability as a teacher eventually led to him start his own school there.

Most of all, Siegfried was grateful to Mr Jackson for helping him catch up on his education. His backwardness in the most important subject of the time, classics, had caused him, on entering the school, to be placed in the fourth of six Latin sets and excluded from any of the three Greek sets, even though he was one of the oldest boys at the New Beacon. So determined was he to make up for lost time that by September 1900, his second term, he had moved up in both Latin and Greek to set two. His response to Mr Jackson's skilful teaching there was immediate, though he failed to share his master's enthusiasm for Euripides. (After he left the New Beacon he continued tuition with Mr Jackson by post, and went on playing cricket and golf with him for even longer. They would still be in touch in 1938.)

Mr Jackson's teaching proved so effective that after only one term with him Siegfried was again moved up, this time to the top sets in both Latin and Greek. Here he came into closer contact with the headmaster, whom he found an equally 'magnificent schoolmaster'. Though Siegfried never shone in either subject, Mr Norman enabled him to reach the standard required for public school entrance and he was awarded prizes in both subjects in his final term.

Siegfried's admiration for his headmaster was based on more than gratitude, however. He clearly responded to Mr Norman's belief that the three pillars of education were a sense of humour, a sense of proportion and the gift of sympathy. Mr Norman stressed that unless boys were interested in their work they would not make progress, a theory he also applied to extra-curricular activities. To give boys a sense of real achievement he used to get the senior boys to help him with gardening and wooding in the school grounds, for example. He was also a pioneer in modern teaching methods which must have been of particular help to someone like Siegfried who found conventional learning difficult. Mr Norman was ahead of his time in emphasizing the importance of co-operation between school and home, a belief which would have comforted

Siegfried's mother. Altogether she had been lucky in her choice of Siegfried's first school. Under Mr Norman's guidance, the New Beacon was disciplined but not repressive; as Rupert Croft-Cooke, who had been both a boy and a master at the New Beacon, put it: 'The boys were neither coddled nor drilled'.[6] Beaconians were allowed more freedom of activity than was usual for the period. The system of dividing boys into four 'companies', for example, whilst sounding somewhat military, in reality encouraged team-spirit without squashing individuality.

Mr Norman seems to have been well aware of Siegfried's individuality and to have appealed to one of his stronger traits, his sense of humour. With teasing allusion to his sudden access of dignity in his last few terms at the school, he had christened his pupil 'Dook Sig', or 'Dook' for short. Siegfried in return referred to his headmaster, who was almost blind in one eye, as 'Cockeye'. (He had the usual schoolboy's relish for others' imperfections.)

Mr Norman probably also encouraged the boy's literary abilities, even though he wrote no actual poetry at the school, since Siegfried was to inscribe a copy of one of his earliest printed volumes to his headmaster long after he had left.[7] Mr Norman's own literary enthusiasms revealed themselves in the exciting 'readings' he gave to the boys in the big schoolroom at weekends. Siegfried remembered *Moonfleet* as one of the choices and Norman's son tells us that others included equally riveting stories by such writers as Anthony Hope, Sir Arthur Conan Doyle, Stanley Weyman, Robert Louis Stevenson and Jerome K. Jerome. Clearly Mr Norman knew his audience even if, as in Siegfried's time, he had occasionally to compete with the distractions of chestnut-roasting at the schoolroom's inviting open fire.

Curiously enough, Siegfried had entered the school in the second set at English, though Michael and even Hamo, were in the first set. After only one term, however, he was next to top in the first set and stayed there, coming top of the whole school in English in the two terms before he left and winning a prize in the subject. He also won prizes in the two remaining exam subjects, Maths and French, though his progress in both was more erratic and he moved uneasily between the second and first sets during his two years at the New Beacon.[8]

Of all Siegfried's extra-curricular activities, there is no doubt that he enjoyed cricket most, probably because it was one of the few things at which he shone. Happily, his arrival at the New Beacon in April 1900 coincided with the completion of a new cricket pitch, which had cost Mr Norman the then large sum of £320 18s. 6d. Siegfried was immediately put into the First Eleven, where he was joined the following year by Hamo. In a 1901 school photograph of the team, taken on the important occasion of their winning the West Kent Preparatory School Cup with the highest score the school was to record until at least the mid-1960s, the two Sassoon brothers tower above their younger fellow cricketers. Siegfried, in an effort to look more nonchalant than perhaps he felt, or as a sign of slight rebelliousness, has his blazer collar turned up. The New Beacon scorebook, which he copied out in his neat hand, shows that by 1901 he was a reasonable all-rounder, third in the batting averages and fourth in the bowling averages. He is described in the school magazine that year as 'a very useful change bowler'. Cricket and Siegfried's other enthusiasm at the New Beacon, golf, were to form a link which kept him in fairly close touch with the school up to the First World War.[9] He displayed less enthusiasm for the many other physical activities included in the New Beacon timetable.[10]

Siegfried seems to have enjoyed life at the New Beacon. Many of the boys brought their bicycles with them and were allowed to ride them after school. Siegfried's anxious mother had let him cycle only after she had discovered her sons driving Grandma Thornycroft's brakeless bath-chair down the steep hill outside Weirleigh. But she would not have enjoyed the sight of up to forty boys careering madly around the school grounds and would have preferred her sons to attend school picnics in Mrs Norman's carriage.

Even long wet walks, when the weather was too bad for games, were made enjoyable by the bars of chocolate and bottles of ginger pop that were provided to keep the boys going. Mr Norman clearly understood small boys and their large appetites. He introduced what Beaconians called the 'Grub-cart', which came once a week to supply them with tuck. To begin with Siegfried met it at the school gate like the other boys and trotted behind it up the drive to ensure his place in the queue. It was a measure of his greatly increased dignity during his final terms that, at the risk of finding his favourite Turkish Delight sold out, he always waited until the wild and unseemly scramble was over. He had, as Mr Norman put it, become too 'Dook'-like to join in the fray.

Siegfried's last term at the school was his least eventful. His first had been almost too dramatic. Ironically, in view of Theresa's extreme anxiety over his health, there had been an outbreak of diptheria at the New Beacon in the summer of 1900. A killer at the time, diptheria was rightly feared and almost a quarter of the pupils had been withdrawn, nearly destroying Norman's new venture at the outset. The mystery is why the solicitous Theresa did not remove her three sons instantly. Returning to school without Michael after the long summer holiday of 1900, Siegfried is elevated from 'Sassoon Minor' to 'Sassoon Major' (one reason perhaps for his increasingly 'Dook'-like behaviour). He discovers the joys of golf while caddying for Mr Jackson and starts to feel more confident about his work. In January 1901, when Queen Victoria dies, it never occurs to him to mark the event in verse as he would once have done. He cannot even remember what 'feeling inspired' is like, though he does occasionally suspect that he has lost something precious. His main response to the momentous death is a fit of giggles when Mr Jackson sits on his bowler hat at the memorial service. Cricket dominates the summer term of 1901, when Siegfried helps win the West Kent Prep School Cup and gains his 'colours'.

After the memorable holiday with Mr Jackson on the Norfolk Broads in September 1901 he returns for his last term at the New Beacon. In spite of his rather slapdash approach to his entrance exam – Mr Norman makes him do it twice and, with rather dubious morality, destroys his first effort – Siegfried gets his place at Marlborough. When he leaves, at Christmas, he is top of the school in one subject – English.

In spite of his evident enjoyment of school life, Siegfried does not appear to have retained any close friends from the New Beacon, though a number of the pupils were subsequently at Marlborough with him. It may be that the company, first of both his brothers, then of his younger one alone, insulated him a little from the other boys and made him seem more self-sufficient than he felt. Possibly they were put off by his slight 'scattiness' – he was nicknamed 'the Onion', he explained, because he seemed to them a little 'off his onion'. The fact that he was considerably older than the majority of the boys may also have made close friendships less likely. The most probable explanation is that he was still struggling to survive in the outside world from which his mother had protected him for far longer than normal. That he was happy at the New Beacon is a sign of his resilience and eagerness to catch up. Theresa herself must also have been pleased with it, since she almost certainly recommended it to her nephew, John Thornycroft, who was to send his two sons there in 1908 and 1911 respectively.

The one boy with whom Siegfried remained in close touch from the New Beacon, the headmaster's younger son, Cecil Norman, was indirectly the cause of his next choice of school, Marlborough College. In fact, neither Siegfried nor his mother had actually chosen Marlborough, it was the suggestion of Mr Norman, who had already entered Cecil for it. Not only did his school already have strong connections with Marlborough, but he also felt that it would suit Siegfried better than Malvern, which had been chosen for Michael. Mr Norman's policy, unusual for the time, was not to send a boy automatically to the school his father had attended, or to the one chosen by his socially aspiring parents, but to try to cater to the boy's individual needs. Siegfried was clearly neither academically brilliant nor was he a hopeless case. In addition his family, in spite of its name, was not wealthy. Marlborough seemed, therefore, the right choice. Siegfried later recorded his gratitude that Norman had succeeded in persuading his cautious mother to agree.

Theresa had probably been helped to decide on Marlborough by Fräulein Stoy, whose star pupil, Nevill Forbes, had gone on there from the New Beacon in 1897. She must also have been reassured by what Mr Norman could tell her of the comfortable boarding-house – Cotton – that he had chosen for his own son. At any rate Theresa had put Siegfried's name down for Cotton House and in January 1902 he left home again, this time for a more distant destination.

Siegfried was not allowed to travel by himself to Marlborough for his first term, but was accompanied by his anxious mother who was still unwilling to let him face the world alone. Though intensely nervous, he would rather she had seen him off at Paddington station and left him to sink into a state of numb apprehension than to have to keep up appearances with her for the whole journey. Like another well-known Marlburian poet, John Betjeman, he probably felt 'Doom! Shivering doom!' as he clutched his small holdall containing night-clothes, sponge-bag, house-slippers, health certificate, Book of Common Prayer and photographs of home.[11] He was pleased to be going to Marlborough and felt rather important about it, even though he suspected that he could never do outstandingly well at either work or games, the two pillars of public school life at that time. He was determined to do his best but very apprehensive about beginning. To make matters worse, his mother had insisted on arriving early so that she could vet both the Master of the College and Siegfried's housemaster.

The first interview, with Marlborough's Head, the Reverend George Bell, seemed mercifully brief to Siegfried. Bell, who was in the penultimate year of his twenty-seven-year rule, simply greeted Theresa politely and told Siegfried to 'be a good boy', with the air of one who had performed this ritual too many times for it to seem meaningful. For his part, Siegfried was abjectly grateful not to have to talk to 'Tup', as the Master was irreverently called. He was also greatly relieved that his mother, probably a little over-awed by the venerable, white-bearded Bell, did not draw his attention to her son's exceptional intelligence and lack of physical robustness. Bell did not, perhaps, invite confidences. His successor, Frank Fletcher, who had reason to appreciate his helpfulness, nevertheless described him as 'a dry, humorous, eminently safe personality'.[12] It is not surprising that Siegfried, whose taste in humour was far from dry, fails to mention Bell after an initial reference in his account of Marlborough.

With Siegfried's house-master, Mr Gould, whom he and his mother visited next, it was quite different. For Gould was the type of eccentric schoolmaster whom boys love and remember. His habit of riding a lady's bicycle at a snail's pace down the Bath Road into College drew fine taunts from his charges – 'You're scorching, Mr Gould' – which Gould dealt with, genially, in his usual style – 'Shut up, you wretched brute!'. It was quite normal for boys to boo him as he entered their classrooms or studies, but the booing was affectionate. He was a deliberate clown who used his buffoonery to win over the boys. Some of his colleagues were shocked by the bursts of disorderly laughter which came from his classroom, but according to Fletcher, the last Master under whom Gould served, 'there was more method about his buffoonery than unsympathetic critics realized'.[13] The boys remembered the Greek constructions he taught as well as his jokes. Out of a staff of nearly forty, generations of Marlburians recalled Gould in particular. Charles Hamilton Sorley, for instance, who arrived only six years after Siegfried, thought that his best days at Marlborough were 'the days under Gould'.[14]

Siegfried's first impression of Gould was that, with his 'majorish moustache', he looked more like a retired military man than a schoolmaster. On closer acquaintance he felt that Gould bore more resemblance to an 'easy-going clubman who had put away a good deal of port in his day'.[15] Looking back on his introduction to Gould, he realized that, instead of dutifully showing the Sassoons round Cotton House and answering Theresa's predictable questions about arrangements for her son's health, he would far rather have been reading a French novel in his comfortable armchair. Siegfried's later analysis of Herbert Marius Gould was that he was more of a Herbert than a Marius. Though an excellent classicist, as his scholarship to Trinity College, Oxford from Marlborough and First Class degree there showed, and in spite of a taste for good food and wine, his resemblance to Marius the Epicurean was limited. He was perhaps too worldly to resemble his namesake.[16]

There was a general feeling at Marlborough that Gould's abilities were wasted as a schoolmaster and that he would have done far better at the Bar or in Parliament. He was very active in the local Tory party, and brought, as Fletcher put it, 'a whiff of the outer world' into the somewhat narrow school community. His contacts with men in public life caused many of them to send their sons to his house. He was in his element at the Saturday evening dinner parties he gave, when his brilliant conversation found a more suitable outlet than in teaching. It is not difficult to imagine him caring less than his colleagues for discipline and rules. His house was run along very relaxed lines – some said too lax – and this helps to explain Siegfried's enjoyment of life there. (After Gould's retirement Cotton House became a far more disciplined place.) Siegfried was to meet Gould a few years after his retirement in 1910, when it was clear that his ex-housemaster was spending most of his time at the Carlton Club and that club life was not agreeing with his constitution, 'for his nose was more blue and bulbous than ever above his tobacco-stained moustache, and he looked so doddery' that his ex-pupil felt 'he would be all the better for country air and a few games of croquet, at which he had been such a reputed expert'.[17]

In 1902, however, when Siegfried arrived at Marlborough, Gould was still playing croquet and only halfway through his fifteen years as housemaster of Cotton. His pronounced paunch indicated a love of the good things in life, but he was also active in caring for his boys. Siegfried had fond memories of him toddling round the dormitories at night murmuring 'Ho, you big fellow', or 'Hullo, you little fellow'. (Another ex-pupil remembered less kindly that when their housemaster took his nightly patrol, he was 'more than a little shaky after that last little nip!'[18]) Clearly Gould was attached to them in his own idiosyncratic way and Siegfried's overall response echoed that of many: 'Good old Gould!'[19]

Marlborough had been founded in 1843 by the Reverend Charles Plater, who saw the need for a good public school which the clergy could afford. It opened in what had originally been a country house built by the Seymour family, which then became the famous Castle Inn on the London to Bath road. Shortly afterwards a New House, Junior House and Dining-Hall had been added and many other buildings followed between 1852 and 1902. The College's prospectus for the year of Siegfried's entry, 1902, proudly draws attention to its fine buildings, the most relevant of which to this story is Cotton House, opened in 1872.

Cotton was one of the first two purpose-built Out-College Houses. The urgent need for more accommodation had been raised by the adverse report of a Sanitary Commissioner in April 1870. His conclusions that there was serious overcrowding and lack of ventilation in almost all the old College buildings had previously been reached by the School's Council as well as many parents. In fact, the Council had already commissioned plans for one new boarding-house, but following the Sanitary Commissioner's report, it decided that two were needed.

The distinguished architect G.E. Street, best known for his design of the London Law Courts, was asked to produce plans for two large but inexpensive buildings, to be called Cotton and Littlefield Houses. Street, whose pupils included Norman Shaw, Philip Webb and William Morris (himself an Old Marlburian), came up with a building characteristic of the Arts and Craft movement popularized by Morris in the late 19th century. In order to minimize costs he made walls out of a concrete compound consisting of flint and chalk excavated from the site. The result was one of the earliest examples of a large-scale concrete construction in a domestic building and, as such, was subsequently listed. Fascinating though this might be to an architectural student, the effect, reinforced by its exposed situation high above the Bath Road, is somewhat bleak and in marked contrast to the warm red brick of the central College buildings. It could not have been a welcoming sight to a forlorn new boy in January 1902.

Cotton House, named after the man who pulled Marlborough back from the brink in 1852,[20] had an historic name but not a long history of its own by 1902. Gould was only its second housemaster, the first, F.E. Thompson, having underwritten almost half the building cost of £5,228. For his outlay of £2,500 Thompson was allowed to run the house as a business, taking fees from parents and sharing in the profits. Since it had been designed as a boarding-house, living conditions were far more comfortable than In-College, but fees were correspondingly higher. The basic annual fee in the four Senior Out-Houses in 1902 was £110 as compared with £85 for the more spartan In-Houses, a difference of 30% which Siegfried's mother paid, no doubt willingly. It was generally regarded as more convenient to be In-College, but more comfortable to be Out.

One of the many advantages of being in Cotton House for Siegfried, of which he was probably unaware, was that he escaped the austerities and horrors of A-House and Upper School. Louis MacNeice likened A-House, the In-College building for juniors, to a prison and is eloquent on the miseries of Upper School, the communal room for boys on first entering a Senior In-College House. Betjeman, Sorley, Beverley Nichols and many others have reinforced the grim picture MacNeice paints of physical discomfort and ritual bullying.

As a Senior boy entering an Out-House, Sassoon would automatically have escaped these trials. His dormitory in Cotton House was one of four and, since there were less than fifty boarders in all, is unlikely to have held more than twelve boys. Long wooden partitions between beds gave each boy relative privacy, unlike the shorter ones which have since replaced them. A central table contained blue and white washing bowls, soap-dishes and tooth-mugs, one for each boy, and, though the water was cold, at least there were opportunities for hot baths.[21] Bedclothes were supplied by the house, including a bright red top blanket known as 'college redders', but Theresa Sassoon, convinced in advance of their inadequacy and possible infectiousness, had taken the precaution of bringing Siegfried his own blankets. Gould, understandably, had been less than enthusiastic about this domestic detail, but the Dame (or Matron), Mrs Bolt, a 'prim but very nice person' according to the embarrassed Siegfried, seemed grateful for the additional bedding.[22] She clearly took Theresa and her son to be 'some of those frightfully rich Sassoons who were always entertaining Royalties'. Not for the first time, Siegfried wished for a more commonplace name, knowing from experience that within a very short time the boys would be calling him 'Stinkweed Bassoon', or something equally awful. (In fact, for some obscure reason, his schoolfellows came up with nothing worse than the nickname 'Gaggers'.[23]) It was probably partly in self-defence that he later adopted a variety of grotesque pseudonyms such as 'Z. Zazzoon', 'Solemn 'Un Sassoon', 'Sashum' or 'Pinchbeck Lyre'.

One of Siegfried's problems in arriving in January, rather than the more usual time of September, was that he found himself the only new boy in Cotton House; the other entrant, Herbert Singer, had come from a Junior House, Upcot, and had already been at Marlborough over a year. The rest of the boys had already paired up. For the first time in his life, therefore, Siegfried was entirely on his own. His memories of this period are of total confusion. The smallest undertaking, such as finding his classroom, or doing up his tie, made him feel panicky. Fortunately Cotton House allowed him a certain amount of privacy. Unlike the In-Houses, it had plenty of studies, arranged over the ground and first floors, most of them shared with only one other boy. These were furnished comfortably, if basically, with bookcases, tables and wicker armchairs.

Sassoon's study-mate in his first term was almost certainly Christopher Teesdale (nicknamed 'Zip') who later wrote to reminisce about their time together: 'I can shut my eyes and see the study at Marlborough'.[24] Once Hamo joined Siegfried at the school, they shared a privileged south-facing study on the upper floor. Sassoon makes no mention in his memoirs of study-mates or other friends, but it may be that the 'good-natured' youth who finally showed a desperate Siegfried how to get his dark-blue tie up into his stiff double collar became a sympathetic friend. If so, he fails to say so.

Another subject Siegfried fails to mention in his description of Marlborough is homosexuality. Yet, like most public schools of the day, the Marlborough authorities clearly feared that the close proximity of teenage boys deprived of female company would result in what they regarded as immoral practices. In an attempt to discourage sexual liaisons and what was known as 'self-abuse' or 'beastliness' (that is, masturbation) there were no doors on the lavatories. Pupils were not allowed to visit dormitories alone in the day and several parts of the school grounds were strictly out of bounds. One housemaster, anxious to stamp out what he called 'impurity', made a close study of the subject and concluded that the most dangerous place was Upper School and that the most tempting times for boys were 'early summer mornings before early school and (most dangerous of all) Sunday mornings when many people are in chapel at early communion'.[25]

Since Siegfried was not In-College, Upper School would not have provided any temptations for him, but he is unlikely to have been entirely free from them. He was to tell a friend sixteen years later that from 'early youth' he had been tortured by the knowledge that women were 'antipathetic' to him and that he could 'only like men'.[26] It is unlikely, however, that his homosexuality found any physical outlet until those same sixteen years had passed. Writing to the sexual pioneer, Edward Carpenter, with whom he appears to have been entirely frank, and echoing the notion implied by his Marlborough masters of sexual innocence as 'purity', he claims to be still 'unspotted' at the age of twenty-four.[27] It is more than likely that his attraction towards his own sex made him both confused and unhappy at Marlborough, all the more so because he was unable to confide in anyone about it. However, since it was, as he put it to Carpenter, 'almost a subconscious thing', he was probably able to repress it and carry on with his everyday routine, which makes his lack of reference to the subject understandable.

A more curious omission in Siegfried's account of Marlborough is a description of the countryside. In those days Cotton House was surrounded by fields for miles around and its country air was counted as one of its many advantages. His mother, with her obsessive concern for his health, would certainly have registered that fact when she decided to pay its higher fees. For many Old Marlburians, notably Sorley, the Marlborough Downs were one of the main attractions of the school. Yet Siegfried, who loved his native Kent passionately and wrote endlessly about the countryside in his early verse, makes only passing references to such features of the Marlborough landscape as Savernake Forest and White Horse Hill. Perhaps it was loyalty to Kent that silenced him. It may also have been that his determination to make up as much ground as possible academically left him time for little else.

One of the disadvantages of being in Cotton House must have dawned on Siegfried in his first full day of school. For 'early school', that barbaric custom of holding one lesson before breakfast, was In-College and involved a cold, dark walk down the Bath Road. Since 'early school' started just after 7 a.m., he had to get up at about 6.30 a.m., wash in cold water in an unheated dormitory, throw on his clothes (he was particularly proud of his new cap and black jacket, but still struggling with his tie) and follow the other boys into school to the tolling of what Betjeman called 'the inexorable bell'. Once at the porter's lodge, however, everyone dispersed to their different forms and Siegfried was left vainly trying to remember the way to his. The experience remained with him for over twenty years as a recurring nightmarish dream: 'It seemed as if I were in a buzzing existence where everyone was bumping about and slamming doors and all noises were unnaturally loud and essentially uncharitable'.[28]

Early school was followed at 7.50 a.m. by compulsory chapel and at 8.15 a.m. by breakfast. For this the ravenous Cotton House boys had to rush back along the Bath Road, to devour their filling if basic meal of porridge, a boiled egg or kipper or something similar, bread and tea. Marlburians, understandably, added their own luxuries to this rather austere meal from their 'brew-boxes'. Siegfried's mother. convinced of the inadequacies of all school arrangements, provided marmalade in 7lb jars, so he is unlikely to have suffered too badly. If supplies ran out he could visit one of the town's two tuck-shops, Duck's or Knapton's, though only in the limited time available to him before lunch.

The first prep. of the day, which involved yet another walk back into college, began at 9.15 a.m. More lessons followed, until noon on what were called Fag Days. On these whole schooldays there were two further periods between 5 and 6.30 p.m. On 'half-holidays' – Tuesdays, Thursdays and Saturdays – there were no afternoon lessons, but an extra morning period at 12.20 p.m. ending just before lunch at 1.30 p.m.

Apart from morning chapel, lunch was the only occasion when the whole school met together. Known as 'Hall', because of its rather bleak venue, it was a more formal affair than other meals. A Latin grace was said by one of the school prefects, who seemed to Siegfried awesome figures in their white ties, before the boys sat down at their own house tables. Cotton House was often unsupervized until quite late in the proceedings, since Mr Gould had a habit of coming in for the cheese course only. Siegfried suspected that his sybaritic housemaster, unable to face college food which was notoriously bad in those days, had dined – and wined – at home. Siegfried himself had some trouble with 'College meat' which was often dubious in both colour and smell. Like most of the boys he probably filled up on puddings such as 'Treacle Bolly'.

Afternoons were devoted to games. Siegfried, who had not played rugger at his prep school, began with hockey. Having had his shin badly bruised in one of his first games, he was rather resentful when Gould swooped down on him one lunchtime and accused him of trying to avoid games by taking organ lessons. Anxious to counteract his housemaster's impression of him as a pampered 'softie', derived no doubt from his affluent surname and his mother's excessive concern for his health, he stood up to Gould who subsequently left him alone. The housemaster's 'choleric performance' towards a new boy, however, had its positive side, since it won him some sympathy and welcome attention from the older boys, who had previously ignored him. He had, in effect, he tells us, created a 'good new Gould joke'.[29]

The cause of the row, Siegfried's ambition to play the organ, had led to an embarrassing interview with the school's organist, Mr Bambridge. Convinced that her son was not only an invalid but also a genius, Theresa had written to tell the music master so. It was only as Siegfried prepared nervously to play 'Venetian Gondola' from Mendelssohn's *Songs Without Words* that he realized what was expected of him. He had, indeed, a real love of music as his mother claimed, but was not yet capable of giving it convincing expression. In fact, in his nervousness he played even less well than usual. Luckily for him Mr Bambridge whose lean, bearded face gave no sign of it, had a good sense of humour. Stopping Siegfried halfway through the first page, he put down Theresa's letter with a smile and arranged a time for organ lessons. No doubt it was not the first occasion on which a boy had failed to live up to his doting mother's description.

Siegfried's modest musical abilities led to another incident with his housemaster. Shortly after his arrival, the boy who usually played the piano at evening prayers claimed to have cut his finger badly and informed Siegfried that he would have to stand in. Protestations were in vain; the boy chose Siegfried an easy tune, apparently at random, and left him to it. As he practised the hymn compulsively at the ancient upright in the panelled hall where meals and prayers were held, Siegfried reminded himself that it was Saturday night, which Gould celebrated with an extra glass or two of port. Still trying to convince himself that no one would notice his fumblings, he waited in a trance-like state for Mr Gould to join the boys and Matron for prayers. When Gould eventually entered through the library, Siegfried had still failed to notice one crucial point – the words of the hymn:

4. 'Harum-Scarum Schoolboy' (1900-1904)

> How blest the matron who endued
> With holy zeal and fortitude,
> Has won through grace a saintly fame,
> And owns a dear and honour'd name.[30]

This perhaps would have escaped censure, even with Matron present, but the second verse, with its reference to a part of matron's anatomy which makes most small boys snigger – 'Such holy love inflamed her *breast*' – and the third, with its direct reference to 'the *flesh* that weigheth down the soul' must have alerted even the pleasantly fuddled Gould. Hymn and prayers were brought to an abrupt close and Siegfried found himself, for the second time, facing an enraged Gould. Fortunately his horrified expression made his housemaster realize that the naïve new boy had been duped. Abandoning his intention of shaking Siegfried violently, Gould merely uttered one of his characteristic remarks as he stormed out: 'You brutes! You wretched brutes!'[31] Also characteristic of Gould was his chuckle on his dormitory rounds that evening as he passed the apparently sleeping pianist.

Siegfried understandably concentrates on such amusing incidents in his autobiography. He says little about his education; it is clear, however, that he carried out his intention of working hard. He still had a great deal of ground to recover in spite of the New Beacon's excellent teaching. Entering the school at fifteen, already two years later than the majority of the new boys, he was placed very near the bottom in the Upper Fourth form of the Lower School. (Scholars, like Sorley and Beverly Nichols, usually entered the school much higher at a much younger age.)

He worked so conscientiously in his first term with Mr Meyrick, however, that he came 8th out of 26 in the form lists and even Gould was pleased with him. Promoted to Shell A at the bottom of the Upper School in the summer of 1902, he spent two terms there with Mr O'Regan, coming 19th out of 27 in the summer term but climbing rapidly to 4th out of 26 in the winter of 1902. After a term's absence in the spring of 1903 he found himself promoted again, to Mr Lupton's class, Remove B, where he came a modest 12th out of 28. Winter 1903 brought further promotion, to the Lower Fifth 2B with Mr England, where he remained until he left in the summer of 1904. Perhaps because he knew that, at nearly eighteen, he was not high enough in the school system to be allowed to stay on, his efforts seem to slacken in this class and his initial position of 19th out of 27 is only marginally improved to 15th out of 28 the term he leaves.

Looking back on his education, Siegfried wondered why he found himself so unable to win academic honours. Rather than blaming his teachers, he arrived at the same conclusion as he had over his difficulties in learning languages, that he had a mind which absorbed information slowly and could only learn easily when its visual imagination was stimulated. There were few if any public schools at the beginning of the twentieth century which concerned themselves with the artistic temperament or boys' latent abilities. Siegfried had to confess that he himself had shown little promise of achieving anything out of the ordinary while at Marlborough. Yet, like most imaginative children, he responded, if not to the academic system at least to stimulating teaching. And there was one man at Marlborough who provided that for him. It is no coincidence that, of his four form-masters and numerous teachers between January 1902 and July 1904, and apart from his eccentric housemaster, he describes only one in any detail – John O'Regan.

Though Siegfried's first form-master, Mr Meyrick (nicknamed 'Murke') was said to be 'a great character' by O'Regan's son and others, he receives scant attention in the memoirs.[32] His third form-master, the Reverend J. M. Lupton ('Luppers'), receives even less, though his post as School Librarian might have been thought to make him more memorable to the budding writer.[33] Siegfried's fourth form-master, Mr England, with whom he spent two terms, is not mentioned directly at all, though his tolerance towards his pupil's increasingly idiosyncratic behaviour is obliquely described.

'Pat' O'Regan, on the other hand, is lovingly recreated by his grateful disciple. After referring briefly to the fact that O'Regan had played hockey for England, Siegfried concentrates on his outstanding abilities as a teacher. He found the small, ebullient Irishman so easy to work for that he wanted to stay in his class as long as possible. O'Regan, a First-Class scholar of Balliol who arrived at Marlborough eight years before Siegfried in 1894, wore his learning lightly. Though Senior History Master, he got on extremely well with the younger boys. Very likeable and unaffected, he was according to his biographers, 'a boy among boys'. One of the few teachers who made a direct appeal to their imagination, O'Regan sometimes held tutorials on the roof of an imitation Roman villa he had built for himself in the town. On Sunday evenings he often read to his form after they had written letters home and had had their tea. Siegfried still remembered, thirty-six years later, the 'subdued gusto' with which his form-master read the passage about the young curate and the lady in Kenneth Grahame's *The Golden Age*, a book which gave his pupil 'a pleasant feeling of being away from school and doing things one wasn't allowed to in a shady garden'.[34] Fletcher remembered O'Regan as 'essentially out of the ordinary' and believed that it was 'good for boys to have masters among them who were out of the ordinary'.[35]

O'Regan made an even stronger appeal to Siegfried's imagination when he read out poetry and then invited the boys to write some themselves, for a prize of half a crown. Siegfried was grateful, not so much for the money, which he nearly always won, but for the encouragement to return to an activity he had begun to look back on with nostalgia. O'Regan had Siegfried's first poem framed and hung on his form-room walls. Though clearly a set-piece, it shows an assurance in the handling of rhythm, form and in particular enjambment that O'Regan must have recognized as unusual in an otherwise backward fifteen-year-old:

> My life at school is fraught with care,
> Replete with many a sorrow.
> When evening shadows fall I dare
> Not think about tomorrow.
>
> The extra lesson doth correct
> My wandering attention;
> And other things which I expect
> It might give pain to mention.
>
> But extra lessons cannot kill,
> And blows don't fall so hard
> That they will end the life of this
> Ambitious little bard.[36]

The same term that Siegfried produced this poem, and possibly as a result of it, he started to write poetry voluntarily again. This reawakening of the poetic impulse had occurred early in the summer term of 1902 in the library of Cotton House. Alone and at a loose end, he had taken down a volume of *Ward's English Poets* and opened it randomly at Thomas Hood's 'Bridge of Sighs', a poem completely new to him.[37] The effect was immediate and lasting:

> I had always preferred poems which went straight to the point and stayed there, and here was a direct utterance which gave me goose flesh and brought tears to my eyes.[38]

It was not so much the subject of the poem which thrilled the dormant poet in him as Hood's powerful expression and memorable word music. This ability to combine two of his great loves remained one of Siegfried's main aims in poetry throughout his life. He had worshipped it in Swinburne as a child, and it was now revived in him by Hood's strongly rhythmical lines.

It is significant that Siegfried stresses the apparent randomness of his action in reading Hood, as though he felt himself guided back to his earlier poetic vocation through a higher, unexplained power. It is also interesting that he refers specifically to his childhood belief in himself as 'a prophetic spirit in the making'. There is little doubt that he believed in the poet as prophet and, therefore, as divinely inspired. Both in his War poetry and in his later work, this prophetic role comes to the fore, a fact he himself linked to his Jewish origins.

In Cotton House library, with the mundane clatter of the servant laying the long wooden tables in the hall next door for tea, his belief in his calling as a poet was restored. The immediate effect was to liberate him both from his surroundings and from his sense of inadequacy in a world that glorified things at which he could never excel – scholarship and team sports. The 'dreaming boy', his own description of himself as a child, could believe once more in his creative power, unrecognized though this was by the majority of those around him. Emboldened by Hood and other poets – Emily Brontë, Dante Gabriel Rossetti, Byron, Matthew Arnold and Arthur Clough – whose works he copied into his diary, he went on to write poems of his own again.

Siegfried's first serious efforts included a 'dirge-like' piece on the illness of Edward VII, which had postponed the coronation in 1902, and a 'Fragment of Poem Written in Jan. 1903', an allegory which began:

> Youth with a joyful heart and mind
> Set out his way through life to find,
> He thought not of the years before,
> But of his childhood left behind.

And ended:

> The dawn saw Youth and Phoebus rise;
> And as 'mid gold and crimson skies
> The sun went down; old age crept home
> And the world faded from his eyes.[39]

He went on to write 'Ballad-Land' and an ode on another king, Richard II, an anticipation of a further regal poem on Edward I.[40]

Siegfried may have derived his inspiration for his ode on Richard II from studying Shakespeare's play in his English lessons. He is unlikely to have come across Richard in his History studies, since these were devoted throughout the Classical side of the school to the Roman period. The rest of his educational diet was standard fare: Latin, Maths, Divinity, French and Greek with options in German, Geography, Science and a few other subjects. He must have opted, somewhat surprisingly, for Science since his signed *Inorganic Chemistry* textbook has survived from 1903 with his manuscript notes, scribbles, engravings of Bunsen burners and a pull-out, coloured spectral frontispiece.[41]

When Hamo arrived at Marlborough the term after his brother, he was entered in the Army Class of the 'Modern' School, where German and French largely replaced the Classics, and Natural Sciences, Maths, History (chiefly modern) and Geography were taught. English Composition, as well as Literature, was compulsory on the Modern side, the assumption being that if a boy was not a Classicist he could not possibly write his own language correctly. Bookkeeping and Shorthand were also offered, presumably to prepare boys for business rather than academia. The Modern School tended to be looked down on by the 'Upper' School, as the Classical side was confusingly called, but this would not have worried Hamo, who went his own imperturbable way to the admiration of his more easily flustered older brother.

Siegfried found it difficult just keeping up with his day-to-day duties, particularly in his first term. These included, apart from lessons and prep, some 'fagging' for senior members of his house. There were strict rules on fagging at Marlborough and his tasks were unlikely to have been onerous. They generally consisted of fetching and carrying for a 'lordly youth', cleaning his football boots or cooking him sausages for tea, perhaps, at 4.30 p.m. Organ practice was, in theory, another of Siegfried's duties, but in reality it turned out to be a blissful escape from school life. Though his feet refused to operate the pedals in unison with his hands, an example it seemed to him of his 'life-long inability to do two things at once', he enjoyed practising Handel's 'Largo' with the *vox humana* stop pulled out. It was almost the only time his mind could lie fallow, an essential requirement for him in writing poetry.[42]

Though Gould had accused him of using organ-playing to avoid games, this was not possible and Siegfried found himself on the hockey pitch most afternoons. By no means an outstanding player, he probably spent the bulk of his time standing around in the cold, apart from the occasional tackle and inevitable blow to the shin. Weather conditions were particularly severe in early 1902. The year had begun with snow and tobogganing at Weirleigh. The cold had also hastened the death of his Aunt Rachel's husband, which meant an icy journey to the Beer Mausoleum at Highgate Cemetery for the funeral. Once back at school, it had turned so bitter in February that, even in such an intentionally spartan régime, it had been thought necessary to suspend 'early school' until conditions improved.[43] One positive aspect of the abnormally low temperatures was the chance to ice-skate on Swindon Reservoir, for which the Midland and South Western Railway laid on three special trains.

Siegfried's enjoyment of skating, as well as his lessons, were abruptly terminated at the end of February by an attack of measles. Though there were strict rules forbidding boys to return to school with an infectious disease, or even if they had been in contact with one, epidemics regularly broke out at Marlborough. If they were particularly serious, the whole school might be sent home.[44] In this case, though the disease was not serious in itself, it had tragic consequences. One of the complications of measles before the advent of antibiotics was secondary bacterial infection brought about by the patient's lowered resistance. The commonest types were ear infections and, as in Siegfried's case, pneumonia. It requires little imagination to envisage his mother's reaction when she was informed by the school that her son, whose life had already been threatened by the disease, now had double pneumonia.

Siegfried himself, after a relatively pleasant week of measles in the sanatorium, was hardly aware of what was happening to him. A sleepless night, in which he had been so thirsty that he had been reduced to drinking from his tepid hot-water bottle, was followed by a blur, punctuated by the dim consciousness of his mother, a large, kind bearded man and frequent sips of strong beef tea. Theresa, rightly afraid that her son might die, had called for the distinguished physician Sir Thomas Barlow and, presumably on his advice, made Siegfried beef tea with her own hands. The school's medical officer, Dr Edward Penny, may not have liked being overruled in this way, but he must have been grateful that Siegfried did not join the list of those boys who died during the epidemic.[45] It is to be hoped that Penny's pet theories on *The Influence of Pure Air on Septic Pneumonia; Diptheria etc.* had not led him to open too many windows in the Sick-House, thus causing Siegfried's pneumonia in the first place.

Theresa, whose activities with beefsteaks in the College kitchens had been considered rather *infra dig.* by the authorities, according to her son, was only concerned for his welfare. She had, as Gould generously acknowledged during an early visit to a convalescent Siegfried, probably saved his life. At any rate Siegfried, who had been prayed for in Chapel, felt very important as he lay blissfully recovering. But it was not until the end of March that he was allowed home, looking forward to a game of cribbage with his brothers and the joys of cricket. He may already have started the professional coaching he had decided on after his success in cricket at New Beacon. (By April 1904 he was certainly being coached by James Seymour, who played first class cricket for Kent from 1902 to 1926, and Edward Humphreys, who similarly played for Kent from 1899 to 1920.[46]) He had clearly improved by the time he returned to Marlborough for the summer term of 1902, when he was put straight into the House Team.

He further distinguished himself by a treble mention in the Lower Games House Matches. On one occasion his batting was said to have helped win a match, but his bowling was thought even more impressive: 'Sassoon and Feiling were the most successful of the bowlers', Cotton House book records. 'The former got 9 for 43 ...' In the next report he becomes 'our only successful bowler capturing 7 wickets for 47'. Yet curiously, under 'Characters of House XI' he is described as 'a disappointing bowler who never found his length till after half-term', though the writer concedes that he 'then took a lot of wickets'. He was listed among the 'promising' young players who should be 'useful in the future'.

Siegfried's achievements in cricket this term were one sign of his increasing confidence and competence. The advent of his self-assured younger brother, sharing a study with him, his delight in Mr O'Regan's teaching and above all his return to poetry, all helped him to feel less apologetic about himself. He is still inclined to make fun of himself in his memoirs of this period, however. The account of his performance in the Rifle Volunteer Corps, which he joined in the summer of 1902, is a case in point.[47] Dressed in what was called the 'Bugshooters' *café-au-lait* coloured tunic with blue facings, small forage cap and cartridge bandolier, which he remembered wearing upside-down on more than one occasion, he maintains that he handled his old carbine with extreme caution. He also records his bewilderment when told to go and fire 'Morris tubes' on the indoor range. Even after learning to shut the correct eye he tells us that he missed the target more often than he hit it and gave up all idea of becoming a marksman. For someone who was later to prove such an intrepid soldier he makes himself seem unbelievably ineffectual.

'Siegfried the Maladroit' is clearly one of his favourite themes and personae in his autobiography and not always an entirely convincing one. Nobody who was as unco-ordinated as he makes himself seem could have played cricket well enough to get into the House team in his first term. He also played rugby well enough to be awarded his House Colours for it, but represents himself in his autobiography as a 'conscientious but confused ingredient of the "scrum"', who got his colours 'more through discomforts endured than actual merit'.[48] While he can never resist a joke at his own expense, the reader cannot help suspecting that accuracy is sometimes sacrificed to humour.

The truth is that, taking into account his extremely late start in conventional education and his own lack of confidence, Siegfried made good progress at Marlborough to begin with. By the winter of 1902, in his second term with O'Regan, he had climbed from nineteenth to fourth in the form. One result of his efforts, ironically, was that he then missed more school time. For by the middle of November his hard work had led to conjunctivitis and what Matron diagnosed as a 'strained heart' and he was sent home. His mother's ever-present anxieties surfaced and, with Dr Neild's backing, she decided to keep him off school for the Spring term as well. Any hopes he had had of catching up must have begun to seem unrealistic by this time.

One positive result of Siegfried's enforced absence from Marlborough, however, was the start of a life-long passion, book-collecting. Bored, no doubt, by his need to continue studying Classics by post with his New Beacon master, Mr Jackson, and prevented from playing golf with him by a spell of bad weather, he conceived the fortuitous idea of making a serious business of books. Until then he had read them enthusiastically but had only collected modern books with coloured illustrations, most of them Christmas presents.

As the sales of his library at Christie's and Sotheby's after his death would show, he succeeded beyond all expectations in building up a superb collection from a modest and haphazard beginning. With virtually no capital and even less expertise, his choice to begin with was fairly random. Motivated more by imagination than business acumen, his goal was 'a large cosy accumulation of leather-bound tomes', what the trade refer to as 'furniture'.[49] Not only did the smell of such books appeal to him, but they also suggested 'leisurely lives in days when authors had odd handwriting and did their work very slowly in panelled parlours while their wives made homemade wine or sang sweetly to the lute'.[50] His two main criteria were that his books should be as old as possible, or else be mentioned in Edmund Gosse's *History of Eighteenth Century Literature*, his sole guide to book-collecting. Grateful for anything which would keep her son occupied, Theresa allowed him to fund his enterprize with the several hundred books left behind by her husband.

So, by a system of exchange and barter, Siegfried launched himself on his new venture. From the start he kept meticulous notes of his undertakings, recording the dates he received booksellers' catalogues, bought books, sent letters and made or received orders. In addition he noted some bibliographical details, commenting on condition as well as prices asked and offers received for books he himself was selling.[51] It is therefore possible to build up a fairly accurate picture of his initial progress as a collector.

By the early and fortunate sale of a first edition of Pater's *Appreciations* (curiously altered to Gissing's *New Grub Street* in his autobiography) he was able to stock his library with at least ten suitably antiquated works of mainly seventeenth- and eighteenth-century writers. Many of them were in numerous volumes and most were bound in calf. He further improved their venerable appearance by brightening up their tooling and lettering with burnishable gold, bought through the Army and Navy Stores mail-order catalogue. But, he failed to find the insides of his purchases as attractive as their outsides and quickly gave up trying to read Rollin's *Roman History*, Sir Dudley Digges' *State Letters*, *The Works of William Penn*, *Burke on the Sublime* or Bacon's *Sylva Sylvarum*. He may have found Dr Johnson's *Works* (in 12 volumes) more attractive, for his next acquisitions have a more literary bias – Moore's *Lallah Rookh*, Cowper's *Poems*, Pope's *Rape of the Lock* and *The Miseries of Human Life*. By now he was more interested in reading what he had bought, including several volumes of Johnson's *Lives of the Poets* and various eighteenth-century poets. Under a list of 'Books read in February' he also noted some Shakespeare plays.

Hamo, who had been likewise kept at home for the Spring term of 1903, does not appear to have become involved in Siegfried's book-collecting, but he did help him with cricket practice as the Summer term approached. Both he and Michael had joined Siegfried in setting up their own cricket team in 1902. With the help of masters and pupils from the New Beacon and local enthusiasts such as Tom Richardson, the Marchant brothers, Fritz Neild (the doctor's son) and assorted villagers, they regularly played other amateur sides, calling themselves, variously 'I. B. Hart Davis's XI', 'Mr Sassoon's XI', 'S. L. Sassoon's XI' or simply 'Weirleigh XI'. With such rigorous practice, it is not surprising that on Siegfried's return to Marlborough in the Summer term of 1903 he was again chosen for the House Team. Once more the Cotton House book praises him, in particular for learning to keep a good length, and describes him in 'Characters of House XI' as 'a very useful bowler who has got a good many wickets during the term'. His best performance, apparently, was 7 wickets for 18.[52] Though his batting fares less well, he is awarded his colours. Curiously enough, this is his last appearance in the House cricket team.

Cricket was also the unlikely means of forwarding Siegfried's literary career in April 1903. Despairing of ever getting his poems into the school magazine, *The Marlburian*, which politely ignored his contributions, he had finally sent a piece to *Cricket*, a weekly publication edited by W. A. Bettesworth. To his great surprise, his parody of Charles Kingsley's 'The Sands of Dee', entitled 'The Extra Inch', was accepted, though no payment was made. One can only assume that it was the topicality of Siegfried's subject matter that led to his first appearance in print, since his poem is little more than a humorous exercise:[53]

> O batsman, rise and go and stop the rot,
> And go and stop the rot.
> (It was indeed a rot,
> Six down for twenty-three).
> The batsman thought how wretched was his lot,
> And all alone went he.

And it ends:

> Full sad and slow pavilionwards he walked.
> The careless critics talked;
> Some said that he was yorked;
> A half-volley at a pinch.
> The batsman murmured as he inward stalked,
> 'It was the extra inch.'[54]

Siegfried's poem must have appealed to *Cricket*'s editor and readers, since he had four more poems accepted by the magazine in the following sixteen months, 'Spring', 'To Wilfred – Bowling', 'Yuletide Thoughts' and 'Dies Irae'.[55]

Siegfried's final year at Marlborough was uneventful. Since by this time it had become clear that he was still too low down the school for his age and would not be able to stay on after summer 1904, he probably felt it was not worth continuing his efforts. Neither Mr Lupton nor Mr England, his new form-masters, were able to perform miracles and he remained low down in both their classes. Marlborough's new Master, Frank Fletcher, who arrived in 1903, was feeling his way slowly towards change and his arrival appears to have made no impression at all on Siegfried.

After another term's absence in spring 1904, the result of his mother's continuing fear of pneumonia, Siegfried did discover something to interest him at school, calligraphy. Mr England, who tolerated what he describes as his 'semi-idleness', was amused and possibly cheered by his pupil's new-found enthusiasm and allowed him to copy out his weekly Latin prose exercise in pseudo-Gothic characters with ornate initial letters in red, though he drew the line at gilding. Calligraphy, which clearly appealed to Siegfried's highly developed visual sense, continued to delight him throughout his life. He would often copy out his own poems in elaborately beautiful writing as presents. Sometimes, as in the case of a variorum edition of three versions of *The Rubáiyát of Omar Khayyam* in three different coloured inks, he simply created the work for his own pleasure.[56] Like his early childhood notebooks, his handwritten books were at times also illustrated.

There were no prizes for such artistic achievements in Marlborough at the turn of the century, however, and Siegfried left without honours. His failure to succeed at almost everything there seemed to him to explain his recurring dream in later life that he was going back to Marlborough for one more term. In his dream he always relished the idea of being there and 'cutting a fine figure'.[57]

In summer 1904, however, Siegfried cut a rather poor one. His final report concluded: 'Lacks power of concentration; shows no particular intelligence or aptitude for any branch of his work; seems unlikely to adopt any special career'.[58] Mr Gould's parting advice to him was 'Try to be more sensible'. He had come to regard Sassoon major, perhaps by comparison with the more diligent and hard-working Hamo, as irresponsible and rather weak. Siegfried's strengths, which were apparent to very few people at that time, could hardly be expected to appeal to an old-fashioned public school master. Their parting was, nevertheless, friendly and Siegfried left regarding his Old Marlburian tie affectionately. More importantly, 'he also saw it as a sign of his emancipation'.

5

The Chancellor's Muddle
(1904-1907)

Siegfried had entered Marlborough College a child; he left it as a young man. Sassoon, liberated, as he saw it, from an experience which he had found 'moderately pleasant [but] mentally unprofitable',[1] he could now look forward to a more independent way of life. Though his disappointing performance at Marlborough meant a year's cramming for Cambridge, his middle-class goal, he could at least expect to be treated like a responsible person. And so it turned out. Instead of being condemned him for what he admitted was rather 'harum-scarum' behaviour at Marlborough, the teachers at his next educational establishment, Henley House, merely regarded him as 'lively and amusing'.[2] This change of attitude had a very positive effect on him and by the end of his three terms there, from September 1904 to July 1905, he had worked harder and to much greater effect than he had ever done at Marlborough. From having been by his own account at least four years behind his contemporaries at the age of twelve, he would make up sufficient ground by his nineteenth birthday to pass Cambridge's entrance exam, the 'Little-go'.

Sassoon's mother, whom he now started to call by her family nickname 'Ash', had had a number of reasons for choosing Henley House. One undeniable advantage was its proximity to Weirleigh. Situated at Frant, less than nine miles away, it was close enough for her son to ride there on the new bicycle he acquired in the summer of 1904 and to return home for visits during the term if he wished. Another advantage, as far as the cyclist was concerned, was that the journey took him through some of his favourite countryside. After only ten minutes on the main road from Matfield to Tunbridge Wells, he could turn off at Kippings Cross on to a narrow lane which wound through the hilly, peaceful woodland where Richardson had taken him riding as a child. Once across the border into Sussex, it was a short pedal through Bells Yew Green to Frant.

Characteristically, Sassoon, in his autobiography, places the advantages of the journey before the more serious reason for choosing Henley House, its excellent academic reputation. He did, however, appreciate its tutoring, which was not quite what might have been expected. For, though Henley House was a full-blown 'crammers', it managed to convey a leisurely, uncompetitive air entirely suited to Sassoon's own dreamy, unworldly temperament. As a result he felt less 'crammed' than he had at school, and worked all the better for it. Whatever its methods, Henley House achieved its ends and succeeded in sending an impressive number of young men to both Oxford and Cambridge, as well as the Armed Forces.[3]

Henley House was already known to the Sassoons; Michael had gone there in 1903 to be coached for Cambridge. And his mother must have thought well of it, since she seems to have recommended it to members of the Thornycroft family. The same term that her second son entered, her nephew Alastair Donaldson also arrived and there were at least two Thornycrofts on the enrolment list for the previous term as well as a Strickland, the family into which her niece Mary had married. As in the case of Sassoon's cousin Alastair, many of the pupils came from some distance and, with very few exceptions, all of them boarded.

In order to accommodate the twenty or so youths needed to make his establishment a profitable concern the headmaster, Henry Malden, had had to find a sizeable building. Henley House had twenty-two bedrooms and a ground-floor room big enough to be used as a schoolroom. It also had a large drawing-room and all the other accoutrements of a gracious country house. Not the least of its attractions was the house itself and its surroundings. Set in twenty acres of rolling countryside just outside the centre of Frant, it looked down on a lake which could be used as a skating-rink in winter.[4]

There was room not only for two tennis-courts and some cricket nets but also a nine-hole golf course, which Siegfried appreciated greatly. His love of golf, born at the New Beacon and kept alive by games in the holidays with Mr Jackson and other friends, was beginning to be something of a passion with him, and Henley House seemed to be ideal in this respect. All four members of staff were keen golfers. Henry Malden's cousin, Eustace, was not only a good player but also an expert in laying out golf courses. As well as the school links, he had helped plan more professional courses at Ashdown, Crowborough and Rye. He also had strong theories about golf-clubs and made his own in a small workshop in the school grounds. Among Sassoon's favourite memories of Henley House was that of Eustace in a pleasant fug of pitch, glue and varnish explaining the finer points of one of his strangely shaped club-heads, or winning a golf-match against all the odds with a seemingly impossible fifty-foot putt on an unmown green.

Eustace, or 'Uncle' as he was affectionately known to the pupils, was deputy head at Henley House. The establishment had been started by his more enterprizing cousin, Henry, who was also Eustace's brother-in-law, having married Eustace's sister. At the age of twenty-five Henry had opened a small school in Tunbridge Wells, but in 1897 he had decided to move to larger premises at Frant. He was joined there by the newly-married Eustace, who was accommodated in Henley House Lodge.[5] The school continued to flourish and by the time Sassoon arrived in September 1904 he noted that there were over twenty young men studying for either the Oxford or Cambridge entrance exam.

'The Boss', as Henry was called, earned his nickname but it was given with affection. His methods of keeping control over his still schoolboyish pupils were low-keyed. According to Sassoon, it was something to do with his imperturbable voice and manner. When he found the Old Marlburian actively directing a sousing campaign against an unfortunate youth who had made himself objectionable, instead of ordering him to stop he merely asked Sassoon if he minded using *metal* jugs to pour water over the victim, since the earthenware ones were 'apt to come away from the handles'. The effect was immediate and the 'ragging', stopped at once without a threat or a raised voice. Henry, a small but well-built man of forty-two with greying hair and moustache, was deliberate and systematic in all he did. Looking back, Sassoon felt that he carried a heavy responsibility on his shoulders and might well have preferred to be indulging his interest in agriculture or stocks and shares rather than running an establishment for often backward or spoilt young men.

His cousin Eustace, on the other hand, seems to have managed to carry out his duties as a teacher and pursue his numerous hobbies at the same time. Besides taking Siegfried through Paley's *Evidences*,[6] and teaching Wellington's campaigns to army candidates, he kept bees and made his own beehives as well as golf-clubs. He was a keen photographer at a time when the art was less commonly practised than today, and took many pictures, on glass, of Henley House. Thanks to him there is a contemporary photograph of Sassoon playing a game of golf near the school lake with two other members of staff. Eustace's own eccentric game sometimes won him the annual Henley House Golf Cup. (Sassoon's even more erratic performance did not, though his golf improved steadily.)

Eustace also excelled at another of Siegfried's passions, cricket, and had, to his pupil's great admiration, kept wicket for Kent twelve times between 1892 and 1893. Over a decade later Sassoon thought he could detect something of the wicket-keeper's slow, meandering walk in his teacher's lean and rather stooping figure.[7] Uncle was also a skilled billiards player and joined the boys every evening at snooker, unlike his more aloof cousin. In knowledge as in sport he was something of an all-rounder. An authority on birds, he taught his daughter Angela, who herself became an expert ornithologist. And her father's knowledge of history was equally inspiring to her brother, who later specialized in the subject.

One of the less predictable activities of this fairly unpredictable man was his job as local weather-officer, though how he found the time to carry out his daily 'readings' was a mystery to his family and friends. Yet with all his talents his daughter insists that 'he never thrust them down your throat'. He was a modest man and a devout Christian. Shattered by the deaths of many ex-Henley House pupils in the First World War, and unable to fight because of a weak heart, he was to be ordained at the age of fifty-one, in order to contribute something to the War effort. With many of its clergy in France, the Church of England had need of reinforcements and he would regularly take the service at the Frant Anglican Church. Though Sassoon does not comment specifically on the side of his teacher's character which would lead him to join the clergy, nor, as Eustace's daughter does, on his thoughtfulness with the boys, he presents a picture of a gentle, kindly man of unusual talents.[8]

Sassoon is equally admiring of the two remaining members of staff at Henley House, George Wilson and Mr Rawsthorne. So much so, indeed, that he asks the readers of his autobiography to forgive him for mentioning so many likeable characters. One of the reasons Henley House looms fairly large in his memoirs, he explains, is that it so effectively illustrates his intention: 'to commemorate or memorialize those human contacts which supported me in my rather simple-minded belief that the world was full of extremely nice people if only one could get to know them properly'.[9] 'The Teacher', for example, was so selfless in his devotion to the boys that he would probably have been surprised had he been identified by his name, Mr Rawsthorne. 'He just taught – quietly, persistently and admirably', Sassoon tells us. Since Mr Rawsthorne taught Sassoon French he probably had need of all these qualities and more. Together they ploughed their way through *Le Voyage de Monsieur Perrichon*, which neither of them wasted time in finding humorous, and 'Le Cid Ballads'. Sassoon found the ballads a great bore but liked Victor Hugo because he was easy to translate. 'The Teacher' characteristically expressed no opinion on the subject. Ten years after Mr Rawsthorne's patient tuition Sassoon told a friend that, while he had been able to read and appreciate French poetry, he could not speak the language at all, since he was hopeless at learning anything factual. His conclusion, that this difficulty in speaking foreign languages was 'typical of my sketchy way of going through my time', underlines his resistance to anything academic. Nevertheless Mr Rawsthorne persisted. He reminded Sassoon of Wordsworth with his simplicity, austerity and high-mindedness. He also put him in mind of a clergyman. Dressed always in a high, single collar even when playing his predictably steady rounds of golf or cycling slowly round the countryside alone, he seemed to Sassoon a reassuring presence at Henley House.[11]

The remaining member of staff, George Wilson, was rather more colourful, and even more admirable as far as Sassoon was concerned. He identifies George as the Classics teacher at Henley House and an excellent all-round athlete who had played rugby for Cambridge and the Corinthians in the mid-Nineties. Though he suspected at the time that George was an unusually fine person, full of courage, humour and intelligence, it was not until after his death that he realized that he was truly 'one of the paragons of my human experience'.[12] To the modern reader George may sound too good to be true, but it is clear that he impressed Sassoon enormously, and not just because he was a good teacher. The two were afterwards to become close friends and thus to preserve a link for Sassoon with Henley House until well into the nineteen-twenties. For 'George', as he was simply known, was to marry Henry Malden's daughter Jane and to retain close ties with the school even after he had left to start up an establishment of his own in Cambridge.[13] Their friendship started at Henley House and marks the beginning of a period in which Sassoon at last seems ready to make and keep friends. It may be no coincidence that it was also the second time in his life that he had had to face the outside world without the protection of either of his brothers. Michael, who had completed his year at Henley House successfully, was about to go up to Cambridge and Hamo was still at Marlborough when Siegfried arrived at Henley House; so for one term in the autumn of 1904 he had to fend for himself. During that short period he formed two of his closest early friendships.

The first of these, with a fellow-student, Norman Loder, is well-documented. Sassoon uses Loder as a model for Denis Milden in *The Memoirs of a Fox-Hunting Man*, to illustrate his theory that for many years he himself was almost a split personality. There was his dreamy, poetical self but also the sporty, physical side to him that loved cricket, hunting and golf. Not only did Loder share his love of sport, hunting and golf in particular, but he also served, in Sassoon's words, as an 'antidote to my poetical-mindedness and indulgence in dreamy sensibility'.[14] Born of an upper middle class Sussex family and educated at Eton, where he did little but hunt with the beagles, Loder represented a class and way of life that both attracted and repelled Sassoon.

It took Sassoon many years to overcome the temptation Loder's company afforded to give in to his hearty, extrovert self at the expense of his poetic side. Nor was the choice at all straightforward. The county set, symbolized for Sassoon from early on by Loder, had its virtues. While he felt that it generally lacked subtlety and rarely had either aesthetic or intellectual interests, he could also admire its positive qualities, as epitomized in Loder. He was simple, direct, conscientious and good-natured. Though blunt and matter-of-fact, this only made him seem more solid and reliable, the kind of person often referred to as 'the backbone of England'. He was in addition an outstanding sportsman, something Sassoon could not dismiss. Matching Sassoon's adult height of over six feet, he was the very picture of an English sporting gentleman, as Sassoon implies: 'tall and limber-built, with his neatly-gaitered legs and deliberate way of walking, his brown felt hat tilted over his eyes and a long-stemmed pipe between his teeth'.[15] At his premature death in 1940 a mutual friend was to sum up Norman as 'the perfect knight of the saddle, a gallant English gentleman'.[16]

After Cambridge, where he failed to take a degree, Loder was to spend most of his life on the hunting-field as master of various packs[17] and Sassoon would continue to seek his friendship for nearly twenty years. It was largely an attraction of opposites, though the sporting side to the poet's character was also a factor. He was eventually to coin a word, 'Loderism', to describe the healthy, decent but animal and philistine existence Loder represented for him, about which he felt so ambivalent. When he finally came to reject the way of life it dictated, his friendship with Loder would gradually decline. In 1904 and 1905, however, their friendship was very much alive. It was to survive Cambridge, though they were at different colleges, and to grow even stronger when Sassoon returned home to live the life of a country gentleman. At Henley House it almost certainly centred round golf, since horses were out of the question, but after that it would be based firmly on a mutual love of hunting.

Another friendship strengthened by golf at Henley House was with Henry Thompson. Ill-health had interrupted Thompson's education and he was struggling to get into Oxford. Whereas Sassoon makes no mention of Loder in his retrospective description of this period, since he had already portrayed him graphically as Denis Milden, he does describe his friendship with 'Tommy', as he called Thompson. (Thompson in return addressed him as 'Sig'.) Again it seems to have been largely an attraction of opposites, Thompson complementing him in almost every respect.

Unlike the slightly older Sassoon, he was mature for his age and got on well with his elders, listening politely to his headmaster, for instance, when he droned on about debentures and chemical manures. A native of Cumberland, Tommy had a certain north-country shrewdness which must have contrasted sharply with Sassoon's naiveté. Physically he was much smaller than his friend and his red hair was more striking than Sassoon's, which was nearer to auburn. His slight build and delicate health gave the more robust Sassoon an advantage in golf, since Tommy simply had not the physique for long, straight drives against a head-wind. But he was usually far more philosophical than Sassoon when something went wrong with his game, though there were occasions when even his patience reached its limit. There was one particular match, played three years after they had left Henley House at Littlestone-on-Sea when what should have been a winning putt by an overconfident Tommy leapt out of the tee and Sassoon refused to allow the shot. Matters were made worse by the fact that, in marching huffily to the next tee, Tommy slithered in undignified fashion on a plank-bridge they had to cross to reach it. Years later Sassoon asked him what he would have done had he fallen into the muddy dyke below: 'I should certainly have returned to Cumberland by the next train', he replied, adding 'with your usual tactlessness you'd have burst into a loud guffaw, and I was already simply paralytic with annoyance at missing the putt, which you'd have given me if you possessed a spark of gentlemanly feeling!'[18]

Besides a passion for golf, Tommy shared with Sassoon what the latter calls a 'delightfully cronyish quality' and they were to spend many happy days in each other's company. They took a number of long golfing holidays together in their early twenties and paid several visits to each other's houses. Tommy got on particularly well with Theresa, who liked him a great deal better than she was to like most of Sassoon's later male friends. They entered so enthusiastically into the relative merits of Kent and Cumberland soil for growing roses that they seemed to Sassoon to become 'like one mind'.[19] When Thompson later contacted Sassoon from Ceylon, where he went to work for a rubber company, he wrote that he often thought of 'the old days at Weirleigh, and how I loved staying with you and listen[ing] to you playing "To a Wild Rose" '. He remembered Sassoon's study, the room above Theresa's studio converted for his adult use, 'a real delight surrounded by your books and smoking a pipe and planning a trip to Westward Ho!'[20]

There was one area of his life that Sassoon did not share with Thompson or Loder, his growing commitment to poetry. Though no poems survive from his time at Henley House, apart from a piece called 'Yuletide' in the *Cricket* magazine, his autobiography suggests that he was planning to write an epic in twelve volumes after he had passed his Cambridge entrance exam. By September 1904 he had apparently written the first two lines, which rather portentously reflect his sense of isolation and approaching adulthood after leaving Marlborough:

> Sundered from earth and utterly alone,
> Upon the heights of manhood stood a soul ...[21]

It is also likely that during this year he started to draft some of the poems which appear in *A Pageant of Dreams*, a handwritten volume dedicated to 'Ash' and given to her as a Christmas present in 1905. One poem in particular – 'Dies Irae', referring to the advent of the Russo-Japanese war in 1904 – suggests that he may have composed at least some of the pieces during his time at Henley House. Another, 'Praise of Spring', may well have been written in the last term of 1905 when, he remembers, 'poetry was awakening [his] senses to ignorant rapture'.[22] After personifying the four seasons in a fairly predictable manner, Sassoon concludes with more specific references to his love of dawn and the wooded countryside of Kent.

Shortly after Sassoon wrote 'Praise of Spring', he was formally admitted to Clare College, Cambridge, though he did not go into residence until the autumn of 1905. On the same day, 29 April 1905, Hamo was also formally admitted to Clare. Their elder brother, Michael, who had been admitted on 13 October 1904 and gone up that term, was still at Clare when Siegfried and Hamo arrived in October 1905. It was, however, his last term there and he left without taking a degree.

In choosing Cambridge for her sons rather than Oxford, Theresa was rejecting her husband's family traditions and supporting recently established Thornycroft ones. The wealthier Sassoons generally sent their sons to Eton and Christ Church, Oxford. Sassoon's own father and his father's younger brother, Frederick, had partly followed their tradition in going to Exeter College, Oxford.[23] Alfred's elder brother, Joseph, had been at Christ Church. When the Thornycrofts started sending their sons regularly to university in Sassoon's generation, they chose Cambridge. His Donaldson cousin, Malcolm, was the first to go, to Trinity in 1902. Hamo's son, Oliver Thornycroft, followed in 1903 and dictated Theresa's choice for her sons by selecting Clare College, which was smaller than Trinity and approximately the same size as King's. When Michael Sassoon entered Clare in 1904, he set the pattern for his younger brothers who both went up to Clare in 1905. At the same time Alastair Donaldson entered Jesus College and in 1907 his younger brother, Eric, followed Malcolm to Trinity.

Sassoon opens his section on Cambridge in *The Old Century* with a description of a family gathering there in June, 1906. A dozen of them, all young, all cousins, had met together for the Trinity Boat Club Ball. Apart from the three Sassoon brothers, there were two, possibly three of Hamo Thornycroft's children and the rest were Donaldsons. It is an interesting confirmation of the close family ties maintained by Thomas and Mary Thornycroft's offspring, connexions which Sassoon himself rarely mentions in his autobiography, where he concentrates far more on his moments of isolation, bewilderment and solitary pleasures.

Theresa's decision to follow her brother's choice of college for his son seems entirely understandable. Clare was, and still is, an attractive place. Founded by the Lady Elizabeth, sister and co-heir of Gilbert, Earl of Clare, in 1326, it is the second oldest of all the colleges. With his Pre-Raphaelite love of the medieval, Sassoon could not have helped but enjoy its architecture and cloistered calm. He filled his low-ceilinged rooms on the third floor of the college with pictures by Burne-Jones and Rossetti, as if to emphasize the point, and one of his first purchases was a six-volume set of Swinburne's *Poems*, which he had had specially bound in half parchment gilt.

Situated between the River Cam and the Market Square and only a few minutes' walk from the University Library, Clare placed Sassoon literally at the centre of Cambridge life. (His rooms actually overlooked the Market Square.) And to some extent he took advantage of his privileged position. His allowance of £80 per term, while not a fortune, was fairly generous for a young man who as yet neither smoked nor drank. Since his love of book-collecting had continued to grow, some of his money went on buying handsome books in vellum bindings, which he rarely read. Some was spent on entertaining. When his uncle Hamo came to visit, for example, he fêted him with lobster mayonnaise, the best College hock and any other luxury he could find.

Having started to make friends at Henley House, Sassoon appreciated the social life that university offered. Looking back on his time at Clare, he saw himself as a fatuous undergraduate 'sprawl[ing] about in other people's rooms, talking my irrepressible nonsense or listening to someone playing Chopin *scherzos* on the pianola'.[24] Apart from his brothers and cousins, he got to know other students, though none of these friendships was to prove as lasting as those with Loder and Thompson.[25] Cambridge also provided him with the opportunity to improve his golf and cricket. Many afternoons when he should have been studying he spent golfing at Mildenhall, Coton or Royston, and he maintained a sufficiently high standard at cricket to feel that it helped conceal his other shortcomings as well as keeping him fit.[26]

Sassoon's greatest inadequacy, he felt, lay in the crucial area of work. Having just scraped into Cambridge with the help of an excellent crammers, he had neither the self-discipline nor the motivation needed to benefit academically there. The problem, moreover, was not simply one of maturity. Throughout his memoirs he argued emphatically that his academic failure lay deeper than that. As he saw it, it had to do with the poetic temperament, which rejected hard facts in favour of a more imaginative existence. Though this may sound like a cliché, it cannot be dismissed as an explanation. There is no doubt that Sassoon was highly intelligent, hard-working and effectual when his imagination was engaged. When forced, by his conscientious and well-meaning guardians, uncle Hamo and the family solicitor, to study Law, however, motivation failed him completely.

Persuaded initially by the fact that a Law degree required less mathematics than most other degrees, Sassoon quickly found himself bogged down in such dry and bulky works as the *Edicts of Gaius and Justinian*. He dutifully memorized vast amounts of information on ancient Roman Law, attended 'droning' lectures and desperately scribbled notes which he afterwards failed to understand. He could find no relevance in any of this and often turned over two pages of his law books without even noticing it. He felt himself becoming a complete absurdity in the eyes of his quick-witted Law Coach, whose patience finally gave out: 'If I were to go out into the street and interrogate the first errand-boy I met,' he exclaimed, 'he couldn't know less than you do about Maine's *International Law*'.[27]

It was almost certainly this remark which decided Sassoon to give up Law. To his great relief, his senior tutor, W.L. Mollison ('Molly'), who admired his poetry, seemed to understand that Law allowed little scope for the poetic imagination and suggested History as an alternative.[28] His head filled with picturesque scenes from his favourite books, Sassoon gladly embraced the idea. With a burst of characteristically disorganized energy, he started to study the reign of Louis XI, but was soon floundering again. After enjoying Philipe de Commines' *Memoirs* in a quaint seventeenth-century translation, he found himself facing Chastellain's *Memoirs* in medieval French. Even if he had been able to understand the language, he soon realized that the only facts he would have been likely to retain were those that appealed to his visual imagination. He wanted history to be like Stanley Weyman's novels or Shakespeare's plays and almost entirely lacked a grasp of its constructive elements and political implications. If he could make a poem out of a subject, it interested him; if not, he instantly forgot it. The career of Joan of Arc, for instance, fascinated him and he planned to celebrate it with a long poem in blank verse. The struggle between the Empire and the Papacy, on the other hand, which his History Coach insisted was more important, had no appeal for him at all.

It was the narrative aspect of history, particularly at its dramatic points, which Sassoon absorbed. His choice of Medieval History, not necessarily a wise one, was clearly linked to his continuing interest in the Pre-Raphaelites. When he should have been studying Thatcher and Schwill's *General History of Europe* in the summer term of 1906, he was spending the time reading William Morris's *Earthly Paradise* in a punt, as Oscar Wilde had before him at Oxford. Whether he would have done any better at Cambridge if he had been allowed to study English Literature formally is an interesting but academic question. The English Literature Tripos was not established at Cambridge until 1917, in contrast to Oxford where the English Honours school had been established in 1893, though only after a struggle.

Sassoon's first year at Cambridge was a time when, to use his own words, he was 'bursting with poetic feeling ... though so immature'.[29] In October 1905 he started to compile an anthology of his favourite poems. Dante Gabriel and Christina Rossetti compete with Swinburne, Browning and Tennyson for top place. A number of minor contemporary poets, such as William Watson, Austin Dobson, Stephen Phillips, John Davidson, Alfred Noyes, Charles Doughty, Robert Louis Stevenson and Ethel Clifford take up most of the rest of the collection. Shakespeare is allowed only one entry, together with Ronsard and Arthur Clough. In keeping with his Romantic tastes at the time, Keats is represented by five sonnets. A less predictable inclusion is Kipling, though his romantic as well as his jingoistic verse is included.[30]

Of his five favourite poets he tells Sassoon that Swinburne was his main influence. Though he still loved Tennyson he was beginning to feel incapable of imitating the older poet's 'distinctness'. Dante Gabriel Rossetti and Browning were now more influential, the latter's *Saul* being his 'prime favourite'.[31] And it was his admiration for Browning's dramatic monologues, as well as a growing interest in blank verse, which led him to attempt his most ambitious poem of this year, 'St Joan'. Written in a state of what he called 'rapt afflatus',[32] it was part of a poetic outpouring that might have resulted from the removal of rigid academic discipline.

The poetic flood had started after he left Henley House in July 1905. By Christmas, apart from this anthology, he had also filled a beautifully bound grey cloth and cream leather notebook tooled in gold with exquisitely handwritten poems of his own for his mother. The bulk of them appear to date from his first three months at Cambridge. The poetry, though still highly derivative, is much more accomplished and assured than that of his childhood notebooks. It is still Romantic in influence, with specifically Pre-Raphaelite emphasis on the medieval in both language and content. Two of the poems appear to be based on Pre-Raphaelite pictures. 'Slow Music' describes a warrior being carried to his grave, while:

> Maidens pace slowly by, and knights well mailed,
> Across wet gleaming sand.

'Love Triumphant' concerns allegorical forms of Love, Mortality and Time, with Joy 'uprising like a prayer' and 'soar[ing] upon the tireless wings of ecstacy [sic]'. There are many similar echoes of Keats and other Romantic poets, the main influences, as the numerous epigraphs indicate, being Keats, Tennyson, Rossetti, Swinburne and their ardent disciple Sir William Watson.[33] Sassoon explicitly states his Romantic creed in 'Canor Canorum':

> How should he sing who knew not the soul of Nature at all,
> And is it not her heart whence all our melodies fall?

Sassoon's subject matter is also predictably late-Romantic – the too-swift passing of time, the arrival of spring, death, creation, the seasons. There is one 'occasional' poem, 'Dies Irae', but for the most part the poems are a vague, generalized examination of the passions. Love is frequently cited, but there is no personal love poetry. One might have expected a great deal from a young man of nineteen, but if he experienced such impulses, as he almost certainly did, he also felt that he must keep them to himself. He was ashamed of his attraction towards men and was still trying hard to suppress such feelings even from himself. There are hints in some of the poems that he was fighting what he saw as defilement and impurity. The tone in these poems alternates between resolution and despair.

The language itself, like the subject matter, is largely lacking in freshness, being full of archaisms and poeticisms, most of them borrowed from other poets: 'darkling', 'laggard', 'westering', 'clad', 'thwart', 'minstrelsy', 'throstle' (three times!) 'clove', 'vernal', 'supernal', 'is't', 'o'er', 'where'er' and so on. Archaic spellings, where they exist, are chosen in preference to modern ones, 'sov'ran' being a particular favourite. Words are sometimes given mock-archaic qualities, 'purpureate' being a lurid example.

There is clearly a striving for originality, as 'vampired clouds' shows, but, as it also suggests, this can lead to an unfortunate straining after effect. All the 'big' things in life are personified, or at least given capital letters, though even this is not consistent. Life, Love, Joy and Hope fight with Death, Hate, Misery and Despair. Ambition and Lust strive to gain control over Honour and Shame. The imagery itself is likewise largely clichéd: Music strikes her golden lyre, Poetry pours in a flood from the poet's lips, Hope is the dawning of a brighter day, Time's myrmidons 'work their wild way no more'. Sometimes the metaphors are exuberantly mixed:

> The unfettered joy, uprising like a prayer,
> Soars upon tireless wings of ecstacy

Occasionally, when the description is of something known personally to Sassoon, it is fresh and stimulating: in 'A Vision of Seasons', for example, a tired allegory of the poet dreaming of Spring, Summer and Autumn in an 'enchanted woodland vale', we are reminded of the orchards of Kent in spring:

> For without the song of many birds
> Fell, as scattered blossoms on the air
> Fall when orchards rock in winds of May.

Under the influence of Swinburne and Watson, Sassoon's passion for alliteration is freely indulged, as in the eighth stanza of 'A Vision of Seasons':

> Shafts of sunlight, striking through the leaves,
> Lit upon their liquid loveliness ...

Sassoon's intoxication with sound extends also to rhythm. He relishes hexameters and experiments freely with odd combinations. Highly experimental and largely unsuccessful lines of eight feet give way to pentameters and trimeters combined within a single stanza. He also tries his hand at the roundel, a medieval convention. His favourite form is blank verse, though he also favours rhymed iambic pentameters. Whilst decidedly more skilful at handling these forms than in previous volumes, he is sometimes forced to resort to padding to make them work.

At the end of *A Pageant of Dreams*, written in quite a different hand and clearly added after it had been presented as a Christmas gift to his mother, Sassoon included five poems, three of which indicate a more vigorous poetic impulse. 'Sea-Faring', for example, is much more personal than anything that appears before it. Though couched in fairly stilted language and conventional metaphor, it deals with Sassoon's own struggle to remain 'pure':

> Adrift upon an ocean tempest-toss'd,
> We cast our manhood to the winds, till fain
> To ask a little mercy of the Main
> That hurls us on the rocks, defiled and lost;

5. The Chancellor's Muddle (1904-1907)

> The sullied hours are number'd, and their cost
> Measured by endless misery; – free from stain –
> The shores of godlihead how may we gain –
> Is not this gulf too turbulent to be cross't?

In 'Doubt', which was almost certainly written as the New Year approached, his mood is far more resolute, and the language reflects this, particularly in its swinging rhythms:

> Doubt not the light of heaven upon the soul,
> Doubt not the lyric passion, giving all
> Desire and Hope Wonder to its thrall;
> Doubt not the goal:
> Doubt not the rapture of the smitten lyre;
> – The fearless hours, magnificence with might;
> – Creation from a chaos of delight;
> Doubt not the fire ...

The final poem in the volume, 'A Thought', is another of the few poems based on personal experience and is, correspondingly, less tired and derivative. This gives it a certain amount of vigour, unlike the majority of the pieces in this his first adult volume.

After presenting his mother with *A Pageant of Dreams* at Christmas 1905, Sassoon continued to write feverishly. By June he had had four poems published in the University magazine, *Granta*, and one in *The Cambridge Review*.[34] Though all were parodies, of Stephen Phillips, Robert Browning, Swinburne and the Psalmist, they are exuberant proof of his love of words and sounds.

Sassoon had fed this love of sounds with Swinburne's *Atalanta in Calydon* and other lush verse. The Pre-Raphaelite poems and pictures in which he immersed himself provided an ideal escape into a dream world which seemed both more attractive and, ironically, more real than either Law or History. He filled a blue notebook, originally entitled 'Roman Law II' with 'Rough Drafts' for his poems rather than lecture notes. By September 1906 he had enough poems to contemplate publication. Either he lacked the confidence, or did not wish to approach a commercial publisher. Certainly he was not at all sure of the worth of his poems. A privately printed volume of modest size but attractive appearance seemed the answer. It could also be anonymous and thus avoid the possibility of hostile criticism. (It was a pattern that was to be repeated with variations throughout his life.)

Sassoon finally made his decision on the 8 September 1906, his twentieth birthday, and tentatively approached the publishers of his favourite magazine, *The Athenaeum*. When they readily agreed to print fifty copies, with no price mentioned, he was so grateful that he sent the manuscript off almost immediately without further enquiry on 20 September. A fortnight later he received the first proofs, added some lines called 'Aspiration' and sent the corrected proofs straight back. By early November he had returned the second set of proofs but it was not until he made anxious enquiries in mid-December that he finally received the book, just in time for Christmas. It numbered thirty-six pages and was bound in thick white cartridge paper, with a tastefully contrasting dark blue satin marker band. The title, simply *Poems*, was printed on both the cover and the title-page, with no name. There were two extra copies on hand-made paper. Its production seemed to Sassoon remarkably cheap at £7.

Most of the information about the composition of *Poems* (1906) and Sassoon's reaction to it come from letters written to a friend made at Cambridge, Everard Leaver Guilford. This friendship, which proves that Sassoon had managed to form relationships outside the close, almost claustrophobic family network that operated even at Cambridge, provided him with a confidant and adviser. He seems to have used Guilford rather as a litmus-paper before braving the opinion of the rest of the world with his work.

Guilford had entered Clare two years before Sassoon in 1903, the same year as Oliver Thornycroft, and may have been introduced to him by his cousin.[35] He was completing the last year of his degree in 1905, but after he left Cambridge for France in 1906 they kept up the friendship by letter for at least another two years. Guilford was reading History when Sassoon met him, another possible influence on Sassoon's choice of second subject. As Guilford's later editing of several textbooks and archives was to show, he was particularly interested in Sassoon's favourite period, the Middle Ages.[36] The two men also shared a passion for golf and cricket, which revealed itself after Guilford had left Cambridge. For Sassoon sent him detailed accounts of lazy afternoons at Coton and Royston Golf Clubs and the scores of matches played for Matfield and Brenchley Cricket Teams, as well as the more illustrious Blue Mantles of Tunbridge Wells.

The friendship was probably cemented by a shared sense of humour, for the most part rather schoolboyish. Addressing Guilford as 'Gussy', 'Gustavus', 'Gustavus Adolphus' and even as 'patient Griselda' on one occasion, Sassoon signs himself variously 'Sarson' or 'your hairbrained and debilitated P. O'E. Taster.' He has, he informs Guilford, 'been "going the noiseless tenor of my way" – as usual – to the cackle of inane merriment – insane epigrams and illimitable alliterations'.[37] For his friend's amusement he jokily invents bad poems in the style of Swinburne and Alfred Austin, among others, and, in turn, anticipates what he calls 'Gussy "wit"'.

More importantly Guilford and Sassoon shared a love of the arts which survived their separation in 1906. Sassoon describes visits to the theatre, concerts and art galleries on his journeys to and from Cambridge through London. His very detailed account of a spectacular production of *Richard*

II, for example, suggests that he knows that his recipient shares his love of the visual too. Guilford's most significant rôle as far as posterity is concerned, however, was as a sounding-board for Sassoon's ideas on poetry during and just after his Cambridge days.

Both men recommend poems to each other and Sassoon clearly trusts Guilford's judgement, though when the latter attempts poetry of his own he is promptly put in his place: 'the feeling is good,' Sassoon writes rather condescendingly, 'but the language and form rather hackney'd, as would be expected with so little practice'. Guilford, nevertheless, carries on advising Sassoon without rancour and Sassoon admits to him on at least one occasion that he needs his friend's praise to prevent him feeling suicidal – 'for of all the unfortunates who may hap to read my lines none dislikes them (at times) more cordially than Sarson itself'.

After a long letter of 12 July 1906, describing and quoting the main piece in *Poems* – 'St Joan' – in great detail, Sassoon sends an even fuller description of his aims in this, his first printed volume, together with an attractive little notebook filled with handwritten copies of his work. When the book itself appears Guilford is the first to receive a copy and, in his enthusiasm, requests a second. By October 1906, when *Poems* is at the printers, Sassoon is able to tell Guilford that it contains about 800 lines, 'not so bad for less than a year's work – including History and Law Tripos'. Though later Sassoon was to invite another friend to laugh at some of their 'poetizings, their naive moralizings, verbal imprecision and auto-intoxication with word-sounds', he also pointed out the main significance of *Poems*: that he was 'doing it all on [his] own steam, with no one to tell [him] how to do it professionally'.[38] He told a third friend that '*Poems 1906* is mostly weak imitation of Tennyson, Swinburne and D.G. Rossetti and is full of didactic moralizing and humbug'.[39] But, looking back, he was thankful that he had not been a 'sophisticated youth' but had really experienced all 'those aspirations and vague upliftments'.[40] *Poems* does not differ substantially from the Romantic outpourings of *A Pageant of Dreams*.

In fact *Poems* opens with four works taken straight from *A Pageant of Dreams* – those pieces that were added after Sassoon presented the book to his mother – and a fifth, 'The Bonds of Speech', has been retitled and adapted from 'Canor Canorum', likewise from *A Pageant of Dreams*. A sixth, 'Dawn-Dimness', has also been retitled from the previous volume. The remaining sixteen are new. One of the first of these chronologically, 'March', suggests that Sassoon's fresh burst of inspiration started in the spring of 1906. Composed as a roundel, 'March' also indicates that Sassoon is still interested in medieval forms. Apart from the main poem 'St Joan', there is less blank verse, and far fewer pieces in hexameters. Experiment continues but the majority of the poems are in a fairly conventional mixture of pentameters and lines of two feet.

Though still reading Swinburne (in particular, tragedies like *Bothwell* and *Chastelard*) and quoting four lines from him on the title page of

Poems, Sassoon is consciously trying to free himself from his intoxicating influence. In doing so, however, he appears only to have changed influences by a decade, his manner now clearly reflecting a hypnotism with the Nineties. Whilst advising Guilford to read Francis Thompson and Norman Gale, among others, he himself begins to adopt something of their languid tone and melancholy (false, in his case) as an extract from 'Vigil' shows:

> Through the night's whole weariness we wait,
> Lifting pale faces and tired eyes, whose sight
> Streams eastward for the breaking of the light;
> For now it is not early, neither late,
> And drowsy Dawn is hastening towards Heaven's gate; ...
> Waited and watched have we the livelong night.

The effect on the language is as enervating as the content itself. Sassoon regretted the loss of urgency and directness in poems like this, as compared with earlier ones like 'Doubt', but he felt powerless to remedy it for a number of years while the infection ran its course. The overall content, like the language of *Poems*, lacks freshness, the same tired themes being regurgitated, in particular the significance of Nature, the mysterious quality of dawn (Sassoon had actually stayed up specially to record this, one fine June morning), the imminence of death. He continues to appeal to God to help him to be 'noble', 'pure' and 'true'. As in *A Pageant of Dreams*, he sometimes takes his subject matter from a suitably mournful Pre-Raphaelite picture, 'Sic Transit' being a case in point:

> Leave him alone as he lies in his perfect repose,
> Neither disturb ye the house whence his spirit hath flown;
> None hath been here save the merciful Healer of Woes;
> Yea – whom the sovran of shadows, all shadows hath shown,
> Leave him alone ...

There are a few moments in the volume when Sassoon's own observations animate the verse. He himself picked out a few lines from 'Among the Hills', written while he was staying in Wales in August 1906:

> ... In the sunlit heights of Heaven
> Lazily sail the sea-birds ...

'Don't that suggest a hot August noon', he asks Guilford on 2 October; 'while "the wrinkled sea beneath him crawls" and the sheep crop and the flaming gorse pricks his backside'. One experiment, 'The Dreamer: A Fragment', the second longest poem in the book, is an allegory about a Christian soul led eventually to Heaven by a small child. Though a failure, it is an ambitious attempt and interesting for what it reveals of Sassoon's conventional piety at this time.

More successful is the most sustained effort in *Poems*, 'St Joan'. A dramatic monologue, written under the spell of Browning and early history, it manages to steer clear of much of the weariness of language in the less original lyrics. It is no surprise to learn that Sassoon wrote its 220 lines almost at one sitting. He told Guilford on 12 July 1906 that it was 'a long way the best thing I have done; ... and it was done before I could turn round – Heaven knows how!' It has a directness and thrust lacking in the shorter poems and is far more powerfully conceived. Spoken by Joan on the eve of her execution, it also has pathos while managing to avoid mawkishness:

> ... I shall not seek the pathless summits more
> When roses strew the road of rising day;
> I shall not from the silence of the hills
> Look down upon the basking vale below
> In the haze of summer noontide; never more
> Young hope shall yearn to scale the western clouds,
> Nor in the dreaming depths of youthful eyes
> Glimmer the light of many dawns to be,
> And many fires of energy unquenched.
>
> With darkness to the valleys we descend,
> And in shadows find our shelter; be it so:
> I have walked the steeps of Life, and at the last
> Whither may I pass but into dark once more
> By the path that all must tread, or soon or late?

Sassoon's friends and relatives responded encouragingly to his first printed volume, but it would probably have seemed churlish to react otherwise to a Christmas present.[41] Had he realized what he acknowledged afterwards, that his ideas in *Poems* 'lacked originality' and that his language was 'hopelessly hackneyed', he might well have stopped writing then and there. As it was, he continued with undiminished energy to pour forth poetry.

While *Poems* was at the printers, for example, he was busily preparing an entry for the Chancellor's Medal in poetry. His uncle Hamo, visiting him at Cambridge in the summer of 1906 and hearing of his poetic activity, had diffidently suggested that his nephew try for it and his senior tutor, Mollison, having admired some of his erratic student's work, also urged him to enter. Introduced by His Royal Highness William Frederick, Duke of Gloucester, who was Chancellor of Cambridge University from 1811 to 1834, the Chancellor's Medal was the equivalent of the Newdigate Prize at Oxford and had been won by some subsequently well-known poets.

In fact, one reason Sassoon wanted to try for it was that it seemed to him his only chance of earning academic distinction. He was comforted by the fact that it had been won by Tennyson, who had left Cambridge without taking a degree. If he could win the Chancellor's Medal, it might, as he put it to Guilford, 'save [me] from being hoofed out if I fail in Trip[os Exams]'. As early as July he was asking Guilford if he knew what the subject for the Chancellor's Medal would be.

By the time the subject was eventually announced in October 1906, Sassoon's *Poems* were ready for the press and he was, therefore, free to concentrate on the prize. Ironically, the subject turned out to be historical – 'Edward the First'. To begin with, Sassoon felt this to be propitious, since his uncle Hamo had made an equestrian statue of the king. With a photograph of the statue on his desk, he set to work enthusiastically to produce the requisite 200 lines. His first instinct was to imitate one of his current favourites, Browning, and he dashed off a rough opening as a dramatic monologue, in which the king mused eloquently on events just before the battle of Crécy. It was only when he bought Professor Tout's monograph the next day that he discovered that Crécy was fought about forty years after Edward I had died. He also realized, not for the first time, that facts, revealed to him through Tout and *The Dictionary of National Biography*, had a decidedly chilling effect on his imagination. As a Romantic his interests lay mainly in exploring emotions and his imagination was dulled rather than fired by learning about Edward's legislative activity, his military career and his sporting prowess. As soon as he tried to put these 'facts' into blank verse – his chosen medium – the results were depressingly flat, an opinion that Guilford unfortunately shared when he sent a sample to him.[42]

Sassoon was hampered by a conviction that the poem would not benefit from his usual Pre-Raphaelite or Nineties treatment, both of which seemed entirely inappropriate to the austere Plantagenet Edward. After rejecting the idea of a soliloquy delivered by the young king on one of his Crusades, he decided on a straightforward retrospect dictated by Edward to an anonymous chronicler towards the end of his reign. Another one hundred flat lines later, however, he realized that he had still not found the correct formula, and put the piece away, consoling himself by seeing his *Poems* through the press.

When Sassoon returned to Edward in December, with most of Tout's indigestible facts forgotten and after further encouragement from his tutor, Mollison, inspiration returned. So, too, did the Pre-Raphaelite influence. In what even he recognized as an echo of Tennyson's rendering of King Arthur's end, he gave Edward the 'death-bed' treatment: 'All his inherent nobility of nature was finding solemn expression in blank verse which almost made me feel as if I were bidding farewell to the world myself'.[43] It was an unfortunate choice of treatment, its lack of originality allowing him to indulge in all his favourite clichés. The opening lines, from a handwritten copy sent to Guilford, give the flavour of the whole:

> I have no strength to urge these Scottish wars
> Further, so here at Burgh-on-the-Sands,

5. The Chancellor's Muddle (1904-1907)

In the last slow surrendering of life
Will pray that I be brought unto repose,
And the valley of the shadows, which is Peace.

Not surprisingly, Sassoon felt that his poem was unlikely to win the Chancellor's Medal. In desperation, weighed down by the heaviness of Stubb's *Constitutional History and Select Charters*, which he was trying unsuccessfully to assimilate during the Christmas vacation, he had made the winning of the Medal his condition for returning to Cambridge at the beginning of 1907. Facing certain failure in his second-year exams, it seemed to him the only possible way to maintain credibility. Since the results were not due until March 1907, he stayed on at Weirleigh after Christmas, making a mild attack of 'flu his excuse for not returning to Cambridge at the beginning of the Lent term.

This was not, however, a simple matter. Sassoon's guardians could not be expected to accept a decision they would certainly consider unwise and irresponsible. The family solicitor, Mr Lousada, caused his charge little concern. Sassoon was used to being reproved by him for his expensive tastes in books and clothes. It was his uncle Hamo, for whom he had great affection and respect, who worried him.

In the absence of Alfred Sassoon, Hamo Thornycroft, the younger of Theresa's two brothers, had become something of a substitute father for Sassoon, the main male influence in his young life. He saw the small, spare man in many ways as a rôle model. Hamo and his wife Agatha (on whom Hardy had partly based Tess in *Tess of the Durbervilles*[44]) frequently visited Weirleigh with their children during the troubled years of Alfred's abandonment of his wife and sons. Sassoon showed his affection for his uncle in a number of ways, notably dedicating what he called his *Red Poetry Book* to him in 1898. He admired his uncle not so much for his outstanding artistic achievements as for his modesty and self-effacing simplicity, describing him as 'a simple enthusiastic soul'.[45]

When detailing the elaborate lunch he gave Hamo at Cambridge in June 1906, Sassoon reflects: 'If I could have the ordering of that meal again I would give him some good Cheshire cheese, a nice brown loaf, and a tankard of home-brewed ale, and possibly a cold gooseberry tart. Simple country things were what he liked best, and he always had the look of an open-air man, as well he might, since he came of a line of thriving gentleman farmers in Cheshire'.[46] Hamo himself had grown up in the country. His father and mother, desperately short of money and struggling to maintain their large family, had reluctantly agreed to send him at the age of four to live with his uncle, William Thornycroft, on his prosperous cheese farm at Great Tidnock, Cheshire. The plan, to pass the childless William's farm on to Hamo, failed because of one quality the adults had not taken into account, Hamo's determination. Though he greatly enjoyed his nine years on the farm and retained a love of rural pursuits and the countryside for the rest of his life, he decided quite early on that he wanted to return to London, 'to be something', as he put it.

Like his father before him Hamo had shown an early and independent talent for modelling and drawing and he finally decided on sculpture. His father, disillusioned by his own lack of success in the field and increasingly drawn towards his eldest son's experiments in engineering, tried hard to deflect Hamo's interests that way. With quiet but iron-willed persistence Hamo went his own way, secretly modelling a figure of a dancing faun which gained him early admission to the Royal Academy School. Taught by Frederic Leighton and other illustrious Academicians there, he quickly established himself as a sculptor in the classical tradition and had won three prestigious prizes before he was twenty-two. Later, under the influence of William Morris, he became something of an innovator, his 'Mower' being the first successful statue of a man in working-clothes. Followed by 'The Sower' and other examples of men and their trades, it portrayed working men with dignity rather than sentimentality, and with an authenticity doubtless gained from his own early experience on a farm.

Edmund Gosse, who became a life-long friend of Hamo's – a connection from which Sassoon was to benefit – greatly helped the young sculptor's career by writing extensively about his art and influencing his many friends to commission work. In addition, and throughout his highly successful life, Hamo received many public commissions, notably for the statues of Oliver Cromwell at the House of Commons, Gladstone opposite the Law Courts, Gordon of Khartoum, now in the Embankment Gardens, and King Alfred at Winchester.

On the face of it, there was not much to encourage Siegfried as he contemplated his uncle's character and achievements. He was, it seemed, all that his nephew was not: effective where Sassoon failed, determined where he vacillated. In addition his own son Oliver, born a few months after Michael Sassoon, had just successfully completed his own BA at Clare. It was true that Oliver himself, with a familiar swing of the pendulum, had disappointed his father by proving keener on engineering than on art, but he had nevertheless achieved what he had set out to do. Sassoon realized how hard it would be for his uncle to understand his own dilemma. Hamo had appeared to sympathize with his poetic aspirations, but his nephew felt that he would seem to him a failure if he were to tell him his plan to leave Cambridge should he miss the Chancellor's Medal. How could such a determined, hard-working and successful man possibly understand his position? His only hope lay in his uncle's sympathy and generosity of spirit, which he trusted would eventually win him over.

As it turned out, when Sassoon heard on 11 March 1907 that he had failed to win the Medal, he felt that he had no choice. After a week's delay he wrote with a mixture of defiance and apology to his uncle:

5. The Chancellor's Muddle (1904-1907)

I must screw myself up to inform you that I intend to give up Cambridge. I see no use in staying there three years and not getting a degree, and am sure I should never pass the exams.

I expect you will be very sick with me about it, but I don't think I should ever do anything there. I admit that it appears rather idiotic, but I have quite made up my mind about it.

Yr. not at all truculent nephew

S. Sassoon

I thought I had better let you know before writing to Mollison.[47]

In desperation, Hamo wrote to Gosse, whose wife was still a close friend of Sassoon's mother, asking him to use all his powers of persuasion on her. (She was in London at the time.) He also wrote to Sassoon with a mixture of exasperation and sorrow familiar to those who try to advise twenty-year-olds:

20 March '07

Dear Siegfried,

I could have wished that you had asked my advice. I should have advised you to stay on until Oct. at any rate, and I certainly think you should do so.

This modern method of 'chucking work' or chucking College as soon as it becomes in any [way] tedious is a poor development.

At the risk of being prosaic I will say that the moral discipline of work we do not quite like is an excellent thing, and as Xtianity gets less and less a guiding influence, will become more and more necessary.

I do not see why your being at Cambridge should not be an advantage to you in every way – even if you do not take your degree.

Yours affectionately,

Hamo Thornycroft.[48]

Sassoon would probably have acceded to Hamo's wishes had he possessed the faintest hope of passing his Tripos exams. He was quite convinced that his uncle was unable to understand his character, which was so very different from his own. It was perhaps a case of his dilettante father's traits confronting solid Thornycroft virtues.[49]

Though deflated when his poem failed to win the prize, Sassoon was more than ever determined to be a poet. He not wanted to take a degree in the first place and now felt himself freed from any obligation to try for one. (He would later describe his time at Cambridge as 'Four terms of boredom and discomfort'.[50]) His mother, who had believed in his poetic vocation from an early age, supported his decision wholeheartedly. She had, in any case, never forced him to do anything he disliked. In her positive way she tried to make the best of it with a joke about the Chancellor's 'Muddle', then said no more. Sassoon himself settled down with relief to live the life of a country gentleman.

POEMS.

—→∙∣∙∣≡→—

"*Our words and works, our thoughts and songs, turn thither,*
Toward one great end, as waves that press and roll.
Though waves be spent and ebb like hopes that wither,
These shall subside not ere they find the goal."

SWINBURNE.

—→∙∣∙∣≡→—

✦❧ 1906. ☙✦

Cover of Sassoon's rare first book.

6

Sporting Squire and Gentleman Writer (1907-1914)

Seven months after Sassoon's decision to leave Cambridge he celebrated his twenty-first birthday alone with his mother at Weirleigh. Nearly two-thirds of his twenty-one years had been spent at home with her and, in contrast to most of his male contemporaries, only just over a third away at school and university. He was now to pass yet another seven years at home, bringing the time spent there up to three-quarters of his life. His own diagnosis of this prolonged childhood was that his 'youthful personality ... had no shape or coherence unless [he] was inside the radius of [his] limited experience'.[1] While knowing at some level that he should leave Kent, perhaps even England, he was still not ready to face the outside world on his own. His father had once promised to take him abroad, but faced with going alone Sassoon found it easier to stay in familiar surroundings and follow accustomed routines.

Though outwardly uneventful, the period between 1907 and 1914 is a crucial one in Sassoon's development, a fact he himself tacitly acknowledged by devoting an entire volume of his three-part autobiography to it. The year 1911, for instance, brings a turning-point both in his poetic fortunes and in his attitude towards his own sexuality. By the end of this period he has gained enough confidence to leave home for London. One of his main problems at this time was how to fill his days. Loving Weirleigh was not quite enough and so gradually he began to adopt the life of a country gentleman, which became almost a full-time occupation. His spring and autumn would be spent golfing, his summer in playing cricket and his winter in renewed pursuit of his early passion, fox-hunting. To these sports he added an even more challenging one, which, like hunting, brought out the daredevil in him so apparently at odds with his timidity – steeple-chasing. Another less predictable enthusiasm during these years was dancing.

In direct contrast to these physical activities, and sometimes conflicting with them, were Sassoon's cultural needs. He continued his book-collecting, made a determined effort to improve his musical skills and added to his store of favourite paintings. Occasional days in London were spent mainly at concerts and art-galleries, though they also included visits to his tailors and bootmakers for smart hunting-clothes. Literature, however, remained his chief artistic outlet, and within that broad category, poetry still dominated. Between 1908 and 1913 he produced nine volumes of verse, as though driven by a need he himself did not wholly understand. He became increasingly aware of himself as two separate selves, one physically daring and outgoing, the other tentative and inward-looking. Thinking back on himself in 1914, he remembered the problems he had amalgamating his 'contrasted worlds of literature and sport'. At twenty-eight he would ask himself:

Why must I always be adapting my manners – and even my style of speaking – to different sets of people? Was it really necessary to exclude one world in order to find diversity in the other? Couldn't one combine them in 'one grand sweet song'?[2]

Sassoon may have ultimately found the conflicting rôles of sporting squire and gentleman writer impossible to maintain, but he had initially set about qualifying for them both in a rather deliberate manner. At the most obvious level, he took to smoking a pipe. (A 'smoking-room' was immediately created for him out of his father's old study.) And in 1908 got himself elected to a London club. Since he had neither the money nor the reputation for one of the more prestigious clubs – that would come later – he had to settle for a less well-known establishment.

Conscious of how obscure it was, Sassoon disdained to name his club in his autobiography, but he did mention it in a letter to his uncle Hamo and occasionally use its headed writing-paper. We know, therefore, that it was the Royal Societies Club and further research reveals that it was founded in 1894, had 3,000 members and charged only one guinea entrance fee. It also had the advantage of being situated in St James's Street just off Piccadilly.[3] Ostensibly for 'Members of Learned Societies', it possessed, to Siegfried's further satisfaction, a large library which was virtually unused. In addition it provided reasonably cheap accommodation for him when he stayed in London overnight. Such occasions were rare, however, and it is clear that he felt obliged to join a club more for social than practical reasons. That being so, he could not fail to be aware of his own club's lack of prestige. His way of handling this in his autobiography, apart from his failure to name it, was to make it appear faintly ridiculous, which to his satirical side it must sometimes have seemed.

Informing his readers that he had once heard it jokingly misnamed 'The United Nonentities' club, Sassoon paints a picture of a sombre, dull but highly respectable place where it took him seven years to become even faintly friendly with one or two elderly members. The club itself was more or less deserted after nine in the evening and made him feel at least five years older than he was. It seemed to him, when hanging up his top-hat in the cloakroom, that he was 'a sort of hybrid product of [his] "double-life"

... One half of [him] was hunting-field and the other was gentleman writer'.[4]

Before Sassoon returned to the hunting-field in 1907 he spent the spring and summer in the two sporting activities he had been able to pursue consistently throughout university, golf and cricket. From 1906 to 1910 he played golf regularly in the autumn, spring and early summer. His main partner was his friend Henry Thompson with whom he had kept in close touch since leaving Henley House.[5] An attempt to combine golf and work at Aberdovy in the summer vacation of 1906 had failed, but once he had formally left Cambridge in March 1907, he could indulge in the game with a clear conscience. As early as 1904 he had set up a mini-golf course in the garden at Weirleigh, and was able to practise his shots whenever he felt like it. From 1907 to 1910 he and Tommy competed annually in a protracted game which sometimes lasted five weeks and took them to Littlestone, Rye, Sandwich, Deal and Westward Ho! (Sassoon's favourite course was Rye.) And on at least one occasion he visited Tommy in Cumberland to continue their game there and at Siloth on the Solway Firth. Since they got on well together and were fairly evenly matched, Sassoon found it a most agreeable way of spending time.

Sassoon also played with Loder or the staff of his old preparatory school and crammers. In between he played many matches at a local golf-course run by Squire Morland at Lamberhurst. His description of its neglected and irregular conditions – it was 'much frequented by sheep'[6] – provided him with an amusing digression in *The Weald of Youth*, yet it is clear that he enjoyed his games there as much as, if rather differently from, anywhere else, in particular its 'idyllic pastoral surroundings'.[7]

Sassoon's love of golf stemmed partly from the physical exercise it offered. He also enjoyed being out of doors in attractive surroundings. And the company was almost exclusively male. Most importantly of all, golf allowed him to be what he called 'ruminative', there being plenty of time between strokes for daydreams. With a handicap of six, he was sufficiently good to enjoy the game without worrying too much if he sometimes lost. He himself found it 'highly significant of human affairs' that someone of strong literary tastes 'should feel an almost equal regard for the sanddunes amongst which he formerly straddled and swung and for those with whom he shared his enjoyment of the game ...'[8]

The same might also be said of Sassoon's love of cricket, though that was to last a lifetime, while his passion for golf faded away in his thirties. Consequently it has been impossible to do full justice to the subject in a few lines. But then there has always been a strong link between cricket and literature. John Squire's 'Invalids' and J.M. Barrie's 'Allahakbarries' are only two examples of a number of teams made up entirely of writers. It is a game which seems to invite literary exploration, as Sassoon himself realized early on in his book-collecting when he bought John Nyren's beautifully written *The Young Cricketer's Tutor* (1833) with its (in Sassoon's words) 'incomparable, brilliant and vivid portraiture of *Cricketers of My Time*'.[9]

Not only would Sassoon's own relatively small but interesting cricket library emphasize the literary interest of the sport, but he himself would contribute memorably to that literature in his description of 'The Flower Show Match' in *Memoirs of a Fox-Hunting Man*. His cricket library suggests that he collected fairly seriously until about 1905. He owned such classics as Christian's *At the Sign of the Wicket* (1894), Daft's *Kings of Cricket* (1893), Gale's *Echoes from Old Cricket Fields* (1871), W.G. Grace's *Cricket* (1891), Lester's *Bat v. Ball* (1900), Pycroft's *The Cricket Field* (1859) and Ranjitsinhji's *Jubilee Book of Cricket* (1897). Not surprisingly he had books on Kent and Cambridge cricket, though he also owned some of the yearbooks for both Somerset and Derbyshire County Cricket Clubs and Spybey's *Annual Register of Nottinghamshire Cricket Matches* (1884, 85 and 86). On the other hand his sets of Wisden and the magazine *Cricket* (where he had first appeared in print) were far from complete, a sign that he was not a totally dedicated collector.

Certainly after 1906 books were added very irregularly and often as gifts. John Arlott's *The Picture of Cricket* (1955), for example, was from a first class cricketer in his own right, Dennis Silk, as also was R.C. Robertson-Glasgow's *Crusoe on Cricket* (1966). His copy of J. May's *Cricket in North Hants* (1906), is signed 'L.J.E. Arlott' and was presumably presented by the great cricket commentator himself.[10] Sassoon probably added Neville Cardus's *Autobiography* (1947), *Second Innings* (1950) and *Cricket All the Year* (1952) to his initial collection as they appeared. Perhaps the most interesting volume from a collector's point of view is W.G. Grace's *Cricketing Reminiscences* (1899); it is initialled 'S.S. 1899', no doubt the year Sassoon acquired it, but with a letterhead of Gloucestershire County Cricket Club laid down, dated 26 September 1901 and signed by Dr E.M. Grace, W.G.'s elder brother. Symptomatic of Sassoon's own linking of cricket with literature is the appearance among his cricket scores of antiquarian books purchased in 1902, the year he started collecting.[11] Both pursuits seem to have been of equal interest to him.

Apart from its strong literary appeal, cricket fulfilled other needs in Sassoon. While helping to keep him fit, like golf, it also brought him into close contact with men of widely varying class and age. In his local cricket teams, Brenchley and Matfield, for example, he played with villagers he would not normally have got to know in the fairly rigid class system of the day. It was impossible to look down on a person who may have served one in a shop the previous day but had just bowled one out. Sassoon was respected in the local teams not because he was the 'gentleman' of independent, if limited, means from Weirleigh but because he was a useful bowler, good batsman and great enthusiast, even willing to help with the scoring. In a typical year (1908), when he played a fair amount of cricket for the official local team, Brenchley, he reported to Guilford in July that he had an average of 26 runs for all matches, one innings of 45 not out (out of a total of 91 runs) and one of 40. He had taken 5 wickets for 12, 5 for 27 and 5 for 29, which made him something of a star. He continued to improve and in 1911 he had a batting average for Brenchley of 35.37 with a highest score of 103 not out and in 1912 he headed the club's batting averages with an average of 23.14 for 8 innings. Not surprisingly he was a valued member of both Brenchley and Matfield teams and some weeks played as many as five matches.

During the Easter 1904 school holidays, Sassoon had attended the Tonbridge Cricket Club nets while being coached by the Kent professional Humphreys. He had subsequently played for the Club when studies permitted and in 1905 had the distinction of averaging 28.33 with the bat. The Kent professionals Hardinge, Humphreys and Hubble headed him, but his average was higher than that of Woolley, the great Kent and England batsman who was to become his ideal.

Sassoon appeared more frequently, however, for the Blue Mantles, who also played on the Nevill Ground at Tunbridge Wells. The Blue Mantles (sometimes styled Bluemantles) was founded in either 1862 or 1864 by the Bluemantle Pursuivant at Arms, to provide cricket for the local gentry and visitors to the then fashionable spa town of Tunbridge Wells. By 1896 it was playing about 36 matches a year and had over 140 members. And by 1904, when Sassoon joined Blue Mantles, it was playing some very good club sides and had several players with some limited first-class experience. Sassoon almost certainly struggled at this level. With characteristic modesty and probably some truth he suggested that his selection had more than a little to do with his ready availability. The cricket, he felt, was a good deal better than he was. But he was a reliable club cricketer and was not completely ashamed of his averages, considering them 'quite a creditable record for a poet'.[12] In 1910 and 1911, presumably his two best seasons, he had 51 innings with ten not-outs and an average of nineteen. He must have been of some value since by 1910 he was playing twenty-three out of thirty-one days in the summer and in 1912 he played an impressive fifty-four matches during the season.

Sassoon may have owed his introduction to the Blue Mantles to Cecil Norman. They had kept in touch when Sassoon left Marlborough for Henley House and Cambridge. They played golf together at Lord Amherst's course, the Wildernesse at Montreal Park, and from about 1904 to 1911, cricket for the Blue Mantles. In spite of knowing himself outclassed by most of the team members, Sassoon liked playing with them greatly. Part of his enjoyment was, as already suggested, literary: he could so easily see his team-mates as 'characters', even at the time. Later he lovingly described them in his autobiography – N.F. Druce, the brilliant batsman who had played five times for England *versus* Australia, the captain, 'Camel' Kelsey, a brewer in private life and a 'tremendous club

cricketer' who played once for Sussex, Captain Disney, resplendent in I
Zingari colours, Sir Arthur Conan Doyle, whose 'artful slows' had lost
some of their effectiveness by the time Sassoon played with him and 'Fred
Buzzaway' (A.P. Braybrooke), an indifferent bat but a singular figure with
his bow-legged run caused by too many seasons on the hunting field.[13] To
these Cecil Norman added, in his own account of the Blue Mantles team,
Jack Le Fleming, an old Kent player, the Hon. Osmond Scott, a valued
left-handed bowler who played twice for Gloucestershire, Sir Cecil Moon,
Colonel Nicholson, cousin to the Duke of Norfolk, and a local doctor,
Elliott. His emphasis on the aristocratic element in the team contrasts
sharply with Sassoon's relish for the eccentrics of whatever class.

One strong appeal the game had for Sassoon was its beauty. Cricket on
a well-tended village green in dazzling whites, with the reassuring sounds
of afternoon tea being prepared by non-participating women in the pavil-
ion, was quite a pleasurable experience. He spent a great deal of his life
looking back to his youth and became extremely nostalgic about cricket.
Even in his twenties he reminisced about the older, more amateurish
cricketers and their idiosyncratic ways. A later cricketing friend of Sassoon's remembered his nostalgia for old Kentish cricketers, especially
Frank Woolley, who had once repaired a puncture for him in his little shop
by the Angel ground at Tonbridge.[14]

While Sassoon undoubtedly appreciated the all-male environment, it
was not the real reason for his enjoyment of the game. Its main appeal for
him was, and continued to be, its essential Englishness. And as the writer
of an article on Sassoon's later cricketing performance argues, 'Cricket
was his game because it gave him space and time'.[15] Cricket became the
epitome of all that was peaceful in his past. It remained for him not merely
a game but a way of life, symbolizing all that he loved most about rural
England in summer.

Winter was another matter. As autumn approached Sassoon's thoughts
turned to fox-hunting. Largely unhindered by the doubts and conflicts
which trouble the sport today, though there were times when he questioned its humaneness, his main problem was finding the money needed
to pursue it. When he was a boy his mother had sold her jewelry to buy
him horses, but as a young man with an allowance of his own he was
expected not only to buy them himself but to pay for their upkeep as well.
His allowance of £400 per annum should have been quite sufficient, since
his mother continued to pay all household expenses from her far less
generous income of £200. It is not surprising that, eighteen months after
he returned home, his uncle had to inform him that his mother's income
in 1908 had proved insufficient; nor that he felt obliged to tell his self-absorbed young nephew that he thought he and his younger brother should
help with household expenses. When Sassoon did finally pronounce himself 'anxious to help in the housekeeping', however, his uncle pointed out

that he could not do that *and* 'do the wealthy patronizing gentleman, subscribing to all the golf clubs etc. and keeping a couple of hunters'.[16] If he, Hamo, had spent '£400 a year on self' at the age of 23, he argued, he would have been 'a fool'.

None of this prevented Sassoon from pursuing his chosen lifestyle, however. Since hunting, unlike cricket, was as much a social as a sporting activity – and Sassoon himself admitted to being something of a snob at this time – he had, in addition to horses, to spend fairly large amounts on riding equipment ordered from the correct tailors and bootmakers. The not inconsiderable hunt subscription had also to be found. The family solicitor, Mr Lousada, the more worldly and stricter of his two guardians, tried hard to dissuade him from such extravagance, but in 1907, shortly after his twenty-first birthday, Sassoon bought himself a hunter and with it a winter's occupation. For the next seven seasons he was to hunt regularly. Even when war intervened and he joined the army, he would go out with the hounds whenever possible, though it was not until the winter of 1920 that he would again have his own horse. In 1923 he was to give up hunting altogether. But, as his *Memoirs of a Fox-Hunting Man* shows, he was never to lose the sense of pleasure hunting had given him and continued to enjoy it vicariously through his extensive collection of books on the subject.[17]

Dame Felicitas Corrigan suggests that the pleasure Sassoon derived from a day with the hounds 'rose out of the aesthetic love for the English countryside of a young poet at the height of his physical vitality'.[18] Hunting in the first half of the twentieth century was, like cricket, a quintessentially English pursuit.[19] Sassoon himself maintained:

> For me hunting is inevitably associated with the pleasant country house life of the past which the Second World War has apparently eliminated. There was a traditional flavour about hunting which has never been the same since 1914. Admittedly, it was an undemocratic flavour, since it was derived from the 'design for living' of a prosperous and privileged upper class society which could still feel secure against the distant agitations of Socialism .
> Those were indeed the days, and delightful they are to remember, though deplorable to the urban-minded politicians of today's Government which aims at reducing us all to equality of income and mediocrity of mind. Nevertheless, I am unable to believe that the material basis of what is called the fabric of existence will alter the mental attitude of people who love horses and hunting. All the essential ingredients will still be there – the behaviour of the animal, the smell of a winter morning, and the sense of personal adventure and physical well-being in the rider.[20]

There was more to it than that for Sassoon, however. Cocooned as he was in his childhood environment, sheltered by an over-protective mother and an independent income from having to face anything uncongenial, he clearly had a need to take risks, to face danger. As an inexperienced child he had followed the Master over the highest jumps and he continued recklessly to do so. It is significant that, on the occasion when he chased forty German soldiers single-handedly from their own trench in the First World War, he did so with blood-curdling hunting-cries.

Sassoon derived an equal amount of pleasure from the less dramatic side of hunting, the early start on a crisp winter's morning, with boiled eggs and cocoa for breakfast, the echo of the horse's hoofs on the frosty road, the gradual dawning of day over the misty countryside and then, after the exhilaration of the galloping, jumping and chasing, the slow ride home on his tired horse, with a break for tea at a country inn by a roaring fire. *Memoirs of a Fox-Hunting Man* is full of such nostalgic details. It also contains more practical accounts of horses bought and sold, meets attended and, of course, descriptions of the more eccentric of his fellow riders, thinly disguised.

As Sassoon explains in *The Weald of Youth*, published fourteen years after *Memoirs of a Fox-Hunting Man*, he deliberately avoided the subject of fox-hunting in his 'real' autobiography because it had 'already been monopolized by a young man named George Sherston' who he admits was 'only me with a lot left out'.[21] He then goes on to give actual names and dates, together with a long description of the peak of his hunting career – a season with Loder at the Atherstone Hunt from September 1913 to March 1914. By that time he had acquired four hunters, Rubicon, Golumpus, Crusader and his favourite, Cockbird. These he transported together with his groom, Richardson, and a stable boy, to Witherley where Norman was living in a cottage while Witherley Lodge was being renovated for him.

Sassoon had already stayed with Norman at Ringmer, Lewes, when Loder was Master of the Southdown Hunt. He had also spent less exciting days with the West Kent Hounds. The Atherstone was quite different. Though only on the edge of 'the real grass countries', and only just 'one of the Shires' as Sassoon puts it, it provided much better hunting. Kent was too densely wooded, particularly the area surrounding Weirleigh, as Richardson had often complained. Both he and Sassoon were delighted at the opportunities Warwickshire offered. In an area approximately twenty-four miles by eighteen, the Atherstone hunted over grassy open pastureland of ridge and furrow relatively free of the huntsman's curse, barbed wire. But it was an extremely expensive undertaking, which Sassoon knew he would be unlikely to afford again. This gave it a unique added piquancy which comes through in both his fictional and autobiographical accounts.

While enjoying almost every minute of his time with the Atherstone, however, Sassoon had learnt by the end of his six-month stay that physical activities alone could not satisfy him. He was extremely fond of Loder and his abrupt, matter-of-fact ways. He also enjoyed the company of Loder's fellow-Etonian friend, Charles Wiggin, and other friends who came to stay. But he could not talk to them of poetry, art or music. Eventually he began to feel that it was possible to have 'too much unadulterated fox-hunting'. It was not Weirleigh he missed; a few days there in February 1914 seemed to him rather dull by comparison with the liveliness of Warwickshire. But by devoting himself entirely to the physical he had lost the precarious balance he was gradually establishing between body and mind. It was a situation that was to recur throughout his thirties and forties, until he managed to find a routine which satisfied both.

Meantime he finished off his season with Loder in style by competing in what had become another addictive sport, steeplechasing, and winning from Loder by not much more than the length of Cockbird's neck. It was the purchase of Cockbird in December 1910 which had first given him the idea of racing. He had bought the eight-year-old horse from the son of his mother's old hunting friend for only £50, but Richardson thought Cockbird capable of winning a point-to-point. Apart from his smooth action, he was a natural jumper and had great staying power. His only fault, as Sassoon discovered, was that he lacked the competitive spirit and did not finish well in a race. With some persuasion, however, from Sassoon who must have been a much better rider than his modesty allowed him to admit, Cockbird won four out of the eleven races he ran between 1911 and 1914, came second once, and third three times. Sassoon proudly commissioned a painting of his horse in 1911, the year he won his first race with the Southdown Members. He describes the thrills and dangers of steeplechasing as vividly as those of the hunt, and it is clear that both appealed to him for similar reasons. It was not so much to do with winning as the excitement of the thing itself. After a particularly disappointing ride in the early 1920s he wrote to a friend: 'It is *something* to be competing at all; I do love racing'.[22] Another advantage point-to-points offered was that they followed the hunting season and prolonged it by several weeks.

Perhaps the greatest benefit Sassoon derived from steeplechasing was that it brought him into contact with someone who was to become the best sporting friend he ever had, Gordon Harbord. Gordon's brother, Kenneth, had been in Cotton House, Marlborough, with Sassoon and may have invited him to stay at his father's rectory in East Hoathley, Sussex, about thirty miles from Weirleigh. Sassoon's fictional version of his meeting with Gordon (as Stephen Colwood in *Memoirs of a Fox-Hunting Man*) places it in 1911 at a local point-to-point. In his diary, however, and in a letter to Lady Ottoline Morrell he dates the meeting as 1908. Whenever the friendship started, it became very close indeed and Sassoon stayed with Gordon and his family on many occasions. All the Harbords, or at least all the males of the household whom Sassoon met, were keen horsemen: Gordon's father, the Reverend Harry Harbord, his brother Kenneth who went into the services on leaving Marlborough, and another brother, Geoffrey the 'lively-minded and humorous ... young Gunner major' referred to in Sassoon's diary.[23] Geoffrey was to remain in touch with Sassoon after the First World War and would be partly responsible for him taking up hunting again in 1920. He may also have helped inspire *Memoirs of a Fox-Hunting Man*, as I shall show later.

Gordon himself was nearly four years older than Sassoon, but he became a closer friend than either Geoffrey or Kenneth, who was almost the same age as well as a fellow Marlburian. The fact that Gordon, like his eldest brother Henry, went to Winchester rather than Marlborough and won an Exhibition to London University suggests that he was academically able, though it was evidently not a path that he wished to pursue. (In 1912 he joined the R.F.A.) Like Sassoon he was sensitive but basically non-intellectual in his approach to life.

Physically Gordon resembled his father, whom Sassoon described as 'a composite portrait of Charles Kingsley and Matthew Arnold'.[24] But he was much taller and, at 6ft 4in, even taller than Sassoon. (When the War came he would remark that the Germans must be 'awful mugs' if they could miss him!) One of his friends attributed his success with difficult horses to his long legs, which he would 'wrap' around the animal and 'ram him along in such a resolute fashion that the most determinedly pusillanimous refuser would find himself jumping'.[25] Another difference between Gordon and his father, according to Sassoon, was that Gordon's meditative air was softened by a humorous, at time, whimsical expression. This sense of humour, together with his sensitivity and passion for horses, explains his instant rapport with Sassoon and the strength of their friendship. He had various names for Sassoon, all of them jokey – 'Sig', 'old cocky', 'Sarsoon' or 'Sarson'. Referring to Sassoon's own jokey manner he claimed that it would take 'a very experienced Sig-ologist to distinguish matter from mocker, or sense from Surtees'.[26]

They were both avid readers of the sporting writer Surtees and shared many private jokes about his characters.[27] One of their favourite pastimes was to address each other in a specialized jargon drawn exclusively from the characters of that mid-Victorian novelist. They were helped by the fact that most of the members of Gordon's local Hunt, the Southdown, could well have stepped straight out of *Jorrocks's Jaunts and Jollities* or *Mr Sponge's Sporting Tour*. Gordon facetiously placed Sassoon in the role of a Surtees character, Billy Pringle, reputed to be very rich, thus magnifying his friend's modest income to £10,000. He rarely tired of referring with some irony to the financially struggling Sassoon as 'the richest commoner in England'. For his part Sassoon never succeeded in finding a satisfactory role for Gordon, though he continued to relish the game.

By a curious coincidence, not long after Sassoon's encounter with Gordon and the Southdown Hunt, his old friend Norman Loder became the Master of it. Gordon learnt to admire Loder's sportsmanship and solid if unimaginative character as much as Sassoon had and the three became good friends. When Sassoon, who lived rather too far from the Southdown for convenience, was unable to stay at the Harbords' rectory overnight, he was invited to keep Loder company in his little house at Ringmer. Whilst he treadled out Dvořák's *New World Symphony* on Loder's ancient pianola after a hard day's hunting, he reflected that his friend was as homely, kind and easy to get on with as ever. His efficiency and thoroughness as Master of Hounds were, however, a new side to his character that could only raise him in Sassoon's already high estimation. He would almost certainly have endorsed what another member of the Southdown said of Loder: 'I was immensely impressed by [his] handling, not only of his hounds, but his field; which I think was the best disciplined I have ever seen, and I never heard Loder swear at anyone'.[28]

During Loder's brief Mastership of the Atherstone, which followed that of the Southdown in 1913 and ended in 1914 shortly after Sassoon's extended visit, Loder met and fell in love with Phyllis Fisher, one of the boldest riders in the Hunt. The effect of his marriage to her, that same year, was blurred by the outbreak of war in September but was to become clearer when he and Sassoon resumed their friendship after the Armistice. Though there is no suggestion that their relationship had been a sexual one, as long as his friend remained unattached Sassoon had been able to ignore the problems marriage posed. It is quite clear from his diaries that even in his late thirties some of his heterosexual friends were still hoping he too would marry. There is little doubt that these expectations started in his early twenties at Weirleigh after he had left Cambridge. In the socially rigid and fairly limited society of the district, a handsome, unattached young man of private income, however modest, was inevitably seen as eligible. He showed no outward signs of his distaste for women in general and none of the clichés attached to homosexuals at the time fitted him. Far from seeming effeminate, he was the very model of masculinity with his lean sportsman's figure and dark good looks. His sensitivity and love of the arts appeared quite natural in the son of a professional painter and talented musician. Not surprisingly, therefore, he found himself invited to numerous dances and balls. He was frequently the guest of the Stirling family at Finchcocks, for example.

As an extension of what he called his 'life of action', to which he thought himself '(spasmodically) suited by temperament', Sassoon enjoyed dancing.[29] An 'earnest rather than a volatile performer', he rarely sat out any dance, not even the Lancers, and was 'hard at it until the band had played its final bar'.[30] He says the more romantic associations usually attached to dancing escaped him completely, but that is hard to believe. It is more likely that, when his partner suggested that some particularly soulful tune to which they swayed was playing 'specially for us', he was not unaware of its intimate implications, as he claims, but merely untouched by heterosexual interests, perhaps even threatened. He felt more romantic about the Queen Anne country houses where the balls often took place and in which he frequently stayed. He enjoyed their elegance, their discreet luxury, but above all their sense of history. His description of one such house in *The Weald of Youth* was based on Finchcocks at Goudhurst, only seven miles from Weirleigh. The daughter of the house, Marjorie Stirling, who had known Sassoon from childhood, was one of his few female friends in his twenties.[31] Once the suggestion of romance or sex was removed Sassoon enjoyed talking to women and was later to make confidantes of a number of them. If he suspected them of a sexual interest, however, he began to see them as voracious harpies. He would have enjoyed dancing with Marjorie because she posed no threat to him in this respect.

Two other popular sports of the time were croquet and clock-golf, both of which Sassoon probably enjoyed. He seems to have conformed to the pattern of the young country gentleman in all bar one respect: that of shooting. Significantly he had never felt able to shoot either animal or bird.

At no other period of his life did Sassoon feel able to compartmentalize his activities so neatly. He was later to argue that too great a concentration on the physical was detrimental to his artistic side:

> How easy it is to be alive when we demand of life only the simple and crude reward of success in a steeplechase. In such a mood art also seems easy, and I feel tempted to lapse into sloppy emotions and luscious derivative cadences – the drawing-room music of poetry, the melody that snares us into easy-flowing sentiment.[32]

Certainly during this period of intense physical activity his tastes in art continued to be romantic. The books he bought for his growing collection reflected his literary tastes as well as his appreciation of fine craftsmanship. In 1906, for example, he acquired two Kelmscott Press publications, a first edition of William Morris's *Poems By the Way*, one of a hundred copies on large hand-made paper, and Tennyson's *Maud*. These joined his collection in his new study-library, the large, well-lit first-floor room over his mother's studio. (To celebrate his coming of age she had had it redecorated in his favourite peacock-blue.)

After a phase of admiring George Meredith for his 'few lyrical masterpieces', he had become intoxicated by Walter Pater, who began to fill his shelves.[33] He was particularly fond of Pater's *Imaginary Portraits*. His mother's old friend Helen Wirgman quite rightly suspected that Meredith would have provided a more useful model, but it was precisely the romantic and enigmatic in Pater which he craved. Largely ignoring the don's impressive learning, he wallowed in his studies of sensitive temperaments in the picturesque past. Pater's deliberately stylized prose did nothing to improve the aspiring poet's already ornate phrases.

Other books added to Sassoon's new library-study in 1907, however, suggest that he was not completely dominated by Pater's influence. He began to collect A. Wright's 1902 edition of Shakespeare, for example, and bought at least two books of contemporary poetry, Herbert Trench's *New Poems* (1907) and Andrew Lang's *Ballads and Lyrics of Old France* (1907).

One aspect of book-collecting which particularly pleased Sassoon and revealed another important aspect of his character was that of arranging his treasures on shelves: 'it is an occupation which appeals to my craving for neatness and order', he wrote in his diary in 1922.[34] 'The books looked much more contented and companionable when I'd finished them'. He had a particular fondness for the imprint of William Pickering, whose fine editions appealed to his highly aesthetic tastes.

These tastes, as well as Sassoon's romantic leanings, were also satisfied by his growing collection of paintings in his twenties. His mother had bought him a reproduction of Burne-Jones's 'The Days of Creation' to hang in his new room and it fitted in perfectly with his other Pre-Raphaelite pictures. He added a Hollyer photograph of Burne-Jones's 'Laus Amoris' which, he remembered, inspired many a 'langorous sonnet'.[35] Even in his thirties he considered his taste in pictures 'a very lop-sided affair, overbalanced by [his] unaesthetic and unintellectual bias towards "literary interest" '.[36] This remark was made on the occasion he bought the photos of the martyrdom of San Lorenzo by Santa Croce, not for aesthetic reasons but for its 'morbidly sexual appeal to my sexually morbid mind':

> I hurry from one San Sebastian to another: from Ganymede to Narcissus and from Narcissus to Apollo. I hunt for beardless Christs and prostrate Abels, and hang about in front of Isaacs quailing at the crises of immolation by Abraham. Abraham, owing to the intervention of the angel, substitutes a ram for his offspring. I wish I could substitute intellect for the lust of the flesh. Also I find myself drugging my visual senses with *colour* instead of cultivating my appreciation of *design*. (The Venetian painters seem to provide the colours I like best.)

Sassoon's bias towards literary interest may partly account for his love of landscape painters such as John Sell Cotman, James Pyne and George Mason, which endured throughout his life, unlike his interest in the Pre-Raphaelites which gradually declined. But his tastes in painting were to remain fairly conservative and as late as 1952 he could refer to the great French Modernist as 'that awful Matisse'.[37] When he did buy something even slightly experimental, such as Henry Lamb's first small oil painting of Lytton Strachey, or three works by Gilbert Spencer, it tended to be for personal rather than aesthetic reasons.

Sassoon's taste in music between 1907 and 1914 was slightly more adventurous, perhaps because he had come to it later and without his mother's dominating influence. Though his impulse was still basically romantic, he was much readier to experiment with contemporary or near contemporary music. Helen Wirgman, who had taught him to love music in the first place, was herself open to new experiences and helped him to explore composers who were still regarded as challenging in the early twentieth century, such as Debussy and Grieg. Grieg was still just alive when Sassoon bought himself a grand piano in 1907. Though he had to resort to hire-purchase – a humiliating necessity as he saw it – his need to play the piano was almost as great as his urge to write poetry, two processes he believed to be closely connected: 'Most of my early verse', he wrote in *The Weald of Youth*, 'was vague poetic feeling set to remembered music. Unintellectual melodiousness was its main characteristic. Rich harmonies and lingering sonorities induced a relaxation of the nerves and acted on me like stimulating oxygen'.[38] Sometimes he would insert bars of music into his poetry notebooks as a guide to metre and a number of his works lent themselves readily to musical settings.[39]

Though Sassoon found Debussy much too difficult for his amateurish technique, he was excited by his 'delicate descriptiveness and his new and sumptuous subtleties of tone'.[40] Helen Wirgman considered it very 'go-ahead' of him to admire Debussy, whose new outlook on harmony and musical structure sometimes presented difficulties to his contemporaries, but it was the romantic melodist in Debussy that attracted Sassoon rather than the experimental technician, as his confessed preference for *Clair de Lune* over *Passepied* indicates. *Clair de Lune* had not, he argued, taken him very far from his romantic poetic tastes but 'merely made me indulge my periodic propensity for echoing the minor poetry of the 'Nineties'.[41]

By 1911 he was again expanding his musical horizons, this time through his renewed friendship with Fräulein Stoy's former pupil, Nevill Forbes. Though Sassoon had initially reacted strongly against his governess's praise of Forbes's musical and linguistic abilities, he had gradually come to share her admiration. Having kept in touch with the Forbes family after he left the New Beacon, he visited Nevill in 1910 at Oxford, where Forbes – who spoke at least fifteen languages – was Professor of Russian. In 1911 Forbes paid a return visit to Weirleigh. Apart from indulging Sassoon in Debussy, he introduced him to other contemporary composers such as Ravel, Reger, Albéniz, Chausson, Scriabin and César Franck, all of whom Sassoon enjoyed despite their modernity.

Sassoon's musical tastes were to be stretched once again in the 1920s, but, as he himself recognized towards the end of his life, they remained essentially conservative and romantic, as in poetry and art. His range was relatively wide, running from Bach, Handel and Gluck to Grieg, Debussy and Franck, but stopping short of highly experimental twentieth century composers. Bartok's work, for example, seemed to him 'dry bones and caricature and discontent and distortion and ungracious ingenuity', much the same words he might have used about most modernist poetry.[42] Above all, he looked for what he somewhat apologetically called 'sentimental melodies' in both arts, a characteristic he found lacking in most music after the early twentieth century.

Music was one of the main themes in Sassoon's poetry of this period. He claimed to have only two real subjects in his apprentice work, music and early morning. (His rough drafts also show some attempts at love poetry.)

The work published privately between 1907 and 1913, while Sassoon practised to become a professional poet, opens and closes with works related specifically to music. The first of these, *Orpheus in Diloeryum* (1908) may well have been influenced by his childhood memories of a picture by G.F. Watts entitled 'Orpheus and Eurydice' at his aunt Rachel's house, when his mother told him their story. It was also at Rachel's house he had heard an act of Gluck's 'Orpheus' sung.

The work began life in late 1906 or early 1907, shortly after *Poems* (1906) had gone to press, as a detailed examination of Orpheus's role as an inspired musician and the power of his music.[43] At this stage great emphasis is laid on Orpheus as a singer. As Sassoon explores the theme, it is clear that he is identifying Orpheus's 'song' with poetry: 'only aim and idea – song – and love – whereby song is elevated ...'[44] Whilst Orpheus's love for Eurydice can inspire him to great art even after her death, Sassoon's love is 'one that dares not speak its name'. Nevertheless, through the Orpheus myth he can highlight his belief in the importance of love as inspiration for 'song', or poetry. He plans to end his first version with Orpheus's 'wild note of grief – upflung arms, and the lyre cast away'. After several further experiments – the notes run to nine pages of 'Rough Drafts' – he arrives at a more restrained treatment of the subject, where Orpheus is used to satirize the false and superficial in art, personified in the characters of the musician Discordia, the poet Dorgrelian and others.[45] Through one note on the lyre Orpheus awakens the music of the natural world, which symbolically drowns even his own.[46]

By March 1908 fifty ordinary copies were bound up by the Athenaeum Press in stiff wrappers of pale grey cartridge paper and five special copies more elaborately produced in quarter vellum with white cloth sides, gold lettering and marbled end-papers. (Sassoon's aesthetic appreciation of fine papers and bindings is a distinctive feature of his privately printed books.) One of the limited editions went, appropriately enough, to a musician's wife, Lady Bliss.[47]

Sassoon himself characterized *Orpheus* as a 'typically juvenile performance', only 'a shade more sophisticated' than his previous volume.[48] He freely admitted that large parts of it were imitative, often deliberate parody of contemporary minor poetry.[49] From an early stage his poetry veered unsteadily between the lyric and the satiric. As a young poet uncertain of his own voice, parody offered him the opportunity to imitate the lyric poets he admired without publicly committing himself to their style. *Orpheus in Diloeryum* contained specific parody of a poet who had strongly influenced him, Swinburne, and may have been an attempt to free himself from his undue influence. At the end of his apprentice years parody was to provide him technically with a way forward, as well as to give him an effective preparation for some of his most powerful war poems.

In 1908, however, the main effect of his parody was to give *Orpheus in Diloeryum* a certain 'exuberance', as Sassoon put it. He was particularly proud of the 'effective dramatic device' by which the eponymous Orpheus nevertheless only makes one brief appearance at the end 'to admonish and stampede a clique of pseudo-artistic persons who had failed to recognize that he was the real thing, though disguised in a shepherd's cloak'.[50]

> Orpheus: Hush! for the dawn grows red beyond the hills;
> The earth is awed with prayer. And now the trees
> Loom dark and clear against the flushing sky.
> Silence, and holy pureness in the air,
> While the sweet land steals out of dusk to day.
> Now do I strike one chord upon this lyre;
> And all the woodland answers, giving praise
> For darkness ended and triumphant light.

Helen Wirgman, to whom he sent a copy, whilst 'smil[ing] considerably at it', could not 'help wishing there was more of Orpheus' himself in the piece.[51]

Edmund Gosse, who also received a copy at Uncle Hamo's suggestion, had fewer reservations than either its author or Wirgie, describing it as a 'delicate and accomplished little masque' which reminded him of the 'strange entertainments of the early Renaissance and of Italian humanism generally'. 'You own richness of fancy and command of melodious verse', he told the gratified Sassoon.[52] It was an important contact and one due largely to Hamo Thornycroft. Having failed to persuade his nephew to finish his degree, he was, with typical generosity, trying to help him succeed as a poet. By appealing to Gosse, one of the most influential critics of the day, he hoped to advance the young poet's career. Hamo himself had always encouraged Sassoon, on one memorable occasion urging him to try on Tennyson's hat and cloak, lent to the sculptor for his commissioned statue of Tennyson. (The hat was too large and slipped down over Sassoon's eyes.) He had also given him sound advice from his own experience in another artistic field: 'Let your thoughts ring true; and always keep your eye on the object while you write'.[53]

While appreciating the wisdom of his uncle's advice, Sassoon was not yet able to follow it and the next three years were spent working and reworking a group of largely derivative poems. Having temporarily satisfied his satiric urge in *Orpheus*, from 1909 to 1912 he devoted himself mainly to lyric poetry. His favourite form during this period became the sonnet.[54] He was probably more interested in the natural confines of a form which encouraged the shaping of a small but significant observation than in technical virtuosity. Equally attractive, from his bibliophilic viewpoint, was the sonnet's ability to fill a whole page yet leave room for elegant margins. The visual effect of poetry was always important to him.

At the same time, Sassoon continued to experiment with other verse forms, though he was neither radical nor revolutionary in his approach, sticking mostly to alternately rhyming lines. In 'Morning-Land', one of the two 'verses' – as opposed to 'sonnets' – that he preserved from his next volume, *Sonnets and Verses* (1909), he inserts an extra line between two quatrains, but the effect only reinforces the simple, traditional nature of the poem:

> ... While hamlet steeples sleepily
> At cock-crow chime out three and four,
> Till maids get up betime and go
> With faces like the red sun low
> Clattering about the dairy floor.
>
> (*CP*, p. 54)

The content of this and the other sixteen 'verses' Sassoon planned to include in *Sonnets and Verses* is mainly pastoral, though not confined quite as closely to sunrise, as Sassoon suggested, at least two of the pieces being devoted to sunset. The content of the eighteen 'sonnets' he planned to include with the seventeen 'verses' also defies his over-simplification. There is, for example, one striking poem 'Villon' on the medieval French poet, another of the poems from the period which he chose to preserve in his *Collected Poems*:

> They threw me from the gates; my matted hair
> Was dank with dungeon wetness; my spent frame
> O'erlaid with marish agues: everywhere
> Tortured by leaping pangs of frost and flame,
> So hideous was I that even Lazarus there
> In noisome rags arrayed and leprous shame,
> Beside me set had seemed full sweet and fair,
> And looked on me with loathing.
>   But one came
> Who laid a cloak on me and brought me in
> Tenderly to an hostel quiet and clean;
> Used me with healing hands for all my needs.
> The mortal stain of my reputed sin,
> My state despised, and my defilèd weeds,
> He hath put by as though they had not been.
>
> (*CP*, pp. 49-50)

It was the publication of this sonnet which led to Sassoon's debut on the London literary scene. Whilst putting the finishing touches to his third volume for private publication, he had also been trying to get some of the sonnets accepted by the better-known literary journals. After a number of curt rejection slips he had tried *The Academy*.[55] Advertized as 'the liveliest of the literary weeklies' and edited by a poet whose sonnets he admired for their polished technical perfection, it was his last resort. When, unexpectedly, the editor wrote to suggest a meeting to discuss publication of some of his sonnets, however, he panicked. T.W.H. Crosland, the editor in question, was known to him only as 'a powerful but repellently pugilistic literary journalist' and he politely declined the invitation, though at the same time indicating his willingness for Crosland to print some of his poems.[56] The result was a characteristically brusque letter from Crosland returning all his work. After a conciliatory telegram from Sassoon, a meeting was arranged and the apprehensive young poet found himself facing the notoriously dour and outspoken Yorkshireman.

Sassoon's later description of Crosland as an 'out and out blackguard' whom he nevertheless 'couldn't dislike'[57] indicates his ambivalence towards him. Polite, restrained and socially inhibited himself, he was both shocked and fascinated by Crosland's deliberate flouting of social conventions. (He particularly noted Crosland's defiant wearing of a hat at all times.) He seemed to him 'a remarkable man ... a human battleground of good and evil'.[58] Accepting Crosland as 'one of the finest journalists of his time', he genuinely admired his literary abilities and was to benefit from his suggestions as an editor who was himself a poet. As the first professional editor to give him meaningful encouragement, Sassoon felt some kind of obligation to him.

When he accepted Crosland's offer to publish nine of his sonnets in *The Academy* for payment of a guinea each, a fee that was extremely low even for the time and which, in any case, never materialized, Sassoon had only the haziest notion of the editor's background. Later on, long after he had severed all ties with Crosland, he was to discover how ferocious and implacable he could be. In 1909, when they first met, Thomas William Hodgson Crosland, who was just over twenty years older than Sassoon, was best known in the literary world for his journalism. His caustic attacks on friends and enemies alike had earned him a reputation for brutal honesty, though some thought that they sprang from perverseness. From 1907 he had helped edit *The Academy* under Lord Alfred Douglas, Oscar Wilde's notorious 'friend'. Together they hunted down all those who had come to Wilde's rescue in his last, sad days. Sassoon admired Crosland's technical achievements but he did not consider him a first-rate poet – a 'vigorous versifier' was all he would concede.[59] By the time he died in 1924, Crosland had written or contributed to over forty books. In 1909, when Sassoon first met him, he was best known for two biting parodies, *The Egregious English* (1903) and *The Unspeakable Scot* (1902). (His incorrigibility and productiveness is perhaps best illustrated by the fact that he wrote his own reply to the latter, under a title which he knew would appeal to his many enemies, *The Unspeakable Crosland* (1902).) Had he known of Sassoon's own attempt at parody in *Orpheus* he would probably have responded even more positively to him. As it was, when Sassoon turned back to parody in 1913, Crosland would be there to publish it and, in doing so, give Sassoon his first real chance in the literary world. Meantime their relationship revolved uneasily around Sassoon's more solemn attempts at lyric poetry.

6. Sporting Squire and Gentleman Writer (1907-1914)

Crosland's choice of Sassoon's 'Villon' as his first publication in *The Academy* was shrewd. Though still suffering from excessive archaisms and stilted inversions, the choice of subject matter is fresher than in most of Sassoon's early work and the technical handling of such matters as enjambment, caesura and rhyme scheme far more assured. Sassoon was right to feel a cautious confidence at his entry into the London literary world, as he contemplated his first publication in an important literary magazine.[60] Diffidence and a fear of being teased by his sporting friends had led him to initial his sonnet only, but that could easily be rectified if success followed.

In a reversal of their roles the previous year, this time it was Gosse who had doubts and reservations about Sassoon's poetry in 1909. Sassoon had followed up *Orpheus in Diloeryum* by sending his would-be patron copies of poems he planned to include in *Sonnets and Verses*. In May 1909 Hamo Thornycroft had written to his friend whom he still considered potentially useful to his nephew:

Just on our leaving the other day – on your doorstep – you almost told us what you thought of young Siegfried Sassoon's attempts at verse.

I am one of his Trustees, and as you can probably see, he is the apple of his Mother's eye, or some such thing.

So I am anxious that he should have any help and encouragement in the difficult path he has sworn to follow. So if you can advise him, do please, if opportunity occurs. He is an interesting personage and spirit. I have been severely calling him to order lately for spending too much on hunting, golf, cricket and expensive editions of books, beyond what his income of £400 will stand. (He lives at home). After letting off some fireworks to me in correspondence – as poets do! – he sends me an affectionate note – as he should!

I confess I have considerable hope that he will achieve something in literature. At present he is too much with the inferior country intellects and I should like him to meet literary men.

Gosse felt obliged to reply as honestly as he could, in the circumstances:

Melbury, Dorchester
May 16, 1909

I want to give you my exact impression of Siegfried Sassoon's verse, and I find it difficult to do so. What he has shown me is what people call 'promising', but one asks one's self what does such work promise?

You will quite understand what I mean when I say that there is no criterion in poetry, as there is in sculpture or painting, by which you can judge whether a young man is, or is not going to be, a good *workman*, whether he is going to be an *artist* or not. The cultivation of the eye and ear is now so general that nobody who is educated at all ought to write bad verses.

One has to look for something else, more subtle, a distinct originality.

Now I cannot truly say that I see as yet much evidence that Siegfried possesses this. So that I think that to arrange his life from the point of view of his becoming a poet would be very rash. The poetry should come as the

147

ornament and the appanage, at all events at present. I think that if I was his Trustee, I should feel that he ought to have the chance of training for some other profession. Of course, if, in five or six years, he should feel his powers as a writer strengthening, and find that his vocation as a poet was irresistible, he could then retire and live on his modest fortune, (as Robert Bridges did after becoming a physician), as a poet.

This is how it strikes me at present. Siegfried seems to be a most attractive and engaging fellow, and to have striking gifts. His charms and his talents will not be diminished by a little of the discipline of the world.

Hamo is unlikely to have shown his nephew Gosse's reply. Had he done so it might have saved Sassoon the seven guineas he spent in June 1909 on the private production of *Sonnets and Verses*, which was to have an extremely brief life-span. Sassoon received copies of his new book from the Athenaeum Press on the day of his fifth appearance in *The Academy* (26 June). He was pleased with the look of the thirty-five ordinary copies, which with his usual eye for detail had been bound in stiff white cartridge paper covers, and the three 'specials' on hand-made paper bound in black buckram.[61] Resolved to do things 'in style' this time, he had instructed the printers to use some red ink on the title-page: 'Sonnets' was in bold scarlet type, and so was 'Verses'. Where his name might have been expected, there was only a quotation from Pliny in the original Latin, to add what he ironically called 'a touch of scholarship'.[62] Another quotation from Meredith on the reverse of the title-page suggests that his mother's favourite poet had had a dominant influence in the composition of the contents. One of the specials was for himself, one for his mother and one was sent to the author he had quoted at the beginning of the 'Verses', Charles Doughty.[63] The first of the ordinary copies was presented to Helen Wirgman, who happened to be staying at Weirleigh.

This was the only copy to survive. Deeply depressed by the discrepancy between the book's elegant appearance and the undoubted failure of some of its lines, and upset by Wirgie's less than enthusiastic response, Sassoon worked himself up into a tantrum and burnt the remaining ordinary copies. Only its tough black buckram binding saved the special copy intended for but never given to his mother. When he confessed to Wirgie what he had done, she gave him one of her searching looks and told him that he sometimes reminded her of his rather unbalanced Aunt Lula. His impetuosity had suffered no real checks from his indulgent mother and there had been no father to discipline him since the age of five. Only Wirgie, who suffered from similar rages, ever indicated how undesirable such behaviour might be.

On reflection Sassoon decided that some of *Sonnets and Verses* deserved a better fate than burning and by August 1909 he had reprinted eleven of the 'Sonnets', heavily revised, together with six new ones, as simply

Sonnets. The fifty copies printed through Messrs. Hatchard were even more sumptuously produced than the previous volume, obviating the need for a 'special' edition. Printed on hand-made paper and bound in grey paper boards with ivory cloth spine, the end-papers were of the same expensive paper as the book.

Significantly, Sassoon does not tell us the cost of this elaborate production. Nor does he mention Gosse's rather ambivalent response. Whilst telling Sassoon that he found *Sonnets* a 'firm advance beyond all verse of yours which I have previously read', he nevertheless spent four more pages of this letter warning him of the dangers of 'a mere misty or foggy allusiveness' and metrical and grammatical inaccuracies.[64] 'I look for great things from you', he enigmatically concluded.

Of the six new pieces in *Sonnets* the first in the book, 'Before Day'(see p. 34), is almost certainly the best and not surprisingly Sassoon chose to preserve it in his *Collected Poems*.

Sassoon's own copy of *Sonnets* has survived, heavily revised in red ink and pencil, in preparation for yet another version of basically the same material.[65] This copy is rather puzzlingly inscribed, two years after publication:

> To the only begetter of Problems
> these ensuing sonnets –
> with ye author's compts.
>
> Feb. 1911

The echo of Shakespeare is unmistakable and it is tempting to assume that this book is similarly being presented to a young man. The addition of the word 'problems' would reinforce this interpretation, since it could only have been a 'problem' for Sassoon in 1911 if this romantic poetry were inspired by a man. The inscription could also be read as self-directed, with Sassoon himself becoming 'the only begetter of Problems', though this seems uncharacteristic and, therefore, unlikely. It is more likely that he first heavily revised his own copy of *Sonnets* in 1909, the year of its publication, and then presented it two years later to a newly-met friend as a highly personal gift. The revisions show no definite change in poetic aims; whilst some eradicate archaisms, others reinstate them. The most likely reason for the changes is either that Sassoon could not resist tinkering with his work, or that he actually enjoyed the process of revision.

A more interesting question is why he chose, for the third time, to repeat large amounts of material already printed. His own explanation is that, in spite of Wirgie's advice that he should write in a more *physical* way, like her hero George Meredith, by 1910 he was aiming at refinement rather than vigour. As he freely admits: 'Poetry was a dream world into which I escaped through an esoteric door in my mind'.[66] This is borne out in his next volume, privately printed in 1911, *Twelve Sonnets*, in which only two of the twelve pieces are new. Of these one survives in *Collected Poems* as 'Goblin Revel'. Far from showing progress towards a more personal voice it is, as he suggests, laden down with 'pseudo-archaic preciosities', curious outdated words such as 'fleering', 'loutings', 'brisk' (as a verb) and 'dulcimers' dominating the text:

> In gold and grey, with fleering looks of sin,
> I watch them come; by two, by three, by four,
> Advancing slow, with loutings they begin
> Their woven measure, widening from the door;
> While music-men behind are straddling in
> With flutes to brisk their feet across the floor, –
> And jangled dulcimers, and fiddles thin
> That taunt the twirling antic through once more ...
>
> (*CP*, p. 50)

The most plausible explanation for Sassoon's compulsive reworking of material is that living at home in Weirleigh, whilst it was comforting and safe, did not provide him with new subjects. There were, perhaps, only so many poems to be written about sunrise and music. Most of his energies seemed to go towards perfecting his technique, a technique that was already being challenged by other young poets as unfitted to the emerging twentieth century.

By turning to myth in *Orpheus*, Sassoon had tried to bring freshness to his work. But he was a poet who wrote best about things he had actually experienced. Nor was he very adventurous in his work, unlike his daring in life. Before the advent of War in 1914, he was to make three more attempts to break away from his usual subject matter, twice into Greek myth in *Amyntas* (1912) and *Hyacinth* (1912), short prose plays laced with lyric poetry, and once, in his most uncharacteristic venture of all, into contemporary low life in *The Daffodil Murderer* (1913).

Meanwhile, in 1911, he persisted with his usual subjects. *Poems*, issued this year, is significant mainly for the fact that its author, emerging cautiously from his anonymity, signed the last piece in the book 'Siegfried Sassoon'. He kept to his usual practice, however, in having thirty-five copies privately printed, this time by the Chiswick Press, who were to remain his printers for some years. Five of the pieces had, unsurprisingly, already been included in the 'Verses' section of his destroyed *Sonnets and Verses* of 1909. In addition to the two from this group preserved in *Collected Poems* ('Morning-Land' and 'Arcady Unheeding'), he was to preserve another three from the new pieces – 'An Old French Poet', 'Dryads' and 'At Daybreak'. Gosse was kind as usual, but advised him ominously to 'work more' and 'write, write, write – even if conscience makes you burn and burn'.[67]

Even Sassoon's prose play, *Hyacinth*, an apparently new departure in

1912, incorporated previous work. For *Hyacinth*, an 'Idyll', drew three of its six verse interludes from a small volume of *Melodies* published earlier that same year. (Gosse had been 'quite pleased' with *Melodies*, but warned its author against spending his whole life 'among moonbeams and half-tones'.)[68] While the poems in *Hyacinth* are predictably pastoral and lyrical, however, the prose subject matter does occupy new territory. In drawing on the Greek myth of the beautiful youth Hyacinth, who is loved by both Apollo and Zephyrus and finally killed by the latter, Sassoon is moving closer to a description of the homosexual love he dared not openly express. His choice of quotation on the title-page from the great exponent of love between men, Plato, reinforces this idea:

> Not all love, nor every mode of love, is beautiful, or worthy of commendation, but that alone which excites us to love worthily.

Sassoon's choice of a similarly beautiful young Greek, Amyntas, for another prose play written the same year as *Hyacinth* but never printed in book form, *Amyntas, a Mystery*,[69] is another sign of Sassoon's homosexual instincts at this time.[70] Sassoon's version has Amyntas, the young shepherd-boy of Greek legend, as someone of higher social standing, perhaps in order that he might identify with him more closely. For Duke Amyntas, a sensitive music-loving youth, who hates the noise and swagger of court life, is searching restlessly for a cause in life, very much like his idealistic creator. When a mysterious male prophet appears on the scene, he longs to escape with him to 'the green hills'. His musicians play, at his command, a song about a duke 'who loved but the lily and the rose./ He led no lady to his hall'. At the end of a rather inconclusive action, Amyntas shares with his faithful servant, Walter, a revelation that Sassoon himself may well have just experienced:

> By love my spirit can be healed and saved from darkness. I do not ask a love so vast as can embrace the whole world and guard all mortal men as one. I desire a love less infinite, a pity more human; eyes that may answer mine, arms that shall hold me fast.

The realization that an ideal love may not be enough sounds a new note in Sassoon's early writing, though it did not satisfy him. After reading a proof copy, produced by the Chiswick Press, he decided that it was not worth printing and two years later was to dismiss it as 'too bloodless! and silly to a degree'.[71] Even the author could see that the long soliloquies in poetical prose were 'rather absurd' for their time.

Significantly it was in 1911, the year before both *Hyacinth* and *Amyntas* were written, that Sassoon first openly declared his homosexuality. In June 1910, while staying with Nevill Forbes at Oxford, he had heard from him of his friend, the great sexual pioneer Edward Carpenter.[72] Almost certainly at Forbes's prompting, he subsequently read at least two of Carpenter's ground-breaking works, *The Intermediate Sex* and *Towards Democracy*, a long, Whitmanesque poem of which the fourth section, 'Who Shall Command the Heart?', was published separately.[73] His immediate identification with Carpenter's proposition that there was an 'intermediate' point in sexuality for both men and women between the wholly masculine and the wholly feminine changed his life.

Carpenter had been almost the same age as Sassoon when he arrived at an acceptance of his own homosexuality through a reading of Walt Whitman in 1869. Like Sassoon, Carpenter had been born into a middle class family and gone to Cambridge. Unlike Sassoon however, he had completed his degree and taken holy orders, serving for a time as curate to the early Christian Socialist, F.D. Maurice. His eventual rejection of the Church and wholehearted espousal of the working-class cause was closely bound up with coming to terms with his homosexuality. The rest of his long life was lived almost entirely among working-class people, with whom he joined in manual labour. The 'love of comrades' referred to so movingly in Walt Whitman's 'Calamus' poems (a passage of which is underlined in Sassoon's copy of James Thomson's *Walt Whitman, the Man and the Poet*) and the camaraderie of the working-classes were inseparably linked for many middle-class homosexuals at the beginning of the twentieth century. Both the plight of the working man and that of the homosexual was seen as that of a minority group trying to free itself from oppression.

Carpenter's first book on homosexuality, *Iolàus: An Anthology of Friendship* was published the year after Queen Victoria's death, symbolically heralding the start of a slightly more enlightened era. There had been, until then, very little published in England on homosexuality, and what did exist was usually disguised as a study of Greek mores. For example, the only other book Sassoon had read on the subject by 1911, apart from Carpenter's, was John Addington Symonds's *A Problem in Greek Ethics*. What distinguished Carpenter was his relative openness and lack of evasiveness, particularly since his books followed closely on the Oscar Wilde trial and the Cleveland affair.

Though his works may seem naive today, they were revolutionary in their time. In addition, as Jeffrey Weeks suggests, Carpenter's works 'had a particular warmth and insight that struck a chord for the young (especially among the middle class) of the period'.[74] Their puritanical emphasis on the 'dignity' and 'comradeship' of male Platonic love tied in neatly with both Christian and public school ethics. Robert Graves, for example, was to write to Carpenter from Charterhouse in 1914, claiming that *Iolaus* and *The Intermediate Sex* 'had taken the scales from his eyes and crystallized his vague feelings'.[75]

In much the same vein, Sassoon wrote to Carpenter on 27 July 1911, long before he himself had met Graves. He enclosed a copy of *Twelve Sonnets* 'to thank you for all that I reverence and am grateful for in you and your writings'.[76] Though unable at that time to sympathize with Carpenter's socialism, his theories on sexuality had been a revelation to Sassoon:

> ... your words have shown me all that I was blind to before, and have opened up the new life for me, after a time of great perplexity and unhappiness. Until I read the 'Inter[mediate] Sex', I knew absolutely nothing of that subject, (and was entirely *unspotted*, as I *am now*), but life was an empty thing, what ideas I had about homosexuality were absolutely prejudiced, and I was in such a groove that I couldn't allow myself to be what I wished to be, and the intense attraction I felt for my own sex was almost a subconscious thing, and my antipathy for women a mystery to me.[77]

Carpenter's sympathetic and open discussion of a problem Sassoon had suppressed, together with his chance discovery that his younger brother Hamo felt exactly as he did, comforted him greatly though it did not entirely solve his problems. As he confided to Carpenter, he still sometimes felt 'bitter agony' at the 'misunderstanding and injustice' suffered by homosexuals. There was also a sense, however, in which he seems to have partially accepted society's prejudices, as his use of the word 'unspotted', to denote his virginity, indicates. It also suggests suspicion on his part of physical desires, the fulfilment of which might somehow sully the purity of love. (He was ever the idealist.)

Whatever the implications of the word, it is clear that Sassoon had not yet experienced a physical sexual relationship by 1911, though he goes on to say that, had he read Carpenter earlier, when he was at Cambridge, things might have been different:

> I am [now] old enough to realise the better and nobler way [he wrote to Carpenter on 2 August 1911], and to avoid the mire which might have snared me, had I known five years ago – I write to you as the leader and the prophet.

These are views that would have been entirely consonant with Carpenter's teachings, which argued that homosexual men were less inclined to 'lust' than others, a convenient way of dealing with activities still frowned on by society and, in any case, prohibited by law.

In reading *The Intermediate Sex* Sassoon must have drawn consolation from the numerous passages which emphasize the artistic nature of many homosexuals, and he was eager to share with Carpenter (himself a poet) his love of poetry and music. His first real knowledge of homosexuality had come through his musical friend, Forbes, and he may also have known of Carpenter's own earlier activity as an Extension Lecturer at Cambridge in the History of Music among other things. Enclosed with the *Twelve Sonnets* he sent Carpenter in 1911 is an extra, handwritten sonnet, 'On Music', which suggests at least one way in which he attempted to sublimate his sexual urges:

Deep voice that through these lands of Life and Time
Forever sings with passion to control
The wayward straying of my human soul,
Leading me up to summits of sublime
Beauty eternal, flushed with golden fire;
O glory of great music, still in thee
I find foreknowledge of the destiny
Sought by all earth-born spirits that aspire.
So through all my days I pass with power to hear
The infinite melody that can atone
For all the sorrow and disgrace of living;
The rapture Life acclaims, forgetting fear;
Light in the night where I have dwelt alone;
Forgiveness when the world has no forgiving.[78]

In an attempt to excuse himself from responsibility for inclinations he still could not wholly accept, Sassoon told Carpenter of his belief that his 'intensely musical' father 'had a strong vein of the homosexual nature in him'. Alfred Sassoon, whose reputation as a 'womanizer' was probably well merited, might have found such an idea surprising.

Carpenter had also emphasized in *The Intermediate Sex* that, although sexuality should be seen as a continuum, with heterosexuals at either pole and homosexuals somewhere near the middle, this did not mean that homosexual men would necessarily appear effeminate. On the contrary he argued that they were often muscular and well-built. Sassoon again hastens to identify himself with this:

I live here mostly, in the country with my mother, cricket in summer, and riding and hunting in winter; and I am thankful to say I am as good as those others in their sports, and have some of their strength and courage.

He ends this first long letter to Carpenter by confessing that he is not religious, but that he has to believe 'that our immortality is *to be* (in those immortals whom our better lives may lead to, and whose immortal ways are marred and kept base by the grossness of unworthy souls)'. The high-flown language points to a spiritual need no longer satisfied by his mother's simple Anglicanism, which he had by now rejected. (He would refer later to 'the torment of his mocking youth that denied the God of priests, and triumphed in the God of skies and waters'.[79]) By denying or ignoring what he sees as the grosser physical element of sex, he attempts to promote his homosexuality into a religious cause. Over the years he was to become more sympathetic towards Carpenter's socialist ideals and by 1918 would be eager to join him near Sheffield at a manual job among the working-classes.[80] Though this plan never materialized, it was to pave the way for other socialist activities after the War.

In 1911, however, Sassoon was still largely out of sympathy with Carpenter's socialism. (He probably found Carpenter's suggestion that he become a stoker on an ocean liner risible.) It was sexual liberation he sought and, when Carpenter replied by return to his first outpourings, begged to be allowed to visit him.[81] Carpenter had told him of his friendship with his uncle Hamo's sister-in-law, Margaret, and her husband, Sidney Olivier. Hamo's brother-in-law, Harold Cox, was also a fervent socialist. Carpenter, Cox and Olivier had met at Cambridge and they remained friends after leaving university. Together with other subsequently well-known figures such as William Morris, Annie Besant and Bernard Shaw, they had started the Fabian Society. By August 1911 Sassoon had not, as he tells Carpenter in reply to his query, met the Oliviers. He was far more interested in meeting Carpenter, whom he felt 'could help him a lot'.[82] Until he resolved his sexual problems he was not ready to engage with political ones.

There is no doubt that Carpenter's influence changed Sassoon's attitude towards himself and had a palpable effect on his work. The year 1911 is a turning-point in his life. As a direct result of his new self-confidence his writing becomes bolder. Instead of clinging to old material and endlessly recycling it, in 1912 he not only writes two works in a different medium and on different subject matter – his prose plays *Hyacinth* and *Amyntas* – but also experiments with yet another form, the ode. His *Ode For Music*, whilst basically on the same subject as many of his sonnets and lyrics between 1906 and 1911, is far more expansive and confident in tone. Written in six stanzas varying in length from fourteen to nineteen lines, its hundred lines are, in the manner of the Romantic ode, an exalted address to spiritual powers.

The religious language used here, as in the sonnet 'On Music' sent to Carpenter in 1911, suggests that music had come to replace conventional Christian faith as the way to God for Sassoon. The skill with which the difficult but rewarding form is handled shows that Sassoon had benefited, at least technically, from his prolonged years of apprenticeship:

I

Angels of God and multitudes of Heaven,
    And every servant of the soul's aspiring,
Be with me now, while to your influence bending
I strive to gain the summits of desiring;
    Grant me in music's name
    Your symphonies of flame;
Come, and with rapture of resistless lyring,
    Where sense with spirit has striven,
    Through stellar spaces riven,
Bring vastness to my human comprehending:
    That I may know you near,
    Let me awake and hear
The rumour of your earthward wings descending.
    The rhythmic, mighty sound

Of heavenly hosts unbound,
And the tumultuous glory there attending!

As this extract suggests, and Sassoon admits, his style in 'Ode for Music' had been influenced by Francis Thompson, and Wordsworth too has left his mark, but the theme sprang from his own deepest feelings. His love of music was a genuine and abiding passion and he had written the poem in a state of 'ecstatic afflatus'.[83] He regarded it as his 'liberation from anaemic madrigals about moonlit gardens thrummed by the lutes of ill-starred lovers'.[84] In spite of the inflated rhetoric, *An Ode To Music* has more life and energy in it than most of his previous works. Whilst Gosse, to whom he sent the first of the fifty copies he had had elegantly printed by the Chiswick Press, failed to register any admiration, Crosland recognized its authenticity.

Crosland had left *The Academy* in 1910 and two of the nine sonnets he had accepted for publication in the magazine had been returned to Sassoon by the next editor. The unstoppable Crosland had, however, then become a publisher under the name of John Richmond Ltd, and the editor of a new monthly magazine, *The Antidote*. Sassoon gratefully accepted his offer to publish *An Ode for Music* in *The Antidote*, though Crosland had warned him that he could not pay for it.[85] Sassoon particularly appreciated Crosland's assessment of the poem, which showed an awareness of both its achievements and failings:

> You may take it from me that it is a good piece of work, and as fine and nobly intended, as anything we have had in this way for a long time. But it suffers from what we may call 'youngness' and want of mellowness and beating out ... but you are a much better poet than I am and I don't want to upset you.[86]

The surly Yorkshireman could be relied upon to tell the truth, whatever else his failings, and Sassoon must have felt more confident of his powers by the end of 1912, as he looked around for new subject matter. He was to find it in an unexpected quarter, yet in a sense it was only another swing of the pendulum from the lyric to the satiric in his work.

Confined to his study in December 1912 by a particularly bad spell of wet weather which prevented hunting, Sassoon searched his bookshelves for something to cheer him up. Though Crosland's praise had helped, he was still rather depressed about his prospects as a poet. Settling, quite by chance, on John Masefield's long narrative poem, *The Everlasting Mercy*, he looked to see if its 'headlong octosyllabics' still seemed as exciting as when he had first read them the previous year. Masefield's revolutionary style, with its emphasis on the colloquial and natural, had attracted both extravagant praise and criticism and Sassoon's own reaction seems to have been ambivalent. Whilst admiring its vitality, he could not help finding this realistic story of the conversion of the villainous Saul Kain by a Quaker woman amusing in a way Masefield had certainly never intended. It had already proved an easy target for the parodists and he could not resist joining in.

With his natural gift for imitation he had very little difficulty in parodying Masefield's distinctive style. By transposing Masefield's protagonist and setting into something nearer home – a Sussex farmhand waiting to hang for the accidental killing of the 'chucker-out' or 'bouncer' at his village pub – Sassoon unwittingly provided himself with the first real 'subject' of his poetic career. So intense was his response to his material that, after the first fifty lines or so, he dropped all pretence that he was improvising an exuberant skit:

> While continuing to burlesque Masefield for all I was worth, I was really feeling what I wrote – and doing it not only with abundant delight but a sense of descriptive energy quite unlike anything I had experienced before.[87]

His parody had turned into a pastiche. With his limited experience of working-class life, he could not claim that his Sussex yokel was entirely convincing but he did feel that he had managed to convey something of the rural Sussex he had absorbed through following the Southdown Hunt.

Never before had he been able to do what Wirgie had advised, to write physically. His new-found ability to describe the commonplace poetically emerges with particular clarity in the passage he himself chose to quote in his autobiography, the moment when the protagonist thinks back on the man he has unintentionally murdered:

> I thought how in the summer weather
> When Bill and me was boys together
> We'd often come this way when trudgin'
> Out by the brooks to fish for gudgeon.
> I thought, When me and Bill are deaders
> There'll still be buttercups in medders,
> And boys with penny floats and hooks
> Catching fish in Laughton brooks ...[88]

Sassoon was so invigorated by his subject matter that it took him only two days to finish a poem of over 500 lines. Though he knew that his composition was far from original, he rightly considered his handling of the story and characterization a decided step forward. His poem offers no equivalent in terms of Masefield's minor characters (the parson and Mrs Blaggard, for example) but his protagonist is a more appealing and more believable creation than Masefield's brutish Saul who turns preacher. Sassoon's portrayal of *his* Saul's resigned acceptance of his fate, as he tells his story to the prison chaplain, is both moving and convincing:

> ... There's one I'd like to have a word with,
> And get a hand-shake to be cheer'd with;

And tell 'im I took no offence
For how he treated me long since.
'Tis certain sure before I die
They'll let Sue in to say good-bye.
She'll have to leave a lot unsaid;
Her face'll be so swelled and red.
Like a good gal she'll make small fuss;
I'll hug her once and gi' 'er a buss;
Because her man she mun be leaving,
Her man as isn't worth the grieving.
She'll have to live with her old mother;
Mayhap in time she'll wed another.

The poem concludes with two stanzas of lyric poetry celebrating the changing seasons, written with a simplicity that had previously eluded Sassoon.

It is an effective end to a skilfully controlled narrative, which moves quickly, within its framework of Saul's confession to the prison chaplain, from his customary journey to the village pub after work, through his argument with a fellow-drinker, his ejection from the pub and his planned retaliation, to the unintentional murder of his childhood friend and the subsequent arrest. This ability to handle a story anticipates by almost sixteen years Sassoon's first novel. It is also significant that his response to an imaginary working-class man in dire circumstances should have appealed to his imagination so shortly before the outbreak of a war which would bring him into real contact with men of similar social class in equally difficult circumstances. Though technically he fell well below Masefield in his handling of the difficult octosyllabic couplet and use of realistic working-class language, *The Daffodil Murderer* shows a distinct increase in Sassoon's powers as a writer.

Sassoon sent his (untitled) poem to Crosland, since he was the only man of letters who had given him any practical help. He was genuinely surprised when Crosland immediately offered to publish it, on condition that the author contributed ten pounds towards expenses.[89] Whilst gladly accepting Crosland's offer, Sassoon rejected his suggested title, 'The Gentle Murderer by Peter Expletive' and the pseudonymous and adulatory introduction his publisher wanted to write. He also rejected Crosland's perceptive criticism, that the poem needed a little more 'parody and suggestiveness', partly because he was squeamish, and partly because he did not know how to provide it. Unaware until then of Crosland's hostility towards Masefield, he had innocently provided him with welcome ammunition. His imitation had been stimulated by admiration and he had no desire to wound Masefield.

However, Sassoon did agree to the title 'The Daffodil Murderer' by Saul Kain', a jokey double reference to Masefield's recently published *The Daffodil Fields* and the protagonist of *The Everlasting Mercy*. In an ironic anticipation of Sassoon's own career, the facetious preface, written ostensibly by 'William Butler' (a jibe at Yeats) but really written by himself, describes the author as a soldier who had 'fought for his country on many a bloody field' but who was 'fonder of poetry than pipe-clay'.[90] The quotation from Chaucer on the title-page deliberately matched the lines by Lydgate which formed the epigraph to Masefield's poem. A thousand cheerful yellow and brown pamphlets, costing just sixpence each, were ready for the publisher only three weeks after Sassoon had finished polishing it under Crosland's expert guidance.

Sassoon's desire to preserve his anonymity, understandable in the circumstances, also served Crosland's ends, since he probably wanted it to be believed that he had written yet another brilliant satire along the lines of his *Unspeakable Scot*. In the event the book was virtually ignored, its one reviewer (in *The Athenaeum*) dismissing it in a few words: 'This is a pointless and weak-kneed imitation of *The Everlasting Mercy*. The only conclusion we obtain from its perusal is that it is easy to write worse than Mr Masefield'. Sassoon later consoled himself with the theory that, since Crosland was a bitter enemy of *The Athenaeum*, the attack had sprung from the assumption Crosland had deliberately fostered, that he was its author. (He had been very cross when he learnt that, in an attempt to promote sales, Sassoon had revealed the book's true authorship to Mr Bowes of Bowes and Bowes, the Cambridge bookshop, where he had so 'rewardingly' overspent his allowance as an undergraduate.)

Though enormously proud of his achievement at the time and hoping for overnight success from *The Daffodil Murderer*, Sassoon was later able to put it into perspective. When Sydney Carlyle Cockerell showed him a postcard from Wilfred Scawen Blunt, which claimed that it was 'better than Masefield, in the same way that Swinburne's parody was better than Browning', Sassoon told a friend:

> I don't agree with that! As you say, it is good stuff where it is serious. But it's main significance is that it was the first sign of my being capable of writing as I did during the war, and the first time I used real experience. It also revealed my gift for parody, which is considerable.[91]

In retrospect Sassoon almost certainly acknowledged the wisdom of Carpenter's judgement:

> It is rather a good imitation of Masefield – though hardly up to his mark. But I really don't see *why* you have done it! ... You have such a good turn for verse, I can't help wishing you would write something solid. Only I expect you ought to go and do something solid first![92]

Gosse was far more impressed by *The Daffodil Murderer*. Sassoon had, almost automatically, sent a copy of the sixpenny pamphlet to his uncle's friend, expecting either the usual bland reply or none at all. Instead Gosse wrote at once to congratulate him. His letter sets the tone for the relationship which was to follow, being cautious as well as encouraging and, above all, honest. Gosse rarely wrote an unconsidered word and, though his carefulness sometimes amused Sassoon, it was a quality he came to value highly. After Gosse's tactful silence over the poetry he could not honestly praise, Sassoon was the readier to believe him when he did write on 13 February 1913:

> My dear Siegfried,
> *The Daffodil Murderer* is a composition which interests me very much, and about which I feel a difficulty in defining my opinion. It is a very clever, brilliant thing, and displays powers which I had not expected from you. But, apart from the 'Preface', which is a very amusing (and well-deserved) bit of satire, what puzzles me about the poem is that it is not really a parody at all. It is a pastiche. It treats a Masefield subject exactly in Masefield's own manner, as if you had actually got into Masefield's own skin, and spoke with his voice. There is nothing comic about it. A tale of rustic tragedy is told with real pathos and power, only – exactly as Masefield would tell it. The end is extremely beautiful ...[93]

Gosse must have found it a great relief to be able, finally, to believe in the young poet. He had been devoted to Sassoon's uncle, Hamo Thornycroft, since 1879. Though they had known each other slightly through Gosse's wife, Nellie, and Hamo's sister, Theresa, it was not until June 1879 that the acquaintance ripened into friendship. Hamo had invited Gosse to join him in a cruise down the Thames on his father's steamer, *The Waterlily*, and Gosse's response to the trip had been ecstatic. Brought up by a loving but stern father, whom he afterwards immortalized in his minor classic, *Father and Son*, he saw in Hamo's carefree but sensitive and passionate response to nature his ideal. As they bathed and sunbathed nude in the lovely backwaters of the Thames, he thought of the Greek sculptures he had secretly worshipped in his Calvinistic childhood. That Hamo himself was a sculptor and an exponent of the New Sculpture, with its emphasis on the beauty of the human body, made it all the more exciting. In August 1879 he asked permission to dedicate his *New Poems* to him. (He had portrayed Hamo as a sculptor, Myron, in one of these poems, 'The Island of the Blest', where he takes the opportunity to say how much he owes him.) His affection for Hamo became a passion not easily distinguished from the sexual. Though happily married since 1875, when Hamo himself announced his engagement to Agatha Cox in July 1883, Gosse was moved to write: '... at this crisis of our lives my one great thought is one of gratitude to you for these four wonderful years, the summer of my life, which I have spent in a sort of morning glory walking by your side'.[94] As Gosse's biographer, Ann Thwaite, remarks of a similar letter from Gosse, 'This is lover's talk'. Gosse is not known to have been a practising homosexual, however, and, if his feelings for Hamo were those of a lover, he suppressed any physical manifestations of it. Lytton Strachey may have analyzed the situation correctly when he was asked if he thought Gosse homosexual: 'No', he replied, 'but he's Hamo-sexual'. Sassoon himself confirmed this view.[95]

When Gosse and Hamo took their first holiday together – there were to be many more, even after Hamo married – Gosse had already established himself in the literary world as a shrewd critic and the friend of Rossetti, Swinburne and Browning. After eight tedious years as clerk at the British Museum, he had in 1875 been offered a much better job as Translator at the Board of Trade, which also left him more time to pursue his literary interests. Though only a year older than Hamo (he had been born in 1849, Hamo in 1850), he was far more established in his chosen field, though he was never to achieve the fame he longed for as a poet. Despite the fact that in 1879 his knowledge of art was as limited as Hamo's was of literature, he dedicated himself to furthering his friend's career, an end he undoubtedly achieved. He did not hesitate to use his influence wherever possible. The fortunate chance of being the brother-in-law of the fashionable Victorian painter, Alma Tadema, for example, enabled him to get Hamo elected to the Royal Academy at an unusually early age.[96]

By the time Gosse wrote his cautious letter of praise to Sassoon in 1913, however, Hamo's career was no longer in need of his promotion, though the writer still watched over him 'like a careful nursemaid', as the sculptor's daughter put it. It seemed the most natural thing in the world for Gosse to transfer his efforts to Hamo's nephew, especially since his wife continued to be close friends with Sassoon's mother. By 1913 he had even more to offer in the way of patronage and influence. Not only had he held the prestigious Clark Lectureship at Trinity College, Cambridge, from 1884 to 1890, but he had also been honoured in 1904 with the position of Librarian to the House of Lords. In addition he had extended his friendships with famous writers to include Robert Louis Stevenson, Henry James and Thomas Hardy, among others. Apart from his autobiography, *Father and Son* (1907) and his innovative work on Ibsen, Gosse was known for his eminently readable critical books, *Seventeenth Century Studies* (1883), *Gossip in a Library* (1891), *Critical Kit-Kats* (1896), *French Profiles* (1905) and *Portraits and Sketches* (1912). H.G. Wells had dubbed him, rather mischievously, 'the official British man of letters'.

In the short time it took Gosse to respond to Sassoon's gift of *The Daffodil Murderer* in February 1913, he had already taken the first practical steps in helping Hamo's nephew, by making sure that the 'choragus' of the new poets, as he somewhat pedantically described Edward Marsh, also had a copy of the bright yellow pamphlet. As he explained to Sassoon, Marsh was the editor of *Georgian Poetry*, an anthology of contemporary verse which had recently made its successful appearance on the literary scene. Since Marsh had expressed a polite interest in Gosse's protégé (it would have been difficult for him to have done otherwise), Gosse advised Sassoon to send him his other booklets:

> I should like you to get into friendly relations with Mr Marsh, who is a most charming man, extremely interested in poetry, and the personal friend of all the new poets. It would be useful to you, I think, as you lead so isolated a life, to get into relations with these people, who are of all schools, but represent what is most vivid in the latest poetical writing. It is time, I think, for you to begin to tilt up the bushel under which your light has been burning.

Rarely have the workings of the literary bandwagon been so clearly exposed.

Gosse's momentous letter was followed by an equally exciting invitation to visit him a few weeks later at the House of Lords. It was to be Sassoon's first private talk with a man for whom he had already formed a profound respect. Nellie Gosse's visits to Weirleigh during Sassoon's childhood had kept her husband alive in his mind and he thought of him during those years as someone 'in ideal association with poets and poetry'.[97] His first serious reading of Gosse's work – *Gossip in a Library* (1891) and *Critical Kit-Kats* (1896) – had not only made him want to read the books so enthusiastically described but had also paved the way for his own excursion into book-collecting a few years later in 1903. That same year he had also seen Gosse for the first time, at a dance given jointly by Nellie Gosse and his Aunt Agatha at Hampstead Town Hall, but he was not to talk to him for another six years.

Meantime, encouraged by his uncle, Sassoon had started to send the critic his work. So he was thrilled to be invited to an afternoon party at the Gosses' in 1909 and again in 1911.[98] Though the latter was in honour of a Dutch writer of whom he had never heard, Maarten Maartens, he hoped to meet one or two better known poets. Gosse's daughter Tessa, whom he knew, did her best to make the shy young man feel at home, but her introductions were all to non- literary ladies. In spite of his smart clothes – dark summer suit and buff linen waistcoat with spats to match – Sassoon felt extremely ill at ease and rather disappointed. But when most of the guests had left, he was consoled by a cosy chat with Gosse, who introduced him flatteringly but rather whimsically to the Dutch writer as 'the very youngest of our unpublished poets, and a veritable centaur among them, since he bestrides his own Pegasus in hunt steeple-chases'.[99] Sassoon was then entertained with one of Gosse's virtuoso speeches and sent on his way feeling that he would have to be very good indeed to be allowed full access to that charmed world. He had continued to correspond with Gosse since then, but it was not until the publication of *The Daffodil Murderer* in 1913 that he was invited to meet him again, this time alone and in private.

In the event Sassoon's first intimate talk with Gosse turned out to be an uncomfortable affair, quite different from the many delightful chats which were to follow. Still socially unsure of himself, as well as constitutionally shy, Sassoon felt that he had made a poor impression. Though small and unprepossessing in appearance Gosse had a fierce manner at times and could be a formidable enemy. (Aldous Huxley called him 'the bloodiest little old man'.)[100] He was also an urbane host, though he failed to put his young guest at his ease on this occasion. Overawed by Gosse and his august surroundings in the House of Lords' library, Sassoon was able to say very little, particularly when his host asked him about Crosland, of whom he clearly disapproved.

Sassoon managed to redeem himself a little by remarking innocently, when given a glimpse of the assembled Lords: 'Anyone would almost think they were all half-asleep!' It gave Gosse a chance to deliver one of his artful, if ponderous, periphrases: 'Some of them, I doubt not, are indulging in a decorous doze. The speaker is one of the most profusely unenlightening of our hereditary legislators!'[101] This humorous note, common to both, helped consolidate their relationship and an invitation to a party on 5 June 1913 followed.

Big London where Poets Live
(May-July 1914)

Sassoon's friendship with Gosse was undoubtedly a crucial step in his literary career. Whether it was a positive one in the long run is open to debate. 'No one has done me greater service', Sassoon was to write to Gosse in 1927. But by identifying with Gosse and his friends in 1913, when a major shift in poetic consciousness was already under way, Sassoon was aligning himself with the old guard in literature. If Crosland's poetic development had stopped short at W.E. Henley in the Nineties, Gosse's had not gone much further. And, though he claimed in his letter to Sassoon of February 1913 that his friend Edward Marsh fostered all that was 'most vivid in the latest poetical writing', Marsh too was suspicious of radical experiment. To begin with, his *Georgian Poetry* anthology represented innovation but it came increasingly to seem highly conservative and by 1922, when the last volume appeared, even Gosse was moved to remind Marsh that 'poetry should not always be "breathing through silver" '.[1]

Sassoon's diffidence and lack of confidence in 1913 made him particularly vulnerable to any type of influence. Whether his later rejection of modernism was a result of Gosse and his friends is impossible to say. What might have happened had his personal introduction to the literary world come through, say, the Imagists, or the Bloomsbury Group, both flourishing in the contemporary London scene? The Imagist movement, influenced by T.E. Hulme's insistence on hard, clear, precise images and encouraged by Ezra Pound during his stay in London just before the First World War, fought against the two things of which Sassoon was most guilty at this time, romantic fuzziness and facile emotionalism.[2] Though the Bloomsbury Group, which was well established by 1913, did not include any major poets at its centre, its aims in both literature and art were ultimately modernist. By choosing Gosse as his mentor, Sassoon chose Gosse's friends, the most influential of whom in terms of poetry was undoubtedly Edward Marsh.

One has only to look at Marsh's advice to Sassoon, in response to the slim volume he sent him, to show how conservative that influence was. Gosse had urged the young poet in 1909 to defend the 'purity of the language'. In 1913 Marsh wrote in very similar terms. Though he criticized Sassoon's sonnets and lyrics for containing 'far too much of the worn-out stuff and garb of poetry',[3] his own criticism sprang from an acceptance of traditions which were already being rejected in England by poets like Pound, Richard Aldington and D.H. Lawrence. (Eliot would follow shortly afterwards and become Sassoon's particular *bête noir*.)

Within its own terms, however, Marsh's criticism was helpful, encouraging Sassoon to resist the 'vague iridescent ethereal' poetry of Rossetti, Swinburne and Dowson and 'to write either with one's eye on an object or with one's mind at grips with a more or less definite idea'.[4] Marsh admired poems which followed this rule, in Sassoon's case 'Dryads', which he found 'exquisite'. The sonnet he admired most was 'Goblin Revel', which he thought 'exactly like the dance of grotesques in the Russian ballet, *Oiseau de feu*'. The allusion to Stravinsky was lost on Sassoon, though he was later to be introduced to Diaghilev's troupe through Marsh himself and to become quite as addicted. The most gratifying part of Marsh's letter was its opening, with an appropriately musical metaphor: 'I think it certain that you have a lovely instrument to play upon and no end of beautiful tunes in your head'.[5] The invitation to visit Marsh in London which concludes the letter was hardly less exciting and Sassoon arranged to do so immediately.

When Sassoon first met Edward Marsh at the National Club in Whitehall in March 1913, Marsh was already a highly successful man. Born twenty-three years after Gosse, in 1872, he himself owed some of his literary influence to Gosse. Introduced to him in 1894 by a mutual friend, Maurice Baring, he then went on to meet others of Gosse's influential circle. It was Gosse's recommendation which enabled him to penetrate the Reform Club, that bastion of social privilege, in 1898. But, by the time Sassoon came to know them both, they were equally powerful in their separate but related spheres, and known jointly to at least one of their friends as 'the oracles'.[6] The two 'oracles' were, however, very different and were to serve different purposes in Sassoon's poetic career. While Gosse encouraged him in fairly general terms and introduced him to 'useful' people, Marsh was to give him more specific help with his work. An outstanding classicist in his generation at Westminster and Cambridge in the 1890s, he became for the younger and less scholarly Sassoon an authority on such technical problems as metre and diction.

Marsh shared other interests with Sassoon beside poetry. At Cambridge he had been friends not only with writers like Baring but also with those involved in the art world, such as Walter Sickert's brother Oswald, and Roger Fry. Fry, who was far ahead of his time, introduced Marsh to the latest developments in art and infected him with an enthusiasm which never left him. By the time Sassoon met him, he had already bought his first picture, 'Parrot Tulips' by Duncan Grant in 1912. (His taste in art was more modern than his taste in literature.) From then on he continued to help struggling young artists by buying their work. Mark Gertler, John Currie, Stanley Spencer and the poet-painter Isaac Rosenberg were all to benefit from his generosity, Marsh becoming known as something of a Maecenas.

Though comfortably placed, with a well-paid job in the Civil Service, Marsh did not have unlimited funds and he supported his young friends in a curious way. His mother's grandfather, Sir Spencer Perceval, had the distinction of being the only English Prime Minister to be murdered while in office and the family was compensated by a Government grant, one sixth of which eventually came to Marsh. It was this 'murder money', as he called it, which financed his young protégés. In addition, when the *Georgian Poetry* anthology became an overnight success in 1912, he scrupulously divided the profits among the contributors. *Georgian Poetry* had arisen partly out of Marsh's close friendship with Rupert Brooke, whom he had met in 1906 on one of his many return visits to Cambridge. When Brooke's first slim volume of poems came out in 1911, Francis Meynell had suggested that Marsh review it for his friend Harold Monro's *Poetry Review*, and the team which was to produce *Georgian Poetry* was born. It needed only a chance remark by Brooke to bring the anthology into being. Monro agreed to be the publisher but it was Marsh who was to find the poets, make and arrange the selection and distribute payment. The first number was an instant success and went into thirteen editions. In all there were to be five volumes of *Georgian Poetry*, keeping Marsh very busy indeed over the next decade. Since he had no wife or children of his own, he treated his contributors as his family and looked after them devotedly. The son of a surgeon and a nurse, as his biographer points out, it was rather like a surgeon and a nurse that he worked among his young friends.

All this had to be combined with his demanding job at Whitehall. By 1913 he was already six years into his close relationship with Winston Churchill. He would twice be Private Secretary to the great statesman, from 1917 to 1922 and 1924 to 1929, and his friendship with Sassoon was eventually to be threatened by that connection.

In March 1913, however, Sassoon was too overwhelmed by Marsh and his world to challenge it. Sitting in the National Club opposite the 'monocled young man of fashion' (Marsh was fourteen years older than the twenty-six-year-old Sassoon but retained his youthful air),[7] he felt that he had truly 'arrived', particularly when they were joined at coffee by Gosse's friend and colleague, Austin Dobson. Too shy to tell the modest old poet and essayist how his 'delicious verses' had been his earliest models when trying to write with delicacy and precision, or that he had saved his shillings to buy Dobson's *Collected Poems* for his mother's birthday in the 1890s, Sassoon simply drank it all in.

At his next meeting with Marsh, however, he began to feel less intimidated and started to confide in him. This was early in 1914, during his week off from his strenuous hunting season with Loder. He had written to Marsh from Witherley Lodge, Atherstone on 23 October 1913 to tell him that he was 'getting terribly fit, but quite unpoetical',[8] and again, on St Valentine's Day, 1914 to say that he was hoping to see him again. 'Eddie', as he now became, obligingly invited him for an evening. After dinner at the Moulin d'Or, they retired to his rooms in Raymond Building, Grays Inn. By contrast with Sassoon's fairly primitive surroundings in Loder's huntsman's cottage and his somewhat philistine friends there, both Marsh and his rooms seemed highly civilized.

After nearly five months of an almost entirely physical existence, Sassoon was feeling culturally starved, which further heightened his appreciation of Marsh's attractively furnished rooms full of modern pictures. The paintings might need explaining to his unenlightened eyes but the overall effect was most desirable. Eddie in his bachelor stronghold provided him with a model of what he himself might be if he ever dared to leave Weirleigh. No sooner had he expressed his discontent with his aimless life in Kent than, according to him, his host had decided on the answer: 'But why don't you come and live in London?' he asked.[9] Sassoon afterwards wrote that he was too excited and insecure to admit that he could not afford it and that in an alarmingly short time Marsh had decided his future. He would organize the whole matter. He was in his element the next day, rushing Sassoon off, after a quick lunch in Whitehall, to view a vacant set of rooms in the same block as his own, and when they turned out to be 'depressingly dilapidated', offering to arrange for their redecoration.[10]

Sassoon almost certainly exaggerated Marsh's part in his decision to live in London; a letter towards the end of February suggests that he was actively urging Marsh to help him find rooms, rather than being pushed into it by his friend:

> My dear Marsh,
>   I have quite made up my mind to live in London a good deal in the future. I shall never do any decent work buried alive among fox-hunters. So I want you to help me to find somewhere to live. I hope you will forgive me bothering you, but I am such an idiot in these matters and I don't want to say anything about it to my people, (at present), as I know they would kick up a fuss and spoil the whole venture! I looked at three lots of rooms in Gray's Inn; the only decent ones appear to be in 1 Raymond Buildings. I wonder if they have any acute disadvantages. I should be eternally grateful if you were to look at them and say what you think ...[11]

This is a rather different version from the one given in Sassoon's autobiography, but in either case it is a measure of his impracticality at this time that he did not seriously work out how, on an income of £400 a year, with the expense of keeping four horses, a groom and a stable boy, he could afford not only to pay an extra £100 a year for rent and rates of a flat, but also have it furnished and redecorated. His own retrospective explanation is that he was 'so desperate to get out of my groove' that he simply ignored the problem. He was probably depending on his mother to bail him out, as usual.

It had been an exciting week in London altogether. Apart from the momentous decision to move there, he also had two other stimulating meetings. The more predictable of these, a dinner on 22 February with Gosse at his house in Hanover Terrace, helped cement their relationship. Sassoon had seen him only once since their meeting at the House of Lords library nearly a year earlier, in March 1913, and Gosse had been too busy on that occasion to say more than a few words to him, but the dinner was different. A cosy affair, it allowed Sassoon to get to know Gosse better, though he was still too uncertain of himself to say much. The only other male guest, the novelist Filson Young, seemed much more self-assured and the evening threatened to become rather dull.[12] It was redeemed, however, by a glimpse of Gosse at his most enthusiastic and appealing. Pulling Max Beerbohm's prose parodies, *A Christmas Garland* down from the bookshelf, he introduced Sassoon to a writer who was to become not only a great favourite but also a close friend. It was Gosse himself who would introduce him to 'dear delicious Max', as he called him.

Sassoon's less predictable lunch with his first editor, Crosland, was equally interesting in its own way. He had met him while filling in time watching a revue at the Hippodrome (chosen deliberately because it was the kind of low-brow entertainment he could satisfactorily describe to Loder on his return to Warwickshire). Shockingly changed, from a formidable but basically genial man with a thick moustache to a physical wreck, whose sunken, clean-shaven face gave both his mouth and eyes a saturnine air, Crosland seemed to Sassoon a pitiable figure. Guiltily aware that he had ignored his request for a 'fiver' a few months previously, he was unable to refuse his invitation to lunch.

Clearly someone else had come up with more than five pounds, for Crosland took him to Paganis, a restaurant Sassoon came to know well in the twenties, for what the Yorkshireman himself might have called a 'slap-up meal'. Even Sassoon's youthful and hearty appetite was sated by what he regarded as one of the largest lunches of his life. They washed down vast portions of hors d'oeuvres, jugged hare and peach melba with a flask of Chianti and by the second glass Sassoon, never a big drinker, felt quite warm towards his host. It was not until Crosland had devoured his meal with the air of a man determined to pack in as much as he could while he could, that he responded to this friendliness.

Over special coffee and Corona cigars he explained to Sassoon his theory that life ought to be 'a Promethean struggle with adversity and injustice'.[13] Perhaps pointedly, he indicated to the rather spoilt young man in front of him that those who had never suffered deprivation could not claim to have lived at all. Neither he nor his guest could have foreseen that in less than a year Sassoon would begin to realize the truth of this for himself. At the time Sassoon took it to be largely a rationalization of Crosland's own intemperate lifestyle, which involved him in periods of great hardship. A heavy gambler, he was rashly generous when winning and an unashamed 'scrounger' when his money ran out. He was not the kind of man Sassoon could possibly understand, though neither could he completely dismiss him. He had had no hesitation in abandoning him the moment Gosse and his far more respectable world beckoned. Yet it is significant that, between Crosland's publication of *The Daffodil Murderer* in February 1913 and their lunch together a year later, Sassoon had written nothing he considered worth publishing.[14] Perhaps Crosland's abrasiveness had had a more stimulating effect on him than Gosse and Marsh's more urbane style. Moreover, it was not until Sassoon's comfortable world was challenged, as the blunt Northener had suggested, that he began to write with conviction. When he did so, it would be in spite of the disturbing effect he knew it would have on Gosse and Marsh's establishment views.

For the time being, however, it was Marsh who became the catalyst. His willingness to help Sassoon move to London had a profound effect. After seven years of life spent trying to satisfy both his physical and aesthetic needs, Sassoon determined to devote himself solely to poetry. His visit to Weirleigh during his week away from fox-hunting had done nothing to change his mind; in fact, so dull and empty did it appear compared with the excitements of London in the spring of 1914 that it strengthened his resolve to leave it. In spite of the fact that he knew he should have been at home consoling his mother for the sudden death of her faithful servant Miriam, particularly as Michael had left for British Columbia and Hamo for Argentina, he could not wait to escape. His five months in Warwickshire had given him a greater degree of independence. 'I was conscious of having somehow outgrown the whole place during my absence', he recorded.[15] Then Marsh had provided the incentive.

Yet Sassoon's bid for freedom was to last less than three months. He moved into his flat at 1 Raymond Buildings, Gray's Inn, in early May and by the end of July he was back at Weirleigh. The reason he gave in his autobiography was financial, but a close reading of it suggests that he was still emotionally unable to cope on his own. To begin with there was the supervision of the decorating and furnishing of his rooms. Sassoon's fourth-floor flat, originally a set of barrister's chambers, was at the noisiest end of the building, but to him it seemed a haven of peace. As he surveyed his immaculate white bedroom, brightly renovated bathroom and two living-rooms, painted in French grey and his favourite peacock-blue, he felt sure that he would produce some very good poetry there. His view of the terraced lawns and tall plane trees of Gray's Inn gardens in their late spring greenery was inspiring and there would be no golf or cricket to distract him. His cooking and cleaning were to be dealt with by a friend of Marsh's famously efficient housekeeper, Mrs Elgy. In describing Mrs Fretter, as she was called, he was moved to compose the kind of facetious jingle he knew his equally jokey recipient, Marsh, would appreciate:

> *To A Baconian*
> I sing you the song of my Fretter,
> Whose cooking grows better and better;
> At frizzling a rasher,
> By G–d! she's a smasher;
> So whatever you do, don't upset 'er.[16]

It was not only Mrs Fretter's admirable cookery which pleased Sassoon to begin with. For the first month at least he woke up 'with a sense of freedom and exhilaration', the kind of feeling he associated with the start of a holiday.[17] Every morning after a cold bath and leisurely breakfast, he would spend between two and three hours at his poetry.

On both Gosse and Marsh's advice, he was studying verse technique with a view to improving his own haphazard methods. Though he found the results disappointing, he kept at it and, in contrast to what he suggests in *The Weald of Youth*, produced at least one poem for his next volume, 'South Wind'.[18] Written at a period when he admitted to feeling 'forlorn' about his future, this first 'town' poem harks back nostalgically to the country. Apart from a few half-hearted attempts at blank verse, it is also the first of his poems to reject the constraints of a rigid rhyme scheme and the variation in stanza length is more adventurous than usual. The opening question and personification, together with the paradox of a violent south wind stealing shyly to the poet at the end, gives the poem greater impact than most of his previous pastoral pieces:

> Where have you been, South Wind, this May-day morning, –
> With larks aloft, or skimming with the swallow,
> Or with blackbirds in a green, sun-glinted thicket?
>
> Oh, I heard you like a tyrant in the valley;
> Your ruffian haste shook the young, blossoming orchards;
> You clapped rude hands, hallooing round the chimney,
> And white your pennons streamed along the river.
>
> You have robbed the bee, South Wind, in your adventure,
> Blustering with gentle flowers; but I forgave you
> When you stole to me shyly with scent of hawthorn.
>
> (*CP*, p. 60)

It may be that Sassoon's struggle to be on his own, though not as

'Promethean' as Crosland would have wished, was bearing fruit. Reading the poem three years later in *The Old Huntsman and Other Poems*, Virginia Woolf was to claim in her *TLS* review of that book:

> Here we have evidence not of accomplishment, indeed, but of a gift much more valuable than that, the gift of being a poet, we must call it ...[19]

Another poem probably conceived at this time, 'Alone', deals specifically with the problem Sassoon was himself facing, loneliness. The mention of 'Bright roofs and towers of towns' suggests that it was also composed at the window of his room in Gray's Inn. A poem about a yearning which neither sight, nor sound, nor thought can satisfy, it might additionally be seen as a comment on his own methods of composition; looking and listening, while not enough, do provide material for his poetry, but thinking obscures it. His emphasis throughout his career would always be on the non-intellectual qualities of his own poetry:

Alone

I've listened: and all the sounds I heard
Were music, – wind, and stream, and bird.
With youth who sang from hill to hill
I've listened: my heart is hungry still.

I've looked: the morning world was green;
Bright roofs and towers of towns I've seen;
And stars, wheeling through wingless night.
I've looked: and my soul yet longs for light.

I've thought: but in my sense survives
Only the impulse of those lives
That were my making. Hear me say
'I've thought!' – and darkness hides my day.

(*CP*, p. 61)

The insistent patterning of this poem, with its pervasive assonance and simple stanza form, is typical of Sassoon's best lyrical poetry. The emphasis on the aural and visual within the poem itself demonstrates his belief in the nature of true poetry, 'the impulse of the lives / That were [his] making' being, of course, visual on his artist mother's side and aural on his musical father's side.

It is possible that Sassoon also composed two other poems for his 1915 volume at Raymond Buildings, 'Tree and Sky', as he looked out over Gray's Inn gardens, and 'Rain in June'. There was certainly torrential rain in June the day he tried to make contact with someone he felt could help him with his problems, the poet Ralph Hodgson. Still suffering from the split between his sporting self (he had been helping Loder sell horses at Tattersalls shortly after his arrival in London) and his poetic side, Sassoon had gradually come to believe that Hodgson had the answer. He had admired his *Song of Honour* when it appeared in 1913 and was intrigued by Marsh's assurance that the bowler-hatted, pipe-smoking Hodgson did not look in the least like a poet. His career as a judge of bull-terriers at Crufts made Sassoon feel that he would understand his own divided loyalties. Sassoon's attempt to visit him at his lodgings in the King's Road, Chelsea, however, were unsuccessful and it would be another five years before he could, as he put it, 'gain admittance to his many-sided and imaginative mind' or congratulate him on the 'startling freshness' of his poetic voice.[20]

Sassoon's failure to contact Hodgson marked a turning-point for him in London. By the time of his abortive visit to the sporting poet in early June he was beginning to find his daily routine unsatisfactory, even boring. The effect of studying technique, rather than wandering about the countryside or browsing through his favourite books, was to stifle his poetic urge. Rightly or wrongly, he felt that his best poetry was 'inspired'. He would often quote the case of 'Everyone sang', which came to him in a flash as he prepared to go to bed one night, and there were many other examples.[21] He might afterwards work on the resulting poem, but without the initial inspiration he felt lost and very depressed. He had come to London not only to counteract cricket and hunting but to lead the kind of existence he thought would give him 'something real' to write about.[22] Ironically, he had found far more subjects for poetry in the country.

Equally ironic was the fact that Sassoon felt lonelier in the busy city than in his big house in the country, now empty of his brothers. In the mornings he could pretend to work and from half past twelve until about half past two he could occupy himself by taking the 19 or 38 bus to Piccadilly and strolling to the club in St James's Street for lunch, but the afternoons and evenings remained a problem. After five weeks he had exhausted his appetite for art galleries, museums and churches and was feeling too poor to distract himself with daily concerts or plays.

His social life was almost non-existent. He did take his great-aunt Mozelle to lunch and a matinée and would no doubt be invited back. He had also met his old friend Helen Wirgman, not once but twice by accident at London Zoo, and had taken her to a concert and tea at his new flat, but this had not been an unqualified success. Marsh was very kind and invited him to the occasional concert, but he was too busy with his work and his other protégés to protect Sassoon from a strong sense of isolation. Several times he had been reduced to the extreme step of taking a bus at random, just to see where it went. (A visit to Hornsey Rise seems to have cured him of this particular habit!) He had even, on one of his aimless walks across Regent's Park, dared to call on the Gosses unannounced, only to find that they were away for a month in Portugal.

Anyone who has lived in London on their own in their twenties will sympathize, but they might also ask why he did not do more to make friends. The Poetry Bookshop, for example, opened since January 1912 and already becoming a central meeting-point for young poets, was just around the corner from him at 35 Devonshire (now Boswell) Street; whilst he was not yet sufficiently well known to be invited to read there, at least he could have dropped in for a browse and a chat. Perhaps he did; if so, he fails to mention it and neither does the owner, Harold Monro. It may be that Sassoon had been put off by Marsh, who was not very close to Monro in spite of their joint publishing venture.[23] It is equally likely that he was too diffident or shy.

Another, even more puzzling question, is why Sassoon did not respond to an invitation from Marsh and Gosse's friend, Robbie Ross, on 13 June to 'look [him] up' any evening at about six o'clock.[24] Ross's letter, with its formal 'Dear Mr Sassoon' opening, indicates that the two were not yet friends, though they had both been at a party given by Gosse a year earlier on 5 June 1913. (So were thirty-three other people, however, and they may not even have talked to each other.) Ross's letter is, however, a friendly one, responding positively to *The Daffodil Murderer* and other early publications sent by the hopeful poet and promising dinner when he can be 'more sure of [his] movements'. Perhaps Sassoon did try calling on Ross, as the latter suggested. If so, he was again unlucky and the friendship, which was later to be so precious to him, and which would surely have made all the difference to his loneliness in June 1914, was delayed for another six months.

According to Sassoon, only two things prevented June and July from complete flatness, the Russian Ballet and a meeting with Marsh's most brilliant and famous protégé, Rupert Brooke.[25] Sassoon was invited to meet Brooke when the poet came to stay with Marsh after an adventurous year abroad. By the time he was formally introduced to him at a small breakfast party, he had already glimpsed the legendary young man walking towards Marsh's flat. Both then and at the breakfast Brooke made Sassoon feel something of a failure. Yet Marsh had presumably brought them together because he felt that they would like each other.

They had a number of things in common. Near contemporaries, both had had a comfortable middle-class upbringing culminating in public school and Cambridge. Sassoon had been starting his second year when Brooke arrived at the university in October 1906, though his premature departure meant that they overlapped by only one term. In fact Sassoon had been impressed then by Brooke, without knowing it, when he had admired the striking Greek herald in *Euripides* that term, the same occasion which had led to Marsh's introduction to Brooke. Most significantly of all, both young men were consciously striving to be poets.

Sassoon, however, was far more aware of their differences. Whereas he was still virtually unknown, Brooke had already achieved fame, or at least notoriety, through his 1911 *Poems*, in particular 'Channel Crossing', and his contributions to the *Georgian Poetry* anthology of 1912. Sassoon admitted in a chapter of his autobiography, which he found difficult to write because of his continuing friendship with Marsh in 1942, that, by the time the two poets met in 1914, Brooke's success had already aroused in him 'an admiring antagonism':

> The unromantic and provocative character of Brooke's 1911 volume had produced a vividly disturbing effect on my mind. Slow to recognise its abundant graces, I was prevented – by my prejudice against what I designated 'modern ugliness' – from perceiving his lovely and never prettified work as it really was. But in those days I didn't read things carefully or bend my mind to meanings. My unagile intellect was confused by his metaphysical cleverness. Interested though I was by the prospect of meeting the much-discussed young poet, I was unprepared to find him more than moderately likeable. Eddie's adoring enthusiasm had put me somehow on the defensive.[26]

In June 1914 his attitude was influenced more by Brooke's personal effect on him. Self-contained and carefree, he made Sassoon feel even more gauche and inadequate than usual. Whereas he had clearly resolved the conflict between his sporting prowess and intellectual powers by simply concealing the former at Cambridge, Sassoon was still struggling with this dichotomy. And while Sassoon had left the university early only to return to his mother, Brooke had left his equally adoring mother to travel half-way across the world. As a result, Brooke had found the vivid subjects for poetry that Sassoon had so far failed to discover.

It was not surprising that Sassoon responded to Marsh's favourite poet with a mixture of jealousy and unwilling admiration.[27] His presence quite overshadowed that of another 'Georgian' whom Sassoon would, in other circumstances, have greatly enjoyed meeting, W.H. Davies (the 'supertramp').[28] As it was Davies seemed rather naive and long-winded by comparison with the sophisticated and very handsome Cambridge graduate. Whether some of Sassoon's hostility sprang from an involuntary physical attraction towards him is also a moot point. He certainly described Brooke's appearance in loving detail, with particular emphasis on his long brown-gold hair, 'living blue' eyes, sunburnt complexion and bare feet.

They were left alone together, after Marsh had departed for Whitehall and Davies for another engagement, but conversation was stilted and Sassoon formed the distinct impression that Brooke was bored with him and merely tolerating his continued presence. Feeling rather like a Lower Fifth form boy talking to the Head of School, he did not dare to discuss the one subject that might have brought them together, poetry. His single attempt to impress Brooke by dismissing Kipling's poetry had failed and he was too ill at ease to add that really he admired Kipling and knew by heart the first eight lines of Kipling's 'Neither the harps nor the crowns amused'. It was both a relief and a disappointment when the meeting came to an end. Thanking Marsh afterwards for the breakfast, Sassoon remembered saying that he hoped to meet Brooke again some day – 'he is absolutely delightful' – but it is hard to believe that he was being quite sincere.[29] In any case, the outbreak of War only two months later was to make another meeting between them impossible.

If Sassoon's meeting with Brooke was really as unsuccessful as he portrayed it, then Marsh had probably been wise not to invite him to meet another future war poet, Isaac Rosenberg, who had visited him at Raymond Buildings earlier, on 8 May. Whilst Sassoon half-shared Rosenberg's Jewishness and his dual interest in poetry and art, their class difference might have made a meeting between them difficult, since both were very class-conscious.

It is, nevertheless, tempting to speculate why Marsh did not introduce them and what might have resulted if he had. Rosenberg's visit occurred shortly after Sassoon moved into number 1 Raymond Buildings, and Marsh must surely have been aware of how lonely his neighbour was feeling. Perhaps he did not think Rosenberg established or respectable enough for the rather snobbish Sassoon. It may be that he thought Sassoon needed time to settle in. As it was, the two poets would never meet, though they were to admire each other's work. (Rosenberg praised the 'power' of Sassoon's verse in *Georgian Poetry* of 1917 and Sassoon respected Rosenberg's sufficiently to write an introduction to his *Collected Works* in 1949.)

Sassoon's lack of contact with Rosenberg, or any of the other aspiring poets known to Marsh by 1914, was unfortunate but not entirely surprising. He was still caught uneasily between at least three worlds, the sporting, the poetic and the social. After a morning studying poetic technique, he continued to don the socially correct uniform of top hat (bowler if it rained), black jacket, wash-leather gloves and, with a rolled umbrella hooked jauntily over his left arm, make his way to his gentleman's club for lunch. At the same time he was secretly yearning for a good game of cricket, one reason he might finally have decided to return to Weirleigh towards the end of July.

The reason Sassoon gives – that of financial necessity – was something of a rationalization. As the family solicitor pointed out when Sassoon appealed unsuccessfully to him for £100 to pay some of his debts, if he had really wanted to live in London and remain solvent he could have done so. The thought of furnished rooms rather than what Helen Wirgman had called his 'swell establishment', decorated and furnished to his own taste, did not, however, appeal to someone who had already acquired expensive tastes and established for himself a certain position in society. Mr Lousada would not have minded Sassoon living in Gray's Inn at all if he had been studying for the Bar, as the address suggested. Had Sassoon really believed that he could write better poetry in London, he should theoretically have been prepared to sacrifice social standing. For all his avowed intentions, he was not yet totally dedicated to his art.

Sassoon demonstrated his order of priorities clearly this summer when he decided to pay a guinea, a great deal of money by 1914 standards, for a ticket to the Gala Performance of the Russian Ballet at the beginning of July. Not only was this something he could not afford, but it was also a further venture into the social world which he professed to despise but still obviously enjoyed. Eddie Marsh, whom Sassoon later came to feel was something of a social butterfly ('dear old Eddie was hollow inside', he agreed with a friend[30]), reflected the almost hysterical response of London 'Society' to the Russian Ballet, when he told his ignorant young friend that it was 'simply the most divine thing in the world!'.[31] Tempted by such enthusiasm, and possibly intrigued by Marsh's comparison the year before of his poem 'Goblin Revels' to a piece in their repertoire, *Oiseau de feu*, Sassoon embarked on a three-week orgy of Russian ballet and opera.

Sergei Diaghilev had formed his permanent company, the *Ballets russes*, in Paris in 1909 in an attempt to integrate the ideals of music, painting and drama into those of dance. The expressive, mimetic dancing of Fokine, Pavlova, Karsavina and Nijinsky, the exotic sets of his compatriot, Leon Bakst, and the explosive music of another young Russian, Igor Stravinsky, brilliantly realized his aims and revitalized contemporary ballet. The troupe was an instant success in Paris and, when it travelled to England in 1911, took London by storm. The *Ballets russes* was in its fourth London season when Sassoon first saw it in July 1914. (By this time Pavlova had left the company and Massine joined it.) The 1914 season was to symbolize for many, in retrospect, the last period of carefree gaiety before the outbreak of War. It came to epitomize, for Sassoon and others, the end of an epoch.

Sassoon's response at the time to the lively and innovative Company was immediate; he was overwhelmed by the lavishness of its decor and the beauty of its sights and sounds. Almost entirely ignorant of ballet, he went to the first performance more out of curiosity than in expectation of enjoyment. A sharply contrasted programme of *Les Sylphides*, *The Legend of Joseph* (its *première*) and *Papillons*, however, turned him into an instant addict. He was particularly enchanted by Schumann's haunting score for *Papillons*, which sent him home charmed, exhilarated and determined to return. He also resolved to visit Diaghilev's Russian Opera Company where the music would be even more important. Though somewhat antagonized by the largely upper middle class audience, who struck him as forming 'an enormous but exclusive party'[32], he realized that he was witnessing a memorable artistic event and continued to make his way almost nightly to Drury Lane for either ballet or opera.

Sassoon's response to Russian opera was less bewildered than to ballet and even more intense. Though almost as ignorant about it (he had previously seen only Bizet's *Carmen* and Mozart's *The Magic Flute*), his

177

appreciation of music was generally less untutored. Whilst still feeling confused about the plots of *Boris Godounov* and *Prince Igor*, which their Russian librettos did nothing to clarify, this only added to their thrill and mystery for him, as did Diaghilev's revolutionary scenic devices. He revelled in Moussorsky's and Borodin's music and found Chaliapin's singing magical. (He heard him eleven times in all.) While London suffered under an oppressive heat-wave, suffragettes got themselves arrested in public places and members of his Club sat reading about the burning 'Ulster Question', he was haunted by and perhaps identified with 'the half-oriental sadness of Russian music' and 'the legendary poetic feeling of all that colour and movement which was nocturnally alluring [him] to Drury Lane'.[33] It was 'a romantic discovery' which appealed to his imagination more than any previous dramatic performance.[34] His only consolation when it ended was to buy the piano scores of both *Boris Godounov* and *Prince Igor*.

It was not only the loss of his nightly 'fix' Sassoon had to face when the Russian season ended in the third week of July; he had also to confront the financial consequences of his indulgence. His compulsive attendance of the ballet and opera had brought his financial difficulties to a head. He owed at least £500 but could see no way of finding such a large sum. Yet he must have known in advance what his extravagances would lead to. Either he was incapable of economizing, or he secretly welcomed an excuse to return home to Weirleigh, where his mother would support him.

Had he been convinced that living in London helped his poetry, he would have found a way of remaining there. But he felt that from September 1913 to July 1914 he had got into a 'blind alley of excessive sport and self-imposed artistic solitude' and that neither extreme had been productive. The one positive result of his stay had been the development of an appreciation of the metropolis. He had grown up regarding London as a place in which the dirt and noise made him grateful to be living in the country, but by the end of his three months there he had grown to love 'its back-street smells and busy disregard of my existence'.[35] He became particularly fond of Holborn and, like his near contemporary Virginia Woolf, began to find a poetry in the dingy city streets which fed his mind and 'created stirrings of expectation'.[36] Unwittingly he was being prepared for another kind of ugliness which likewise had its own poetry, life in the trenches.

8

The Happy Warrior
(August 1914-November 1915)

The outbreak of the First World War on 4 August 1914 came at exactly the right moment for Sassoon, who felt almost as if he had been waiting for it to happen.[1] Initially the War fulfilled a number of urgent needs for him. Practically, it resolved the problem of his mounting debts, by forcing him to economize and providing him with a small additional income. Emotionally, it finally freed him from his prolonged dependence on his mother and presented him with the cause for which his idealistic nature craved. Even more importantly, it gave him a genuine subject for poetry, something which had continued to elude him, even in London. During the four harrowing years between 1914 and 1918 he produced poems conspicuously superior to the work which had preceded them and published his two most successful verse volumes, *The Old Huntsman* (1917) and *Counter-Attack* (1918). The War also benefited him socially, bringing him into contact with people who were to have a powerful effect on him: Robert Graves, Robbie Ross, Lady Ottoline Morrell and Sir Sydney Cockerell, besides less well-known but equally significant figures.

Sassoon's attitude towards the First World War was to change profoundly during its course and to become increasingly complex, a process reflected faithfully in the development of his poetry at this time. To begin with his views were broadly those shared by the majority of English people, that the War was both necessary and just and that he was bound by honour to serve in it. It was an attitude, as he himself later noted, 'uncomplicated by intellectual scruples'.[2] There was also the added incentive of being given a sense of direction, or rather a feeling that he no longer needed to look for one. He had arrived back in Weirleigh from London in the third week of July 1914, heavily in debt and extremely doubtful of his abilities as a poet, so that it was almost a relief to learn from a visiting family friend, Mab Anley – the mother of two colonels on the Active Service List – that war was unavoidable and that young men were needed to fight in it.

Mab Anley's arrival on 25 July followed the announcement of an ultimatum from Austria-Hungary to Serbia on 24 July. The ultimatum had been provoked by a long-standing tension between the two nations which had culminated in the assassination of the Austrian Archduke Ferdinand by a Serb on 28 June. What began as a localized hostility reached international dimensions when Germany, with its own barely concealed global ambitions, took sides with Austria, and France with Serbia. Obliged by her informal alliance with France and Russia to help protect them, Britain was more or less forced to join in when on 4 August Germany, having officially declared war on France as well as Russia, invaded Belgium, a country whose neutrality Britain was pledged to preserve.

Sassoon's own realization of the inevitability of Britain's involvement came, like many other people's, when he read *The Times'* leading article of 31 July. Though he had suspected the truth for at least a week (his two-day cricket match with Blue Mantles on 29 and 30 July had been interrupted by the recall of several players to their naval and military stations), it was not until he read *The Times'* grave predictions that he fully accepted the situation and its personal implications. His immediate reaction was to set off on a punishing bicycle ride of sixty miles, to Rye and back, ostensibly to consider his next move. In reality he had already accepted the fact that he would have to enlist: the physical exertion, as so often with him, was merely a form of outward release. Far from feeling heroic, he was rather embarrassed by his decision but also very relieved. As he wrote later, it freed him from 'any sense of personal responsibility'.[3] Given his background and upbringing, his decision comes as no surprise. Even Charles Hamilton Sorley, who experienced serious misgivings about the War from the outset, demonstrates that for a middle-class young man with a public school background there was really very little choice.[4]

Sassoon's impetuosity probably makes him the first War poet to have enlisted. Certainly by 1 August he had been given his Army Medical and at the official outbreak of War on 4 August he was in ill-fitting khaki. Like the majority of British people, who were almost completely ignorant of the War's complicated origins and the strength of Germany's ambitions, he believed that it would last no more than eighteen months. His main reaction was not fear, though he was apprehensive, but indignation. As he was subsequently to admit, he had lived to the age of almost twenty-eight with unquestioning confidence in the stability of the world and his own place in it. Without the intervention of War, it is very likely that he would have continued in the same calm but unstimulating assumptions until his death. As with so many other young men and women of the period, it was the subsequent turmoil and conflict which drove him in self-defence to attempt to shape his experience into art.

To begin with, however, Sassoon was more concerned with practicalities than with poetry. He had already written to his friend Gordon Harbord, a regular soldier in the Artillery since 1912, asking him how to enlist in the Cavalry should the need arise. Whether under Gordon's directions or not, his first choice (a hasty one which he later regretted) was the Sussex Yeomanry, an old county regiment. It is clear from his later description of cavalry officers that he did not regard the Yeomanry as a satisfactory substitute for the regular Army equivalent, being all too conscious of the cavalryman's 'superior social connections'.[5] He was also aware, however, of the money usually needed to belong to such an élite group and, even more importantly, the time required to go through various formalities. In his impatience to act, he was probably unable to contemplate the delay involved in such a move. Joining a local yeomanry regiment would have been a much faster route into the Army.

When Sassoon enlisted in the 1st/1st Sussex Yeomanry – later to become the 16th (Sussex Yeomanry) Battalion of the Royal Sussex Regiment – it was a relatively new body. Raised as a Volunteer Force in the closing months of the Boer War, for the first five or six years of its existence it was not brigaded with any other units. On the formation of a Territorial Force in 1907-8 – part of a wider effort to improve the army – it was amalgamated with the South-Eastern Mounted Brigade, under Brigadier-General Fowle. Brigadier-General Briggs took over the command in 1911, a year which saw increasingly strenuous training in preparation for a War which the army rightly anticipated.

The Sussex Yeomanry itself was commanded by Lieutenant-Colonel the Earl of March when Sassoon joined it in August 1914. Its Adjutant, Captain Blakiston Houston of the 11th Hussars, was the officer in charge of mobilization, not an easy task as the regimental historian points out, 'in a country which did not believe in the possibility of war'.[6] The regiment, whose headquarters was in Brighton, mobilized by squadrons at Lewes, Brighton, Chichester and Eastbourne. (Sassoon reported to Lewes and became part of C Squadron.) Mobilization went very much to plan, with the notable exception of the supply of horses which broke down very badly. Sassoon, who brought his precious hunter Cockbird with him must therefore have been doubly welcome to the Sussex Yeomanry staff who, in their desperation to keep the few horses they had managed to requisition, are reputed to have hidden them in cellars.

One of Sassoon's main motives in joining the cavalry had been to avoid separation from Cockbird and his choice of the Sussex Yeomanry seems on the surface to have been the right one. However, because he felt unable to face the responsibility of being an officer, he made the mistake of enlisting as a private (known in the cavalry as a 'trooper'), a position which cut him off almost completely from men of his own class and culture. Though initially attracted by the 'jokes and jollity' of the 'good chaps' in the ranks[7] (condescending phrases which belie any truly democratic impulse behind his decision), he quickly began to miss the conversation of his peers. Just as quickly he realized that, in order to save Cockbird from the enormous weight of equipment a trooper's horse was expected to carry, he must accept his squadron officer's request to buy him. Though he subsequently enjoyed seeing his former hunter looking unburdened and professionally groomed, his motivation for joining the yeomanry was irreparably undermined. At about the same time his remaining two hunters, Jim Murphy and Golumpus, were requisitioned from Weirleigh. It was the end of an important era in both Sassoon's and his groom Tom Richardson's existence.

Life in the ranks of C Squadron, 1st/1st Sussex Yeomanry – popularly known as 'the jolly Yeo-boys' – had been fun to begin with, rather like an overgrown scout-camp, or, as Sassoon put it, 'a mounted infantry picnic in perfect weather'.[8] After mustering in Lewes Corn Exchange, where they had slept their first two nights on the bare floor, the recruits of C Squadron rode *via* Brighton to Hode Farm, only a mile and a half from Canterbury. (Tom Richardson had brought Cockbird by train to Lewes for the journey.) There they slept, twelve to a makeshift bivouac, training daily for the feared German invasion of the South Coast.

Sassoon, whose incompetence in practical matters contrasted oddly with his skill at sports, found the training arduous and had to struggle hard to get through the daunting business of preparing himself and his horse for routine inspection. Accustomed to both leisure and servants, the dawn start with mucking out of stables before breakfast must have come as an unpleasant shock. Though he joked about his 'rough' accommodation, he must have missed his comfortable bedroom at Weirleigh, particularly as the weather turned colder. Even having to groom his own horse after years of Richardson's unobtrusive care would have been exhausting. Then the training, designed mainly for raw recruits, was tough, including such unwelcome features as 'dawn alarms', when the men were expected to 'saddle-up' and 'stand-to' an hour before sunrise. Sassoon's small, well-thumbed, maroon *Yeomanry and Mounted Rifle Training Manual* shows that it included not only 'Equitation' and 'Mounted Drill' but also 'Drill on Foot', with numerous sub-sections to each discipline.[9]

Sassoon was saved from complete ignominy by his superiority once in the saddle and protected, to some extent, by his acquaintance with a number of the officers, who had hunted alongside him with the Southdown. At the same time, as Tom Richardson had predicted, knowing some of the officers also made his position rather uneasy. His refusal of a commission in the Yeomanry puzzled his superiors, but he himself felt 'safe' where he was.[10] Yet he had also refused the offer of an eminently 'safe' job as Captain in the Remount Service, a non-combatant unit whose main duty was to requisition suitable horses for the army. Evidently his use of the word 'safe' cannot be taken at its face value. It was not fighting of which he was afraid – he had 'serious aspirations to heroism in the field' – but responsibility.[11] He was still unwilling to assume an adult role and it is no coincidence that he compared his 'safe' life in the ranks of the Yeomanry to life at school.

Sassoon had earned himself some kudos by volunteering for the Service

Squadron when this had been formed three weeks after mobilization. As a Territorial Regiment the Yeomanry had not, technically, pledged themselves for foreign service. Once War seemed inevitable they had been asked to volunteer for overseas and those who did so were regarded, for a short time, as an élite.[12] Sassoon, who was rapidly tiring of the monotonous daily routine, hoped to be sent to Aldershot in preparation for a posting abroad. In a letter written only two weeks after enlisting, he begged Marsh to reply as soon as possible, 'as I am so terribly bored here, only one gent. in the ranks'.[13] It may have been this letter which produced the offer of a captaincy in the Remount Service, since Marsh, though not working at the War Office at this stage in his Civil Service career, had many friends in high places.

Sassoon's 'escape' (his word) from increasing tedium came unexpectedly. At the end of September his mount had gone lame and, since he was known to be a good horseman, he had been sent out on the chargers of various men in the Squadron, such as the Quartermaster. One morning early in October the farrier-sergeant asked him to take his horse out and give it a little 'sharpening up'. Sassoon's interpretation of this order was to find as many jumpable fences as possible and pretend that he was out hunting again. Ironically, on this occasion he suffered a far worse fall than any he had experienced on the hunting-field and his brief career in the Sussex Yeomanry ended with a badly broken arm when his horse rolled on top of him.

Sassoon's decision to leave the Sussex Yeomanry was not a sudden one. The three months spent recovering from his fracture, which initially refused to knit and had to be operated on, gave him time to realize his mistake. As he mooned around in his lodgings at a doctor's house in Canterbury he obsessively balanced the pros and cons of his current situation.[14] He no longer had Cockbird to ride and, though life in the ranks was mercifully devoid of responsibility, it was correspondingly boring. In addition Gordon Harbord had been telling him for some time that he would be 'an awful mug' if he missed the chance of a commission, though he made it quite clear that he hoped Sassoon would not be sent out to France. The deciding factor for Sassoon was almost certainly his belief that, as a cavalry unit in a predominantly infantry War, the sleepy Sussex Yeomanry would never be sent overseas and, therefore, never see fighting. He had been disgusted by the fact that only twenty per cent of them had volunteered for foreign service, quite forgetting in his unmarried and financially independent state that many had wives and families they were loath to leave, as well as businesses they could not simply abandon.

Would Sassoon's decision have been different had he been able to look into the near future and seen the Sussex Yeomanry in action at Gallipoli as dismounted cavalry?[15] Probably not, for by October 1914 he had already decided that he wanted a change. Though continuing to enjoy the weekly visits of friends from the 'jolly Yeo-boys', particularly that of a farmer's son with whom he had previously hunted, he was mentally separating himself from the regiment, so much so that he was unwilling even to visit them in their new quarters only a short walk away.

Sassoon's desire to see action was almost certainly increased by news from the Front during his convalescence between October 1914 and January 1915. Writing to Marsh on 10 November, for example, he says that he will be very upset if he misses the Battle of the Meuse. By January 1915 self-respect demanded of most able-bodied young Englishmen that they fight to prevent an increasingly threatening situation. Though English newspapers had boosted public morale with glowing reports of the 'Russian steam-roller' (the Russians had scored notable early successes for the Allies in East Prussia and Galicia), their subsequent reports of enormous losses of British and French troops at the battles of Mons, the Marne and Ypres from late August to late October 1914 had made most people realize that this War was on a wholly different scale from previous ones and was likely to continue far longer than first anticipated. Though Paris had been saved and the Germans forced to fall back at the Battle of the Marne in September, they had quickly returned to the offensive just over a month later, at Ypres. By Christmas the opposing armies had dug themselves in along a line from the Belgian coast to Switzerland, a line that was rarely to move more than ten miles either way during the next four years.

By February 1915, back in Weirleigh for the end of his long convalescence with his arm finally healed, Sassoon reluctantly made up his mind to leave the Sussex Yeomanry and apply for a commission in an Infantry Regiment. This decision was reinforced by the news that Tom Richardson, had lied about his forty-four years and had volunteered for service overseas in the Army Veterinary Corps: 'It wasn't the first time that Tom … had given me a quick hint as to what was expected of me', Sassoon records in his fictionalized account of this period.[16] Nevertheless, it took him some time to carry out his secret resolution. His mother's understandable wish that he should remain in what she saw as a comparatively safe posting, together with the pleasures of mild spring days at the end of February, were undeniable deterrents, as was an invitation to visit his Thornycroft cousins on the Isle of Wight that spring.

Another factor which helps to explain Sassoon's delay was a resurgence of the poetic impulse. Dampened by his initial period of recruitment and training in harsh physical circumstances, it began to reassert itself during the solitude of his convalescence in Canterbury at the end of 1914. Writing in his diary in September 1922 of 'those mystics', Emily Brontë and John Clare, he would reveal that he had 'never approached that state of mind, except, perhaps, in the winter and early spring of 1915 when my broken arm was slowly mending'. His return to Weirleigh, which had been one of his favourite subjects for poetry since childhood, the lovely spring weather and a strong sense of uncertainty about the future provided the final stimulus. He described his return to poetry as 'almost like a recovery of the vernal raptures' of his youth.[17] By 27 February he was sending Eddie Marsh two poems written some time between October 1914 and February 1915 – 'Storm and Rhapsody' and 'Wisdom'. Marsh, whose suggested corrections about excessive capitalization and titles Sassoon immediately adopted, admired both pieces. This seems to have given Sassoon the confidence he needed to bring out another private collection of poems.

Discoveries, as Sassoon named his slim volume in green paper wrappers, was printed, like his four previous private productions, by the Chiswick Press in a limited edition.[18] Each of the thirteen poems, however brief, appears on a separate page, giving the book an air of luxury and elegance. By contrast with most of his earlier productions, only one poem in the book had appeared before.[19] An even stronger contrast to earlier volumes is that Sassoon thought all but two of the thirteen pieces worthy of inclusion in his *Collected Poems*.

On reading *Discoveries* it is immediately clear why so many of its poems were preserved. It is the first work of Sassoon's maturity. No longer heavily Ninetyish – though still basically romantic in theme and treatment – it reflects both Gosse and Marsh's advice to Sassoon. By persuading him to think more carefully about both subject matter and technique, they appear to have stemmed his earlier gush of undigested emotions. It is significant that *Discoveries* follows a long period of silence on the lyric front. Between *Melodies* (June 1912) and this new volume lies a period of nearly three years, suggesting a greater degree of discrimination on Sassoon's part. Whether he himself saw it as a result of Marsh and Gosse's strictures or not, he was certainly 'conscious of a newly-acquired technical control' and an 'exultant sense of verbal freshness' in it.

With Marsh's advice in mind it is possible to see Sassoon now writing for the most part either with his eye on an object or with his mind at grips with a more or less definite idea. (One of the two subsequently rejected poems was the vague 'Romance', from *Amyntas*.) Many of the poems contain closely observed descriptions of nature: 'Daybreak in a Garden', for example quoted on p. 34 for the detailed and precise picture it gives of the garden at Weirleigh. In addition – and this is where the most noticeable improvement lies – the poems usually have a 'more or less definite idea' at their centre. It may be a simple structural device, as in 'Companions', where the bird 'sings' and the clouds 'tell a story', or a more self-conscious Wordsworthian 'epiphany' (the 'discovery' of Sassoon's title) as in 'Wonderment':

> Then a wind blew;
> And he who had forgot he moved
> Lonely amid the green and silver morning weather,
> Suddenly grew

Aware of clouds and trees
Gleaming and white and shafted, shaken together
And blown to music by the ruffling breeze.

Like flush of wings
The moment passed: he stood
Dazzled with blossoms in the swaying wood;
Then he remembered how, through all swift things,
This mortal scene stands built of memories, –
Shaped by the wise
Who gazed in breathing wonderment,
And left us their brave eyes
To light the ways they went.

(CP, p. 58)

Both in 'Wonderment' and in the majority of other poems in this volume, Sassoon has moved away from the security of the sonnet form he had favoured for so long. He experiments freely with a number of verse forms, ranging from simple couplets and rhymed quatrains to both blank and free verse. His years of apprentice work have given him a noticeable assurance in the handling of these.

Sassoon had continued to write copiously between June 1912, when *Melodies* was produced, and May 1914, when he left Weirleigh for London, as his MS notebook for the years 1911 to 1914 shows. However, the bulk of the poems in *Discoveries* date from a relatively short period between June 1914 and February 1915.[20] The most interesting poem in the volume, partly because it gives Sassoon's early reaction to the War, is 'To-day'. Ostensibly it is a strikingly simple personification of Time and Nature:

This is To-day, a child in white and blue
Running to meet me out of Night who stilled
The ghost of Yester-eve; this is fair Morn
The mother of To-morrow. And these clouds
That chase the sunshine over gleaming hills
Are thoughts, delighting in the golden change
And the ceremony of their drifting state.

(CP, p. 57)

But the poem also touches on a theme clearly evoked by the thought of War, the possibility of the poet's own imminent death:

This is To-day. To-morrow might bring death, –
And Life, the gleeful madrigal of birds,
Be drowned in glimmer of sleep ...

(CP, p. 58)

As a result, the poet's appreciation of the moment – 'To-day' – is strengthened and the poem ends with the pantheistic plea:

> ... To-day I know
> How sweet it is to spend these eyes, and boast
> This bubble of vistaed memory and sense
> Blown by my joy aloft the glittering airs
> Of heavenly peace. Oh take me to yourselves,
> Earth, sky, and spirit! Let me stand within
> The circle of your transience that my voice
> May thrill the lonely silences with song.
>
> (CP, p. 58)

Sassoon's thoughts on War may as yet be generalized, but significantly he has already started to see it as a fit subject for poetry.

The language of 'To-day' and the majority of the poems in *Discoveries* is, in keeping with their more sharply focused observation, less archaic and derivative. Though the tone is still frequently elevated, it is an elevation more akin to the heartfelt simplicities of Wordsworth than the deliberate artificialities of Swinburne, as if the poet is more genuinely absorbed in his message. Under Marsh's tuition he is already sounding more like a Georgian. While alliteration still abounds, it is used more skilfully to reflect the thing described rather than to intoxicate with sound.

The suspicion that Sassoon had been reading Wordsworth is reinforced by the title of the longest poem composed in spring 1915, for 'The Old Huntsman', as he called it, is the sub-title of Wordsworth's early ballad, 'Simon Lee'. Though almost certainly the best poem of this period, it is not difficult to see why Sassoon did not include it in *Discoveries*. Quite apart from its length, 'The Old Huntsman', a colloquial narrative poem of nearly 200 lines of blank verse in which the narrator remembers better days, has more in common with *The Daffodil Murderer* of 1913 than the romantic 'discoveries' of the young nature-worshipper of 1915. Though not without its lyric passages, these are much tougher and written in very different language from the shorter pieces, perhaps a self-conscious attempt by Sassoon to emulate Wordsworth's 'language really used by men'. In one sense the poem can be seen as Sassoon's farewell to his privileged pre-war days in the hunting-field; in another as an indirect tribute to his long-standing friend, Norman Loder, to whom the poem is dedicated; and in yet another as a further manifestation of a satiric impulse which contrasted oddly with his lyric vein but which was to feature significantly in his War poetry. (It is no coincidence that 'The Old Huntsman' would head his first book of war poems, to which it would also give the title.)

Whether Cecil Roth is right to claim that 'The Old Huntsman', like *The Daffodil Murderer*, started as a skit on Masefield or not, Masefield even more than Wordsworth's influence lies behind the colloquial speech, which is more vigorous and less uneven than in Sassoon's previous narrative.

Ironically, by avoiding *The Daffodil Murderer*'s excessive 'realism' Sassoon has made his narrator more realistic:

> I've never ceased to curse the day I signed
> A seven years' bargain for the Golden Fleece.*
> 'Twas a bad deal all round; and dear enough
> It cost me, what with my daft management,
> And the mean folk as owed and never paid me,
> And backing losers; and the local bucks
> Egging me on with whiskys while I bragged
> The man I was when huntsman to the Squire.
>
> (*CP*, p. 3)

The authenticity of such language is reinforced by minutely observed details of the hunting-field, details which Sassoon was to use again to great effect in *Memoirs of a Fox-Hunting Man*:

> ... And I've just pulled the terrier out and left
> A sharp-nosed cub-face blinking there and snapping,
> Then in a moment seen him mobbed and torn
> To strips in the baying hurly of the pack ...
>
> (*CP*, p. 4)

Another characteristic which has no chance to express itself in Sassoon's lyrics but will reappear in his fiercest War poems is his grim humour, nicely illustrated by the agnostic old huntsman's concept of hell in terms of a bad day's sport:

> Hell was the coldest scenting land I've known,
> And both my whips were always lost, and hounds
> Would never get their heads down; and a man
> On a great yawing chestnut trying to cast 'em
> While I was in a corner pounded by
> The ugliest hog-backed stile you've clapped your eyes on ...
>
> (*CP*, p. 6)

As the reviewer from *The Cambridge Magazine* argued when 'The Old Huntsman' finally appeared in print in 1917, it sums up in many ways Sassoon's main characteristics, his 'broad humanity and sympathy, his keen sense of the poetry of country life, and a touch of that grotesque cynicism which comes out so strongly in his shorter War poems'.[21]

By the time *Discoveries* arrived from the printers in April 1915, Sassoon was about to leave for his new regiment. He had finally taken action at the end of February, after sending his poems to the printers. There is some-

---

* The Golden Fleece a public house

thing of a puzzle surrounding the incident. He himself suggests in his closely autobiographical *Memoirs of a Fox-Hunting Man* that his first step was to consult an old family friend in the neighbourhood, Captain Ruxton, yet other facts make this seem unlikely.[22] Nevertheless, it makes a good story and is probably true to the extent that one of his family friends used his influence to smooth the young man's path. Like Captain Ruxton it would probably have been someone who had known him since birth and regarded him as an unofficial godson, someone also who lived near Weirleigh. It could even have been Ruxton himself with the details of his army career slightly altered.

Ruxton, who reminded Sassoon irresistibly of a little brown partridge, had retired from an army career to work a moderate-sized farm overlooking the neighbouring village of Brenchley. Though well into his seventies, he was still extremely active. Chairman of the local Bench and a church warden, he was a solid, respectable figure in the district. Theresa, who shared his love of gardening and sport, ice-skating in particular, had enjoyed his gallantry towards her ever since Sassoon could remember. It does seem natural that, in the absence of a father, he should turn for advice to this 'brisk, freckled, God-fearing, cheerful little man' as he says he did.[23] There seemed to Sassoon a certain irony in the fact that the last thing Ruxton wanted was that his friend's son should be killed, but that his belief in 'honour' over-rode all other considerations: 'To him as to me,' Sassoon wrote, 'the War was inevitable and justifiable. Courage remained a virtue'.[24]

As a result of their talk, Captain Ruxton, or whoever it was, wrote recommending Sassoon for a commission in the Royal Welch Fusiliers. Though he had retired from the army many years before, the Adjutant there happened to be the nephew of a former brother officer of Sassoon's sponsor and the old-boy network ensured Sassoon an instant and positive response. Within a week he was instructed to make a formal application for a Special Reserve commission. The Special Reserve was a new name for the old Militia and a temporary commission in the New Army would have come to much the same thing.[25] Sassoon's sponsor was, however, an old-fashioned snob, of the rather harmless variety in Sassoon's eyes, and could not help looking down on Kitchener's New Army.

Sassoon, while poking gentle fun at his old friend afterwards, nevertheless went along with his suggestion at the time and a number of his subsequent actions and comments suggest that he himself was not immune from a similar snobbishness. His first act on receiving confirmation of his commission, for example, was to go straight to the best military tailors available to order a very different uniform from his former ill-fitting tunic and breeches, an exercise which reminded him strongly of his previous acquisition of hunting clothes. Both the army and the Hunt, he seems to be reminding his reader, were equally class-ridden worlds. And his account of his first visit to the army tailor, whilst humorously deflating his own snobbishness – 'I became as wax in his hands' – tacitly acknowledges his complicity in the class system.[26]

Sassoon's choice of regiment the second time around also illustrates his anxiety to do the 'correct' thing, at least as far as his limited means would allow. The Royal Welch Fusiliers had a long and honourable history. It was originally raised in 1689 to help William III fight the deposed James II and his Irish and French Catholics in Ireland in 1690. Urgently in need of reinforcements, William had given Lord Herbert of Chirbury a warrant 'by beat of drum or otherwise to raise volunteers for a Regiment of Foot' in the border counties of Wales, to be quartered at Ludlow. The resulting eight companies of the '23rd Foot' were then taken over by Lord Herbert's cousin, Colonel Charles Herbert, and known for the first few years as 'Herbert's Regiment'. In 1702 they were honoured by selection as one of the three Fusilier Regiments, formed originally to protect the artillery and distinguished by the light 'fusils' they carried instead of the heavier, more awkward musket. Renamed several times, on the accession of George II in 1727 they finally became The King's Own Royal Regiment of Welch Fusiliers.[27]

From their first engagement at the Battle of the Boyne in 1690, when their commander, Major Toby Purcell, distinguished himself, the Royal Welch Fusiliers were at every one of the numerous wars Britain fought over the succeeding two centuries. Their battle honours read like a crash course in British military history, including such famous names as Namur, Blenheim, Ramillies, Corunna, Salamanca, the Peninsula, Waterloo, Inkerman, Sebastopol, Lucknow and the Relief of Ladysmith. As Robert Graves, who was proud to belong to the Regiment, points out in *Goodbye to All That*, not only did the Royal Welch Fusiliers have twenty-nine battle honours when he joined them in 1914, but 'they were all good bloody battle honours'.[28] He also reveals that they considered themselves second to none, even where the Guards were concerned. When offered the choice of becoming the Welsh Guards after the Boer War, they indignantly turned down a change which would have made them junior in the Brigade even to the recently formed Irish Guards.

Like all venerable institutions the Royal Welch had its own insignia and rituals. The most distinctive of these, the wearing of a 'Flash' consisting of five black ribbons attached to the collar of all ranks, a recognition of the fact that in 1805 when the army had abolished the wearing of the pig-tail (protected in a black leather bag), the Royal Welch Fusiliers were at sea and thus the last regiment to carry out the order. Another ritual, shared with several Welsh regiments, was the custom of being led on parade, and even into battle, by a white goat with gilded and ornamented horns. St David's day, as might be expected, was particularly rich in special rites, which one hopes for Sassoon's sake were suspended during the First World War. It is difficult to imagine him enjoying the eating of a raw leek, one foot on the table, while the drums rolled behind him, though easier to envisage him at the conclusion of this ceremony drinking a toast to 'Purcell of the Boyne' and 'Toby Purcell, his spurs and St David'.

The contrast between this ancient regiment with its elaborate rituals and the recently formed company of mainly part-time amateurs which made up the Sussex Yeomanry when Sassoon had joined it in August 1914 could hardly have been greater, and his immediate pride in the Royal Welch Fusiliers is understandable. (Gordon Harbord thoroughly approved of his choice, though he made it quite clear that he hoped Sassoon would not be sent out to France: 'I must have some one left to hunt with me when peace comes along'.)

When War broke out in 1914 the Royal Welch Fusiliers consisted of two Regular battalions – the 1st and 2nd; one Special Reserve battalion – the 3rd; and four Territorial Units – the 4th, 5th, 6th and 7th. The 2nd Battalion left immediately for France in August, and the 3rd left barracks at Pembroke on 9 August and returned to Headquarters at Wrexham, while the 4th, 5th, 6th and 7th were put on War footing. The 1st Battalion went straight out to Flanders in October 1914. Within one year the original seven battalions had swelled to twenty-one, so enthusiastic had been the initial response to Kitchener's call to arms. After conscription was introduced in 1916 the Regiment again expanded and the final tally of battalions reached was forty-two, eighteen of which saw active service.

By the time Sassoon joined the Regiment in May 1915 the 1st and 2nd Battalion between them had fought bravely in all the major battles in France and Belgium – Mons, Le Cateau, the Marne, the Aisne, Ypres, Neuve Chapelle and Aubers. After Turkey's entry into the War on Germany's side in late October 1914, the 5th, 6th, 7th Battalions and in June 1915 the 8th were sent out to Gallipoli, where the Allies were planning their ill-fated attempt to gain control of the Dardanelles, Turkey's lifeline to Europe.

Sassoon's own inexperience in matters of War was uppermost in his mind when he reported to the 3rd Battalion of the Royal Welch Fusiliers at its Wartime Training Depot near Liverpool.[29] Though now technically of the officer class – he had been gazetted Second Lieutenant on 28 May 1915 – he felt something of a fraud. Nothing in his brief period of training as a trooper with a non-combatant cavalry unit seemed to have fitted him for a position of command, however lowly, in a fighting infantry regiment. Whilst he felt that he was beginning a fresh and untarnished existence, he was also decidedly apprehensive. As he made the tedious journey by train from Paddock Wood to Charing Cross, Euston to Liverpool and Liverpool to the dingy suburb of Litherland, he must surely have debated the wisdom of his choice. Once in the taxi, which took him through a rash of recent housing developments near Seaforth and Litherland station, over the Leeds and Liverpool canal to the wilderness of an industrial estate, he was probably longing to return to the genteel comforts of Weirleigh and the beauty of the undulating Kent countryside. The tin huts of Litherland Camp, situated between the 'hell-workshop' of Brotherton's Ammunition Factory (an extension of their Tar Works) and a large Roman Catholic cemetery, with the smoking chimneys of Bryant and May's match factory half a mile away, could not have been a cheering sight.[30]

During this journey through the dreary industrial suburbs Sassoon found some consolation in the company of another newcomer, Norman Stansfield, an overweight, middle-aged Canadian who, in rather ripe language, grumbled amusingly about the £800 a year job he had just given up. Nevertheless Sassoon felt completely lost on arrival at the camp. Used to the rolling and lush Weald of Kent, he was inordinately depressed by the features of the surrounding countryside with its stunted houses and sparse vegetation. Even the nearby canal seemed to him 'disconsolate', a revealing example of the pathetic fallacy at work.[31] In the comfortless hut where he tried clumsily to assemble his folding bed, he felt entirely cut off from his previous life. His months with the Sussex Yeomanry at Canterbury, conveniently close to his home, and even his brief bid for independence in London had not prepared him for such feelings of complete isolation. His only comfort appears to have been Palgrave's *Golden Treasury* which he had brought with him.

The majority of Sassoon's fellow-officers were probably experiencing similar reactions. With an average age of twenty-one, many of them had come straight from public school and were younger than the men they were being trained to command. Though Sassoon's own room-mate was not very communicative, the atmosphere at the Camp was friendly, even aggressively cheerful, perhaps to compensate for the rising number of men being killed in action. Some of the new officers, like Stansfield, had come from well-paid jobs in civilian life and were part of what were called Special Battalion Commissions. With his socially superior Special Reserve Commission and his socially correct uniform ('You can't have [your shirts] too dark' his tailor had warned Sassoon, a remark he had remembered when he first saw the unfortunate Stansfield's straw-coloured ones), Sassoon was part of the Establishment, with reservations.

Like Graves, also a Special Reserve officer, Sassoon was almost certainly reminded on arrival of his great good fortune in being granted the privilege of fighting with one or other of the regular battalions, if the War lasted. In peacetime a candidate for a commission had not only to distinguish himself in the Sandhurst examinations and be strongly recommended by two other officers of the Regiment, but also to possess a guaranteed independent income that would enable him to play polo, hunt and generally keep up the social reputation of the Regiment. But in wartime these requirements were waived. Great stress was laid on the fact that Special Reserve officers were not temporary, like those of the New

Army, but held permanent commissions. On the other hand they must not expect to be recommended for orders or decorations, since these were considered to be not personal but representative awards for the whole regiment and, as such, the rightful preserve of professional soldiers on their upward climb.

Nevertheless Sassoon's Special Reserve Commission would have ensured him a privileged position. And, together with his youthful air, would probably have placed him, in others' eyes, among the public schoolboys and ex-Sandhurst cadets. Though his twenty-eight years theoretically separated him from these younger men, his lack of worldly experience and his public-school background enabled him to identify with them quite easily. Within a few days he began to feel one of this outwardly light-hearted group, whose only purpose, he tells us, was to 'get sent out' as soon as possible. ('Getting out to the Front', he wrote, 'had been an ambition rather than an obligation' at that time.)[32]

Sassoon's first overt War poem, written between April and September 1915, just before and just after joining the Royal Welch Fusiliers, shows quite clearly that he shared the group's attitude to begin with. For his initial response to the War was one of unquestioning idealism not easily distinguishable from that of his contemporary, Rupert Brooke:

> *Absolution*
> The anguish of the earth absolves our eyes
> Till beauty shines in all that we can see.
> War is our scourge; yet war has made us wise,
> And, fighting for our freedom, we are free.
>
> Horror of wounds and anger at the foe,
> And loss of things desired; all these must pass.
> We are the happy legion, for we know
> Time's but a golden wind that shakes the grass.
>
> There was an hour when we were loth to part
> From life we longed to share no less than others.
> Now, having claimed this heritage of heart,
> What need we more, my comrades and my brothers?
> (*CP*, p. 11)

The lack of originality, together with the inflated and clichéd language of these, to use Sassoon's own words, 'too nobly worded lines',[33] suggests that his response in mid-1915 was still largely unconsidered and untested, the conventional response of a member of the ruling-classes. He himself later saw them as typical of 'the self-glorifying feelings of a young man about to go to the Front for the first time'.[34]

Adrian Caesar argues that 'Absolution' reveals both sadism and masochism in Sassoon's attitude to War, an attitude based largely on earlier War poetry, where sacrifice and the brotherhood of man is glorified.[35] It is true that Sassoon knew poems like Tennyson's 'Revenge' and 'The Defence of Lucknow' by heart, but the imagery of the title, 'Absolution', together with such words as 'anguish', 'scourge' and 'wounds' and the notions of purification through suffering and laying down one's life for others are essentially Christian and come as no surprise in the work of someone who has only just begun to question his Christian faith. Even after he abandoned Christianity Sassoon continued, like so many other First World War poets, to use its imagery, notably in 'The Redeemer', 'The Prince of Wounds', 'Golgotha', 'Stand-To: Good Friday Morning' and 'Christ and the Soldier'. While Dame Felicitas Corrigan takes this as a sign that Sassoon was still 'strangely Christian',[36] it seems clear to me that the Christian imagery and concept in these poems are being used either conventionally or with satiric intent rather than from concealed sadistic or masochistic impulses.

A note Sassoon later added to 'Absolution' states that 'People used to feel like this when they "joined up" in 1914 and 1915', and that was no doubt true of the majority of recruits who unthinkingly accepted that 'honour' demanded 'sacrifice'. Yet Charles Hamilton Sorley, whose approach was far more objective, had questioned this attitude from the outset and it was he who wrote of Rupert Brooke, when he died on 23 April 1915 (perhaps the very day Sassoon started to write his poem):

> He is far too obsessed with his own sacrifice, regarding the going to war of himself (and others) as a highly intense, remarkable and sacrificial exploit, whereas it is merely the conduct demanded of him (and others) by the turn of circumstances, where the non-compliance with this demand would have made life intolerable … He has clothed his attitude in fine words: but he has taken the sentimental attitude.[37]

These are words which could equally well be applied to Sassoon's first War poem.

It is clear that in his first days at Litherland Sassoon was an unquestioning part of the 'happy legion' (an echo perhaps of Wordsworth's 'happy warrior'), eager to leave for the Front. However, he was already beginning to register the complacency and unawareness of those who were in no danger of being sent out, in particular the staff at the camp. Made up mainly of permanent officers from the pre-war Special Reserve Battalions, their job was to prepare the younger men as efficiently as possible for their almost certain death at the Front, a situation Sassoon was later to satirize fiercely in War poems very different from 'Absolution'. Whilst the regulars could look forward to a comfortable life of good dinners at the best hotel in Liverpool (the Adelphi) and battalion cricket or rugby matches, the younger men could only try not to think about the grim casualty lists from abroad.

Meanwhile they naturally distracted themselves as much as they could with all available diversions. Apart from dinners at the Adelphi with fellow officers, Sassoon particularly enjoyed battalion cricket. The Regiment had been given the use of the local cricket ground and he played as much as possible through the bright summer weather of 1915, an activity which must have reminded him of his pre-war life at Weirleigh. At weekends and sometimes even on weekdays he indulged in another of his favourite sports, golf, by courtesy of the Formby Golf Club, which had made all officers of the Royal Welch Fusiliers honorary members for the duration of the War. After a short ride on the electric railway from Seaforth to Freshfield station, he would spend hours on the links, generally alone, and often have a meal at the cosy club-house where Wartime austerities were kept at bay by the members, most of whom were local businessmen.[38] He also hoped in the autumn to get in some days hunting across the Mersey in Cheshire. He was to discover throughout his army career that to be known as a hunting man to regular officers was as decided an advantage as wearing the right coloured shirts.

In the meantime he often simply took a walk down to Seaforth Sands, where the sight of the sea and the flocks of seagulls helped offset the drabness of the Litherland depot. And, he actually hired himself a Bechstein piano – which rapidly went out of tune – and spent an occasional hour playing the music he had loved so much the previous summer, Borodin's *Prince Igor* – probably, as he noted, the first and possibly the last performance given in Litherland. In addition he attended every concert he could, with varying degrees of pleasure.

Side by side with these leisure activities, rigorous daily training went on. Young officers arriving in camp were instructed by efficient N.C.O.s, who would teach them, among other things, how to form fours, slope arms and so on, until they could drill a company of recruits with rigid assurance, a state Sassoon felt himself unlikely ever to reach. Whilst senior officers busied themselves with company accounts, kit inspections and other routines, raw recruits like Sassoon would have to learn the rudiments of musketry and field training, the use of Lewis guns, rifles, hand-grenades and mortars. Most of these skills had their own manual and Sassoon spent many hours trying to master such mysteries as the mechanism of the rifle, or the precise order of Company drill. He noted down on several occasions an alliterative mnemonic on what qualities were needed in a Company Commander, a typically literary response to the situation.[39] Headed 'C's and their Consequences', it lists 'care (of Men)' as its top priority, a concern he was to demonstrate throughout his three years with the Royal Welch Fusiliers.[40]

Gradually, in spite of his natural resistance to dry knowledge, Sassoon mastered the contents of his Infantry Training Manual. Learning to be a Second Lieutenant, however tedious, was in some ways a relief. Ironically, it kept his mind off the War and made it seem further away. Only when news came from the 1st and 2nd Battalions in France was he unable to forget his own approaching fate. In April, when the Germans used poison gas for the first time, the 1st Battalion of the Royal Welch Fusiliers lost large numbers of officers and men at Festubert. Meanwhile, another three of their battalions were still in Gallipoli. The first phase of the fighting there had ended in early May with heavy Allied casualties, but the campaign was to be renewed. The continuing threat of Turkey in the Middle East, Bulgaria's alliance with the Central Powers and trouble in Africa from Germany's colonies in 1915 made huge demands on the Allies, who had to withdraw large numbers of troops from the Western Front as a result. By the autumn they were in urgent need of reinforcements there.

The threat of departure had overshadowed Sassoon's summer, but it had nevertheless been one of the happiest of his life. Living in an all-male environment was not the least of his pleasures. (As he noted in his diary, the only merit of hut life was that there were 'no women about'.[41]) With the departure of his first, rather taciturn room-mate had come the arrival of someone who was to mean a great deal to him and who was, indirectly, to change his attitude towards War profoundly – David Cuthbert Thomas. It is clear from the language Sassoon uses in his diary and in his thinly-disguised account of Thomas as 'Dick Tiltwood' in *Memoirs of a Fox-Hunting Man* that he fell deeply in love with the young Sandhurst subaltern, whom he nicknamed 'Tommy'.[42]

Ten years Sassoon's junior, Tommy seemed to the older man the embodiment of youth and beauty. The emphasis on his 'slender' figure, 'yellow' hair, 'kind grey' eyes, 'young ... warm' hands and 'brilliant' smile makes the reader aware of Sassoon's physical attraction towards Thomas. Yet one is also aware of his need to idealize the love object, as though to purify the attraction of any grosser elements. (Sassoon had assured Carpenter in 1911 that he was still 'unspotted' and there is no evidence to suggest that any significant change had occurred in the intervening three years.)

The picture Sassoon paints of Thomas is almost too good to be true. From the 'candour and freshness' of his face, the 'radiant integrity' of his expression, his 'simple and reassuring' tone of voice, his 'bright countenance of truth' and strong 'reticence and modesty' the reader is led to imagine a paragon of all the virtues; Sassoon actually called him 'as good as gold'. (Robert Graves's less inflated claim, that Thomas was 'a simple, gentle' fellow, 'fond of reading', is more convincing.[43]) Sassoon emphasized how old Thomas made him feel, but he was clearly attracted to him partly because of his youth and innocence. Though there is no suggestion of a physical relationship in this particular case, Thomas is the first in a long line of younger men with whom Sassoon became infatuated. All his subsequent sexual relationships were with people at least ten years younger than himself, often more.

At a rational level there were obvious explanations for Sassoon's attraction towards Thomas. Thomas, like Gordon Harbord, was the son of a well-to-do clergyman and came, therefore, from a similar middle-class background to Sassoon's own.[44] He was also a good sportsman and joined Sassoon at the nets of the neighbouring cricket ground on long summer evenings. On at least two occasions they played cricket against the local teams, Bootle and Wallasey, making a highly effective pair of opening batsmen. (Sassoon, first in the batting order, was the top scorer and Thomas, second in the order, was joint second highest scorer.)

Though Thomas had hunted very little, he thought it 'immensely important' and listened to Sassoon's hunting stories eagerly, just as another young friend, Glen Byam Shaw, was to do years later. Since Gordon Harbord's letters to Sassoon, written from France, were full of nostalgic hunting references, he would often read them aloud to Thomas, thus linking indirectly his two greatest friends at that time. Perhaps most importantly of all for Sassoon, Thomas took a keen interest in his poetry, though his rather awed tone suggests that he was not altogether at home with literature:

> Now for your works [Thomas wrote on 26 August 1915]. I think the poems rightly named 'Discoveries' are lovely. You seem to have struck a splendidly lyrical strain in them. 'Hyacinth' is, as you say, real poetry, and to one who has been privileged to know a small part of your mind, this playlet shows you yourself and your ideas. I can recognise old Sassons himself, as it were, living in the piece, as things are introduced which I know to be your own experiences. I've read 'The Daffodil Murderer' and am very curious to know about it.

In more practical terms, Thomas, with his Sandhurst training, proved extremely helpful to Sassoon and patiently guided him through the numerous training manuals. Above all, his cheerful and unquestioning acceptance of his patriotic duty which Sassoon shared at this time, gave the older man a sense of security in a manifestly insecure world.

August brought the two men a month in 'Paradise', as Sassoon saw it. In his description of their four-week training course at Pembroke College, Cambridge, he tells his readers that the room he and Thomas shared had the name of its previous occupant – 'Paradise' – still on the door.[45] Whether this was literally true or not is beside the point; Sassoon's symbolic intentions are clear. To him it *was* paradise. Though barred from attempting a physical relationship with Thomas by his own moral code, he nevertheless enjoyed every moment of his company, an enjoyment sharpened by his sense that it might be their last time together. Though Thomas did not share Sassoon's sexual inclinations, he clearly enjoyed his company. After the day's training was over, they spent long evenings together at the Red Lion pub, enjoying their relative freedom.

It is impossible to recapture Sassoon's precise feelings on returning to

Cambridge ten years after his first stay there. However, since Thomas was approximately the same age as he had been then, it is reasonable to suppose that his presence made Sassoon very conscious of his younger self and all that it had taken for granted. He may even have experienced regret at having so precipitately left the University. The town would certainly have been at its most attractive in the fine summer weather of 1915, though strangely denuded of students under Wartime conditions.[46] While he never publicly stated regret for his previous abrupt departure, in later life he was to attempt to make Cambridge his centre again, an indication of his affection for it.

One of the main reasons Sassoon appreciated Cambridge the second time round was that he was introduced to a number of interesting people there. His visit was marked by the beginning of several important relationships which must have put his Officer's Training programme firmly into the background. The most enduring and richest of these was with Sydney Carlyle Cockerell.

Born in 1867 Cockerell had had an extraordinary career by the time he met Sassoon in 1915. Following the early death of his father, he felt obliged to relinquish a scholarship at St Paul's School to enter the family business as a coal merchant in the mid-eighties. But his close friendships with John Ruskin and William Morris from 1885 onwards led him to give up this job in 1891 to become secretary to Morris and, eventually, to the Kelmscott Press. After Morris's death in 1896, he became secretary and factotum to the poet Wilfred Scawen Blunt, to whom he would introduce Sassoon in 1919. A period in process-engraving with Sir Emery Walker in the early 1900s was followed by the position which made his name, Director of the Fitzwilliam Museum in Cambridge. Bringing his enormous energy and business acumen to bear on a traditionally sleepy and conservative occupation, Cockerell transformed a dreary and ill-hung provincial gallery into a fine display of treasures. (Fund-raising was one of his many talents.)

Sassoon had been introduced to the well-known connoisseur by a letter from Edmund Gosse, who had himself first become acquainted with Cockerell earlier in the year.[47] No doubt at Gosse's suggestion, Sassoon wrote to Cockerell on 30 July and again on the 31st and was invited to dine with him the next day at Jesus College, of which Cockerell was an honorary fellow. (Was there an unconscious pun in Cockerell's description of Sassoon on that occasion – 'a very nice fellow he seems to me'?)[48]

Just under a week later, on Saturday 7 August, Sassoon was again invited to dine with Cockerell, this time at his house, Wayside Cottage in Cavendish Avenue on the outskirts of town. There, in Cockerell's candle-lit study, he was allowed to look at some of the collector's many treasures. Though Cockerell's speciality was medieval illuminated missals and psalters, he chose initially to appeal to Sassoon's more contemporary taste for the Pre-Raphaelites, a taste which he had indulged to the detriment of his studies during his original stay in Cambridge. After an evening handling original manuscripts by such adolescent heroes as William Morris, Francis Thompson and Dante Gabriel Rossetti, Sassoon returned to his camp-bed in Pembroke College in a 'trance of stimulation'.[49] So successful had the visit been that it was repeated the next day and the remaining two Sundays of Sassoon's stay in Cambridge. There were also several visits to the Fitzwilliam to look at beautifully illustrated books by Cockerell's wife, a tactful move on the younger man's part.

Sassoon initially perceived Cockerell as an almost supernatural being – 'a bearded and spectacled magician'[50] – and he was subsequently surprised by his kindly interest in a far from expert enthusiast twenty years his junior. Though somewhat brusque and uncompromising, with austere light blue eyes, his plain-spoken manner belied an innate gentleness and tolerance. To Sassoon's relief most of his mistakes were greeted with an indulgent laugh. When Cockerell related to him the occasion on which he had advised Thomas Hardy to stop waxing his moustache, he positively guffawed. (Sassoon later nicknamed him Sir Sydney Conundrum.) Cockerell was a connoisseur of friendship as well as manuscripts, friendships which Sassoon described from his own experience as 'tender yet astringent – brusque but adoring'.[51] He particularly admired Cockerell's insistence on truth and the 'unexpected intransigence of [his] opinions'.[52] Another close friend, T.H. White, referred to Cockerell's 'loyalty, kindness and industry'.[53]

For his part Cockerell found Sassoon very entertaining company and admired his poetry greatly. They were to remain friends for the next forty-seven years. Their common interests, numerous even at the start, were to increase with time. To a love of the Pre-Raphaelites, fine books and pictures, they were to add a shared enthusiasm for such cult figures as Max Beerbohm, Charles Doughty, Charlotte Mew, Wilfred Scawen Blunt and T.E. Lawrence, and a love of Thomas Hardy which bordered on hero-worship. Both generous by nature, they would frequently send each other lavish presents and collaborate several times to help struggling writers or their families.[54] Sassoon, who retained his admiration for Cockerell in spite of later reservations, cast him as a kind of Crabb Robinson (the friend and helper of the Romantic poets), 'a man who had been born to become, through his practical abilities, the trusted adviser of great writers'.[55] Without creating works of art himself, Sassoon saw Cockerell as 'causing creativeness in others',[56] and he was conscious of having benefited greatly from their friendship.

One way in which Cockerell tried to help the virtually unknown Sassoon in 1915 was to introduce him to people he might find either interesting or useful. The most important of these, from several points of view, was Edward Dent. Sassoon may already have heard of him from Marsh, whose protégé Rupert Brooke had known him as a Fellow of King's in the early 1900s; Marsh himself knew Dent well.[57] Nine years Cockerell's junior and only ten years older than Sassoon, Dent was already established as a respected musicologist when he and Sassoon met. He had already written books on Scarlatti and Mozart by 1915 and was to become Professor of Music at Cambridge University in 1926. When he met Sassoon at Cockerell's on 15 August (he came to tea, Sassoon to supper) his immediate response was to invite the younger man to dinner.

In replying to the invitation on the 18th Sassoon made it clear that he saw music as an important aspect of their friendship: 'Music is a thing I can't do without for long! – though I am no performer myself.'[58] He felt particularly deprived of music in the army. In England he was still able to get to occasional concerts, but once in France he was to feel 'starved' of anything worth listening to and it was Dent, his 'dear old music-man' to whom he would turn. 'I wish you could send me a tube of melody', he was to write to Dent less than a year after their first meeting. 'The musical part of me is at the last gasp for a drink. Someday I will kill the man who wrote keep the home fires burning – they play it in the hottest weather, too'.[59] Despite Dent's wide knowledge and talent (he had himself composed a number of pieces), he was the opposite of self-important and he and Sassoon quickly became firm friends. While Sassoon's close relationship with Cockerell remained fairly formal for some time, he became intimate with Dent almost immediately. When on leave in February 1916 it was Dent, not Cockerell, he hoped to meet 'to do something together, lunch off macaroni, and look at some pictures and talk, talk'.

One explanation for this intimacy emerges in Sassoon's numerous letters to Dent following their initial meeting – their very similar sense of humour. Alluding to Dent's fondness for Italian food, Sassoon addresses him as 'Dear Bolognese', and sending Dent a copy of an ancient Egyptian glass-cup on 15 October 1915 he cannot resist punning 'My cup is thy cup'. When he follows this with a present of stem ginger in March 1916, his next letter begins: 'My dear Ginger'. After Dent has given him some fatherly advice on his health and practical help in publishing his poetry, he addresses him on 30 April 1916 as 'My dear Marius! Advocate of Beecham's Pill!', a facetiousness to which Dent readily responds.

Sassoon and Dent shared an even more fundamental bond than their sense of humour and love of music, however – their homosexuality. While Sassoon was only just beginning to come to terms with his, Dent was part of a circle of intellectuals at Cambridge who accepted their sexuality with far more confidence and were able to discuss it frankly among themselves. It was probably Dent who introduced Sassoon to members of this circle, including E.M. Forster, Goldsworthy Lowes Dickinson and A.T. Bartholomew. Certainly Dent made the ideal confidant and his must have been one of the few relationships at the time which did not involve Sassoon in concealment. For Sassoon's own conflicts and the legal position of the time made it virtually impossible for him to discuss his sexual preferences with many people. He was unable to reply honestly to an army friend, for instance, who asked him why there were 'no women' in his verse.[60] And though Cockerell was clearly a 'man's man' – he spent at least five nights a week eating, drinking and sleeping at Jesus, an all-male college in 1915, regarded women as inferior to men and was an open admirer of male beauty – he would probably have been shocked if Sassoon had attempted to discuss his homosexuality with him. He is unlikely even to have suspected Sassoon's preferences, since he invited a young woman to dinner especially to meet him. It must, therefore, have come as a great relief to be able to talk freely to Dent, who was entirely frank about his numerous homosexual liaisons and kept a flat in London mainly for that purpose. It was not Dent, however, but one of the least-known and temporary members of his circle, Gabriel Atkin, who was to have the greatest effect on Sassoon's attitude. Posted to Cambridge for Officer Training just before Sassoon in 1915, he had already left by the time the latter arrived and it would be three years before Dent managed to bring them together and transform Sassoon's life.

For the time being Sassoon had to be content with nostalgic memories of Cambridge and falling chastely in love again, this time with a young man he had known slightly before the War, Robert Hanmer. Hanmer arrived at the Litherland depot in September and, as Sassoon confided to his new confidant, Dent, immediately became his new 'angel'. The need for 'purity' in sexual matters is clearly still paramount. Whilst his love is denied physical expression, it remains 'pure' and it is significant that he is attracted to young men he knows to be heterosexual. (Tommy, for example, is 'very much intrigued with a young nurse in Liverpool', he tells Dent.) Like David Thomas, Hanmer seems to Sassoon the very model of English youth, cheerful, bright-eyed, fair-haired, shining-faced, healthy, simple and good. The picture, as with Thomas, is too good to be true and Graves's more objective description is, again, a salutary corrective: 'a perfectly charming boy of a rather conventional type but absolutely unlike the usual run of Sandhurst subalterns in his nice manners and simple tastes'.[61]

Deprived of the possibilities of sexual gratification with 'Bobbie the Beautiful', as he christens him, Sassoon feels that his only means of satisfaction would be to save his life – 'a Gorgeous idea!'.[62] In the interim, however, he sublimates his feelings in hero-worship and attempts to get closer to 'Bobbie' by the more conventional means of getting close to his sister, Dorothy. He had met the Hanmers while staying with Norman Loder in the winter of 1913 to 1914.[63] According to Sassoon, Dorothy was one of the Belles of the Atherstone Hunt; but his efforts to fall in love with her, as an extension of Bobbie, and their eventual engagement early in 1916 were, understandably, to be a failure. As he wrote in his diary for 16 July 1916, when he finally decided to end the 'flimsy' engagement:

I must go out into the night alone. No fat settling down; the Hanmer engagement idea was a ghastly blunder – it wouldn't work at all. That charming girl who writes to me so often would never be happy with me. It was my love for Bobbie that led me to that mistake.[64]

It was more than love for Bobbie that prompted Sassoon to propose to Dorothy Hanmer. He told Ottoline Morrell that he had become engaged as 'he felt he ought to be as all his brother officers had a girl', but he soon found it impossible as he really only liked men and 'women were antipathy to him'. He did not enjoy the prospect of living on his own, but could not contemplate defying social and moral conventions at this stage of his life. At twenty-nine he was also beginning to want children, a need which was to become more pronounced once he embarked on his first sexual relationship.

Meanwhile Sassoon attempted to sublimate his feelings in ceaseless physical activity. Life at Litherland Camp, after his return from Cambridge on 22 August, continued as before, except for new recruiting marches through Liverpool. Daily training and as much sport as he could squeeze in kept his body healthy, and he enjoyed feeling fit. To celebrate his twenty-ninth birthday on 8 September he borrowed a captain's horse and rode along the bleak sands from Litherland to Southport, a solitary, unfestive outing in keeping with the times.

Only two days earlier, word had come of Bulgaria's entry into the War on the side of the Central Powers and with it the need for more Allied troops on the Eastern Front. From Gallipoli, where Sassoon's younger brother, Hamo, was serving with the Royal Engineers, the news was no more cheerful. In August the Allies had landed at Suvla Bay but during the long, hot summer sickness had seriously weakened the troops and the Allies were beginning to consider withdrawal. At the same time there was an urgent need for reinforcements on the Western Front, where the British were beginning to plan an attack on Loos in support of the French at Souchez. (The 1st, 2nd, 4th and new 9th Service Battalions of the Royal Welch Fusiliers were to be involved.) It could only be a matter of weeks before Sassoon himself was sent abroad.

When Sassoon's draft finally came it was not, as he had feared, for the Balkans or the Dardanelles but for France. He was delighted to find himself going out with David Thomas but very sad to be leaving Robert Hanmer behind. ('I don't like to think what it will be like, when I leave him, because I know he will miss me frightfully', he wrote to Dent in early November.) One consolation was a week's leave, granted by custom before embarkation and called, rather ominously, 'last leave'. Sassoon's took place in mid-October and he spent part of it in London with Marsh, Dent and Gosse. It was at Gosse's that he met someone who was to become more important to him than either Cockerell or Dent – Robbie Ross.[65]

Sassoon and Ross had both attended a party given by the Gosses in June 1913 but Ross, who was under a cloud at the time, had not felt able, as he rather quaintly put it, to 'offer the hand of friendship' to Sassoon in the circumstances.[66] Though Sassoon had sent him *The Daffodil Murderer* and other works in June 1914 and been invited to visit him then, the outbreak of war had delayed their first real meeting for yet another year. When he eventually met Ross at the Gosses' on 17 October 1915, he would certainly have known of him, and not just from his friendship with Gosse and Marsh. For Ross's involvement with Oscar Wilde still marked him out, particularly among homosexuals. Ross, who had been a friend, some said more than a friend, to Oscar Wilde from the mid-1880s, had, at the cost of his own reputation, stood by him throughout his trials in 1895. Afterwards he had devoted himself to rehabilitating Wilde's name and paying off his debts, both seemingly impossible tasks. He was also responsible for the transfer of Wilde's remains to Père Lachaise cemetery in Paris and Epstein's magnificent memorial there. (He had requested that his own ashes should be buried with Wilde's.) His devotion had earned him the undying hatred of Lord Alfred Douglas, anxious to prove his own change of heart, and he had been remorselessly hounded in the press and the courts by Douglas and his ally, Crosland. Through all these troubles Gosse had, in spite of his anxiety to remain respectable, unexpectedly stood by Ross. (To some, his sympathy smacked of fellow-feeling.) By October 1915 it looked as though Douglas's spite had exhausted itself, and Ross felt able to respond to Gosse's renewed offer of an introduction to Sassoon.

Ross and Sassoon immediately liked each other, not surprisingly since they had a number of interests and experiences in common. Like Sassoon, Ross had left Cambridge without a degree. He had then started his career as a literary journalist before turning to another of Sassoon's interests, art. After running the Carfax Gallery with his friend More Adey from 1901 to 1909, he had become first an art critic on the *Morning Post*, then Adviser to the Inland Revenue on picture valuation, an unlikely post for someone who enjoyed shocking the Establishment. He had spent his time since War broke out trying to get official status for War artists, an initiative which eventually led to the founding of the Imperial War Museum.

In spite of being seventeen years older than Sassoon, Ross had an almost schoolboyish sense of humour and seemed to Sassoon like 'a benevolent and impulsive bachelor uncle with whom one could feel on easy terms of equality'.[67] Sassoon, who himself could rarely resist a pun however bad, was delighted on one occasion by Robbie's reply to his wondering what had caused a fire at the house of the Poet Laureate, Robert Bridges: 'Dry rot, I expect'.[68] Ross shared Sassoon's acute sense of the absurd, which once caused him to describe Sacheverell Sitwell, who was growing unexpectedly tall, as 'now a few inches higher than the Great Pyramid but slightly shorter than the Eiffel Tower'.[69] Ross also greatly admired another humorist Sassoon was to worship, Max Beerbohm, and had risked public censure when he mounted an early exhibition of Max's caricatures in 1901. A dapper little man with his light grey alpaca suit, soft black hat, large scarab ring, ebony cane and jade cigarette-holder, Robbie attracted Sassoon both physically and mentally. It was not just his wit and taste in literature and art he admired but also, and especially, his loyalty to his friends. When he came to write Ross's elegy it was this aspect of his character he stressed above all, thus inviting the criticism of Michael Thorpe for his admittedly flowery last line:

O heart of heart! O friend of friends![70]

Yet everything Sassoon wrote about Ross emphasizes the same point. His loyalty was remarkable and he gained his greatest pleasures in life, it seemed, in helping his friends, from Wilde onwards. In Sassoon's case there was much he could do. Unlike Marsh and Gosse, he was not anxious for the approval of the Establishment, in fact he enjoyed opposing it, and he encouraged Sassoon from the start to express his views honestly and directly, especially in his poetry. With his strong anti-War feelings, it was Ross, more than any other single person, who was to help bring about the distinctive change in Sassoon's War poetry during 1916. Arnold Bennett's remark to Sassoon, that Ross was 'the most indirectly creative person [he had] known',[71] is very similar to what Sassoon said of Sydney Cockerell. Both men delighted in helping younger, more creative men, perhaps as a way of expressing homosexual feelings. In Cockerell the attraction, if it existed, was not admitted, whereas in Ross it was very much in evidence.

Though Sassoon was afterwards to tell Dame Felicitas Corrigan that he had never talked to Ross about Oscar Wilde, it is clear from contemporary letters and later remarks to friends that this was an evasion of the truth. Why otherwise would Sassoon have told Cockerell in 1944, whilst writing the third volume of his autobiography, that he had to be 'extremely careful' about his description of Ross, 'but as he very seldom spoke about Wilde to me I have been able to avoid all that without any loss of veracity'.[72] There is a distinct difference between 'very seldom' and 'never'. He and Ross certainly discussed homosexuality, both their own and others'. Ross, for example, was to tease Sassoon about Lady Ottoline Morrell's attraction to him later on, and he was anxious to know more about Sassoon's brief contact with Alfred Douglas. Sassoon had received a letter from Douglas in answer to his query on the whereabouts of his former editor, and Douglas's friend, Crosland. To Sassoon's relief Ross accepted his former business dealings with Douglas's partner, Crosland, calmly, though it must have seemed unfortunate to the poet in retrospect that he had unwittingly chosen to send Crosland's publication, *The Daffodil Murderer*, as a first example of his work to Robbie Ross in 1914. Whereas Gosse and Cockerell are unlikely to have broached the subject of homosexuality, however much they secretly sympathized, Ross and Dent allowed Sassoon to articulate feelings he had had to suppress for many years. In practical terms Ross was part of a group of influential men who could exert influence in the literary world for Sassoon when the need arose. At least part of Sassoon's success as a War poet would be due to the efforts of this band of admirers and supporters. Sassoon himself was to acknowledge Ross's prime role in the process by dedicating his second volume of War poetry 'To Robbie Ross'.

In October 1915, however, Ross's influence lay in the future and Sassoon continued to write poetry in the same martial vein with which he had begun a few months earlier. The most extraordinary example of this occurs after the death of his brother Hamo at the beginning of November. Hamo, the only one of the Sassoon brothers to get a degree, had worked for several years in the family engineering firm, Thornycrofts, before going out to Argentine in 1913 as a structural engineer in the River Plate area. (Sassoon carefully preserved his brother's maps of the region till his own death half a century later.) He had been there just over a year when War was declared, and returned to England to enlist in May 1915. Sassoon, who was waiting to join the Royal Welch Fusiliers, had overlapped with him at Weirleigh for three days, his first sight of his brother for two years. He may have taken the last photograph of Hamo in the garden with his mother, a sombre scene in which Theresa's apprehensiveness appears clearly on her face.

Hamo was then gazetted Second Lieutenant with the Royal Engineers and sent out to Gallipoli in August without being able to say goodbye to his brother, who was in Cambridge. The situation in the Dardanelles was critical by the time he arrived and by the end of October it seemed hopeless. After eight months of fighting 25,000 Allied troops had died, another 12,000 were reported missing and 75,000 were wounded. The final figures were to be even more devastating. Hamo himself was among those evacuated in late October, but died of wounds on board a hospital ship on 1 November 1915. It seemed appropriate to Sassoon that his brother, who had always ridiculed the pomposity of funerals and undertakers, should be buried at sea: 'I know he would have liked the idea of his body being given to the sea', he was to write to Hamo's old form master at Marlborough, John Bain. 'He was a strong, slow patient swimmer'.[73] Sassoon was also able to emphasize Hamo's 'underlying wisdom and imperturbable judgement of men and things. He always seemed to be smiling to himself at the queer ways of the world. And he went his ways alone and serene'.[74]

It was Hamo's humour and self-possession, which Sassoon had noted even as a child, together with his passion for climbing, that Bain brought out in his poem 'In Memory of Lieut. H.W. Sassoon, R.E.'[75] That poem depends for its effect on an acceptance of the public-school athletic-military code of honour, to use John H. Johnston's phrase, and Sassoon's own tribute to Hamo appeals to the same code. Both are curiously impersonal. Though addressed 'To My Brother', Sassoon's conveys no sense of intimacy, contains no revealing touches. It is, rather, a rallying cry to battle, as 'Absolution' had been:

> Give me your hand, my brother, search my face;
> Look in these eyes lest I should think of shame;
> For we have made an end of all things base.
> We are returning by the road we came.
>
> Your lot is with the ghosts of soldiers dead,
> And I am in the field where men must fight.
> But in the gloom I see your laurell'd head
> And through your victory I shall win the light.[76]
>
> (*CP*, p. 12)

Poeticisms such as 'lest', the padding of 'the field where men must fight', the vagueness of 'we are returning by the road we came', the cliché of 'the laurell'd head' in the 'gloom' and the emulation of Brooke in 'For we have made an end of all things base' make this a tired poem which gives no sense of Sassoon's personal loss. Perhaps he was anxious to emphasize a larger 'brotherhood' than that of blood ties. The notion of comradeship, so vital to both Whitman and Carpenter in elevating homosexuality, was certainly important to Sassoon and it is interesting that he originally entitled this poem 'Brothers', thus allowing it to embrace all comrades in arms. 'Absolution' had ended with an appeal to 'my comrades and my brothers'. It may be that he had to convince himself of the validity of War in order to make Hamo's death meaningful and, therefore, more acceptable.

Another possible explanation for the lack of convincing grief in Sassoon's poem to his brother may lie in an initial failure to grasp the reality of his death. If, as seems likely, the death of 'Stephen Colwood' (a character based on Gordon Harbord) in *Memoirs of a Fox-Hunting Man* is really a description of Hamo's death, then Sassoon was in a state of numb disbelief after he heard the news. (Gordon Harbord was to die in August 1917, not November 1915; but since Sassoon had made his self-portrait, George Sherston, an only child in *Memoirs of a Fox-Hunting Man* he could not very well describe the death of a brother, so he substituted that of the character based on Gordon in the story – Stephen.) Sherston is about to carry out his routine round of inspection as orderly officer when a telegram is handed to him announcing 'Stephen's' (i.e. Hamo's) death: 'It was queer to be doing [my duties], with that dazed feeling and the telegram in my pocket', he tells the reader.[77]

Writing to Dent shortly after Hamo's death, Sassoon makes it clear that he associated his brother primarily with his early childhood, when they were at their closest, 'hunting moths and playing cricket on summer evenings'.[78] In a sense his death, more than anything else, signalled the real end of Sassoon's childhood. He had finally been exiled from the garden, symbolized so perfectly by Weirleigh. 'And I am far from the garden', he was to write in his diary after a particularly intense memory of childhood and Hamo in their own paradisal garden.[79] It is no coincidence that his thoughts turn frequently to it, especially after the horrors of Wartime France. The day before he actually pens his poem to Hamo on 18 December 1915, and after his first experience of the trenches, he writes:

> Lovely now seem the summer dawns in Weirleigh garden; lovely the slow music of the dusk, and the chords of the piano-music. Loveliest of all, the delight of weaving words into verses; the building of dream on dream; oh the flowers and the songs, now so far away. The certainty of my power to touch the hearts of men with poetry – all faded now like a glorious sky. And then the July days, the afternoons of cricketing, and the silly joy I had when I managed to stay an hour or two at the wicket.[80]

Sassoon's lament for Hamo is inextricably bound up with his sorrow for the loss of childhood and in this wider grief he fails at first to feel the particularity of Hamo's death. It would take another six months for it to become real to him, and when it did it would contribute significantly to his change of attitude towards the War and the consequent shift in his poetic technique.

Meantime, as Sassoon confessed to Dent, he felt a 'general inclination towards sentimentality',[81] an inclination strengthened by the thought of his imminent departure for France. Hamo's death made him even more conscious of the possibility of his own. It must also have caused him to worry even more about his mother who was entirely alone. (Her eldest son, Michael, had been in Canada since 1910 and showed no signs of returning.) Her response to her youngest son's death had been predictably intense. Since her husband's abandonment of her twenty-five years earlier, she had relied wholly on her sons for emotional fulfillment. Now one of them was dead, one about to leave for the Front and the third 6,000 miles away. Her grief was terrible. Refusing to accept Hamo's death, she preserved his room exactly as he had left it and insisted on showing it to unwary visitors.[82] Her attempts to contact him through Spiritualism were to make Sassoon deeply unhappy and to cause a serious rift with one of his closest friends.

It was, therefore, with a guilty sense of relief that Sassoon finally left Victoria Station on 17 November 1915 after what one can only imagine to have been an almost unbearable leavetaking. Perhaps this is the reason he fails to describe it in his War diary, which begins the same day. However, he does give us some idea of the pain experienced by both mother and son as the train left for Folkestone: his fictionized Aunt Evelyn's 'last, desperately forced smile' as she sees Sherston off for France in *Memoirs of a Fox-Hunting Man* is surely Theresa Sassoon putting on a brave face as her favourite son starts for the Front.[83]

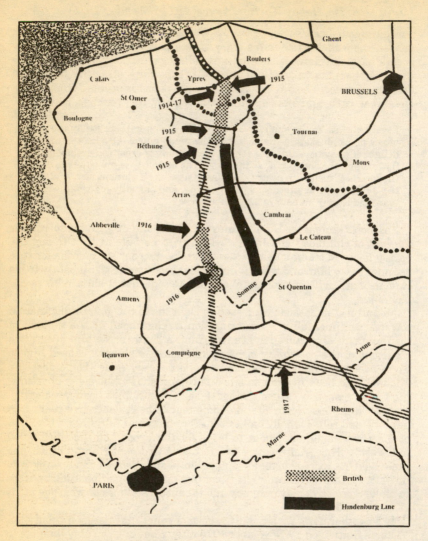

Part of the Western Front in Belgium and France (1915-17).

'Goodbye to Galahad'
(November 1915-March 1916)

Remarkable though it may seem, Sassoon, who was in the army from the day War broke out to the day it ended and had the reputation of being a fire-eater, spent barely a month out of a possible fifty-one in the Front Line. There were a number of reasons to account for this and chance also played a part. His early riding accident in the Sussex Yeomanry and subsequent change of regiment delayed his active service for well over a year and it was not until November 1915 that he embarked for France. There followed yet another four months of 'resting', home leave and duties as a Transport Officer before he joined his battalion in the trenches at the end of March 1916. During the next three years trench-fever, two serious but not life-threatening wounds and an anti-war protest kept him in England for an additional seventeen months. It is also possible that his bold exploits at the Front, whilst gaining him a justifiable reputation for great courage, made his superiors hesitate to include him in particularly delicate operations. Even he was ready to admit that he became 'inefficient and excitable ... when in close combat with Germans'.[1]

Largely because of Sassoon's late arrival at the Front, he maintained his 'happy warrior' outlook for at least eighteen months after War began. His first contact with the trenches in November 1915 and February 1916, even before he was directly involved in the fighting, brought about a change which began gradually but accelerated rapidly after the death of a close friend in mid-March of 1916. With his own entry into Front Line action at the end of March 1916, and the full realization of his brother Hamo's death, came the final loss of his initial idealism. His increasing bitterness expressed itself forcibly in his poetry, which closely reflects the whole process of disillusionment.

When Sassoon first set out for France on 17 November 1915, however, it was to some extent a relief. The boredom of life in Litherland Depot, the tension of waiting to be drafted and the guilt and inadequacy he was experiencing over his mother's sufferings were at least brought to an end. 'To have finished with farewells; that in itself was a burden discarded' he remembered many years later, when describing this period in fiction.[2] Everything negative seemed behind him and only positive action ahead.

There was also the excitement of his first arrival on foreign soil. The lunchtime train from Victoria had deposited him on Folkestone pier at 6 p.m. and by 7 p.m. he was on the reassuringly named *Victoria* steaming out to sea. He and Thomas sat in bright moonlight waiting for their first glimpse of France but, like most events in the Wartime army, it was an anti-climax. Not until one in the morning did they stumble ashore at Calais, having been diverted from their real destination, Boulogne, by the sinking of a hospital ship in mid-Channel. After a night spent on a hotel floor at Calais, they eventually left for Boulogne at 11.15 a.m. next day, probably rather less wide-eyed about France.

In Boulogne there were more aimless hours spent waiting for orders and it was not until 11.30 at night that they reached the Base Camp at Etaples only fourteen miles away. This was, according to one veteran, 'a hellish dump without a single redeeming feature', and Sassoon's experience there appears to confirm his statement.[3] Altogether there were 320 newly arrived officers at the camp and it is not difficult to imagine the confusion and desultoriness of the next four days while Sassoon waited for his posting. He dealt with this partly by cycling with his usual vigour into nearby Le Touquet to visit a friend in hospital, but the bike broke down and he was forced to take a taxi back. The laconic diary entries during his stay in the transit camp reflect his frustration and boredom: three whole days are conveyed by two telling sentences: 'very cold and dry; nothing doing. Fed in Etaples at rotten café'.[4] On the fourth day relief appeared, first in the weather, which became milder, then in the news of imminent departure to the Battalion of his choice, the 1st. Best of all was the knowledge that his request not to be separated from Thomas had been heard, or at least fulfilled.

As the oldest battalion in the Royal Welch Fusiliers, the 1st enjoyed the greatest status. When Sassoon joined it near Béthune on 24 November, many of its original members at the outbreak of War were dead or wounded. They had landed at Zeebrugge with the 7th Division in 1914 and marched through Belgium to Ypres where they had scored a decided victory against the Germans. In their subsequent struggle to help keep the enemy from seizing the Channel ports, however, they had been decimated. (In twelve days, and despite reinforcements, they had been reduced from 1,150 to 90 men.) Restored by more drafts to its proper strength, the 1st had again distinguished itself at the Battle of Neuve Chapelle in March 1915, but had once again lost the greater part of its men at the Battle of Festubert two months later. In September 1915 it had suffered further casualties in another great massacre, the Battle of Loos. Sassoon and his fellow officers were being sent out to make up for heavy losses in the Givenchy trenches on the La Bassée canal. He was fortunate enough to join the Battalion at Béthune just as it was preparing for a long rest in the back area.

Béthune is less than fifty miles from Etaples, but it took Sassoon, Thomas and Stansfield, who had also been assigned to the 1st, nearly five hours to reach it. They had had to parade with kit at two o'clock that morning, though the train had not left for at least another three hours, so that they were already tired at the start of the long, roundabout journey, which was interrupted by frequent unexplained stops. It was not the best introduction to the French countryside and to Sassoon's weary eyes it looked lifeless and unattractive, no good for hunting in, even if that had been possible. The area round Béthune was particularly desolate after months of heavy fighting.

Nevertheless, almost anything was better than the wastes of Litherland and Sassoon gradually became stimulated by the change of scene. He also liked his new fellow officers, apart from his Commanding Officer, Colonel Minshull Ford, whom he commemorated not entirely kindly as 'Winchell' in *Memoirs of a Fox-Hunting Man*. (Robert Graves described him under his nickname 'Scatter', short for 'Scatter-Cash', given him because he had spent his allowance so lavishly when he first joined the Army.[5]) Though Sassoon was to switch battalions twice more before the end of the War, he would remain close friends with a number of the survivors from the 1st.

On arrival at Béthune Sassoon had been told to report to 'C' Company, which was particularly short of officers, and was delighted to learn that 'Birdie' Stansfield and Tommy were again to stay with him. Together they marched the final three miles to their billet at Le Hamel on the Béthune-Le Touret road, where they met their Company Commander, E. J. Greaves.[6] Greaves, like all the battalion officers except Colonel Minshull Ford, his second-in-command, the quartermaster and four or five subalterns from Sandhurst, was not a regular soldier and made a pleasant introduction to the army in France. Sassoon, who portrayed him as 'Barton' in *Memoirs of a Fox-Hunting Man*,[7] found him good-natured and easy-going, not at all what he had imagined a Company commander to be like. His very presence, big, burly and *pince-nezed*, made the Front Line seem positively cosy.

Educated at Harrow and fairly well-off, Greaves seemed to him entirely out of place in the cramped, smoky little room which constituted C Company's headquarters; Sassoon could much more easily have imagined him in front of a bright fire sipping a glass of vintage port. With his love of the good things of life and his vague appreciation of the arts, Greaves longed for a pleasant, sedentary job after the War, such as cathedral organist – a remark Sassoon came to appreciate in time as he was gradually exposed to a number of famous French cathedrals. (He was careful to emphasize that it was not love of music that prompted Greaves's ambition.) Older than most of the officers, whose average age was twenty-five, and married, which many were not, Greaves was clearly something of a father-figure to the five platoon commanders under him. He was frequently referred to as 'Father' Greaves. His age was further accentuated by the fact that he had a younger brother, Ralph, in the same regiment.

Sassoon grew very fond of Greaves, but he became even more attached to the two other officers who were new to him in C Company – Julian Dadd and Edmund Leslie Orme.[8] He particularly admired Dadd and was to praise him in both prose and verse in terms which Dadd's family thought showed great understanding and affection.[9] He celebrated Dadd's unassertive courage and goodness in *Memoirs of a Fox-Hunting Man* under the pseudonym 'Durley', a name taken from Dadd's home address in Stamford Hill, London. With modesty Dadd, whose conscientiousness made him feel he could always have done better, was to protest later, in verse:

> Dadd, though early, was not like Durley
> In the matter of stomach for the fight;
> And, when in security, into obscurity,
> Dadd sank rapidly out of sight.
> Later on Kangar,* in Homeric anger,
> His thoughts on the war beginning to write,
> A friend when in France painted well with romance,
> And so 'twas Durley saw the light.[10]

Dadd's unselfishness and concern for his men were an example Sassoon quite consciously tried to follow in France, though he was less impressed by his jokes, which reminded him of a bus conductor trying to cheer up his passengers on a wet winter's day.

Like Sassoon, Dadd had two brothers, one of whom had been killed at Gallipoli, though unlike Sassoon his remaining brother, Edmund, was with him in the 1st Battalion (A Company).[11] Their father, Stephen Dadd, was a black and white sporting artist and their great-uncle the painter Richard Dadd. The older members of the family were ashamed of the latter connection because of what Julian called 'the tragic and gruesome termination of his career as a free member of society' when Richard had killed his own father. (When Sassoon himself came into possession of a Richard Dadd picture later on, he was to donate it to the Tate Gallery in memory of Julian and his two brothers.) Julian's younger brother, Gabriel, had shown outstanding artistic talent before his death in Gallipoli, but Julian himself had been a clerk in Somerset House when War broke out. One of Sassoon's few regrets about their relationship was that his friend, though a fine swimmer, had never hunted, almost certainly as a result of his rather different social background.

The remaining platoon officer in C Company, E.L. Orme, seems to have been equally attractive to Sassoon, though in a very different way. In

---

* 'Kangar' was a name given to Sassoon by his friends in the 1st Battalion, possibly because of his ungainly movements when excited. He had also owned a horse called Kangaroo, which may have suggested the name to his friends in the first place.

Memoirs of a Fox-Hunting Man, which Dadd himself felt gave a 'true and kindly' picture of the Royal Welch Fusiliers,[12] Sassoon portrays Orme as 'Ormond', a 'sturdy little' youth straight from public school, who made no secret of his wish to avoid a hero's death. 'He wanted life', Sassoon writes, 'and he appeared capable of making good use of it, if allowed the opportunity'.[13] With his large round eyes under dark eyebrows, 'young Worm', as his friends called him, was a lively presence in C Company, sometimes too lively. His taste for mawkish popular songs, which he played constantly on his portable gramophone, made Sassoon long for Handel's violin sonatas, or even his mother playing 'The Harmonious Blacksmith' not very skilfully on the piano.

Nevertheless he was glad when Orme later accompanied him on his transfer to another battalion, the only officer from the 1st to do so. As Charles Hamilton Sorley remarked, the wartime 'friendships of circumstance' were unpredictable and could prove surprisingly strong.[14] When Orme died a year and a half later, Sassoon was to make him the subject of his poem 'To Any Dead Officer', composed in mid-June 1917, the very time at which he also wrote his anti-war protest. It was almost certainly Orme's death, among other factors, which precipitated his statement. He was not to know, when he joined C Company in November 1915, that of its six officers, two would be dead and the remaining four wounded by May 1917.

Another even closer friendship formed in November 1915, which was to inspire Sassoon to more than one poem, was with a young officer from A Company of the 1st Battalion, Robert von Ranke Graves. His meeting with Graves is one of the best-known literary encounters of the First World War, partly because it has been described in detail by both participants – fictionally by Sassoon in *Memoirs of an Infantry Officer* and autobiographically by Graves in *Goodbye to All That*.[15] There have also been a number of books and articles dealing with this meeting. It has also been remembered too, perhaps, because, like Sassoon's other famous encounter with Owen at Craiglockhart several years later, it seemed almost predestined. For, while it was entirely natural that Graves should have enlisted in a Welsh regiment near his parents' holiday home at Harlech, there appeared no compelling reason for Sassoon to choose the same unit. It seemed mere chance that directed him there. And, having joined, it was again chance, or fate, which sent him to the 1st Battalion at that particular time and place in France.

Graves himself had started his service abroad in the 2nd Battalion of the Royal Welch Fusiliers and it was again chance, or fate, that led to his transfer to the 1st at approximately the same time as Sassoon. (Rumour had it that Graves was transferred out of the 2nd Battalion because he put his very large foot on a kitten, but the truth is probably more mundane.[16]) Once there, however, it was entirely natural that they should have come together, even from their different companies. For, as Graves pointed out, it was an unusual experience to encounter, in a group of forty to fifty officers, one seriously literary person.[17] So it was not surprising, when Graves discovered a copy of Lionel Johnson's essays among the usual clutter of military manuals and 'trashy' novels on a visit to C Company's mess, that he should seek out the owner. Glancing round for someone who looked both literary and Jewish (he had only Sassoon's signature to go on) he had no difficulty in identifying him. So immediate was their rapport that a short time later they were walking into Béthune together to indulge in cream cakes and talk.

Sassoon's diary entry on that occasion suggests that his initial reaction to Graves was both condescending and intrigued: 'An interesting creature, overstrung and self-conscious, a defier of convention' he wrote on 28 November 1915.[18] He may already have been aware of Graves's existence during his three days with the 1st Battalion prior to their encounter, since he also notes that he was 'very much disliked' in the unit. Or Graves himself may have told him this on their walk.

Though Sassoon's immediate reaction implies a sense of superiority and difference, in fact, he and Graves had a number of things in common. Apart from the superficial and unfortunate one of having a German name in the British army, both were from cultured middle-class backgrounds which encouraged interest in the arts. Graves's father was the popular poet and song-writer, Alfred Perceval Graves (whom Sassoon knew but secretly thought very 'bad'). They had both been educated at public school, though Graves's career at Charterhouse had been more regular and academically more successful than Sassoon's, culminating in a (deferred) Exhibition to St John's College, Oxford. Both wanted to be poets and had already written a great deal, though neither was yet established, in spite of the efforts of Marsh, their mutual friend. Another important link was their similar attitude towards the War at that time. (Whether they would have responded so positively to each other after Sassoon's change of heart in 1916 is doubtful. They were to disagree strongly over his public protest in 1917, though Graves himself was also against the prolongation of the War by then.) Finally, and this too was to change with time, they were both what might be called idealistic homosexuals. Though Sassoon's attitude towards sex had almost certainly been influenced by his correspondence with Carpenter and his meetings with Dent and Ross, it was still basically puritanical, as was Graves's. Graves, who had himself written to Carpenter in 1914, had had an idealistic relationship with a boy at Charterhouse, but none of any significance with women by 1915. When his sexual interests changed later and he married, it was to be another cause of tension between the two men.

Looking back on their relationship in 1930 Graves claimed that Sassoon had been sexually attracted to him, a charge that the latter flatly denied: 'For you I felt affection, but physical attraction never existed'.[19] Yet eight years before this statement, in June 1922, he had written about Graves in his diary 'there was some vague sexual element lurking in the background of our war-harnessed relationship. There was always some restless passionate nerve-wracked quality in my friendship with R.G., although he has been one of my most stimulating companions'.[20] This 'vague sexual element' had undoubtedly helped bond their friendship in November 1915.

There, however, the similarities ended. Temperamentally they were very different. In spite of being nine and a half years younger, Graves seemed to Sassoon far more confident than he, the natural leader of the two and something of an oracle to him when they first met. Deeply introverted himself, Sassoon appears to have been fascinated by Graves's extrovert personality. Where he was diffident about his talents, Graves bragged unashamedly of his modest achievements, probably one reason he was not popular with his fellow-officers. While Sassoon was conventional and conformist in both social and artistic matters, Graves gloried in rebellion. 'He is a strange person, full of ideas and originality', Sassoon reported to Marsh shortly after their first meeting.[21] He felt that it was Graves's originality, rather than his brashness, which provoked hostility in the 1st Battalion.[22] Unlike Sassoon he made no real effort to conform to army standards in manners or dress and seemed slovenly and careless beside his friend. On one occasion, when Sassoon admitted to knowing 'von Graves', as Graves was called with direct reference to his partly German origins and middle name, he was told by a fellow officer:

> ... he's quite dotty. He used to sit up till one o'clock at night writing with dozens of candles lit all round his bed, and in the morning he used to shave with one hand and read a book with the other.[23]

While Sassoon struggled to become a good officer, Graves appeared to care little for such matters. According to Colonel C.I. Stockwell, who was to take over the 1st Battalion shortly after Graves joined it, he was 'an average officer who did his work neither well nor ill – but he lacked something – He did not instil confidence or moral [*sic*]'.[24] By contrast he found Sassoon an excellent officer.

Even Graves's and Sassoon's physical appearances highlighted their pronounced difference. It was almost as though Graves's inner irregularity was symbolically represented by his outward aspect. (Sassoon talked of Graves's 'twisted, grieving face'.) Though both were over six feet tall Sassoon was normally graceful, while Graves was, according to both of them, 'clumsy'. And, though both had prominent noses, Sassoon's lent distinction to his face while Graves's took it away. It was not surprising that Lady Ottoline Morrell, who was to get to know them both, would compare Sassoon romantically to a 'stag or faun' and Graves, less flatteringly, to a prizefighter.

Pronounced as the physical differences were, however, the mental ones were greater. Sassoon's approach to both art and life was, by his own

admission, emotional and non-intellectual. Indeed, he was deeply suspicious of the intellectual, a suspicion which Graves would inadvertently
strengthen in time. For Graves was assertively intellectual, revelling in
the play of ideas, often at the expense of emotions. It was no coincidence
that he embraced the difficult, strange and modern in art while Sassoon
lingered nostalgically in the past, another distinction which was to cause
problems in the future.

For the time being, however, their difficulties provided welcome stimulation for them both. As they talked avidly, more of literature than of War,
Sassoon discovered that Graves despised most of the books he venerated,
including, to his disbelief, *Paradise Lost*. Graves's hero at this time was
the controversial author of *Erewhon*, Samuel Butler, whose iconoclastic
impulses he shared. Though both fusiliers loved music, Graves provoca-
tively insisted that Northern folk ballads were superior to Beethoven's
Fifth Symphony, a typically absurd claim which Sassoon was too timid to
refute. It was only when Graves argued that 'fox-hunting was the sport of
snobs and half-wits', doubtless a deliberate bait, that Sassoon grew angry,
accusing him of being a 'fad-ridden crank'.[25] One crucial difference between them, which again was to change with time was their approach to
War poetry. While they both basically accepted the necessity of the War,
Sassoon wanted War at that time to be 'an impressive experience –
terrible, but not horrible enough to interfere with [his] heroic emotions'.[26]
Graves, on the other hand, distrusted sublimation and seemed to Sassoon
to want the War to be 'even uglier than it really was'.[27] (He deliberately
'shocked his venerable sire', Sassoon told Nellie Gosse, 'with violent
French lyrics about lice and corruption. Father retaliates with impassioned hymns in the *Observer*'.[28])

Such divergent attitudes revealed themselves most clearly in their
work at that time. While Sassoon's idealism gave rise to 'Absolution',
Graves's realism manifested itself in the poems he had prepared for his
first volume, *Over the Brazier*, (to be published on 1 May 1916). Some of
these pieces initially repelled Sassoon, who characterized them as 'very
bad, violent and repulsive'[29], though they almost certainly influenced him.
Graves was equally critical of Sassoon's work. 'Siegfried Sassoon is here
and sends his affectionate remembrances', he wrote to Marsh on 10
December 1915: 'a very nice chap, but his verses, except occasionally, don't
please me very much'.[30] Recalling their meeting nearly fifteen years later
he claims that Sassoon showed him his poem 'To Victory' at their first
meeting. Since this had not yet been written, he is more likely to mean
'Absolution', which was very different from the kind of verse he himself
was writing.

In spite of these pronounced differences, perhaps partly because of
them, the relationship flourished. As Sassoon himself pointed out, until he
met Graves in 1915, he had known no writer of his own age, or anywhere
near it.[31] Apart from Graves's entertainment value – he blew expert double

smoke rings and did an extremely funny imitation of an excitable Welshman – Sassoon found him a great help with his poetry. Graves, in turn, welcomed Sassoon's advice and sometimes left whole poems or even books unpublished at his suggestion.[32]

In conscious emulation of another great literary friendship, that between Coleridge and Wordsworth, they even planned to bring out a modern equivalent of *Lyrical Ballads* together. Sassoon, who adopted a fatherly attitude towards Graves at times, in recognition of their age difference, often made generous gifts of money to him. such as a witty £23 for his twenty-third birthday in 1918. He was to settle an annuity of £250 on Graves in his will, a sum which would be increased, rather curiously, to £300 after their relationship deteriorated in 1927. Graves, who seemed unembarrassed by Sassoon's generosity, occasionally gave him books, but his real contribution to the relationship appears to have been intellectual.

With direct reference to his Jewish blood, of which he was becoming increasingly conscious, Sassoon would quip: 'You have given me so many valuable tips about poetry that I may surely tip you in return with some of my semitic sovereigns none of which I have the least right to call my own'.[33] One such 'tip', which Sassoon was to take up enthusiastically, concerned another War poet whom Graves greatly admired, Charles Hamilton Sorley. Like Sorley, they planned to travel to exotic places after the War, but together. Taking up the Oriental theme and with deference to Sassoon's love of Fitzgerald, Graves was to write in his verse 'Letter to Sassoon from Mametz Wood':

> In old Baghdad we'll call a halt
> At the Sâshun's ancestral vault;
> We'll catch the Persian rose-flowers scent
> And understand what Omar meant.[34]

A year later Sassoon, not to be outdone, would suggest New Zealand and Polynesia. It was a stimulating and fruitful relationship which began at Le Hamel on 28 November 1915, only four days after Sassoon's arrival in France.

Less exciting but equally important to Sassoon was his relationship with the soldiers under him. Though he had already been in a position of command at Litherland, he had never felt fully responsible for his men's welfare there, as he came to feel he was in France. His platoon, exhausted and reduced in number by its recent experiences in the Givenchy trenches, accepted him 'apathetically' at first, caring only for thoughts of the forthcoming 'Divisional Rest'.[35] In spite of this, he gradually won them over with his growing concern for them.

Only a day after he took charge he was ordered to lead a working-party up to the trenches at Festubert, where a new defence scheme was under way. As he marched the men through the ruined town, across a marsh and up the muddy communication trench in the rain and darkness, he began to realize how unglamorous the reality of War was, particularly for the ordinary soldier. Two nights later, this time in brilliant moonlight and a frost of ten degrees below zero, he again led a patrol through the treacherous area; as the men staggered and slipped beneath their burdens of hurdles and planks, they seemed to him 'inhuman forms going to and from inhuman tasks'.[36] Two more working-parties followed on the two subsequent nights, one of them bitterly cold, the other very wet and, though Sassoon himself returned home soaked, his concerns were already more for his platoon: 'A shocking night for the men, whose billets are wretched'.[37]

Sassoon's increasing involvement with his men comes through very clearly in a poem written between the second and third of these nightmarish sorties (and revised the following March), 'The Redeemer':

> Darkness: the rain sluiced down; the mire was deep;
> It was past twelve on a mid-winter night,
> When peaceful folk in beds lay snug asleep;
> There, with much work to do before the light,
> We lugged our clay-sucked boots as best we might
> Along the trench; sometimes a bullet sang,
> And droning shells burst with a hollow bang;
> We were soaked, chilled and wretched, every one;
> Darkness; the distant wink of a large gun.
>
> I turned in the black ditch, loathing the storm;
> A rocket fizzed and burned with blanching flare,
> And lit the face of what had been a form
> Floundering in mirk. He stood before me there;
> I say that He was Christ; stiff in the glare;
> And leaning forward from His burdening task,
> Both arms supporting it; His eyes on mine
> Stared from the woeful head that seemed a mask
> Of mortal pain in Hell's unholy shrine.
>
> No thorny crown, only a woollen cap
> He wore – an English soldier, white and strong,
> Who loved his time like any simple chap,
> Good days of work and sport and homely song;
> Now he has learned that nights are very long,
> And dawn a watching of the windowed sky.
> But to the end, unjudging, he'll endure
> Horror and pain, not uncontent to die
> That Lancaster on Lune may stand secure.
>
> He faced me, reeling in his weariness,
> Shouldering his load of planks, so hard to bear.
> I say that He was Christ, who wrought to bless
> All groping things with freedom bright as air,

> And with His mercy washed and made them fair.
> Then the flame sank, and all grew black as pitch,
> While we began to struggle along the ditch;
> And someone flung his burden in the muck,
> Mumbling: 'O Christ Almighty, now I'm stuck!'
>
> (*CP*, pp. 16-17)

In strong contrast with 'Absolution', this is a work full of concrete details of Front-Line conditions and it is probably significant that it was started the very day that he met Graves. His realism may be noticeably less shocking than Graves's, but it marks a distinct change of direction for him. The word 'darkness', which opens and closes the first stanza, sets the tone for a poem which no longer deals in abstractions but draws attention to the realities of trench warfare, the 'mire', the 'clay-soaked boots', the 'droning shells', the 'soaked, chilled and wretched' soldiers and even their 'woollen caps' (or Balaclavas). If the comparison between the soldier 'floundering in mirk' with his heavy burden and Christ carrying His cross smacks somewhat of the heroic tradition, this is undercut by the irreverent colloquialism and direct speech of the last two lines, with their snatch of convincing blasphemy from the exasperated soldier – a device Sassoon was to repeat in later poems. Here at last is War poetry based on actual experience rather than literature. Years of apprentice-work at verse forms has paid off in a simple but effective nine-line stanza of neatly interwoven rhyme scheme, in which the slight and matching variation in rhyme-pattern of the first and last verses helps round off the poem and gives Sassoon the benefit of two concluding couplets with which to drive home his satire.

Language too is varied to good effect between the deliberately elevated ending to verse three where the soldier's Christ-like heroism is being emphasized. Sassoon wisely changed the last two lines which read originally 'And dimly in his pain he hopes to die / That Brummagem be safe beyond the seas', to the equally calculated colloquialism of the concluding verse, all the more effective for the contrast. Otherwise, apart from the onomatopoeic neologism 'mirk' and the insistent repetition of 'I say that He was Christ', the language is simple and unrhetorical, conveying directly the narrator's emotional involvement with the common soldier, particularly in the first four lines of verse three. Wilfred Owen told his sister in 1917 that 'The Redeemer' was a poem that he had been wanting to write every week for the past three years.

In *Memoirs of a Fox-Hunting Man* Sassoon states that his concern for his men was inspired by Julian Dadd, but there were clearly other factors at work. Apart from his active imagination, which could envisage only too vividly how they suffered in the quagmire trenches and cramped cold billets, he also found himself at last in a position where his preference for men could legitimately express itself without the disapproval of society or the law. Whilst it is true that the vast majority of officers, whatever their sexual concerns, became emotionally involved with their men and were, in turn, often idolized by them, Sassoon's feelings undoubtedly went beyond the paternalistic and platonic.

Paul Fussell, who believes that the War gave homosexuals 'a fresh impetus', has argued that 'in Great War diction there are three degrees of erotic heat attaching to three words: *men* is largely neutral, *boys* is a little warmer; *lads* is very warm'.[38] At least two of the authors he quotes in support of the theory, Whitman and Housman, were known to Sassoon by 1915 and he was probably not unaware of the connotation of 'lads'. It is significant, therefore, to find him less than a year after taking over his first platoon in France writing the following lines 'To My Soldiers':

> I have pitied you, shattered with wounds, and dying, and killed, –
> Lads that I've loved and will never change eyes with again:
> But Oh my dears, did you know I was proud as a king,
> When I heard you grumble and joke, and chatter and sing?[39]

Even if we reject Fussell's theory, the vocabulary here betrays an unusual warmth of feeling. Sassoon's later description of a young private, Jim Linthwaite, about whom he was also to write a short story, suggests that he became erotically involved with at least one of his men, though there is no evidence that such feelings were given physical expression.[40] There are other references in his diary to the physical attraction he felt for his men, an attraction he was to resist resolutely throughout the War.[41]

Part of the ordinary soldier's appeal for Sassoon may have lain in their working-class origins. Except for cricket there had been very few occasions in his past life when he had come into contact with this end of the social scale. As Peter Parker points out in his biography of another, less reticent homosexual, Joe Ackerley, 'the trenches were to show these men at their very best'. Paul Fussell has discussed at some length the attraction of many middle-class homosexuals for both the working-classes and men in uniforms, and in First World War France Sassoon found the two combined. It is important to note, however, that he never subsequently, in his active homosexual phase, took a working-class lover and the point must not be exaggerated. What is significant is the way in which he channelled his passions into caring for his men as well as possible. (Eventually they were to become his main reason for returning to the War in late 1917.) This made him an excellent officer, as Colonel Stockwell would corroborate, and quickly won the affection of his platoon. One of its members, V. King, was to write to him later: 'I wonder if they will really know what kind of officer you were[,] always thinking about your men[,] our food and feet, and seeing that we got a few cigs'.[43]

Vivian de Sola Pinto, when he became Sassoon's second-in-command later in the War, could not praise him sufficiently: 'It was not merely that he was kind and considerate: he seemed to radiate heroic energy and generosity ... like every man in [the] company, I at once became his devoted servant ...'[44] Towards his actual servant in C Company in 1915, R. Molyneux, a former railway signalman, Sassoon was particularly kind. He fully appreciated his affection – 'he told me he loved me like a brother – very nice of him; he *is* a dear' he noted in his diary[45] – and wrote to him on leave. His description of him as 'Flook' in *Memoirs of a Fox-Hunting Man* shows that he found Molyneux entertaining as well as endearing, especially his broad Lancashire accent and expressive use of expletives, which appear in his verse.

Sassoon had ample opportunity to show his concern for Molyneux and the rest of his men in late 1915. At the beginning of December the gruelling working-parties were succeeded by an almost equally punishing journey behind the lines for the eagerly awaited Divisional Rest. The move began with a five mile march northwest out of the La Bassée sector to more comfortable billets at Gonnehem.[46] After two days of rest there the Battalion marched westwards another three hours to Bourecq, a village two miles west of Lillers. Though the countryside was theoretically ideal for marching, its very flatness made it dreary and its roads were awash with liquid mud. After another day's rest the 1st Battalion marched into Lillers, where it entrained for Sadeux, a village just beyond Amiens. The forty-mile journey south took ten hours and it was dark on arrival.

By the time the men disembarked, unloaded their equipment and drank their tea it was past twelve and they had to march all night to reach their final destination in the Picardy uplands, Montagne. It had taken seven hours to march sixteen miles, the last two of which were very steep indeed. After what Sassoon describes with great restraint as a 'wretched' meal, he and his men crawled into their billets at 10.45 a.m. and slept till five in the afternoon.[47] A journey of approximately sixty-five miles, which would have been an easy three hour drive for the Divisional General in his staff car, had taken them from 30 November to 6 December, a whole week – a fact which underlines one of the less dramatic but pressing problems of the First World War, the simple logistics of moving large groups of men and equipment even short distances.

Sassoon himself, fit and unencumbered as he was, had found the last stage of the journey exhausting, but in a curious way it revived his flagging War-zeal. It may have been the sight of the men marching hour after hour with their heavy packs and inadequate boots often through torrential rain – 'the men that do the dirty work and keep us safe'[48] – that inspired his 'happy warrior' outburst on the fourth day of the journey:

Everything out here goes past me like a waking dream. My inner life is far more real than the hideous realism of this land of the war-zone. I never thought to find such peace. If it were not for Mother and friends I would pray for a speedy death. I want a genuine taste of the horrors, and then – peace. I don't want to go back to the old inane life which always seemed like a prison. I want freedom, not comfort. I have seen beauty in life, in men and in things; but I can never be a great poet, or a great lover. The last fifteen months have unsealed my eyes. I have lived well and truly since the war began, and have made my sacrifices; now I ask that the price be required of me. I must pay my debt. Hamo went; I must follow him. I will. Bobbie [Hanmer] will come out soon. I will be happy with him for a few months. And in the spring – who knows?[49]

There seems little doubt that Sassoon's willingness to sacrifice himself was closely connected with his homosexuality, either as it related to Bobbie or to his men. In an almost Christ-like gesture he appeared ready to suffer for them, as though suffering might bring the fulfillment he was denied. At the same time he seems to have seen the harsh conditions as a welcome punishment for some unspecified sin, perhaps that of homosexuality. For, in spite of Carpenter's reassurances, he was still unable to accept it without guilt. This might explain a puzzling statement in his diary that same month: 'I slew the dragon in my heart when the war began, and it was only a little wheedling thing after all'.[50]

If Sassoon wanted suffering there would be plenty of opportunity for it in France, though not just yet. For life at Montagne was reasonably comfortable. Compared with Béthune his duties were light and not entirely uncongenial. Since Minshull Ford believed, according to Graves, that the enemy's defences would be quickly penetrated and open warfare would ensue, he insisted on training them like a peacetime army.[51] Battalion drill and musketry training alternated with field-days and, although the whole exercise seemed rather irrelevant to men already experienced in the realities of trench-warfare, it was not unenjoyable, particularly the days spent out in the unspoilt Picardy countryside. Twenty miles behind the Front Line, Sassoon and his men could only faintly hear the sound of guns in the distance.

When Sassoon had to instruct them, two or three evenings a week, he tried to keep things as pleasant as they seemed. Confining himself to asking them easy questions from the Infantry Training Manual, he would insist that 'we had got to win the War (and were certain to)' and then read out the League Football news.[52] Another distraction for both men and officers were games of football and rugby, which Graves and Thomas joined in, as full-back and inside three-quarter respectively. Though Sassoon played neither rugby nor football, and it was the wrong season for cricket, he did have a chance to enjoy another of his favourite sports, riding.

Since transport at this stage of the War was largely dependent on animals, the 1st Battalion had a number of horses. One of these, the 'little black mare' of *Memoirs of a Fox-Hunting Man*, had been blinded in one eye and become almost unmanageable. With great patience and gentleness, however, Sassoon won her over and, with it, the right to ride her whenever he could, which was normally two or three afternoons a week. She became, as far as any horse could, a replacement for Cockbird in his affections and a welcome distraction. His skill with horses, as well as his reputation as a hard rider to hounds, was standing him in good stead in France.

It is little wonder that Sassoon described himself as happy in Montagne. Surrounded by rolling countryside which he could explore on horseback, his imagination began to revive. His diary entries, which had started in November 1915 as terse and mainly factual, gradually expanded and became positively lyrical as he responded to the surrounding scene. Compared with the 'soul-clogging' flatness of Flanders,[53] and even in its own right, Picardy seemed to him very beautiful. Its unfenced ploughlands, dotted with dark woods and a few villages, reminded him of East Kent and the Tickham hills. Even the sky seemed to him different, dominating the earth in a way it had never seemed to do in Flanders, perhaps because he knew that it was 'the sky of freedom, not a death-haunted appendage'.[54] Time and again his descriptions reveal the influence of his mother's training as he mentally 'composes' the landscape into a painting by one of his favourite artists:

> Walked through the woods beyond Le Fayel after lunch. Beautiful country – sat on edge of wood, under beech and cypress trees, looking across a valley of ploughland to grassy hills crowned with long dark lines of pine-covert – like a picture by Wilson Steer – a faint golden light over all, austere and yet delicate in tone and outline.[55]

It seemed to him as though he were walking through 'a living masterpiece of landscape-painting'.[56]

Despite a determination to avoid 'fine writing', Sassoon could not help comparing Montagne to Arcadia, particularly when he saw the old men and boys at the plough and flail, or watched the windmills spinning, or an old shepherd driving his sheep and goats home; even when a nearby cock woke him up at 6.30 a.m. Sitting in the small, tiled kitchen of his billet (a cottage abandoned by a Frenchman of fighting age), in front of an open fire with a book on his knee, he could not help enthusing to his mother's old friend, Nellie Gosse, about it all, though he did not forget to ask her to visit Theresa, too.[57] He was still missing serious music – he could hardly count the 'squeaks and shrillings' of the battalion's fife and drum band as such – but he had his books and was grateful for Nellie's offer to send him more. Whilst unable to specify exactly what he wanted, he suggested something 'old-fashioned' and 'quietly written'. (He may have had Lamb in mind.)

There is no record of what Nellie Gosse decided to send, but we do know some of the books Sassoon found consolation in that winter. Apart from his copy of Lionel Johnson's essays, which had betrayed his presence to Graves, he had brought to France A.E. Housman's *Shropshire Lad*, which he was to carry with him throughout the War.[58] Like many other soldiers, it suited his mood and offered its own austere comfort. Housman's belief that poetry should 'transfuse emotion', not 'transmit thought' agreed completely with his own view of the art.[59] In addition, he was reading *Nostromo* by Conrad, whose fatalistic outlook seemed also to suit his attitude. Quotations from Robert Bridges and Henry Vaughan in his diary suggest that he had some of their works with him too, perhaps in an anthology. He usually had at least one with him and, in late 1915, probably more, since, in addition to his own copy of Palgrave's *Golden Treasury*, he had asked Dent to send him Sidgewick and Jackson's *Anthology of Modern Verse*, and Marsh had given him the second volume of his *Georgian Poetry* anthology. He must have read this at Montagne, since he reported finding 'nothing new' in it.[60] Its greatest effect on him was to make him long to get back to his own versifying.

Another incentive to start writing poetry again at Montagne was the peacefulness of his surroundings. For, while he filled in his War-diary whatever the circumstances, he needed relative calm to compose verse. His first Montagne poem, 'To My Brother' (see page 206) a direct result of his revived 'happy warrior' mood, is disappointing, particularly after the promise of his November effort, 'The Redeemer'.[61] His second, 'The Prince of Wounds' is little better, though it does begin to question accepted notions of the link between religion and war in its closing lines:

> Have we the strength to strive alone
> Who can no longer worship Christ?
> Is He a God of wood and stone,
> While those who served him writhe and moan,
> On warfare's altar sacrificed?[62]

Like the later, more successful 'Stand-To: Good Friday Morning', this poem was probably intended, to use Sassoon's own words, to be a 'wholesome shocker'. Since he chose not to include it in either *The Old Huntsman* or his *Collected Poems*, we can assume that he recognized its weaknesses. Full of clichés, such as a road 'dark with blood' or 'warfare's altar', and based on tired religious imagery, it casts little new light on its subject. Nevertheless, it does contain a small personal detail of biographical interest. By Christmas 1915, when this poem was written, the things Sassoon was missing most were 'Music and colour and delight'. It is a theme he was to take up more successfully in his next two poems.

Meantime Christmas was celebrated with reasonable success. It was to be Sassoon's only Christmas in France and he marked the event in his favourite way by riding his little horse out by Warlus and back through the woods near Méricourt. He also mentions joining his fellow-officers round a large log-fire in the evening, but makes no reference to sharing Christmas dinner with them which he would certainly have done. Yet this was probably an even more luxurious affair than that described by an officer of the 2nd Royal Welch Fusiliers a year later, when conditions were more austere:

> This year H.Q. made sure of its goose and turkey; we've been fattening them for a month. We had paté de foie gras, julienne, curried prawns, roast goose, potato and cauliflower, plum-pudding, anchovy on toast, dessert; Veuve Cliquot, port, cognac, benedictine; coffee.[63]

The same officer's description of the men's Christmas meal suggests that, though this was very good by their usual standards, it was markedly less exotic than the officers':

> One o'clock dinner was soup; roast meat with potato, carrot, turnip and onion; plum-pudding; an apple, or orange, and nuts.

However, the men at Montagne were also allowed a little 'disciplined insobriety' for the event, and the village was full of 'maudlin sergeants' and 'paralysed privates', all trying, no doubt, to forget what was in store for them.

A week later New Year's Day was doubtless an occasion for both men and officers to take more sober stock of what lay ahead in 1916. Though the fighting had quietened down for the winter, the situation was far from hopeful. Sydney Cockerell, who took a close interest in events, voiced the anxieties of many when he wrote in his diary on 1 January 1916:

> The British losses, though far less than those of the French, have been enormous. Our campaigns in the East have been unsuccessful and very costly. In the West we remain where we were 15 mths ago. We can only hope for a turn of the tide when the winter is over and a forward move can again be attempted.[64]

It was, of course, the 'forward move' that the soldiers feared. Already the Germans were planning a massive attack at Verdun, where almost 420,000 French and Germans would die, and beyond that lay the British counter-offensive on the Somme, another appalling massacre in which 623,000 Allied troops would be casualties. Both battles were to drag on to the end of the year, leaving the situation looking no more hopeful than at the start. In view of such uncertainties, it is not surprising that Sassoon held his own personal stocktaking on this New Year's Day. In 'A Testament', as he called this, he tried to come to terms with the strong probability of death in the near future. The setting for this poem appears to be a deserted château he passed regularly on his rides:

> If, as I think, I'm warned to pack and go
> On a longer journey than I've made before,
> I must be taking stock of what I leave,
> And what I stand to lose, of all my store,

Cries for completion. Things, that made me weep
For joy of loveliness, come shining back
Dazzling my spirit that prepares for sleep.

Hushed is the house that once was full of songs.
In stillness rich with music that has been,
I wait death's savage hour that shall deliver
My soul and leave the soaring night serene.

There was a narrow path from glade to glade
Threading the golden forest, like a story
Planned to no certain close; a path that went
From morning to a sundown spilt with glory:

My home was safe among the slender trees;
There, on the blossomed slopes of time and sense,
Birds flocked and days came delicate and cold;
But now the tempest stoops to bear me hence.

The arches of the air are mighty songs
That tell me of a wide-flung radiance spread
Across the world; my feet roam with the tides,
And I am crowned with the triumphant dead.[65]

Still in his mood of heroic renunciation, Sassoon fails to provide any central tension to this poem, which is little more than an unconvincing acceptance of death in vague romantic terms. The true interest of the poem lies in its insistence, as in 'The Prince of Wounds', on the importance of music and visual beauty to the poet, a theme which becomes central in his next poem, 'To Victory'.

Blessed for once on 3 January by a sunny day, which lit up the Somme Valley and the rooftops of Airames on its opposite side, Sassoon felt a return of his joy in nature, all the more precious in the face of possible death. Playing on the treble function of Apollo as the bringer of sunshine, the god of his two favourite arts (music and poetry) and Admetus's shepherd, and reminded of him perhaps by the manly youth and beauty of many who marched beside him, he exclaims:

The ghost of Apollo is on these cornlands – Apollo in Picardy; it was here that he ground the kern and plied the flail, and lived at the farm.[66]

However lovely the moment, it was soon gone and the next day Sassoon poured out his longing for the old life of beauty. The image of a garden, based undoubtedly on his childhood experience at Weirleigh, symbolizes something sacred and apart, a complete contrast to the ugliness of War. Apart from a neat conjuring with colours and a growing technical confidence, the poem is interesting mainly as an insight into Sassoon's state of mind at the beginning of January 1916, when his greatest fear in war was of being blinded:

> *To Victory*
> Return to greet me, colours that were my joy,
> Not in the woeful crimson of men slain,
> But shining as a garden; come with the streaming
> Banners of dawn and sundown after rain.
>
> I want to fill my gaze with blue and silver,
> Radiance through living roses, spires of green
> Rising in young-limbed copse and lovely wood
> Where the hueless wind passes and cries unseen.
>
> I am not sad; only I long for lustre.
> I am tired of the greys and browns and the leafless ash.
> I would have hours that move like a glitter of dancers
> Far from the angry guns that boom and flash ...[67]
>
> (*CP*, pp. 13-14)

Sassoon himself pointed out that this poem was 'a much more conventional and unrealistic production' than most of his subsequent War poems.[68] It seems, therefore, appropriate that he should have dedicated it to Edmund Gosse, whose views on the War were predictably conventional.[69] He later told Gosse's son, Philip, that he did not think 'too well' of the poem in 1933, but Gosse himself admired it greatly when it was sent to him and managed to get it into *The Times* for 15 January 1916. Sassoon had insisted that only his initials be given, but Lady Ottoline Morrell, a colourful patron of the arts to whom its high-flown sentiments appealed, discovered his identity through Gosse and wrote him a glowing letter.[70] Though the two did not meet for another seven months, it was the start of an intriguing relationship which ended only with Ottoline's death in 1938.

'To Victory' was the last poem Sassoon wrote at Montagne. By January there was already a sense of impending departure which may well have prevented the return of his muse. Though the Battalion was not due to leave until the end of the month, there were rumours of change of plans, and everyone started preparing themselves mentally for the move. They were also issued with gas-masks, clumsy devices at that stage in the War which emphasized its grotesqueness and seemed to bring the fighting nearer. The Quartermaster, Joe Cottrell, a seasoned campaigner much respected in the Battalion, gloomily forecast that they were bound for the Somme, a prediction which did nothing to raise spirits. In the face of such possibilities, it is understandable that Sassoon took refuge in an almost mystic mood of supreme self-sacrifice. He seems deliberately to have tried to strengthen this state, which was partly induced by his renewed joy in Nature, with a visit to Amiens Cathedral towards the end of the month, and a further reading of the mystic poet Henry Vaughan. Quoting lines from Vaughan's 'Song to Amoret':

> For I not for an hour did love
> Or for a day desire,
> But with my soul had from above
> This endless holy fire,

he declares:

> I am fortunate in having come to the blessed state of mind when earth and light are one; I suppose it is what the mystics call finding Reality. I am part of the earth, which for me is soaked in the glory of sunlight and past seasons ...[71]

His retrospective comment on this state is more down to earth: 'I used to persuade myself that I had "found peace" in this new life'.[72]

At a daily level life itself was fairly mundane. Training continued even more rigorously, and so did Sassoon's rides. Sometimes, when Thomas accompanied him, he pretended he was out hunting, much to his friend's entertainment, and could forget for a while the realities of his situation. He also rode occasionally with the Battalion's Transport Officer, R. Ormrod, with whom he was billeted, and was sad when Ormrod left for England on 18 January. In his absence Sassoon was the natural choice for Transport Officer, a relatively safe job which, in his elevated mood of self-sacrifice, he did not want. It seemed ironic to him that, while he yearned almost masochistically for danger and hardship, he should have been given such a post.

Sassoon's friends rejoiced for him and, since there was no choice, he made the best of it. It was certainly more fun than being a company officer and brought him into even closer contact with horses. Always an individualist, in spite of his conformist exterior, he enjoyed the freedom and took on the responsibility with a confidence impossible to imagine at the beginning of the War when he had shied away from a commission. In the days before motorized vehicles had become the norm, 'Transport' involved a surprisingly large number of animals and men, for all of whom he was technically responsible (though he suspected that Joe Cottrell and the Transport Sergeant could have managed perfectly well without him). There were drivers, officers' groom, brakesmen and the men who looked after the nine pack animals. On the next rung up were the transport sergeant, his corporal and a farrier-corporal, as well as a shoeing-smith, saddler, carpenter and cook. The vehicles themselves included a General Service wagon, a mess-wagon for carrying officers' kits, some company cookers, a watercart, a 'Maltese' cart for the Quartermaster's special use and, not least importantly, limbers which carried machine-guns and ammunition. All these had to be mobilized for frequent journeys and were vital to the Battalion's well-being.

Sassoon took his responsibilities very seriously and filled a whole army notebook with details of his job. He made a list of 'NCOs and Men Employed in Transport', which came to over sixty and included their marital status. There was also a list of 'Officers' Chargers', which he classified variously as 'slight whistler', 'bad wind-sucker' or 'bad side-bones'. His copious 'Veterinary Notes (for grooms)' included advice on 'Cracked Heels', 'Mud Fever', 'Saddle Galls' and 'Diseases of the Feet'. Less relevantly, but of equal if not greater interest, his 'Army Notebook 152' also contained the draft of a poem which suggests that he had plenty of free time and was still in 'happy warrior' mood:

> The silver moment showed him lashed with rain
> Unhappy in his labour: one whose voice
> Must swell the dying roar of legions slain
> That in the end, bright victory may rejoice.[73]

One of the greatest advantages of Sassoon's new job seemed to him his closer contact with the Battalion Quartermaster. He had met Joe Cottrell shortly after joining C Company at Béthune, when his Company Commander had invited Cottrell and Ormrod to a dinner which turned out to be particularly unpalatable. Sassoon had admired then the tactful way in which Cottrell had praised its only passable course, the toasted cheese, and had looked forward to working with him.

Though Sassoon remained in his own billets while they were at Montagne, he knew he would be sharing quarters with Joe, as everyone called him, once they returned to the Front. Between the small, balding, middle-aged, disillusioned, working-class Quartermaster from Lancashire and the tall, young, idealistic ex-public schoolboy from the Home Counties there developed an unexpected friendship which was to survive the War. Sassoon himself tried to explain what attracted him to Cottrell in a Kiplingesque poem more interesting for its content than its technique:

> *The Quarter-Master*
> Bad stations and good liquor and long service
> Have aged his looks beyond their forty-five;
> For eight and twenty years he's been a soldier;
> And nineteen months of war have made him thrive.
> He's got a face to match his breast of medals,
> All stained and veined with purple and deep red.
> His heart is somewhat bigger than his body,
> And there's a holy anger in his head ...[74]

Sassoon was not the only officer in the 1st Battalion to admire Joe. Julian Dadd also thought him 'a wonderful old man' and praised Sassoon's description of him in *Memoirs of a Fox-Hunting Man*.[75] And Colonel 'Tibbs'

Crawshay of the 2nd Battalion, who had been 'bosom pals' with Joe at Youghal in Ireland before the War, told Sassoon that he had 'never known a man so loyal – despite his Red talk'.[76] When Joe had been brought before their Commanding Officer for 'making a Book', Crawshay had managed to persuade him not to treat the case as harshly as the C.O. had intended. 'Poor old Joe Cottrell,' Crawshay concluded: 'It's really sad. He deserved so much'. It was almost certainly Joe's lack of education, as well as a pronounced sense of independence, which had prevented him from rising above the position of Quartermaster in spite of his ability and long service.

Though Sassoon was to be transferred from the 1st Battalion before the end of 1916, he would remain in close touch with Joe, who was to write him long letters detailing the progress of mutual friends, or grimly reporting their deaths. In spite of his lack of education, Joe had a lively, natural style which delighted Sassoon, who replied faithfully. Cottrell's letters are full of 'old soldier' phrases, such as 'all the boys [i.e. officers] send their chin-chins', or 'what a game - oh - my masters - what a game', highly evocative of Wartime France.[77] Whenever Sassoon was in England he would send Joe presents of kippers, or cakes, and when he thought there was a danger of being killed or wounded he gave his friends Joe's name to write to for information. Cottrell, who was not easily impressed, came to regard Sassoon as one of the bravest soldiers he had ever known. (Joe himself had a D.S.O., rarely awarded to an officer of his rank.)

So that it was, on the whole, a pleasure being Joe's right-hand man in Transport. Even when the time came to organize the Battalion's return to the Front, Sassoon managed his part of things without undue panic. As the wagons lumbered across the Somme at Picquigny his main regret was that he would be out of the fighting and therefore unable to protect his young friend, Tommy. Otherwise he enjoyed riding along on his little black mare, whilst his friends trudged at the head of their platoons. On the first day, 30 January, the Battalion marched thirteen miles in raw and foggy weather to Vaux and on the second, another ten miles in equally bad weather to Pont Noyelles, describing a wide arc round Amiens to the north. On the third and final day they marched yet another ten miles to Morlancourt, a village approximately fifteen miles northeast of Amiens and five miles south of Albert. Occupying a strip of undulating land between the Somme and Ancre rivers, Morlancourt had not yet suffered shellfire, and would not do so for another two years. Centred on the meeting of five roads round a little farm and pond, with a church at each end, it still retained its rural atmosphere and was to provide a strong contrast to the trenches in the coming months. Sassoon had comfortable canvas billets near the transport lines and enjoyed waking up to the sound of birds every morning. The majority of the men had no time to enjoy the relative calm of Morlancourt, however, for the day after they arrived they had to leave for the Front Line trenches five miles away, near enemy-occupied Fricourt, where they were due to relieve the 12th Middlesex.

9. 'Goodbye to Galahad' (November 1915-March 1916)

Trench systems varied considerably in different parts of the line. At the beginning of the War, troops on the Western Front had simply dug ditches in which to shelter from enemy fire, but by February 1916 trenches were far more sophisticated. Much wider and deeper passageways were constructed, usually in several roughly parallel lines, so that if a section of the Front Line were taken, reinforcements could be moved up from the rear *via* communication trenches. Each line was zig-zagged irregularly to prevent the enemy from firing along it, as well as to reduce the impact of bombs, and small 'dug-outs' were excavated in the back of the trenches to provide room for shelter, sleep and even cooking. Sandbags added further protection against enemy fire, as well as support for the sides of the trenches.

Since mud was one of the most unpleasant features of the Western Front, good trenches were paved with 'duck-boards' to walk on and avoid slipping. In front of the first line tangled masses of barbed wire were laid to prevent enemy penetration and narrow passages, or 'saps', ran out to observation posts in the neutral area between the two forces. Known as No Man's Land, this was usually pitted with deep craters left by exploding shells from both sides. Since German and Allied trench systems stretched from the Alps at one end to the English Channel at the other, a distance of approximately 475 miles, outflanking was impossible. In an attack, therefore, the 'poor bloody' Infantry had to 'go over the top', in other words climb out of their own trenches – generally at dawn – cross No Man's Land and rush the enemy, officers with revolvers, men with .303 Enfield rifles with bayonets fixed. As they followed so-called 'safe' routes up to the enemy trenches, they would throw hand-grenades into them, another hazard of trench warfare. Their attack was generally preceded by heavy artillery bombardments which would theoretically kill some of the enemy and destroy their barbed wire, but in practice the far from accurate howitzers often missed, leaving enemy and wire intact and destroying both the surprise element and No Man's Land itself, which was frequently churned up into a sea of mud. As the heavily-laden troops floundered towards the enemy line, they were more often than not mown down by a murderous hail of bullets. Sometimes they were held up by their own gas attack, which drifted back in their faces as the wind changed. Of all these hazards, mud seems to have featured most largely in the soldiers' lives, closely followed by noise and smell.

The trenches occupied by the Royal Welch Fusiliers in the Bois Français sector near Fricourt were particularly bad. As their Commanding Officer observed on his first tour of them, they were situated on a bare rolling down of chalk. About 500 yards of the Front consisted of a continuous row of craters. In places the Germans were less than sixty yards away and had established bombing posts within forty yards of the British Front Line. But at least the chalky soil made for relatively dry and well-drained trenches at a time when the French winter could be calculated to turn most trenches into mud baths. Even so, the mud was 'beyond belief', according to Sassoon,[78] and the sludge was ankle-deep beneath the duck-boards. 'Trench-foot', brought about by continually wet and cold feet, was one of the many undramatic curses of First World War France. Another was lice, a third rats and a fourth, more seriously, pneumonia. Sassoon had a constant sore throat, but tried to impress on his men the importance of looking after their feet.

In contrast to the British trench system the Germans' was a model of efficiency. Since their High Command tried to keep its units in the same place in the line, there was usually a competitive spirit between compan-ies, battalions and regiments in constructing and improving trenches. Each separate trench system was strongly wired in and contained deep dug-outs at regular intervals. The great strength of their Fricourt sector was the linking up of the first and second line systems by a series of fortified positions: each wood and village had been prepared for defence, every advantageous piece of ground had been entrenched, often provided with dug-outs and wired. It was virtually impregnable, except perhaps against massed artillery, prepared for by lengthy bombardments.

Though Sassoon felt himself to be only an onlooker as Transport Officer, he became very familiar with the trenches at Fricourt. During the Battal-ion's six-day stint there he would ride up regularly every afternoon with the food and water-wagons. After spending a morning attending to the horses, while the cooks prepared dixies of stew and tea, he would accom-pany Joe and the rations up to the line. To begin with they started at 2:30 p.m., but as the days lengthened they were forced to wait a little longer, since they could not go beyond Bray after dark, for fear of attack. They also had to take a more devious route than the soldiers, which increased the five miles to seven. The whole journey took never less than seven hours and was extremely hazardous, but Sassoon cared very little for danger, even seemed to relish it, as he had on the hunting-field. He regularly visited C Company in the Front Line and listened avidly to their reports of trench-mortar attacks and machine-gun fire. Though he was glad to get back to Joe's comfortable billets, which were shared by the French inter-preter, Monsieur Perrineau, he longed to be with his Company. Physically fearless and hardened as he was, the trenches held very little terror for him. In his semi-mystical, heroic mood, half-longing for death to resolve his inner conflicts, trench warfare seemed to offer the possibility of both sacrifice and resolution.

Unable to alleviate his men's sufferings in any practical way, apart from bringing food, Sassoon expressed his sympathy in what he called his first 'outspoken' War poem, 'In the Pink'. This was composed on 10 February, during the Battalion's rest from its first tour of the trenches, when his own duties were accordingly lighter. He was almost certainly inspired by the sight of the Machine-Gun Officer shivering in his blankets on the floor from a combination of alcoholic poisoning and cold feet, though he denied this. Nevertheless, he noted the circumstances and conceded that his verses refer to 'some typical Welshman who probably got killed on the Somme in July, after months and months of a dog's life and no leave'.[79] He could not have been very surprised when the *Westminster Gazette* refused it for publication on the grounds that it might prejudice recruiting. The poem's harsh criticism of fighting conditions distinguishes it sharply from any of his previous War verses, except 'The Redeemer', and it anticipates in both content and technique the works which were to make him famous:

> *In the Pink*
> So Davies wrote: 'This leaves me in the pink.'
> Then scrawled his name: 'Your loving sweetheart Willie.'
> With crosses for a hug. He'd had a drink
> Of rum and tea; and, though the barn was chilly,
> For once his blood ran warm; he had pay to spend.
> Winter was passing; soon the year would mend.
>
> But he couldn't sleep that night; stiff in the dark
> He groaned and thought of Sundays at the farm,
> And how he'd go as cheerful as a lark
> In his best suit, to wander arm in arm
> With brown-eyed Gwen, and whisper in her ear
> The simple, silly things she liked to hear.
>
> And then he thought: tomorrow night we trudge
> Up to the trenches, and my boots are rotten.
> Five miles of stodgy clay and freezing sludge,
> And everything but wretchedness forgotten.
> Tonight he's in the pink; but soon he'll die.
> And still the war goes on – *he* don't know why.
>
> (*CP*, p. 22)

Here already is the foundation of a formula for Sassoon's bitter War-satires. The verse form is simple, with no pyrotechnics to distract from the content, and the six-line stanza ends with a rhyming couplet to drive home the ironic point. The language is also simple and largely colloquial, partly to help create the soldier's working-class background, but also to express more bluntly the nastiness of War. The phrase 'in the pink', which is used three times in all, ironically underlines the fact that the soldier is not 'in the pink of health' and, even if he were, it would be short-lived. His boots are frankly 'rotten', rather than politely 'inadequate'. And as the narrator concludes in a phrase which does not quite avoid the charge of sounding condescending, he echoes the uneducated soldier's thoughts, whilst at the same time emphasizing his bewilderment – '*he* don't know why'. The few rhetorical flourishes are kept deliberately simple: the man imagines himself as nothing more sophisticated than 'cheerful as a lark' and the narrator repeats 'in the pink' for his own ironic ends.

In spite of some shortcomings, the poem is an important one. It is the first of its kind, showing more clearly than 'The Redeemer' Sassoon's need to escape the subjective lyric approach, largely inadequate in the face of the horrors of the Western Front, to a more objective, dramatic one. In doing so, he is forced to find a different vocabulary, which gives the poem a freshness lacking in most of his earlier work. His previous attempts at the colloquial, *The Daffodil Murderer* and 'The Old Huntsman', were no doubt helpful to him in a way he could never have anticipated. As in so many later poems, a little scene is set and a brief character sketch presented by an apparently detached narrator, who nevertheless makes his irony felt by the end. Sassoon described his method as 'composing two or three harsh, peremptory, and colloquial stanzas with a knock-out blow in the last line'.[80]

Sassoon's lyric impulse was never far away, however, as his next poem, 'The Dragon and the Undying' shows. Inspired perhaps by his regiment's red dragon insignia, he organizes this poem around a not entirely convincing contrast between the dragon of war, 'sing[ing]' his battle-song, and the souls of the slain, absorbed back into nature, 'vocal[izing]' their own thoughts through streams and trees. The fifth and sixth lines of the sonnet's sestet, describing the dragon lusting 'to break the loveliness of spires, / And hurl their martyred music toppling down', are almost certainly a reference to the half-destroyed but defiantly surviving statue of the Virgin on the church spire at Albert, which Sassoon could see from Morlancourt.[81]

On the whole, however, the poem is of slight interest, significant mainly because it shows Sassoon tempted back into the lyric mode. Since it is dated only 'February 1916', it is possible that it was not even written in France and that the true horror of the trenches was not as fresh in his mind as when he wrote 'In the Pink'. For he was given ten days' leave unexpectedly on 23 February and spent the end of the month and the beginning of March in England.

It took Sassoon twenty-four hours to reach London. The 9.30 a.m. train from Méricourt made its leisurely way to Amiens and Le Havre, where he caught the night boat for Southampton. After a shorter train journey to Waterloo he arrived in London at 10 a.m. on 24 February and spent the night with his Uncle Hamo and Aunt Fanny at the family house they shared in Melbury Road. He cannot altogether have relished the idea of seeing his mother, who was still very bitter and unhappy about Hamo's death, but he dutifully spent the next few days at Weirleigh with her. His subsequent stay in London must have seemed much more enjoyable, since he passed it visiting friends and attending at least one concert. He had kept up a regular correspondence with Gosse, Marsh and Dent, all of whom he saw during his leave. Gosse celebrated his return by inviting Max Beerbohm and his wife, as well as Robbie Ross, to meet him at a dinner given in his honour at Hanover Terrace on 2 March.

There seems to have been some competition between Sassoon's four mentors, Gosse, Ross, Marsh and Dent, to entertain him, particularly between the two latter. 'I never knew it was you who had snatched Sassoon away from me that day,' Marsh wrote to Dent on 14 March. 'I had two very pleasant meetings with him in spite of you'.[82] Both of them seemed anxious to influence his poetic development. Marsh cautiously approved of the direction he was taking, but did not want him to 'throw away the gift of melody'. He preferred to see him using it in the service of his 'more direct and simple' manner, a wish that Dent almost certainly shared.

The greatest influence on Sassoon's poetry at this time, however, came from neither Marsh nor Dent, but from his more recently made acquaintance, Ross. During his visit to London he stayed with Ross at 40 Half Moon Street, off Piccadilly, and it was not simply convenience which dictated his choice. There had been an instant *rapport* between the older, more care-worn but essentially lively art connoisseur and himself when they had met at Gosse's the previous October. Since Sassoon had then been about to leave for France, there had been no time to get to know each other. Now, as he saw Robbie in his own elegant milieu surrounded by loyal friends, he began to appreciate him more fully. Ross showed himself as fearless in his attitude towards the War as he had in his defence of Oscar Wilde.

Sassoon quickly realized that he was far more hostile to it than the more conservative Gosse or Marsh, who had both shown that they preferred what he called 'idealized soldier-poems'.[83] It was during his stay with Ross that his own views, which had already begun to change, responded to the older man's influence. He would certainly have shown Ross his satiric 'In the Pink', which would have appealed to the latter's taste for the lively and the new, particularly if it were calculated to annoy the Establishment. For, as Sassoon quickly realized, there was an element in his friend's nature which delighted in provoking opposition: 'He hated the war and was unable to be tolerant about it and those who accepted it with civilian bellicosity and self-defensive evasion of its realities'.[84] One of the results of Sassoon's stay with Ross was a hardening of his attitude to what Ross called 'screaming scarlet Majors', a phrase which Sassoon was to make memorable. It was probably for this reason that he entrusted Ross, rather than Gosse, Marsh or Dent, with a manuscript book of his recent poems.[85]

From this time Ross's rooms became Sassoon's centre when he was on leave in London. Not only did they delight his eye with their subdued half-Italian, half-Oriental tones and exquisite pictures and furniture, but they also allowed him access to an aesthetic world to which he too aspired. While partly listening to one of Ross's erudite conversations with his Burlington Fine Arts Club cronies, or his old friend More Adey, he could browse through his eclectic collection of poetry and *belles lettres*, savouring the matured artistic judgement which informed it all.

One of the choicest pieces in Ross's collection, according to many friends, was his housekeeper and her, too, Sassoon learnt to appreciate on this visit. The former lady's maid of Robbie's mother, Nellie Burton had taken to letting rooms to 'single gentlemen' after her employer's death. She had naturally offered her protection to Robbie when he needed it in 1914. Known variously as 'Nellie', 'Dame Nellie' or simply (and 'chicly' according to Anthony Powell)[86] as 'Burton', she was an unforgettable character.

Part of this was Nellie's remarkable appearance. Small and stout, with an alarming number of double chins accentuated by what Sassoon's American playwright friend, Sam Behrman, was to call her 'minaret' hairstyle, she was not afraid to draw attention to herself with innumerable pieces of jewellery in both hair and clothes. As Behrman recalled, it was 'a congeries of ornaments and unclassifiable styles, but somehow I was soon aware that Miss Burton securely dominated her effects so that she had a style of her own'.[88] Her prominent blue eyes and benevolent smile added charm to the effect. It was an effect which stimulated the imagination of more than just Behrman and gave rise to a number of pungent comparisons. Robbie's close friend, Squire Sprigge, coming upon Nellie in a mauve dressing-gown, cigarette in hand, supervizing the gilding of Robbie's rooms (he was her favourite tenant), compared her lovingly to 'a bad character from a Hogarth print'.[89] Anthony Powell, who was taken to tea with her by Osbert Sitwell, could not help thinking of her as a younger version of Rosa Lewis, proprietress of the infamous Cavendish Hotel, where Dukes and Princes took their mistresses. Though Nellie and her rooms were eminently respectable, her colourful appearance made him feel that there was something 'a shade *louche*' in the background.

Yet Nellie was also a motherly figure to the gentlemen she petted and pampered. Respectful, chatty and infinitely understanding – though she could be outspoken at times – she created a home for a number of lonely men, most of whom had no wish to marry and create a home for themselves. Sassoon himself would become one of her tenants and a great favourite. So, too, would Osbert Sitwell and the composer Lord Berners. The actor and director Glen Byam Shaw, though he never took rooms at 40 Half Moon Street, would also become an admirer through his friendship with Sassoon. And Wilfred Owen, recommended by Sassoon, would stay in her rooms on his last leave in London. Dame Nellie became a legend in her own life-time and when she died the *Manchester Guardian* was to celebrate her vivid personality in an article entitled simply 'Miss Burton of Half Moon Street'.[90]

Nellie's one weakness, which fortunately chimed in with most of her tenants', was a suspicion of women: 'fair to the eye and rotten to the core' was how she summed them up to Behrman.[91] Powell relates an Osbert Sitwell anecdote in which an unfortunate gentleman attempted to introduce a female element into Half Moon Street. This had greatly incensed Nellie, who had shouted in her strongest Hampshire accents: 'I won't have any Tondelayos here', Tondelayo being a dusky seductress in a contemporary stage hit, *White Cargo*.[92] The story which perhaps best brings out Nellie's tendency to seem larger than life comes from Glen Byam Shaw, who, after visiting her in the 1930s, told Behrman:

> Her new house is lovely but somehow everything about it is huge; the tomatoes are huge, the sunflowers are huge, the sofa in the drawing-room is huge, and the lunch was huge. I don't know how we ever got through it. But she's always wonderful ... I always kiss her when I see her. It's like kissing a large, wet gooseberry.[93]

Sassoon, who described Nellie all-embracingly as 'Shakespearean', quickly fell under her spell.[94] Anything that distracted him from the War was welcome. Similarly, when, contrary to his fears, the snow melted and allowed the possibility of hunting, he seized it. One of the things he had most missed in France, he gladly sacrificed the last few days of his leave to hunt with an old friend who was valiantly keeping the Southdown going.[95] He spent three days at Middleham, Ringmer, near Lewes, and took back with him to France memories of 'woods and fields in Sussex, in clear sunlight of early March, and the scarlet-coated huntsman galloping his jaunty little grey nag, cheering his hounds to a find or casting them across the wet ploughs'.[96] As he had remarked to his hunting friends when stretching his legs to a glowing fire and munching a muffin after a hard day's hunting, it had been 'bloody Bliss!'[97]

Sassoon was back in France on 6 March. He had been seen off by his friends at Waterloo and was to remember their, presumably anxious, faces for weeks afterwards. The rest of the journey had been uneventful, a reverse process of night crossing from Southampton and long train ride to Méricourt. He found the country round Morlancourt as he had left it, deep under snow. Most memories of his leave, strong at first, faded before the exigencies of the present.

Sassoon's new Commanding Officer, Colonel Stockwell, who had arrived to replace Minshull Ford the day before Sassoon's departure for England, was a strict disciplinarian and demanded extremely high standards from his men.[98] He made Minshull Ford seem positively easy-going by comparison. Since it had been clear for some time that Minshull Ford was seeking promotion, the 1st Battalion was not sorry to see him go, but it was apprehensive about his replacement. Stockwell had the reputation of being a first-rate soldier but he was also known to be hard on his men, who nicknamed him 'Buffalo Bill'. Cottrell, who had known him since he had been a subaltern, more affectionately called him 'Stocky' and Sassoon gave him the pseudonym 'Kinjack' in his fiction, perhaps to suggest keenness and fierceness. Though critical of Stockwell's harshness – he would threaten to shoot any man who did not obey to the letter – Sassoon immediately acknowledged his merits: 'He is aggressive efficiency, very blatant, but knows the job' he wrote in his diary the day Stockwell arrived.[99] He also appreciated his sense of humour. Another of Stockwell's officers, Julian Dadd, summed him up as 'crude but kindly'.[100] Stockwell himself recognized Sassoon's potential, though he was rightly wary of his rashness, and thought him wasted as a Transport Officer. Only two weeks after the latter's return from leave he was to transfer him back to the line.[101]

Meantime Sassoon carried on with his job in Transport. The wintry weather which had greeted him on his return to France gave way within a week to spring. Sitting in the sunshine reading Shelley in small doses from Robert Bridges' anthology, *The Spirit of Man*, he felt hope revive in him.[102] In spite of the ceaseless gunfire and the exhausting daily journey to the trenches he was happy. David Thomas had welcomed him back warmly and he had written a poem attempting to capture his friend's youthful appeal:

> *A Subaltern*
> He turned to me with his kind, sleepy gaze
> And fresh face slowly brightening to the grin
> That sets my memory back to summer days,
> With twenty runs to make, and last man in.
> He told me he'd been having a bloody time
> In trenches, crouching for the crumps to burst,
> While squeaking rats scampered across the slime
> And the grey palsied weather did its worst.
> But as he stamped and shivered in the rain,
> My stale philosophies had served him well;
> Dreaming about his girl had sent his brain
> Blanker than ever – she'd no place in Hell ...
> 'Good God!' he laughed, and slowly filled his pipe,
> Wondering 'why he always talks such tripe.'[103]

Not one of Sassoon's most successful poems, this sonnet fails fully to capitalize on its Shakespearean form; its three quatrains lead to no particular conclusion in the final rhyming couplet. Thomas, with his 'kind ... fresh face slowly brightening to [a] grin', 'his pipe', his gratefulness and modesty, is idealized beyond credibility. The description of the trenches, refracted through Thomas's eyes, is far less powerful than in 'The Redeemer' or 'In the Pink', and the use of direct speech at the end is rather clumsy.

The piece does, however, convey the type of person Thomas was, through echoes of the language he might have used, that of a typical ex-public-schoolboy; even his swearing is genteel. It also helps the reader to understand his appeal for Sassoon, who clearly associated him, in a phrase taken straight from Newbolt's 'Vitaï Lampada', with golden summer days of cricket and adored his slight bashfulness and near inarticulateness.

'A Subaltern' was written about 8 March, three days after Sassoon had returned from leave. Ten days later Thomas was dead. Sassoon had unwittingly written his epitaph. In his attempt to explain the circumstances of this painful loss in *Memoirs of a Fox-Hunting Man*, Sassoon appears to blame Stockwell to some extent. With his 'new broom' energy and exacting standards, the Colonel had insisted that the Battalion attempt to bring its sector of the English Front Line up to German standards. His first report had read: 'Wire rotten; parapet everywhere bad and nowhere bullet-proof'.[104] He was particularly concerned about the barbed-wire, which he told Greaves was not strong enough to stop a wheelbarrow. So he ordered the whole of their Front Line to be re-wired. This meant extra work for the already exhausted men, who had to go out nightly on wiring-parties in addition to their other duties. On the evening of 18 March Thomas had taken his turn, been wounded in the throat by a stray bullet and died a few hours later. Robert Graves, who was back with 'A' Company after eight weeks at Base Camp, was in the trenches that night, busily sandbagging a section of the Front Line. When news of Thomas's wound reached him, it was reassuring, since Thomas was reported able to walk to the dressing-station. The Battalion doctor, Kelsey Fry, a throat specialist in civilian life, assured Thomas that he would be all right, as long as he lay still for a while. In defiance of his orders Thomas raised his head to take a letter from his pocket for his girl-friend and died instantly. To Sassoon and Graves, both deeply suspicious of women at the time, this must have seemed the final irony.

It was not the only irony in the case. Sassoon, whose strongest motive for wanting to be in the trenches had been to protect his 'little Tommy',[105] was due to return there only two days after his death. Did he ask himself whether he might not have averted that death if he had been present? The recent advent of spring, with its invigorating promise of renewed life, must also have seemed to him a mockery. And, although his recent poems had suggested that Thomas needed him more than his girlfriend, at least in France, in reality it was she who had prevailed. It was his concern for her which, according to Graves, had killed him.

Without exaggeration, Sassoon found the loss almost unbearable. While his brother Hamo had died in a faraway place during Sassoon's mood of greatest heroic idealism, he had seen Thomas only the day before his death. Notebook in hand, he had been reading Sassoon's last poem, presumably the one written about himself. As Sassoon watched the sack containing his friend's body being lowered into the ground, he felt that he 'knew Death' for the first time.[106] His initial reaction was extreme grief, which he vented in a little wood alone. His second was a longing for 'the bodily presence that was so fair'.[107] His third, which was to prove transitory, was acceptance in a mood of exalted self-sacrifice:

Grief can be beautiful, when we find something worthy to be mourned [he

239

wrote in his diary for 9 March]. To-day I knew what it means to find the soul
washed pure with tears, and the load of death was lifted from my heart. So
I wrote his name in chalk on the beech-tree stem, and left a rough garland
of ivy there, and a yellow primrose for his yellow hair and kind grey eyes,
my dear, my dear ... So Tommy left us, a gentle soldier, perfect and without
stain. And so he will always remain in my heart, fresh and happy and
brave.[108]

It was in this mood that he wrote a quatrain to his departed love two days
after his death, lines which emphasize how much he missed Thomas's
actual physical presence:

> For you were glad, and kind, and brave;
> With hands that clasped me, young and warm;
> But I have seen a soldier's grave,
> And I have seen your shrouded form.[109]

Just over a fortnight later Sassoon was again attempting to express his
horror and grief in 'Memory', a poem which was never published. Its last
stanza returns obsessively to Thomas's spilled blood, an image suggesting
Christlike sacrifice, and gives the first hint that such memories would
eventually create in Sassoon a desire for revenge:

> I thought of him, and knew that he was dead;
> I thought of his dark hour, and laughter killed,
> And the shroud hiding his dear, happy head –
> And blood that heedless enemies have spilled –
> *His* blood: I thought of rivers flowing red,
> And crimson hands that laid him in his bed.[110]

With a swing back to a more resigned mood Sassoon then wrote 'The
Last Meeting', a semi-mystical poem in which he attempts to accept death
as a transformation rather than an end. Based on his efforts to recall
Thomas's presence a month after his death, it describes Sassoon's journey
to another wood in search of his friend. Failing to find him in an empty,
half-built house there, he turns back to Nature:

> Ah! but there was no need to call his name.
> He was beside me now, as swift as light.
> I knew him crushed to earth in scentless flowers,
> And lifted in the rapture of dark pines.
> 'For now,' he said, 'my spirit has more eyes
> Than heaven has stars; and they are lit by love.
> My body is the magic of the world,
> And dawn and sunset flame with my spilt blood.
> My breath is the great wind, and I am filled
> With molten power and surge of the bright waves
> That chant my doom along the ocean's edge.'
>
> (*CP*, p. 38)

The poem continues in this mystical vein for another thirty-nine lines, when the narrator, won at last to acceptance of irrevocable loss, concludes:

> And, as it was in life, his name shall be
> Wonder awaking in a summer dawn,
> And youth that, dying, touched my lips to song.
>
> (*CP*, p. 40)

It is interesting to note that, in an earlier, franker version of the poem which was subsequently censored, possibly by the more worldly Ross or Marsh, Sassoon referred to Thomas 'wait[ing] to feel my fingers touch his face' and, even more specifically, finished his poem with a direct reference to their stay together in the same Cambridge room with the name of the previous owner, Paradise, on the door – 'And lips that touched me once in Paradise'. This emphasis on the physical was completely omitted in the final version.[111]

Whichever way the last line reads, Thomas had indeed touched Sassoon's lips to song, but neither here nor in the last poem he wrote about him, 'A Letter Home', does that song rise above the tired, inherited language of his Romantic and Nineties models.[112] Fortunately for poetry it was not a mood which would last. The reaction, when it came, was violent and stimulated Sassoon to write some of his best poems of the War.

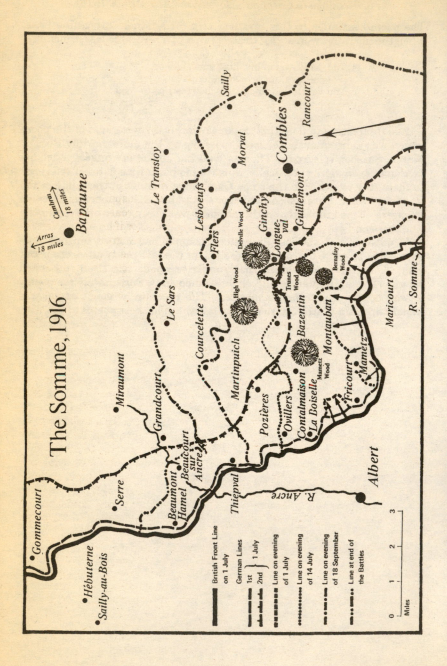

The Somme, 1916

Gommecourt

Hébuterne
Sailly-au-Bois

Serre

Miraumont

Grandcourt

Beaumont
Hamel   Beaucourt
sur
Ancre

Thiepval

R. Ancre

Albert

Pozières

Ovillers

Contalmaison
La Boiselle

Martinpuich

Courcelette

Le Sars

Le Transloy

Grandcourt

Bapaume

Arras
18 miles

Cambrai
18 miles

Flers

Lesbœufs

Morval

Sailly

Rancourt

Combles

Guillemont

Ginchy
Longue-
val

Delville Wood

High Wood

Trones Wood

Bernafay
Wood

Bazentin

Montauban

Mametz
Wood

Fricourt

Mametz

Maricourt

R. Somme

N

British Front Line
on 1 July

German Lines
1st } 1 July
2nd

Line on evening
of 1 July

Line on evening
of 14 July

Line on evening
of 18 September

Line at end of
the Battles

Miles
0   1   2   3

10

'At the Edge of the World'
(March-July 1916)

During the four months which followed David Thomas's death in March 1916, Sassoon's mood fluctuated wildly. His initial despair and resignation was followed closely by anger, an anger which increased his recklessness and made many people, including himself, wonder if he was trying to get killed.[1] As the reality of his brother Hamo's loss grew on him and first-hand experience of the trenches brought home the random destructiveness of War, his hatred of the Germans was re-directed towards those in authority on his own side, the politicians, army staff and 'yellow-press' journalists he began to hold responsible for the continuation of the conflict. At the same time, and alternating curiously with such bitterness, he still had moods of almost mystical exaltation in which he longed to sacrifice himself for his country. Paradoxically, but not surprisingly, the more he wanted to die, the sweeter life seemed to him and this produced other, more familiar moods of joy in nature.

With the romantic's intense response to extremes of feeling Sassoon's impulse was to record these wild mood-swings in words, as the prose and poetry of this period demonstrates. The poetry faithfully reflects in changing modes his turbulent feelings, for which it also provides a safety-valve. At times, indeed, he finds poetry the only thing that gives his life meaning at the Front. Recognizing the very different nature of some of his poems, he separates the lyrics off into another of his privately printed booklets and sends the satires from early April onwards to one of the most outspoken anti-war reviews of the day, the *Cambridge Magazine*. His prose, too, is equally varied as he describes now some idyllic pastoral landscape in Picardy, now the grotesque aftermath of battle, or the death of a close friend.

The backdrop to the period is the Battle of the Somme, with its long build-up as the Allies prepare to mount their most massive attack so far, and the opening of the battle itself. Always in the picture, though never at the centre as he would have wished, Sassoon witnesses unforgettable scenes of carnage as the 1st Royal Welch Infantry joins in the long drawn out battle of Mametz Wood.

In March 1916, however, all that lay ahead and the Allies were still preparing for the Somme. For Sassoon the month was marked not only by the death of David Thomas, but also by his first real experience of the trenches. Officially transferred back from Transport to his platoon on 20 March, a change he welcomed, it was not until 26 March that he set out on his first tour of them. He spent his first night there engaged in nothing more dramatic than helping pile sandbags on the crumbling parapet, but the place reminded him forcibly of Thomas, who had been fatally wounded in those same trenches only eight nights earlier. By an odd coincidence he was also reminded of Hamo's death on his second day there. Attracted no doubt by his striking surname, a friend of his brother from Cambridge, a Royal Engineer officer named Sisson, came into his gloomy steel dug-out to talk to him about Hamo, in particular his intensely humorous way of looking at things. (His reminiscences made Hamo seem 'much more real' than he had been since his death, Sassoon told Dent.)[2] It was as if this vivid reminder of Hamo so soon after the loss of Thomas finally brought home to him the reality of his brother's death and, with it, a belated desire for revenge. As soon as he has time to think clearly, on the first day of his rest period at Morlancourt, he tells his diary:

> I used to say I couldn't kill anyone in this war; but since they shot Tommy I would gladly stick a bayonet into a German by daylight. Someone told me a year ago that love, sorrow and hate were things I had never known (things which every poet *should* know!). Now I've known love for Bobbie and Tommy, and grief for Hamo and Tommy, and hate has come also, and the lust to kill.[3]

Longing for 'Peace', at this time he writes a poem of that name in which the middle stanza nevertheless reads:

> In my heart there's cruel war that must be waged
> In darkness vile with moans and bleeding bodies maimed;
> A gnawing hunger drives me, wild to be assuaged,
> And bitter lust chuckles within me unashamed.[4]

Two days later, still resting at Morlancourt, and now in billets with an officer called Anscombe, Sassoon asks himself what all 'this rancour' is about. He realizes that it may simply be the effects of a disturbed liver, but he can hardly wait to get out to the Front Line again. Not content to sit tamely in the trench hoping to avoid death, he prefers the excitement and challenge of night raids in No Man's Land. Stockwell has made it clear that he wants a prisoner, but Sassoon knows very well that this is not the reason he goes looking for Germans, bludgeon in hand. In an uncharacteristically violent outburst he confesses:

> I want to smash someone's skull; I want to have a scrap and get out of the war for a bit or for ever. Sitting in a trench waiting for a rifle grenade isn't

fighting: war is clambering out of the top trench at 3 o'clock in the morning with a lot of rum-drugged soldiers who don't know where they're going – half of them to be blasted with machine-guns at point-blank range – trying to get over the wire which our artillery have failed to destroy. I can't get my own back for Hamo and Tommy that way. While I am really angry with the enemy, as I am lately, I must work it off, as these things don't last long with me as a rule. If I get shot it will be rotten for some people at home, but I am bound to get it in the neck sometime, so why not make a creditable show, and let people see that poets can fight as well as anybody else? And death is the best adventure of all ...[5]

Out of such mixed motives of revenge, boredom, recklessness, pride in his calling and what Virginia Woolf has described as the need for 'the danger emotion',[6] emerged 'Mad Jack', a nickname given him by his companions for his complete fearlessness in the Front Line. Sassoon confessed to Dent that he 'thoroughly enjoyed' his first tour of the trenches, particularly when he bombed a German working party out of a freshly made mine crater.[7] His modest claim, that he 'got rather famous for a day or two', probably conceals the origin of the 'Mad Jack' legend. He certainly relished the need to take risks in what one sergeant described graphically as 'a pretty 'ot shop'. Since he was quite sure that he would be killed, as he told Dent in a second letter from this period, he made no effort to protect himself and went out on raiding parties whenever possible, a military equivalent of Russian roulette.

Crawling up to the German trenches, revolver in one hand, knob-kerrie in the other and three hand-grenades in each pocket, was an exhilarating experience. It reminded him of the start of a steeple-chase and he was just as determined to win as when he raced. Insisting that there was nothing brave about it, he assured Dent that 'it's only lack of control'. Added to that was his fascination with the nightmare landscape of No Man's Land, which he visited nightly with a fellow daredevil, Corporal O'Brien, a man for whom he was later to risk his life.[8] Together they would lie flat as the snipers shot at them, watching the white rocket-lights going up and laughing with sheer delight when the danger was over. Another companion on these raids was Private Morgan. As a fellow-member of C Company, V. King, wrote to Sassoon after the War: 'You were always doing something out in No Man's Land with Pte. Morgan. You had our Captain worried when you were out.'[9]

Whilst Sassoon took his own courage for granted, he admired O'Brien and Morgan for theirs. And they were not alone in this. For one of the many results of this first tour of trenches was the increased admiration it brought for his platoon. In elevated but heartfelt cadences he exclaims: 'Their temper is proven, the fibre of their worth is tested and revealed; these men from Welsh farms and Midland cities, from factory and shop and mine, who can ever give them their meed of praise for the patience and tender jollity which seldom forsake them?'[10]

Under the influence of such extreme feelings, Sassoon's prose takes wing. His descriptions of the trenches at this time, at once concrete and poetic, are among his finest writings. Sights, sounds and emotions are all vividly evoked:

> As I sit in the sun in a nook among the sandbags and chalky debris, with shells flying overhead in the blue air, a lark sings high up, and a little weasel comes and runs past me within a foot of my outstretched feet, looking at me with tiny bright eyes. Bullets sing and whistle and hum; so do bits of shell; rifles crack; some small guns and trench-mortars pop and thud; big shells burst with a massive explosion, and the voluminous echoes roll along the valleys, to fade nobly and without haste or consternation.
>
> Bullets are deft and flick your life out with a quick smack. Shells rend and bury, and vibrate and scatter, hurling fragments and lumps and jagged splinters at you; they lift you off your legs and leave you huddled and bleeding and torn and scorched with a blast straight from the pit. Heaven is furious with the smoke and flare and portent of shells, but bullets are a swarm of whizzing hornets, mad, winged and relentless, undeviating in their malicious onset.
>
> The big guns roar their challenge and defiance; but the machine-guns rattle with intermittent bursts of mirthless laughter.
>
> There are still pools in the craters; they reflect the stars like any lovely water, but nothing grows near them; snags of iron jut from their banks, tin cans and coils of wire, and other trench-refuse. If you search carefully, you may find a skull, eyeless, grotesquely matted with what was once hair; eyes once looked from those detestable holes, they made the fabric of a passionate life, they appealed for justice, they were lit with triumph, and beautiful with pity.[11]

Living as he was at the highest pitch of emotion, Sassoon believed that he was at last learning to observe things with more receptiveness and accuracy than he had in his undisciplined past. His poetry bears this out. With first-hand experience of the Front Line, it gains in immediacy and, more gradually, in technical skill. His first trench poem, 'The Redeemer', started four months earlier, is now revised. Writing to Eddie Marsh on 16 March 1916 he encloses the amended version but adds that he wants to change the last two lines to provide a more shocking and less ambiguous conclusion.[12] He also writes three new poems, of which 'Golgotha' is almost certainly the first.

> Through darkness curves a spume of falling flares
> That flood the field with shallow, blanching light.
>   The huddled sentry stares
>   On gloom at war with white,
>   And white receding slow, submerged in gloom.
>   Guns into mimic thunder burst and boom,
>   And mirthless laughter rakes the whistling night.
> The sentry keeps his watch where no one stirs
> But the brown rats, the nimble scavengers.[13]

(CP, p. 14-15)

Dated simply 'March 1916' and placed by Sir Rupert Hart-Davis before 'A Subaltern' in *The War Poems*, 'Golgotha' can nevertheless be traced to the end rather than the beginning or middle of the month, since the phrase 'And mirthless laughter rakes the whistling night' echoes the diary entry for 30 March ('machine guns rattle with intermittent bursts of mirthless laughter').[14] The phrase 'mirthless laughter' and all that it implies about the indifference of the universe to man's plight may be the first sign of Hardy's influence, which Sassoon himself acknowledged in his War poetry.

On the surface a straightforward description of one sentry's impression of the trenches, 'Golgotha' manages to convey a sense of menace and nightmare, of 'gloom at war with white' in which the white, symbolic of goodness and hope, though at the same time a literal reference to the bleached sandbags, is 'submerged in gloom'. The very title 'Golgotha', with its reference to the extreme agony of the Crucifixion, means 'skull' in Aramaic and takes the reader back again to the diary entry for 30 March: 'If you search carefully you may find a skull'.[15] Ending as it does with scavenging rats, there is no reprieve from the relentless horror of the scene. Even the verse form is disturbing, shifting uneasily from a five-beat to a three-beat line and back again, to reflect the instability of the situation. The final feminine ending takes away any sense of certainty or closure and is in direct contrast with the insistent alliteration of 'falling flares / That flood the field' or the guns that 'burst and boom'. The diction, while simple, is carefully chosen and the personification of the machine guns' 'mirthless laughter', with the added metaphor of raking the night, sinister and highly effective.

Where 'Golgotha' is concentrated, 'A Working Party', also written during Sassoon's first tour of the trenches, is discursive. And 'Golgotha's' tight rhyme-scheme is replaced by less demanding blank verse. A curious piece, which seems to fall naturally into two halves, it would almost certainly have been improved by such a division. As it is, the last four stanzas, which start with a near repetition of the first line, read almost as a self-contained poem. They continue Sassoon's practice of 'In the Pink' by giving a deft thumbnail sketch, of 'a young man with a meagre wife / And two small children in a Midland town.' Whilst remaining impersonal – no names are given – it creates a poignant picture of all the young men with their undernourished wives and children ('pale' rather than 'small' in the original), who have died and will die senselessly and needlessly in the War, simply doing their duty. The man's thoughts are sketched in by way of vivid detail of trench life (which Sassoon had now experienced for himself):

> He thought how slow time went, stamping his feet
> And blowing on his fingers, pinched with cold.
> He thought of getting home by half-past-twelve,
> And tot of rum to send him warm to sleep

In draughty dug-out frowsty* with the fumes
Of coke, and full of snoring weary men.

(CP, p. 20)

The end, though sudden, is prepared for in the fourth stanza ('Now he will never walk that road again'):

> He pushed another bag along the top,
> Craning his body outward; then a flare
> Gave one white glimpse of No Man's Land and wire;
> And as he dropped his head the instant split
> His startled life with lead, and all went out.

The transferred epithet 'startled' and the staccato alliteration of 't's mimicking the gun which is responsible are particularly effective in the last two lines of this extract. In fact the moment Sassoon moves from the detailed narrative description of the man stumbling up the trench to the mini-drama of his death, the poem comes to life, though the first three stanzas are nevertheless important as one of the earliest examples of realistic description of trench conditions. The whole piece was rigorously revised in its final version, the most significant change being the omission of a last stanza which in the original version diffused the tension with its prolix and redundant 'message'.[16]

Sassoon wrote 'The Working Party', and probably 'Golgotha' too, while he was actually carrying out his first tour of the trenches. He was undoubtedly encouraged to write in such a way by having read Graves's assertively realistic poems the previous November. When it came to the actual composition, however, he had to do without Graves's advice, since his friend had left for England just before the tour started. Though unwilling to forfeit Graves's company, Sassoon had cheered him on his way, generously writing a note to Nellie Gosse on 22 March asking her to invite Graves to tea.[17] With his protective attitude towards the younger man, which was not without a hint of patronage at the time, he no doubt thought it would help Graves's literary career if he met Gosse. He could not have anticipated that, just over ten years later, he would have reason to regret the introduction. For the moment it seemed a useful move and one which Graves evidently welcomed.

Once in England Graves stayed on for an operation to reset his broken nose, which was difficult to breathe through and made wearing the primitive gas-masks of that era impossible. He was not, therefore, to share Sassoon's next two tours of the trenches which took place in April. 'I am missing Robert very much', Sassoon wrote to their mutual friend Marsh on 19 April: 'there is no-one else to fill the gap'.[18] (His old friend Gordon Harbord had written to him from a few miles north of the 1st Royal Welch

---

* 'stuffy' in the original

Fusiliers' sector, hoping that they could meet, but this had proved impossible.)[19] His wish to protect Graves triumphs, however, and he continues: 'But I am equally delighted to think that he's safely out of it all for a bit ... It gives me enormous satisfaction to think of him enjoying things, after the rotten times he has had out here'.

While Graves made full use of his rest, Sassoon continued to go in and out of the Front Line. By 23 April, Easter Sunday, he had done eighteen days' trench duty altogether and was feeling the strain. He became increasingly sure he would be killed, and for once Nature seemed unable to cheer him up. Though the sun shone frequently, since the death of Thomas most days appeared to him dark and unhappy. Even writing poetry became an enormous effort and of the few short pieces he produced only one seemed worthy of publication, 'Stand-To: Good Friday Morning'.[20] Written, in fact, the day after Good Friday, this poem successfully conveys his frustration and depression in a colloquial style which contrasts sharply with his lyrics of the period:

> I'd been on duty from two till four.
> I went and stood at the dug-out door.
> Down in the frowst I heard them snore.
> 'Stand-to!' Somebody grunted and swore.
>> Dawn was misty; the skies were still;
>> Larks were singing, discordant, shrill;
>> *They* seemed happy; but *I* felt ill.
> Deep in water I splashed my way
> Up the trench to our bogged front line.
> Rain had fallen the whole damned night.
> O Jesus, send me a wound today,
> And I'll believe in Your bread and wine,
> And get my bloody old sins washed white!
>
> (*CP*, p. 24)

Sassoon uses his own experience directly here: he had indeed been 'on duty from 2 till 4' on Good Friday, 21 April, and had gone to rouse his platoon for 'stand-to', the early morning ritual of standing with weapons in readiness for action. (There was another 'stand-to' at dusk.) Out of this routine event he versified, as he himself noted, 'a jaunty scrap of doggerel' which anticipated his later successes in condensed satire.[21] What surprised him, as much as it shocked many of his readers, was his talent for satirical epigram. Nothing in his previous work had led him to predict such a turn and he could think of no precedents for it, though he was able to trace the influence of Hardy's *Satires of Circumstance* in some of his longer War poems.

The laconic tone of the piece, however, is all Sassoon's own and deliberately introduced in conjunction with the sacredness of the day, Good Friday, and the event it marks, the Crucifixion, in order to shock by its irreverence. It is produced partly through the abrupt, matter of fact statements, contained in all but one case in short, end-stopped lines, and partly through the echoes of soldiers' blasphemous language. In view of the day, the reader is led to reflect on the ironic comparison and contrast between Christ hanging on the cross to save mankind through His literally 'bloody' wounds and the soldier-narrator demanding a wound, or 'Blighty one', before he will believe in Christ and His message. As Michael Thorpe points out, this is 'calculated to affront one of the most dearly cherished convictions at home – that the War was a contest sanctioned by Heaven and that the British were God's favourite team'.[22] The blasphemy is a deliberate attempt to shock the reader into making the connection between the apparently pointless blood and wounds of the front line and the claims made for Christ's sufferings. And by extension, the soldier who suffers such wounds is equated with Christ as in 'The Redeemer', though it is an ironic comparison.

In a truncated sonnet which mirrors the abruptness of the language the poet sets the scene, drawing a contrast between the apparently happy larks and the narrator, as well as between the joyful, though to the narrator discordant, birdsong and the snoring, grunts and curses of the exhausted men, then leads the reader in the sestet to the narrator's defiant and outrageous plea.

Part of the poem's effect depends on the deliberate ordinariness of the diction, which avoids 'poetic' or archaic words. When an unusual words is introduced, such as 'frowst' in line 3, it is in an attempt realistically to convey the sordidness of the trenches. When 'Stand-to' was reprinted in *The Maoriland Worker* in 1921, it caused the editor to be prosecuted for publishing a blasphemous libel, though he was subsequently acquitted.[23] Sassoon maintained that it summarized the feelings of thousands of other platoon officers besides himself and was one of his most effective war poems.

The day after 'Stand-to' was written, Sassoon was on a bus speeding away from the War-zone. Possibly because of his exploits in No Man's Land, he had been one of two officers chosen from his battalion to join subalterns from other units for a month's course at the Fourth Army School. 'Lucky Kangaroo – to be hopping away for a holiday!' he reports his company commander as saying.[24] Situated at Flixécourt, halfway between Amiens and Abbeville and thirty miles from the Fricourt trenches, the Fourth Army School was a complete, if temporary, escape from the Front Line. As Sassoon rolled along through the French countryside on a fine Easter Sunday, he too could hardly believe his luck:

> Coming away from it all [he wrote in his diary for 23 April 1916] – to find the world outside really acknowledging the arrival of spring – oh it was a blessed thing – the journey on a sunny morning, pleasantly blown by a north-west wind … the landscape looking its best – all the clean colours of late April –

the renewal of green grass and young leaves – and fruit-trees in blossom – and to see a civilian population well away from the danger-zone going to church on Easter morning – soldiers contented and at rest – it was like coming back to life, warm and secure – it was to feel how much there is to regain. Children in the streets of towns and villages – I saw a tiny one fall, to be gathered up and dusted, soothed, comforted – one forgets 'little things' like those up in the places where men are killing one another with the best weapons that skill can handle.[25]

Flixécourt also appeared to be putting itself out to 'flatter and soothe' him. With its jumble of whitewashed houses, glossy chestnut trees and burgeoning apple-blossom it seemed homely and welcoming, as did its inhabitants. Above all it was peaceful. Several large châteaux and quaint farms added charm to the picture, which promised at every point rest and renewal. Even his billet, a small clean room with tiled floor and shuttered windows in one of the cottages, appeared part of the conspiracy to help him forget War.

Space to spread out his belongings and a table for his books seemed luxuries after the cramped squalor of the trenches. Sassoon viewed his reading-matter with pleasurable anticipation – Lamb's *Essays*, Surtees' *Mr Sponge's Sporting Tour* and Hardy's *Far From the Madding Crowd* in particular. For there would be that further indulgence denied him in the trenches, time to read, and he intended to reinforce the illusion of escape by reading only books that seemed to him quintessentially English. In the unlikely event that books palled, there was the nearby Mess shared by fourteen other officers, all of them pleasant. From the Commandant of the School downwards, everyone seemed determined to be as friendly as possible. The head of Sassoon's 'class' – the 300 or so officers were divided into groups of twenty-eight – was particularly likeable. It reminded Sassoon of starting at Marlborough, only without the new boy's dread of doing the wrong thing and being punished.

There were, of course, duties to be attended to at Flixécourt, but to Sassoon these also seemed agreeable, in spite of their exacting nature. Every day there was practical training in some aspect of Warfare, followed at 5.30 by lectures on various subjects. Since the army school instructors were as obsessed with Open Warfare as Colonel Minshull Ford had been, both the lectures and the practical exercises often appeared irrelevant. While Regular Army Officers, still dogged by their peace-time training, emphasized the need to think in terms of 'mobility', Sassoon would have preferred to be given a few practical hints on how to patrol the God-forsaken mine craters in the Fricourt Sector. When a famous big-game hunter gave enthusiastic lessons in the art of sniping, Sassoon could not help thinking that he would have been better employed using his skill actually to shoot the enemy, perhaps because he himself felt that he was 'no good' with a rifle.[26] It was all very well being an expert on telescopic sights, but those were a luxury seldom enjoyed in the trenches.

One lecture Sassoon could not dismiss as impracticable affected him deeply. Given by a massive Highland Scot, Major Campbell, who would afterwards be awarded a D.S.O. for his murderous eloquence, it centred simply on a few lines from the *Manual of Bayonet Training*. Impressed by the lively performance of the genial, sandy-haired major and his tall, sinewy assistant, who demonstrated each move of the homicidal drill with machine-like efficiency, Sassoon was nevertheless profoundly disturbed by this public acknowledgement of the soldier's one aim – to kill. Though he had admitted to himself the murderous impulses and intentions induced in him by the deaths of Hamo and Tommy, the major's cold, logical exposition of the killing process seems to have greatly shocked him. The final words of the lecture: 'Kill them! Kill them! There's only one good Boche, and that's a dead one!' rang in his ears as he walked up a nearby hill to a little wood of hazel and beech trees. But the peace of the spring-time scenery failed to eradicate the insistent voice: 'The bayonet and the bullet are brother and sister'. 'If you don't kill him, he'll kill you'. 'Stick him between the eyes, in the throat, in the chest, or round the thighs'. And so on.

In his diary entry written shortly after the event, Sassoon makes it clear that he was repelled by the public gloating in violence he had just witnessed:

> I told the trees what I had been hearing; but they hate steel, because axes and bayonets are the same to them. They are dressed in their fresh green, every branch showing through the mist of leaves, and the straight stems most lovely against the white and orange sky beyond. And a blackbird's song cries aloud that April cannot understand what war means.[27]

The juxtaposition of nature's beauty and peace with the brutality of the major's message is intentionally significant. A later poem written in January 1919 about his brother's sword, which Theresa had hung on the wall to commemorate her son, suggests that Sassoon shared the same loathing for steel:

> ... The sword is her idea of glory,
> Who, hating cruel things, can feel
> A secret passion for cold steel.
> (Perhaps that's why she voted Tory).
>
> I too am proud of my slain brother.
> But, when I see that murderous blade
> Kept bright for honour, I'm afraid
> That Wilson's Points have failed, – with mother.

To argue, as Robert Graves does, that the poem which emerged from Major Campbell's talk was originally meant to be taken at its face value as a celebration of violence, and only later offered as satire, is to ignore both Sassoon's contemporary and later descriptions of his reaction.[28] To state, as Adrian Caesar does, that 'The Kiss' 'articulates a sadistic wish, in overtly sexual language' and 'suggests both a self-hating fear of male sexuality and a fear and hatred of women' is to carry psychoanalysis too far, as well as to ignore Sassoon's increasingly satiric impulse at the time.[29] The poem is meant to shock the reader into a rejection of the major's murderous message by its apparently enthusiastic embracing of it:

> To these I turn, in these I trust –
> Brother Lead and Sister Steel.
> To his blind power I make appeal,
> I guard her beauty clean from rust.
>
> He spins and burns and loves the air,
> And splits a skull to win my praise;
> But up the nobly marching days
> She glitters naked, cold and fair.
>
> Sweet Sister, grant your soldier this:
> That in good fury he may feel
> The body where he sets his heel
> Quail from your downward darting kiss.
>
> (*CP*, pp. 15-16)

Read as satire the poem fits convincingly into Sassoon's development in that genre; taken seriously, as a blood-thirsty celebration of killing, it shows a puzzling inconsistency with both his own reaction and the poems he was writing at the time. As a satire it achieves its aims, but as a straight poem it seems little more than clever doggerel organized around the major's banal 'brother/sister' metaphor. Sassoon himself was quite clear as to his intention in writing the poem and continued to be irritated by its misinterpretation. As late as 1965 he wrote to the critic Michael Thorpe:

> I am tired of telling people that The Kiss was intended as a satire on bayonet fighting, which I loathed – Graves's statement is one of his many inaccuracies. Campbell's lecture was an absolute horror. Surely I indicated in The Infantry Officer that I was shocked by it. Can you do *something* to correct this?[30]

Four days after 'The Kiss' was written, Sassoon's first trench poem, 'The Redeemer', was published in its revised form in the *Cambridge Magazine*. It was the beginning of an important partnership that would last beyond the end of the War. Sassoon had sent the poem to Dent on 11 March, together with 'The Subaltern', wondering if he would 'like my Christ poem' and it is quite clear that Dent did. On 5 April Sassoon gave him permission to submit it to the *Cambridge Magazine*, with which Dent was intimately connected. Supported by a group of Cambridge scholars, most of whom were close friends of Dent, in particular the University Librarian Theo Bartholomew and Fellow of King's College, Goldsworthy Lowes Dickinson, this paper was the obvious choice. One of the few anti-war journals of the day, it welcomed poems which would certainly have been rejected by its more conservative counterparts, such as the *Westminster Gazette*.

Edited by the originator of Basic English, C.K. Ogden, it was uncompromisingly pacifist, so much so that its offices were more than once attacked by outraged patriots during the War.[31] Sassoon, who had already been introduced to Bartholomew and, probably, Lowes Dickinson by Dent, was to have a steady correspondence with its editor, Ogden, until after the War had ended and to become familiar with many of his other contributors, including Edmund Blunden, Walter de la Mare, John Drinkwater, John Masefield and Edith Sitwell. The *Cambridge Magazine*'s publication of 'The Redeemer' on 29 April 1916 marked the beginning of his public recognition as a poet determined not to glorify War. The following month his poem was issued as number two in a series of seven *Cambridge Magazine* 'reprints', supervized by Bartholomew, priced at twopence each and sold by Heffers of Cambridge. Sassoon did not say whether he was pleased to have his talents thus finally given public recognition in his own University town.

By the time 'The Redeemer' appeared, however, Sassoon was no longer in the same mood as the one which had produced it. Once away from the trenches, it was hard to sustain the feelings of bitterness and anger which came naturally there, perhaps as a defence mechanism. Soothed by the absence of palpable suffering and horror, his impulses turn once more towards lyric poetry, his more habitual means of expression. Something of the early patriotism and heroic idealism creeps back into his poetry in the peaceful, almost idyllic surroundings of Flixécourt. Now it seems to him, in 'France', that:

> ... they are fortunate, who fight
> For gleaming landscapes swept and shafted
> And crowned by cloud pavilions white;
> Hearing such harmonies as might
> Only from Heaven be downward wafted –
> Voices of victory and delight.
>
> (*CP*, pp. 12-13)

As he wrote enthusiastically to Dent a week after his arrival: 'The 4th Army School is a blessed loaf. And I get the blessed evenings to myself and great waves of lyrical delight sweep along the pounding shores of my beautiful bright brain. No one can possibly kill me until May 21st'.[32] Whilst at the Front it had seemed to him irrelevant whether he had his poetry published or not, though he had been enthusiastic when Marsh suggested that Harold Monro should produce a slim volume of thirty-two pages for the Poetry Bookshop. In the midst of such 'distracted times' he had resolved, however, not to have his work produced privately any more, perhaps because it seemed frivolous in such a context. But once settled at Flixécourt with what he calls 'glad things' pouring out of him, he asks Dent to have his poems typed because he plans to produce another of his privately printed books.[33]

Even David Thomas's death can be accepted, almost joyfully, in the little copse 'of hazel twigs / With misty raiment of awakening green', where Sassoon goes 'to find the face of him that I have lost'.[34] It is a temporary reprieve but one which lasts until the Battle of the Somme, over a month later, brings him sharply back to the reality of War, and to satire. Meantime, he allows himself to dream, knowing it to be a dream, as he admits to Graves, his friend with the 'crooked smile and baffling laughter', in a verse letter written from Flixécourt:

> Robert, there's a war in France;
> Everywhere men bang and blunder,
> Sweat and swear and worship Chance,
> Creep and blink through cannon thunder.
> Rifles crack and bullets flick,
> Sing and hum like hornet-swarms.
> Bones are smashed and buried quick.
>> Yet, through stunning battle storms,
>> All the while I watch the spark
>> Lit to guide me; for I know
>> Dreams will triumph, though the dark
>> Scowls above me where I go.
> You can hear me; you can mingle
> Radiant folly with my jingle.
> War's a joke for me and you
> While we know such dreams are true![35]
>
>> (*CP*, pp. 42-3)

Thomas's death, which he knows has affected Graves as deeply as himself, is now referred to in dreamy terms of the fairytales and legends so loved by Graves:

> You and I have walked together
> In the starving winter weather.
> We've been glad because we knew
> Time's too short and friends are few.
> We've been sad because we missed
> One whose yellow head was kissed
> By the gods, who thought about him
> Till they couldn't do without him.
> Now he's here again; I've seen
> Soldier David dressed in green,
> Standing in a wood that swings
> To the madrigal he sings.

He's come back, all mirth and glory,
Like the prince in fairy story.
Winter called him far away;
Blossoms bring him home with May.

(*CP*, pp. 41-2)

One reason for Sassoon's apparent acceptance of Tommy's death, apart from the soothing influence of springtime Flixécourt, may have been his meeting there with another young officer, Marcus Goodall. Though there is no suggestion that Goodall replaced either Tommy or Bobbie Hanmer in his affections, he was certainly attracted to him and made plans to travel with him, as with Graves, after the War.

Almost the same age as Graves (he had been born the month before Graves in 1895), Goodall had a stronger initial link with Sassoon: they had both been at Marlborough. (Goodall had joined in January 1909, the term after Charles Hamilton Sorley, whom he knew.) Sassoon, who continued to be rather shy, saw this as a great advantage. If there were any awkward pauses in their conversation, 'Marlborough talk bridg[ed] the gaps'.[36] Goodall had had a far more successful career at the school than Sassoon – he had been a Foundation Scholar, Junior Scholar and Prefect – but had not gone on to University when he left in July 1913, nine years after Sassoon. He had been working as a solicitor's pupil when War was declared and, like Sassoon, had joined up at once. By the time they met he was a Captain in the Yorkshire and Lancashire Regiment. (His father was a Canon at Rotherham in Yorkshire.) Sassoon described Goodall both in his diary and, by a neat pun on his name and nature, as 'Allgood' in *Infantry Officer*. Yet there is no real indication in either of the depth of his feeling for this quiet, scholarly youth who loved birds and history. It is only in Sassoon's franker letters to Dent and in his unpublished poetry that this comes through clearly. Writing to Dent on 6 May about his 'dear Marlburian', he includes an extract from one of two sonnets he has already written to his 'Marlborough Marcus':

... I looked at you
And caught your side-long glance, unboding, gay, –
Your whimsical fleet smile, and queer, pale blue
Eyes like the blown rifts of a rainy day.

This is undoubtedly a romantic poem and helps to explain Sassoon's extreme happiness at Flixécourt. It casts a new light on his comment in *Infantry Officer*, when he describes his memories of Flixécourt as haunting – 'almost as though I were remembering a time when I'd been in love'.[37] It was almost certainly a time when he *had* been in love but could not say so: his love was of the wrong sex.

Sassoon particularly enjoyed Goodall's response to the countryside and took two trips with him during their month together, one to Amiens, the other to Abbeville. In the midst of officers who struck him as mostly insensitive and unaware, it seemed miraculous to be sharing his love of nature with a kindred spirit. This comes through clearly in his description of the two of them travelling into Abbeville on a bus together and nudging each other, often simultaneously, if they saw something they wanted to share.[38]

As Sassoon prepared to leave Flixécourt the day after this excursion, 21 May, he felt that Goodall's was the only face out of hundreds that he would remember – 'his is a real personality which responds to mine. The others make military (and unmilitary) noises with their mouths; he talks, and answers with his eyes'.[39] In spite of the coming separation, and with no certainty of meeting again in a Wartime situation, he was happy, perhaps with the happiness new love brings:

> But let anyone who reads this [i.e. his diary entry for 20 May 1916] know that I was four weeks at Flixécourt, and four weeks happy and peaceful – and free, with my books and my work and the heaven of spring singing all around me over the whole country, and lighting the skies with magnificence.

When Sassoon arrived back at Morlancourt the contrast with Flixécourt could hardly have been greater. Preparations for the Somme summer offensive were building up and everywhere there was feverish activity. The Front to be attacked, from Maricourt to Serre, formed a great salient with Fricourt at the apex, and preparations in this sector were particularly busy. Between the rivers Somme and Ancre observation on the enemy Front Line was good, mainly because it generally lay above the British trenches, but practically nothing could be seen of its rear systems, the second of which was between 3,000 and 5,000 yards away on the summit of the high ground in front of the Fourth Army.

Since the coming fight would depend largely on a frontal assault by the infantry, massed artillery and huge stocks of shells were needed, as well as extra dugouts for shelter, medical aid and storage. After strengthening their own sector of the line, as Stockwell had demanded, men of the 1st RWF were involved, like many others, in the work this entailed. Vast stocks of ammunition and stores had to be accumulated within a convenient distance of the British Front, which meant laying many miles of new railway, as well as trench tramways.

All available roads were improved, others created and long causeways built over marshy valleys. Scores of miles of deep communication trenches had to be dug, as well as trenches for telephone wires, assembly and assault trenches and numerous gun emplacements and observation posts. Mining operations were crucial, to ensure that charges were laid at various points beneath the enemy's lines. Even something as apparently simple as water created a huge amount of work, since numerous wells and borings had to be sunk and over a hundred pumping stations installed, in order to supply even the basic needs of the thirteen British and five French Divisions and their horses destined for this area.

It was little wonder that, in the midst of such frantic preparations, Stockwell should have been incensed by a new and absurd demand from Staff Headquarters. Before leaving Morlancourt on 23 April Sassoon heard that Brigade had ordered Stockwell to organize a raid on the enemy Front Line, ostensibly to capture and examine a portion of enemy trench, take prisoners, bomb dugouts and kill some Germans. In reality everyone suspected that it was simply an expensive morale-boosting exercise, inspired by a recent and successful effort by some tough Canadian soldiers. Knowing the dangers and difficulties of the sector and unwilling to risk his men needlessly, Stockwell had not hesitated to give the 'brass-hats' at Brigade Headquarters his candid opinion, but to no avail. A month later the raid was imminent and was one of the main topics of conversation on Sassoon's return from Flixécourt.

Once back at the Front Sassoon had reverted to martial mood and was, therefore, extremely disappointed to hear that Stockwell had appointed Stansfield, not himself, to lead the raid. Whilst he recognized that the burly Canadian had more common sense, he nevertheless rightly believed himself to be the superior man when it came to crawling among shell-holes in No Man's Land. Stansfield's bulk and lack of experience in night patrols made him less suitable than the bolder and more agile Sassoon. Stansfield frankly admitted that he did not want to risk his life in such a foolhardy enterprise, whereas Sassoon was once more longing for the excitement and risk it would bring. This was probably the main reason Stockwell had not put him in charge of it.

In addition Sassoon wanted specifically to earn himself an M.C. (Only the Battalion doctor, Kelsey Fry, had so far won one.) Just as he had been determined to win steeplechases before the War, he now wanted a medal to prove himself the equal of his contemporaries. Significantly, he no longer actively wished to die, in fact he seems to have feared death on this occasion; but he was already bored by the monotonous drudgery of most trench activities and longing for adventure.

Still hoping that he might persuade Stockwell to change his mind, Sassoon carried on with his usual duties. On 23 May C Company was sent up to the reserve trench. Known dryly as '71.North' (most trenches had more fanciful names like 'Piccadilly' or 'Haymarket'), this was a relatively safe assortment of dug-outs and earth-covered shelters about a thousand yards from the Front Line. Hidden by sloping ground behind a steep bank, it seemed to Sassoon rather like a busy suburb, and life there was fairly relaxed in spite of occasional shells. But the road which passed it, once the way to Fricourt, now led only to the British Front Line, a constant reminder of the coming conflict. For three days he waited there, then on the evening of the 25 May prepared to join the raid.

10. 'At the Edge of the World' (March-July 1916)

Anticipating disaster, Sassoon writes a farewell letter to his mother, strips off his tunic, dons his leather waistcoat and old raincoat – it is raining hard – and with steel helmet on and nail-studded knob-kerrie in hand goes to find the raiding-party. Twenty-five blackened faces greet him, reminding him grotesquely in their burnt cork make-up of a negro minstrel band and hiding their nervousness with jokes and a little whiskey. Once at the Colonel's headquarters, 400 yards from the front line, Sassoon begs to be allowed to accompany the raiders. Stockwell's emphatic negative brooks no argument, however, and Sassoon finds himself with the less exciting job, or so he thinks, of 'counting the men in' when the raid is over. After being led up the support trench by Stockwell's second-in-command, Major Compton Smith, the four parties of five men and their 'evacuating party' with ladders and flashlamps prepare to cross the sixty yards to the German trench. Pitted with deep mine-craters, this is a precarious undertaking in the dark and Stansfield, helped by Sergeant Lyle and Sassoon's daredevil friend, Corporal O'Brien, has already been out to lay a guiding trail of lime across No Man's Land. Since Sassoon's only means of following events is by sound, he listens anxiously. He knows that the British wire has been cut, but fears that the Germans' has not, in spite of preparatory bombardments. After fifteen minutes he can contain himself no longer and, strictly against orders, goes out with the rearguard to join the evacuating party twenty yards into No Man's Land.

After another tense five minutes he is convinced that the raiders have been held up by the German wire, a suspicion confirmed by one of the bayonet-men, who returns to report this. He says that the raiding-party's only choice is to throw bombs and retire. Minutes later a rifle-shot rings out, followed by the explosion of several bombs. What follows is chaos and complete confusion as the Germans, who have been cunningly waiting for the raiders in silence, open fire and send them helter-skelter back across the treacherous ground. Sassoon counts sixteen men in, then goes out once more to investigate. He finds Stansfield, wounded but safe, and other injured men crawling in. Only O'Brien, his 'dear bombing corporal', and another man are absent down one of the deep craters.[40]

In the face of continuing rifle shots and bombs, Sassoon searches the craters. ('The bloody sods are firing down at me at point-blank range', he thinks incredulously as five or six Germans concentrate their fire.)[41] Expecting every moment to be his last, he works his way slowly and painfully around the bottom of the twenty-five foot crater until he finds O'Brien and his companion. O'Brien is badly wounded and so heavy – Sassoon describes him as 'a huge Irishman' – that Sassoon has to crawl back twice more to the British trench for help, the second time in dangerously light conditions. By the time he has finally got O'Brien in from the crater, he is dead and all Sassoon can do is to write an epitaph for his 'fine lad':

Corporal Mick O'Brien (who often went patrolling with me) was a very fine man and had been with the Battalion since November 1914. He was at Neuve Chapelle, Festubert and Loos.[42]

Of the twenty-eight men who went out, eleven were wounded, of whom one died, and one was killed. As Stockwell noted in his diary, the raid had been a failure and it was 'largely owing to Sassoon's bravery' that it had not been a complete disaster.[43] Sassoon's action in bringing O'Brien in, as Julian Dadd later pointed out, was only the 'conclusion of a remarkably well co-ordinated piece of work' on his part.[44] Stockwell had no hesitation in recommending him for an M.C., which Sassoon received a month later, the first Special Reserve Officer in his regiment to do so. The citation read: 'For conspicuous gallantry during a raid on the enemy's trenches. He remained for one and a half hours under rifle and bomb fire, collecting and bringing in our wounded. Owing to his courage and determination all the killed and wounded were brought in.' Sassoon later wrote in an 'Autobiographical Outline', now at the Beinecke Rare Book Library, that he 'did not believe in decorations' and was, therefore, never 'decorated with M.C. by king for this reason'. He did, however, proudly wear his white and purple M.C. ribbon which the Battalion doctor took from his own tunic the day confirmation of the honour came through, and sewed to Sassoon's uniform with his own hands.

Sassoon himself admitted that he was lucky that Stockwell had refused to allow him to go out with the raiding party, as he 'meant to get through that wire somehow, and it seems to have been almost impossible'.[45] Had he succeeded, however, he realized that the Germans would have been waiting for him. Not unnaturally, he experienced a severe sense of anti-climax after the failed night raid and tried to keep up the excitement. Ignoring the extreme danger he had already undergone, he was out in No Man's Land the next night collecting equipment abandoned in the confusion. Three axes and one knobkerrie seemed scant reward for the risks involved in retrieving them, but he was lucky not to have been killed. His moods, noticeably unstable at this time, fluctuated even more wildly. One moment he was longing, uncharacteristically, for a 'Blighty one' to take him safely home to England, the next glowing in the notion of valour and sacrifice and ready to throw his life away:

And, as for dying, I know it's nothing, and there's not much for me to lose except a few years of ease and futility. What I'm doing and enduring now is the last thing anyone could ask for; I'm being pushed along the rocky path, and the world seems all the sweeter for it. The world seen from exile; I can't see things in proportion at all to-night. Death seems the only fact to be faced; the rest all twaddle and purposeless energy. Lord Kitchener is drowned – there's another shock to everyone's tender hearts.[46] And yet, why shouldn't he die? We're all dying. And the war will go on and on till we can't stick it any longer, and Victory will greet us with a very wry smile and a 'dud' shell in each hand. I suppose I'm feeling what Robert Graves felt when he wrote

'Is this Limbo?' Shut in; no chance of escape. No music; the quest for beauty doomed. But I *must* go on finding beauty *here* and now; not the sort of beauty I used to look for.[47]

Whilst Sassoon's duties as a Company Officer did not allow him sufficient leisure to write poetry about the curious kind of beauty he was finding in France, neither were they stimulating enough to provide an alternative source of excitement, consisting as they did mainly of reinforcement work and wiring parties.

He did not, however, welcome a change of job, as might have been expected. When he was made Sniping Observing Officer on 7 June, he worried about his qualifications for the post. Yet it was probably less demanding than being a company officer and may well have been given to him by Stockwell as a reward for his courage. His misgivings about it seem to have been a symptom of a more general angst, apparent in many passages of his diary at that time. Even when leave was granted to him on 9 June, a week earlier than expected, he was not sure whether he really wanted it, as his jaundiced diary-entry suggests:

> There'll be the tedious train-journey down to Havre, and the boat waiting in the twilight, and chatter of officers going home like me. Then the beastly hours of trying not to feel ill; and Southampton, and the sentimental thrill as one sets foot on an English railway-platform ... Then London, and luxury, and being clean and tidy, and going down to Paddock Wood, and the Weirleigh garden in the June sunset; and poor old Mother trotting out to meet me. It's all so nice, but do I really long for it (to keep me safe) as much as I long to keep my freedom here? For it *is* freedom, even when it rains and I get the blues. And I *have* been most awfully slack in every way till I had to be a soldier.[48]

The reason Sassoon was sent on leave on 9 June, rather than the 15th as previously planned, was almost certainly the imminence of the Battle of the Somme. The authorities were anxious to have all officers back in France well before the offensive was due to open at the end of June. So Sassoon left for England on the evening of the 9th and arrived, exhausted, in Southampton nearly two days later. Sitting peacefully in the London house shared by his Aunt Fanny and Uncle Hamo in Melbury Road the same evening, with a piano tinkling across the road, seemed to him a strange and rather disturbing contrast to his recent experiences. Much as he loved being back among books, pictures and comfortable furniture, he felt almost entirely detached from his surroundings, perhaps already anticipating the misery he would feel when he had to leave it all again.

It was the same at Weirleigh, his next port of call. He had dreamed in France of enjoying his books and piano under the influence of its clustering roses, green trees and 'bird-sung' dawns,[49] but there was also the continuing unhappiness of his mother to spoil his pleasure. Proud as she was of his M.C., having lost one son she quite understandably worried about the dangers he had risked to win it and much of his time at home was spent reassuring her. It was a relief to leave for London again, where his literary friends were all clamouring to see him.

Sassoon had encouraged Dent to come down from Cambridge for a lunch or concert, and Marsh, too, had his claims. Gosse invited him to dine, with only Ross for company, an occasion almost certainly set up to discuss his poetry. For, with the Allies' 'Big Push' ahead, both Sassoon and his friends were anxious to prepare for the not unlikely eventuality of his death. (The greatest casualties in the First World War were predominantly among junior officers.) Marsh, one of the keenest to see him published, had suggested to Harold Monro at the Poetry Bookshop and had approached him with the idea in March 1916, at a time when Monro was preparing Graves's first book of poems for publication.

By April Sassoon was wondering if Marsh had settled anything with Monro, since he would 'like to see [his poems] out, or in proofs anyhow, before these beastly battles begin'.[50] To this end he asked Marsh to select the poems he liked best. Seeing them in print, he reasoned, would be 'a link with ones reasonable existence which seems lopped right off' in France.[51] One of the problems was that Monro could only commit himself to thirty-two pages, including prelims, whereas Sassoon had enough material for a larger book, which he favoured. By 30 April, irked no doubt by such restrictions, Sassoon had decided on another private production by the Chiswick Press. In May, however, he was agreeing with Marsh and Ross, who both felt by that time that it was better to wait.

In the event, the matter was decided by Monro, who by 5 June had decided not to publish Sassoon at all, a decision he must later have regretted. Gosse, who wanted Sassoon to get his juvenilia out of his system, regretted Monro's decision, and his dinner for Ross and Sassoon on 16 June was almost certainly intended as an occasion to discuss the matter further. Ross, who admired Sassoon's anti-war poems most, was keen for him to write more in the same vein before publishing. Gosse, who was dubious about the satires but admired the lyrics, wanted the latter published. A compromise seems to have been reached: that Sassoon should siphon off his lyrics into another private production (which was to become *Morning-Glory*) and concentrate on writing more of the satires Ross admired, so that the latter could approach a respectable commercial publisher with them. Dent, meanwhile, though not present at this discussion, was also encouraging Sassoon to write more of his satires for the *Cambridge Magazine*. It is interesting to see the influence of Gosse and Marsh, so powerful at the start of Sassoon's entry to the literary world, diminishing under the 'alternative' views of Ross and Dent, who prove to have been the shrewder critics.

One friend Sassoon was not able to see during his brief leave was Graves, who was with the 3rd RWF at Litherland, but he looked forward to seeing him back in France, which Graves now regarded as his true 'home'. It was one of a number of reasons why Sassoon was not sorry when his leave ended. Like Sorley, and no doubt many others, he had found a curious freedom in the apparently constricting conditions of trench-life. After the first strangeness of being transported back so suddenly from his comfortable bed and clean clothes to his 'flea-bag' on a hard floor and muddy army uniform had passed off, he looked forward like most of his companions to some action, however dangerous.

The 1st Battalion had been moved, in Sassoon's absence, for a last 'rest' behind the lines at Bussy-le-Daours, a pleasant little village on the marshy banks of the River Hallue, a tributary of the Ancre. C Company was billeted in buildings situated round a friendly farmhouse and everyone seemed relaxed. With no duties save a little easy field training, there was time for Sassoon to enjoy the countryside, different as it was from the Kentish Weald. Sitting by the river, all seemed smooth and peaceful, the long green weeds 'swaying with the current like nosing fishes slowly curving their way upstream'.[52] Further up the river, along the marsh, there were yellow irises among the reeds, thousands of tiny dark-green and golden frogs and waterside birds 'crying and calling and swinging on the bullrushes and tufted spires, by the smooth grey-green pools and creeks'. Appropriately, he was reading *Tess of the D'Urbervilles* and there is something of Hardy's glowing description of the lush dairy-country of Talbothays in his own enthusings, which culminated in the poem 'Before the Battle'. Written six days before the Battalion returned to the Front, it underlines the calming effect of Nature on him, even as he contemplated the possibility of his own death:

> Music of whispering trees
> Hushed by a broad-winged breeze
> Where shaken water gleams;
> And evening radiance falling
> With reedy bird-notes calling.
> *O bear me safe through dark, you low-voiced streams.*
>
> I have no need to pray
> That fear may pass away;
> I scorn the growl and rumble of the fight
> That summons me from cool
> Silence of marsh and pool
> And yellow lilies islanded in light.
> *O river of stars and shadows, lead me through the night.*
>
> (*CP*, p. 33)

When Sassoon wrote this poem and when, the next day, he marched the eleven miles back to Morlancourt, he was expecting to be in action within forty-eight hours. Morlancourt itself was crowded with troops and a new Main Dressing Station had been erected in his absence. As he lay once more in his old billet, even the garish pictures on the walls, of the Eiffel Tower and 'jocular Jesus',[53] must have seemed precious details of a life he was about to risk.

Sassoon might have spared himself the emotional strain, since the order was changed and the action delayed by another forty-eight hours. Instead of the excitement of a 'show', there was the familiar trudge up to the trenches on the evening of the 28th to relieve the 7th Borderers on the Battalion Front opposite Fricourt Cemetery and Station. Since it had been, to quote his Colonel, 'a filthy wet morning', the trenches were swimming in mud and he spent an uncomfortable night there. The English bombardment, intended to destroy the enemy wire, continued noisily as it had done for the past twelve days, but Sassoon's C Company had a quiet night in '85th Street' trench. For all his wet feet, trench mouth and lack of sleep Sassoon was happy, thinking back to the Southdown Hunt stables and his friend Gordon's welcoming house in particular. They seemed so safe and solid in his precarious situation. He was still reading the idyllic Talbothays section of *Tess*, though it must have seemed decidedly inappropriate in the trenches. Perhaps that is why he also took up Hardy's *Dynasts*, with its searching questions about the Immanent Will and its Designs and its stoical view of Fate. At any moment he himself might become the victim of a plan too vast for his comprehension and completely beyond his control. Such a plan was about to be put into effect.

In essence the scheme was that General Rawlinson's 4th Army, supported by five divisions of the French on its right and two divisions of the 3rd Army round Gommecourt on its left, would attack on a fourteen-mile front between Maricourt and Serre, with the initial objective of breaking the German Front Line in that sector. It was, however, a badly flawed plan. The original intention had been for the Allies to attack on a much larger front, with forty French divisions taking the area from Lassigny to the Somme and the British throwing twenty-five rather than eighteen divisions into battle. The Germans' ferocious attack on the French at Verdun in the spring and the consequent drain on French resources had forced the change. It had also marked a turning-point in the War, since from the Somme onwards the British were to take up the main burden of the Western Front Campaign.

Another problem, which could not be avoided, was that since the Germans had the high ground, the Allies had to attack mainly uphill, both a physical and psychological disadvantage for the troops if not for the artillery. Furthermore, the assault, which was frontal, was spread evenly across the whole line without special regard to the enemy's weak points or, indeed, to the Allies' own resources. For the British, attacking on a front almost twice as long as the French, had only half their heavy guns – one to every fifty-seven yards – and only one gun of any kind in every twenty yards.

In fact, the Staff placed altogether too much faith in a preliminary bombardment. Intended to wipe out the German defences, it not only failed conspicuously in this aim but also warned the enemy of the coming attack. As a result the Germans had accelerated the strengthening of their defences, which by 1 July were virtually impregnable. Consequently, when the British Infantry, fatally slowed down by equipment weighing more than half their body weight, lumbered across No Man's Land in stiff formations, German soldiers, still in many cases secure in their dug-outs, were ready to mow them down with their deadly machine-guns.

Sassoon's 7th Division, together with the 21st (both part of the XV Corps) were involved in a smaller battle within the grander scheme, the Battle of Albert. Centred on Fricourt, their front was approximately two miles long, of which 800 yards was the responsibility of the 1st RWF and one of their partners in the 22nd Brigade, the 20th Manchesters. By 28 June, Colonel Stockwell already knew that their action was to be 'subsidiary' and that 'Scatter' Minshull Ford's Brigade, the 91st, would bear the brunt. Not only that, but the 1st RWFs would be in support only, so that they were even less at risk.

Sassoon's own Company, C, was to be split up into groups for carrying ammunition and would, therefore, not be called upon to fight at all. It was intensely disappointing to Sassoon, who could never resist the lure of danger when he was near it. As it was he had to be satisfied with some hazardous wire-cutting and spent most of the night of 29 June occupied in this task. It was difficult work, since the English wire was deliberately thick, and it had to be carried out under constant shelling from both the Germans and the English, whose own shells often fell short. Nevertheless he was out again on the 30th in broad daylight frantically making gaps for the next day's attack. The official confirmation of his M.C. the same day no doubt spurred him on to even more daring efforts than usual.

When the great day dawned, Sassoon found himself left ingloriously in the support trench with his fellow-officer, Garnons-Williams, his company officer, Greaves, and no men. All he could do was to observe the progress of the battle from a safe distance, approximately five hundred yards behind the line. In spite of the anti-climax, he had a sense of being 'irrevocably involved in something bigger than had ever happened before'.[54]

After a hasty breakfast at 6 a.m. on a beautiful summer morning Sassoon witnesses the start of the action when 'all hell is let loose' at 6.30 a.m. as the English bombardment theoretically prepares the way for the troops. Since the slight breeze is in the wrong direction, the smoke-screen has had to be cancelled and he can see clearly all that follows, as far as the lie of the land allows. By 7.45 a.m. the artillery barrage is working to the right of Fricourt and he watches the 21st and 7th Divisions advancing to the left of it, with some Germans apparently surrendering about three-quarters of a mile away.

After a quick shave in the dug-out at 9.30 a.m., Sassoon continues to watch the men going across the open with no sign of casualties, though German trench-mortars are wreaking havoc on the ground where his neighbours in the support trench, the Manchesters, are due to attack. The morning drags on, with surprisingly little drama. Men still file across No Man's Land in twenties and thirties, and – except for an occasional explosion in German-held Fricourt, some English observation balloons and aeroplanes overhead and the confused fluttering and cries of bewildered birds – it is difficult to believe that one of the biggest battles in history is underway. 'I am looking at a sunlit picture of Hell', Sassoon records. 'And still the breeze shakes the yellow charlock, and the poppies glow below Crawley ridge ...'[55] The weather is cloudless and hot. A lark is singing overhead.

By 1.30 p.m. Sassoon hears that Mametz and Montaubon are taken, a fact he is unable to verify for himself because of the rising ground towards Mametz. At 2.30 p.m. the Manchesters are finally instructed to advance. He can see about 400 of them cross No Man's Land, many walking slowly with sloped arms. In spite of intense firing there are only forty or so casualties on the left and he is proud of the risks he has taken to cut the English wire for them. Simultaneously the Germans start shelling his dug-out, but he bears a charmed life. At 5 p.m. he watches men from A Company of the 1st RWF going across to help the Manchesters, who have been held up in the Bois Français support, their Colonel dead. By 8 p.m., he learns that the 7th Division has finally reached its objectives, except on his own Brigade Front where the 20th Manchesters are still in trouble. Eventually, with the help of the 1st RWF's A and B Companies and parties of bombers, they reach Fricourt which, in defiance of Headquarters, Stockwell orders them to take. By 2.30 p.m. on 2 July it is reported captured. Rumour has it that over 2,000 prisoners have been taken by the 7th Division, 200 of these by the 1st RWF alone, clearly a gross exaggeration since history records that the whole of the XV Corps took only 517 prisoners altogether. Not one officer of the 1st Battalion has been killed.

Other sectors of the line were not so fortunate, however, and Sassoon's experience on the first day of the Somme was by no means typical. Situated as he was at Fricourt, on the right centre, he was at the very turning point of the battle. The French, south of the Somme and north of it as far as Maricourt, had gained all their objectives with slight losses. Between Maricourt and Fricourt the British XIII Corps had reached its objectives, though with heavier losses. On its left the XV Corps, of which Sassoon had formed an infinitesimal and passive part, partially achieved its aim of pinching out the stronghold of Fricourt village and wood. But this marked the boundary of success. All to the north was failure – La Boiselle, Contalmaison, Thiepval and Beaumont Hamel. The French might justifiably have claimed success, but for the British, whose thirteen divisions had taken a small tract of land and less than 2,000 prisoners against only six German divisions, it was a disastrous failure. Of the quarter of a million men who went into battle, on the first day alone 20,000 were killed, the heaviest British loss of any single day's fighting in the War, and one which gave the lie to Haig's optimistic faith in massed artillery.

Still unaware of these terrible facts, though news was slowly coming in, Sassoon's initial reaction was mainly personal: he felt 'a bit of a fraud'.[56] Not only had he been in a relatively safe sector, but he had played a largely passive part, not an experience he enjoyed. In spite of his disappointment, however, he relished the victory, particularly when he was able to lie in front of what had previously been his Front Line, 'basking in the sunshine where yesterday there were bullets'.[57] Fricourt itself was full of troops looking for souvenirs and what had formerly been a ruin had become a dust heap. It was an odd experience seeing people moving about freely in previously alien territory.

Early on the morning of 3 July, nearly sixty hours after they had marched up to the support trench, C Company left it to join the battalion at 71.North. Their destination was a grassy hollow south of the Carnoy-Mametz road. Here, together with three other battalions of the 22nd Brigade – 20th Manchesters, 2nd Warwicks and the 2nd Royal Irish – they were to spend the day resting in preparation for an attack on Mametz Wood the following day. As Sassoon lay listening to the contented chatter of officers and men, and contemplating his own good luck in the recent event, he once again found consolation in Nature and in poetry:

> *At Carnoy*
> Down in the hollow there's the whole Brigade
> Camped in four groups: through twilight falling slow
> I hear a sound of mouth-organs, ill-played,
> And murmur of voices, gruff, confused, and low.
> Crouched among thistle-tufts I've watched the glow
> Of a blurred orange sunset flare and fade;
> And I'm content. To-morrow we must go
> To take some cursèd Wood ... O world God made!
> 3rd July 1916   (*CP*, p. 22)

Sassoon's forebodings about the 'cursèd Wood' turned out to be fully justified. Of tactical importance to the British in their push forward to the German second line, Mametz Wood proved far more of an obstacle than anticipated. A rumour had started, and been accepted by the staff, that the Wood was unoccupied and the 1st Battalion, together with the 2nd Royal Irish, was ordered to 'go and make a position' on its southern edge. Armed with trenching tools, barbed wire and other equipment, the Royal Welch Fusiliers started out after some hours' delay on the evening of 3rd to 4th July, through Mametz village and up a long communication trench to Bottom Wood. Stockwell had refused to move until the bewildered guide had found his bearings and it was nearly 2 a.m. before the exhausted men set off.

For the first time Sassoon found himself among the debris of a fierce attack, rags and shreds of bloody clothing, bullet-riddled boots and abandoned equipment. This both horrified and fascinated him. Passing about thirty of the British dead laid out by the side of the road, 'their fingers mingled in blood-stained bunches', he reflected that these Gordon Highlanders, Devons and South Staffordshires were finally beyond regimental rivalry in the companionship of death.[58] As he reached the old German Front Line in his slow progress towards Mametz, he was conscious of a 'sour pervasive stench' which differed from anything he had previously experienced: it was the smell of corpses nearly three days old. Some of these strewed the communication trench out of Mametz, their badly mangled bodies deeply shocking in their distorted attitudes. Though he had been with the 1st Battalion in France for nearly eight months, these were the first newly dead Germans he had seen.

When the Royal Welch Fusiliers arrived at their destination at 3 a.m., Stockwell was disgusted to find that it was an impossible place to consolidate. A piece of rising ground only fifty yards from the wood, it was clearly visible to the enemy in the dawn light and, in any case, his men were 'dead-beat' after their wearying crawl uphill from Mametz. When, therefore, a bombing fight broke out at the edge of the supposedly empty wood, Stockwell had no hesitation in ordering his men back to camp. Meanwhile, the Royal Irish, who had been sent up ahead of the Royal Welch to consolidate trenches close to the south end of Mametz Wood and to clear its outskirts, ran into enemy machine-guns, bombers and snipers. When they tried to bomb the Germans out of the wood they suffered sixty casualties and were only saved from further losses by the English guns firing heavy shells, which enabled them to retreat. It had been eleven hours of muddle and mismanagement caused largely, Sassoon believed, by bad staffwork at Divisional Headquarters. Yet, elated by the promise of action at last and stimulated, as always, by danger, he could still describe the events of the previous forty-eight hours as 'great fun'.[59]

Revising their plans only slightly, Headquarters sent orders on the morning of 4 July that the line which the two battalions had been instructed to consolidate the previous night should now be attacked. Since it was raining hard – an added misery for the men in their inadequate bivouacs – the company commanders could see little of the ground on their afternoon reconnaissance trip and, in any case, the enemy line was not normally visible from the British line at Bottom Wood. So that it was in some ignorance and with pardonable trepidation that the 1st Battalion got into position at 12.30 a.m. on 5 July, with the depleted Royal Irish on their right and the 7th Northumberland Fusiliers on their left. Preparations for the battle had been poor and, though the wire in front of Quadrangle Trench was reported 'well gapped', that in front of Wood Trench had only one opening. In addition the heavy rain had made the ground a quagmire. Under these unfavourable conditions the attack was launched by the 1st Royal Welch Fusiliers on a two-company front of 600 yards at 12.45 a.m.

Once again Sassoon was thwarted of a good fight, since Stockwell had decided to send up B and D Companies, with A Company in reserve and C Company, as before, split up into carrying parties. By 1.15 a.m., with B Company in difficulties, A Company was sent up in support, but still Sassoon waited. At 2.10 a.m., with the news that A and D Companies were under extreme pressure from the Germans, Stockwell finally ordered the remnants of C Company (only twenty-six men) up to the line and Sassoon's moment seemed to have arrived. Once again he was to be disappointed, however, for with the report a few minutes later that only bombs and bombers were needed, not more men, Stockwell countermanded the order and C Company was recalled. What followed is typical of Sassoon's impetuousness, hunger for excitement, physical courage and highly emotional nature.

Frustrated by the lack of action Sassoon ignored Stockwell's order, though he sent his men back. As he crossed the 500 yards from the support trench at Bottom Wood to the newly captured Quadrangle Trench, dawn was breaking. Eager to be involved, he started to investigate the trench to the right, where communication with the Royal Irish had failed. The trench itself offered little protection, since it was still only half-finished, and the enemy was also firing down Quadrangle Alley, the communication trench from Mametz Wood. The greatest threat, however, came from a German sniper at the end of Wood Trench, which the Royal Irish had failed to capture. Not far from where Quadrangle Trench finished, it provided an ideal sniping post and already British soldiers were lying killed and wounded as Sassoon made his way to the trench end. Whether he was enraged by the general carnage and the death of one of his own favourites, Lance-Corporal Gibson, in particular, as he suggests in *Infantry Officer*, or whether he craved some excitement of his own after his frustrating inactivity of the previous five days, or whether he simply gave way to one of his many impulses, he suddenly decided to put an end to the sniper who was wreaking so much havoc.

Rushing across the little valley and light railway line which separated him from the Germans in Wood Trench, he pulled the safety-pins out of two Mills bombs as he went and, mounting the bank on the opposite side, threw them into the hidden trench. His own words to Marsh convey vividly what happened next: 'Eddie, I chased 40 Bosches out of a trench by Mametz Wood all by myself. Wasn't that a joyous moment for me? They ran like hell and I chucked bombs and made hunting noises'.[60] His amazement at this unexpected success could only have been equalled by that of the Germans had they realized that they were fleeing from a single officer. It was the sheer foolhardiness of his action, together with covering fire from his own side, which had saved him. As he confessed to Marsh, he wondered if he would 'ever be able to take soldiering seriously'. It is a remark which might help explain why Stockwell was so reluctant to allow Sassoon responsibility.

The attack itself had not achieved very much. Once occupying the roomy German trench Sassoon had no idea what to do next. Unable to consolidate his position he did not relish the idea of the enemy's return. Graves's story, that he simply pulled out a book of poetry and settled down to read, however attractive, is almost certainly apocryphal and not mentioned by Sassoon in either his autobiographical or fictional accounts. It is far more probable that he tentatively explored the trench, like George Sherston in *Infantry Officer*, and then 'took a deep breath and ran headlong back'.[61]

Unlike Sherston, however, his action, far from earning him a reprimand from his Commanding Officer, caused him to be recommended for a further decoration, either a bar to his M.C. or a D.S.O. However annoyed Stockwell was by his initial disobedience, he believed that Sassoon, like his friend Julian Dadd and another bomber, Stevens, had done 'splendidly'.[62] The decoration was to be disallowed, on the grounds that the overall attack had been a failure, though the Royal Welch Fusiliers had gained their objectives.

One of the most interesting things to emerge from this well-documented incident, apart from the further light it throws on Sassoon's character, is the poem which arose from the day's adventure. Whilst exploring Quadrangle Trench at dawn he had come across the body of a young German, clearly killed whilst digging. His gentle, good-looking face, undisfigured by wounds, and his fresh blond hair seem to have made Sassoon particularly aware of the waste and futility of War. Wiping the mud from the youth's eyes and mouth, he carefully propped him up against the side of the trench.

On his return later the same day, however, Sassoon found him trodden into the mud by a careless English boot. It is significant that, out of the many incidents of what he calls 'The Night Attack', he chose to describe, not his own courage, but the pathos of the young German soldier. By revealing genuine sympathy for the enemy the poem indicates a further shift in Sassoon's attitude towards War at the very moment when he is most enjoying it. After describing the British soldiers' relief as they lie resting twelve miles behind the lines, Sassoon continues:

> One says, 'The bloody Bosche has got the knock;
> And soon they'll crumple up and chuck their games.
> We've got the beggars on the run at last!'
>   Then I remembered someone that I'd seen
> Dead in a squalid, miserable ditch,
> Heedless of toiling feet that trod him down.

10. 'At the Edge of the World' (March-July 1916)

He was a Prussian with a decent face,
Young, fresh and pleasant, so I dare to say.
No doubt he loathed the war and longed for peace,
And cursed our souls because we'd killed his friends.

...
                    I found him there
In the gray morning when the place was held.
His face was in the mud; one arm flung out
As when he crumpled up; his sturdy legs
Were bent beneath his trunk; heels to the sky.[63]
July 1916

In *The War Poems* (1983) Rupert Hart-Davis reprints the version of this poem published in *Stand* magazine in 1970-71, which does not appear to be Sassoon's first version. In the original manuscript,[64] written on 6 July 1916, the day after this incident occurred, apart from including more details about the young Prussian's probable home-sickness, Sassoon has added an extra twelve lines underneath the date. These emphasize his sympathy for the German youth and his increasing sense of the futility of war:

I lifted him, a heavy lump of death, –
Wiped mud from mouth and eyes, and beardless cheek,
And showed that sullen mask to the blank sky:
I propped him safely up beside the trench,
Till he looked tidy for a hostile corpse!

But in the afternoon I passed and found him
Sprawling ungainly on his back: his face
Green and disfeatured where a British boot
Had trod his skull deep into the gray ooze.

Such is defeat, not beautiful nor kind;
And this was ugly death, a shameless thing,
Stripped of the sable hood that cloaks his grin.

Ultimately Sassoon decided not to include this poem, in any version, in his collections of War poetry, almost certainly because he thought it too personal.

Sassoon's sense of the ugly wastage of War was further strengthened the same evening that this incident occurred, as the 1st Battalion was relieved by the 14th Royal Welch Fusiliers, a unit of inexperienced, half-trained civilians. Watching a little platoon officer trying to settle his nervous men down 'with a valiant show of self-assurance', and suspecting the hell and carnage that awaited them, he realized then 'for the first time, how blindly war destroys its victims'.[65] Two days later the 38th (Welsh) Division, of which the 14th Battalion formed a part, was to be massacred in one of the most fiercely fought engagements of the War.

By that time Sassoon himself was resting gratefully at Heilly-sur-l'Ancre, twelve miles away. The 1st Battalion had marched there over-night on 5 July, and, after long delays in congested Fricourt, had reached their camp by the river Ancre at about 8 a.m. on the 6th. In spite of the rain, which made the marshy ground even muddier, the Battalion spent an enjoyable five days there. They had suffered only fourteen dead out of 132 casualties in the seven days since the great battle started and considered themselves extremely lucky.[66]

Sassoon even managed to get into Amiens on 7 July for a luxurious lunch at Godberts with Greaves, Reeves, Cottrell and Julian Dadd, riding the first four miles on horseback and being driven the other seven in Cottrell's friend's car. On the 9th he had another treat, when he made contact with his pre-war hunting friend, Norman Loder, who was Assistant Provost Marshall to the XIII Corps Headquarters and lived in a very comfortable billet at Corbie. Perhaps Sassoon told Loder of his instinctive 'view-holloas' when chasing the Germans out of their trench, a detail that would not have surprised his more sober but equally hunting-mad friend. Riding home in sunshine through a peaceful Sunday afternoon, he stopped to let his horse graze and to take in the beauty of the scene, very conscious that he might not see it again. On arrival back at camp he learned that the 7th Division was moving up to the line again the next day. Mametz Wood had still not been taken.

At 4 p.m. on 10 July the 1st Battalion, reinforced by five officers and fifty-seven men from the 20th RWF, started back to their camp at the Citadel just south of Fricourt. Between Méricourt and Treux they were passed by the Commander-in-Chief of the British Armies in France, Sir Douglas Haig, a privilege they are unlikely to have appreciated. And at Morlancourt Sassoon noted a solitary doctor in a white coat standing at the church-door, perhaps because it seemed to him an ominous conjunction. They arrived at the Citadel about 9 p.m. and, after a brief rest, were standing-to at 10.45 p.m. At 11.30 p.m. they set off for Mametz, but were brought back, without explanation, after only a quarter of an hour and spent a peaceful night sleeping under the stars.

The next day Sassoon learnt that once again he was to be left out of the action, placed in reserve with Julian Dadd and five other officers. Of these five he found two – Dobell and Newton, fresh from Sandhurst – cheery and attractive, two others – Hawes and Hanmer-Jones – hearty but harmless, and the fifth not worthy of comment. Together they were sent to the Transport Lines three-quarters of a mile away near Méaulte, a chaotic place of horses and wagons, tents and bivouacs, red poppies and blue cornflowers, a 'caravanserai for supplies and men and munitions', according to Sassoon.[67] He does not appear to query why he had once again been left out of the action, but an outsider cannot help wondering if this was Stockwell's delayed reaction to his most recent act of impetuosity. In his fictionalized account Sassoon has Sherston's Colonel threaten good-humouredly to leave him out of the 'next show' as a punishment for his impulsive and unconsolidated attack on Wood Trench,[68] and perhaps that really was the explanation. In any event Sassoon was to remain for the next eleven days in a state of limbo, while the rest of the battalion fought the Battle of Bazentin Ridge. Whatever his personal feelings, he seems to have been extremely lucky, since at least two officers of the 1st Battalion were killed and three wounded in the fierce fighting. Even when C Company's Commander, Greaves, was hurt, it was Hawes, not Sassoon, who was chosen to replace him.

Only later did Sassoon appreciate how fortunate he had been. At the time he suffered from both boredom and suspense: as long as the battle continued he could be called on at any moment. In an effort to deal with the mental stagnation which overcame him in such an 'arid and irksome place',[69] he spent much of his time reading Hardy, whose fatalistic outlook suited his state of mind more than ever. He was finishing *Tess* and starting *The Return of the Native*, neither of them calculated to give him much hope, but both totally unsentimental and highly evocative of the English countryside which he longed to revisit. Above all Hardy helped him to avoid what he thought of as the 'unreasoning mechanical outlook' of his companions, who irritated and endeared him by turns.[70] Often, as he watched them huddled up asleep, they reminded him of the corpses he had recently seen, giving him irrational fears that they might be dead:

> For at any hour I may come upon them, and find that long silence descended over them, their faces grey and disfigured, dark stains of blood soaking through their torn garments, all their hope and merriment snuffed out for ever, and their voices fading on the winds of thought, from memory to memory, from hour to hour, until they are no more to be recalled.[71]

Memories like these would haunt his own sleep for many years to come. One of the few enjoyments in this period of suspense and boredom was an unexpected meeting with Robert Graves. When Graves had left for England in late March on a leave prolonged by an essential nose operation, both he and Sassoon expected him to return to the 1st Battalion. They had kept in close touch during Graves's absence and continued to fantasize about all the places they would visit and the poetry they would write together after the War. Graves had sent 'Sassons', as he affectionately called him, an advance copy of his first book of poems, *Over the Brazier*, in May, another incentive for Sassoon to think seriously about publication. He had also confided to Sassoon his misery over an enforced separation from his Charterhouse 'friend', Peter. There was, therefore, a great deal to be discussed when, as they hoped, Graves rejoined the 1st RWF. They were, understandably, very disappointed when he was assigned instead to the 2nd Battalion, which he joined at Givenchy on 5 July. Their delight was all the keener, therefore, when the 2nd Battalion was then sent to join the 1st at Mametz Wood. Sassoon heard of his friend's arrival in the neighbourhood on 12 July and sent him a note asking him to visit immediately. When Graves did so on the 13th, he was unable to find Sassoon and it was not until the following day that they finally met.

Sassoon's protective attitude towards Graves in his absence – he noted in his diary for example that he was 'unpopular, of course, poor dear'[72] – gave way to feelings of great excitement in his presence. As they sat talking in the darkness, surrounded by their sleeping men, he thought wildly of 'travels, and adventures, and poetry; and anything but the old groove of cricket and hunting, and dreaming in Weirleigh garden'.[73] When the War ended he would be 'at the crossroads' and he now knew which path to choose. He must 'go out into the night alone'; there could be 'no fat settling down'.

Graves, whom Sassoon found 'as whimsical and queer and human as ever', made his old life seem conventional silliness. And it is no coincidence that he went on to say in the same diary passage that he could never marry Bobbie Hanmer's sister, an idea which he had been seriously considering. Even his new role as a soldier, which had to some extent liberated him, seemed shallow and unreal under the intoxicating influence of Graves's vivid imagination and total commitment to art. The dissatisfaction he expressed forcibly in his diary a few days later was undoubtedly a result of this meeting with Graves:

O God, when shall I get out of this limbo? For I'm never alone here – never my old self – always acting a part – that of the cheery, reckless sportsman – out for a dip at the Bosches. But the men love me, that's one great consolation. And some day perhaps I'll be alone in a room full of books again, with a piano glimmering in the corner, and glory in my head, and a new poem in my notebook.[74]

At the time of writing this Sassoon was busy copying Graves's latest poems into his notebook. He was also composing one of his own in response to Graves's visit, 'The Crown'. The first of its two stanzas reinforces the view that this visit had had an unsettling effect on him:

Ask me what I long for most;
Not my old life; that's dead; –
And dead lips make no boast
When eyes are dull like lead.
Ask what I loved; I'll say –
'Things that are here to-day;
'Friends who go forth to die
'Proud as the evening sky.'[75]

Curiously, Graves either forgot or deliberately omitted to describe this meeting, which had been so important to Sassoon, and it is not mentioned in *Goodbye to All That*. It may be that he meant more to Sassoon than Sassoon to him. It was certainly something Sassoon came to suspect over the next few years. For the moment, however, the relationship seemed equally intense on both sides. Graves, who moved up to Mametz Wood with his men the next day (15 July), nevertheless found time to write a verse letter in reply to Sassoon's May epistle from Flixécourt. This shows quite clearly that he, as much as Sassoon, envisaged a closely shared future travelling together:

> ... And doing wild, tremendous things
> In free adventure, quest and fight,
> And God! what poetry we'll write![76]

Graves, in the 2nd Battalion, was part of the same attack as the 1st Battalion, and had already been in action with the 7th Division by the time he arrived at Mametz Wood. Rawlinson, commanding the 4th Army, frustrated by the 38th Division's failure to take the Wood, had devised a plan to break through the German defences along a four-mile front between Delville Wood on the right and Bazentin-le-Petit Wood on the left. Since direct attack had proved ineffective, he decided on a surprise night attack. With the 9th and 3rd Divisions of the XXII Corps on the right and the 7th and 21st Divisions of the XV Corps on the left, troops would break through at dawn on 14 July and take the German second line. In this they succeeded, the 1st Battalion helping the 7th Division clear Bazentin-le-Petit Wood and push up the slopes beyond towards High Wood. By 15 July, Sassoon could report: 'The 7th Division have reached their objective'. Graves, who arrived at the new Front Line the same day, had to sit waiting in shell-holes for the next stage of the battle. On the 17th he moved up to a position just north of Bazentin-le-Petit to relieve some Irish troops, and that night he supervised the digging of several strong-points.

On the evening of the 19th Graves's Battalion, reduced by casualties to 400 men, was pulled out of the Line and told that they would be in reserve for the major assault on High Wood the next day. (The 1st Battalion would, once more, be in the Line.) Ironically, it was while Graves was waiting in reserve in a relatively safe position that he was injured. The Germans had put down a barrage on the ridge where he was sheltering and, as he tried to escape, an eight-inch shell burst just behind him, wounding him badly in the leg and chest. The Battalion M.O., Dr Dunn, having announced that there was 'no chance' of him surviving, he was assumed dead.

A shocked Sassoon was informed of Graves's 'death' the following day. (Julian Dadd was later to write to him: 'Do you remember sitting under a sort of tarpaulin bivouac, discussing Graves's death, just after the report had reached us, and your saying that one of the worst features of the war was that people were beginning to lose any sense of the value of human life?')[77] His thoughts turned back to David Thomas and forward to his own, possibly similar, fate:

> So he and Tommy are together, and perhaps I'll join them soon. 'Oh my songs never sung, And my plays to darkness blown!' – [Graves's] own poor words written last summer, and now so cruelly true. And only two days ago I was copying his last poem into my notebook, a poem full of his best qualities of sweetness and sincerity, full of heart-breaking gaiety and hope. So all our travels to 'the great, greasy Caucasus' are quelled. And someone called Peter will be as sad as I am. Robert might have been a great poet; he could never have become a dull one. In him I thought I had found a lifelong friend to work with. So I go my way alone again.[78]

By the time the news of Graves's supposed death reached Sassoon, the 1st Battalion was reunited with its Reserve Officers and Transport on a hill south-west of Dernancourt. Sassoon had helped prepare for the returning men on 21 July and had waited six hours with Cottrell to welcome them back. Though they had suffered relatively few casualties in the general carnage (less than a hundred), they arrived back in an exhausted and subdued state after what Sassoon described as 'eight days in hell'.[79] A day later, following a good sleep and a shave, they were a great deal more cheerful and on their way to La Chaussée, a mile from Picquigny, for a fortnight's well-earned rest. The journey was an easy one of approximately twenty-three miles, most of it by train, and Sassoon should, theoretically, have been able to relax. Instead, by 23 July, he was feeling extremely ill with a temperature of 105°, and by the next morning was in the New Zealand hospital at Amiens.

The initial diagnosis was dysentery, which Sassoon suspected he had caught from the new billets at La Chaussée, left in a far from sanitary state by their previous inhabitants. It is more likely that dysentery was in fact only one of the symptoms of trench fever, since his temperature was so high.[80] At first he felt too ill to care about anything, simply appreciating the luxury of a clean bed away from the Front. But gradually, as his temperature returned to normal, the full impact of Graves's death hit him. He had been too busy with battalion business at Dernancourt fully to register this loss. Now, with time on his hands and the news of the death of yet another friend, Marcus Goodall, he felt it necessary to express his sorrow, to pin it down. To Dent he wrote, on 29 July:

> There was something of bitter charm in [Graves], a sort of sallow, victimised, faithful Jester in the storm – quite impossible to describe – queer twisted smile – ungainly lankiness – rather goggling eyes – and all that's been dumped into a shell-hole and blathered over by a parson (if he was so 'lucky' as to get that last piece of patronising attentive impudence thrown at him) ... His rare gaiety was like a young animal hopping in a daisied field. The other one, Goodall – you remember my dear Marlburian – ... He too had planned all sorts of travels and adventures with me *après la guerre* ... lying

276

1. Siegfried Sassoon, *c.* 1916.

2. Siegfried's great-grandfather, David Sassoon, with three of his eight sons (*l. to r.*:) Elias, Abdullah and Siegfried's grandfather, Sassoon David ('S.D.'), the first member of the family to wear Western dress.

3. Siegfried's maternal grandfather, Thomas Thornycroft.

4. Siegfried's maternal grandmother, Mary Thornycroft, seated in the drawing-room at Weirleigh.

5. The *Waterlily*, a steam yacht designed by John Thornycroft for his father, Thomas, *c.* 1863. Thomas is at the wheel.

6. Siegfried's father, Alfred Sassoon, inscribed on the back 'With love to Michael, Siegfried and Poggie [i.e. Hamo]'.

7. Siegfried's mother, Theresa Thornycroft, before her marriage.

8. Siegfried's uncle, Hamo Thornycroft, and his fiancée, Agatha Cox, taken at John Thornycroft's house at Bembridge, Isle of Wight, *c.* 1884.

9. Siegfried's aunt Agatha, after her marriage to Hamo Thornycroft. Inscribed on the verso, '... T[homas] H[ardy] himself told me that while writing Tess [i.e. of the d'Urbervilles] he had her face in mind more than any other. This photograph ... seems to me a veritable picture of Tess'.

10. Siegfried's paternal aunt, Rachel Beer (née Sassoon).

11. Siegfried's great-aunt Mozelle, the youngest child of David Sassoon, inscribed by Siegfried 'Dear Aunt Mozelle'.

12. The earliest photograph of Siegfried, *c*. 1888.

13. Siegfried's elder brother, Michael, *c*. 1892, aged about ten. Note the miniature violin, in emulation of his father?

14. Siegfried's younger brother, Hamo, '*c*. 1890'.

15. Siegfried on his first horse, in the nursery at Weirleigh, inscribed 'SS – circa 1891'.

16. Weirleigh, bereft of its 'tower'.

17. Theresa Sassoon and her three sons in the dog-cart near Weirleigh.

18. Siegfried at the age of eight.

19. Theresa Sassoon and (*l. to r.*:) Siegfried, Hamo and Michael 'artistically' posed, *c.* 1890.

20. Alfred Sassoon shortly before his death at thirty-four, with (*l. to r.*:) Michael, Siegfried and Hamo at Eastbourne.

21. The last known photograph of Alfred Sassoon, inscribed on the verso 'With love to Michael, Siegfried and Hamo'. (Courtesy of the late Mrs Leo Sassoon)

22. (*l. to r.*:) Hamo and Siegfried up to no good in the garden at Weirleigh, inscribed on verso 'S.S. & Hamo. 1899 (taken by C.H. Hamilton)'.

23. Tom Richardson ('Dixon' of *Memoirs of a Fox-Hunting Man*) in front of the stables where he and his family also lived at Weirleigh.

24. The village carrier, Tom Homewood ('John Homeward' of *Memoirs of a Fox-Hunting Man*).

25. Matfield cricket team: back row (*l. to r.*:) Alec Read – unknown – Mr Moon – Tom Richardson – Richard Marchant – William Larkin – Sam Butler; front row: 'Scunger' Austin – unknown – Tom Homewood – Siegfried Sassoon – unknown – Harry Fuller – Ned Farris.

26. Siegfried (*centre, holding cricket ball*) at the New Beacon, *c*. 1901.

27. Study at Cotton House, Marlborough College,
c. 1903. (Courtesy Mrs Pat Robertson)

28. Siegfried at Marlborough College.

29. Staff of Marlborough College, 1903. Back row (*l. to r.*) Tuckett – Lupton – Prior – Sandford – Alsop – O'Regan – Gaul; next to back row: Bain – Preston – Wood – Abbott – Hughes – Hewitt – Bambridge – Cummins – Hardy – Emery – Wall; middle row, seated: Meyrick – Madden – Leaf – MacDonald – Bell – Richardson – Drury – Alford – Gould; front row (on the grass:) England and other young masters.

30. Staff of Henley House: early 1900s; seated (*l. to r.*:) E.B. Rawsthorne ('Teacher') – pupil – Henry Malden ('Boss') – Eustace Malden ('Uncle') – George Wilson – pupil.

31. Sassoon in the grounds of Henley House (*l. to r.*:) E.B. Rawsthorne – unknown – Sassoon – George Wilson.

32. Sassoon and his prizewinning horse, 'Cockbird', April 1911. (Courtesy of the late Mrs Leo Sassoon)

33. Sassoon on 'Rubicon', who came second in the Sussex Heavyweight Point-to-point in 1912.

34. Norman Loder (centre), Master of the Atherstone Hunt, at Measham, Leicestershire, in March 1914, while Sassoon was staying with him at Witherley.

35. Edmund Gosse, Sassoon's first patron. (Courtesy Miss Jennifer Gosse)

36. Edward Marsh, 1912, another important patron.

37. Sassoon at the Army School, Flixécourt, May 1916.

38. David Cuthbert Thomas ('Dick Tiltwood' of the *Memoirs*), *c*. July 1915.

39. Theresa Sassoon and her youngest son, Hamo, in the garden at Weirleigh on his embarkation leave for Gallipoli.

40. Theresa Sassoon alone in the garden at Weirleigh.

41. 'Dame' Nellie Burton with 'Siegfried'.

42. Robert Ross, 'friend of friends', 1916. (Courtesy Robert Baldwin Robertson)

43. (*l. to r.*:) Lady Ottoline Morrell, Dorothy Brett and Sassoon at Garsington in November 1916.

44. Lady Ottoline Morrell from Robert Gathorne-Hardy's photograph album. (Courtesy Lady Anne Hill)

45. Sydney Carlyle Cockerell, Sassoon's 'bearded and spectacled magician'.

46. Robert von Ranke Graves, taken near the time he met Sassoon in November 1915. (Courtesy William Reese)

47. Officer Cadet Wilfred Owen, 1916.

48. Captain W.H.R. Rivers, R.A.M.C.

49. Foot inspection.

50. Vivian de Sola Pinto, on sick leave, Hampstead Heath, 1917.

51. Lena Ashwell Concert Party, Y.M.C.A., Egypt. (Courtesy Philip Guest)

52. John Masefield in a photograph inscribed 'for Siegfried Sassoon from John Masefield. Nov. 9. 1918', two days before the armistice.

53. Lennel House, Coldstream, as it was when Sassoon was there. (Courtesy Miss Grizel Kennedy)

here one sees war in a new light: the callous uselessness of it – and oh the dullness – when I'm there I'm a *beast* – nothing more – healthy and full-fed on coarse filth – with no desire but to rest and smoke a pipe. Now I get away from it all and my brain begins to work again.[81]

The poem which emerged from this sorrow, 'To His Dead Body', originally dedicated to Graves, was subsequently retitled 'The Traveller', revised and rededicated to Marcus Goodall when it emerged that Graves was alive after all. This suggests that it was not so much a personal tribute to one particular soldier but an elegy for all the promising young men who were dying so pointlessly in the War, a theory borne out by the fact that the final two lines come from a cancelled manuscript poem called first 'Elegy: for R.G.', then 'Elegy: for Marcus Goodall':[82]

> *To His Dead Body*
> When roaring gloom surged inward and you cried,
> Groping for friendly hands, and clutched, and died,
> Like racing smoke, swift from your lolling head
> Phantoms of thought and memory thinned and fled.
>
> Yet, though my dreams that throng the darkened stair
> Can bring me no report of how you fare,
> Safe quit of wars, I speed you on your way
> Up lonely glimmering fields to find new day,
> Slow-rising, saintless, confident and kind –
> Dear, red-faced father God who lit your mind.[83]

Sassoon's grief at the death of two of his dearest friends within a week of each other was made even worse by haunting memories of the putrefying corpses he had seen at Mametz. His state of mind was not helped by the presence of a young officer in the bed opposite his, whose serious condition was concealed by red screens which glowed with deceptive cheerfulness at night. As the dying soldier grew more delirious, he started to rave about a wood which he cursed for the miseries he had experienced there, including the loss of a close friend. His disjointed phrases contained for Sassoon 'all the horror of the Somme',[84] as well as reminding him of his own nightmare experience in Mametz Wood.

Sassoon's first version of the poem, written the day he woke to find the boy's bed empty, was much longer than the final version. By cutting the first two and the last of the original seven verses and reducing his stanzas from five to four lines, he greatly improved the poem, condensing it to its barest and most telling details. His substitution of the official phrase 'Died of Wounds' for the title, in place of the original 'In Hospital', is also an improvement. And his use of fragmented snatches of direct speech is particularly effective:

Died of Wounds

His wet white face and miserable eyes
Brought nurses to him more than groans and sighs:
But hoarse and low and rapid rose and fell
His troubled voice: he did the business well.

The ward grew dark; but he was still complaining
And calling out for 'Dickie'. 'Curse the Wood!
'It's time to go. O Christ, and what's the good?
'We'll never take it, and it's always raining.'

I wondered where he'd been; then heard him shout,
'They snipe like hell! O Dickie, don't go out' ...
I fell asleep ... Next morning he was dead;
And some Slight Wound lay smiling on the bed.[85]

(*CP*, p. 28)

In spite of Sassoon's mental suffering, his physical state slowly improved and he fully expected to be back in his unit by the end of July. 'Not lucky enough to be wounded' as he put it frankly to Dent on 29 July, he nevertheless still felt very weak and it later emerged that he was anaemic. More significantly for his future, he was also thought to have shadows on his lungs, possibly a legacy from his childhood bouts of pneumonia. Sassoon himself thought that his M.C. influenced the doctor's decision, though there is no proof of this. Whatever the truth of the matter, instead of being sent to join his battalion at La Chaussée, as they prepared for another engagement at Ginchy, he found himself first on a train for Rouen, then, more miraculously, on a hospital ship for Southampton. By an extraordinary coincidence, Graves too had been sent to Rouen when he was found to be alive after twenty-four hours presumed dead, and was still there recovering from his wounds when Sassoon arrived at No. 2 Hospital, Rouen, on 30 July. They also landed in England within a day of each other, Sassoon on 2 August, Graves on 3 August. Yet Sassoon still believed that Graves was dead, having been told this both by his Colonel and his Adjutant.

Nevertheless, Sassoon could not help rejoicing as he lay in the hospital train taking him, he thought, to London. Whilst he felt guilty at forsaking his men and believed that three or four weeks' convalescence in France would have enabled him to rejoin them, he longed for a break from the almost unrelieved horrors he had recently witnessed. His thankfulness shows itself in an uncharacteristically mild description of his arrival in England, so mild in fact that it was accepted for publication by the *Westminster Gazette*.[86]

Virginia Woolf used the last four lines of 'Stretcher Case' to argue that Sassoon's realism was 'of the right, the poetic kind. The real things are put in not merely because they are real, but because at a certain moment of emotion the poet happened to be struck by them and is not afraid of spoiling his effect by calling them by their right names'.[87] Looking at the lines in question, it is hard not to believe that Woolf wrote more from a desire to please Ottoline Morrell, who had asked her to write the review, than from poetic sensibility:

> There shone the blue serene, the prosperous land,
> Trees, cows and hedges; skipping these, he scanned
> Large, friendly names, that change not with the year,
> Lung Tonic, Mustard, Liver Pills and Beer.
>
> (CP, p. 30)

Even taking Sassoon's own description of the poems as 'mildly satirical' into account, it is still a disappointing performance, though it does underline how far he had come from his Romantic beginnings. Dedicated to Edward Marsh, who had tried hard to alleviate Sassoon's grief over Robert Graves, 'Stretcher Case' was written at Oxford, the new 'paradise' in which Sassoon found himself safely installed on 2 August 1916.

11

'My Killed Friends Are With Me
Where I Go'
(August 1916-January 1917)

August 1916 to January 1917 is among the most eventful as well as the most productive years of Sassoon's life, but it begins fairly quietly. Outwardly, its first five months are one of the least dramatic periods of the War for him. Passed wholly in England, they appear to be a time of rest, recuperation and gentle socializing. Inwardly, however, it is a period of great change as his attitude towards the War hardens. Encouraged by the colourful and influential Lady Ottoline Morrell, whom he meets in August, he begins to find intellectual grounds for what had been an emotional rejection of the fighting and this, in turn, affects his poetry. Many of the most powerful poems in *The Old Huntsman*, which is more or less ready for publication by February 1917, are written during this period.

When Sassoon arrived back in England at the beginning of August 1916 the battle of the Somme was still raging and would do so until 1 November. On the opening day alone, as he knew, the British had suffered enormous losses and in the space of four months were to see 400,000 dead and wounded for severely limited gains. The failure of the Somme offensive would be the start of a fresh series of crises for the Allies, which would include the Battle of Arras in the spring of 1917 and culminate in the nightmare of Passchendaele in the second half of that year.

The collapse of the Russian Army following the February Revolution of 1917 would lead most observers to anticipate the eventual peace treaty between Russia and Germany, which did in fact follow the October Revolution the same year and freed large numbers of German troops from the East to fight on the Western Front. America's entry into the War in April 1917, though heartening to the Allies, was to be of no immediate practical help, since they would need time in which to raise and train the army of a million men promised for the late spring and summer of 1918. It is hardly surprising that Sassoon's faith in the so-called 'year of victory', was to grow very dim indeed during the course of it. Eventually he would come to believe that there was no justification at all for the continuation of a War which was claiming so many lives and causing so much suffering to ordinary men and women.

In August 1916, however, Sassoon was not yet seriously disaffected. He was simply happy to be back in England, away from the horrors of the Somme and not even wounded. The so-called 'spots' on his lung which had helped bring about this miracle had either quickly disappeared, or been misdiagnosed in the first place. His vigour, undermined by trench-fever and a more long-standing anaemia, was gradually returning under strict medical care, in a situation which made none of the demands of trench life. Delivered from his one great fear in battle, that of being blinded, he feasted his eyes on the beauty of his surroundings which contrasted sharply with the ugliness of the War zone.

Life at No. 3 Southern General Hospital in his little cream room on the ground floor of Somerville College, with its view of tranquil lawns and trees was positively as well as negatively enjoyable. Though the college was a relatively new building by Oxford standards – it was founded in 1879 and therefore only thirty-seven years old when Sassoon arrived there – architecturally it was very similar in style and feel to the more ancient and august foundations. Curiously enough Sassoon does not seem to have minded being in an all women's college, though he was not unaware of the irony. (Writing to Graves at Somerville on 14 March 1917, he was to joke: 'How very unlike you to crib my idea of going to the Ladies' College at Oxford!'[1]) It also seemed to him ironic that he should be in Oxford exactly one year after spending a month in that other great seat of learning, Cambridge. He loved the Oxford bells chiming the hour, the sound of a piano from across the lawn and the tall chestnut trees swaying against the blue sky. Better, even, than the physical advantages were the mental ones. There was now time to read and his choice of Fanny Burney's *Evelina* suggests that he gladly embraced the chance to escape the harshness of trench life. He also felt ready to pour out all the poetry which had been bottled up in him. As he himself observed, it was not easy to be both poet and platoon commander. Relieved of the latter responsibility, he felt overflowing with accumulated impressions and emotional reactions to the extraordinary events he had experienced.

Only one thing seriously marred his happiness, the death, as he be-lieved, of his friend Robert Graves. The relationship had seemed to promise so much in so many ways that, though it was nearly two weeks since Graves's death had been reported to him, he was still unable to come to terms with it. His joy, therefore, when Edward Marsh telegraphed him the news that Graves had actually survived was unbounded.[2] Writing to Dent less than two days after his arrival in Oxford, Sassoon could hardly control his emotions, let alone his punctuation:

> You dear old music-man, I'm so glad in my heart; Robert has come back! He is in hospital at Rouen and going on quite well; Everyone said he was killed; I asked both Colonel and Adjutant of his Battn. Isn't that wonderful and splendid? And I've been sent to England with spots on my lungs or some rot,

and I've been lying on the lawn in sun and breeze and and Oxford bells – oh paradise for the poet!³

While Sassoon was writing joyfully to Dent in Cambridge, still believing Graves to be in Rouen, Graves was addressing a letter to Sassoon in France from his hospital bed in Highgate. It was a comedy of errors which was quickly resolved and three days later Graves, now correctly informed of Sassoon's whereabouts though still incorrectly believing him to be wounded, writes again. After expressing both concern and relief (that Sassoon is 'out of it') and also regret that he did not get himself sent to Oxford ('what a missed opportunity'), he invites Sassoon to go with him to Harlech, which should speed up both of their recoveries:

> Advantages besides those already enumerated – sea air; skilled and certifi-
> cated nurses – (my sister and mother); a piano not too much out of tune and
> my sister plays exquisitely and so do you, don't you?; some younger brothers
> to liven things up; Snowden; the complete works of Samuel Butler and
> Middleton and other amusing books; Gwuthdy Bach [Graves's cottage], oh
> and lots more.⁴

Not content with this exuberant letter, and still rejoicing in his renewed contact with Sassoon, Graves follows it with a second, verse, letter, playfully describing in classical terms his escape from Lethe through the help of Proserpine and some morphia, with which he drugs Cerberus.⁵ If anything, his narrow escape from death strengthens the affection between him and Sassoon. They continue to plan a joint volume of verse, in the manner of Wordsworth and Coleridge's *Lyrical Ballads*, another reason why Graves believes it is vital Sassoon should visit him in Harlech.

Meantime, relieved of his greatest anxiety, Sassoon starts to write his own poetry again. In a letter to Dent he includes an 'absurd' poem which he is sure will 'tickle' Dent's 'cynical old gullet' – 'The Father'. Lightweight though this is (Sassoon admitted it had a touch of the *Spoon River Anthology* about it)⁶, it is interesting for what it reveals of Sassoon's attitude as well as his working methods. Since his diary at this time is both sparsely written and not very revealing of his state of mind, his verse is a particularly important source: 'it was only when I was writing verse that I tried to concentrate and express my somewhat loose ideas', he wrote of this period.⁷ 'The Father' shows that he has lost none of his growing cynicism about the War. It also demonstrates clearly how an apparently trivial episode of everyday life can be turned by him into scorching satire. As he lay relaxing in the grounds of Somerville College he had noticed a tall, well-preserved man pushing his rather sallow and sulky son across the lawn in a long, wheeled bed. The son had lost a leg and the father appeared all solicitude, but Sassoon suspected that they had not got on well together before the War. From this fleeting impression he builds up a bitter picture of mutual loathing and distrust:

> ... I wheel him slowly out in his long bed, while nurses
> watch my stooping tenderness;
> then he smiles up at me, shifting his head: and what's
> between us there they never guess.
>
> For when my boy gets well and finds his legs, and the War
> ends with 'no one quite the same',
> We shall renew – as sure as eggs are eggs, – our bitter
> feud: but he'll be walking lame.

'The Father', with its condensed narrative, colloquial language and deliberately simple stanza and rhyme scheme, is as effective in its own way as others Sassoon allowed to be published. The reason it remained unpublished was almost certainly its challenging of one of the most cherished of ideals, particularly in wartime, family loyalty.

By the time Sassoon sent Dent 'The Father', he had already completed the poem he dedicated to Edward Marsh, 'Stretcher Case'. A day later, in full flow, he finished a third poem, 'Christ and the Soldier'. Described by Sassoon himself as an 'ambitious failure',[8] this remained unpublished until Dame Felicitas Corrigan included it in her spiritual biography of Sassoon, together with his retrospective comments.[9] Apparently he had intended it to be a commentary on the mental condition of most Front Line soldiers, himself included, 'for whom a roadside Calvary was merely a reminder of the inability of religion to co-operate with the carnage and catastrophe they experienced'. As far as he could remember, no one at the Front had ever talked to him about religion. Since it is a long poem and, as Sassoon recognized, a not entirely successful one, it seems sufficient to quote only the last verse, in which a disconsolate soldier finally abandons his attempt to find comfort in the crucified Christ-figure:

> 'Lord Jesus, ain't you got no more to say?'
> Bowed hung that head below the crown of thorns.
> The soldier shifted and picked up his pack,
> And slung his gun, and stumbled on his way.
> 'O God', he groaned, 'why ever was I born?'
> The battle boomed, and no reply came back.

The same ironic play between the suffering and wounds of Christ and those of soldiers at the Front, together with blasphemous and irreverent phrases like 'O Christ Almighty, stoop this bleeding fight' as in 'The Redeemer' and 'Stand-To: Good Friday Morning' probably ensured that, even if Sassoon had decided to allow publication, it would not have been easy.

Two more poems followed in quick succession, 'The One-Legged Man' and 'The Hero'.[10] Both pieces were to become very popular with reviewers, almost certainly because each epitomizes in its own way Sassoon's satiric method at its most effective. In both Sassoon almost gleefully set out to provide 'a thoroughly caddish antidote to the glorification of "the supreme sacrifice" and such like prevalent phrases'.[11] In order to do this he had deliberately chosen two deeply ironic situations. In 'The One-Legged Man' a badly wounded soldier, instead of raging against the loss of a leg, is grateful for the amputation which restores him to safety. In 'The Hero', where even the title is heavily ironic, a 'brother officer giv[es] a white-haired mother [a] fictitious account of her cold-footed son's death at the front'.[12] In both poems the mini-drama is played out rapidly in only three verses, though 'The Hero' has a more discursive six-line stanza, and rhyme forms an important part of the satiric thrust. The one-legged man, having come home to what is recognizably Sassoon's own Kentish Weald, seems delighted with life, rather oddly so in view of his amputation:

> And he'd come home again to find it more
> Desirable than ever it was before.
> How right it seemed that he should reach the span
> Of comfortable years allowed to man![13]
>
> (*CP*, p. 48)

In the last verse the savage meaning, anticipated in the title, becomes all too clear:

> Splendid to eat and sleep and choose a wife,
> Safe with his wound, a citizen of life.
> He hobbled blithely though the garden gate,
> And thought: 'Thank God they had to amputate!'[14]

The use of direct speech and, in particular, the careful choice of diction, are both features of Sassoon's most successful satires. They figure prominently in the second of these two pieces, 'The Hero'. The poem opens with the poor old Mother's quavering words, 'Jack fell as he'd have wished' ..., 'The Colonel writes so nicely'..., 'We mothers are so proud / Of our dead soldiers'. These phrases are then contrasted ironically in the following two verses with the thoughts of the brother officer as he thankfully escapes, his duty done:

> Quietly the Brother Officer went out.
> He'd told the poor old dear some gallant lies
> That she would nourish all her days, no doubt.
> For while he coughed and mumbled, her weak eyes
> Had shone with gentle triumph, brimmed with joy,
> Because he'd been so brave, her glorious boy.

He thought how 'Jack', cold-footed, useless swine,
Had panicked down the trench that night the mine
Went up at Wicked Corner; how he'd tried
To get sent home, and how, at last, he died,
Blown to small bits. And no one seemed to care
Except that lonely woman with white hair.

(*CP*, p. 29)

The contrast in viewpoints between the two anonymous archetypes, the Mother and the Brother Officer, is complete and the reader has been let into a secret. Sassoon's powers of condensation and his telling use of cliché are strikingly illustrated by the word 'cold-footed', which deftly boils down the phrase 'to get cold feet' to a single dismissive adjective.

Sassoon himself came to feel later that there was something rather dubious about the pleasure he derived from perfecting poems based on other people's suffering.[15] At the time, however, he felt it was his duty to disturb civilian complacency, knowing that the average Englishman would hate this poem precisely because it set out to destroy the myths built up in Wartime for the protection of civilians' peace of mind. When it first appeared in the *Cambridge Magazine* on 18 November 1916, he would not therefore have been surprised to find an irate reader by the name of Charles Geake writing in to say that 'at least one Englishman [was] pained not to say disgusted by the poem'. Sassoon saw a resemblance in both 'The Hero' and 'The One-Legged Man' to Hardy's *Satires of Circumstances,* which he had read with amusement in 1914.

Both poems seemed to Sassoon to resemble satiric drawings designed to shock with deliberately crude lines. Just as he would later come to find Hardy's *Satires* 'unworthy of his greatness', so he would reach the conclusion that his own two pieces were too purely savage and lacked the graphic sincerity of a poem such as 'Died of Wounds', which he felt made it ultimately more effective.[16] Sassoon almost certainly made no attempt to have either 'The One-Legged Man' or 'The Hero' accepted by such establishment journals of the day as the *Westminster Gazette*, the *Saturday Review*, the *Spectator*,the *Nation, Today, Art and Letters* or *Land and Water*, though all of these were to publish his less controversial Warpoetry. Fortunately, Dent's contact with the *Cambridge Magazine*, which had become the main literary mouthpiece for the anti-war faction, ensured him an audience, both poems appearing there.[17] At least twenty-six of his satires were to be accepted by the editor, C.K. Ogden, during and immediately after the War. The introduction to Dent at Cambridge in August 1915 had been very timely indeed.

Sassoon denied that 'The Hero' was based on anyone he had known, but both 'The Road' and 'Died of Wounds', probably completed during the same period, were entirely autobiographical.[18] 'The Road', differs markedly from other poems at this time. Its largely descriptive account of the road up to Mametz, whilst starkly realistic, reveals a more tender, less ironic side to

Sassoon, which he would develop later in such poems as 'Break of Day' and 'Prelude: the Troops':

> You in the bomb-scorched kilt, poor sprawling Jock,
> You tottered here and fell, and stumbled on,
> Half-dazed for want of sleep. No dreams would mock
> Your reeling brain with comforts lost and gone ...
> Too tired for thoughts of home and love and ease,
> The road would serve you well enough for bed.
>
> (*CP*, p. 32)

It is likely that Sassoon wrote most of these poems during his first week in hospital, since he was confined to the grounds of Somerville College during that time. Once allowed out, and from his favourable vantage point in the Woodstock Road close by St Giles, he began to explore the city. After a few days browsing through bookshops and picture-galleries, however, he began to want company and was, therefore, delighted when Robbie Ross telegraphed his intention of visiting him. But when he saw the dapper, little man in his light grey suit, jaunty black hat and ebony cane approaching him across the College lawn, he was concerned to note how exhausted he looked. Always somewhat careworn for his age, Ross's face was already reflecting further harassment from the implacable Lord Alfred Douglas, who was mounting yet another campaign against Oscar Wilde's staunchest friend. In spite of this Ross's gaiety appeared undiminished and together they planned the afternoon's outing.

Sassoon's autobiographical account of their trip seems to be either disingenuous or a revealing example of the effects of time on memory. According to *Siegfried's Journey*, when Robbie asked where he would like to go, he innocently enquired about the identity of Lady Ottoline Morrell who, he remembered, lived somewhere near Oxford. Yet 'To Victory', the poem which had first attracted Ottoline's attention to Sassoon when it was published anonymously in *The Times*, had appeared nearly seven months earlier on 15 January. Since then Sassoon had paid a number of visits to the man who had revealed his identity to Ottoline, Edmund Gosse, as well as exchanging several gifts and further letters with the mistress of Garsington. It is difficult to believe that Gosse would not have told him of Ottoline's well-known position as half-sister of the Duke of Portland, wife of a Liberal MP who had taken an extreme pacifist line and a lavish patroness of writers and painters, even if Sassoon had not already heard of it from other sources. (Both Ross and Marsh knew her well.) It is also unlikely that Ottoline, who was very conscious of her position, would not herself have made Sassoon aware of her credentials. Of course, Sassoon's version, that he still believed her to be 'a romantic-minded young lady living in the depths of the country', makes for a better story, but it does alert the reader to the dangers of accepting all his autobiographical writings literally.

In essence, however, Sassoon was right to cast Ottoline Morrell as a romantic-minded young lady. Even though she was already in her forty-fourth year when they met (and thirteen years older than the poet), her sprawling handwriting, 'an arabesque of dots and flourishes' and, even more, her high-flown idealism expressed in gushing language, seemed more appropriate to a less mature woman. When she wrote to Sassoon in France that 'it was such a delight to find – in these dark prison-like days – a sympathetic desire to fly out beyond into the beauty and colour and freedom that one so longs for …'[19], she could have been echoing Sassoon's younger self which was still apparent in his early War poetry. But when Lady Ottoline confided that 'it was only through poetry and wild days in the country that one could escape', he seems to have felt that it was a solace in which he could no longer indulge as the realities of War grew grimmer. Nevertheless he jumped at Robbie's suggestion of a visit to this exotic being.

Sassoon's first view of Ottoline's country retreat, Garsington Manor, which he and Ross reached by taxi from St Giles, only confirmed his romantic impression of her.[20] From the moment they arrived at the tall wrought-iron gates and stood in the shadow of some lofty elms, he felt that he was in enchanted and enchanting territory. Within the gates was a green forecourt, flanked on either side by high yew hedges, and across it a paved path which led to the mellow Tudor manor house. On this first occasion he was to see only the Monastery studio, where the Hon. Dorothy Brett [21] was painting Ottoline's portrait, and the celebrated Italianate gardens where the unexpected guests were invited to have tea with their hostess and her M.P. husband, Philip. Later he would discover the charms of the house itself, which was a testimony to Ottoline's strongest gift, her innate decorative flair and tact.

Ottoline's decorative abilities also revealed themselves dramatically in her dress, as Sassoon's first meeting with her confirmed. Nothing could more solidly have reinforced his initial diagnosis of romanticism than her costume of voluminous pale-pink Turkish trousers, orange tunic and, to top her already striking six-foot figure, purple hat on purple hair. (Sassoon claimed that his first sight of her was of the aforesaid baggy pink trousers coming backwards down the studio loft-ladder.) On this occasion she had the excuse of sitting for her portrait, but she had always a tendency towards theatrical dress, an inclination which was to cause the conventional Sassoon acute embarrassment at times. It may have accounted partly for his shyness at their first meeting.

It was perhaps his endearing diffidence which attracted Ottoline, who was already half-inclined to fall in love with the next handsome young man she met, since her long affair with Bertrand Russell and shorter one with Henry Lamb, among others, were more or less over. According to her most recent biographer, Miranda Seymour, her private papers show that she fell deeply in love with Sassoon, but as Ottoline's descendants have denied further access to these papers since Ms Seymour's biography, we must take this on trust. However, there is more than a hint of infatuation in Ottoline's published account of their first meeting, which is also worth quoting for the vivid picture it gives of Sassoon at this time:

> While he and Philip and Robbie Ross were talking I watched him. He sat up very erect and turned his head in a peculiar stiff movement to one side. Although he talked a good deal he had a trick of hesitating over his sentences as if he were shy, but still he was full of humour and laughed and was gay, always keeping his head erect and looking down, Perhaps it was his way of turning his head, and the lean face with green hazel eyes, his ears large and rather protruding, and the nose with the wide nostrils, that was not exactly *farouche* but he seemed very shy and reserved, he was more *sauvage*; and, as I looked at his full face I said to myself, 'He could be cruel'.[22]

Ottoline found Sassoon, unlike many of her more intellectual friends, 'sympathetic and wonderfully intimate' to her and was intensely moved at meeting someone whose thoughts seemed so akin to her own, 'simple, yet imaginative'.[23] Whilst Sassoon might have agreed with her diagnosis of him as more imaginative than intellectual, he would certainly have been nervous had he read the frustrated longing which concluded it, that someone would 'enter into that chamber of my being whence springs the fountain of romance, where a strange and magical coloured light played upon the intruder'.

Almost certainly in pursuit of that romance, Ottoline suggested another meeting to Sassoon as he and Ross left, clutching the peacock feathers she had given them as souvenirs. Sassoon, who viewed the proposed meeting as largely cultural – a visit to the Ashmolean Museum – upset her by his casual lateness, but then *he* was not in love. The 'start of joy' she felt when he did eventually appear reinforces the impression that *she* was. It was a situation which was to cause her a great deal of pain, wholly unintentional on Sassoon's part. Though he knew of Ottoline's reputation as a 'man-hunter' (she was nicknamed 'Lady Utterly Immoral' by unkind people), it was some time before he suspected that she had designs on him. Since he had, from the start, made it clear that he was fonder of men than women and had first appeared in the company of a well-known homosexual, Ross, it was not an unreasonable assumption. When he accepted Ottoline's invitation to visit Garsington for a stay in September, therefore, he did so in all innocence. For him their bond was poetry and things spiritual; for Ottoline things spiritual had a way of leading on to things physical.

At their first meeting, however, none of these complications had become apparent and Sassoon thoroughly enjoyed his visit to Garsington. He also enjoyed another outing, this time alone, to meet his Uncle Hamo at Burford on 11 August. Sassoon appreciated seeing his simple, unpretentious uncle as much as, if not more than, the exotic chatelaine of Garsington. The journey in itself was a pleasure, particularly by contrast with the grim troop-trains he had recently taken through France. Oxfordshire on a fine August day still appears quintessentially English and it must have seemed even more so eighty years ago. Sitting in the dilatory train which took him from Oxford to Shipton and then in the even slower horse-bus which completed the twelve miles to Burford, Sassoon felt such serenity was worth all the sacrifices demanded at the Front. The ripe harvest fields, the little stone bridge over the Windrush, Burford's steep street of grey houses and the quaint old inn where his uncle greeted him seemed like a welcome home from the War, so completely different was it from France.

Under such tranquillizing effects, Sassoon's nagging doubts vanished. He enjoyed Uncle Hamo's quiet pride in his nephew's M.C. and relished the one or two local 'characters' he was taken to meet, though he was disappointed that Hamo's old friend Thomas Hardy had not been persuaded to visit as hoped. He also liked hearing about his uncle's harvesting work which he suspected was rather amateurish, and his successful fishing trips to the nearby river. However, when he was finally taken up the steep little street for tea with a local dignitary, Mr Horniman, his doubts began to return.[24] Though genuinely enjoying his visit to the distinguished old gentleman and fully appreciating the treasures with which his lovely house was filled, he could not help remembering the men he had left behind on the Somme. Yet he felt that it would have been quite impossible to convey the reality of that carnage to his uncle and his charming old friend. Fond as he was of Uncle Hamo and much as he admired Mr Horniman's fine taste, he realized fully for the first time that they, and their like, were incapable of facing the truth about the War. 'Their attitude was to insist that it was splendid to be in the front-line. So it was – if one came out of it safely' he concluded.[25]

Exposed to the sufferings not only of himself but more particularly of others on the Somme, Sassoon found himself resenting their patriotic suppression of the unpleasant aspects of War, in a way which was new to him. His friendship with Ross, who was almost recklessly critical of the handling of the War, had shown Sassoon that there were civilians capable of confronting the unpalatable truths about it. It was mainly due to his friend's encouragement that he had started to write candidly about them. Now, in the gentle environment of the sleepy little Oxfordshire village in the company of his well-meaning uncle and friend, he felt an urge to go even further. It was another important step towards his public protest.

The most immediate results of his fresh dissatisfaction were three more poems underlining the distance between civilian perceptions of life at the Front and the reality of it, all of them unpublished in his lifetime. The first two emphasize the fact that his sympathies were no longer confined to his own side. While 'For England' contrasts the miserable end of an English soldier – 'something smashed his neck; he choked and swore' – with the interpretation his civilian relations place upon it:

> A glorious end; killed in the big attack.
> His relatives who thought him such a bore,
> Grew pale with grief and dressed themselves in black;[26]

'The Stunt' describes the unfeeling slaughter of some German soldiers by a gung-ho Englishman who receives a medal for his callousness:

> 'How splendid. O how splendid!' his relations said,
> But what the weeping Saxons said I do not know[27]

In this second poem there is also an ironic dig at the idea that 'God is on our side', for it is 'Gentle Jesus' who keeps the Englishman safe while he slaughters the Germans. In the third piece, 'Via Crucis' Christianity is again invoked to suggest that, whilst Christ's suffering and death had at least a purpose, the soldier's equally agonizing lot has not even that with which to dignify it:

> Mangling crumps and bullets through the brain,
> Jesus never guessed them when He died.
> Jesus had a purpose for His pain,
> Ay, like abject beasts we shed our blood,
> Often asking if we die in vain.
> Gloom conceals us in a soaking sack –
> Mud and rain.[28]

While none of these poems is wholly successful, they do show Sassoon's increasing anger and determination to force ignorant civilians to face the truth about the War.

Sassoon himself argued, only half-jokingly, that a great deal of his bile arose literally from leading an unhealthy life. Once away from the temptation to over-indulge in food and drink, and under the strict régime of daily physical exertion imposed on him in France, his doubts generally subsided. 'It is impossible to remain cynical when one's liver insists on being utterly in order', he wrote to Dent; 'only heavy luncheons in London Clubs can produce the genuine ironic vein of the critical pacifist'.[29] This is clearly an oversimplification, but it is true that he needed strenuous physical activity to keep him cheerful. Since Oxford offered him the possibility of neither horse riding, golf nor cricket and as his health rapidly returned, he took to a new sport, canoeing. It demanded all his formidable energy, for the River Cherwell, where he spent most of his afternoons during his last week of convalescence, had been sadly neglected during the War and was full of weeds. Reaching Water Eaton, only a few miles upriver, seemed to him convincing proof that he was fit enough to be discharged from hospital. While his doctors approached the question in a rather more scientific fashion, they came to the same conclusion and by 18 August he was back home.

One of the first things Sassoon did when he arrived at Weirleigh was to incorporate his idyllic days on the Cherwell into a striking poem, which Wilfred Owen was to call 'a perfect piece of art'. Based also on his memory of hospital at Amiens, 'The Death-Bed' is a new departure for Sassoon. Abandoning heavy satire for a method closer to his more lyrical early War poems, he nevertheless does not revert to his earlier glorification of war. Perhaps he felt, as he had with 'Died of Wounds', that graphic sincerity could sometimes be more effective than dextrous sarcasm.

The subject, the death of an innocent young soldier, is certainly very similar to 'Died of Wounds', though the narrator's pity is far more overt in the later poem. Much of the effect is achieved through shifts in the point of view. The first six stanzas are an imaginative reconstruction of the dying soldier's gradual descent into the waters of oblivion, expressed appropriately through imagery taken from Sassoon's days on the Cherwell:

> He drowsed and was aware of silence heaped
> Round him, unshaken as the steadfast walls;
> Aqueous like floating rays of amber light,
> Soaring and quivering in the wings of sleep.
> Silence and safety; and his mortal shore
> Lipped by the inward, moonless waves of death.
>
> Someone was holding water to his mouth.
> He swallowed, unresisting, moaned and dropped
> Through crimson gloom to darkness; and forgot
> The opiate throb and ache that was his wound.
> Water – calm, sliding green above the weir.
> Water – a sky-lit alley for his boat,
> Bird-voiced, and bordered with reflected flowers
> And shaken lines of summer; drifting down,
> He dipped contented oars, and sighed, and slept.
>
> (*CP*, p. 34)

In the seventh verse the narrator steps forward and openly invites compassion for this young man who symbolizes all the unnecessary loss of life in War, drawing the reader directly into the drama:

> Light many lamps and gather round his bed.
> Lend him your eyes, warm blood and will to live,
> Speak to him; rouse him; you may save him yet.
> He's young; he hated War; how should he die
> When cruel old campaigners win safe through?

In the eighth and final stanza the point of view shifts again:

But death replied: 'I choose him.' So he went,
And there was silence in the summer night;
Silence and safety; and the veils of sleep.
Then far away, the thudding of the guns

This less savage but still heartfelt condemnation of the War was refused, without comment, by the *Westminster Review*, as 'In the Pink' had been six months earlier.

'The Death-Bed' concluded Sassoon's compulsive need to put his Somme experiences into verse, at least for the time being, and he spent most of his stay at Weirleigh mooning about in the overgrown garden and neglected stables. It seemed hopeless to attempt to restore the tennis court to serviceable condition and there were no longer any local cricket matches to occupy the summer days. His mother, still unreconciled to Hamo's death ten months earlier, was indifferent company. He was, therefore, guiltily relieved when Graves's promised invitation to Harlech materialized.

Graves, whose autobiographical version of this period is highly inaccurate, claims that he and Sassoon travelled up to Wales together at the end of August and gives a detailed picture of Sassoon reading an account of the 1st Battalion's massacre at Ginchy on 3 September while they waited for their train at Paddington Station, clearly a chronological impossibility. In fact Graves travelled up to Harlech on 26 August with his sister and Sassoon followed on 29 August. He and his dog Topper, an affectionate little fox-terrier of whom he was very fond, were met at Harlech station by Robert and his younger brother, Charles.

Both Sassoon and his dog made a good impression on the Graves clan, particularly on Robert's father, who described Sassoon in his diary as 'a fine, tall manly modest fellow'.[30] Everyone enjoyed his stories which according to Robert's youngest brother, John, were extremely humorous and related in 'a nervous but entrancing way'.[31] John remembered one anecdote which ended with someone – Sassoon, he thought – hurling an overripe pear at an odious man of the Profiteer type as he sat in his enormous motor-car. A slight story in itself, it suggests that Graves was for once accurate when he claimed that at Harlech he and Sassoon were becoming increasingly unhappy about the continuance of the War. They had both begun to see it as 'merely a sacrifice of the idealistic younger generation to the stupidity and self-protective alarm of the elder'.[32] Later on they would differ as to how this unhappiness should express itself, but for the moment they were in complete agreement.

Sassoon's fortnight at Harlech went well. Almost fully recovered physically, he enjoyed numerous games of golf with Charles Graves, a fellow-enthusiast, and went on several outings into the beautiful surrounding hills with the family. Most of his time, however, was spent with Robert in his little cottage, Gwuthdy Bach. Newly pink-washed and hung with fresh blue curtains, it made an attractive retreat. It was here they carried out the main purpose of their visit, to work on their poetry together.

They were still planning a joint publication along the lines of *Lyrical Ballads* and were as close as Wordsworth and Coleridge in the support and help they gave each other. Both perfectionists in their very different ways, they had already started suggesting emendations to each other's work, mainly in letters. Graves, for example, when sent Sassoon's 'Stand-To: Good Friday Morning', had asked 'can't you "splash" next time instead of "sploshing"? It's more fitting for Good Friday', a suggestion Sassoon had happily accepted.[33] Graves, in turn, was ready to trust his friend's judgement.[34] They now applied this practice to the respective collections which they hoped to co-ordinate.[35] One of the guiding principles of this collaboration, Graves claimed, was that they should define War 'by making contrasted definitions of peace'.[36] With Sassoon it was hunting, nature, music and pastoral scenes, whereas with Graves it was children. Having already considered Marsh's copious comments, they aimed to have a manuscript ready for Ross's inspection by the middle of September, with a view to publication later in the year.

Before travelling to London to see Ross, however, they seem to have stopped off in Oxford for a night or two with the Morrells at Garsington. This version of events contradicts what Sassoon himself and both Graves's and Ottoline Morrell's biographers claim. All of them clearly imply that Sassoon spent a full week at Garsington in September, but the dates simply do not tally. Sassoon was at Harlech with Graves from 29 August to 11 September, in London from 13 to 15 September, at Weirleigh from 15 to 20 September and again from 28 September to at least 5 October. From 20 to 28 September he was at Loder's house near Peterborough. The only days unaccounted for are the 11 and 12 September. Further evidence that these were probably spent with Graves at Garsington comes in his first surviving letter to Ottoline Morrell in the Harry Ransom collection at Austin, Texas. Writing from Harlech on Monday, 4 September, he tells her that he will be coming to Oxford with Graves the following Monday (i.e. the 11th) and would like to bring his friend to Garsington, which presumably he did. Her diaries show that they visited her together some time in September. By 20 September Sassoon was in Peterborough, by 23 September Graves was in Llandrindod and by 30th September she was in Harrogate.

The point of this apparent carping about dates is that Sassoon's autobiography is clearly not factually reliable. Since it was written after his break with Graves, not only does he entirely omit any reference to his stay at Harlech, but also any mention of the fact that Graves went with him to Garsington. In his version his visit, extended imaginatively to a week, becomes an excuse for a full description of Ottoline, Garsington and its mainly Pacifist inhabitants. The week's stay probably did take place but later than he suggests.

Whenever the visit occurred it made a deep impression on Sassoon, who devotes five pages of his autobiography to it.[37] Though he had seen Ottoline at least once since his introduction to her by Ross, he had not previously been inside her house. When at last he did so his imagination was stirred by what he aptly called its 'sumptuous homeliness'.[38] It was the combination of its ancient charm and irregularity, moderate proportions and Ottoline's exotic decoration which struck not only him but most of those who saw it. Many have commented on the panelled drawing room painted a rich lacquer red and furnished with fine Italian furniture, and he was no exception. He had a general impression of faded silks and velvets, of dusty browns and purples tinged with glints of tarnished gold from coffers and cabinets.

It was an effect Ottoline had consciously cultivated in her house and herself, as though both had stepped out of the Renaissance. While Sassoon remained nervous about being seen with a walking period piece outside her setting, inside it he fully appreciated the effect. As Ottoline sat embroidering of an evening in a Velasquez-like gown of rich brocade, or as he himself sat reading the *Oxford Book of English Verse*, given him by his hostess, in his mullion-windowed room with its four-poster bed, he felt the instinctive tact and harmony of his surroundings. It was an escape, of a kind he had frequently enjoyed in his pre-war existence, into a peaceful and gracious past. For the next ten years he was to regard Garsington as one of the few houses where he could feel free to do as he pleased, and he would return to it on many occasions.

However much of a refuge Garsington seemed, it did not allow Sassoon to escape thinking about the War as he had hoped. Philip Morrell's pacifist views were passionately shared by his wife and they had filled Garsington and its out-buildings with conscientious objectors. Since farm-work was considered a legitimate alternative to fighting, they had been able to offer their house and farm as a haven for a number of friends. Many were writers or artists, the more famous including Ottoline's long-time philosopher lover, Bertrand Russell, the critic John Middleton Murry and the painter Mark Gertler. (Not surprisingly the farm was not run very efficiently and many of the intellectuals appeared rather ungrateful for the escape route so generously offered them.)

When the day's work was over and the pacifists came in for an evening by the fire, Sassoon was exposed to an entirely different view of the War from any previously offered him, except perhaps by Ross. Though he had himself been highly critical of its handling at the Front, especially after the Somme, he had never before heard the Government criticized so roundly and so articulately. Philip Morrell's parliamentary connexion gave him an insider's authority and this lent weight to his claim that the Germans had already made tentative peace overtures through neutral channels, which had been turned down. While it suited Sassoon to believe that the soldiers had real cause for dissatisfaction, it was nevertheless a genuine revelation to him and one which contributed significantly to his eventual public protest. It was one thing to sacrifice men idealistically in a necessary War, but quite another to continue to do so for cynical, self-serving reasons. Though he was at times to deny the influence of the Garsington pacifists, there is little doubt of their effect on him. They brought him one step nearer to rebellion and were to help him in a quite practical way to express it. From being a largely emotional reaction to his own and others' gruelling experiences, his dissatisfaction acquired a firm intellectual basis.

Ottoline herself, unlike the majority of his other friends, was to encourage Sassoon's impulse to protest and it was during this first stay at Garsington that the foundations were laid. Ottoline's initial impression that Sassoon, like herself, was more imaginative than intellectual, was reinforced and gave her hope of an even deeper *rapport*. They also shared a love of nature and a generosity of quixotic proportions. From the start Ottoline showered gifts on Sassoon. Valuable copies of her favourite poets, a beautiful orange-vermilion vellum manuscript book for him to write out his current collection of poems, silk scarves, precious stones and hand-embroidered tapestries were only some of the presents she was to bestow on her handsome new friend in the next six months. Sassoon responded with copies of his poems, elaborately illustrated, and, an ultimate gesture of trust, was eventually to send her his diary to read.

Another characteristic shared by the poet and his hostess was their idealism. Ottoline's was, however, of a more intense kind than that of the essentially reserved Sassoon and he was nervous of her excessively high expectations of him. Still deeply suspicious of women, whom he regarded largely as potential predators, he was probably already beginning to suspect that Ottoline wanted more than friendship. He was to entertain Ross in March 1917 with an account of another homosexual friend, Nevill Forbes's visit to Garsington, when not so discreet enquiries were made about Sassoon's 'previous career as an amorist'.[39] Sassoon humorously but sincerely expressed a wish that *The Times* 'would find someone else to write a poem and draw the fire of Ottoline's too ardent eyes elsewhere'. He found it highly embarrassing to be 'crowned as a sort of Keats-Shelley-Blake-Tagore-Nijinsky-Rupert Brooke' (a phrase which anticipated Wilfred Owen's impression of him) and begged Ross to find a substitute, one who could 'tackle the problem and storm the Messalina fortress once and for all'.[40]

Apart from his nervousness about Ottoline's amorous intentions, Sassoon also realized, after long talks with her, that she was altogether too intense and perhaps too humourless for his taste. Reading her lofty aspirations in the privacy of his perfect bedroom, he seems to have found what he calls those 'touchingly amateurish pages' a little comic, in spite of their unquestionable sincerity:

> Come then [she had written] gather here – all who have passion and who desire to create new conditions of life – new visions of art and literature and new magic worlds of poetry and music. If I could but feel that days at Garsington had strengthened your efforts to live the noble life: to live freely, recklessly, with clear Reason released from convention – no longer absorbed in small personal events but valuing personal affairs as part of a great whole – above all to live with passionate desire for Truth and Love and Understanding and Imagination.[41]

Sassoon was to become genuinely fond of Ottoline, once she had accepted him as a comrade rather than a potential lover, and was to recommend her to at least one friend as 'a jolly good sort'.[42] The more he saw of her the more he came to appreciate her genuine desire to share the imaginative life of her artistic friends and to promote it whenever possible. Unlike D.H. Lawrence, Aldous Huxley, Osbert Sitwell and others, he resisted the temptation to caricature such an easy target in his work. In fact, he was unintentionally to hurt Ottoline by not alluding to her at all in *Memoirs of an Infantry Officer*, though he was to describe her at length in his official autobiography. Apart from a few mild jokes he limited his criticism to the observation that she was 'in some ways an idealist, essentially generous but deficient in constructive comprehension of the problems which she contemplated with such intensity. At that period her idealism was still in the full flush of its immaturity'.[43]

Sassoon is unlikely to have been quite so restrained when he met Ross in London shortly after his first stay at Garsington. He and Graves had to be there for examinations by their respective chest specialists on 13 September but also to show their revised joint manuscript to Ross. They had already booked rooms with Nellie Burton at 40 Half Moon Street and during their two days there discussed their *Lyrical Ballads* plan with Ross. So involved had they become in the idea of a collaboration that they were very surprised when Ross rejected it outright. From his more objective standpoint he probably saw that it would do neither of them any good.

Sassoon needed a publication of his own and had enough strong poems to warrant one, while Graves, who had only recently put all his worthwhile poetry into *Over the Brazier*, needed more time to build up another collection. Writing to Ross two days after accepting his advice Graves acknowledged its wisdom, but also registered his regret:

> … I am deeply indebted to you for helping me to make up my mind about the proposed 'Lyrical Ballads' which I now see could not have answered at all. I'm sorry, rather because old Sassoon's such a dear and we took some pains over coordinating the two sets of verses: and I'm disappointed at not having enough myself for printing after having polished them to the verge of disgust.

Sassoon's letter to Ross, if there was one, has not survived but he was almost certainly excited by the change of plan. He could not have found it entirely easy to accept that his much younger friend had already had a volume of War poems brought out by the publisher who had eventually turned his own poems down, Harold Monro. Sassoon admired Graves's work and liked him as a person sufficiently to rejoice in his good fortune, but it must have left him with an ambition to see his own poems published in book form. Private productions brought some satisfaction, and he already had another one with the Chiswick Press, but the time had come for wider recognition. It is a measure of his increased confidence that he was at last ready to face public exposure on his own.

Instead, therefore, of working with Graves and Ross, Sassoon found himself working with Ross alone on an initial selection to show first to Gosse, then to the publisher William Heinemann. Gosse had been anxious for Sassoon to get his early poems out of his system by publishing them and this almost certainly influenced the selection, which was fairly comprehensive, ranging from his early sonnets of 1909 to his most recent War-satires. It was eventually to include poems not even written at the time of submission to Heinemann in late September and was to become, in effect, an early *Selected Poems*.[44]

Directly the selection had been made and dispatched to a typist and, after another month's leave had been granted to Sassoon by his chest specialist, he took Graves down to Weirleigh to return his hospitality. What happened next was the cause of one of the more famous literary disputes. It was not the event itself which caused the trouble, but Graves's description of it over thirteen years later in *Goodbye to All That*. His account there is so inaccurate that it is difficult to unravel what actually occurred, particularly since Sassoon omitted the whole incident from his own autobiography; he limited himself to a manuscript note in *Goodbye to All That* to the effect that Graves's remarks were 'unforgivable' and 'almost entirely apocryphal'.[45] The 'almost entirely' does, however, suggests that there was some truth in Graves's version and it is likely that Sassoon himself was suppressing a great deal of painful knowledge about the affair.

It had all started on the evening of Graves's arrival at what he obliquely (and inaccurately) refers to as the house of 'a recently wounded First Battalion friend'.[46] After describing in some detail the way in which the friend's mother (Theresa Sassoon) tried to keep the memory of her dead son alive by preserving his room exactly as it had been, Graves related how he had been continually woken up the first night by sudden rapping noises, followed by sobs, shrieks and laughter which made sleep impossible. According to him, his friend explained that it was his mother, who had been reading the spiritualist Sir Oliver Lodge's *Raymond, or Life After Death*, and was trying to get in touch with her dead son. Sassoon himself was to confirm the truth of at least this part of Graves's account and his own irritation with his mother, when he wrote in his diary only four months later:

> Stuff like *Raymond* repels me utterly. Having discovered the fatuity of it in my own case, and watched that pathetic, foolish clinging to the dead which goes on among so many women who (like my own mother) have nothing else to distract their minds from war and wretchedness. It is the *worst* confession of weakness ... [47]

It was not, therefore, what Graves said which angered Sassoon but his disloyalty in retailing such private confidences to the world at large in his characteristically exaggerated and inaccurate fashion.

There was one part of Graves's account which was entirely untrue, however, and that was the claim that he told Sassoon after the first night, 'I'm leaving this place. It's worse than France'.[48] In reality, not only did he stay for nearly another week but he also described Weirleigh to Ross, two days after his arrival there (that is, *after* his disturbed first night) as having 'a congenial atmosphere'.[49] Having accepted Ross's rejection of the *Lyrical Ballads* project, he was attempting to start a prose work , a novel based on his War experiences, and he found Weirleigh the right place for this, in spite of Mrs Sassoon's nightly vigils.

Though Graves may not have made the remark about Weirleigh being worse than France, that country was very much on both their minds, particularly the battalion Sassoon had recently left. And whilst the news of the 1st Battalion's horrifying experiences near Ginchy could not possibly have reached them, as Graves claimed, on their way up to Harlech at the end of August, it certainly had by the time they arrived at Weirleigh on 15 September. The carnage was well over by then and there had been time enough for them to have learnt the real facts, so carefully concealed by the official accounts. Sassoon already knew something of the 1st Battalion movements from his old friend, Joe Cottrell, who had written to him on 8 August. Haig, having failed to carry out the third phase of his original Somme plan – to roll up the German Front northwards – had decided to continue his main pressure with his right flank from Guillemont to Bazentin-le-Petit. On his left General Gough aimed to take the Pozières-Thiepval end of the ridge.

As part of one of the three Corps of the Fourth Army chosen to carry out Haig's scheme, the 1st Battalion of the Royal Welch Fusiliers had been involved in bitter fighting throughout August and had moved forward only a few miles from their original position by the end of the month. Their engagement at Delville Wood near Ginchy at the beginning of September was part of a holding operation to prevent the Germans firing into the backs of troops attacking the main objective, Guillemont. (For nearly two months Division after Division had failed to capture it.) Though the 1st did all that could be expected of it in what – with good reason – became known as 'Devil's Wood', and Guillemont itself was finally taken, the engagement as a whole had been unsuccessful. The Manchesters had failed to take Ginchy, which it would require another week of hard fighting to capture, and the troops, to quote one commentator, were little better than 'compressed cannon-fodder'.[50]

Sassoon's friend and fellow-officer in C Company, Julian Dadd, had been severely wounded in the throat at Ginchy and his last surviving brother, Edmund, killed. Years later, after a series of nervous break-downs, Julian was to tell Sassoon that Ginchy had always been 'a plague spot' in his mind. One of a number of his 'horrific memories' of Ginchy was when two shell holes were bombed, killing almost all those sheltering in them, their bodies 'looking somehow like dead fish'.[51] Though he said he was 'satisfied that, so far as I was concerned, I did the best I could have done', citing their Colonel, Stockwell, to support this, it is clear that he felt he had not fully done his duty and that he had found it much worse than the 'bad business' he admitted to.[52] (This delusion almost certainly led to his suicide in January 1937.)

Another casualty of Ginchy was the young dark-haired bombing officer, V.F. Newton, described as 'Fernby' in *Infantry Officer*, who died of wounds shortly afterwards.[53] Only two officers out of the whole Battalion had not been hit. Even the doctor, Kelsey Fry, had been buried under debris in a nightmare incident when the aid-post was blown in, killing five already wounded men and five stretcher-bearers. Hundreds of other had been killed or wounded, leaving the 1st Battalion once more badly depleted.

Sassoon had learnt many of these details through Cottrell. Shaken out of his usual sang-froid, the old Quartermaster had sent a graphic account to another 1st Battalion officer invalided to England, 'Birdie' Stansfield, with instructions to pass his two letters on to Sassoon.[54] It was almost certainly at Weirleigh in mid-September that Sassoon read them. Twelve years later, when he came to describe the event in *Infantry Officer*, he was to base his description on these two letters, and a detailed account of the officers concerned, written at his request by Julian Dadd.[55]

It seems ironic that, with the knowledge of such bloodshed to fuel his mounting anger against the handling of the War, Sassoon should this same month have brought out another private booklet with the Chiswick Press of the escapist pre-war variety. Of the eleven poems in *Morning-Glory* (a fourteen-page volume on hand-made paper bound in dark-blue) only four – 'To Victory', 'To His Dead Body', 'Brothers' and 'The Dragon and the Undying' – deal with War, and none of them criticizes it. If anything, they promote the romantic view he appeared to have rejected. Clearly he wished to preserve them in some form, however modestly (and only eleven copies of these eleven poems were printed, in imitation of a cricket team apparently).

The remaining seven poems are even more reminiscent of Sassoon's pre-war poetry, though most show a marked improvement in technique. It comes as no surprise to find that at least two of these – 'Wind in the Beechwood' and 'A Poplar and the Moon' – were written during his peaceful interlude at Flixécourt in May. 'Wind in the Beechwood', which he told Dent had been entirely rewritten as a sonnet during his time there, describes the copse at Flixécourt which had also provided the setting for his elegy on David Thomas, 'The Last Meeting'. It is an unashamed plea for a return to the consolations Nature had afforded him before the outbreak of War:

> O luminous and lovely! Let your flowers,
> Your ageless-squadroned wings, your surge and gleam,
> Drown me in quivering brightness: let me fade
> In the warm, rustling music of the hours
> That guard your ancient wisdom, till my dream
> Moves with the chant and whisper of the glade.
>
> (*CP*, p. 63)

It is almost certain that the equally unwarlike title-poem, as well as 'A Child's Prayer' and 'Dream-Forest' were also some of the 'glad things' written at Flixécourt. Even 'To His Dead Body', composed originally as an elegy to the supposedly dead Graves and subsequently re-dedicated to Marcus Goodall, takes a romantic view of death far removed from the brutalities of his more recent 'The Hero'.

Only one poem stands out rather puzzlingly in this collection, 'Ancestors' (see p. 14) Why, it might be asked, has Sassoon chosen this particular moment to reflect on his exotic Jewish forebears? The answer lies possibly in a story told by a surviving member of the Ashley Park branch of the family, Jacques Sassoon.[56] He distinctly remembers being told that, when the news of Siegfried's M.C. came through, the Sassoon family broke its long, self-imposed feud with Alfred's widow and invited her son to visit. 'But it was an invitation to tea, not dinner', Jacques Sassoon points out, indicating how suspicious the Sassoons still were of their half-Gentile relative. Though Sassoon himself made no reference to such a visit, he did state later that his only communication from his father's brother, Joseph, was a poem of an assertively patriotic nature in June 1917, which suggests that his uncle felt it necessary to make a point:

> O piteous grave! – and black, untimely loss!
>   And laughing eyes, too soon acquaint with tears!
> Still the loved greetings faintly steal across
>   The waste of years.
>
> A hero's shade now takes the grand adieu;
>   His meed of praise in stately numbers ranged;
> And 'there's a war in France, my kinsman true!'
>   And 'men are changed'.
>
> June 1st 1917   J. L. Sassoon

It is important to remember that, when Sassoon came to make his public protest only a month after receiving his uncle's poem, he did so in the full knowledge that it would antagonize the closest of his Sassoon relatives. The Sassoons as a whole were far more likely to approve of another family member, Sir Philip Sassoon, who was on the Army's General Staff and took the Establishment position towards the War.

'Ancestors' and the other ten poems of *Morning-Glory* were all to be included in Sassoon's next volume and, more significantly, in his *Collected Poems* over thirty years later. This suggests that he was at least as proud of them as of his more celebrated anti-war poems. Certainly they were to be more typical of his poetic output as a whole and the kind of work for which he would prefer to be remembered.

At Weirleigh in September 1916, with one collection of poems safely in print and another being typed for Gosse's comments, Sassoon took a short break from poetry, to spend nine days cub-hunting with his old friend Loder's wife, Phyllis. Loder himself was still in France but his job as joint-Master of the Fitzwilliam was being carried out ably by his wife, herself a skilled horsewoman. The contrast with poetry and other mental activities was one Sassoon continued to need throughout his life, though this must not be exaggerated. Phyllis, for example, besides taking him out cub-hunting, also provided him with musical recitals in the evening, since she was almost as good a pianist as she was rider. Sassoon was rarely single-mindedly 'sporty', whatever he liked to suggest in *Memoirs of a Fox-Hunting Man*. Nevertheless, he did indulge himself during this leave in as much sport as possible, knowing that he would shortly be deprived of it in France. He had barely returned from Peterborough on 28 September when he was off again for a week's hunting with the Southdown at Ringmer, followed by a week's golfing at Rye with another old friend, David Ayton. Then he spent a further week with the Southdown Hunt from 17 to 24 November, as though cramming in as much as possible before his leave expired.

These strenuous physical activities, however, did not prevent Sassoon from writing at least eight more poems during the autumn. Spurred on by Heinemann's offer on 1 October to publish a selection of his poetry, he settled down to work at Weirleigh, possibly the same day.[57] Having hit on a fruitful vein of satire, he now set about producing more of the same for inclusion in Heinemann's book. He knew that it was the sort of poetry to please his sponsor, Ross, who was, ostensibly, to make the final selection. (In fact, Ross told Sassoon on 11 October: 'You need not take my advice. I will of course adopt *your* own choice as mine in order to pacify the Oracles' [i.e. Gosse and Marsh].)[58] Ross had indicated that there were not enough poems of the kind he admired and Sassoon was clearly trying to remedy this. In doing so he was to produce one of the most successful of his satires, and it was no coincidence that he was staying with Ross when he did so on 31 October.

Before then, however, Sassoon produced three other poems. The first of these, 'The Tombstone-Maker', is a savage satire on a stonemason who complains about the effect of the War on his 'trade'. The language convincingly, if somewhat condescendingly, echoes his uneducated speech:

> 'You'd think so much bereavement would have made
> Unusual big demands upon my trade.
> The War comes cruel hard on some poor folk;
> Unless the fighting stops I'll soon be broke.'
>
> He eyed the Cemetery across the road.
> 'There's scores of bodies out abroad, this while,
> 'That should be here by rights. They little know'd
> 'How they'd get buried in such wretched style.'
>
> (CP, p. 27)

Sassoon implies, as in previous poems, that Christianity is fairly meaningless when he has the callous stonemason lean his head against 'a sorrowing angel's breast' in the first verse, and puts pious words into his mouth to underline his hypocrisy in the last, where the narrator concludes mischievously:

> I told him with a sympathetic grin,
> That Germans boil dead soldiers down for fat;
> And he was horrified. 'What shameful sin!
> O sir, that Christian souls should come to that!'

('Souls' was originally 'men', but changed for the better.) The diction in this poem shows Sassoon's customary concern for the exact nuance, which leads him to give unusual functions to quite ordinary words. The tombstone-maker, for example, '*primmed*' his loose red mouth, the striking verb deriving from the simple adjective 'prim', and condensing a vital aspect of the man's character, his hypocrisy, into one word. Like Sassoon's other harsh satires, 'The Tombstone-Maker' was not easy to place. When it was sent to the *New Statesman* the editor, J.C. Squire, replied: 'The poem has entertained me so I am glad you sent it. But it is a bit thick for a respectable paper: besides, all our undertaker subscribers would protest'. As usual, the *Cambridge Magazine* came to the rescue and published it on 25 November 1916 and Sassoon was to include it in *Collected Poems*.

The second poem, written in October 1916, also to be included in *Collected Poems*, was of a rather different kind. It may have been written between the 17th and 23rd of the month, when Sassoon was again at Weirleigh in between hunting at Ringmer and golfing at Rye. Almost certainly a result of reading back over his War diaries, it deals with a less harsh aspect of the conflict. On 3 June 1916, hardly more than a week after his dramatic retrieval of Corporal Mick O'Brien's body, which won him his M.C., he had reflected on the possibility of the spirits of the dead men surviving, in spite of his dismissal of his mother's flirtation with Spiritualism:

> If there are ghosts, then they will be all over this battle-front forever ... I can imagine that, in a hundred or two hundred or two thousand years, when wars are waged in the air and under the ground, these French roads will be haunted by a silent traffic of sliding lorries and jolting waggons and tilting limbers – all going silently about their business.[59]

From this simple, imaginative premise the poem 'Two Hundred Years' stems. There is more pity than anger in this sonnet where the narrator, like Charles Hamilton Sorley in 'Le Revenant', imagines the ghosts of the First World War. Apart from the possibility of Sorley's influence, it is interesting as an example of the way Sassoon constantly reworked his material, relying heavily on his original diary entries in both his poetry and his prose.

Unusually, Sassoon wrote his third poem this month during a golfing trip. Apart from his dog Topper, smuggled illicitly into his lodgings at Dormy House, Rye, he was accompanied by a retired Scottish professional, David Ayton, who reminded him strongly of a music-hall comedian, especially when cleaning the ball with his tongue. It may have been his friend's jokey influence which caused Sassoon to produce a piece of doggerel which falls well below his usual standard. Called simply 'A Ballad', it adopts a deliberately sing-song metre reminiscent of Kipling's *Barrack-Room Ballads* to tell the story of a captain who shot himself in the foot after only a week at the Front and was invalided home. The irony comes predictably in the last line of the last of the three quatrains:

> Now the Captain's at the Depot, lame, but happy as a lark;
> And in billets out in France, the men who knew him tell the story
> Of "the bloke that 'ad an accident when walking in the dark" –
> While the Captain teaches raw recruits the way to blood and glory.

Sassoon wisely decided not to attempt publication of 'A Ballad' and waited till he was back in London before writing his fourth and last poem that month. It was to prove one of the most popular satires he ever produced. Composed at Ross's house late one night after a long evening in which Ross had been criticizing the Bishop of London, 'They' seemed to Sassoon to write itself. When he showed it to Eddie Marsh, whose taste was still for the more heroic type of War-poetry, Marsh had exclaimed 'It's *too* horrible', but Ross instantly recognized its power. Consisting simply of two six-line stanzas, in which an initial quatrain is followed by a couplet, the form allows Sassoon to maximise the effect of rhyme and to throw emphasis on the most ironic word, especially in the second stanza. As he noted himself in *Siegfried's Journey*, 'it went its wicked way to the twelfth and last line'.[29] His usual device of putting direct speech into the mouths of his characters makes for further irony as the privileged Bishop, with his platitudinous mouthings, is contrasted sharply with the uneducated private soldiers, who relate in a matter-of-fact way the stark results of the Bishop's support of the War. The inadequacy of Christianity and its representatives to deal with the horrors of War emerges with shock effect:

> The Bishop tells us: 'When the boys come back
> They will not be the same; for they'll have fought
> In a just cause: they lead the last attack
> On Anti-Christ: their comrades' blood has bought
> New right to breed an honourable race,
> They have challenged Death and dared him face to face.'
>
> 'We're none of us the same!' the boys reply.
> 'For George lost both his legs; and Bill's stone blind;
> 'Poor Jim's shot through the lungs and like to die;
> 'And Bert's gone syphilitic; you'll not find
> 'A chap that's served that hasn't found *some* change.'
> And the Bishop said: 'The ways of God are strange!'
>
> (*CP*, pp. 23-4)

Sassoon claimed actually to have met the Bishop of London on his return from showing this poem to Marsh, and that the Bishop 'turned a mild shining gaze on me and my M.C.'[60] It is to be hoped that such a good story is true. Even the *Cambridge Magazine*, which readily published the poem on 20 January 1917, found the word 'syphilitic' too bold for the time and omitted it.

In addition to poetry and sport Sassoon managed to fit in a visit to Cambridge in October. Both Dent and Cockerell wanted to see him, but it was Dent with whom he stayed when he arrived there after his week's golfing on Saturday, 28 October. Not only did he feel closer to Dent by this time but Cockerell, his original sponsor in Cambridge, was preoccupied with his invalid wife Kate. Since Sassoon's first visit to them in August 1915 her multiple sclerosis had grown so bad that Cockerell was unable even to invite him home for a talk. Having admired the two books of poetry Sassoon had sent him in August, particularly *Morning-Glory*, he would have 'begged' Dent to spare him for an hour or two had it not been for his wife's health. (It is significant that Cockerell, who had originally introduced Sassoon to Dent, should have felt it necessary to 'beg' Dent to let him see Sassoon.)

Sassoon did, however, pay a visit in Cambridge and one which is of greater interest to posterity. Either on Saturday 28th or, more probably, on Sunday 29 October, he met the father of a War poet he had grown greatly to admire, Charles Hamilton Sorley. Graves had introduced him to Sorley's poetry shortly after the young poet's death at the Battle of Loos in October 1915 and he had become so fond of it that Graves had eventually to insist that he return his copy of Sorley to him. For both of them he had become a standard of excellence and undoubtedly influenced their own attempts to tell the unsentimental truth about the War. When the Somme was at its worst for Sassoon, he wrote in his diary: 'I've still got my terrible way to tread before I'm free to sleep with Rupert Brooke and Sorley and all the nameless poets of the War',[61] as though identifying himself more closely with his fellow Marlburian. It was, therefore, not surprising that he should wish to pay homage to Sorley when he learnt that the poet's family lived in Cambridge and was willing to see him.

Sassoon's visit to Professor Sorley must have gone well, for when Sassoon left he was presented with a collection of Sorley's *Letters from Germany and the Army*, recently edited and privately printed by the professor. Less than two months later, inspired and cheered by the lucidly intelligent and highly entertaining letters, he was to acquire his own copy of Sorley's *Marlborough and Other Poems*, which had gone into a third edition. What he particularly admired about the young poet was that he was 'so ready for all emergencies, so ready to accept the "damnable circumstance of death" – or life'.[62] In the face of yet another trip to the Front he was to find strength in Sorley's philosophical acceptance of death, expressed most vividly for Sassoon in the opening lines of his last poem:

> When you see millions of the mouthless dead
> Across your dreams in pale battalions go,
> Say not soft things as other men have said,
> That you'll remember. For you need not so.[63]

It was a reaction to Brooke and his heroics which Sassoon himself could second. He had come a long way since writing 'Absolution'.

Sassoon continued to read Sorley's letters and poems throughout and after the War and was undoubtedly influenced by him. He would have responded to Sorley's humour and, equally, to his love of nature; on one wet day in France he was to refer to 'the rain (that Sorley loved)'.[64] He was to compare the popular War poet, Robert Nichols, unfavourably with Sorley and, when he went to lecture in America in 1920, would use Sorley's 'To Germany' to point up the failure of other soldier poets – 'who had used *not* their experience *but* their feeling of what they *ought* to say'.[65]

Perhaps the most intriguing reference of all to Sorley occurs in Graves's letter to Sassoon of May 1916, which reveals more about the two living poets than the dead one. When Sassoon met another Marlburian, Marcus Goodall, that month at Flixécourt, Graves asked him what Goodall had said about Sorley: '… and was he 'so'?', that is to say homosexual. As Sorley's poetry contained no conventional love-lyrics by the age of twenty, Graves concluded that he must be. Clearly he wished to include his favourite poet in a category to which both he and Sassoon assigned themselves at that time. In fact, Sorley, in his brief life, had shown convincing proof that he was attracted by women, but it is interesting to see Graves's attempts to cast him otherwise. It also confirms that he and Sassoon confided in each other and made reference to their own sexuality.

Professor Sorley and Dent were not the only people Sassoon visited in his last precious weeks of leave. Knowing that his Medical Board was coming up on the 17 or 18 November and that it would almost certainly find him fit, he squeezed in a visit to his great-aunt Mozelle in Hove, as well as several more stays with Ross at 40 Half Moon Street. His great-aunt was still very sprightly at sixty-one and he enjoyed seeing her sufficiently to want to return fairly often after the War. She was the only other member of his father's family apart from his aunt Rachel with whom he kept in regular touch. It was probably because, unlike the rest of the Sassoons, she appears not to have disapproved of his anti-war poetry.[66]

Much as Sassoon enjoyed his visit to Aunt Mozelle at the seaside, he undoubtedly preferred staying at 40 Half Moon Street. By 31 October, when he paid the second visit of his leave there, Ross's lodgings had become his London base and Nellie Burton would increasingly be asked to reserve rooms for him there. Since he enjoyed the company of both Ross and Burton, he found it far more congenial to stay with them than at the more impersonal Royal Societies Club on the other side of Piccadilly. He was also getting to know a number of Ross's friends, in particular Roderick Meiklejohn. Though he does not refer to Meiklejohn in his autobiography, they were to become quite close over the next fourteen years. Not quite a father-figure, Meiklejohn became more like an indulgent uncle to Sassoon. Barely ten years his senior, he was outwardly far more sober than the irrepressible and often deliberately outrageous Ross. (Sassoon confessed to finding Meiklejohn's company 'slightly dreary', like 'talking to the family solicitor'.)[67]

Meiklejohn's career, first at St Paul's School, then Oxford and finally in the Civil Service was, like most things about him, eminently respectable. From the War Office he had gone into the Treasury, where he had risen to the rank of Deputy Controller of Supply Services. In 1928 he was to become the first Civil Service Commissioner and in 1931 he would be knighted for his services. By the time Sassoon met him in 1916 he had been Private Secretary to such elevated figures as Sir Edward Hamilton, the Duke of Devonshire and Asquith, a sign of his trustworthiness, ability and discretion. His homosexuality, though less openly displayed than Ross's, was suggested by his bachelorhood and his preference for male company, particularly that of younger men, and much of his time was spent either in his own clubs (Brooks and the Beefsteak) or those of his friends. He also gave dinner parties at his home, first in Holland Road, later in Connaught Square, and was to invite Sassoon to them frequently over the years.

Though not a practitioner of the arts, Meiklejohn was a connoisseur and something of a patron to the younger men he adopted and discreetly adored. From November 1916 onwards, he was to write constantly to Sassoon, who normally replied by return but was grateful that Meiklejohn did not expect a reply. These letters, which were to become less regular after Sassoon's marriage in 1933 but nevertheless continued until the 1950s, indicate a faithfulness and devotion which Sassoon undoubtedly appreciated in the early years. Like Graves, he thought Meiklejohn 'a dear'[68] and quickly penetrated the stiff Civil Servant exterior. Meiklejohn's fondness for Sassoon was to express itself in a number of ways apart from his invitations to lunch or dine. He was to send Sassoon almost as many books as his other adoring friend, Ottoline Morrell, and, like her, to make the arduous journey to Edinburgh in an attempt to cheer him up later on. Sassoon often listed the books he was reading for Meiklejohn's interest.

In some ways Sassoon and Meiklejohn were fairly similar. Both shy and, at least in Sassoon's case, sexually repressed, they both found relief in humour. It is no coincidence that, when Sassoon dedicated a poem to Meiklejohn a few months after their first meeting, it would be a facetious one on 'Liquor Control'. Though Sassoon did not find Meiklejohn nearly as stimulating as Ross, he did appreciate him as a kind of Roger de Coverley figure. His elaborate jokiness with Meiklejohn has an old-fashioned feel to it that would not have been out of place in the eighteenth century. While in Edinburgh, for example, he describes the young women he surprises with their soldier sweethearts in the gorse bushes as 'trollopes' and 'doxies', two quaint terms which also indicate a distaste for the sex he clearly assumes Meiklejohn will share.[69] Such assumptions were common to most of Ross's friends and were comforting to Sassoon in a situation which sometimes made him very unhappy.

At one of his first dinners with Meiklejohn, on 16 November 1916, Sassoon would almost certainly have discussed with him his reluctance to return to France. No friend of Ross's could possibly have been completely in sympathy with the handling of the War, and there is little doubt that Meiklejohn was critical of it. Sassoon was expecting his final Medical Board the following day and already dreading the inevitable result. As he had done with many other unpleasant experiences in Wartime, however, he managed to turn the occasion to positive use. For his visit to the Medical Board at Caxton Hall, Westminster, gave him material for both a poem and an entertaining prose passage in *Infantry Officer*.[70] The poem, written soon after the event, makes full use of the macabre humour of a notice in the desolate waiting-room, advising amputees on how to get government replacement limbs free of charge, though the irony is a little laboured. Sassoon nicknames his thinly-disguised self 'Captain Croesus', either because he is rich in the full complement of limbs and health, or with an allusion to the wealth implied in the name Sassoon; the Colonel who sends young officers out to risk their lives or possible amputation is, not very subtly, called 'Sawbones'; and the poem's title, 'Arms and the Man', is almost certainly an ironic reference to the famous opening lines of Virgil's *Aeneid*:

> Young Croesus went to pay a call
> On Colonel Sawbones, Caxton Hall:
> And, though his wound was healed and mended,
> He hoped he'd get his leave extended.
>
> The waiting-room was dark and bare.
> He eyed a neat-framed notice there
> Above the fireplace hung to show
> Disabled heroes where to go,
>
> For arms and legs; with scale of price,
> And words of dignified advice
> How officers could get them free ...
>
> (*CP*, pp. 27-8)

Conscious of the need to add to his collection before the final choice was made and also before his leave expired, Sassoon wrote three more poems in November. The first of these, 'Decorated', hinges on the irony of rewarding soldiers for 'murdering' other soldiers, but, as Sassoon admitted to Dent, was '*not* up to the usual form'.[71]

The other two are more interesting, since both show a fluctuation in feelings which had become almost a commonplace for Sassoon by this time. It is significant that, when he decided to include 'A Mystic as Soldier' in his *Collected Poems*, he placed it among his early, largely idealistic War poems, though chronologically it belongs much later. After a brief description in stanza one of the 'fair songs' of his pre-war days, in stanza two the poet resolves to seek God, whom he believes to be 'in the strife', and in the third and final stanza concludes:

> I walk the secret way
> With anger in my brain
> O music through my clay,
> When will you sound again?
>
> (*CP*, p. 15)

There are a number of puzzling factors in this short poem. What was it, for example, that changed Sassoon's attitude towards God so abruptly and so soon after the blistering scorn of 'They'? When had he become a mystic? And what precisely did he mean by 'the secret way'? One critic has seen the phrase as a reference to 'the life of Sassoon the homosexual artist'.[72] But it is more likely to refer to his sense of being separated from ordinary men by his poetic vocation and his feelings about the War, since a diary

entry written two months after the poem reads: 'When I go out again I will
be mad as ever. And the others will laugh at my secret frenzy'.[73] Moreover
his use of the word 'secret' in a rather similar poem less than a month later
also suggests that it is not a coded reference to homosexuality. 'Secret
Music', as it is called, seems to be using the word 'secret' to refer again to
his sense of being different because of his poetic vocation and attitude
towards the War:

> I keep such music in my brain
> No din this side of death can quell;
> Glory exulting over pain,
> And beauty, garlanded in hell.
>
> (*CP*, p. 32)

Both 'A Mystic as Poet' and 'Secret Music' were composed in sudden
surges of renewed idealism which did not last long. In Sassoon's third and
last poem, written in November, 'The Poet as Hero', he describes a very
different mood. From the ironic use of the word 'hero' in the title onwards,
this poem seems genuinely engaged with its subject; that is, the poet's
reasons for rejecting his former chivalric values for a harsher, less beautiful truth. It is a process which Yeats had already described in similar
terms in 'All Things Can Tempt Me', though it is doubtful that Sassoon
knew this when he came to write his own. What adds vigour to Sassoon's
treatment is the easy, conversational tone of his reply to an imaginary
companion who has questioned his change from 'silly sweetness' to 'an
ugly cry'. Using an extended metaphor from Arthurian legend, the poet
explains in the final sestet of this sonnet:

> But now I've said good-bye to Galahad,
>   And am no more the knight of dreams and show:
> For lust and senseless hatred make me glad,
>   And my killed friends are with me where I go.
> Wound for red wound I burn to smite their wrongs;
> And there is absolution in my songs.[74]

The 'absolution' of the last line will come not through sacrificing his life
for his country, as in the earlier poem of that title, but in telling the grim
truth about war in his poetry. Curiously, 'The Poet as Hero' was not
included either in *The Old Huntsman* or in *Collected Poems*. Its only
appearance was in the *Cambridge Magazine* on 2 December 1916.

Sassoon was to make another attempt to describe his change of poetic
technique in 'Conscripts'. Written at the end of two months spent training
raw recruits for France at Litherland Depot in early 1917, it uses the
metaphor of army conscripts to show how inadequate his former lush
descriptiveness has proved in the face of War's harsh realities. In a
striking opening to the poem, the narrator addresses his former poetic

attitudes as though he were shouting at a bunch of clumsy conscripts on the barrack square:

> 'Fall in, that awkward squad, and strike no more
> Attractive attitudes! Dress by the right!
> The luminous rich colours that you wore
> Have changed to hueless khaki in the night.
> Magic? What's magic got to do with you?
> There's no such thing! Blood's red, and skies are blue.'
>
> (*CP*, pp. 30-1)

In the fourth of the five stanzas, having drilled and lectured his bored conscripts, the narrator ships them off to France:

> Where most of those I'd loved too well got killed.
> Rapture and pale Enchantment and Romance,
> And many a sickly, slender lord who'd filled
> My soul long since with lutanies of sin,
> Went home, because they couldn't stand the din.
>
> (*CP*, p. 31)

Sassoon was amazed, but also amused, when Gosse, who was Librarian at the House of Lords, took his reference to 'many a sickly lord' literally and reprimanded him.[75] Sassoon thought that he had made his meaning quite clear in the last verse, where he praises the 'kind, common' techniques that he had previously despised but Gosse failed to grasp his metaphorical intent and had to be placated. The lines, Sassoon explained, were meant 'as a joke at the expense of his own pre-war precocities', otherwise he would never have used such clichés as 'lutanies of sin'.[76]

Sassoon passed his last weeks of freedom in other ways beside writing poetry. He spent another week hunting at Ringmer from 17 to 24 November and a few more days in London. Whether he managed to squeeze in a last day with the Southdown Hunt, as he suggests in *Infantry Officer*, or not, he was certainly back at the Litherland depot by 2 December. His return to the bleak camp was made easier by Graves who had been there for nearly a fortnight.[77] It was not just the knowledge of Graves's presence, however, that reconciled Sassoon to Litherland. Graves, in an enthusiastic letter of 30 November urging Sassoon to join him as soon as possible, had offered another incentive – Bobbie Hanmer. He had found the young officer just as enchanting as Sassoon had and not nearly as 'conventional' as he had expected, 'only rather charmingly ignorant on certain subjects'.[78]

Graves saw a distinct likeness between Hanmer and David Thomas and would have made friends with him at once, he claimed, even if he had not known that he was Sassoon's 'particular intimate'. To tempt Sassoon further he told him that he could share a hut with Bobbie, even if it meant Graves having to give up his own place for him. A further attraction was the presence of several old friends from the 1st Battalion, 'Bill' Adams[79] and C.D. Morgan among them, and 'a jolly nice crowd of other folk including Hubert Jones the bloke who plays piano quite pleasantly'.[80]

Beside being welcomed by old friends at Litherland, Sassoon was given a much more respectful reception by those in charge than on his first arrival. With his prestigious purple and white M.C. ribbon and his reputation for daring, he seemed a very different man from the one who had entered the Camp so diffidently in May 1915. His confidence was increased by the conviction that he had also made progress as a poet and was about to have his first important book published by a well-known house.

None of this helped very much when it came to the boredom of camp life. His duties were light and unexacting, but constant interruptions by well-meaning friends made it almost impossible to use his plentiful free time in the way he wanted, writing poetry.[81]

A less frustrating way of passing time till the inevitable call to France came lay in sport. Sassoon's weekends and some of his afternoons were, consequently, spent either at Formby Golf Club,[82] or hunting with the Cheshire Hounds when the weather permitted.[83] Though he still enjoyed the physical side of these activities, he was increasingly disgusted by the other participants. Most of them belonged to the class he was beginning to regard as a ripe target for his satire, the wealthy non-combatants who profited by the War. Fat businessmen gorging themselves on unheard-of delicacies at the Golf Club, rich socialites dancing wildly in country houses after a day's hunting in Cheshire, but above all the women who seemed to glory in the sacrifice of human lives, all repelled him.

It was a world which Sassoon found increasingly suspect. After a particularly pleasant day hunting near Tarporley, for example, he stayed the night at Wistaston Hall, dancing at Alvaston, and wrote in his diary the following day:

A few hours in the pre-war surroundings – 'Loderism' and so on. Pleasant enough; but what a decayed society, hanging blindly on to the shreds of its traditions. The wet, watery-green meadows and straggling bare hedges and grey winding lanes; the cry of hounds and thud of hoofs, and people galloping bravely along all around me; and the ride home with the hounds in the chilly dusk – those are *real* things. But comfort and respectable squiredom and the futile chatter of women, and their man-hunting glances, and the pomposity of port-wine-drinking buffers – what's all that but emptiness? These people don't reason. They echo one another and their dead relations and what they read in papers and dull books. And they only *see* what they want to see – which is very little beyond the tips of their red noses. Debrett ['s *Peerage*] is on every table; and heaven a sexless peerage, with a suitable array of dependents and equipages where God is ...[84]

A page of the diary is torn out at this point, suggesting that Sassoon's scorn had carried him beyond acceptable limits. The War was having a palpable effect on his conservative pre-war view of society.

Nevertheless, when it came to occupying his evenings, Sassoon found, like most officers, that the most effective antidote to the spartan camp was a trip into the society he despised. Over an expensive dinner at the Adelphi Hotel, where he was gaining a reputation as a *bon viveur*, he was again confronted with people who looked as though they were either unaffected by the War, or doing well out of it. He was conscious of his own dissipation in all this and longed to be alone, either in the garden at Weirleigh or his little study there:

> ... I dream of a small firelit room
> With yellow candles burning straight,
> And glowing pictures in the gloom,
> And kindly books that hold me late.
> Of things like these I choose to think
> When I can never be alone:
> Then someone says, 'Another drink?'
> And turns my living heart to stone.
>
> (*CP*, p. 14)

This was written on 8 January 1917, nearly five weeks after Sassoon's arrival at Litherland. Bored as he was, he was determined not to go out to France until the harshest weather had passed and was extremely relieved when he was given another month's home service on 27 December. Ironically, Graves had been so convinced by Sassoon's initial belief that it was their duty to maintain the reputation of poets by going back to France, that he had persuaded his Medical Board to pass him fit for overseas service on 18 December. In the event he did not leave for France until 22 January and Sassoon enjoyed another three weeks of his company. When he finally left Sassoon agreed to see his small collection of poems, *Goliath and David*, through the press for him.[85]

Sassoon also continued to add to his own collection. Two days after checking Graves's proofs on 21 January, for example, he wrote a poem on hearing Elgar's *Violin Concerto* for the first time. He almost certainly attended the concert alone, since most of the other officers preferred to play the popular songs of the day interminably on their gramophones. Elgar's *Enigma Variations*, also on the programme, gave him 'as much pleasure as usual, which is a lot' he wrote to Dent the following day, and he found Ravel's *Spanish Nocturne* 'exquisitely delicate and brilliant', but it was Elgar's *Violin Concerto* which moved him most.

Returning to his bleak hut he was still filled with the visions which had come to him during the 'noblest' passages. In spite of himself he kept seeing 'the suffering mortal figure on a cross, but the face is my own'.[86] His startling identification with the Christ figure, which he omitted from

another account of the evening in his autobiography, suggests that he felt
ready to sacrifice his life for his men in France. He had been reading
George Moore's fictional life of Christ, *The Brook Kerith* and had admired
it far more than he had expected. It is significant that it was not conventional religious practices which inspired in him visions of Christ:

> I have seen Christ, when music wove
> Exulting vision; storms of prayer
> Deep-voiced within me marched and strove.
> The sorrows of the world were there ...[87]

The Brook Kerith, which may have left its mark on 'The Elgar *Violin
Concerto*', was one of a number of books Sassoon read at Litherland in an
attempt to escape his surroundings. When Meiklejohn sent him Curzon's
Visits to Monasteries in the Levant for Christmas, he dutifully ploughed
through it, though Doughty's *Arabia Deserta* had spoilt him for such
works. In contrast, he devoured Sorley's *Letters from Germany and the
Army* and continued to dip into his poetry. He also carried on reading
Conrad (*Nostromo*) and Hardy (*The Dynasts*). Another consolation was
17th century poetry, Donne and Herrick in particular. Whilst he could not
change his circumstances, he could escape from them, though escape is
hardly the right word everything he read dealt with the subject which was
most on his mind – death.

Sassoon's greatest consolation, however, remained his own poetry,
which he continued to write in the face of all difficulties. Including the four
poems already mentioned, he produced at least eleven poems during his
nine weeks at Litherland Depot. 'Secret Music' probably came first in early
December and 'A Whispered Tale' second in the middle of the same month,
after Julian Dadd's visit to Liverpool. Dadd's throat wound at Ginchy had
left him virtually mute and the death of his last surviving brother,
Edmund, in the same battle had driven him to the edge of sanity. As
Sassoon listened to the grim details of Dadd's 'Whispered Tale' he could
not help contrasting it with the bragging account 'fool-heroes' might have
given. Unusually for a sonnet, it is written in couplets, though it retains
the traditional break after the octet:

> I'd heard fool-heroes brag of where they'd been,
> With stories of the glories that they'd seen.
> But you, good simple soldier, seasoned well
> In woods and posts and crater-lines of hell,
> Who dodge remembered 'crumps' with wry grimace,
> Endured experience in your queer, kind face,
> Fatigues and vigils haunting nerve-strained eyes,
> And both your brothers killed to make you wise;
> *You* had no babbling phrases; what you said
> Was like a message from the maimed and dead.
> But memory brought the voice I knew, whose note

> Was muted when they shot you in the throat;
> And still you whisper of the war, and find
> Sour jokes for all those horrors left behind.[88]
>
> (*CP*, p. 21)

The idea of Dadd's distorted speech being 'like a message from the maimed and dead' is simple but vivid. Of the five officers who listened to Dadd's account in December 1916, two would be dead and one wounded by May 1917, and Dadd himself would finally take his own life.

Sassoon dedicated 'A Whispered Tale' to Dadd, whose visit almost certainly sent him back to his diary entries for the time they spent together at Morlancourt early in 1916. The result was 'The Distant Song', an almost entirely descriptive poem which experiments not altogether successfully in unrhymed stanzas of five and nine lines. A contrast is made between the sordidness of trench-life and the miracle of spring:

> ... Down by the splintered trees of Hidden Wood,
> Beyond the German line a blackbird sang;
> And suddenly he was aware of Spring –
>   So he stood staring from his ghastly ditch,
>   While Paradise was in the distant song.[88]

Sassoon had already handled the same material more successfully in 'Stand-To: Good Friday Morning' and the real interest of this December version is that he was to use a phrase or two from it for the end of *Fox-Hunting Man*.

Even on Christmas Day, traditionally one of rest, Sassoon was writing verse. He had spent most of the day at Formby Golf Club and, though he had enjoyed the enormous cold spread of goose and turkey for lunch, the sight of such excess in a time of general deprivation increased his anger at those who were having a 'good War'. Among these he certainly included the Army Staff. Reading back over his trench diary had reminded him of 'old wine-faced Rawlinson' taking the salute of 200 officers and NCOs at Flixécourt the previous May: 'and how many of them are alive and hale on Christmas Day?' he asked himself.[89] The result was, in his own words, 'a grim, jeering, heart-rending' poem, 'The March-Past', which ends:

> 'Eyes right!' We passed him with a jaunty stare.
> 'Eyes front!' He'd watched his trusted legions go.
> I wonder if he guessed how many there
> Would get knocked out of time in next week's show.
> 'Eyes right!' The corpse-commander was a Mute;
> And Death leered round him, taking our salute.[90]

The idea of making his Corps-Commander a 'corpse-commander' (a rather obvious pun he could not resist) and a mute, almost certainly came to Sassoon from his recent meeting with the virtually voiceless Julian Dadd. Thoughts of his previous Christmas at Montagne had made him very conscious of death, for of all the officers there then, seven had been killed and ten wounded, leaving only four of the original contingent with the Battalion.

Revived memories of Montagne and Morlancourt brought back a more specific loss to Sassoon, that of David Thomas and the deaths he had inflicted in his rage at this death. By 6 January 1917 he had produced the first version of yet another poem about him, 'Enemies':

> He stood alone in some queer sunless place
> Where Armageddon ends. Perhaps he longed
> For days he might have lived; but his young face
> Gazed forth untroubled: and suddenly there thronged
> Round him the hulking Germans that I shot
> When for his death my brooding rage was hot.
>
> He stared at them, half-wondering; and then
> They told him how I'd killed them for his sake –
> Those patient, stupid, sullen ghosts of men;
> And still there seemed no answer he could make.
> At last he turned and smiled. One took his hand
> Because his face could make them understand.[91]
>
> (*CP*, p. 26)

As Edmund Blunden noted on the manuscript of this poem, now in the Harry Ransom collection, Texas, there is an affinity between Sassoon's 'dream' and that of Owen's 'Strange Meeting'. It seems likely that 'Enemies' was at least one source for Owen's poem, which was written after Sassoon's. The idea of enemies meeting in hell almost certainly came from 'Enemies', just as Owen's tunnel setting which becomes hell is probably indebted to Sassoon's 'The Rear-Guard'. Owen also appears to have echoed the word 'sullen', used to describe the Germans in 'Enemies', and applied it to the 'sullen hall' of hell in 'Strange Meeting'. Certainly Blunden believed that both poems had 'the voice of that hour, of the war-spirit we were living with'.[92]

Three more poems followed in January, only one of which, 'When I'm Among a Blaze of Lights', was published in his lifetime. Of the other two, 'England has many Heroes' is another sarcastic jibe at the Army Staff:

> Ten thousand soldiers, tabbed with blue and green,
> Who, if they heard one shell, would crouch and bolt.[93]

The other, more unusually, attempts a description of the surrounding countryside to which he was evidently becoming reconciled. He had already explored the beach, but on 23rd January he walked out into the 'starved, colourless fields' which bordered the camp and was made unexpectedly happy by the experience. Unlike the Kentish Weald though it was, the northern farmland nevertheless brought back memories of home and childhood, which in turn reminded him of his dead brother. The result was as unpredictable as his pleasure in the landscape, for it was 'Serenity', not misery he felt.[94]

Two weeks later, and in a very different mood, Sassoon produced his most successful poem of his stay at Litherland, just a few days before taking his final leave. Ostensibly the result of an evening spent at the Liverpool Hippodrome with a fellow-officer, 'Blighters' is also another angry reaction to the thought of his own probable death in the face of civilian complacency and unawareness. Its success lies in his ability deftly to sketch in a situation and to echo the banalities of non-combatants' rationalizations in colloquial speech. Above all, he chooses exactly the right words for the horror he sees just below the surface; 'cackle', 'shrill' and 'prancing' make the audience and the chorus seem particularly nasty.[95] The 'riddled corpses' of the last line allows no evasion of the realities of War:

> The House is crammed: tier beyond tier they grin
> And cackle at the show, while prancing ranks
> Of harlots shrill the chorus, drunk with din;
> 'We're sure the Kaiser loves our dear old Tanks!'
>
> I'd like to see a Tank come down the stalls,
> Lurching to rag-time tunes, or 'Home, sweet Home',
> And there'd be no more jokes in Music-halls
> To mock the riddled corpses round Bapaume.
>
> (*CP*, p. 21)

From the indictment of the punning title onwards – those who remain in 'Blighty', or England, are 'Blighters', or rogues – the narrator's venom is unmistakable. His violent wish to see a tank come 'lurching' down the stalls, killing the complacent civilians, shocks the reader and forms a grotesque link between two very different worlds. The description of the chorus girls as 'harlots' is both an accusation and a suggestion of his continuing distaste for women. and his use of popular music is a neat, if snobbish, shorthand which indicates the low-brow character of the audience.

Sassoon himself thought it worth making an extra effort to include 'Blighters' in *The Old Huntsman*, as his Heinemann collection was to be called. He had already read proofs of the book by the time 'Blighters' was completed on 4 February, but he seems to have pleaded for its inclusion, possibly at Ross's suggestion. Apart from a rather jokey piece about a drunk who staggers into a chapel and thinks he has reached Heaven,[96] and an equally facetious piece about a Special Constable, this completes the work included in *The Old Huntsman*.

Three days after finishing 'Blighters', Sassoon was back at Weirleigh on leave, his last before returning to France. He had spent nine weeks at Litherland, nearly seven of them with Graves.[97] The time had passed pleasantly enough, but he was far from happy. In spite of all his efforts to distract himself there were many occasions when thoughts of France had impinged. It was neither possible, nor did he want to put off returning indefinitely. In fact, it was quite a relief when he was passed fit for General Service on 27 January 1917. His moods still fluctuated between a desire to sacrifice himself and anger at those he believed had made such a sacrifice necessary.

During Sassoon's stay at the Depot his loss of belief in the War had shaped itself from 'a ferment of disturbing and disorderly ideas'[98] into a more coherent form, bringing his public protest that much nearer. His contact with the pacifists of Garsington in September and the continuance of Ross's anti-war views had been followed by disappointment at Romania's defeat by Germany in November. By December he felt completely disillusioned about the 'Great Advance' promised by the Allies. Having expected too much of the Battle of the Somme, he had been keenly affected not only by his own experience in it, but more particularly by the virtual massacre of his old Battalion at Ginchy on 3 September. Young Fernby, Edmund Dadd and others were yet more added to the list of friends whose violent deaths had made him profoundly unhappy. Early in January 1917 he had read a Danish magazine which increased his growing doubts:

> The sons of Europe are being crucified in the barbed wire enclosures [it claimed] because the misguided masses are shouting for it. They do not know what they do, and the statesmen wash their hands. They dare not deliver them from their martyr's death.[99]

Ottoline kept the Garsington influence going with long letters accompanying the exotic gifts she sent to cheer up his drab surroundings and Sassoon increasingly found himself agreeing with her. She echoed his own feelings precisely when she wrote that the 'spirit and purpose of the war, that kept it fine and clean at first, dwindles and gets fainter, leaving it utterly ghastly'.[100] Like her, he was beginning to believe that it was the 'brutal fury of L[loyd] G[eorge] and politicians like him' which allowed it to continue, though he admitted that his own fate as an individual 'about to be involved once again in the crass chancefulness of battle' made him readier to criticize.[101]

Sassoon's most powerful revelation, however, came from a new novel by H.G. Wells, which illuminated the whole background of the War for him and confirmed his worst suspicions. He had started to read *Mr Britling Sees It Through* on 27 December, the same day that he was given another month's home service. Though deferred, the Front still threatened and whereas death had seemed 'a noble and inevitable dream', it now seemed to him 'horrible'.[102] Wells's words struck a nightmarish chord:

> Everywhere cunning, everywhere small feuds and hatreds, distrusts, dishonesties, timidities, feebleness of purpose, dwarfish imaginations, swarm over the great and simple issues ... It is a war now like any other of the mobbing, many aimed cataclysms that have shattered empires and devastated the world; it is a war without point, a war that has lost its soul, it has become mere incoherent fighting and destruction, a demonstration in vast and tragic forms of the stupidity and ineffectiveness of our species.[103]

By the time Sassoon's orders for France had come through a month later, his feelings had changed again, perhaps in self-defence. He felt now 'as if a load had been lifted' from his 'sullen' heart and another chance been given him to die a 'decent' death.[104] Whilst his body cries out against it, something within him 'lifts adoring hands, something is filled with noble passion and desire for that benison of promise and freedom'. (The language sounds suspiciously like Ottoline's.) All the 'greatness' that was his in 1916 would be his again. It is an unnerving shift in mood and one that will be repeated a number of times before the end of the War.

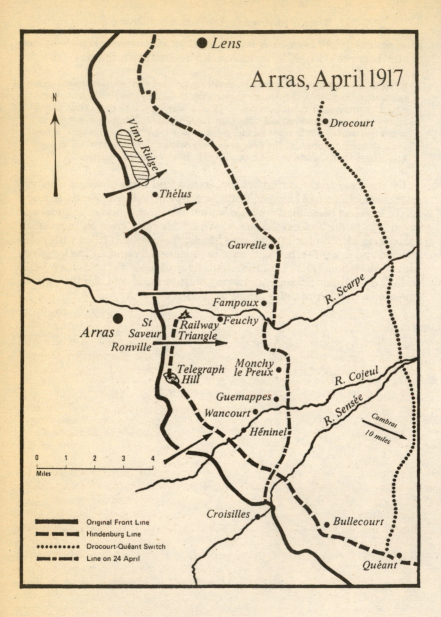

Arras, April 1917

Lens

Drocourt

Vimy Ridge

Thélus

Gavrelle

R. Scarpe

Fampoux

Feuchy

Arras

St
Saveur

Railway
Triangle

Ronville

Monchy
le Preux

Telegraph
Hill

R. Cojeul

Guemappes

R. Sensée

Wancourt

Héninel

Cambrai
10 miles

| 0 | 1 | 2 | 3 | 4 |
Miles

Croisilles

Bullecourt

Quéant

▬▬▬▬▬ Original Front Line

▬ ▬ ▬ ▬ Hindenburg Line

•••••••••• Drocourt-Quéant Switch

▬·▬·▬·▬ Line on 24 April

12

The Wounded Hero
(February-April 1917)

After more than six months of peaceful convalescence in England Sassoon was propelled once more into action in France. For the Battle of the Somme was followed by Arras, an equally costly engagement which prompted at least three Generals to protest to Haig. Though officially in reserve throughout the battle, Sassoon was drawn into it by one of the chances of War. What he saw there would be sufficient to galvanize him into making public his profound concern about the conduct of the War.

Sassoon left for France on 15 February 1917 after a week's leave divided equally between Weirleigh and Half Moon Street. Weirleigh, which he both longed for and dreaded, came first from 7 to 10 February. Most of his time there was spent revising the galley proofs of his poems which had arrived from Heinemann's. Dreading his mother's reaction he delayed telling her of his return to France until the last moment:

> February 7
> This evening I was playing Elizabethan lute songs, so gay and full of tenderness. I have got to break it to poor mother that I'm going out again but haven't had the heart to do it yet. She was so pleased and unconscious of it when I arrived last night.

It must, therefore, have been with some relief that he left Kent for London on the 10th. His frantic socializing during his five days there shows how far he had come from the lonely young man of summer 1914. Ross wanted to introduce him personally to Heinemann, which he did at dinner on Monday, 12 February. Ottoline Morrell and Meiklejohn also demanded his company. He lunched with Ottoline at one of her favourite restaurants, the Eiffel Tower in Percy Street, then accompanied her to the National Gallery where they met another of her circle, Lytton Strachey. A visit to Tower Bridge followed and finally tea in Ottoline's lodgings at 38 Bloomsbury Street. Ottoline found this a depressing experience, Sassoon confiding to her about the future when she had hoped for something more personal.[1]

Sassoon's older friends, Marsh and Gosse, were equally anxious to see him during what might prove to be his last few days ever in England. On

Sunday, 11 February he outdid himself, taking breakfast with Marsh at Raymond Buildings to discuss his proofs, lunch at the Reform Club with Meiklejohn and Ross, tea with Dorothy Brett to inspect her vast portrait of Ottoline, and dinner at the Gosses'. Only Dent, unable to get down from Cambridge it seems, was missing. The base for all these activities remained Ross's lodgings at Half Moon Street, for the influence of his early 'oracles', Gosse and Marsh, was continuing to give way to the more stimulating, less establishment views of Ross. This was partly due to Sassoon's own changing attitude to the War, which had grown something of a challenge to the more conventionally patriotic pair.

It comes, therefore, as no surprise to find that it was Ross who accompanied Theresa Sassoon to Waterloo Station to see her son off to France on Thursday, 15 February. Sassoon's frantic socializing in London had exhausted him – he claimed that his friends had talked him to death – but it had helped put off thoughts of his uncertain future. As he boarded his train at Waterloo he began to feel 'nervous and rattled',[2] yet once aboard the *Archangel* at Southampton the worried feeling wore off. He himself noted that people seemed to become happy 'in a bovine way' as soon as they were relieved of all responsibility for their future, and he was no exception. The usual self-protective change in attitude took place as the boat left the dock, though he felt rather like a cabbage going to Covent Garden Market and did resent the fact that someone stole his greatcoat en route. Resigned as he was to his fate, he could not prevent thoughts of death impinging. It must have seemed cruel to be so near worldly success at last, yet to have it threatened by powers outside his control with whom he did not agree.

One source of comfort, as always, were his books. Anticipating nightmarish conditions at the Front he had chosen not just the writers he most admired, but those who seemed to him quintessentially English and, therefore, of greatest consolation in France. Hardy was chief among these; apart from a selection of his poems, he had *The Dynasts* and asked Meiklejohn to send him *Far from the Madding Crowd*. Beside bringing out the landscape for him, he found that Hardy's irony helped him 'to fight against the inevitable homesickness for things which really don't matter, such as comfortable rooms and blameless domesticity'.[3] In a different way Lamb's Letters and Essays promised an escape from the grim surroundings, as did Chaucer's *Canterbury Tales*. For the trenches themselves he was saving Shakespeare's tragedies, perhaps the only literary equivalent he could imagine for the horrors to come. He was still trying to finish Conrad's *Nostromo* and *A Set of Six* and, though he could not have regarded these works as either very English or very consoling, the Pole's tragic vision undoubtedly seemed to suit the situation.[4]

Sassoon would have had ample time for reading on his way to the 5th Infantry Base Depot at Rouen, since the journey took well over a day. He did not arrive at the camp, which was situated a few miles from the city, until the evening of 16 February. In his fictionalized account, his arrival at the bleak depot was made worse by the fact that he learnt immediately of his transfer to the 2nd Battalion of the RWF, 'for I wanted to go where I was already known [i.e. to the 1st Battalion], and the prospect of joining a strange battalion made me feel more homeless than ever'.[5] Yet his letters to Ross and others show quite clearly that in reality he was still expecting to be posted to the 1st Battalion for another three weeks and suggests that he predated it in his fiction to underline his sense of desolation. This was not helped by another event which almost certainly *did* occur on his arrival and which gave rise to one of his bleakest satires.

Stumbling around in the dark looking for the store-room, Sassoon found himself instead in a Guard Room, where a man, naked to the waist, was kneeling in the middle of the floor, clutching at his chest and weeping uncontrollably. A patient but unpitying sergeant explained to Sassoon as he guided him to the blanket-store that the man had been under detention for assaulting the military police 'and now 'e's just 'ad news of his brother being killed. Seems to take it to 'eart more than most would. 'Arf crazy, 'e's been, tearing 'is clothes off and cursing the War and the Fritzes'.[6]

When Sassoon came to deal with the incident in his poetry, instead of using the sergeant's working-class speech, as he had in 'In the Pink', he chose to make a middle-class narrator the vehicle for his satire. The inability of the insensitive and unsympathetic officer-narrator to comprehend the man's suffering achieves the shock effect Sassoon intended:

> *Lamentation*
> I found him in the guard-room at the Base.
> From the blind darkness I had heard his crying
> And blundered in. With puzzled, patient face
> A sergeant watched him; it was no good trying
> To stop it; for he howled and beat his chest.
> And, all because his brother had gone west,
> Raved at the bleeding war; his rampant grief
> Moaned, shouted, sobbed, and choked, while he was kneeling
> Half-naked on the floor. In my belief
> Such men have lost all patriotic feeling.
>
> (*CP*, p. 76)

The last line, as in most of his successful satires, carries the weight of the charge, though it is hinted at earlier in the euphemistic cliché 'And, all because his brother had gone west'.

Sassoon found life at the 5th Infantry Base Depot altogether very depressing. The Mess was awful, the food bad and Mess charges high. When officers were not on the training-ground – known as the 'Bull Ring' – they sat around playing cards, cursing the bitterly cold weather or talking tediously about the War. It was like being in a Military Sorting Office, where everyone waited with ill-concealed anxiety to discover their final destination. And since it was just possible to hear the distant grumble of the guns, there was no escaping the fact that the rumoured 'Spring Offensive' was already underway.

After a whole day of this Sassoon realized that it was not just the camp that was making him feel low; he also had a fever. And when he reported sick on the morning of Sunday, 18 February, German measles was diagnosed. If anything his billet in the isolation hospital, a barbed wire enclosure about 300 yards from the main camp, was worse than his first bed in a narrow segment of a low canvas shed. There were already six patients in the small hospital tent to which he was assigned and his arrival caused further crowding. He felt unwelcome, bored and disaffected.

Instead of joining in with the eternal games of bridge which occupied at least four of his fellow-inhabitants, Sassoon simply read and observed. (One of his few pleasures was Chaucer who, he told Meiklejohn, 'tickled [his] palate like a glass of rum punch at Brooks'.[7]) The card-players he seems to have dismissed instantly as capable of only the dullest obscenities. He was less dismissive of a young Territorial Captain, whom he found both sensible and humorous. His main interest, however, was reserved for a young Scot in the Gunners, whose charming youthfulness no doubt reminded him of both David Thomas and Bobbie Hanmer. Fresh from Edinburgh University, the nineteen-year-old surprised and delighted Sassoon by quoting Milton and Keats in a broad Scots accent. But even he could not prevent Sassoon from losing faith in the human race; apart from providing him with future material for fiction, his fellow-patients made little difference to his mood of resigned despair.

'I loathe the sacrificial imbecility of war', Sassoon wrote to Ross four days after arriving in hospital, 'and the whole scheme of things as one sees it out here. I could never have believed that things could be so meaningless and so contemptible'.[8] He admitted to lying awake at night 'in unholy terror at the thought of losing my life in that organised inferno of mud and misery "up the line"', though he knew from experience that when he got there he would only be 'angry and defiant – not afraid'.[9] But much as he hated the War, he was unable to face the idea of returning to England without being 'scarred and tortured once more'.[10]

In this muddled, hopeless state his main comfort was not literature but nature. The only advantage the squalid, little compound offered him was the huge pine-forest which surrounded it. He would frequently slip through the barbed-wire fence and walk among the sweet-smelling trees, thankful for their 'quiet stems and slowly waving crowns of branches' and the rooks cawing and flapping above.[11] By 23 February he was writing to tell Dent that the worst of his 'blackest horrors' were over.[12] One result, as he knew from past experience, was that he would soon be feeling 'heroic and optimistic' again. It seemed impossible to remain neutral. 'I came out here longing to scarify war', his letter to Dent continues, 'but I know I shall be writing rhapsodies long before Easter-Day, and *that* will probably produce "An Ode on the Eucharist in a Shell-Hole", or "The Peace that Passeth Understanding", a Paschal Play for Devout Sergeants, or some drivel like that ...'

Though half-joking, Sassoon really did long for the kind of simplicity he saw in Bobbie Hanmer, who could kneel down every night to say his prayers and fall asleep, content to lose an arm or a leg, or even die for England. At home with his pacifist friends, it had seemed easy to criticize the mindless stupidity of War, but once in France he was drawn back irrevocably into the machine. Dull acquiescence, if not willing self-sacrifice, seemed inevitable.

Apart from possibly keeping him out of the trenches for another ten days, Sassoon's German measles made no real difference to his fate. When he returned to the main camp on 27 February he was still destined for the Front and his fellow officers seemed just as boring. There were very few, he told Ross scathingly, whose ideas rose above a five franc prostitute: 'Poor weary old harlots', he fantasized, 'how tired they must be of the Welsh dialect and the Lloyd George embrace!'[13] Having heard a number of the younger officers describing their experiences in lurid detail, he almost wished he had the courage to visit the local brothel, the orgies there seemed such a good subject for satire. Relying on Ross's unshockability, as well as their mutual distaste for women as sexual objects, he tried him out with an extempore verse, begging him not to show it to the more staid Meiklejohn:

> She met me on the stairs in her chemise;
> I grinned and offered her a five franc note;
> Poor girl, no doubt she did her best to please;
> But I'd have been far happier with a goat.

The suggestion that the Welch Fusiliers would prefer sex with their regimental goat to a woman is a particularly virulent manifestation of Sassoon's distaste for heterosexual activity, as well as a reference to rumours that circulated on such practices in Wartime.

Sassoon felt isolated in other ways too. He had no inclination to join in the never-ending card games and he despised the popular songs that were churned out incessantly on the gramophone. While waiting to be posted, which he still thought would mean being sent back to the 1st Battalion, he tried to make the most of his stay. He paid at least one overnight visit to the centre of Rouen, where he enjoyed a hot bath, a gourmet dinner and a comfortable bed for the night.[14] He told Dent on 8 March that he was trying to get good material for his poetry in France, but this was not easy while he remained at the base. Rouen, on the other hand, provided material for at least two satires. The first of these, written on 4 March, was inspired by lunch at the Hôtel de la Poste the same day. In a third person prose description of the event he used many of the phrases which were to make his poem on the subject memorable, a revealing glimpse into his creative processes, in particular his dependence on telling words and phrases. After describing a young subaltern (presumably himself) enjoying a second glass of wine, he continues (the italics have been added):

Grey-haired colonels with fierce eyebrows lingered over a chicken casserole with the tenderness of a lover ... A Brigadier-General came and sat down a few feet away. He had the *appearance* of a man with a liver who spends most of the year sitting in London clubs. He began *guzzling* hors d'oeuvres as though his life depended on the solidity of his meal.

The cynical subaltern who was staring at him from the next table felt an almost irrepressible desire to walk across and pour a plate of soup down his neck. 'O you bloody Brigadier! you bloody Brigadier! you are a professional soldier: I am not. Why can't you go and show the Germans how to fight instead of *guzzling at the Base*. You have never been within thirty miles of a front-line trench, and yet you call yourself a general. And *you* will be alive, over-eating yourself in a military club, when I am dead in a shell-hole up on the Somme. *You* will *guzzle* yourself to the grave and gas about the Great War, long after I am dead with all my promise unfulfilled.

'O damn all these *bald-headed* incompetent belly-fillers!' he thought. And he glanced at a Gunner Colonel with a D.S.O. who was cutting himself a big slice of cheese, hoping that he at least might be a brave man. But all the really brave men were dead, or else maimed or *up the line*.[15]

Sassoon himself pointed out that the phrase 'scarlet Majors' came from Robbie Ross,[16] but the rest of the poem which resulted from the incident, 'Base Details', can be traced directly to this prose passage and to Sassoon's inimitable way of sketching in a character and giving that character a voice. (In this case there are two 'voices', that of the complacent Staff Officer and that of the scathing narrator, which undercuts it):

> If I were fierce, and bald, and short of breath,
>   I'd live with scarlet Majors at the Base
> And speed glum heroes up the line to death.
>   You'd see me with my puffy petulant face,
> Guzzling and gulping in the best hotel,
>   Reading the Roll of Honour. 'Poor young chap,'
> I'd say – 'I used to know his father well;
>   Yes, we've lost heavily in this last scrap.'
> And when the war is done and youth stone dead,
> I'd toddle safely home and die – in bed.
>
> (*CP*, p. 75)

The opening pun of the title as well as being, literally, details about the Infantry Base, it is a poem full of 'base details' of War and a comment on the 'base', or lowly, soldiers, or 'details', who are sent to fight is echoed in the multiple word-play of 'scarlet Majors'; this implies not only that they are wearing the red tabs of the General Staff on their lapels with red bands round their caps, and that their faces are red from the high blood-pressure induced by over-indulgence in food and drink, but also that they are 'scarlet' with sin and, possibly, from 'screaming', as Ross saw it.

Both phrases illustrate Sassoon's remarkable powers of condensation, as do the unexpected conjunctions of '*glum heroes*' and 'up the line *to death*' (my italics). The alliterative addition of 'gulping' to his diary word 'guzzling' matches that of 'puffy petulant face' and lends weight to the phrase. The emphatic 'stone dead' of line 9, though unlikely to have been used by the euphemistic Staff Officer, makes an inescapable point, which is rounded off in the last line by Sassoon's inspired device of the colloquial 'toddle', which makes the 'scarlet Major' seem more than a little childish and faintly ludicrous. His original choice was 'waddle' which he wisely changed after the poem's publication in the *Cambridge Magazine* on 28 April 1917, since 'toddle' is more the kind of euphemism which the Staff Officer might himself have used for his presumably inebriated state.

The fact that the Scarlet Major plans to die 'in bed', rather than at the Front with the men he has sent there, underlines the discrepancy between his sybaritic lifestyle and their sufferings. By using the opening conditional 'If', the narrator implies a scornful, though unuttered comment at the end – 'but I'm not'. His choice of just the right euphemisms for his complacent speaker – 'Yes, we've lost heavily in this last scrap' – underlines his growing anger with unaware non-combatants still cosily ensconced in the old boys' network ('I knew his father well'). Though this had already expressed itself powerfully in 'The Tombstone-Maker' and 'Blighters', it seems all the more forceful when applied to people within the army itself. Sassoon was to continue this line of attack in 'The General' less than two months later.

Another poem written the same day as 'Base Details' shows that Rouen inspired very different moods in Sassoon. The beauty of its cathedral and, more especially, the church of St Ouen, made him yearn for the consolations of religion, particularly in view of what lay ahead. His poetry, accordingly, becomes more lyrical and elegiac:

> ... My spirit longs for prayer;
> And, lost to God, I seek him everywhere.
>
> ...
>
> But where I stand, desiring yet to stay,
> Hearing rich music at the close of day,
> The Spring Offensive (Easter is its date)
> Calls me. And that's the music I await.[17]

The third poem inspired by Rouen, not necessarily on the same visit, was another satire, 'The Optimist', which Sassoon sent to both Dent and Ross on 8 March.[18] He allowed it to be published in the *Cambridge Magazine* on 21 April 1917, but, wisely, did not include it in his *Collected Poems*.

It was the last poem Sassoon was able to write at Rouen, for after waiting aimlessly for nine days at the Base, he finally received orders to join the 2nd Battalion at Chipilly, a rest camp on the Somme. It was a bitter disappointment to him not to be returning to the 1st Battalion as he had hoped. Even his expectation of at least joining Graves in the 2nd Battalion was dashed when the younger man was invalided back to England just before Sassoon's orders came through.[19] Though most of the officers he had known from the 1st were either dead or wounded by March 1917, he had longed for the comfort of a few familiar faces. His attempts to have the orders changed, however, were a failure.

It was, therefore, with a heavy heart that Sassoon set off from the 5th Infantry Base Depot, Rouen, at 4 p.m. on Sunday, 11 March. The first leg of the journey, an eight-hour train ride to Corbie near Amiens, was tedious and he passed part of it trying to express his mixed feelings on returning to the War-zone. As he approached the area around Amiens, which had held him physically and emotionally since December 1915, he became increasingly conscious of the friends who had died there. While reluctant to return, he nevertheless felt he was back where he belonged, with his men, past and present:

> *Return*
> I have come home unnoticed; they are still;
> No greetings pass between us; but they lie
> Hearing the boom of guns along the hill,
> Watching the flashes lick the glowering sky.
>
> A wind of whispers comes from sightless faces;
> 'Have patience, and your bones shall share our bed.'
> Their voices haunt dark ways and ruined places,
> Where once they spoke in deeds; who now are dead ...[20]

In one of those violent mood-swings so common to him at the time, Sassoon condemned this poem only eighteen days after writing it, as an example of 'entirely artificial emotionalism'. 'The dead are underground all right', he added cynically, 'but they don't care whether I come back or not. This is the sort of poetry I'm always trying to avoid writing'.[21] Nevertheless, it is the sort of poem which crops up periodically in his work.[22]

After an uncomfortable night's sleep on the floor at Corbie, minus his kit which had been left on the train, Sassoon walked the final seven miles to Camp 13 at Chipilly, a few miles from his old camp at Morlancourt. Though safely behind the Line and in a spot he had once found attractive, it now seemed to him an abominable place. Established only a few months earlier, Camp 13 was already a sea of mud. The food was disgusting and the one hut, in which all the Company Officers were herded together, full of smoke from the adjoining kitchen. There was never a moment of silence or peace, only the sound of whiskey-loosened tongues gabbling War-shop as the officers played their endless card-games. Under such circumstances he found it difficult to think, much less write. The mental attitude of his companions, he told Ross after more than a fortnight of their company, was 'like a lead coffin for any sparks of the imagination one [could] muster'.[23] To make things worse, the weather had been wet and windy. He could hardly have joined the battalion under less attractive conditions.

For at least the first week at Chipilly, Sassoon hoped to be transferred back to the 1st Battalion, his 'spiritual home' in France,[24] and continued his efforts to bring this about. After three weeks, however, he resigned himself to staying with the 2nd Battalion, who were about to leave for the Front. On 1 April, their last day in Camp 13, he wrote to Ross: '*We* [my italics] are off to some battle very soon'. It is a small sign that he was beginning to identify with his new unit, which his account in the Battalion history confirms.[25] By 7 April, when a formal request from the 1st for his transfer back to them came through, he had already decided to stay with the 'good old 2nd'.[26] Not only had he found friends among the officers there, but he had, more importantly, begun to bond with his men.

When Sassoon met the 2nd Battalion at Chipilly they had recently returned from two months in the Cléry sector of the Somme front, where they had suffered some of the worst weather of the War and buried 200 of their number. They were a very different unit from the one Robert Graves had encountered nearly two years earlier when he went to join them at Laventie. One of the few regular infantry battalions still more or less intact at that time, the 2nd had seemed to Graves then a hot-bed of snobbishness and élitism and very tough even on Special Reserve officers, let alone New Army ones. They had addressed all new subalterns as 'wart' for at least six months after their arrival, put them through gruelling riding lessons if they were not already first-class horsemen and run a Battalion rather than a Company Mess as a sign of their distinction.

As Graves had quickly realized, however, they were highly professional and extremely good soldiers and he grew proud of belonging to such an efficient battalion. By the time he rejoined them a year later on the Somme, none of the old regular officers remained except the Quartermaster, but the atmosphere had still been far from friendly. When he returned for the third time at the beginning of 1917, however, he found them noticeably changed: 'No riding-school, no battalion mess, no Quetta manners, no regular officers except for a couple of Sandhurst boys'.[27]

Nevertheless they still seemed to Sassoon in March 1917 stiff and unfriendly by comparison with the 1st Battalion. Captain W.W. Kirkby, the Officer in Command of B Company, to which he was assigned, repeatedly referred to him as a 'bloody wart', obviously intending him to overhear. Though relations with Kirkby were to improve once they were on the move, Sassoon could never really understand this initial coldness, but it was probably left over from the tough era Graves describes. Kirkby, who had been a Special Reserve officer with the Battalion since before the War, represented the Old Guard. An upholder of regimental traditions, he clearly believed that it was only right that newcomers should be treated like dirt for the first six months, or until they 'proved' themselves; rather like new boys in the public school system to which the Regular Army was closely allied. He struck Sassoon as a man who enjoyed standing on his dignity, behaviour which seemed to his subordinate entirely inappropriate on active service.

Apart from complaining to Graves, Sassoon must also have written to Joe Cottrell about Kirkby, since Cottrell wrote to say that the recent C.O. of the 2nd Battalion, 'Tibs' Crawshay, had told him that Kirkby was 'a Capital S---'. Another officer from the 2nd described him as a 'potent deteriorating influence'.[28] Dadd, who feared Sassoon would find his new unit 'a somewhat snooty lot', observed that Kirkby *seemed* 'to have a courtly, genial way with him' which made debate very difficult. He advised Sassoon to regard him simply as 'something to study'. Fortunately Sassoon listened to Dadd's advice and the fruits of his careful study of his Company Officer emerge amusingly as Captain Leake in *Infantry Officer*.

Reading other people's comments on 'Uncle' Kirkby – a reference both to his age and his length of service – it is clear that he was considered 'a bit of a character'. A short, red-faced, extremely heavy man of thirty-three, he presented irresistible material for satire. Sassoon drew a vivid sketch of him 'in undisputed occupation of a horse which looked scarcely up to his weight',[29] and a later second-in-command observed that, though on one occasion riddled by fire from two directions, he was 'so large that he could harbour a good many missiles without any important part being touched'.[30]

In spite of such ridicule, Kirby also inspired respect for his professional ability and affection for his outspoken ways. His language when finding himself in the same hospital as the tank-commander who had inadvertently fired on him was thought worthy of mention in the battalion memoirs, but too ripe to be printed. In spite of his initial rebuff, Sassoon learnt to get on with him, as he almost always did with fellow-officers, and there is an entertaining account in both *Infantry Officer* and *The War the Infantry Knew* of 'a convivial evening' drinking bad champagne with Kirkby (among others), which ended with him swearing 'eternal fealty' to Kirkby at the door of his poky little billet.[31] In the more colourful fictionized version, they shake hands 'sholemnly' and Sassoon swears to 'blurry well do [his] damndest' for him.[32]

Sassoon also learnt to get on with the other officers in B Company, some more easily than others. As second-in-command he had three subalterns under him, each of them, like himself, commanding a platoon. The most experienced of these came from a well-known establishment family, the Soameses, and seems to have had problems with discipline. Soames, an old Etonian, had started as a sergeant in the 5th Dragoon Guards early in the War, gone through the Mons retreat and the fighting up to May 1915 with them, then joined the 2nd Battalion as a 2nd Lieutenant. Leaving after only one tour of the trenches, he had become a Flight Commander but after a row with the Royal Flying Corps had returned to the 2nd Battalion, still as a 2nd Lieutenant. Given his family connections, there was probably some not very flattering reason for his chequered career and relatively lowly rank. Though Sassoon refrained from giving it, his omission of Soames from *Infantry Officer* almost certainly reflects the lack of warmth which comes through in his diary account.

Sassoon did include his other two subordinates in B Company, Casson and Evans, however, who seemed to him to provide a 'typical War contrast' of the kind which was becoming more familiar as the fighting claimed increasing numbers of the originally mainly middle-class officers. For while Casson, a refined youth of twenty-three, had been at Winchester and Christ Church, Evans, at about the same age, had not enjoyed similar social advantages. Rather ape-like in appearance, he licked his thumb noisily when dealing cards and invariably answered 'Pardon' to any remark, a habit Sassoon snobbishly found rather trying. As it turned out, both young men were to prove equally reliable when tested under fire. Sassoon understandably felt more at ease with Casson than with the garrulous, working-class Welshman whom he could not help regarding as rather uncouth. He found the Wykehamist an amusing gossip and was to turn to him for company at the Front. 'Shirley' and 'Rees' in *Memoirs of an Infantry Officer* are based largely on the two men. Whatever their differences, Casson and Evans were to die together on 26 September 1917 at Polygon Wood in the Third Battle of Ypres.

Apart from those in his own unit, Sassoon also got to know officers from the three other Companies. He had a particular *rapport* with the O.C. of A Company, Ralph Greaves. Not only had he known Greaves slightly in Kent before the War,[33] an excuse for many nostalgic reminiscences, but Greaves' older brother, E.J. Greaves (the 'Barton' of *Infantry Officer*) had been his Company Commander in the 1st, forming a comforting link with his old battalion.[34] Ralph, who was only three years younger than Sassoon, also shared his love of music. He had studied under Vaughan Williams at Cambridge and played the piano well, as Sassoon discovered on the same drunken evening which witnessed his sentimental reconciliation with Kirkby. This had undoubtedly been an emotional occasion; Greaves, Sassoon remembered, had 'played as though he were saying good-bye to all music for ever'.[35]

Sassoon had already spent a similarly convivial evening with Greaves at the Godbert Restaurant in Amiens on their last day at Camp 13 and his memories of that occasion were equally alcoholic. Though he retained no clear recollection of the evening itself, he did have a record of what he euphemistically called 'the beverages consumed', not including the wine they would certainly have drunk with dinner:

2 John Collins	1 Japanese ditto	1 Oyster Cocktail
1 Sherry and Bitters	Pommard Eclatante, trois verres	
1 Benedictine		

What the 'Japanese ditto' was we are unlikely to discover, but we still have a photograph of Sassoon, Greaves and two friends taken the morning after the night before. Looking surprisingly perky, they face the camera with determined gaiety. While Sassoon appears, as he puts it, 'every inch the soldier', Greaves seems jauntier, more debonair, an effect added to in real life by his monocle and whimsical stammer. Sassoon believed that the whimsy illuminated a half-melancholy temperament which saw life as a tragi-comedy, a view which was to be borne out forcibly in his own case.[36] The two remaining men in the group photograph, also good friends of Sassoon, were Lieutenant T.R. Conning, a 'happy-go-lucky fellow' of 'natural jollity'[37] who appears as 'Dunning' in *Infantry Officer*, and 'kind-hearted' Captain Coster, of D Company. Conning was to die in the coming Battle of Arras, which would also deprive the passionate pianist Greaves of one of his arms and render the other virtually useless. (Coster would be killed later at the 3rd Battle of Ypres.) It was an irony which Sassoon was to make much of in his portrayal of Greaves in *Infantry Officer*, to help underline the random cruelty of the War.

There were many other cases Sassoon might have cited to reinforce his criticism. Captain J.C. Mann, one of whose letters to Sassoon has survived, is a case in point. Typical of the kind of officer Sassoon got to know in the 2nd Battalion, Mann was young, keen and efficient. His initial gaiety, not quite destroyed by the time Sassoon met him during Mann's second year in France, gradually turned to taciturnity under the pressures of continued Front-Line experience. His ability won him rapid promotion to the position of Adjutant, but he never took advantage of this relatively safe job at Headquarters. When the situation was bad, which it frequently was for the Battalion, he often voluntarily risked his life in order to help matters. An added incentive for his recklessness was almost certainly the death of his only brother at about the time Sassoon joined the Battalion. This made him hate all Germans, though he continued to treat their prisoners humanely.

Another bond between Mann and Sassoon besides the loss of a brother was a shared sense of humour. The Battalion doctor, who fortunately enjoyed a good joke too, identified Mann as Father Christmas when he found a tin of rat poison in his sock during the festive season. Extremely popular with the men, Mann was just as popular with his fellow-officers, once resistance to his early promotion had died down. Sassoon, who towered above the short but athletic Mann, described him affectionately as 'our conscientious and efficient little Adjutant'[38] and included him briefly in *Infantry Officer*. He would have been as sad and angry as Dr Dunn, the compiler of the Battalion memoirs, when Mann died in the slaughter at Polygon Wood on 26 September, the same day as Casson and many others. (There were to be 140 casualties that day, 100 of them occurring in one hour alone. Only one officer in action would escape alive and unhurt.)

Sassoon's closest friend amongst the younger officers, Leslie Orme, would be dead already by the time Polygon Wood claimed its toll. He was to be a victim of an earlier but no less bloody engagement at 'Plum Lane', Arras on 27 May, when Battalion casualties were to number ten officers and 155 men, half of whom died.[39] Orme had been with Sassoon in the 1st Battalion, where Sassoon had learnt to admire the sturdy little ex-public schoolboy. (See pp. 212-13) A cheerful, if hot-tempered friend, he had an unashamed determination to save his life if he could and an ability to enjoy what little might be left of it if not. His youthful good looks and the location of a particular skirmish in which he had fought had earned him the intriguing nickname 'the Angel of Crawley Ridge', with which he signed his letters to Sassoon. He may have preferred it to his other nickname, 'Young Worm'. The two shared trips into Amiens and almost certainly paid a visit to their old rest camp at Heilly sur l'Ancre together.[40] Though Sassoon would not have described their friendship as profound, Orme's death was to affect him deeply and lead to one of his most moving War poems. (See pp. 374-5)

Apart from Orme, another link with the 1st Battalion was the Quartermaster, Captain Yates, 'Bates' of *Infantry Officer*, who was an old friend of Joe Cottrell.[41] The two shared many characteristics and Sassoon described Yates as simply 'a burlier prototype of Joe ... with fewer political prejudices'.[42] Graves, on the other hand, thought Yates very different from Cottrell: 'A thing few people realize is what a jolly good fellow (though quite unlike "Young Joe") Old Yates is: always grumbling and very much on his dignity but he's got a kind heart and won't be bullied'.[43] Whatever the truth, there were undeniable similarities. Like Cottrell, Yates had been a regular with the Royal Welch Fusiliers for many years, almost forty by the time Sassoon met him. Like Cottrell too, he was completely dedicated to his battalion. The only officer, apart from a man called Radford, to have been with the 2nd since the outbreak of War, he would do almost anything to ensure its well-being. When stores were low he would, as he euphemistically put it, 'scrounge' new supplies from wherever possible. When he found his stock of horseshoes running low early in the War, for example, he had simply stolen new ones from every smithy he passed. If a Company cooker was defective, he would 'borrow' a new one from another unit, making sure to erase any identifying marks. His ingenuity and resourcefulness stopped at nothing in the service of his battalion.

Yates was a real 'fixer' and could always arrange transport for 'jollies' when the officers needed it. His complaint, when an upright new Transport Sergeant succeeded a more malleable one, caused some amusement: 'He's so honest and truthful that you can't trust him'.[44] (Apparently the young sergeant had butted in with a higher figure than Yates had declared when a Remounts Officer came to comb out horses 'surplus to establishment'.) He was very hard on anyone who failed to do his job properly and could be very stubborn if crossed. Yet for all his unscrupulousness and some character flaws, perhaps even because of them, Yates was a first-class Quartermaster. He would brave anything to get rations through to those in the Line, often disregarding commands in order to do so. His servings of rum, before rum was forbidden by Major-General Pinney in a misguided attempt to improve the efficiency and morality of the troops, were always very generous. He was also ingenious and on St David's Day he always miraculously had a leek for everyone's cap, however desolate the spot.

Officers returning from leave would usually go straight to Yates for all the news and gossip, 'some philosophy and much grousing, and a thundering good tea'.[45] Like Cottrell, he came from the North of England and his diluted Lancashire accent made his humorous remarks particularly pungent. He was, in effect, a 'character', appreciated by everyone in the Battalion from the Colonel downwards. His strongest link with Sassoon was through horses. Early in the War he had acquired from the Cavalry a wounded mare, whom he adored. As 'Girlie' grew stronger he started to race her and, when Sassoon appeared, invited him to ride her in the Corps Sports. Though the Sports were cancelled, the bond had been formed and Yates, like Cottrell, became for Sassoon a sterling type of 'old soldier'.

Another 'old soldier', though of a quite different type, was the Battalion Medical Officer, Captain J.C. Dunn.[46] Colonel 'Tibbs' Crawshay, who had just left the 2nd Battalion, thought Dunn 'one of the most wonderful men' he had ever met. 'He should have had a Brigade', he told Sassoon later. 'He was a born soldier'.[47]

Sassoon, who gave Dunn the pseudonym 'Munro' in *Infantry Officer* to emphasize his nationality, had already heard of the tough Scot by the time he arrived at Chipilly, probably from Graves. Graves had met Dunn during his second period with the Battalion in mid-1916, Dunn having joined it in autumn 1915. On that occasion Dunn had almost certainly saved Graves's life, even though he had initially given him up for dead, but it was more than gratitude which prompted Graves's glowing description:

> Dunn, a hard-bitten Scot, had served as a trooper in the South African War, and there won the Distinguished Conduct Medal. Now he was far more than a doctor: living at battalion headquarters, he became the right-hand man of three or four colonels in succession. Whoever failed to take his advice usually regretted it afterwards.[48]

12. The Wounded Hero (February-April 1917)

As Graves also points out, in a version which is, as usual, both colourful and inaccurate, Dunn was to distinguish himself again at Passchendaele in the autumn of 1917. Graves claims that when 'a shell burst among the headquarters staff, knocking out colonel, adjutant and signal officer', Dunn had 'no hesitation in becoming a temporary combatant officer of the Royal Welch, resigning his medical duties to the stretcher-bearer sergeant'.[49] In fact, the inhabitants of HQ had included neither the Colonel nor the Adjutant, though the second-in-Command, Major Poore, and the Assistant Adjutant, (Sassoon's friend) Casson, had been there. Moreover Dunn had become a 'temporary combatant officer' only to the extent of going out under fire to bring back the Adjutant, Mann's body, a deed closely resembling Sassoon's action in bringing back Corporal O'Brien. Like Sassoon, Dunn was awarded an M.C. for his courage.

Courage was not the only quality that the two men shared, though it was the first thing Dunn commented on in Sassoon. Writing to Graves shortly after his arrival at the 2nd Battalion, Sassoon complained of 'a beast of a stiff arm where old Dunn inoculated me today – sticking his needle in, and saying "the toughest skin of the lot – but you're a tough character, I know." (Not so tough as he thinks!)'.[50] On that occasion Dunn had given Sassoon a double dose of anti-typhoid injection, commenting as he did so: 'That'll keep you quiet for forty-eight hours'. The grim humour of this remark was evidently appreciated by Sassoon, who repeated it in *Infantry Officer*.[51] It was one of a number of reasons why Sassoon wanted to know Dunn better.

Another reason was his love of books, which Graves had no doubt reported to Sassoon. Inured though he was to the hardships of war, Dunn's one serious complaint was that enforced periods of inactivity became 'most boring when a very limited kit [left] no room for books'.[52] It is the kind of remark Sassoon might have made. When Dunn conceived the idea of a collection of first-hand accounts of the Battalion's War-service in 1926, he was to write a great deal of it himself. He was also to appeal to Sassoon, who would provide the longest continuous narrative, in fact a whole chapter for him. (By the time the book was eventually published in 1938, Sassoon had already used an amplified version of his contribution in *Memoirs of an Infantry Officer*.)

It is clear from the many perceptive comments that Dunn makes and includes in *The War the Infantry Knew* that he was a highly intelligent observer of the human scene. The book was justly described by one authority as 'arguably the foremost narrative account of the British Infantry experience on the Western Front'. It ranges from detailed first-hand accounts of individual battles to entertaining asides, such as the way different nationalities named their trench systems. (While 'Piccadilly' remained a favourite with British units, there was always a 'Grafton Street' with the Irish, and a 'Cowcaddens' with the Scots.) Dunn is also quite witty at times, a characteristic which would have appealed to

Sassoon: 'The C-in-C tells me "our backs are to the wall," ' he reports; then adds: 'His men are asking, "Where's the ------- wall?" '[53] On one particularly gruelling day, noting that a single, rare jar of rum had arrived with the mail, he exclaims: 'One! Many of us were not tantalized with a knowledge of this meagre windfall until it was, at most, only an exhalation from the lucky'.[54]

Apart from a good sense of humour and a love of books, as well as music and golf, Dunn shared Sassoon's critical attitude towards the War. Nine years after their first meeting, and six and a half years after Sassoon's detention at Craiglockhart for protesting publicly against the War, he wrote to him: 'Sometimes when I am in the western outskirts of Edinburgh [i.e. where Craiglockhart is situated] I think of you incarcerated for saying what so many of us said – but you said it publicly'.[55] Dunn was particularly critical of the remoteness of the General Staff, for example. Impressed by the visits of both an Australian Brigadier and Australian Chief Medical Officer to the Front, he asks: 'Was one of ours ever within the shelled zone when there was the greatest need for him to know how things were being done, and what might be needed?'[56] It could have been Sassoon speaking.

Sassoon admired Dunn greatly. When the doctor wrote to ask for a contribution to his planned Battalion history in February 1926, the poet replied:

> We'd got a Doctor with a D.S.O.
> And much unmedalled merit. In the Line
> Or out of it, he'd taught the troops to know
> That shells, bombs, bullets, gas, or even a mine
> Heaving green earth toward heaven, were things he took
> For granted, and dismissed with one shrewd look.
> No missile, as it seemed, could cause him harm.
> So on he went past endless sick-parades;
> Jabbed his inoculation in an arm;
> Gave 'medicine and duty' to all shades
> Of uninfectious ailment. Thus his name
> Acquired a most intense, though local, fame.[57]

Sassoon was to remain friends with Dunn till long after the War, not only agreeing to contribute to Dunn's history but also asking the doctor to help him with his medical expertise when he needed a tactful description of his Aunt Rachel's syphilitically induced dementia in *The Weald of Youth*. Dunn was to write him a series of 'enormously long' letters, to meet him regularly in London during the 1920s and to stay with him at least once in 1940. It was only in 1947, after a particularly rambling missive, in which it was clear that increasing age was making Dunn rather 'grumble-some' and 'cussed', that Sassoon would try to end their correspondence. Even then his comment was affectionate: 'The poor old boy can't bear getting old'.

One member of the Battalion who was already rather old and fussy by the time Sassoon joined it was the second-in-Command, Major Poore, brother of General R.M. Poore. Described kindly but briefly by Sassoon in *Infantry Officer* as a 'gentle middle-aged country solicitor',[58] Poore consoled himself by reminiscing about cricket and hunting with Sassoon. With his mannered speech and slow, deliberate ways, he seems to have been rather a figure of fun among his junior officers, who often mimicked him behind his back. But he was also respected for his keenness and efficiency in training, an area largely neglected by the Battalion's Commanding Officer. It would be Poore, not the C.O., directing operations at the Battle of Polygon Wood in September 1917 when a shell landed on Command Headquarters and killed him outright. 'One of the good men who died on September 26th' was Sassoon's epitaph on him.

The Commanding Officer himself, Lt.-Col. W.B. Garnett, who had replaced Col. C.H.R. Crawshay shortly before Sassoon's arrival, was hardly a popular figure in the Battalion. It was not simply that the 2nd had loved 'Tibs' Crawshay so much that he had seemed irreplaceable, but that Garnett appeared almost too indulgent and conciliatory. According to Sassoon, who had his previous Colonel, Stockwell, in mind, greater aggressiveness would have been preferable.

Garnett had got off to an unfortunate start with his new officers by showing off his superior powers of spelling, a 'rare accomplishment' which had merely harassed and embarrassed them according to Sassoon.[59] Sassoon was probably not the only one to enjoy the CO's discomfort when he was ordered to dismount while saluting his Corps Commander.[60] He certainly enjoyed retelling the incident, with Garnett as 'Easby' in *Infantry Officer*, particularly the part where the General bellowed 'Are you stuck to that bloody horse?' Garnett's anxiety to prove that his G.O.C. should 'be able to depend on him at all times' was interpreted by his Battalion as a sign of ambitiousness rather than conscientiousness.[61] Captain Dunn was consistently sarcastic about Garnett in the Battalion memoirs. He noted the times his CO chose to stay safely out of the Line, his lack of any effective training programme and the severe 'intellectual strain' he suffered after only two weeks as Acting Brigadier. He had no parting praise for Garnett when he eventually fulfilled his ambitions and left to command a brigade in May 1918. Privately he told Sassoon that 'Garnett never knew or cared what, if anything, his company officers did'. He felt that Garnett, like Kirkby, was 'a potent deteriorating influence'.

Garnett notwithstanding, Sassoon felt sufficiently at home with his companions by 1 April, the 2nd Battalion's last day at Chipilly, to accept his future with them philosophically. It would, he feared, be a 'squalid' one, since 'some battle' was imminent, though details were still unsure. Cheered by the technical arrival of Spring, the creative urge returned to him. Since poetry was difficult to write in the crowded, uncomfortable camp, he concentrated on prose, sending a piece of what he ironically described as 'fine writing' to Ross. Though ostensibly dismissive of the late 19th century, Royal Academy 'Dream Pictures' he advocates for 'homesick officers in the Field', the nostalgic tone of his piece suggests that he found consolation in such memories himself. It is an insight into his own conservative tastes in art, as well as the influence of his early Kentish background.[62]

Though Sassoon concludes his description of 'Dream Pictures' with the words 'what tripe', his own longing for the English countryside and the calm life it symbolizes shows through. He was also yearning for news from home and complained to Ross that Graves had not written to him since his arrival in France. He was worried that Graves was 'annoyed' that he had changed some of his poems in *Goliath and David* while seeing it through the press. He had no need to be, for Graves had already written to him on 26 March, thanking him for editing the book so successfully, a letter which had not yet reached him by the time he wrote to Ross on 1 April.

Like Sassoon, Graves was taking advantage of his stay at Somerville College Hospital to see a lot of the 'Garsington people'. He was also getting to know the Oxford writers, Aldous Huxley, Harold Childe and Thomas Earp, whom Sassoon in turn would meet. Responding to a 'heartcry' about his new unit from Sassoon, who had not yet become reconciled to his Company Commander, Kirkby, Graves replied: 'Poor old Sassons / Isn't it a bloody battalion? But you can imagine what it was like when it consisted *entirely* of Kirkbys and Superkirkbys'.[63] He was relieved that at least one mutual friend from the 1st Battalion, 'young Orme', was with Sassoon and tried hard to be positive: 'Never mind, cheer up – remember my tip – make friends with Old Yates … Isn't jolly old Garnett a cypher? "Doctorr" Dunn really commands the "battaalion": but he's a good chap, the old doc'.[64] He confessed to being 'much flattered' that Sassoon wanted to hear from him 'after your famous dictum that you forget about people as soon as you're away from them'. This is a puzzling statement, which is probably not true, but suggests that Sassoon was trying to impress his younger friend with his aloofness.

Letter-writing and 'fine' prose passages gave way to scribbled diary entries when the Battalion set off on 2 April for Arras and the Front. The year 1916 had ended in a sense of defeat for the Allies: the Somme offensive had failed, Russian morale was at a low ebb, Roumania had been overrun and, at sea, Jutland had been, at best, a negative encounter. Only the capture of Baghdad (Sassoon's 'ancient family residence' as he described it in a letter of 18 March 'celebrating' the event) could really be counted as a victory and that seemed to most people too far away to be of much interest. One result of the growing dissatisfaction was a change of political leadership in England, where Lloyd George's Government replaced that of Asquith on 11 December 1916, and a switch in military leadership in France, where General Nivelle (of Verdun fame) replaced Marshal Joffre as Commander-in-Chief of the French Armies. While Lloyd George and his fellow politicians on the Allied side were rejecting German peace proposals in December as insincere, Joffre had been drawing up plans for one more great battle, in the belief that this would finally defeat the enemy.

Since Allied troops in France numbered about 3,900,000 men (one-third of them British) to the Germans' 2,500,000, he had calculated that a concerted attack on them in spring 1917 should exhaust their reserves and bring the War to an end. When Nivelle took command in early 1917, whilst accepting Joffre's plan of a renewal of the Somme offensive on a widened front, in principle, he made several significant changes. He proposed to attack on both flanks of the Lens-Noyon-Rheims salient, with the French striking the greatest blow in Champagne after Allied attacks north and south of the Somme had claimed the Germans' main attention. His plan to avoid the old Somme battlefields but attack each side of it reduced the frontage of the British, who were ordered instead to take over the French Front south of the Somme as far as Roye, in order to release more French troops for the main attack in Champagne. In spite of Haig's reservations, the battle was fixed for 1 April, an unfortunate date.

It was an ingenious scheme, but even before it got under way (slightly later than planned) on 9 April, the Germans had disrupted it. Ludendorff, anticipating the Allies' move and anxious to avoid the Somme experience, had already ordered a new, massively fortified line of defence to be built across the base of the Lens-Noyon-Rheims arc. This new line, completed early in 1917, was known as the Hindenburg Line to the Allies, but the Siegfried Line to the Germans, an irony on which Sassoon did not comment. As the Germans retired behind it in good order during the second half of March 1917, they systematically devastated the area they were leaving. This simple but effective device disrupted British plans and delayed preparations for the main attack. Only the area round Arras, a German-held bulge of which Gommecourt formed the most westerly point, remained unchanged and was, therefore, chosen as the starting point of the spring offensive. The VI and XVII Corps were on the left and on the right the VII Corps, of which Sassoon's 2nd Royal Welch Fusiliers formed a part.

The reaction of the 2nd Battalion to the Arras plan, if Dr Dunn's comments are representative, was sceptical. 'The Battle of Arras, and its brood', Dunn wrote, 'was the B[ritish] E[xpeditionary] F[orce] share of the ambitious scheme which British and French Governments had accepted from the new Commander-in-Chief of the French Armies [Nivelle]. Converging Franco-British attacks were to envelop the German centre'.[65] The first stage of the Battalion's involvement was a march of fifty miles to the battle area, which took seven days, including a full day's rest on Easter Friday.

The first leg of the journey, a three-hour march of seven miles westward to Corbie, was familiar to the many who had passed through it on their way into Amiens, and relatively easy. The second day's longer march, northwards to Villers-Bocage, a distance of about thirteen miles, however, took its toll. Sassoon, who had started the day with a hangover after his convivial evening with Kirkby and Greaves, had difficulty in keeping B company up to strength.

It was only as the journey got underway that Sassoon had become fully aware of his own men. On arrival at Camp 13 in March he had been put in charge of no. 8 Platoon of B Company, a sorry collection on the whole. Several of them had been part of a recent draft of conscripts and seemed to him physically and, in some cases, mentally unfitted for the army. A number of his platoon were barely capable of carrying the weight of their equipment and in one case a new recruit did not even know how to load a rifle. (After teaching him, Sassoon felt 'that the poor devil would have been a less perilous ingredient of his command had he been left in his primordial ignorance'.[66]) The total strength of the platoon, including two sergeants, one corporal and six lance-corporals, was thirty-four, but since eight of these were Lewis gunners, the unit shrank considerably on parade, seldom mustering even twenty men. A further problem for their officer, this being a Welsh unit, was the presence of *eight* Private Joneses. He had tried to interest them all at rest camp with novel platoon exercises suited to their limited abilities, such as hide-and-seek, but remained convinced that the majority of them should not have been in the army at all.

It was on the second day's march towards Arras that Sassoon's doubts were confirmed. Several of the weaker members of his little band with others from B Company were 'beat to the world' by the time they reached Villers-Bocage and he covered the last lap trundling two of them in front of him, while another hung on to his belt behind. The Company Sergeant had to carry their rifles. Not one of the three stood more than five feet high. Even those who had marched under their own steam were suffering badly, as a foot-inspection revealed. It stirred all Sassoon's latent love and compassion for what he later called, in a Whitmanesque phrase, his 'brave brown companions',[67] to see the patience with which they endured their badly blistered feet, as a poem written the same day makes clear:

> Foot Inspection
> The twilight barn was chinked with gleams; I saw
> Soldiers with naked feet stretched on the straw,
> Stiff-limbed from the long muddy march we'd done,
> And ruddy-faced with April wind and sun.
> With pity and stabbing tenderness I see
> Those stupid, trustful eyes stare up at me.
> Yet, while I stoop to Morgan's blistered toes
> And ask about his boots, he never knows
> How glad I'd be to die, if dying could make him free

12. The Wounded Hero (February-April 1917)

From battles. Shyly grinning at my joke,
He pulls his grimy socks on; lights a smoke,
And thinks 'Our officer's a decent bloke.'[68]

In spite of Sassoon's Christ-like willingness to sacrifice himself for his men, all he could really do for them was to send a large batch of excruciating boots to the Battalion cobblers, knowing that they would come back roughly botched at best. But the incident added fuel to his growing anger with 'profiteers and "Society people" who guzzled their way through the War'.[69]

Fortunately for Sassoon's platoon, the longest march of the journey was over and the next lap, a straightforward eight miles north along the Amiens-Doullens road to Beauval, brought nothing worse than some unseasonal snow. As they marched, they passed out of one 'Army area' (Rawlinson's Fourth) into another (Allenby's Third), slowly but surely approaching their final destination. Sassoon had spent the previous evening drinking again, this time with A Company, a sign of his growing *camaraderie* with the officers as well as men in the face of imminent danger.

Passing through Doullens on the fourth day of the march, 5 April, Sassoon noted – presumably with some apprehension – the sign 'Arras 32km', a fact reinforced by the sound of heavy firing from the battle area. The journey had not started until 4 p.m., so that it was already 8 p.m. by the time the Battalion arrived at its destination, Lucheux, a few miles north-east of Doullens. Sassoon enjoyed dining in the moonlight round a brazier with a plate on his knee. The next day, 6 April, was Good Friday and a complete rest day. Sassoon woke to the sight of the sun streaming in at his hut door and the sound of broad Scots being shouted by some Scottish Rifles in the neighbouring hut. There were also bagpipes being practised at the edge of the woods where he was billeted.

A slightly longer march of nine miles in cold wind and sunshine on 7 April brought Sassoon and his men to Saulty, further to the north-east. They were now only twelve miles from Arras and began to notice clear signs of the Offensive, from ammunition and food dumps to the tents of the Casualty Clearing Station. There was also a large Y.M.C.A. canteen, which delighted the men and gave Sassoon a chance to stock up for them: 'Twelve dozen packets of Woodbines in a pale green cardboard box', he reminisced, 'were all I could store up for the future consolation of B Company'.[70] His own consolation was to sit in the peaceful park of a nearby château enjoying the sunshine, a few small deer and the various birds, whose song punctuated the thudding of the guns. He reflected, not for the first time and with no great originality, that the threat of death, though terrifying, also made everything seem vivid and valuable:

I don't suppose anyone would believe me if I said I was absolutely happy and contented. Of course this is written after a good meal of coffee and eggs. But the fact remains that if I had the choice between England tomorrow and the battle, I would choose the battle without hesitation. Why on earth is one such a fool as to be pleased at the prospect? I can't understand it. Last year I thought it was because I had never been through it before. But my feeling of quiet elation and absolute confidence now is something even stronger than last summer's passionate longings for death and glory.[71]

His retrospective interpretation of his attitude was that he had 'to play at being a hero',[72] but it felt quite genuine at the time. Among the troops too, he had observed a growing, almost eager expectancy. Paradoxically, the nearer they got to battle, the more cheerful they seemed. Were they, he wondered, always at their best when they knew they were 'for it'?[73] Perhaps they really believed that the Battle of Arras would end the War, unlike Ottoline Morrell, who thought the Spring Offensive 'pure devilry' and had told him so in one of her numerous letters.[74]

The Battalion had been informed that it would move into its 'final concentration area' on 8 April, Easter Sunday. This was an irony which did not escape Sassoon as he marched his men the last six miles eastwards to Basseux, only a few miles from Arras itself. Having made a relatively early 9 a.m. start the men were installed in their billets by midday and he had time to inspect the old Front Line, from which the Germans had retreated. He was struck, as most British soldiers were, by the superiority of the German trench system. Basseux itself had not suffered badly from shells and its relative calm was enhanced, for the officers at least, by their lodgings in an old château. Seated in one of the attics, his feet sticking out of the window, Sassoon watched some of his friends playing cricket and felt again how good life seemed under threat:

Cheery voices; glorious sunshine; pigeons flapping about over red and grey roofs. A small church with pointed tower a little way down the street.[75]

The Battalion was still at Basseux the next day, 9 April, for the opening of the Battle of Arras. This was, on the surface, a brilliant success. Virtually the whole of the German Front Line was taken within three-quarters of an hour and the second line within two hours. Even part of the third, the massively fortified Hindenburg Line, was penetrated by nightfall. (Part of this dramatic opening victory was due to a new artillery strategy, the 'creeping' barrage, in which the artillery moved its fire steadily forward while the infantry followed closely behind.) A few miles away at Basseux the 2nd Battalion talked very loudly about the reported successes but, as Sassoon noted, with 'forced uneasy gaiety'.[76]

For once the rumoured 5,000 German prisoners was an underestimate, the Allies having taken at least 5,600 on this first day. For Sassoon the excitement was marred by his own physical condition. He had gastritis, a sore throat and several festering scratches on each hand. Fastidious by nature, he minded almost as much that he had no clean handkerchiefs or socks left. Minor discomforts as these all were in the context, they coloured most soldiers' experience of the War, though often omitted by military historians, as Sassoon pointed out. He had to confess that a large opium pill, 'to promote constipation "suitable for open warfare" ' was of more consolation than Ottoline's present of Keats's poems, a little india-paper edition bound in green vellum which arrived in the post.[77] Nevertheless, he took the opportunity of a full day's rest at Basseux to write to thank Ottoline for the book and also for the opal she had sent him for good luck.[78]

After describing the hardships of War and praising his fellow-officers for their courage, Sassoon concentrated on the real interest they had in common, and a 'safe' subject, literature. Like him she had been experimenting with prose and he suggested, tactfully, that she should try to condense her rather florid style. He also told her that, having had to reduce his baggage in preparation for the Front, one of the few books he had kept was *Far From the Madding Crowd*, which was helping him survive the uneasy wait for further orders. Though the weather had turned even colder – a deterrent to the most resolute of 'happy warriors' – he was keeping himself calm and independent with Hardy's vision of the rural England he loved.

By the time the 2nd RWF was ordered up to the Front in the late afternoon of 11 April, British success was already beginning to seem less certain. The Germans' third line held firm against renewed attacks and British tanks, which were meant to precede the Infantry and break through the wire, were held up by a combination of mechanical faults and mud. As the Germans brought up reinforcements Allenby's Third Army found itself making a direct attack on a rapidly strengthening resistance without the help of its artillery, whose horse-drawn guns were delayed by the difficulties of crossing the German trench-system. Though the Canadians scored a famous victory further north at Vimy Ridge, an achievement consolidated by the capture of Fampoux a little further south, the River Scarpe marked the limit of real Allied successes. To the south of the Scarpe German resistance, first at Railway Triangle and Telegraph Hill, then on the Wancourt-Feuchy line, was so strong that it badly delayed British advances in that part of the Line.

It was to this area, to the right of Héninel, that the 2nd Battalion, having been 'lent' to the 21st Division for the occasion, was ordered. (The 21st was to relieve the 30th Division.) They had been marching only half an hour when snow started to fall, concealing whole villages which had already been reduced to rubble by the fighting. (One such village was Ficheux, which the men christened 'Fish-hooks'.) The snow had stopped when, after eight miles, they bivouacked by a sunken road near Mercatel, only a few miles from the Front. But conditions were still very bad. Sassoon and his young friend Casson considered themselves very lucky indeed to be able to huddle round a brazier in a tiny coke-filled dug-out with a trench-mortar Sergeant-Major and four others. The misery of B Company was alleviated by Sassoon's thoughtful emergency ration of cigarettes from Saulty.

Not surprisingly daylight found everyone bleary-eyed and dejected. The snow had melted, turning everything to mud, a scene of desolation which intensified the nearer they drew to the Front, and by the afternoon they were less than two miles from it. For a march of about three miles in the rain had brought the Battalion to St Martin-Cojeul, a ruined village north-west of Croisilles and south-west of Wancourt, where the Germans had just counter-attacked. The 2nd Royal Welch Fusiliers, who were relieving the 17th Manchesters in reserve, occupied an old German reserve trench near the Hindenburg Line.

As second-in-command Sassoon was entitled to a place in 'Company Headquarters', but this grand-sounding accommodation turned out to be the nearest thing to a rabbit-hole he had ever experienced. Kirkby's considerable bulk did not help; it left just enough room in the dug-out for Sassoon and a small stove. Rations were short and Sassoon risked damaging his already painful fingers further by fishing his precious half-slice of bacon from the flame which threatened to claim it. He shared his last orange (one of his favourite foods in the trenches) with Casson. Then, since sleep seemed impossible in the cramped, icy conditions, tried to keep himself warm by enlarging the dug-out to make room for Casson and Evans. Kirkby, perhaps because of his cushioning of flesh, showed his usual infuriating ability to sleep soundly wherever he was.

When day eventually dawned there was nothing to do except sit in the dug-out and wait for orders. Rumours abounded. Héninel was said to have been taken by the 56th Division, though Sassoon doubted that it could be held. He was aware that the 62nd Brigade was attacking Fontaine-les-Croisilles and Fontaine Wood from a hill three-quarters of a mile away and, by the end of the day, an ominous Friday 13th, he knew that the attack had failed through lack of support on the left flank. He also knew, as he surveyed the numerous corpses scattered over the hillside by the late afternoon, that his own Brigade would be attacking the same targets the next day at 5.30 a.m. Fortunately he was to remain in reserve again.

At 9 p.m. on Saturday, 14 April, an evening which reminded Sassoon irresistibly of spring twilights in England at the cricket nets, the 2nd Battalion, being in support to the 1st Cameronians, set off to relieve the 13th Northumberland Fusiliers in Hindenburg Support. It had been a day of such carnage that, as Martin Gilbert points out, 'three British generals defied Army tradition by protesting directly to Haig at the mounting casualties'.[79] Yet once again Sassoon found himself relegated to a passive role, or so he thought.

Though the distance was less than two miles, the Northumberland

Fusiliers guides, who had come to fetch B Company, managed to lose their way. Kirkby decided to sit down and wait for daylight, but Sassoon, with his usual mixture of recklessness and courage, tried to rectify the situation. Stumbling off into the darkness he came across – by what he modestly called 'a lucky accident' – a small party of Sappers in a sunken road, one of whom was able to lead B Company to their Battalion rendezvous. It was 4 a.m. by the time they arrived at the cavernous underground communication trench assigned to them and 5 a.m. by the time Sassoon finally got to bed.

Sassoon had spent the intervening hour arranging for his depleted Company to mount sentries along its 900-yard front and, in the absence of anyone sufficiently experienced, had gone out to patrol No Man's Land himself, in a fit of temper at the unawareness of Battalion Headquarters when they issued such orders. The trench itself, lined with grotesque figures of dead or sleeping men – he could not distinguish which – had seemed to him a nightmarish place worthy of a new infernal vision by Dante, Milton or Blake, but No Man's Land was far worse. Alone and unprotected by wire of any kind, since he was now behind the enemy's third line, he could think of nothing more defiant than to relieve himself in the direction of the Germans, an action he found curiously comforting. He was, however, in more danger from his own nervous sentry, as he carefully measured his paces back to the trench, than the enemy, and he was glad to regain the company's left-hand post unharmed as 'a dull, red, rainy dawn rose'.[80] Descending into the chill of the tunnel beneath the support trench he lay, frozen to the bone on his wire-netting bunk, unable to sleep and already anticipating his own death in those diabolical surroundings. He was to remember the scene vividly nine years later and to describe it in a passage reminiscent of Henri Barbusse, whose *Under Fire* he greatly admired:

> For it was a dreadful place we had come to. But it was our business to make the best of it, and I don't suppose that anyone else in the Company felt its dreadfulness as fully as I did. The fact that it was an experience of a pattern which was shared by millions of men does not make it seem any less strange and awful and inhuman to me ... Stage by stage we had marched to this monstrous region of death and disaster. From afar it had threatened us with the blink and din of its bombardments. We groped and stumbled along a deep ditch to the place appointed for us in that zone of human havoc. The World War had got our insignificant little unit in its mouth; we were there to be munched, maimed or liberated.[81]

After only one day in the Hindenburg Trench Sassoon believed that he had seen the most ghastly sights of his life, ones which would haunt him till he died; dead bodies lying about, both inside the tunnel and just in front of it, gruesome beyond belief after the rain. Everywhere he saw mangled Germans or British soldiers in various states of dismemberment, and smelt their decaying bodies. In one of his many attempts to exorcize such memories he wrote 'To the Warmongers':

> I'm back again from hell
> With loathsome thoughts to sell:
> Secrets of death to tell;
> And horrors from the abyss.
> Young faces bleared with blood,
> Sucked down into the mud,
> You shall hear things like this,
> Till the tormented slain
> Crawl round and once again,
> With limbs that twist awry
> Moan out their brutish pain,
> As the fighters pass them by.
> For you our battles shine
> With triumph half-divine;
> And the glory of the dead
> Kindles in each proud eye.
> But a curse is on my head,
> That shall not be unsaid,
> And the wounds in my heart are red,
> For I have watched them die.[82]

It was 'the horrors from the abyss', particularly the suffering and carnage witnessed at Arras, which were finally to provoke Sassoon into making his feelings about the War public: 'You *shall* hear things like this' he threatened those who remained behind, safe and unaware in England. But the experience was evidently too raw for finished verse and he chose not to publish these lines.

After an hour's sleep on the morning of Sunday, 15 April – he had not slept for more than an hour at a time since the previous Tuesday – Sassoon was up again and in charge of a carrying party. In order to encourage the equally exhausted men, he himself lugged loads of heavy trench-mortar bombs between St Martin-Cojeul and Croisilles. It rained all day and the trenches were like glue. To Sassoon, sodden and exhausted, the experience seemed typical of infantry life at the Front. He was among ruins of an intense bombardment of two weeks before, which had left concrete emplacements smashed and tilted sideways, the chalky soil pitted with huge shell-holes and dead bodies everywhere:

I can remember looking down, as I blundered and gasped my way along [he was to write] and seeing a mask-like face floating on the surface of the flooded trench. This face had detached itself from its skull. I can remember two mud-clotted hands protruding from the wet ashen soil like the roots of a tree turned upside down; one hand seemed to be pointing at the sky with an accusing gesture.[83]

12. The Wounded Hero (February-April 1917)

It was nightmare visions like these which were to haunt him later as he walked along Piccadilly, or followed equally innocuous pursuits. His attempt to describe the carnage in 'The Effect' gives an even more vivid impression than the diary account, in spite of the fact that it was written a few months later. Taking up the inept phrase 'he had never seen so many dead before' from the report of a War Correspondent, he uses it as an ironic refrain throughout the poem. It opens the first stanza, where the narrator, like Sassoon, 'lugged his everlasting load / Of bombs along what once had been a road', and also introduces stanza two:

> 'He'd never seen so many dead before.'
> The lilting words danced up and down his brain,
> While corpses jumped and capered in the rain.
> No, no; he wouldn't count them any more …
> The dead have done with pain:
> They've choked, they can't come back to life again.
>
> (*CP*, p. 73)

The War Correspondent's phrase is as dead and meaningless as the corpses, as the contrast between his words (again in direct speech) and the narrator's reactions (in indirect speech) reveals. In the third and final stanza, however, the narrator himself breaks into direct speech; ignoring polite social boundaries he describes the nightmarish truth in harsh imagery from the world of commerce to emphasize how cheaply life is held:

> 'How many dead? As many as ever you wish.
> Don't count 'em; they're too many.
> Who'll buy my nice fresh corpses, two a penny.'

When William Heinemann was shown this poem, he thought the last line 'quite impossible'.[84]

After six and a half hours in the mud and the rain, Sassoon returned to Company Headquarters, only to be informed by Kirkby, snug and dry himself, that he had been detailed to take command of a hundred bombers; they were to act as a reserve for the 1st Cameronians the next day. Though the full strength of the 2nd Royal Welch Fusiliers was only 270, he was to take twenty-five men from each Company for the assignment. That same day, 15 April, Haig had ordered an end to the opening offensive, but the fighting continued. As part of what became known as the Battle of the Scarpe, the 1st Cameronians (to the right of the 2nd Royal Welch Fusiliers) were to negotiate a barrier which blocked both the deep tunnel under the support trench and the Hindenburg Trench itself. They were then to attack the Germans, who were known to be on the other side of the 'block', as it was called. The objective was to clear the trench and tunnel for 500 yards, while other battalions on their left went over the top to attack Fontaine-les-Croisilles. Sassoon's unenviable task was to tackle the Tunnel, if the Cameronians failed. Though the friendly Cameronian officers who explained the plan believed that there was little chance of Sassoon being called on to support 'the Cams', he was decidedly apprehensive. The thought of bombing along a tunnel in the dark against an unknown enemy made him understandably nervous. He was even more alarmed by the need to present a coherent battle plan to his Adjutant, since technical details made him feel inadequate in a way that direct action never did. Clutching the few smudgy notes he had made, and longing for Dr Dunn to advise him, he made his way to Battalion Headquarters along the Tunnel.

A few inches higher than a tall man and fitted with bunks and recessed rooms, this was an eerie place, reeking of foul decay. Once, when he tripped and recovered himself by grabbing the wall, his torch revealed someone half-hidden by a blanket. It was only after shaking and even kicking the apparently sleeping body that he discovered the truth; it was a dead German he was trying to rouse, his fingers still clutching a blackened gash on his neck.[85] Sickened and even more unnerved he stumbled on until he reached Mann at Battalion Headquarters. To his great relief he learnt that the underground part of the operation had been cancelled, though the trench attack on the 'block' would still go ahead. On his way back he was fortunate enough to discover Ralph Greaves sitting in A Company headquarters and was soon supplied with the required organization scheme by his imperturbable friend. While he waited with Greaves between 10 and 12 p.m. for his orders to come through, they reminisced peacefully about the Kentish and Sussex border they both knew well. Nothing could have been further from the grim midnight scene than their mental bike ride on a fine summer's afternoon past some of their favourite spots.

The attack on Fontaine-les-Croisilles began at 3 a.m. on Monday, 16 April. As Sassoon waited nervously at the 1st Cameronians' Headquarters in the Tunnel, ready but not anxious to be summoned, he felt intensely self-conscious. He found it difficult to believe that anyone thought him capable of helping, a modesty which seems to have been entirely genuine. With his hundred bombers lining the fifty steps which led up to the trench he felt something of a charlatan. Yet when the order finally came at 6 a.m. for him to dispatch twenty-five of his weary, chilled men to help the Cameronians' struggling B Company, he insisted on taking them up to the 'show' himself. Stopping only to put on his steel helmet, he led A Company, which happened to be at the top of the steep stairs, into the sunlit but noisy morning of the support trench.

Headed by Sergeant Baldwin ('Baldock' in *Infantry Officer*), an admirably impassive man who 'never ceased to behave like a well-trained and confidential man-servant',[86] the contingent consisted of fifteen bombers, four rifle grenadiers and five carriers, who also acted as bayonet men. Dodging and stumbling up a narrow communication trench to the wide main trench, at the head of this little group, Sassoon says he had not the slightest idea what he was going to do. Fortunately, he was able to conceal his confusion and managed to convince not only his own men but also the retreating Cameronians that he was in full control of the situation. On learning that the latter, after taking several hundred yards of the trench, had run out of bombs and been driven back, he reassured their young Captain (Wright) and set off recklessly to regain the lost ground. As he freely admitted in his detailed account for Dunn's subsequent history:

> ... I never pretended to be a professionally efficient soldier. My methods were always amateurish and unsystematic. I always failed to take necessary precautions and, on the occasion I am trying to describe, my only effective quality consisted in an unreasoning resolve to rush in where The Cameronians were no longer willing to tread. Anyhow my ignorance simplified the situation, and was for the time being an advantage. I knew nothing except that I was in the Hindenburg front trench, outside Captain Wright's Company H.Q. dug-out with my twenty-five men. I also knew that our objective was 'to clear the trench for 500 yards'. The sun was shining in a sky full of large drifting clouds. A few of our own shells were dropping short. It was half-past six on a fresh mid-April morning ... I was excited and mettlesome. The Cameronian crowd had been legging it, and I was out to show them how easy it was to deal with the Germans.[87]

The most interesting aspect of Sassoon's part in the Battle of Arras, for a biographer, is his own attitude toward it. Nowhere is his upper-middle-class background more apparent. For he consistently portrays himself, in true English fashion, as an amateur who nevertheless succeeds where the professionals have failed. Sassoon might dismiss his behaviour, including what followed next, as 'foolhardy', but it was also, without doubt, courageous. Accompanied by Sergeant Baldwin he climbed over the Block and advanced a hundred yards up the trench, without meeting anyone. He then sent Baldwin back to arrange for the collection of small heaps of precious Mills bombs which he had noticed at twenty yard intervals, and continued alone. Rounding a corner with some apprehension, he encountered a small man, fortunately from his own side. This turned out to be a Cameronian Corporal, still on guard, a bag of bombs slung over his left shoulder.

In complete silence Sassoon joined him, his own bag of bombs at the ready, and together they advanced round the next bend. What Sassoon saw there helps to explain his subsequent recklessness. Propped against the wall of the trench, in a pool of his own blood, was a fair-haired Cameronian private staring vacantly at the sky. Enraged by the sight of the badly-wounded man, Sassoon slung a couple of bombs in the enemy's direction, receiving in reply an egg-bomb which exploded harmlessly behind him. Now completely mindless of danger he advanced without caution until he noticed the corporal darting into saps, or side-tunnels, as he threw his bombs. Impressed by his artfulness and efficiency, Sassoon followed suit and between them they drove the Germans back nearly 400 yards, until they reached their objective.

It was only then that the aptly named Corporal Smart spoke to Sassoon, who had forgotten about their 'objectives'. He had caught an occasional glimpse of retreating Germans, but the whole exercise had seemed to him, in his excitement, so absurdly easy that he wanted to push on. Following one of his frequent impulses, he started to explore a narrow sap which ran out from the place where they had stopped. A second impulse, prompted by an apparent lull in the attack going on overhead, nearly cost him his life. Sticking his head out of the sap to look at the surrounding country-side, he received what felt like a tremendous blow on the back, between the shoulders. In reality, a sharp-eyed sniper had shot him through the right shoulder from the front. Sassoon firmly believed throughout the War that his luck never deserted him, and this was a case in point. The bullet had missed both his jugular vein and his spine by a fraction of an inch.

At the time Sassoon was convinced that his end had come and, leaning against the wall of the sap, shut his eyes. When he opened them again, Sergeant Baldwin was beside him, discreet and sympathetic, and he realized to his great surprise that he was still alive. After helping him to the main trench and dressing his wound, which had luckily not bled much, Baldwin went off to fetch more men. By the time he returned with Sassoon's fellow officer, Conning, who had been sent to relieve him, Sassoon had recovered sufficiently to want to carry on fighting and was busy organizing a fresh attack. (He was now, as he observed, not only a hero but a wounded hero.) Only Conning's calm behaviour and written order from the Cameronian Colonel, Chaplin, telling him not to advance further – the attack had failed elsewhere – quelled his offensive spirit.

With a distinct sense of anti-climax Sassoon observed the further order to hand over to Conning and, at 9.45 a.m., only three and three-quarter hours after he first set out, was back at Battalion H.Q. After receiving both the Colonel's and the Adjutant's congratulations on his courageous action, he made his way slowly to the Aid Post. From there he was directed first to the Advanced Dressing Station at nearby Hénin, to be officially labelled 'walking wounded', then to Boyelles, an exhausting walk of three miles through the mud. Fortunately his batman, Mansfield, a quiet, clumsy, middle-aged man, went with him to carry his kit and it was he who put him on a bus for Warlencourt.

An uncomfortable one and a half hours later, for the roads were very bad, he found himself sitting in the 20th Casualty Station hospital, destined for England. His wound was 'hurting like hell', his anti-tetanus injection was making him feel 'very chilly and queer', he was 'half-dead for lack of sleep' and still in the 'same old clothes' he had worn for a week, but he was safe. 'For I've sped through. O Life! O Sun!' he marvelled, quoting in this moment of extreme emotion the words of his friend Robert Graves.[88]

13

'Love Drove Me to Rebel'
(April-July 1917)

The beginning of 1917 proved outwardly more dramatic for Sassoon than the end of 1916 and seemed ready to threaten his anti-war feelings. His exhilaration at playing a part in the Battle of Arras, however, did not last and his disillusionment when Arras proved no more conclusive than the Somme was correspondingly greater. It was a continuation of the doubts which had been building up in him even before the fiasco of the earlier battle. His failure to win the medal which had been recommended for his courage in the Hindenburg Trench was another contributory factor, since it freed him from any lingering sense of loyalty to the army, a disaffection nurtured by the growing influence of Lady Ottoline Morrell and her pacifist friends. The success of his first volume of war poems, *The Old Huntsman*, in May 1917 also helped to give him the confidence he needed to protest. Widely reviewed, and championed by some of England's most eminent critics, this led on to friendships with such literary giants as H.G. Wells and Arnold Bennett, as well as less famous but equally influential figures like J.C. Squire and other literary editors. The publication of *The Old Huntsman* also set in motion another relationship, which was to become one of the most important in Sassoon's life, his friendship with Thomas Hardy, to whom the book was dedicated. June and July were almost wholly taken up with the composition and delivery of his protest.

Sassoon's immediate reaction on being told that he was destined for England in April 1917 was extreme relief. This lasted as long as his rather protracted journey home, via Doullens, Abbeville and Camières, where he waited two days. While his pain and exhaustion continued he still felt like a wounded hero and his attitude remained warlike: 'I know it would be best for me *not* to go back to England', he wrote in his diary on 17 April. But once in England, comfortably installed in the 4th London Hospital at Denmark Hill, his self-absorption gave way to thoughts of those he had left behind. He already knew that, in spite of his own modest success, things were going badly at Arras, and all the subsequent news from the 2nd RWF was to confirm his sense of lives wasted in a pointless exercise.[1]

Only two days after his arrival at the 4th London, he was trying to describe the incident which most forcefully expressed for him the horror of Arras – his experience in the Hindenburg Tunnel. Unusually, the poetic version, 'The Rear Guard', preceded the prose account, which was to follow in *Infantry Officer* many years later:

> Groping along the tunnel, step by step,
> He winked his prying torch with patching glare
> From side to side, and sniffed the unwholesome air.
> Tins, boxes, bottles, shapes too vague to know;
> A mirror smashed, the mattress from a bed;
> And he, exploring fifty feet below
> The rosy gloom of battle overhead.
>
> Tripping, he grabbed the wall; saw some one lie
> Humped at his feet, half-hidden by a rug,
> And stooped to give the sleeper's arm a tug.
> 'I'm looking for headquarters.' No reply.
> 'God blast your neck!' (For days he'd had no sleep,)
> 'Get up and guide me through this stinking place.'
> Savage, he kicked a soft, unanswering heap,
> And flashed his beam across the livid face
> Terribly glaring up, whose eyes yet wore
> Agony dying hard ten days before;
> And fists of fingers clutched a blackening wound.
>
> Alone he staggered on, until he found
> Dawn's ghost that filtered down a shafted stair
> To the dazed, muttering creatures underground
> Who hear the boom of shells in muffled sound.
> At last, with sweat of horror in his hair,
> He climbed through darkness to the twilight air,
> Unloading hell behind him step by step.
>
> (*CP*, pp. 69-70)

Sassoon successfully conveys the nightmare quality of the Hindenburg Tunnel through this one small but unforgettable incident. The experience itself was a fairly common one (his own C.O. had a similar encounter) and it is only through an extremely careful choice of words and imagery that he manages to make it memorable. A comparison of this final version with his rough draft written the same day suggests that he worked hard at this. Apart from the division of an originally continuous poem into four irregular but carefully rhymed stanzas, the changes are mainly to the language. While keeping phrases he liked, such as 'sweat of horror in his hair' and 'Dawn's ghost that filtered down a shafted stair', he made his second version both more evocative and more specific. Thus 'tiny torch' is personified into 'prying torch' and 'whitening glare' becomes 'patching glare'. The 'rosy dusk of battle', in line seven, is changed to 'rosy gloom of battle', presumably in the interests of accuracy, since battles start at dawn not dusk. Sometimes the changes promote a sense of greater restraint, the 'hateful air' of the tunnel becoming 'the unwholesome air', for example, and the 'foul, hunched mattress' becoming simply 'the mattress', as though the narrator himself is restrained by his fear from more elaborate language.

In only one instance is the narrator's emotion made more overt, when he shouts at the apparently sleeping corpse, 'God blast your neck', rather than as originally, 'Wake up, you sod', the effect being heightened by the fact that the soldier has died from a neck wound. Rather than keeping the gruesome phrase 'Bloody fingers clutched a hideous wound', however, Sassoon alters it to the more restrained but more specific 'And fists of fingers clutched a blackening wound'. The dead man's suffering is emphasized by the simple device of throwing 'Agony that died ten days before' into the present and more immediate tense: 'Agony dying hard ten days before'. In a similar way 'clammy creatures' becomes 'dazed, muttering creatures', where the de-humanizing effect of the tunnel is preserved in the word 'creatures' but more specific detail is introduced in the adjectives. With the addition of the last line to the final version – 'Unloading hell behind him step by step' – Sassoon not only spells out his message but also brings the rhyme scheme neatly back to where it started, so rounding off the poem.

Scott-Moncrieff described 'The Rear-Guard' as 'an amazing piece of War photography'.[2] Sassoon himself thought it succeeded and when Edmund Gosse, who visited him in hospital shortly after the poem was written, told Hamo Thornycroft that he believed his nephew was suffering from severe shock, Sassoon pointed to 'The Rear-Guard' as evidence that he was not. 'If so', he argued, 'could I have written such a strong poem?'[3] He did not deny that he had been strongly affected by his recent experiences, but he saw his poems as a way of exorcizing them rather than manifestations of severe shock. 'To the Warmongers' (see p. 346), written on 23 April, powerfully expresses in grim detail the horrors of Arras and his anger at those who condoned the situation.[4] And in 'The General', also written in hospital, this anger is focused on those most directly responsible for the soldier's fate. The germ of that brief but highly effective satire seems to have come from an incident in Sassoon's journey to Arras, when the 2nd RWF had passed their Corps Commander, Lt.-Gen. Maxse (see p. 337). In Sassoon's poem the unsuspecting soldiers' praise of their General's cheerfulness is contrasted starkly with the results of his incompetence. The use of generic names – 'Harry' and 'Jack' – which both personalizes and depersonalizes the soldiers, and the General's breezily repeated greeting, together with Harry's unwittingly ironic comment and the shock ending, convey the situation far more vividly than a more discursive piece:

> 'Good-morning; good-morning!' the General said
> When we met him last week on our way to the line.
> Now the soldiers he smiled at are most of 'em dead,

And we're cursing his staff for incompetent swine.
'He's a cheery old card,' grunted Harry to Jack
As they slogged up to Arras with rifle and pack.
...
But he did for them both by his plan of attack.

(CP, p. 75)

The colloquial 'did for them both', which follows unexpectedly on what appears to be the concluding rhyming couplet, is all the more shocking in its euphemism. It is certainly more effective than his original 'murdered them both', to which several of his mentors had objected.

When Sassoon was not writing poetry in hospital he was attempting prose descriptions of Sambrook Ward, with its grey-green walls, forty white beds, three large red-draped lamps and masses of spring flowers. (Many of these had been sent by Ottoline Morrell.) He noted in passages which anticipated *Sherston's Progress*, how morning rag-time on the vacuous gramophone changed to more sentimental favourites in the lamplit glow of evening. While other patients played cards, he attempted to describe them – the 'lean flying-man in his usual grey dressing-gown', the young man who was shot down by the Germans behind Arras and spent three days in a dug-out with Bavarians and Russians, or the 'burly, swarthy, wide-faced Canadian' who looked like a criminal.[5] The morning was a quiet time for the men, spent mostly in reading or preparing for the visitors allowed in between 3 and 6 p.m., while the rest of the day was filled mainly with card-games and war-talk. In some ways it seemed a blissful escape, or 'Lotus-land', as Sassoon described it, no doubt with Tennyson in mind. And when the Head Sister asked the rising young poet for a verse in her album he dutifully wrote, in his most facetious vein:

> Good luck to the Hun
> Who got out his gun
> And dealt me a wound so auspicious;
> May a flesh-hole like mine
> Send him home from the Line,
> And his Nurses be just as delicious.

His effort, he observed sarcastically, 'aroused delighted simpers of female gratification', but its implications were simply not true. Not only did he fail to find the nurses 'delicious', he found it difficult to appreciate his situation in any way at all. The droning and crashing of machinery from the munitions factory opposite the hospital got on his nerves and he was unable to unwind.

It seemed essential to tell the truth about Arras while it was still fresh in his mind, but the effort exhausted him. Then there were too many letters to answer. On 23 April, for example, he was writing to thank

354

Heinemann for an advance copy of *The Old Huntsman*, which was finally ready, and on the same day he was probably replying to Graves's sympathetic letter which had arrived on the 22nd. ('Poor old Sassons', Graves had opened, ' "Blessé pour la patrie" and according to Robbie rather too slightly to serve any useful purpose'.) He was certainly writing to encourage Dent to come, though already overwhelmed by visitors. That, of course, was part of his problem; when he was not talking to his fellow-patients about the War, he was trying to answer questions from the many friends who visited him.

'My brain is screwed up like a tight wire', Sassoon noted in his diary towards the end of April. On one afternoon alone, the 26th, he was visited by Meiklejohn, Ross *and* Gosse, which may explain why he wrote to Ottoline the same day asking her not to visit. Both Graves's sister, who was working at the hospital, and his father had been to see him, as well as Julian Dadd. Though Theresa Sassoon was not well enough to leave Weirleigh, the family had been represented by his Donaldson aunt and cousins. Over-excited and still not fully recovered physically, he was unable to sleep. Instead his nights were filled with visions of the horrors he had so recently left behind:

> ... when the lights are out, and the ward is half shadow and half glowing firelight, and the white beds are quiet with drowsy figures, huddled outstretched, then the horrors come creeping across the floor: the floor is littered with parcels of dead flesh and bones, faces glaring at the ceiling, faces turned to the floor, hands clutching neck or belly; a livid grinning face with bristly moustache peers at me over the edge of my bed, the hands clutching my sheets. Yet I found no bloodstains there this morning. These corpses are silent; they do not moan and bleat in the war-zone manner approved by the War Office. They are like dummy figures made to deceive snipers: one feels that there is no stuffing inside them. That is always the impression given by the genuine article; here of course there is no stench; the hospital authorities probably made that a stipulation when they admitted these intruders. I don't think they mean any harm to me They are not here to scare me; they look at me reproachfully, because I am so lucky, with my safe wound, and the warm kindly immunity of the hospital is what they longed for when they shivered and waited for the attack to begin, or the brutal bombardment to cease. One boy, an English private in full battle order, crawls to me painfully on hands and knees, and lies gasping at the foot of my bed; he is fumbling in his tunic for a letter; just as he reaches forward to give it me his head lolls sideways and he collapses on the floor; there is a hole in his jaw, and the blood spreads across his white face like ink spilt on blotting-paper. I wish I could sleep.[6]

Experiences like this revived Sassoon's anti-war feelings, which he inflamed by reading Bertrand Russell's *Justice in War-Time*.[7]

There were, however, opposing pressures at work. By the end of April he had received a letter from his Adjutant, Mann, telling him that he had been recommended for another decoration. And in letters to Ottoline, John

Bain and Dent[8] he claimed that the medal suggested was a Distinguished Service Order (D.S.O.), a very high honour indeed for a lieutenant. Yet his only other reference to the recommendation, in *Infantry Officer*, implies that the decoration was not specified in Mann's letter, though he makes it clear that the two most likely ones were a D.S.O. or a bar to his Military Cross.[9] The important point is that, had either materialized, Sassoon believed that it would have 'queered [his] criticisms' of the War.[10] As it was his failure to win another medal, because of the failure of the action as a whole, freed him from any vestiges of loyalty to the army.

With the publication of *The Old Huntsman* now imminent, Sassoon hoped to make his criticism of the War unavoidable and he looked forward to it eagerly. Its printing had been delayed by a war-time rationing of paper, but by 23 April he finally held it in his hands. Its sombre grey and black dust-jacket enclosed the seventy-two poems that he had chosen to represent him between 1909 and the beginning of 1917, when the book had gone to press. Though he did not find it as elegant as his own private productions, particularly the typeface, he was grateful for it. Heinemann had printed a modest thousand copies, of which 260 were sent in sheets to E.P. Dutton of New York. (Reprints of 350 in August 1917 and 500 in January 1918 would follow.) Publication had been set for 3 May, though in the event it would be delayed until the 8th.

To Sassoon, whose only trade publication, *The Daffodil Murderer*, had sunk almost without trace, it was a heady moment. In celebratory mood, the moment he was allowed out of hospital on 1 May, he lunched with one of his staunchest admirers, Roderick Meiklejohn, at the Reform, then again with Meiklejohn and Ross there on the 2nd. Still expecting his book to be out the following day, he enjoyed talking to two already well-established writers, H.G. Wells and Arnold Bennett, as well as the future Foreign Editor of *The Times*, Harold Williams.[11]

At this time, as Leonard Woolf noted, Wells and Bennett, together with Bernard Shaw, stood 'at the zenith of the literary heavens'.[12] Wells, who was the slightly senior of the two novelists, was twenty years older than Sassoon and was to treat him at times like a son. In spite of their differences in both age and background – Wells, the child of an unsuccessful tradesman, had pulled himself up by his bootstraps and was more interested in the sciences than the arts – they formed an immediate *rapport*. Wells, Sassoon remembered, 'behaved as though my opinions were worth listening to, which seemed remarkable in one whose talk was so stimulating and humorous and full of ideas'.[13] Wells's response seemed all the more gratifying in one who was already famed for his uncertain temper and whose celebrity allowed him to choose virtually any company he pleased. By 1917 he had written many of his most successful novels, including *The Time Machine* (1895), *The Invisible Man* (which Sassoon had read as a boy of eleven when it came out in 1897 and had found 'triffically exciting'[14]), *The War of the Worlds* (1898), *Love and Mr Lewisham*

(1900), *Kipps* (1905) and *The History of Mr Polly* (1910). His most recent work, *Mr Britling Sees It Through* (1916) was a bitter criticism of a War which he had initially welcomed as 'the war to end war'. As I have shown, it was a revelation to Sassoon and may well have formed the basis of their first conversation. Certainly Wells would have fuelled Sassoon's mounting anger. His response to his anti-war protest two months later was to be among the few that were positive.

Their strongest link, however, was one Sassoon shared with a number of his friends, humour. Looking back in his fourth, unpublished volume of autobiography at a weekend spent with Wells and his wife, Sassoon would write: 'H.G., as usual, was incomparably communicative, entertaining us with a series of amplified anecdotes about literary figures and really humorous rememberings of less well-known characters ... He seemed the embodiment of a saying I'd acquired from Gosse – humour, the love child of literature'.[15] Later in their friendship Sassoon became more critical of Wells. While remaining 'grateful to (and full of admiration for) the bristling pugnacious little man for the way he succeed[ed] in influencing (and creating) public opinion in the direction of sanity', he could never quite forget a remark of Wells', that 'Poetry has no particular importance; every man ought to compose his own poetry – in the morning, while he is shaving'.[16] Sassoon recognized that such a philistine remark originated in a laudatory desire to 'improve the world quickly', but it antagonized him, making him feel 'uncomfortably aware of [his] own drifting sort of existence in pursuit of "poetry" and artistic excellence'.[17] He would never lose his admiration for Wells' socialism, or his stimulating personality, however, and they were to remain friends until the end of novelist's long life. Wells presented at least ten of his books to Sassoon on publication, one pithily inscribed, after waiting in vain for a letter from the poet, 'To Siegfried the Silent'.[18] When Wells died in 1946 Sassoon would write to a mutual friend, H.M. Tomlinson, 'Odd – isn't it – how when the best people die they become more alive in one's mind than ever'.[19]

Sassoon's relationship with Arnold Bennett was even closer, perhaps because he had more in common with him than Wells. Beside coming from a more middle-class background – his father had been a solicitor – Bennett shared Sassoon's love of music and art, as well as literature. Though he never pretended to be an expert on poetry, he never dismissed it, as Wells did, and admired almost all of Sassoon's work in that field. He was, if anything, even more impressed when Sassoon trespassed onto his own ground, the novel. Sassoon was not able to return the praise quite so enthusiastically; he found Bennett's novels merely 'quite pleasant stuff'.[20] Nevertheless, Bennett had firmly established his reputation with his 'Potteries' novels, *Anna of the Five Towns* (1902), *The Old Wives' Tale* (1908), *Clayhanger* (1910), *Hilda Lessways* (1911) and *These Twain* (1916) and was also a successful playwright by the time they met. About his plays Sassoon was even less complimentary:

The trouble about Bennett [he wrote in his diary for 22 March 1922] is that he 'fancies himself' as being on the same plane as Tchekov and George Moore and Flaubert. Yet his new play [*The Love Match*] ... is on the same plane as Lord Northcliffe's 'travel articles' in the *Daily Mail*. Not only devoid of originality but permeated by the cheapest conventionalities ..

Nor could he resist satirizing Bennett's marked mannerisms. When they first had lunch together, a week after their introduction, he noted:

A trick of pausing in the middle of a remark and finishing it quickly.
    e.g. Shall ... we ...
        (Slow drawl   pause   go upstairs?
        Largo)   (Allegro)
Habit of pursing up mouth – very middle-class. Air of finality.[21]

For all his portentousness Bennett was charming and Sassoon quickly grew very fond of him. Ten years after their first meeting he would call him the 'dearest of men',[22] though whether he 'adored' him, as Sam Behrman claimed, is less certain.[23] There is no doubt that Bennett was very fond of Sassoon, treating him, as Wells did, like a recalcitrant son at times. He started to write to Sassoon soon after they met and would continue to do so until his death. He was generous with invitations to lunch and dinner and with presentation copies of his books. Sassoon took Bennett's inscription of his *Books and Persons* – 'To Siegfried Sassoon, though it is only from Arnold Bennett' – as being characteristic of his 'invariable generosity towards the younger writers'.[24] He reciprocated by sending presentation copies of his own books, together with a signed photograph which Bennett treasured.[25]

There was a sharper side to Bennett, which Sassoon also appreciated. He enjoyed his studied outspokenness, even when it was critical of Sassoon's own work and ideas, because it was usually so witty. 'But dare I ask', Bennett wrote to him in acknowledgement of a volume of poems he did not, for once, admire, 'when you intend to emerge from what I am now decided to call "the carping school"?'[26] On another occasion after observing that he would probably see Sassoon when the latter had 'nothing else to do', he concluded:

It must have crossed your mind that you are a pig in this matter. However, we are all God's creatures – except J[ohn] M[iddleton] Murry when he drags in Katherine [Mansfield]. What dreadful taste.[27]

Apart from Bennett's humour, which makes his letters to Sassoon delightful reading, Sassoon appreciated his genuine concern for his welfare. From the start Bennett promoted his poetry in his influential newspaper articles and introduced him to anyone he thought might help in his career. And in 1918 it would be Bennett, not Wells, who put his name forward for membership of the Reform Club. Strictly heterosexual himself, he was nevertheless to be deeply sympathetic over the problems Sassoon's homosexuality would create for him in the 1920s. Their one great area of disagreement at the start of their friendship lay in their attitudes towards the War. Whereas Wells had become highly critical of its handling by 1917, Bennett, who was head of French Propaganda at the Ministry of Information, still approved of it. His response to Sassoon's anti-war protest would be very fierce indeed. But their friendship survived the crisis and they were to remain close until Bennett's early death at the age of sixty-four in 1931.

One of the first books Sassoon presented to Bennett was a copy of *The Old Huntsman* when it eventually came out, five days late, on 8 May.[28] He had quickly added Bennett's name to the presentation list he had drawn up for Ross. Apart from his original mentors, Gosse and Marsh, he had included his more recent friends, Graves and Ottoline, as well as his mother and great-aunt Mozelle. The most significant name on his list was his current hero, Thomas Hardy. Though he had never met Hardy, he felt he knew him through his uncle Hamo's long friendship with him. Encouraged by this connection, and also by Gosse's assurance that 'True Thomas' would like it, Sassoon had written to ask Hardy if he might dedicate *The Old Huntsman* to him. It was his first direct contact with the writer, whom he was not actually to meet until eighteen months later. (The dedication was very simple: 'To Thomas Hardy, O.M.')

Not only did Hardy give immediate permission but, after reading just half of his presentation copy, wrote via Hamo Thornycroft to praise a number of its poems.[29] In a volume which contained less than a dozen satires in its 109 pages, it was the satires he mainly admired, and not just because of his own influence on them. Writing to Graves a fortnight after publication Sassoon reports jubilantly: 'Hardy of Wessex ... praises "The Hero", "Blighters", "They", "When I'm Among a Blaze of Lights", "The Working Party" and "the Tombstone-Maker", which is satisfactory. I did not expect him to be very excited, but to appreciate the grim humour which he is so capable of judging'.[30] Hardy also admired the 'pathos' and 'reticent poignancy' of some of the anti-war poems.[31] Ross, who had encouraged Sassoon's satiric bent in the face of criticism from Gosse and Marsh, found Hardy's letter 'charming' and promised to show it to Heinemann.[32] Knowing Hardy's tastes, he would not have found the praise unexpected.

Indeed, it was the satires which drew the public's attention as a whole to *The Old Huntsman*. And though the reviewers were equally divided between those who dealt with both the war-poetry and lyrics, they were far more inclined to quote the former. To some extent this was inevitable; the epigrammatic nature of the war poems lent itself to quotation and the ordering of the book drew more attention to them. After the title poem (put in, according to Wilfred Owen, 'to catch the hunting-people and make 'em read the rest'[33]), the first thirty-six pieces and the last three in the book were about war, with the lyrics sandwiched uneasily between. The earliest poems of all, dating from 1909, were further buried, in the middle of the lyrics. Sassoon himself would have liked to cut out the early verse to make room for 'stronger stuff' but he recognized that its presence illustrated 'the development accomplished by the War'.[34] In the event his juvenilia were largely ignored, though the later lyrics received warm praise from some critics.

Virginia Woolf, whose review in the *Times Literary Supplement* was almost certainly a result of Ottoline's log-rolling efforts,[35] while praising Sassoon's 'realism' as being 'of the right, of the poetic kind', continued:

> But we might hazard the guess that the war broke in and called out this vein of realism before its season; for side by side with these pieces there are others very different and not so effective perhaps, not particularly accomplished, but full of a rarer kind of interest, full of promise for the future. For the beauty in them, though fitful, is of the individual, indefinable kind which comes, we know not how, to make lines such as we read over each time with a renewed delight that after one comes the other.[36]

Woolf then quoted 'South Wind' in support of her theory (see p. 171-2). Her glowing review was the second to appear in *The Times Literary Supplement* in two weeks, probably because Sassoon had complained about the much briefer first one. It had, he told Ottoline, ignored his war poems in favour of quoting one of his weaker lyrics, 'Morning Glory'. The impression created seemed to him that of an 'amiable amateur' and he could only hope that the *Nation* would quote some of the poems Hardy liked. It did, and the review, written by the editor, H.W. Massingham, for whom Sassoon was to work briefly later, was one of the most perceptive he received. (Sassoon thought it 'glorious'.[37]) Unlike Woolf, Massingham admired the poetry not for its 'realism', which he considered 'one of the supreme artistic failures' of contemporary writers, but for its 'truth':

> It is no reflection upon [Mr Sassoon] to say that these war-verses are not poetry, that they have nothing to do with poetry, because we dare venture that he would probably agree with us. Nor are they (to go to the other extreme) simply a convenient instrument for vehement rhetoric and declamation. In a word, they are epigrams – modern epigrams, thrown deliberately into the harsh, peremptory, colloquial kind of versification which we have so often mistaken for poetry. And, to our mind, Mr Sassoon is quite right to select this method to fulfil a purpose in which every line throbs and of which every line is acutely conscious. For into this epigrammatic content, he is able to discharge the hot fluid of honest rage and scorn, heartfelt bitterness and indignation, which must read so very unconventionally, so very disagreeably to those civilians, who have been comfortably nurtured upon the war-poem of the past ...[38]

Massingham went on to quote, either whole or in part, five of the satires, including the one Sassoon pinpointed as the critics' favourite, probably because it was among the most shocking, 'They'.

Only one critic, Scott Moncrieff, dismissed Sassoon's war poetry as 'regrettable', though had it been published a few years earlier in the hey-day of Rupert Brooke and Julian Grenfell it would certainly have roused almost universal anger. But Scott Moncrieff's reason for dismissal was not just that he objected to Sassoon's handling of the war material, but that, like Woolf, he thought his lyrics more truly poetic:

> These are the brave poems, in the latter end of the book, and I wish Mr Sassoon had left out the others. Again and again, in the short lyrics and the sonnets ... he touches perfection.[39]

Sassoon wrote at once to complain to Scott Moncrieff – ironically, for Sassoon later came to believe that his lyrics were superior to his war poetry. And only five days after the review appeared in the *New Witness* Scott Moncrieff replied:

> I enjoyed your book much more than I have said, but I do confidently think that you are too 'good at' poetry to waste your talents on such London Mail storyette effects as you have secured in 'The Hero'. If I had written it I should talk about myself for years after, on the head of cleverness. But that is another matter.[40]

Scott Moncrieff's climb-down may well have stemmed from a desire not to lose Ross's friendship. For Ross had made it quite clear that he thought Sassoon's war poetry very good indeed. Together with the publisher, Heinemann, he promoted *The Old Huntsman* as hard as he could, buying multiple copies of the book to give away to friends and acquaintances. (Nellie Burton joined in and sold two copies 'to a lady upstairs'.) Sassoon fully recognized Ross's efforts, writing to him on 8 March: 'You have been a dear about my book; I shall dedicate the next one to you'.

Though Gosse had, as Sassoon put it, 'been terribly windy' about the outspoken war poetry, he too did his best for the book. In his long article on 'Some English Poets' for the *Edinburgh Review* of October 1917 he managed to remain sitting on the fence, or, as Ross more colourfully described it, 'sitting on the hedge'. In literature, specially poetry, Ross argued, Gosse 'waits for the tide: though in all other things he is a pioneer'.[41] After dealing with the poetry of Rupert Brooke, Julian Grenfell, Wyndham Tennant and other war poets more to his conservative taste, Gosse concluded his review awkwardly with an attempt to be both honest and kind about his embarrassing protégé:

> The bitterness of Lieut. Sassoon is not cynical, it is the rage of disenchantment, the violence of a young man eager to pursue other aims, who, finding the age out of joint, resents being called upon to help mend it. His temper is

not altogether to be applauded, for such sentiments must tend to relax the effort of the struggle, yet they can hardly be reproved when conducted with so much honesty and courage. Lieut. Sassoon, who, as we know, has twice been severely wounded and has been in the very furnace of the fighting, has reflected, more perhaps than his fellow-singers, about the causes and conditions of the war. He may not always have thought correctly, nor have recorded his impressions with proper circumspection, but his honesty must be respectfully acknowledged.

Though in later years Sassoon was to agree more with those who, like Gosse and Moncrieff, had questioned his war-poetry, than with those who had admired it at the expense of his lyrics, at the time he was delighted by the many reviews which praised his satires.

Sassoon was equally pleased by the letters of praise which poured in from friends. Bennett had written with characteristic sincerity that the book had 'much pleased him': 'The general spirit, choice of subject, energy and "don't care-a-damness", and youthfulness, give me deep satisfaction'.[42] Even Gosse wrote to say that he thought his recent pieces 'solid, vigorous and full of substance'[43] and that the Poet Laureate, Robert Bridges, a 'rare and grudging praiser', believed that Sassoon had 'got more of the real stuff' in him than almost any other poet of his generation.[44] Another doubter, Edward Marsh, was 'quite enthusiastic' according to Ross,[45] but he must have been keener than that since he was to write less than two months later inviting Sassoon to contribute an impressive number of poems to his next *Georgian Poetry*.[46]

Graves, who had encouraged Sassoon to publish the book despite his own disappointment, had written on 27 April from Oxford to report that he had tried to persuade all the booksellers in the town to buy it and had got his father to review it in the *Observer*. As well as praising it publicly, A.P. Graves wrote privately to congratulate his son's friend, in a verse letter of the kind Sassoon and Graves themselves indulged in:

> May 22 / 17
> ... The Hindenburg line
> By bombardment and mine,
> We may wear through,
> Or tear through
> Or powder quite fine,
> But I – Donner-wetter!
> I know of a better
> And mightier line!
> None other can shape it, ...
> 'The Siegfried' we call it.

Yours *really delighted* with The Old Huntsman and other poems,
A.P.G.[47]

Graves had also persuaded his uncle Charles (Graves) to review *The*

Old Huntsman in *The Spectator*, and hoped to get E. Osborne to do so in the popular *Morning Post*. (He succeeded.) On 19 May he wrote again to predict that Sassoon would 'out-Rupert Rupert [Brooke]'. The most pleasing letter of all was probably from Hamo Thornycroft, whom Sassoon had feared offending with his criticism. Not only did Uncle Hamo find the little book 'stunning' but, more surprisingly, 'especially' admired the war poems. Though Sassoon had written somewhat cynically to Ross on 18 March, 'I think the Thornycroft-Harold Cox-Sidney Olivier [i.e. Hamo and his brothers-in-law] clique will be useful', he genuinely cared about his uncle's opinion.

With such influential friends to support it, *The Old Huntsman* could hardly fail to be a success. The only near-disaster was that Ottoline and Dent were not sent signed copies. Dent was easily dealt with and Heinemann's 'women clerks' were blamed, but Ottoline was more of a problem. Ross, who discovered the omission from Clive Bell twelve days after publication, urged Sassoon to put the blame on him, so worried was he that they would lose what he cynically called 'the Garsington stunt, quite valuable on these occasions'.[48] In the event, Sassoon shifted the responsibility to Heinemann's female clerks again and Ottoline's wounded feelings were soothed. It was a novel situation to find his friends clamouring for copies of his work. As Ross wrote to him on 18 May, 'The tide has obviously turned'; after years of struggle, he had become famous overnight.

Suddenly everyone in the literary establishment seemed anxious to know him. The poet John Drinkwater, to whom Sassoon had been writing hopefully since 1915, told him that *The Old Huntsman* contained 'the real excitement of poetry' and invited him to stay.[49] And on the day after publication Arnold Bennett asked him to lunch with J.C. Squire, another useful contact in the literary world. John (known as 'Jack') Collings Squire, a friend of both Bennett and Marsh, was only two years older than Sassoon but already well-established. A poet, critic and parodist by 1917, he was best known for his literary editorship of the *New Statesman*, which he had held since 1913. Later he would become even better known as the founder and editor of the *London Mercury*, a monthly magazine of some repute for which he would also write. His intriguing pen-name was 'Solomon Eagle'. Sassoon's first impression of him was both amused and positive:

Squire – vegetarian – sad-looking type of poetical person with hair rather long brushed tidily over right eyebrow. Slouching gait, hands in pockets. Distinct charm in face when lit up. Looks more like an actor. Seemed amused by some of my remarks (pacifist cussedness about the conduct and effect of the war).[50]

To Leonard Woolf, who came into frequent contact with Squire at the *New Statesman*, Squire was 'the best type of gay, carnal, good-tempered, generous Bohemian, a literary gent of the kind that has been about Fleet

Street since the eighteenth century'.[51] Squire had had at least four collections of poems published by the time he met Sassoon. While thinking him 'a fine poet technically', however, Sassoon could not help suspecting that his work needed 'stirring up a bit'.[52]

Sassoon was not surprised to find Squire defending Bridges against his criticism of dullness. Squire himself, Sassoon came to believe, was 'incurably conventional'.[53] He was already regarded in 1917 as part of a conservative clique which included Gosse and Marsh. Virginia Woolf, less kind than her husband, described him as 'the very spit and image of mediocrity' and the Sitwells were to attack him and his magazine as boring, pompous and complacent. Nevertheless he was both pleasant and influential and Sassoon was to remain on good terms with him throughout the twenties and early thirties, happy to have access to at least two magazines which would seriously consider his poetry for publication. Squire was also to include him in a number of anthologies he would edit.[54] Though he did not personally review *The Old Huntsman* in May 1917, when Sassoon was 'hanging [his] tongue out for a favourable review by Squire',[55] he did publish one by his friend Shanks in the *New Statesman* and would make up for it in 1918 with his review of *Counter-Attack*.

Sassoon was to lunch with many other literary editors as his reputation increased, but Squire was the only one he had time to meet in early May. The same evening that Bennett introduced him to Squire he moved from Denmark Hill Hospital to the Princess of Wales Convalescent Home for Officers, temporarily housed at the Great Central Hotel, Marylebone, and three days after that he was convalescing at Chapelwood Manor in Sussex. It had not been easy to get the military authorities to agree to such a move, but he had shamelessly used a letter from a titled lady recommending him for one of the country houses in her organisation. Though a sadistic doctor (so it seemed to him) had blocked his first attempt, his persistence was rewarded and he eventually found himself on a train bound for Sussex. He had three weeks in his favourite countryside to look forward to.

Chapelwood Manor was at Nutley, only sixteen miles as the crow flies from Weirleigh and half that distance from his old crammers, Henley House. Grey-timbered and many-gabled, it seemed to Sassoon the most perfect house he had ever stayed in. As he was ushered up to his fragrantly named 'Clematis Room' by a discreet manservant he could hardly believe his luck. From the beautiful view of formal gardens, meadows and the Sussex Downs beyond and the delicate freshness of his room, to the graciousness of his host and hostess, Lord and Lady Brassey, and their splendid dinner, it seemed, as he told Dent, almost too 'heavenly'.[56] Nothing could be more peaceful and harmonious than his first evening, listening to Gluck and Handel played by one of the gentlemanly fellow-officers also staying there.

Thomas, the first Earl Brassey, was an urbane host. Though over eighty and crippled with rheumatism he was still a lively conversationalist and Sassoon listened respectfully while he held forth on public matters. Having served in Government for many years, he spoke with the kind of authority that a young officer would find hard to question. Yet there was also something pathetic in the sight of a once powerful man reduced by time, as Sassoon noted in his diary on the third day of his stay:

> ... serene old age going down-hill too fast to keep its tranquillity: he has not far to go with his dragging feet and body bent double with rheumatics. Sometimes he is querulous, and almost childish. And at times he is the oracular proconsul, with snatches of urbane oratory, as he sits huddled at table, his chin on his chest and his red-rimmed eyes almost closed. His face, once gravely impressive, has become puffy and loose. Death presses him hard; he is losing his grip on life, in spite of his indomitable resistance. A pattern Englishman, no doubt, very wise in the ways of his generation, a useful servant of the State, but a strange figure to Youth in Revolt and Youth torn by sacrifice.[57]

Lady Brassey, born Sybil de Vere and herself the daughter of an Earl, presented no such decline. A second wife, she was considerably younger than her husband and still very alert and good-looking. Gracious, sympathetic and beautifully-mannered, she represented for Sassoon 'the patrician distinctions that he had fought for – the climbing woods and green fields that soldiers learn to love when death is over them'.[58] Impulsively he confided his problems to her. He had been to the Front twice, twice been invalided home and his friends were now trying to persuade him to take a safe job as a Cadet Training Officer at Oxford or Cambridge.[59] Possibly as a result of his serene and safe surroundings, he seems to have been contemplating this seriously for the first time. He told Lady Brassey with complete honesty of 'his longing for life and the take that lay before him, setting against it his mystical joy in the idea of sacrifice and the disregard of death'. But her response – that 'death is nothing' and that those who die are helping to win the War from 'up there' – shocked him. He realized that he had appealed to an alien intelligence, which could not begin to understand the way his mind worked. He was still a Romantic, but of a very different kind from the dreamy, religious boy he had once been:

> She was a good woman as well as a Great Lady. But her mind dwelt in another kingdom from his. He was the starry wind on the hills, and the beast writhing in the mire, the strange traveller who had come to her gates and had been suffered to sit by the fire and rest his tired limbs. What was this 'other world' that she spoke of? It was a dream he had forgotten years ago – the simplicity of his childish prayers, the torment of his mocking youth that denied the God of priests, and triumphed in the God of skies and waters.[60]

He was even more shocked when Lady Brassey concluded the argument: 'It isn't as if you were an only child with a big place to inherit. No; I can't see any excuse for your keeping out of danger'. Such assumptions, however much he had sympathized with them before the War, now antagonized him and pushed him one step nearer to public protest. The very comfort and harmony of his surroundings, which he had appreciated so much at the start, began to oppress him and make him even more conscious of the huge contrast with the trenches. There was no one to whom he could speak frankly at Chapelwood, not even his fellow-officers, who were too full of polite acquiescence and gratitude to remind the Brasseys of the reality of the War. Lady Brassey's spiritualism, like his own mother's, protected her against uncomfortable thoughts. Nothing could penetrate such a barrier.

For a time Sassoon distracted himself with the sheer beauty of his surroundings. Though he was still having problems sleeping, it seemed miraculous to hear English birds singing their 'maytime madrigals' at dawn, for the first time since 1915, cocks crowing and an owl hooting away in the woods. It reminded him of getting up at dawn for a cub-hunt, with cocoa and boiled eggs to set him on his way. Typically his mornings at Chapelwood started with the sound of a gardener whetting his scythe beyond the yew-hedges, something which made him think of Marvell's 'The Mower to the Glow-worms'.[61] After breakfast he would sit out in the garden under the oaks and beeches, browsing through Morley's Life of an 18th Century Frenchman,[62] 'the kind of book where one can read a page or two and then turn to the morning sky and the garden and the distant line of downs as infinitely preferable, like listening to a bird singing outside the church during a dry sermon'.[63]

In the afternoons he became a country wanderer again, climbing gates and staring through tangled hedges at the mossy boughs of apple-trees covered with blossom, or listening to the noise of a tiny brook as it forced its way through its narrow channel. He wanted nothing more than a leisurely chat with an old man mending hedges, or the village parson as he leant over his garden gate. For a time the world became, as it had been in youth, 'a leafy labyrinth with clouds floating above the silence of vivid green woods and clean meadows bright with cowslips and purple orchis'.[64]

His contentment could not last. Front-line experiences had imprinted themselves too deeply on his imagination to allow him more than a brief respite. 'A Quiet Walk', written at this time, describes how, after an idyllic three-mile ramble through lanes lined with flowering hawthorns, 'old ugly horrors' came 'crowding back' as he caught sight of a corpse-like figure:

> A man was humped face downward in the grass,
> With clutching hands, full-skirted grey-green coat,
> And something stiff and wrong about the legs.
> He gripped his loathing quick ... some hideous wound ...
> And then the stench ... A stubby-bearded tramp
> Coughed and rolled over and asked him for the time.[65]

War even invaded the garden and marred his pleasure in the daily miracle of the dawn chorus, as another poem, 'Death in the Garden', written on 25 May records:

> I never thought to see him; but he came
> When the first strangeness of the dawn was grey.
> He stood before me, a remembered name,
> A twilight face, poor lonely ghost astray.
> Flowers glimmered in the garden where I stood
> And yet no more than darkness was the green.
> Then the wind stirred; and dawn came up the wood;
> And he had gone away: or had I seen
> That figure in my brain? for he was dead;
> I knew that he was killed when I awoke.
> At zero-hour they shot him through the head
> Far off in France, before the morning broke.[66]

The ghostly visitor described here almost certainly refers to Sassoon's young hunting friend from Litherland, R. Brocklebank, whose death Cottrell had recently reported.[67]

When Hamo died Sassoon had felt banished from the garden they had shared as children. Now, attempting to return to the garden, its innocence has gone. Sitting there in the afternoons nibbling cucumber sandwiches with Lord and Lady Brassey's neighbours, thoughts of War tormented him. While remaining outwardly polite to these undeniably pleasant and well-meaning people, he inwardly raged at what seemed to him their criminal unawareness. Even a war-widow, who might reasonably be expected to share his views, did not escape his scorn. In a poem which anticipated his two blistering attacks on women – 'Glory of Women' and 'Their Frailty' – he wrote:

> 'Life is *so* wonderful, so vast! – and yet
> 'We waste it in this senseless war,' she said,
> Staring at me with goggling eye-balls set
> Like large star-sapphires in her empty head.
>
> I watched the pearls that dangled from her ears,
> Wondering how much was left for *her* to buy
> From Time but chattering, comfortable years,
> And lust that dwindles to a jewelled sigh.[68]

The complacency of such people and the smugness of the Conservative press they read daily, goaded him towards action, though of what kind he was not yet certain. His discontent was now 'simmering rebelliously'.[69]

Another incentive came from France itself. During his stay at Chapelwood, Sassoon read a copy of a letter Cottrell had sent to Dadd, describing the heavy losses suffered by the 1st RWF during April and early May, and another letter directly from Cottrell full of harrowing details of the 2nd RWF's bloody engagement at Plum Lane, Arras, on 27 May. Two of Sassoon's favourite young officers, Orme and Conning, had been killed, and with one exception all officers in action had become casualties.[70] Lady Brassey's response when he repeated the grim news to her seemed entirely unacceptable, if predictable:

> I told her our Battalion'd got a knock.
> 'Six officers were killed; a hopeless show!'
> Her tired eyes half-confessed she'd felt the shock
> Of ugly war brought home. And then a slow
> Spiritual brightness stole across her face …
> 'But *they* are safe and happy now,' she said....[71]

As he wrote to Graves 'It makes all the placid loveliness of this country of wood and gardens seem like a bit of music by our old friend Mendelssohn, whose sloppy works I perform on the piano of an evening to the huge delight of aged Earls and Countesses, who have outlived their austere emotions'.[72] The War was destroying his romanticism more effectively than Graves had been able to.

Though Sassoon had gone back to writing anti-war poetry, it had begun to seem an inadequate way of protesting. Of all the poems he produced at Chapelwood between 25 May and 2 June, he found only two worthy of inclusion in future collections – 'The Hawthorn Tree' and 'In an Underground Dressing-Station'. The second of these, though published later, had been started first in April, when the memory of 'two bad cases – abdomen (hopeless) and ankle' he had seen at Hénin Underground Dressing-Station was still fresh in his mind.[73] He may have abandoned the poem temporarily as being, in his own words, 'too horrible', but taken it up again after hearing about the 1st and 2nd Battalions' losses because, as he also said, 'these healthy shocks do people good'.[74] In relating the incident he combined the 'two bad cases' into one to emphasize the suffering:

> Quietly they set their burden down: he tried
> To grin; moaned; moved his head from side to side.
>
> 'O put my leg down, doctor, do!' (He'd got
> A bullet in his ankle; and he'd been shot
> Horribly through the guts.) The surgeon seemed
> So kind and gentle, saying above that crying,
> 'You *must* keep still, my lad.' But he was dying.

Though Sassoon had made several improvements to this poem,[75] the final impression is of pathos rather than tragedy. Neither the soldier's nor the doctor's words seem as significant as Sassoon's direct speech often is and the irony lacks bite. Yet Sassoon wanted it published in the *Cam-*

bridge Magazine in preference to another poem he had just completed, a satire on the press entitled 'Editorial Impressions'.[76]

'The Hawthorn Tree' on the other hand makes a deep impression through its very restraint and understatement. Michael Thorpe uses this poem to illustrate his point that, though on the whole Dennis Enright was right to claim that 'Sassoon's most interesting poetry is composed of what have been called the "negative emotions" – horror, anger, disgust' – there are exceptions.[77] In 'The Hawthorn Tree' Sassoon allows a soldier's mother to express as far as she can and with a moving simplicity reminiscent of Wordsworth and Hardy, her love for her absent son:

> Not much to me is yonder lane
>   Where I go every day;
> But when there's been a shower of rain
>   And hedge-birds whistle gay,
> I know my lad that's out in France
>   With fearsome things to see
> Would give his eyes for just one glance
>   At our white hawthorn tree.
>
>   …
>
> Not much to me is yonder lane
>   Where *he* so longs to tread:
> But when there's been a shower of rain
>
> I think I'll never weep again
>   Until I've heard he's dead.

(*CP*, p. 80)

If 'A War Widow' is an anticipation of Sassoon's scornful 'The Glory of Women' and 'Their Frailty', then 'The Hawthorn Tree', as Thorpe points out, is a welcome antidote. The language and form are kept apparently very simple to demonstrate the unsophisticated nature of the rural narrator, allowing the strength of the suppressed emotion to come through all the more powerfully. It is an everyday, natural occurrence, a shower of rain, which sparks off the speaker's ominous announcement in the last two lines.

The contrast between the apparent weeping of Nature and the speaker's inability to weep is made particularly striking in these final lines by a departure from what started out as a near repetition of the first stanza. And, while the form, with its opening eight lines and turning-point at line nine, leads the reader to expect a Petrarchan sonnet, the cutting off at line 13, rather than 14, makes the ending seem abrupt, as though the speaker is too choked with emotion to continue. The curious mixture of formal with colloquial language is convincingly awkward in someone clearly unused to expressing emotions verbally.

The word-play on 'give his eyes' introduces the idea that the son might literally have to give his eyes, or even his life, not for the sight of the hawthorn-tree but for his country and that, if so, he will never see the tree again. It also emphasizes the contrast, which is present throughout, between the 'fearsome things' he is seeing in France and the hawthorn-tree he longs to see, its innocence symbolized simply through its whiteness. It is very likely that it was the sight of so many lovely haw-thorn-trees in flower round Chapelwood Manor which gave Sassoon the germ of this poem in the first place. He found colour highly symbolic, noting for example that the sunsets at Chapelwood were 'yellow and serene – never dyed with crimson',[78] and the hawthorn-tree's whiteness is a deliberately ironic contrast to the evil being committed in France.

By the time Sassoon left Chapelwood Manor on 4 June he had completed eight anti-war poems. He had also more or less decided not to try for a safe job in England, though he had yielded to his friends' pressure to the extent of arranging an interview about a cadet-training post at Cambridge for the second week of June.[79] He believed that there were only two honourable courses of action open to him – either to go back to the Front as soon as possible, or to make a formal protest about the War – and he had three weeks' leave in which to choose. In order to consider the matter objectively he refrained from staying with Ross on his return to London and deliber-ately avoided his company. While Ross shared his views and had encour-aged him to make his criticisms felt in poetry, Sassoon sensed that he was too fond of him to want to see him in trouble with the authorities. By staying at his club, the Royal Societies, he could give himself the space and time he needed to make a decision.

Sassoon engaged in only one other activity during this time, but it was one which, far from interfering with his deliberations, probably helped them. Ross had arranged for him to have his portrait done by a fashionable artist of the time, Glyn Philpot. (Sassoon had sent Philpot a signed copy of *The Old Huntsman* in May in preparation.) The original commission had been for Sassoon to have his head drawn for fifty guineas, all he could afford, but when he presented himself at Philpot's studio flat in The Tower House, 28 Tite Street in early June, he was flattered to find that Philpot thought him such a good subject that he wanted to do a half-length portrait in oils for the same price. This would normally have cost £500 and Philpot made it clear that his generosity stemmed also from affection for Ross, whom he had probably met through two of their mutual friends, Ricketts and Shannon.

Both these well-known artists had influenced Philpot's early style, but by the time Sassoon met him in 1917 he had established his own reputa-tion. As early as 1909, three years after showing his first portrait, he was exhibiting not only with the Society of Portrait Painters, the New English Art Club and the Royal Institute, but also with the break-away Modern Society of Portrait Painters.[80] His career had been partially disrupted by enlistment in the Fusiliers at the outbreak of War, though his poor health dictated a home-service job in the War Office which allowed him to continue some painting. In fact it was while he was still in the army in 1915 that he was elected an associate of the Royal Academy at the early age of thirty. The same year his commission as 2nd Lieutenant had come through, but by early 1917 it was clear that his poor health made him unsuitable for the army. He had just been invalided out when he met Sassoon in June. He had wasted no time in resuming his career and by June 1917 was already busy following up commissions arranged before the War, such as portraits of the 4th Marquess of Salisbury, the Marchioness of Bath, her daughter, Lady Mary Thynne, and a double portrait of the daughters of his life-long friend, the Hon. Lady Packe. Robin Gibson, in his catalogue notes to a 1984/5 exhibition of Philpot's works, argues that the three latter paintings show that in 1917 Philpot was 'modifying his style ... to a more fluent and rather Sargent-like manner'.[81]

Though Sassoon knew very little about Philpot as a painter, he found him immediately attractive as a man:

> Responsively impersonal, he encouraged my communicative questionings, receiving my exuberance with amused and gentle gravity. From the first I had found him a delightfully modest and likeable companion. A couple of years older than I, he was good-looking in a rather Italian way.[82]

He was particularly struck by Philpot's dark, heavy-lidded eyes and his description makes him seem rather exotic, an impression reinforced by his surroundings:

> He had what might be called a still-life temperament; ... This was shown in his paintings of silks, velvets and brocades and in anything which evoked his sensuous joy in surface qualities and harmonious arrangements of colour. Too subtle and fine to be accused of preciosity, his taste was superbly artificial. The interior he had designed for himself was a deliberately fastidious denial of war-time conditions, a delicate defence against the violence and ugly destruction which dominated the outside world.[83]

The rather self-conscious elegance of Philpot's interiors and his passion for beautiful furniture, elaborate Oriental screens and carefully chosen pieces of Greek, Egyptian and Gothic sculptures, is reminiscent of his friend Ross and places him in a line of aesthetes who featured in Sassoon's life from Edward Marsh onwards. He himself was to introduce Philpot to another such connoisseur, Frankie Schuster. It was a side to Sassoon which conflicted very sharply at times with his equally pronounced puritanism.

Sassoon came to feel that Philpot had just missed being 'first-rate',[84] but in June 1917 he was very impressed by him. Far more assured in his chosen art than the slightly younger man, Philpot nevertheless shared his enthusiasm and wholeheartedness. His niece, Gabrielle Cross, described him as 'full of fun', the kind of person who made everything 'light up' when he entered a room.[85] Though his schooling had been limited by ill-health, he was well-read and, like Sassoon, loved music.[86] Brought up a strict Baptist, he anticipated Sassoon by many years in entering the Roman Catholic Church at twenty-one. Both were sensitive, romantic and handsome young men, physically attracted to their own sex, when they met at the age of thirty-two and thirty respectively, and it might be asked why a more intimate relationship did not develop between them. Philpot had, however, already found his life-long partner, Vivian Forbes, and in any case Sassoon was still uncomfortable about his sexuality, still suffering great guilt over his physical preference for men. He was not yet ready to give way to his feelings; it would take an event as dramatic as the end of the War to propel him into his first affair.

Nevertheless, it is clear from Sassoon's autobiography that he very much enjoyed his leisurely afternoons with Philpot. The artist, who was something of a dandy himself, had chosen to paint him in a soft grey silk shirt open at the neck, in three-quarter profile, his eyes gazing soulfully into the distance. When the portrait made its first public appearance, the *Tatler* critic was ecstatic:

Philpot has painted rather beautifully the soldier-poet man Siegfried Sassoon – in a very 'artistic' soft grey silk shirt, open to show a youthful neck à la cinema hero, and with no detail left out of fine and sensitive nostril, curved mouth, delicate features, and wavy brown hair. In the deep eyes and on the mouth of this young poet one may see those marks of war on a fine spirit that have led him to protest in verse almost too awfully true and tragic to be borne.[87]

Sassoon himself was less enthusiastic about his undeniably glamorous portrait, which seemed to him just a little 'popular', more suitable for a posthumous volume (he may have been thinking of Rupert Brooke) than a living poet. When, on its completion, he told Philpot he found it rather 'Byronic', the painter simply replied, 'You *are* rather, aren't you?'[88] Neither Ottoline, who had already compared Sassoon romantically to a stag or a faun, nor Ross, who had translated this into an 'offended deerhound', would have been surprised by Philpot's interpretation. Another poet, to whom Philpot would be introduced by Sassoon and whose portrait he would also paint, Robert Nichols, thought Sassoon looked more like a 'sullen falcon', but the imagery is equally romantic and Philpot clearly captured the dominant impression Sassoon made at that time.[89]

Sassoon thought his portrait 'almost scornfully serene and speculative, giving no indication of the conflict that was being enacted behind that mask of physical prosperity'.[90] The *Tatler* critic, however, claimed to have seen in it 'those marks of war on a fine spirit' which had led Sassoon to criticize it and he was almost certainly planning his protest during the peaceful afternoons he spent in Philpot's flat. Though the painter never mentioned war and Sassoon later wrote that the quiet studio flat was 'a perfect place in which to forget about it',[91] it is unlikely that he did so.

On 7 June, only three days after his return from Chapelwood, he was lunching with H.W. Massingham ('Markington' in *Infantry Officer*),[92] the editor of the liberal weekly *The Nation*, a pale, earnest man who looked as if he had ceased to find human follies amusing. Sassoon wanted to discuss with him the possibility of publishing 'something outspoken' on the War. And three days after that he was at Garsington consulting the pacifist Morrells. Whilst Ottoline urged him to make a public statement, Philip, a Liberal M.P. with a wider knowledge of the world, advised against it. But Sassoon, who had been appalled by Massingham's revelation that England's aims were essentially acquisitive, and that she had refused to state her War Aims to the new Russian Government in April or to publish the secret treaties made between England and Russia early in the War,[93] resisted Philip's advice. He gratefully accepted Ottoline's offer of a meeting with the philosopher Bertrand Russell, a pacifist who would go to prison for his beliefs in 1918.[94]

Two days later, on 12 June, Sassoon was lunching with them both at the Eiffel Tower in Percy Street, having visited Massingham in between for further discussion. Ottoline had also invited another outspoken pacifist, John Middleton Murry, who offered to help Sassoon draft his protest. Sassoon gratefully accepted and went to Murry's Kensington flat for that purpose, possibly the same evening. (Katherine Mansfield was there but hardly spoke.) By 14 June he had a draft ready for Russell, who had offered to act as his 'impresario'. Russell wrote approvingly the next day, asking whether he had begun to write out the statement and, perhaps as a result, Sassoon completed it the same day. A week later, having seen the final version, the philosopher wrote again to say that he liked it *very much indeed*' and to promise to help publicize it.[95] One of his ideas was to introduce Sassoon to a pacifist M.P. interested in his case, H.B. Lees-Smith,[96] who would try to bring his case to the attention of the House of Commons. All this was taking place within the same fortnight that Sassoon was sitting to Philpot for his portrait. The completion of his picture coincided with that of his statement.

Sassoon maintained in his fictionalized version of events that it was Massingham's revelations about the political background which had finally provoked him to protest. It is true that his statement lays most of the blame at the feet of the politicians, while letting the military off conspicuously lightly[97]:

> I am making this statement as an act of wilful defiance of military authority, because I believe that the War is being deliberately prolonged by those who have the power to end it. I am a soldier, convinced that I am acting on behalf of soldiers. I believe that this War, upon which I entered as a war of defence

and liberation, has now become a war of aggression and conquest. I believe that the purposes for which I and my fellow-soldiers entered upon this War should have been so clearly stated as to have made it impossible for them to be changed without our knowledge, and that, had this been done, the objects which actuated us would now have been attainable by negotiation.

I have seen and endured the sufferings of the troops, and I can no longer be a party to prolonging those sufferings for ends which I believe to be evil and unjust.

I am not protesting against the military conduct of the War, but against the political errors and insincerities for which the fighting men are being sacrificed.

On behalf of those who are suffering now, I make this protest against the deception which is being practised on them. Also I believe that it may help to destroy the callous complacence with which the majority of those at home regard the continuance of agonies which they do not share and which they have not sufficient imagination to realise.[98]

There were, however, factors other than the political which led Sassoon so uncharacteristically to this open defiance. The military situation, in spite of a spectacular success at the Battle of Messines on 7 June, was still deteriorating. Prospects on the Russian Front had worsened considerably since the February Revolution and Sassoon was not the only person to fear that the Allies were 'losing the War heavily'.[99] He no longer thought that 1917 would mark the end of the fighting, but that it would continue for at least another two or three years, with all the suffering and loss of life that would involve. He now believed that the politicians actually *intended* the War to continue, since 'to carry out [their] scheme of "crushing Kaiserism and Prussianism" by means of brute force, the War *must* go on two more years'.[100]

Sassoon's own personal experience of the Front, and the recent loss of so many men he knew from both the 1st and 2nd Royal Welch Fusiliers, made it impossible to ignore the consequences of more fighting. When he thought of the 'vast anonymity of courage and cheerfulness' represented by a typical Royal Welch Fusilier at his best, and contrasted it with the gross profiteer whom he had heard boasting that 'If the War continued another eighteen months he'd be able to retire from business', he felt he had no choice but to protest.[101] He could still remember the exact tone of voice in which his friend Orme spoke, so vividly in fact that he wrote the whole of his tribute to him, 'To Any Dead Officer', in that voice.

This poem, which came to him in a flash and almost wrote itself, was composed the same day as his finished statement and seemed to Sassoon to prove the sincerity of his protest. When he first learnt of Orme's death in the 2nd RWF's 'hopeless dud-attack' at Plum Lane, it must have seemed to him particularly cruel since, by rights, Orme should have been back with the 1st Battalion by the time it took place.[102] A further irony was that Orme, who had been taken ill at the beginning of April and ordered to England, was forced to remain in France because the leave boat was full.

He had recovered in time to be sent back to the Line, and be killed at the end of May.

Like the pianist, Ralph Greaves's loss of an arm, the situation crystallized for Sassoon the cruel irony of war. In his poem on the subject Orme himself becomes an archetypal subaltern, cut off in his cheerful prime with all his life before him, his very ordinariness an appeal to our pity. By refusing to sentimentalize the young man, Sassoon makes him all the more convincing. His own strong sense of loss is very evident in the last stanza of 'To Any Dead Officer' which leaves little doubt that Orme's death provided one strong incentive to protest against the War. The narrator has been trying to reach the dead officer by telephone in Heaven, an innovative approach which Graves later thought put some people off:

> Good-bye, old lad! Remember me to God,
>   And tell Him that our Politicians swear
> They won't give in till Prussian Rule's been trod
>   Under the Heel of England ... Are you there?...
> Yes ... and the War won't end for at least two years;
> But we've got stacks of men ... I'm blind with tears,
>   Staring into the dark. Cheero!
> I wish they'd killed you in a decent show.
>
> (*CP*, p. 85)

Graves also thought that the poem contained too much slang, but Sassoon defended his choice. He told Ottoline that it was an elegy on a subaltern 'written in the language of subalterns, yet tragic and glorious'.[103] The slang was deliberate. He believed people ought to read it because it was 'so different to the countless elegies that [had] been written'.[104] So strongly did he believe this that he was prepared to pay for its printing as a *Cambridge Magazine* pamphlet.

Another strong incentive for his protest came from certain of his friends. Since his experiences on the Somme, Sassoon had gravitated towards those who were critical of the War, Ross and the Morrells in particular. Though Sassoon himself doubted that he had been influenced by these people, it is unthinkable that he would have made his protest public without them.[105] His reading, too, had fuelled his anger. H.G. Wells' *Mr Britling Sees it Through* had been followed by Bertrand Russell's *Justice in War-Time*, and by June he had almost certainly begun Henri Barbusse's harrowing account of the suffering of soldiers at the Front, *Le Feu*, which had just been translated into English.[106] Weeklies such as the *Cambridge Magazine* and the *Nation* not only gave him a platform for his own verse, but also kept him informed of current anti-war views. Even the Conservative press, by its very smugness and hypocrisy, added to his discontent. He had been particularly enraged by it during his weeks at Chapelwood, perhaps because Lord and Lady Brassey themselves seemed so infuriatingly complacent. It was almost certainly with Lord Brassey in mind that he wrote in his diary only a fortnight after leaving the house and four days after completing his statement:

> Of the elderly male population I can hardly trust myself to speak. Their frame of mind is, in the majority of cases, intolerable. They glory in senseless invective against the enemy. They glory in the mock-heroism of their young men. They glory in the mechanical phrases of the Northcliffe Press.[107]

And he undoubtedly had women of Lady Brassey's type in mind when he fulminated, in the same diary entry:

> Poor heroes! If only they would speak out; and throw their medals in the faces of their masters; and ask their women why it thrills them to know that they, the dauntless warriors, have shed the blood of Germans. Do not the women gloat secretly over the wounds of their lovers? Is there anything inwardly noble in savage sex instincts?[108]

Apart from revealing Sassoon's extremely low opinion of women, this passage is interesting because it shows him already anticipating, perhaps even mentally rehearsing his own action in throwing his personal medal, if not 'into the faces of his masters', then into the River Mersey. At least by the time it was written in mid-June he was certain that he had not been awarded another medal to pressure him into complicity and silence.

A vital factor in Sassoon's protest was his temperament. Someone equally critical of the War but less impulsive would have thought longer and harder about the consequences, which included the likelihood of a Court Martial and the possibility of being imprisoned for sedition, like Bertrand Russell, or shot for cowardice, before taking action.[109] In his retrospective analysis of his protest, which seemed to him 'the climax of a progression of ideas and emotions which had begun almost a year before', Sassoon pointed out that his behaviour was 'in accordance with the temperament which had led [him] to perform reckless exploits in the front line'.[110] Ironically it was that same recklessness, or courage, which would make it so difficult for the military authorities to know how to deal with him.

Sassoon was well aware that his action would be particularly difficult for his fellow-officers to understand. Whilst accepting that it did not stem from cowardice, some of them would regard it as a disgrace to the Regiment and others would assume he had gone mad. How many of them, he wondered, would give him credit for having done it for the sake of the troops at the Front? For that, ultimately, was his strongest motive:

> It was for the fighting men that my appeal was made [he wrote in his autobiography], for those whose loyalty and unthinkingness would have been betrayed whatever acquisitions the Peace might bring to the British Empire.[111]

Forty-eight years after the event, complaining to Dame Felicitas Corrigan about being labelled 'less compassionate' than Wilfred Owen, he claimed 'I was bursting with [compassion], wasn't I, when I made my famous and futile protest which many now consider reasonable?'[112] His contemporary notes for the statement in any case clearly show that it was the suffering of the troops which was foremost in his mind: 'Fighting men are victims of conspiracy among (a) politicians; (b) military caste; (c) people who are making money out of the war'. Although the final version departed considerably from such a simple formula, it kept the emphasis on the exploitation of the ordinary soldier.

Curiously, Sassoon did not send his statement out as soon as it was finished. He simply waited for events to come to a head. Dreading the consequences, he may have wanted to delay them a little. He was due back at Litherland Depot on 27 June, but had no intention of reporting then, since part of his protest would be to refuse to serve in the army. He would wait until he was summoned, then send his statement to his Commanding Officer, who, he felt, should see it first.

He decided to spend the interval at Weirleigh, where there was only his mother from whom to hide his intentions. (That, in itself, proved to be no easy matter and would provide him with material for a lengthy passage in *Infantry Officer*.[113]) Part of the reason he was not ready to show his protest to anyone until it had been seen by his military superiors was that he rightly suspected that most of his friends would try to dissuade him from such a rash course of action. They would certainly urge him to take the post of Cadet Training Officer which he had been offered at Cambridge when he went for an interview there on 13 June. (This was the day fourteen German bombers, flying at 12,000 feet, attacked London, dropping more than 100 bombs and killing 162 civilians, and Sassoon had been lucky to escape unhurt when the area between his bank and Liverpool Street Station had been targeted.[114])

By the end of June, however, the strain had become so great that Sassoon needed to confide in someone. Since he and Graves had freely shared their criticisms of the War less than a year previously, he chose Graves as his confidant, though he did not send even him a copy of his statement. Graves had already responded to an earlier letter on 30 June and posted it, when he received a second letter hinting at Sassoon's intentions. Clearly alarmed, he wrote again immediately, urging Sassoon to visit him at Osborne on the Isle of Wight where he was convalescing:

> Do say you're coming: I want to know what characteristic devilment this is. Are you standing as pacifist M.P.? That's the most characteristic thing I can think of next to your bombing Lloyd George.[115]

Unable to confide in Graves further for the moment, Sassoon continued to wait. The weather was as oppressive as his thoughts, and he longed for refreshing rain. He could not get the War out of his mind, particularly when the faint thud of guns could be heard across the Channel. Everything reminded him of it:

> Now light the candles; one; two; there's a moth;
> What silly beggars they are to blunder in
> And scorch their wings with glory, liquid flame –
> No, no, not that, – it's bad to think of war,
> When thoughts you've gagged all day come back to scare you;
> And it's been proved that soldiers don't go mad
> Unless they lose control of ugly thoughts
> That drive them out to jabber among the trees.
>
> (*CP*, p. 89)

These lines were the beginning of a poem written in early July which he retrospectively titled 'Repression of War Experience'.[116] Continuing the dialogue with himself, the narrator wishes restlessly for a thunderstorm, then tries to settle down to read, but concludes:

> and yet
> You sit and gnaw your nails, and let your pipe out,
> And listen to the silence: on the ceiling
> There's one big, dizzy moth that bumps and flutters;
> And in the breathless air outside the house
> The garden waits for something that delays.
> There must be crowds of ghosts among the trees, –
> Not people killed in battle – they're in France –
> But horrible shapes in shrouds – old men who died
> Slow natural deaths – old men with ugly souls,
> Who wore their bodies out with nasty sins.
>
> ...
>
> You're quiet and peaceful, summering safe at home;
> You'd never think there was a bloody war on! ...
> O yes you would ... why, you can hear the guns.
> Hark! Thud, thud, thud – quite soft ... they never cease –
> Those whispering guns – O Christ, I want to go out
> And screech at them to stop – I'm going crazy;
> I'm going stark, staring mad because of the guns.

A strong sense of foreboding is created by what is in effect a study in contrasts between the ostensibly 'peaceful' England and war-torn France, where the narrator's thoughts keep straying. (It may be a Freudian slip, created by the line-breakage, when he announces three lines from the end 'I want to go out'.) The strain of trying to 'listen to the silence', the ominous sense of waiting 'for something that delays', the suffocation of 'breathless air', the ugliness of old men who die 'slow natural deaths' rather than fighting in France and the sinister deceptiveness of 'soft ... whispering' guns all help to create a nightmare scenario. It is clearly a description of

Sassoon's own experience. His nightmares after Arras had not gone away; on the contrary they had begun to invade his waking hours. If he had been tempted to forego his protest in the tranquil surroundings of Weirleigh, his memories would not let him.[117]

When the expected telegram requesting him to 'Join at Litherland immediately' arrived at last on 4 July, Sassoon still delayed two days before responding with a copy of his statement and an explanatory letter to his Commanding Officer, Colonel Jones Williams. The letter is worth quoting because it shows how unwillingly Sassoon entered his martyrdom; he had always known that the hardest aspect of it would be risking the misunderstanding of his fellow-officers:

> I am writing you this private letter with the greatest possible regret. I must inform you that it is my intention to refuse to perform any further military duties. I am doing this as a protest against the policy of the Government in prolonging the War by failing to state their conditions of peace.
> I have written a statement of my reasons, of which I enclose a copy. This statement is being circulated. I would have spared you this unpleasantness had it been possible.
> My only desire is to make things as easy as possible for you in dealing with my case. I will come to Litherland immediately I hear from you, if that is your wish.
> I am fully aware of what I am letting myself in for.[118]

While waiting for a response to his letter and statement, Sassoon occupied himself by sending copies to a list of people he had drawn up. (In the days before photocopying machines he had almost certainly spent a great deal of time at Weirleigh making these copies.) Apart from friends like Marsh, Bennett and Wells, the names were mainly of people he hoped would be sympathetic to his cause, such as the editors of the *Cambridge Magazine*, *Nation* and *Westminster Review*, (Ogden, Massingham and Spender) and the M.P.s Lees-Smith, J.F. Hope, Lord Henry Bentinck (Ottoline's brother) and Harold Cox (his uncle Hamo's brother-in-law). The two names at the top of the list were there probably from a sense of duty: Thomas Hardy, who, he felt, ought to know his position exactly, and Lord Brassey, for similar reasons. It is difficult to know why he also decided to send a copy to the sportsman Horatio Hutchinson, who wrote prolifically on golf, cricket and a variety of other subjects. Perhaps it was simply out of admiration for his work. People not on the list also received copies, their names too obvious to need noting down, Robbie Ross, Ottoline Morrell, Roderick Meiklejohn and Bertrand Russell. In addition he sent his statement to Hamo Thornycroft, though he told Harold Cox that he was afraid his uncle would never forgive him. He almost certainly did not send a copy to Gosse, who nevertheless was to hear of it and involve himself.

To a large extent the reactions were predictable. Bertrand Russell had already approved and Ottoline wrote enthusiastically to congratulate him on 'the value and splendour of such a True Act'.[119] His old friend Edward Carpenter, himself a rebel, replied biblically 'Well done, good and faithful!'[120] and Wells, whose own disillusionment had influenced Sassoon, wrote to agree 'that the War was going on through the sheer stupid inability of the responsible people to crystallize out in a plain statement the peace wishes that were practically the same in the minds of reasonable persons everywhere'.[121] He would like, he added, to find some way of backing Sassoon. C.K. Ogden, whom Sassoon thought useful, had obviously responded positively too.

The disapprovers were equally vociferous. Bobbie Hanmer, primed by Graves (who knew how much Sassoon liked the handsome young officer), wrote briskly from his hospital bed to ask: 'What is this damned nonsense' and to urge, with not a little emotional blackmail: 'For Heaven's sake man don't be such a fool. Don't disgrace yourself and think of us before you do anything so mad'.[122]

Marsh wrote more reasonably, expressing surprise that America's entry into the War had not made Sassoon more hopeful of an early resolution and begging him not to be 'more of a martyr than he could help'. Whilst admiring Sassoon's courage, he could not himself 'see any future for decent civilisation if the end of the war [was] to leave the Prussian autocracy in any position of credit and trust'.[123] Bennett was characteristically more forthright, saying that he thought Sassoon 'very misguided', in no position to judge the situation and guilty of 'spiritual pride'. He concluded his closely argued letter by predicting: 'the Army will ultimately lay it down that you are "daft" '.[124] To Sassoon's disappointment Harold Cox, whom he had hoped to have as an ally, also wrote to disagree, though with regret: 'to cease fighting now', he argued, '[would mean] a Victory for the German military party'.[125] Lord Brassey's reply, if he made one, is not recorded – it may have been unprintable.

The most interesting responses came from those who shared Sassoon's unhappiness about the conduct of the War, but feared for him personally. Chief among these was Robbie Ross, who had already seen the son of his great friend, Sir Squire Sprigge, Court-Martialled for a lesser offence[126] and was frightened at what might happen to Sassoon. Writing from Brighton, where the statement had reached him, he made it quite clear that his reaction stemmed from practical rather than philosophical considerations:

Dearest Siegfried, I am quite appalled at what you have done. I can only hope that the C.O. at Litherland will absolutely ignore your letter. I am terrified lest you should be put under arrest. Let me know at once if anything happens.[127]

Unlike Carpenter, Ross's own experience of defying established views had made him more anxious to protect his younger friend, who, he suspected, was still very naive. For the next fortnight he was in constant touch with Graves and Gosse as to the possible outcome. He was able to report to Gosse, whose disagreement did not prevent him wishing Sassoon well, that he had 'promise of powerful help if necessary at the War Office'.[128]

Ironically, Sassoon seemed more concerned about Ross and other friends than himself in the situation: 'Have you recovered from the shock, dear Robbie?' he wrote on about 9 July while still waiting to hear from his Colonel. 'I talked to Roderick [Meiklejohn] for hours, trying to make him less worried about it, but fear he thinks me utterly irresponsible'.[129] Hamo Thornycroft was as anxious as Meiklejohn and Ross. Far from casting his nephew off, as Sassoon had feared, he went to see if Ross could advise him how to help. Apart from giving him a detailed account of events, Ross could only sympathize, since his own feelings were very similar to those of an affectionate uncle. He told Hamo that Sassoon was 'hurt' with him for not agreeing with his 'insane action'.[130] Another person who went to see Ross was Hamo's daughter's husband, Herbert Farjeon, who was himself fighting his case as a conscientious objector. Ross told him that, although 'he agreed with every word of Siegfried's protest', he thought things were 'better left as they are – one man can do so little'.[131] A man with a German name like 'Siegfried', he added, was particularly unlikely to do much with a protest of this kind.

The most surprising response came from Joe Cottrell, Quartermaster of the 1st Royal Welch Fusiliers, to whom Sassoon had also sent his statement. Instead of condemning it roundly, like Bennett, Joe trod a more difficult line. Fearing a Court-Martial for one of his favourites, he tactfully concluded his reply: 'I'm afraid the time is not yet ripe for this. I showed this to [fellow-officers] Reeves and Brunicardi. They, like me, admire your motives but are not so sure of the opportuneness of your action'.[132] Joe had seen too many young officers die unnecessarily to condemn Sassoon's protest outright, as Graves had predicted he would.

The most practical response came from Graves himself, who first heard of Sassoon's statement from Ross on 9 July (his own copy of it was not sent out till 10 July), when he replied from the Isle of Wight:

It's awful about Siegfried: and he did it without consulting his friends or saying anything about it to anyone sane. In strict confidence, I may tell you that as soon as I heard I wrote to the dear old Senior Major at Litherland imploring him not to let the Colonel take S. seriously but to give him a special medical board and more convalescent home till I can get an opportunity for getting hold of him to stop him disgracing himself, his regiment and especially his friends.[133]

As usual Graves's own account in *Goodbye To All That* is rather garbled; he claims not to have heard of the protest until the end of July, when Sassoon sent a copy of it published in the *Bradford Pioneer* of 27 July, yet he was already writing to Ross about it on the 9th.[134] His account of his own feelings about Sassoon's actions in the same book is, however, authentic, since it was a point of view he repeated to Sassoon himself at the time:

> I entirely agreed with Sassoon about the 'political errors and insincerities' and thought his action magnificently courageous. But more things had to be considered than the strength of our case against the politicians. In the first place, he was in no proper physical condition to suffer the penalty which the letter invited: namely, to be court-martialled, cashiered and imprisoned. I found myself bitter with the pacifists who had encouraged him to make this gesture. I felt that, not being soldiers, they could not understand what it cost Siegfried emotionally.[135]

Graves did not hesitate to point out to Sassoon, however, that it was not 'good form', nor was it the act of 'an officer and a gentleman', a piece of emotional blackmail Sassoon managed to resist, though he realized that most of their fellow-officers would endorse it.[136] To their mutual friend, Marsh, Graves wrote on 12 July, 'It's an awful thing – completely mad – that he has done'.[137] Whilst Graves thought Sassoon's actions quite wrong, he was sympathetic to his views and was relieved to learn that Marsh did not regard him as a criminal. He desperately wanted to help Sassoon, and Marsh's attitude made it easier to ask his advice. Like Ross, Marsh regarded the War Office as their best hope, though he was unfortunately no longer working for it. Graves claimed in his autobiography that he immediately wrote to a friend there, the Hon. Evan Morgan, Private Secretary to one of the Coalition Ministers, but in fact the letter was not written until the worst of the crisis was over. What he did do, however, was extremely effective. After receiving a sympathetic reply from the 'dear old Senior Major' at Litherland, Major Macartney-Filgate, assuring him that Sassoon would be ordered a Medical Board rather than a Court Martial, he persuaded his own doctors to pass him fit for home service in spite of the fact that he was not yet fully recovered.

Sassoon meantime had been ordered to rejoin the Regiment at Litherland and did so on 13 July in a state of understandable trepidation. (His promotion to full Lieutenant on 1 July could not have helped matters.) His kind reception by Major Macartney-Filgate, who was acting C.O. in Colonel Jones Williams' absence, made it all the more difficult for him to refuse to withdraw his ultimatum, as gently requested. He felt he was committing 'a breach not so much of discipline as of decorum'. Hoping at least to be arrested, to draw attention to his cause, he was further disconcerted to be told simply to book himself in at the Exchange Hotel in Liverpool while his superiors decided what to do about him.

For the next three days Sassoon waited for developments, his anxiety preventing him leaving the hotel. He may have managed to complete a poem or two[138] but he was in no fit state to settle down to anything satisfactory. After three days spent mainly memorizing poems in preparation for the imprisonment he felt was certain, he was summoned to a Medical Board at Crewe. After a brief struggle with himself he tore up the railway warrant he had been issued, to remove the strong temptation to give in and attend it. As his perplexed C.O. explained the next day, when he came in person to try to persuade him to change his mind, a Royal Army Medical Corps Colonel had come all the way from London for the Board Sassoon had cut. It was shortly after this visit that Sassoon took the train to Formby and in a fit of frustration and anger threw his M.C. ribbon into the Mersey, the most extreme act of rebellion against the army he could conceive.

Sassoon had been alone just over a week when Graves arrived at the Litherland depot on 18 July. Passing through London the previous day Graves had spoken to both Marsh and Ross and promised to do his best to save Sassoon. His arrival was crucial. Since Sassoon had already rejected the army's face-saving offer of a Medical Board to pronounce him shell-shocked, the situation had reached crisis point. Graves's method was simple but effective. In order to take away Sassoon's motivation for continued rebellion, he merely lied to him about the consequences, assuring him, on an imaginary Bible, that if he refused to be medically boarded, the military authorities would shut him up in a mental hospital for the rest of the War.[139] There would be no martyrdom. Thoroughly defeated by the prospect of such an anti-climactic end to his dramatic gesture, Sassoon finally gave in and agreed to attend a Medical. Ignoble as his capitulation seemed to him, he was nevertheless aware of a huge sense of relief, since he had fully expected to be sent to prison. Even after he learned of Graves's lie much later, he was still able to write appreciatively of his act and to admit: 'No doubt I should have done the same for him had our positions been reversed'.[140]

The Medical Board, which was instantly arranged for the next day, had of course been fixed. Whether, as Graves claimed, he 'rigged' it himself with his tearful evidence,[141] or, as seems more likely, Ross's contact at the War Office had given instructions that Sassoon was to be diagnosed as 'shell-shocked', the Board conveniently found him in need of treatment. Sassoon derived what amusement he could from the sight of 'two elephantine R.A.M.C. Colonels' being dissuaded by 'a very sensible nerve specialist' from treating him as either 'insane' or 'pro-German'.[142] The decision was based not on grounds of health but of expediency and seemed the best way of avoiding the publicity both the Government and the army feared. H.G. Wells, who sympathized with Sassoon's stand but had advised him not to 'get locked up' or 'do anything excessive', was clearly relieved[143]:

> Take your discharge for 'shock' [he wrote] and then let every action show that it was a mere excuse, that you are a grave and balanced man, set upon the peace of the world. Don't develop into a 'case'.

Sassoon, therefore, allowed himself to be sent to a convalescent home for neurasthenics at Craiglockhart near Edinburgh. Reporting to Ross the same day, 19 July, Graves was understandably proud of his own part in the affair:

> After superhuman efforts I have arranged everything about Siegfried quietly – struggling first with the people here for a free hand then with [Sassoon] ... Result: he is suffering from nerves and the medical board are sending him to some unpronounc– or spell-able place in Edinboro' ... He is quite reconciled and is going cheerfully. I wish to Hell I could go too. I'm quite worn out. His views on the War are of course unchanged.

Graves would, in fact, be asked to escort Sassoon to Craiglockhart. Meantime, Julian Dadd, who had also been very worried about the possible consequences of Sassoon's action, was full of admiration for Graves. Writing to Sassoon about it twelve years later, and in spite of severe reservations about *Goodbye to All That*, he pointed out that Graves 'was the master of the situation, and I thought that, for a man of his age [22], his ability and tact were wonderful'.[144]

Graves and, through the War Office, Ross had saved Sassoon from the imprisonment meted out to other objectors,[145] but they could not prevent the publicity which the Government was trying so hard to avoid. In spite of Sassoon's referral to Craiglockhart War Hospital, Lees-Smith went ahead with his speech to the House of Commons, in which he read out the whole of Sassoon's statement. J.L. Macpherson, Under-Secretary for War, in his response to the M.P., did what he could to limit the damage, ending his moving account of the brave young officer's supposed shell-shock with the hope 'that Hon. Members would hesitate long before they made use of a document written by a young man in such a state of mind, nor did he think their action would be appreciated by the friends of the officer'.[146]

Macpherson's plea produced cheers in the House, but the Press were clearly unmoved by it, since the statement, or references to it, appeared in at least twelve newspapers. The *Bradford Pioneer* had already jumped the gun, publishing the statement in full on 27 July. The day after Lees-Smith's speech on 30 July, *The Times* also reported it in full, as did the *Manchester Guardian*. Popular Conservative papers, such as the *Morning Post* and the *Daily Telegraph* headed their briefer accounts 'Officer's Strange Letter' and 'Officer's Remarkable Letter' respectively, while the

Daily Chronicle concentrated on Sassoon's family background. Their potted history of the Sassoon clan was taken up a day or two later by provincial papers like the *Burton Evening Gazette* and the *Southampton Echo*. All three failed to observe that a prominent member of that clan, Sir Philip Sassoon, was on the staff of the British Army in France. Nor did they point out the further pronounced irony that, on the maternal side of Sassoon's family, his uncle John Thornycroft was busily supplying lorries and other *materielle* for the Front.

Only two papers came out in open support of Sassoon, the *Labour Leader*, which headed the piece 'Lieutenant Sassoon's Defiance', and the *Herald*, which ended its article on 'An Officer as C.O.' with the subversive suggestion 'but those who know him appear to think he is quite as sane and in good health as ever he was'. Curiously, though Sassoon preserved all the press-cuttings he could find, the only one mentioned by him in his autobiography is the harsh judgement of the *Army and Navy Gazette*: 'It is obvious that soldiers, even if they have reached the exalted rank of Second Lieutenant, cannot be permitted to decide when the time has come for them to discontinue fighting, and the military authorities would appear to have taken a commendably mild view of the case of the young officer in question in adopting the medieval suggestion that his extraordinary action is due to the fact that at the time he entered upon it he was suffering from shell-shock rather than from a sudden impulse of insubordination of a particularly grave kind'.[147]

There was a curious sequel to this saga. Six months after Sassoon's Liverpool Medical Board, a typewritten copy of his statement was discovered by a Mr S. Sullivan of Saltley, Birmingham, in the luggage-rack of a Birmingham-Preston train. It differed slightly from the Hansard version and the one Sassoon was to include in his *Memoirs of an Infantry Officer*. Sullivan sent the statement to Lord Derby, the minister responsible for army recruitment, who in turn handed it over to the War Office Intelligence Service. The protest was annotated 'Lieutenant Sassoon was undoubtedly the author but when it was written he was a lunatic. It seems possible that some pacifists are circulating Sassoon's insane efforts'. (When Sassoon's papers were released in February 1998, the Public Records Office made a completely unfounded claim that this copy was the original version of his protest.) Sullivan's discovery seems to have drawn attention to Sassoon's verse which had hitherto escaped the censor's notice; the deputy director of Military Intelligence, Brigadier General George Cockerill, was so disturbed that he wrote to H.W.M. Massingham, the editor of *The Nation*, 'If Lieutenant Sassoon is now writing verse such as appeared on page 394, issue of July 13, 1918 [i.e. 'I Stood with the Dead'], it would appear that his mind is still in chaos and that he is not fit to be trusted with men's lives'. The intelligence service was particularly upset by the contents of 'Counter-Attack', which had not been submitted for the censor's approval. But Massingham was deliberately vague about its date of composition and the case was dropped.

Sassoon never regretted his action, though he did later acknowledge that it was unrealistic. He had made his protest in all seriousness, fully prepared to accept the consequences, however grave. Yet looking back on events from 1945 he found it 'difficult to believe that a Peace negotiated in 1917 would have been permanent ... nothing on earth would have prevented a recurrence of Teutonic aggressiveness'.[148] Nevertheless his willingness to be sacrificed for his ideals, however impractical, remains as impressive today as it was then.

14

Strange Meeting
(July-November 1917)

Though Sassoon did not welcome a stay in a convalescent home for neurasthenics and was at times deeply unhappy there, his four months at Craiglockhart War Hospital proved to be a very positive experience. On a purely practical level he finally found himself with time to write the poetry which was still demanding an outlet. With his protest behind him and none of the responsibilities of active service to distract him, he could devote himself to expressing those views which had led him to protest, views that were, if anything, intensified by the authorities' attempt to muzzle him. By the end of his stay he had produced the bulk of the work for his next book of War poems, *Counter-Attack*, a collection he was to complete in the following two months.

Sassoon's own conclusion, many years later, was that the poems produced at Craiglockhart were among the best in *Counter-Attack*, and he linked this indirectly with another benefit of his stay there, his 'incalculably helpful friendship' with the psychiatrist, Dr Rivers.[1] As he further pointed out, the period at Craiglockhart also 'brought Wilfred O[wen] in[to] my Life (for the last 15 months of *his*)', another factor which was to influence his work.

By the time Sassoon arrived at Craiglockhart on 23 July 1917, Haig was about to embark on what one historian has called 'the gloomiest drama in British military history',[2] the 3rd Battle of Ypres, known otherwise as 'Passchendaele'. The Allied victory at Messines at the beginning of June had provided a much-needed morale booster and Haig planned to follow it up with a single-handed defeat of the Germans in Flanders. He had already decided in May 1917, as the Battle of Arras drew to its doleful end, to transfer the main weight of his offensive northwards to Flanders, hoping to distract the enemy's attention from both the trouble-ridden French and the crisis caused by the submarine campaign at sea. He also trusted such a move would support the offensive still hoped for from Russia, though by the time his campaign was launched on 31 July such considerations seemed irrelevant. Ignoring both his weather forecasters, who predicted only three weeks of fine weather at most, and his engineers, who warned him that to destroy the drainage system of the low-lying area with an initial bombardment would turn the battlefield into a swamp, he pressed on with an attack for which the Germans had had two months to prepare. Long before his empty victory of 4 November, when the British finally reached their objective, Passchendaele, the battleground had become a sea of mud and blood.

In pressing on to the bitter end, Haig used up valuable reserves which might have saved the Allies from the humiliating reverse at Cambrai that followed. Had Sassoon returned to the 2nd RWF when his leave expired in July, he would have marched with them to the Ypres battlefield in August and fought with them there near Polygon Wood in September, when six of his fellow-officers were killed in one day, together with at least sixty other ranks. Had he rejoined the 1st RWF he would not only have had to face the horrors of Ypres but also the rigours of the Italian Front, where the Allies had lost 600,000 men at Caporetto and were being pushed back relentlessly by the enemy. Russia's withdrawal from the War after a second revolution in November and the failure of American troops to make their presence felt as quickly as had been hoped would also add to the Allies' low morale at the end of 1917.[3] Allenby's entry into Jerusalem on 11 December might set the churchbells ringing but there would be no real expectation of peace in Europe as the year drew to its close.

In spite of the hopelessness and dangers of life on the Western Front, however, Sassoon would far rather have been there with his men than facing what he regarded as imprisonment in a mental hospital. He was to pass his time at Craiglockhart with a suppressed awareness that he was 'shortening the War' for himself every week he remained there.[4] His protest had been genuine enough, but unless he could believe it to be still effective, he felt he was there under false pretences, 'merely skrimshanking snugly along', as he put it.[5] And there were other concerns. One of his closest friends from the 2nd RWF, Dr Dunn, on hearing of Sassoon's fate a fortnight after the event, expressed some of Sassoon's own fears on arrival at Craiglockhart, as well as revealing the mixture of admiration, agreement and doubt which his protest had aroused among his colleagues:

> Sassoon's quixotic outburst has been quenched in a 'shell-shock' retreat. He will be among degenerates, drinkers, malingerers, and common mental cases, as well as the overstrained. It is an astute official means of denying our cold-blooded, cold-footed, superior persons the martyr they are too precious to find from their own unruly ranks. Sassoon gave a moral flavour to a gibe everywhere current at the front for a couple of years, that a lot of individuals in cushy jobs don't care how long the War lasts. It used to be said laughingly, now it is said bitterly. But for one in the Army with an interest in the prolongation of the War there are now hundreds of 'indispensables' at home in well paid war-jobs. The affluence and the squeals of the indispensables have made it hard for the serving-men's families, and exasperated the serving men, many of whom have been taken from increasing affluence for service. But I have not heard any stop-the-war talk among front-line

troops, whatever may be spoken among the Base tribe ... On that point Sassoon did not speak the feeling of those with most to lose by the War.[6]

Sassoon would probably have agreed with Dunn's final sentence, but might well have pointed out that he also had felt war-like at the Front. It was only in England, brooding on the sufferings of his men and listening to highly intelligent pacifist friends that he had become sufficiently distanced from the War to criticize it in the terms he did, and even then he had let the Army off lightly.

So there he was, arriving at a shell-shock hospital in a state of unmilitant defiance of military authority. It was, as he himself pointed out, 'an experience peculiar enough to stimulate [his] speculations about the immediate future',[7] and he had thought about it continuously during his journey up to Edinburgh from Liverpool on 23 July. He was all the freer to do so since his official escorts, Graves and another RWF officer, S.W. Harper, had missed the train at Lime Street, leaving him to travel by himself.[8] On reaching Princes Street Station he decided to carry on alone to Craiglockhart War Hospital, which was situated just over two miles from the centre of Edinburgh at Slateford, a name he was to use to conceal the hospital's true identity in his fiction.[9]

A twenty-minute taxi ride south-west through respectable suburbs took him all too quickly to his final destination. Seeing Craiglockhart for the first time on a fine July afternoon, his reactions were mixed. He found the place itself, a heavy Italianate-baronial building of decayed grandeur, rather depressing, while its views struck him as 'prodigiously' beautiful.[10] Set into the side of Wester Craiglockhart Hill, 400 feet above sea-level, it was a very healthy spot. Built in 1880 as a Hydro for wealthy invalids but converted into a war hospital by the Red Cross in October 1916, the house overlooked both the Forth Valley and the Pentland Hills. Renowned for their beauty, the green and rolling Pentlands were full of inviting footpaths. 'I leap on their ridges like a young ram', Sassoon was to write biblically to Ottoline only a week after his arrival,[11] and his appreciation of the landscape grew even keener during his four months there.

His impression of the institution itself did not improve. While admitting to Dent that it was not a bad place, he continued to find it 'gloomy' and 'cavernous'.[12] The pomp of its yellowish-grey façade and three huge towers was echoed in its black and white tiled entrance hall and marble staircase, but that was as far as it went. Whether as a result of conversion or original planning needs, the patients' rooms on the upper three floors led off windowless corridors, which narrowed down claustrophobically on the top floor to a few feet in width. As Sassoon ironically observed, the War Office had 'wasted no money on interior decoration'.[13] It was not a suitable place to house 160 depressed, often traumatized officers. Even less ideal was the need to fit two of them to a room. Many had hideous nightmares and some could not sleep at all for fear of having them. Sassoon found it the worst aspect of the place. As he pointed out in his thinly disguised account of Craiglockhart in *Sherston's Progress*, the doctors dealt more or less successfully with Craiglockhart's disadvantages by day:

> But by night they lost control and the hospital became sepulchral and oppressive with saturations of war experience. One lay awake and listened to feet padding along passages which smelt of stale cigarette-smoke; for the nurses couldn't prevent insomnia-ridden officers from smoking half the night in their bedrooms, though the locks had been removed from all doors. One became conscious that the place was full of men whose slumbers were morbid and terrifying – men muttering uneasily or suddenly crying out in their sleep. Around me was that underworld of dreams haunted by submerged memories of warfare and its intolerable shocks and self-lacerating failures to achieve the impossible. ... By night each man was back in his doomed sector of a horror-stricken Front Line, where the panic and stampede of some ghastly experience was re-enacted among the livid faces of the dead. No doctor could save him then, when he became the lonely victim of his dream disasters and delusions.[14]

The last two sentences carry the conviction of one who had himself suffered such nightmares, as indeed Sassoon had. But he was never to be reduced to the state of those he described so bitterly at Craiglockhart as 'Survivors':

> No doubt they'll soon get well; the shock and strain
>   Have caused their stammering, disconnected talk.
> Of course they're 'longing to go out again,' –
>   These boys with old, scared faces, learning to walk.
> They'll soon forget their haunted nights; their cowed
>   Subjection to the ghosts of friends who died, –
> Their dreams that drip with murder; and they'll be proud
>   Of glorious war that shatter'd all their pride ...
> Men who went out to battle, grim and glad;
> Children, with eyes that hate you, broken and mad.
> *Craiglockhart, October 1917*   (*CP*, p. 90)

Sharing a room with such human wrecks could not have been easy, but an even greater disadvantage for Sassoon was that it prevented him from writing. He had many ideas for poems, but needed time alone to work them out. The after-dinner hours between eight and eleven were what he jokingly called his 'brainy' time, but it was also the time when his companion, a young Scots Captain in tartan breeches, wanted to retire to their joint room. It is a measure of Sassoon's conviction and determination that he produced as many poems as he did at Craiglockhart under such circumstances. Ideally he would simply have changed his routine and written his poetry during the day, which was largely free. But he did not find it easy to change habits once formed. (The only concession he made as he grew older was to delay the start of his writing time to an hour when everyone else was going to bed.) As it was, he struggled on with his poetry in the evenings and filled the day, as he liked to do, with mainly physical pursuits.

The staff at Craiglockhart, as part of the therapy, offered a wide choice of activities; what mattered was to keep the patients busy, preferably in ways that would help reconnect them to the world around them. Golf, badminton, bowls, croquet, billiards, tennis, swimming and cycling were only some of the options available. Patients could even rear their own poultry, garden or help the local farmers bring in the hay. Those less physically inclined could pass the time making model boats, develop their own photographs, join the Debating Society, take French classes or go botanizing. There was also a hospital magazine, a theatre company and an orchestra, all run by the patients.

It was not unlike boarding-school or university, and Sassoon's choices remained similar to those he had made at Henley House and at Cambridge. After passing the first week in long, solitary walks over the Pentland Hills, he spent a large part of most days playing golf. It seemed a natural choice in a city surrounded by fine golf-courses, particularly in the absence of his usual summer favourite, cricket. It also kept him fit, something he still cared about. Most importantly, as he reported to Graves halfway through his stay at Craiglockhart, it enabled him 'to escape from the truly awful atmosphere of this place of wash-outs and shattered heroes'.[15] (He did not altogether escape the shattered heroes, however. His golfing partner, a talkative Royal Army Medical Corps officer, was a fine player but easily unbalanced, and on the rare occasions when he failed to win was liable to threaten Sassoon with his golf clubs.)

Sassoon's freedom to play golf daily was due largely to the encouragement and co-operation of one man at Craiglockhart, his case doctor, W.H.R. Rivers.[16] 'Doc Willie', as he was popularly known, quickly realized Sassoon's need for strenuous physical activity to balance his active mental life, and one which took him away from the hospital and its disturbed inhabitants seemed ideal. He therefore arranged his thrice weekly meetings with his patient rather unusually for the early evening, leaving Sassoon's day free.

Sassoon had met Rivers within minutes of his arrival, a tall, heavy-jowled, bespectacled man in his early fifties, with a thick moustache and bushy eyebrows but thinning hair. Both were already known to each other by name. 'Rivers will look after you', the neurological member of the Medical Board at Liverpool had assured him after his destination had been decided,[17] and Sassoon had realized even then that Rivers was an important man. Rivers would certainly have been aware in advance of the identity of a patient who had already proved to be so awkward. Sassoon's own account of their relationship, though narrated largely in *Sherston's Progress*, is more reliable than fiction usually is, since Rivers was dead by the time it came out in 1936. 'If he were alive', Sassoon wrote, 'I could not be writing so freely about him. I might even be obliged to call him by some made-up name, which would seem absurd'.[18] He not only gave Rivers his real name, but also stuck very closely to the facts. So much so that, instead of repeating his account of the doctor in his official autobiography, he merely referred his readers to *Sherston's Progress*.

As Sassoon realized, Rivers was already an eminent man by the time he started work at Craiglockhart in 1917.[19] A fellow of St John's College, Cambridge, his central interest was the biological reaction of man to his environment, which led him into the fields of anthropology, neurology and psychology in its widest sense. His research had taken him as far as the South Seas and involved him in daring experiments on the human nervous system,[20] but it was not until the War that he found his true vocation, a remarkable aptitude for treating psychoneuroses. His war work, Rivers believed, brought him into contact with 'the real problems of life'.[21] It certainly brought together his various skills and called on his whole area of knowledge. He had begun it as a temporary Major in the Royal Army Medical Corps at Maghull War Hospital near Liverpool and had been transferred to Craiglockhart not long before Sassoon's arrival there.[22] When they met he was already in charge of a hundred of the hospital's 160 patients, while the other three doctors, Captain Brock, Major Ruggles and Lieutenant MacIntyre, had only sixty patients between them.

Building on his peace-time experience and drawing on Freud's work on dreams, though not entirely agreeing with his conclusions, Rivers had gradually evolved a method for treating shell-shocked soldiers, whose basic problem he saw as a conflict between fear and duty. His pioneering work was crucial in gaining acceptance for a condition which had previously been regarded with deep suspicion by most military authorities as either insanity or a form of malingering. Rivers was to write about his work at Craiglockhart in *Conflict and Dream*, a series of lectures published posthumously in 1923, in which Sassoon features as 'patient B'. In these lectures he isolates the war dream from other types of dream in a way which ties in closely with Sassoon's own account of Craiglockhart by night:

A characteristic feature ... is that it is accompanied by an effect of a peculiarly intense kind, often with a special quality described as different from any known in waking life. The dream ends suddenly by the patient waking in an acute state of terror directly continuous with the threat of the dream and with all the physical accompaniments of extreme fear, such as profuse sweating, shaking and violent beating of the heart. Often the dream recurs in exactly the same form night after night, and even several times in one night, and a sufferer will often keep himself from sleeping again after one experience from dread of its repetition.[23]

Interestingly, it was not Sassoon's dreams Rivers analyzed when he came to discuss him as 'patient B', but his own dream in relation to his patient. For Rivers, as well as Sassoon, the relationship was to produce, in the words of his own title, dreams as well as conflict. It was also to create guilt on both sides.

Rivers' guilt related to his dual role as scientist and army-officer. In his dream he was talking to Sassoon in both capacities. The dream had followed his reading, at Sassoon's suggestion, of some anti-war literature (Barbusse's *Under Fire* and an article in the *English Review*) during which he remembered wondering what would happen 'if my task of converting a patient from his "pacifist errors" to the conventional attitude should have as its result my own conversion to his point of view'.[24] This particularly worried him, since self-interest might well encourage him to wish for the end of the War to enable him to return to his academic research. His main concern in analyzing his dream was to establish whether he was in uniform:

> ... [this] had a definite connection with the conflict which I suppose[d] to underlie the dream, and especially with my relations to patient B. So long as I was an officer of the R.A.M.C., and of this my uniform was the obvious symbol, my discussions with B. on his attitude towards the war were prejudiced by my sense that I was not a free agent in discussing the matter, but that there was the danger that my attitude might be influenced by my official position. As a scientific student whose only object should be the attainment of what I supposed to be the truth, it was definitely unpleasant to me to suspect that the opinions which I was uttering might be influenced by the needs of my position, and I was fully aware of an element of constraint in my relations with B. on this account. So long as I was in uniform I was not a free agent.[25]

Rivers's uniform was not the only constraint in the relationship. He was almost certainly homosexual by inclination and it must quickly have become clear to him that Sassoon was too. Yet neither is likely to have referred to it, though we know that Sassoon was already finding his sexuality a problem. At the same time, as an experienced psychologist Rivers could reasonably expect Sassoon to experience 'transference' and become extremely fond of him. Paul Fussell suggests in *The Great War and Modern Memory* that Rivers became the embodiment of the male 'dream friend' who had been the companion of Sassoon's boyhood fantasies.[26] Sassoon publicly acknowledged that 'there was never any doubt about my liking [Rivers]. He made me feel safe at once, and seemed to know all about me'.[27]

But Sassoon's description of the doctor in *Sherston's Progress*, lingering as it does on Rivers's warm smile and endearing habits – he often sat, spectacles pushed up on forehead, with his hands clasped round one knee – suggests that it was more than liking he felt. And privately he was rather franker, telling Marsh, whom he knew would understand, that he 'loved [Rivers] at first sight'.[28] He quickly began to regard him as a father-confessor, as well as something of a father-figure. Twenty-two years his senior, Rivers was certainly old enough for the latter role and, since the slight cooling-off in relations between Gosse and himself as a result of his anti-war views, Sassoon was in need of a more tolerant replacement. Who better than the man he was later to call his 'fathering friend'?[29]

One qualification of the ideal father is wisdom and Rivers seemed to Sassoon a 'Very Wise Man', the title of one of the poems he was to write about him:

> ... You understand my thoughts; though, when *you* think,
> You're out beyond the boundaries of my brain.
> I'm but a bird at dawn that cries 'chink chink' –
> A garden bird that warbles in the rain ...
>
> (*CP*, p. 106)

In 'Revisitation', written many years after Rivers's premature death in 1922, an event which would leave Sassoon devastated, he was also to emphasize Rivers's selflessness and ardour, endowing him with a saintliness the doctor himself would have found highly embarrassing. As Sassoon confided to Marsh, Craiglockhart, 'that horrible Hydro, ... would have been hell itself without [Rivers]', a statement he was to repeat to other friends.[30]

Rivers was no plaster saint, however. He had a well-developed sense of humour that saved him from being pompous, as well as endearing him to his new patient. In one of their first 'friendly confabulations', as Sassoon called his sessions with his psychiatrist, he asked Rivers whether he thought he *was* suffering from shell-shock, as the authorities claimed:

'Certainly not,' he replied.
'What *have* I got, then?'
'Well, you appear to be suffering from an anti-war complex.' We both of us laughed at that. Rivers never seemed elderly ...[31]

Rivers's case notes, the bulk of which appear to have been taken during his initial consultation with Sassoon on his first morning at Craiglockhart, make it clear that he was telling Sassoon the truth. After outlining his military career between August 1914 and July 1917 and giving a concise account of how Sassoon himself viewed his recent actions, his notes continue:

> The patient is a healthy-looking man of good physique. There are no physical signs of any disorder of the Nervous System. He discusses his recent actions and their motives in a perfectly intelligent and rational way, and there is no evidence of any excitement or depression. He recognises that his view of warfare is tinged by his feeling about the death of friends and of the men who were under his command in France. At the present time he lays special stress on the hopelessness of any decision in the War as it is now

being conducted, but he left out any reference to this aspect of his opinions in the statement which he sent to his Commanding Officer and which was read in the House of Commons. His view differs from that of the ordinary pacifist in that he would no longer object to the continuance of the War if he saw any reasonable prospect of a rapid decision.[32]

Was Rivers right to dismiss the notion of shell-shock in Sassoon's case? Both Eileen Showalter in her article on Rivers and Sassoon, 'The Inscription of Male Gender',[33] and Adrian Caesar in *Taking it Like a Man*, make cases for the possibility that Sassoon was indeed shell-shocked. Both refer to the nightmares and hallucinations he had experienced in April, common symptoms of shell-shock. Caesar also reminds his reader of a letter written the same month in which Sassoon had referred to being very near 'the snapping point' and the 'considerable mental anguish' shown in his diary entries for May.[34] By June and July, he argues, some of Sassoon's friends thought him mentally unstable, Graves and Ross among them. And a diary entry for 9 May 1918, referring to Rivers as 'the only man who can save me if I break down again' constitutes, Caesar believes, an admission by Sassoon of aberrant behaviour in July 1917. Showalter interprets his letter declaring the War a 'deliberately prolonged ... war of aggression and conquest' as a 'bizarre aberration from one whose daredevil valor in combat had earned him the nickname Mad Jack and won him the Military Cross'.[35]

There are, however, as many if not more signs that Sassoon's behaviour was the result of an almost too rational response to the hysteria of patriotism and war-mongering, not shell-shock. Quite apart from the fact that he had none of the physical symptoms of that condition, we have Rivers's expert opinion to that effect. Sassoon himself pointed to one of his most critical anti-war poems, 'The Rear-Guard', as a sign of his complete sanity in May 1917 and a letter to Ottoline, admitted by Caesar as 'conflicting evidence', has this to say:

> My doctor is a sensible man who doesn't say anything silly... But his arguments don't make any impression on me. He doesn't *pretend* that my nerves are wrong, but regards my attitude as abnormal. I do not know for how long he will go on trying to persuade me to modify my views.[36]

This, surely, is the letter of a man in a rational state of mind? He was certainly right to anticipate an attempt by Rivers to 'persuade' him to modify his views, an attempt which was to make him very miserable indeed.

For the first few weeks, however, Sassoon seems to have been relatively happy at Craiglockhart. Golfing by day and reading or, when possible, writing poetry at night, he managed for the most party to suppress memories of France and the Front. His thoughts turned to pre-war days, perhaps as a refuge, and in the third week of August he started to write a hunting poem, to his old friend Gordon Harbord. Ironically the poem had been started, without his knowing it, the day after Gordon's death. Writing to Ottoline on 5 September, to ask her forgiveness for not replying sooner, he told her:

I ... have been knocked flat once again by the best sporting friend I ever had getting killed on August 14 – in France. He was indeed my greatest friend before the war – a Winchester boy named Gordon Harbord, whom I met in 1908 and saw constantly afterwards.[37]

Sassoon had kept in touch with Gordon when he left Sussex in 1912 to become a 2nd Lieutenant in the Royal Field Artillery (RFA) and the letters had become more frequent once Gordon left England for France at the end of 1914.[38] Gordon sometimes copied his replies to Sassoon to his brother Geoffrey ('Geoff'), who was also friendly with Sassoon. The three of them were very different types, but they all shared a passion for hunting. (Writing to Sassoon from France in October 1916, when Sassoon was safe in England, Gordon argues: 'Of course the lists are bloody – and everyone at home is very uncomfortable, broke and miserable but if hunting is off ... one might just as well be out here'.[39]) Geoff, like Gordon, was in the RFA and remained quite near him in France until he was sent out to Mesopotamia with the Middle Eastern Force in 1916. He, too, reported to Sassoon in letters which are as 'horsey' and facetious as his brother's, a style Sassoon evidently appreciated and probably reciprocated.

One of Gordon's first letters from the Western Front in December 1914 refers to taking pot-shots at a German machine-gun post which he hopes will turn out to be 'the officers' latrine of the 26th Jaegers or 32nd Pants', a rather childish pun on 'Jaegers' as a type of long woollen underpants and 'Pants' perhaps for Panzers, the German for tanks. A more revealing letter from him a few months later informs Sassoon that Geoff is very disturbed by their brother Kenneth's marriage: 'he has written me earnest and pitiful appeals not to follow suit. So I've told him that if he'll take a pack, take me as joint-master and huntsman, and pay all expenses I'll be – well, I'll take such precautions as will prevent me from ever getting married –'.[40] The coy allusion here to castration and the attitude towards marriage are typical of the schoolboyish humour and suspicion of women they all shared.

In spite of their jokiness, however, both brothers were very serious when it came to fighting and as fearless in battle as on the hunting-field. By May 1915 Geoff had been wounded twice and by early 1917 Gordon, having gained promotion to Captain, then Adjutant, won an M.C. Each of them was prouder of the other than of himself. On one occasion, after hearing of a particularly brave action by Geoff, Gordon wrote to Sassoon in language reminiscent of the hunting field and their favourite writer,

14. Strange Meeting (July-November 1917)

Surtees: 'Of course a crammin' cock that can get a ruddy bad horse across a ruddy impossible countryside like he can is bound to do these great things'.[41] Geoff, too, in his bluff way, expressed his admiration – and fears – for his brother in August 1917, when Gordon was fighting at Ypres, the area to which Sassoon would have been sent had he returned to the 2nd RWF. The tone of the letter is perceptibly graver than earlier ones, reflecting his fully justified concern for his favourite brother:

> Just think of those sods throwing shells at old Gordon, the best-natured fellow in the world, who never did anybody any harm. What a truly amazing thing war is. I wish to God it was all over.

This letter, in which strong affection shows through the clichés, was written only the day before Gordon's death on 14 August. Another month was to elapse before Geoff, who evidently found it difficult to write in anything but a jokey way, managed to express his grief to Sassoon:

> ... it is an irreparable calamity to every soul who knew the old lad. I know you'll feel it a lot. He was awfully fond of you as you know and I think you were easily his best friend ... His last letter enclosed one of yours, both rhapsodising on hunting and talking about your [planned?] cottage at Milton. Can't write any more .. We shall never again meet such a sportsman with such an extraordinary personal charm and such a loveable old creature in every way.[42]

As Sassoon observed in his letter to Ottoline about Gordon's death: 'When the *un*intellectual people go it is much the worst – one feels they've so much to lose'. He might also have added, that when their unintellectual brother tries to express his feelings in words it is almost unbearably poignant. His one consolation, he told Edward Carpenter, was that Gordon 'died at once'.[43]

Sassoon had learnt of Gordon's death – sometime after his letter to Ottoline of 19 August but before 24 August when he completed a poem on the subject – possibly from *The Times*.[44] Writing to Dent on 29 August, he described himself as still being 'in a state of misery' about 'the greatest of my pre-war sporting friends'. Gordon's death momentarily roused him from an attempt to turn his back on the War and in his bitterness he reminded himself that the War was 'a sham and stinking lie'.[45] Since he had killed off his fictional version of Gordon ('Stephen Colwood') in November 1915, to express his grief at his brother Hamo's death (see p. 206), he would be unable to describe Gordon's death properly in *Sherston's Progress*, as he would otherwise have done.[46] And since there is no surviving diary for this period, the only detailed evidence of Sassoon's feelings comes from the three poems he wrote on the subject. The one written when he first heard the news, 'The Wooden Cross', is full of angry self-pity, self-dramatization and melodramatic phrases, as the opening shows:

My friends are dying young; while I remain,
Doomed to outlive these tragedies of pain ...[47]

The most successful of the six stanzas is the last, based on Sassoon's final
view of Gordon and their shared passion for fox-hunting:

... Only I hoard the hours we spent together
Ranging brown Sussex woods in wintry weather,
Till, blotting out today, I half-believe
That I shall find you home again on leave,
As I last saw you, riding down the lane,
And lost in lowering dusk and drizzling rain,
Contented with the hunt we'd had, and then
Sad lest we'd never ride a hunt again.

Sassoon's second attempt to write about Gordon's death, 'The Investiture', reverts to the same shared love of hunting. Though better digested,
it is still not entirely successful and was to appear only in the *Cambridge
Magazine* (3 November 1917). 'God with a Roll of Honour in His hand / Sits
welcoming the heroes who have died', but Gordon, one of those 'heroes', is
made to feel homesick for the hunting-field:

If I were [there the narrator assures his dead friend]
we'd snowball Death with skulls;
Or ride away to hunt in Devil's Wood
With ghosts of puppies that we walked of old ...[48]

The same nostalgia for what they both regarded as the true heaven, also
informs the last, and most successful, of the three poems on Gordon,
'Together', which Sassoon did allow into his *Collected Poems*. Its success
may partly be explained by the fact that, unlike the first two, it would be
written after a fresh experience of hunting, which Sassoon took up again
in December 1917, the month he composed the poem.[49] The fact that it was
with Gordon's own hunt, the Southdown, helps explain the form the poem
took. Stripped of the melodrama and rhetoric of 'A Wooden Cross' and the
rather elaborate conceit of 'The Investiture', it is a simple account of the
way hunting brought back the reality of Gordon to Sassoon:

Together
Splashing along the boggy woods all day,
And over brambled hedge and holding clay,
I shall not think of him:
But when the watery fields grow brown and dim,
And hounds have lost their fox, and horses tire,
I know that he'll be with me on my way
Home through the darkness to the evening fire ...
(CP, pp. 95-6)

14. Strange Meeting (July-November 1917)

Gordon's death left an emotional void in Sassoon's life and he was glad to welcome a new friend into it the same month. For it was in August that his celebrated relationship with Wilfred Owen began.

When Sassoon and Owen first met, on 18 August, however, Sassoon was still unaware of Gordon's death and his reception of Owen, while cordial, was hardly warm. Owen, who had arrived at Craiglockhart nearly a month before him, had waited another three weeks before daring to knock on his door. The reason for his visit, he explained, was the hope that Sassoon would be kind enough to sign copies of *The Old Huntsman* for himself and a few friends. Sassoon, who had been sitting on his bed cleaning his golf clubs, was naturally flattered and chatted with his reticent visitor as he signed, ending with a fairly lengthy explanation of his motives in writing the poems. It was only as he was showing his visitor to the door than Owen confessed, rather diffidently, to being a poet himself. 'It amused me to remember', Sassoon wrote retrospectively, 'that I wondered whether his poems were any good!'[50]

There are a number of other possible explanations for Sassoon's slight condescension towards Owen at this first meeting. Sassoon was six and a half years Owen's senior, though he looked to Owen the same age as himself, that is just under twenty-five. He was also physically more imposing; over six feet tall, his lean figure literally looked down on Owen's stockier 5 feet, 5½ inches. He also impressed Owen as 'stately' and 'noble-looking' with 'a fine, firm chisel'd ... head'.[51] After their second meeting on 21 August, when Owen took some of his poems to show Sassoon at his suggestion, he detected a general expression of boredom on Sassoon's face which added to the sense of haughtiness he conveyed. As their contact rapidly grew to almost nightly meetings the bored expression was to give way to something far more animated as Sassoon became increasingly interested in and admiring of Owen.

At their first meeting, however, Sassoon freely admitted that he had felt somewhat superior to Owen, who had struck him as a 'rather ordinary young man, perceptibly provincial, though unobtrusively ardent in his responses to my lordly dictums about poetry'.[52] His own social standing, though relatively obscure by comparison with his rich and titled Sassoon relatives, had given him the confidence to dismiss Owen as 'provincial'. It was a subject on which Owen felt particularly sensitive. Though his mother's family had had money and a certain position in society, his father, as a poorly-paid railway clerk, was on the lowest rung of the middle-class ladder, and Wilfred's childhood had been passed against a background of struggle to maintain respectability. Without money to pay for a 'good' education, he had had to attend local schools (the Birkenhead Institute, followed by Shrewsbury Technical School) while secretly longing for a public school. He had also dreamed of Oxford, but had failed even to win a scholarship to Reading University. Sassoon, on the other hand, had been to Marlborough and Cambridge and, though not very successful at either, the experience had certainly added to his social confidence.

It was not surprising, then, that at their first meeting Owen's manners should have struck Sassoon as 'modest and ingratiating', 'he stood at my elbow, rather as though conferring with a superior officer'. Since they were both somewhat snobbish, these social differences gave Sassoon an initial advantage. He vigorously rejected Owen's later suggestion that he was Don Quixote to Owen's Sancho Panza, but he undoubtedly looked down on him, at least to begin with. When Stephen Spender later asked him what Owen was like, Sassoon replied 'He was embarrassing. He had a Grammar School accent'.[53] The remark may have been a reaction to Spender's desire to know about Owen rather than himself, but it is significant that he could make it at all.

Psychologically Sassoon also had the advantage of Owen. While the latter still stammered slightly and continued to suffer bad dreams, both results of the shell-shock for which he was being treated, Sassoon showed no sign of that condition, as Rivers had noted. More importantly, Owen still felt himself under suspicion of cowardice for his inability to deal with his traumatic experiences at the Front, whereas Sassoon had already won an M.C. for his courage under fire and was widely known as a fearless 'Mad Jack', a nickname Owen himself was to use of him.[54]

By far the most important reason for Sassoon's initial condescension, however, must have been his established reputation as a poet and Owen's complete obscurity at that time. Even before the numerous reviews of *The Old Huntsman* had appeared, Sassoon's contacts in the literary world had enabled him to place most of his work in reputable papers, and his name was already familiar to the reading public. Owen, on the other hand, had had no publications at all and felt understandably humble in the company of a poet whom he admired greatly. (It was the reason he had delayed three weeks before approaching 'the great man'.[55]) While determined to succeed as a poet, he believed that he had written only three lines which 'carr[ied] the stamp of maturity' by the time he met Sassoon in August 1917.[56] His praise of Sassoon's work, particularly in a letter written to his mother on 15 August 1917, three days before their first meeting, shows which aspects of it he admired most:

> I have just been reading Siegfried Sassoon, and am feeling at a very high pitch of emotion. Nothing like his trench life sketches has ever been written or ever will be written. Shakespeare reads vapid after these. Not of course because Sassoon is a greater artist, but because of the subjects, I mean, I think if I had the choice of making friends with Tennyson or with Sassoon, I should go to Sassoon.[57]

It was this aspect of Sassoon's poetry, his choice of subject matter and the adjustment of language required by that choice, which was to influence Owen's own work profoundly.

14. Strange Meeting (July-November 1917)

Owen's reference to Tennyson in relation to Sassoon indicates the kind of poetry he had been writing up to August 1917. Like Sassoon he had grown up on a diet of mainly Romantics and Pre-Raphaelites and his style when he met Sassoon was not unlike Sassoon's Swinburnian cadences before the War. 'We have followed parallel trenches all our lives', he told his mother, 'and have more friends in common, authors I mean, than most people can boast of in a lifetime'.[58] Only recently Owen had started a pseudo-medieval ballad of which Sassoon would probably have approved before his own dramatic change of technique. But when it was shown to him at their second meeting, with other poems, he preferred Owen's 'Song of Songs', which he admired for its simple lyricism and dextrous play with words and sounds:

> Sing me at morn but only with your laugh;
> Even as Spring that laugheth into leaf;
> Even as Love that laugheth after Life.

It was almost certainly this common ground, their shared love of the lyrical, which enabled Owen to take the leap he did under Sassoon's influence.

'The Death-Bed', for example, which he thought Sassoon's finest poem, offered him lyricism while also making the kind of statement he too wanted to make about the War. Though Owen was not a pacifist, he was very critical of the conduct of the War and particularly moved, as was Sassoon, by the suffering of his men at the Front. Under Sassoon's influence his attitude was to harden noticeably. (This may have been encouraged by Sassoon's suggestion that he read Barbusse's savage anti-war book, *Under Fire*.) 'The Redeemer' with its blend of lyricism and anger and its haunting refrain, 'I say that he was Christ', struck Owen as the poem he had been 'wishing to write every week for the last three years'.[59]

It was, however, Sassoon's starkly realistic trench-life sketches, such as 'The General' and 'They', which Owen tried initially to copy, their second meeting stimulating him to write his own satire, 'The Dead-Beat'. (Was this a typical word play on 'The Death-Bed'?) Sassoon approved of the opening and closing stanzas which in strong contrast to Owen's previous war poetry, could well have been written by himself:

> He dropped, more sullenly than wearily,
>   Became a lump of stench, a clot of meat,
>   And none of us could kick him to his feet.
> He blinked at my revolver, blearily ...
>
> I've sent him down at last, he seemed so bad,
>   Although a strongish chap and quite unhurt.
>   Next day I heard the Doc's fat laugh: 'That dirt
> You sent me down last night has died. So glad!'[60]

But the highly facetious middle three stanzas seemed to Sassoon 'out of keeping' with the rest.[61] Though Owen worked on the poem, it never really succeeded. Nor did any other of his attempts to copy Sassoon's methods slavishly, as 'The Letter', with its self-consciously colloquial language ('Yer ruddy cow!') demonstrates. It was only when he had fully absorbed Sassoon's subject matter and technique and adapted it to his own genius that the full benefit of his influence would be felt.

The first real sign Sassoon had that his 'little friend was much more than the promising minor poet [he] had initially adjudged him to be'[62] was when, some time towards the end of September, he brought him the sonnet which was to become 'Anthem for Doomed Youth'. Even then, Owen felt in need of Sassoon's help in perfecting it and it must have pleased Sassoon greatly in later life to think that he had been responsible for some of its more exquisite touches. The title itself, for example, is almost solely due to Sassoon. Under his guidance too 'Only the solemn / Monstrous anger of our guns' became 'Only the monstrous anger of the guns' and the 'tenderness of silent / Sweet white minds' in Owen's fourth draft became the memorable 'tenderness of patient minds'.[63] Owen was grateful for these and other suggestions and adopted nearly all of them, in contrast to his response to Robert Graves a few weeks later. (Graves was to visit Sassoon at Craiglockhart in mid-October, when he was introduced to Owen and shown his 'Disabled', which he then proceeded to correct with his usual aplomb. Owen was to ignore all his suggestions save one.)

Sassoon later dismissed his contributions to 'Anthem' as 'slight'.[64] Even at the time, in spite of difficulties of judging manuscript poems which, as he pointed out, could be 'deceptive when handed to one like school exercises to be blue-pencilled',[65] he had realized that Owen's verse 'with its sumptuous epithets and large-scale imagery, its noble naturalness and depth of meaning, had impressive affinities with Keats'. He was the first to recognize Owen's true potential and the most important catalyst in helping him to realize it.

Between the first poem written under his spell, 'Dead-Beat', and his discharge from Craiglockhart at the end of October 1917, Owen drafted over a dozen poems, at least four of which were among his best work. Sassoon was proud of his influence, particularly since he was inclined to think Owen the superior poet of the two in later years. When responding to D.J. Enright's letter about his war poetry on 23 November 1960, for example, he hoped that Enright had 'indicated that the essence of my war poems was fellow feeling for the troops, whose sufferings were so remote from the comprehension of many civilians. In this I was one with Wilfred Owen, though on a lower plane of poetic expression'.[66]

In thinking of Sassoon's relationship with Owen it is easy to overlook the fact that the traffic was not all one way. Sassoon, too, benefited from the extraordinary coincidence of their meeting at Craiglockhart, just as he had profited from his chance encounter with Graves in France.[67] While *his* influence on Owen's poetry has been frequently cited, Owen's on his is rarely mentioned. Yet not only did Owen's comments hearten and help him, as Sassoon acknowledged, but his method of approach began gradually to change his own. 'To remind people of [War's] realities was still my main purpose', he would write in summer 1918, 'but I now preferred to depict it impersonally, and to be as much "above the battle" as I could. Unconsciously, I was getting nearer to Wilfred Owen's method of approach'.[68] The beginnings of this change can be seen at Craiglockhart.

There was, of course, common ground between them, which explains Sassoon's praise of Owen's 'Song of Songs'. It also helps to explain why Owen asked if he could publish the first poem Sassoon wrote at Craiglockhart, 'Dreamers', in the hospital magazine. Owen had taken over the editorship of *The Hydra*, as it was called, in mid-July,[69] and he was delighted to think he might be able to publish a poem by his hero in the fortnightly paper. Sassoon agreed to this, but insisted that Owen also included his own 'Song of Songs'. The unassuming editor did so, but reluctantly and anonymously, and the two of them appeared in print together on 1 September. Rarely can a hospital magazine have witnessed such an august literary event. (Later on Sassoon would try to help Owen 'put some life into' the magazine by writing to influential friends like Wells, Bennett and Drinkwater for contributions to the October anniversary issue.)[69a]

Like two of the three other poems Sassoon allowed Owen to publish in *The Hydra*, 'Dreamers' shows affinities with Owen's technique. Reading his 'sumptuous epithets' and 'large-scale songs' had given Sassoon a renewed appreciation of verbal patterning and music. This is particularly noticeable in the opening octet of the sonnet:

> Soldiers are citizens of death's grey land,
>> Drawing no dividend from time's tomorrows.
> In the great hour of destiny they stand,
>> Each with his feuds, and jealousies, and sorrows.
> Soldiers are sworn to action; they must win
>> Some flaming, fatal climax with their lives.
> Soldiers are dreamers; when the guns begin
>> They think of firelit homes, clean beds and wives.
>>> (*CP*, pp. 71-2)

The final sestet, however, reverts to Sassoon's fiercer manner in which the use of the first person narrator, harsh details of trench conditions and mundane details of everyday life prevent the reader from losing sight of the reality of War:

> I see them in foul dug-outs, gnawed by rats,
>> And in the ruined trenches, lashed with rain,

Dreaming of things they did with balls and bats,
  And mocked by hopeless longing to regain
Bank-holidays, and picture-shows, and spats,
  And going to the office in the train.

The mixing of the two styles is not entirely successful, though 'Dreamers' became one of Sassoon's most anthologized poems, and this may have prompted him to concentrate on what he, as well as Owen, believed he could do best, trench-life sketches. For his next twelve poems, with one or two exceptions, are in his most sardonic manner. They range from a description of a wiring party by a callous officer, which ends:

Young Hughes was badly hit; I heard him carried away
Moaning at every lurch; no doubt he'll die today.
But *we* can say the front-line wire's been safely mended.[70]

and an equally unfeeling report on 'How to Die',[71] to what feels like a less successful version of 'Base Details', 'The Fathers'. In this two non-combatants discuss their soldier sons' fates – 'But Arthur's getting all the fun / At Arras with his nine-inch gun' – and the narrator concludes bitterly:

I watched them toddle through the door –
Those impotent old friends of mine.[72]

The last line, Sassoon admitted, was written in 'sheer temper'[73] and caused consternation when he submitted it to the *Cambridge Magazine*. These attacks on callous officers, self-righteous Christians and complacent non-combatants are all familiar themes. So too is a more successful assault on journalists and M.P.s, which Rivers thought 'very dangerous'[74]:

Fight to a Finish
The boys came back. Bands played and flags were flying,
  And Yellow-Pressmen thronged the sunlit street
To cheer the soldiers who'd refrained from dying,
  And hear the music of returning feet.
'Of all the thrills and ardours War has brought,
  This moment is the finest.' (So they thought.)

Snapping their bayonets on to charge the mob,
  Grim Fusiliers broke ranks with glint of steel,
At last the boys had found a cushy job.

I heard the Yellow-Pressmen grunt and squeal;
  And with my trusty bombers turned and went
To clear those Junkers* out of Parliament.

(*CP*, p. 77)

---

*The original meaning of 'Junker' is 'young German aristocrat', but here it is clearly meant to imply a militarist.

'Fight to a Finish', an allusion to Lloyd-George's famous phrase, epitomizes both the strengths and limitations of Sassoon's satires. Its initial impact is considerable, the scene is deftly portrayed and the language subtly modulated, ranging from simple colloquialism to heavy irony. The weak point of such a poem, however, is its obsessive tone which inevitably becomes less forceful with repetition and the passage of time. Sassoon himself thought it 'fairly effective in its way'.[75]

Nowhere is this obsessiveness more clearly seen than in two other poems written at Craiglockhart, 'The Glory of Women' and 'Their Frailty'. What, if anything, provoked the virulence of the pieces, especially the former, remains uncertain. The fact that the narrator of 'The Glory of Women' feels sympathy for the 'German mother dreaming by the fire', unaware that, while she knits her son socks, his face 'is trodden deeper in the mud', suggests that Sassoon's scorn was not provoked by all women. He seems to have been thinking of women who visited him admiringly in hospital, or remembering the vacuous visitors to Lady Brassey's teas. And his increasing closeness to Owen, who shared his distrust of most women, with the exception of his mother, may have stirred up his own latent hostility.

There are passages in letters to another homosexual friend, Meiklejohn, at this time which suggest other possible reasons for Sassoon's antagonism toward the sex. In them he refers to meeting 'soldiers in the gorse with trollopes' and the 'embarrassment of disturbing amorous soldiers and their doxies among the ferns'. He also refers pityingly to a 'fond lady', who has written to him on his birthday and wants to see him when she comes to Edinburgh, and concludes: 'I wish I could find a charming young fox-hunting squire for her, poor dear'. Whatever the reasons for his hostility, it did not make for satisfactory poetry, mainly because his accusations, based on enormous generalizations, are so blatantly unfair:

> You love us when we're heroes, home on leave,
> Or wounded in a mentionable place.
> You worship decorations; you believe
> That chivalry redeems the war's disgrace.
> You make us shells. You listen with delight,
> By tales of dirt and danger fondly thrilled.
> You crown our distant ardours while we fight,
> And mourn our laurelled memories when we're killed ...
>
> (*CP*, p. 79)

Women here are portrayed as wide-eyed, coy, sadistic and empty-headed, generalizations which are also found in 'Their Frailty', though the tone is not quite so scornful:

> ... Husbands and sons and lovers; everywhere
> They die; War bleeds us white

Mothers and wives and sweethearts, – they don't care
So long as He's all right.

(CP, p. 80)

Sassoon thought 'The Glory of Women' a *'very good* sonnet'[76] and if, as he argued, its purpose was to 'give [women] beans' it certainly achieved its aim.

Yet the success of Sassoon's satires usually depends on his ability to avoid generalizations. Instead he sketches in a specific situation or scene, a character or two and some snatches of actual speech. The failure of 'The Glory of Women' and 'Their Frailty' can be partly explained by his failure to follow the usual practice, perhaps because he was unable to distance himself sufficiently from the subject. Whereas the most successful satire in this group, 'Does It Matter?', gives us three clear-cut situations – a soldier who has lost his legs, another his sight and a third his senses – sets each briefly in a vivid scene and throws in a few clichés to highlight the inadequacy of the average person's response to such tragedies. This poem was almost certainly Sassoon's own response, in the first instance, to at least two specific events, as well as his own fear of being blinded. The first was Ralph Greaves's loss of an arm, which Sassoon reported to Ross on 25 September 1917 shortly before 'Does It Matter?' was written, an irony he must have had in mind when he portrayed another amputee in the first stanza, a keen huntsman who has lost his legs. The second was the news that Julian Dadd, who had lost both his brothers in the War as well as his voice, had suffered a mental breakdown. (Sassoon also reported this to Ross, on 17 September 1917.) He was probably also thinking of the haunted patients of Craiglockhart when he referred to 'those dreams from the pit' in stanza three:

Does it matter? – losing your legs? …
For people will always be kind,
And you need not show that you mind
When the others come in after hunting
To gobble their muffins and eggs.

Does it matter? – losing your sight? …
There's such splendid work for the blind;
And people will always be kind,
As you sit on the terrace remembering
And turning your face to the light.

Do they matter? – those dreams from the pit? …
You can drink and forget and be glad,
And people won't say that you're mad;
For they'll know you've fought for your country
And no-one will worry a bit.

(CP, pp. 76-7)

Each of these three stanzas starts with a similar question, followed by an obviously unsatisfactory answer. Each has five lines, with the regular masculine-ended lines of the quatrain interrupted by a longer, unrhymed line. This longer line, with its less certain, feminine ending, introduces a note of doubt and nostalgia into the poem ('As you sit on the terrace remembering'), undercutting the certainty and insensitivity of the speaker. Such patterning sets up certain expectations and the questions themselves touch on situations so distressing – amputation, blindness, madness – that the speaker is condemned out of his own mouth for even asking if they matter.

The effect is to alienate the reader, who is nevertheless unwillingly drawn into the poem by those same rhetorical questions. The reader's shock at the speaker's callous and inadequate response in the second line of each verse provokes the outraged indignation Sassoon aims to elicit from complacent civilians. A similar effect is achieved by the irony of the final line which, though said ostensibly to reassure the man who has gone mad, underlines a general lack of concern for the victims. It is just possible that another heavily ironic line in the poem – 'They'll know that you've fought for your country' – influenced Owen when he came to write 'Dulce et Decorum Est' a few weeks later, though he brands it more straightforwardly 'the old lie'. During the same period Owen produced another poem which suggests the influence of 'Does It Matter?', at least in subject matter, 'Disabled'. Whilst he explores in depth the suffering of his amputee, however, Sassoon makes his treatment an excuse for another attack on civilian callousness.

Despite their different approaches, perhaps even because of them, Sassoon and Owen were to grow increasingly close during the two and a half months they spent together. Owen dated the start of this, for him, as mid-September: while Sassoon still regarded him as 'a tiresome little knocker on [his] door' at that time, he had begun to regard Sassoon 'as Keats & Christ & Elijah & my Colonel & my father-confessor & Amenophis IV in profile'.[77] In other words, as he put it to his mother, he had started to admire Sassoon not only as a poet, but also 'as a man, as a friend'.[78] That phrase was written on 11 or 12 September and it is likely that the change had occurred a few days earlier on 7 September, when Sassoon had called Owen to his room.

After criticizing some of his poems, amending others and praising a few, Sassoon did him what Owen considered the great honour of reading him his latest works, one of which struck Owen as 'the most exquisitely painful war poem of any language or time'.[79] 'I don't tell him so', Owen added for his mother's benefit, 'or that I am not worthy to light his pipe ... No wonder I was happy last night'. The evening had ended with Sassoon inviting Owen to lunch at his golf club the next day, followed by tea at the Astronomer Royal's house in the Observatory.

Though Owen waited until after he left Craiglockhart to tell Sassoon how he worshipped him, it is clear that he had done so even before they met. It is also highly likely that at his first sight of Sassoon, sitting on his bed in a purplish-blue dressing-gown, his hero-worship had tipped over into romantic love. Certainly he was to regard that first meeting as an epoch in his life, and to replay the scene frequently in his head, as lovers do. Writing to Sassoon from Scarborough on 27 November 1917 he tells him: 'We have had some strong sunshine; and when it strikes anything blue I see you sitting by the bedside as on That Morning in September'.[80]

When, towards the end of October, he spent a whole day with Sassoon, sharing breakfast, lunch, tea and dinner with him, he enjoyed himself so much that he failed for once to write to his mother. And when he heard, the morning after, that he was to have a Medical Board the following Tuesday (30 October), he told her that he was 'rather upset about it' because he was 'so happy with Sassoon'.[81] In the same letter, whilst reassuring his mother of her power over him, he refers to 'all the charm of Edinburgh, and all the love that it has thrown about me'. Though the 'love' is unlikely to refer only to Sassoon, it undoubtedly included him in a very special way. The fact that Sassoon destroyed some of Owen's letters, which he had initially promised to show Harold Owen, suggests that there may have been something compromising in them, something at any rate which Sassoon considered very private.[82]

It is less easy to say exactly how Sassoon felt about Owen, since he was not so effusive about his feelings as the younger man. Writing to his mother in early September, Owen reports that, while his 'friend' is 'intensely sympathetic' with him about 'every vital question on the planet or off it, [he] keeps all effusiveness strictly within his pages. In this he is so eminently *English*'.[83] He tells Sassoon himself that he wishes he 'were less undemonstrative, for I have many adjectives with which to qualify myself. As it is I can only say I am / Your proud friend / Owen'.[84]

It was not just a difference of temperament: by Sassoon's own admission it took him longer to appreciate Owen than vice versa. As the older, more confident, more successful of the two, he only slowly realized that 'he could give me as much as I gave him'.[85] Though his appreciation of Owen's poetry came fairly early, his personal appreciation of the man started a full month after Owen's, that is half-way through October. (He attributed this to the fact that he had by then achieved a room of his own, which meant that their talks 'were no longer liable to be obstructed by the presence of a fellow patient'.[86]) And while there are many signs of his appreciation of Owen's qualities – his 'unassumingness', his 'selflessness', his far more 'compact and coherent personality' and particularly of his 'beautifully sympathetic nature' at a time when he badly needed support – there is not the same suggestion of romantic attachment as there is with Owen. His reference to Owen's 'calm velvety voice' in *Siegfried's Journey* sounds a slightly romantic note, but his description of Owen's other physical attributes seems too detached to be that of someone in love:

He wasn't a fine-drawn type. There was a full-blooded robustness about him which implied reserves of mental energy and solid ability. Under ordinary conditions it wasn't a spiritual face. It was of the mould which either coarsens or refines itself in later life. I cannot say that I ever saw what is called 'a look of genius' in it. His mouth was resolute and humorous, his eyes long and heavy-lidded, quiescent rather than penetrating. They were somewhat sleepy eyes, kind, shrewd, and seldom lit up from within. They seemed, like much else in his personality, to be instinctively guarding the secret sources of his inward power and integrity.[87]

For the most part Sassoon's appreciation reads like that of one fellow-poet for another. Though he missed Owen after his departure, he did not write to him nearly as often as Owen wrote to him. They would both certainly have understood each other's sexual preferences, but in Sassoon's case at least those tastes seem not to be engaged by his new friend. I cannot therefore agree with the claim made by one critic: 'My guess is that Owen fell head over heels in love with Sassoon, but Sassoon wouldn't let himself fall in love with Owen, then came to regret it'.[88] It may be that after losing first David Thomas, then more recently Gordon Harbord, Sassoon simply could not allow himself to feel deeply about Owen. At the same time it is likely that he found Owen something of an emotional substitute for Gordon. Years later, in 1954, he was to dream that Owen had come back and that he was very 'happy at his return and taking charge of him'.[89] That 'taking charge of him' is significant, for it was as a mentor rather than a lover that he saw himself in relation to Owen.

However he perceived himself, Sassoon was not invariably mentor in their relationship, as I have indicated. While pursuing a mainly satiric line during his first few months at Craiglockhart, for example, he experimented with two poems which show the effect Owen was having on his technique. 'Sick Leave' and 'Attack', both written by mid-October, differ significantly from the other poems of this period.[90] Both thirteen lines long, they leave the reader with a sense of something unfinished, perhaps because of an unfulfilled expectation of a completed sonnet. 'Sick Leave' deals with a subject Sassoon had already touched on at Craiglockhart, dreams, and heralds his growing unease at his own comfortable, relatively contented existence at Craiglockhart. Reminded of the battlefield by the 'bellow ... drone and rumble' of a midnight storm, the narrator dreams of his men, some of them dead:

> They whisper to my heart; their thoughts are mine.
> 'Why are you here with all your watches ended?
> From Ypres to Frise we sought you in the Line.'
> (*CP*, p. 85)

In 'bitter safety', the narrator wakes up, 'unfriended', made conscious by the 'slashing rain', which follows the storm, of 'the Battalion in the mud'. (Both the 1st and 2nd RWF were near Ypres at this time.) The poem ends with the voices of the dead, quite different from the harsh colloquial tones of previous poems:

> 'When are you going out to them again?
> Are they not still your brothers through our blood?'

It is clearly the voice of Sassoon's uneasy conscience which speaks.

Sassoon said that the second of these two poems, 'Attack', was based on a note made in his diary while observing the Hindenburg Line attack; it is quite likely that it was something he had also dreamt about at Craiglockhart as his thoughts turned increasingly to the men he felt he had abandoned. The note itself shows how useful Sassoon found his diary entries in recalling details of trench-life:

> On April 14 the 19th Brigade attacked at 5.30 am. I looked across at the hill where a round red sun was coming up. The hill was deeply shadowed and grey-blue, and all the country was full of shell-flashes and drifting smoke. A battle picture.[91]

Sassoon's painter's eye has already noted the telling details of shape and colour, light and shade. In converting it to poetry he fills in his picture with other details – tanks, shovels, the noise of the barrage – and humanizes the scene by conveying vividly what he so clearly remembered, the fear of going into battle. His usual irony is missing, though the poem does end with one of his typical soldier's curses. Masefield considered it Sassoon's 'best war-poem'[92]:

> At dawn the ridge emerges massed and dun
> In wild purple of the glow'ring sun,
> Smouldering through spouts of drifting smoke that shroud
> The menacing scarred slope; and, one by one,
> Tanks creep and topple forward to the wire.
> The barrage roars and lifts. Then, clumsily bowed
> With bombs and guns and shovels and battle-gear,
> Men jostle and climb to meet the bristling fire.
> Lines of grey, muttering faces, masked with fear,
> They leave their trenches, going over the top,
> While time ticks blank and busy on their wrists,
> And hope, with furtive eyes and grappling fists,
> Flounders in mud. O Jesus, make it stop!

> (*CP*, p. 71)

With its abundant imagery, alliterative and assonanced patterning, personification and elaborate rhyme-scheme, 'Attack' is nearer to Owen's than Sassoon's technique at this time. The same is also true of 'Thrushes', which suggests that Sassoon was not entirely preoccupied with the War at Craiglockhart.[93]

Indeed it would have been difficult for Sassoon to remain angry all the time. Unlike regimental life, he was under no one's orders at the hospital. Instead of the hectic duties of a platoon commander, he enjoyed a daily round of leisurely golf. Whatever his initial inclinations had been, by mid-October he had also begun to build up a social life in Edinburgh. Thanks to his friends' efforts he had met Herbert Grierson, Professor of English Literature at Edinburgh University, had had tea with its rector, Sir A. Ewing and lunch with the Astronomer Royal of Scotland, R.A. Sampson, at the nearby Observatory.[94] Lady Margaret Sackville,[95] a minor poet in her own right and daughter of the 3rd Earl de la Warr, had also invited him to lunch.[96] Though he suspected her verse was 'fairly rotten', Sassoon was intrigued: 'A rival to Lady Ottoline', he joked with Ross 'and quite ten years younger!'[97] More to his taste was the occasional dinner out with Wilfred Owen, or a meal at the Scottish Conservative Club, of which Rivers had made him a temporary member. Sassoon, who used its headed writing paper, had altered it to read:

> 'I am *not* SCOTTISH
> or CONSERVATIVE [CLUB, crossed out] thank God'

But he enjoyed its facilities. Free to come and go as he chose, he sometimes took day-trips to places like North Berwick or Glasgow.

Sassoon also had visitors, Meiklejohn making the long journey north to see him in mid-September and Graves returning for his second visit in mid-October. (On the latter occasion Owen remembered being sent to meet 'the big, rather plain fellow' at Waverley Station because 'nothing could keep [Sassoon] from his morning's golf'.[98] Graves seemed to Owen 'the last man on earth apparently capable of the extraordinary, delicate fancies in his books'.) Sassoon wrote frequently to both Meiklejohn and Graves before and after their respective visits, as well as to other friends. Apart from Ottoline and Ross he wrote most often to 'Theo' Bartholomew, the Cambridge University librarian who helped him with his contributions to the *Cambridge Magazine*, to which he was still submitting on average one poem a week. (He would get to know Bartholomew even better later on and be introduced to his great friend 'Enrico', Henry Festing-Jones after the War.) He also kept in touch with Dent, who had probably introduced him to Bartholomew at Cambridge, and who was now anxious to put him in touch with another young man, Gabriel Atkin, a soldier stationed at Margate.

One unexpected source of amusement for Sassoon at Craiglockhart, were his fellow-patients. While he avoided making fun of the really severe cases, he derived some entertainment from the more mildly afflicted. His second room-mate, who came to replace the young Scots captain, was particularly good value, if *Sherston's Progress* is to be believed. A tall, handsome man with iron-grey hair and a monocle, the 'Theosophist', as Sassoon dubbed him, was outwardly quite normal. It was only when he opened his mouth that his dottiness became apparent. In a good mood he would address Sassoon in stilted language reminiscent of Shakespeare or Rider Haggard. If Sassoon complained that the rattling bedroom window was enough to keep one awake all night, for example, he might respond: 'True, O King', or 'Thou hast uttered wise words, O great white chief'. When Sassoon grumbled about the War and the general state of society one evening, his companion reassured him that we were 'all only on the great stairway which conducts us to higher planes of existence'. When Sassoon then asked him what he thought about 'conscripted populations slaughtering each other' on the aforesaid 'great stairway', he simply replied, 'Ah, that is the Celestial Surgeon at work upon humanity'. In the unusual event that Sassoon managed to floor him with some particularly irreverent repartee, the Theosophist would retire into a dignified silence, studying his teeth intently in the shaving-mirror. Sassoon's apology would almost inevitably follow and be graciously received.

In spite of such distractions there were still times at Craiglockhart when life at the Front seemed more real to Sassoon than his daily existence. When this happened he turned to his safety-valve, poetry, to express his frustration and guilt. Having his own room had made writing easier and the three poems which followed this luxury are more developed than his earlier satires. Owen may also have inadvertently influenced him in that direction by choosing Sassoon's longer, narrative poem, 'The Rear-Guard', for his second publication in *The Hydra*.[99] Nostalgia is the keynote of 'Break of Day', where the narrator, waking at dawn on a cold autumnal morning in the trenches, retreats into a dream of happier autumn days on the hunting-field:

> ... Beyond the brambled fences where he goes
> Are glimmering fields with harvest piled in sheaves,
> And tree-tops dark against the stars grown pale;
> Then, clear and shrill, a distant farm-cock crows;
> And there's a wall of mist along the vale
> Where willows shake their watery-sounding leaves,
> He gazes on it all, and scarce believes
> That earth is telling its old peaceful tale;
> He thanks the blessed world that he was born ...
> Then, far away, a lonely note of the horn ...
>
> (*CP*, pp. 82-3)

Autumn at Craiglockhart had clearly brought back memories of an activity which was always to epitomize for Sassoon the innocence of youth and the freshness and purity of nature, hunting. By juxtaposing it to the 'hell' of the narrator's 'dark, musty' dug-out and the 'outcast immolation'

of the doomed men in trenches waiting for a hopeless attack, he emphasizes the foulness of War. While the narrator experiences the 'clean' thrill
of past autumn dawns in his poetic daydream, in the trench the soldiers
are 'far from clean things', both activities being drawn together by the
sound of the horn or bugle. It is a skilful adaptation of a theme he had
always favoured, dawn.

The second of these longer poems, 'Prelude: the Troops', is also nostalgic, but for 'the troops' rather than the hunting-field. Dominic Hibberd
believes that Owen was referring to the last stanza of this poem when he
described having Sassoon read him 'the most exquisitely painful war poem
of any language or time'. The aptness of the description is undeniable,
although the dates do not tally exactly.[100] It is certainly the nearest
Sassoon ever came to Owen in technique, particularly in the last line,
where the phrase 'the unreturning army' brings to mind both Owen's title
'The Unreturning' and his alternative sestet to 'Happiness' which opens:
'But the old Happiness is unreturning'.

Like Sassoon's poem too, 'Happiness' concentrates on the 'boys' who
were sent to war. The influence of Walt Whitman, another admirer of
'boys' and 'comrades', is also evident in the exclamatory opening line of
Sassoon's last stanza: 'O My brave brown companions'. It is an unashamedly Romantic poem, almost certainly drawing on Keats, not only for its
blank verse and verbal music, but also for what Edmund Blunden called
its 'Greek drama beginning',[101] which echoes Keats's moving description of
the fallen gods at the start of *Hyperion*:

> Dim, gradual thinning of the shapeless gloom
> Shudders to drizzling daybreak that reveals
> Disconsolate men who stamp their sodden boots
> And turn dulled, sunken faces to the sky
> Haggard and hopeless. They, who have beaten down
> The stale despair of night, must now renew
> Their desolation in the truce of dawn,
> Murdering the livid hours that grope for peace.
>
> Yet these, who cling to life with stubborn hands,
> Can grin through storms of death and find a gap
> In the clawed, cruel tangles of his defence.
> They march from safety, and the bird-sung joy
> Of grass-green thickets, to the land where all
> Is ruin, and nothing blossoms but the sky
> That hastens over them where they endure
> Sad, smoking, flat horizons, reeking woods,
> And foundered trench-lines volleying doom for doom.
>
> O my brave brown companions, when your souls
> Flock silently away, and the eyeless dead
> Shame the wild beast of battle on the ridge,
> Death will stand grieving in that field of war

Since your unvanquished hardihood is spent.
And through some mooned Valhalla there will pass
Battalions and battalions, scarred from hell;
The unreturning army that was youth;
The legions who have suffered and are dust.

(*CP*, p. 67)

This may, as Adrian Caesar claims, be a 'consolatory Romanticism',[102] but it seems to have been one which both Sassoon and Owen needed in late 1917. As Caesar recognizes, it must have been extremely painful for Sassoon to recreate conditions of trench-life in any detail, which helps to account for the scarcity of longer dramatic narratives in his war-poetry.[103]

Yet Sassoon continued his attempt to be realistic about the trenches. There is nothing vaguely 'Romantic' or 'consolatory' in the last of his three longer poems written in Craiglockhart, 'Counter-Attack', as its first stanza shows:

... The place was rotten with dead; green clumsy legs
High-booted, sprawled and grovelled along the saps
And trunks, face downward, in the sucking mud,
Wallowed like trodden sand-bags loosely filled;
And naked sodden buttocks, mats of hair,
Bulged, clotted heads slept in the plastering slime
And then the rain began, – the jolly old rain!

(*CP*, p. 68)

While such unflinching realism is an important milestone in the development of First World War poetry, there is more than that to admire in 'Counter-Attack'. Sassoon had been working on it since July 1916, when the said 'counter-attack' had occurred,[104] and the effort shows. The narrative opens with a general scene of exhausted soldiers holding a trench they had gained 'hours before'. It appears to be a straightforward description of a counter-attack, but a sense of unease is created by the narrator's ominous 'Things seemed all right at first'. In stanza two the focus narrows down to a 'yawning soldier', who wonders 'when the Allemands would get busy', at which point the narrator interposes ironically 'And then, of course, they started'. The stanza ends with a detailed description of the soldier's reaction, which takes us still further away from the general opening:

He crouched and flinched, dizzy with galloping fear,
Sick for escape, – loathing the strangled horror
And butchered, frantic gestures of the dead.

The reader's attention is next directed to another participant, an officer, whose 'blundering' descent into the trench underlines the mounting ten-

414

sion of the situation. An incisive account of developments follows, its technical detail lending authenticity to the scene:

> Then the haze lifted. Bombing on the right
> Down the old sap: machine-guns on the left;
> And stumbling figures looming out in front.

Suddenly the focus shifts back to the soldier who, in the confusion, has forgotten to use his rifle. The closing description of his death, with its simultaneously external and internal view of the event is one of Sassoon's most vivid pieces of writing.

It is interesting to note the similarities with Owen's description of a gassed soldier in 'Dulce et Decorum Est', in particular the imagery of 'smothering', 'choking' and 'drowning'. There is no conclusive evidence to prove that either poet was influenced by the other in this respect, but if they were, then it is more likely that Owen influenced Sassoon. His piece was written about mid-October, whereas Sassoon's appears to have been completed later. Wherever it originated, Sassoon's is highly effective:

> ... then a bang
> Crumpled and spun him sideways, knocked him out
> To grunt and wriggle: none heeded him; he choked
> And fought the flapping veils of smothering gloom,
> Lost in a blurred confusion of yells and groans ...
> Down, and down, and down, he sank and drowned,
> Bleeding to death ...

The narrator need only add:

> ... The counter-attack had failed

and the poem is skilfully rounded off.

Poems like 'Counter-Attack' suggest that, however much he tried to forget, Sassoon dwelt a good deal on his War experiences at Craiglockhart. And this, in turn, increased his guilt at being safely out of the trenches. He felt particularly guilty about his men, a feeling spelt out in 'Sick Leave', and further explored in what appear to be the last three poems written at Craiglockhart. In 'Twelve Months After' the narrator imagines meeting his very Welsh platoon again:

> Young Gibson* with his grin; and Morgan, tired and white;
> Jordan, who's out to win a D.C.M. some night;
> And Hughes that's keen on wiring; and Davies ('79)
> Who always must be firing at the Bosche front line.
>
> (*CP*, p. 74)

---

* 'Gibson' was Sassoon's pseudonym for Pte Kendal.

The sing-song rhythms lead naturally to his memory of the reassuring song they used to sing, 'Old soldiers never die', but the poem refuses its optimism and concludes bleakly:

> That's where they are today, knocked over to a man.

In 'Autumn' the poet is reminded by the fall of the leaves of his men's deaths:

> ... Their lives are like the leaves
> Scattered in flocks of ruin, tossed and blown
> Along the westering furnace flaring red.
> O martyred youth and manhood overthrown,
> The burden of your wrongs is on my head.
>
> (*CP*, p. 88)

With its echoes of Shelley's 'Ode to the West Wind', in particular its metaphor of autumn for dying, this poem is far from original, yet it is clearly heartfelt, as the last poem in this group, 'Banishment', shows. It is a crucial work, marking a definitive turning point in Sassoon's attitude. Beginning with his sense of banishment 'from the patient men who fight', as though he, not they, is being deprived of a valuable experience, the sonnet turns at the end of the octet to describe the dreams which had started to trouble him again and the decision he has finally reached:

> The darkness tells how vainly I have striven
> To free them from the pit where they must dwell
> In outcast gloom convulsed and jagged and riven
> By grappling guns. Love drove me to rebel.
> Love drives me back to grope with them through hell;
> And in their tortured eyes I stand forgiven.
>
> (*CP*, p. 86)

There, in the final three lines, was his problem in a nutshell. He felt guilty if he was away from his men and he felt guilty if he was with them, since that meant fighting in a War he no longer believed justified.

It was a guilt that Dr Rivers consciously or unconsciously exploited, though doing so made him feel guilty too. In a letter written to his pacifist friend, Ottoline, on 11 October, Sassoon notes that Rivers, who has just returned from a fortnight's much-needed rest,[105] has become very 'war-like', asserting that the Germans 'will admit defeat suddenly in the face of superior American power'.[106] Since Rivers's arguments were usually indirect, it must have shocked Sassoon to hear his doctor arguing that to make peace as Sassoon wanted would constitute a victory for Pan-Germanisation.

Sassoon, feeling guilty anyway, though not for Rivers's reasons, said that he was now prepared to return to the Front. He was frightened, however, that if he agreed to go before a Medical Board for a reappraisal of his mental state, the War Office would merely 'shunt him off' to some home-service job.[107] 'If I can't be passed for G[eneral] S[ervice] I won't be passed for anything at all', Sherston tells Rivers.[108] Rivers, delighted with the concession, implied that he would 'wangle' things with the War Office. His absence had probably given his patient time to think without the sense of pressure his presence imposed. Sassoon, now guilty in a different direction, hastened to explain his decision to Ottoline. Worried by signs of his resolution crumbling, she had written to remind him that the war situation looked more hopeless than ever and to urge him to do something else 'outrageous' to highlight the situation. A wiser and a sadder man after twelve weeks at Craiglockhart, Sassoon replied:

> I am afraid I cannot do anything 'outrageous'. They would only say I had a relapse and put me in a padded room. I am at present faced with the prospect of remaining here for an indefinite period, and you can imagine how that affects me. Apparently nothing that I can do will make them take me seriously (and of course it is the obvious course for them to adopt). I have told Rivers that I will not withdraw anything that I have said or written, and that my views are the same, but that I will go back to France if the War Office will give me a guarantee that they really will send me there. I haven't the least idea what they will do. But I hope you and others will try to understand what I mean by it.
>
> After all I made my protest on behalf of my fellow-fighters, and (if it is a question of being treated as an imbecile for the rest of the war) the fittest thing for me to do is to go back and share their ills. By passing me for General Service (which Rivers says is 'the only thing they can do') they admit that I never had any shell-shock, as it is quite out of the question for a man who has been three months in a nerve-hospital to be sent back at once if he really had anything wrong. If the War Office refuse to promise to send me back I shall let the people here pass me for General Service and then do a bolt to London – and see what course they adopt. Oh I wish I could talk to you about it. It's so hard to say what one means. ... You *must* see how futile it would be for me to let them keep me here in these intolerable surroundings.[109]

Sassoon had not changed his mind in the least, he assured Ottoline, as his poems still appearing in the *Cambridge Magazine* should show. The reasons for his decision were complex and had been building up over a period of time. Apart from his guilt at being safe and comfortable at Craiglockhart, he felt marginalized. His protest had failed and there seemed to him no justification for his current position. In addition, a long letter from Joe Cottrell on 19 October describing the appalling conditions the 1st RWF were suffering at Polygon Wood – 'Three miles of morasses, shell-holes and dead men and horses through which to get the rations up' – made him strangely nostalgic for the old Front Line. Surrounded by the human wreckage of Craiglockhart, the 'functional nervous disorders', as they were politely called, there seemed to him something fine about the trenches, for all their physical discomfort. It was the comradeship, he supposed, yet he knew full well that most of his old fellow-officers and men were either dead or invalided out of the army. It was being exiled from the troops as a whole rather than particular friends that he missed. Though the idea of going back was 'indeed like death', it seemed preferable to spending the rest of the War at Craiglockhart. Exasperated by the people who pitied his 'wrong-headedness', he reasoned, with his own particular brand of irony:

> How else could I get my own back on them ...? Killed in action in order to confute the Under-Secretary for War, who had officially stated that I wasn't responsible for my actions. What a truly glorious death for a promising young pacifist! ...[110]

In a perverse way he rather enjoyed the idea. So Rivers agreed to arrange things as best he could and Sassoon waited apprehensively to hear the date of the Medical Board he had agreed to attend. He was fully aware of what he would be sacrificing by his apparently quixotic gesture.

Life was pleasantly busy at the time Sassoon made his decision to return to France and he did not entirely welcome Rivers's news that he had managed to arrange a Medical Board for him a few days later, on 23 October. It is unlikely, however, that he deliberately missed it because he could not face giving up his social life. More probably he walked out of the waiting room, as he did, in a fit of pique at being made to wait. (He *said* it was because he had an appointment for tea with the Astronomer Royal.) Whatever his motive, he had to face Rivers's rare anger on his return. But the worst part of the ensuing interview was that the doctor looked miserable as well as stern, though he seemed relieved to know that Sassoon's action had nothing to do with his changing his mind. With his customary tolerance he promised to arrange another Board.

In the month which intervened Sassoon stopped worrying about the future and threw himself into his social activities. Having failed to put off Ottoline's threatened visit on 9 November – 'It isn't worth while your coming all the way to Edinburgh in this awful weather. Wait a bit' he wrote tactfully; then, when she insisted, 'It would be jolly to see you; but it seems a terrible long way for you to come'[111] he made the most of her stay. Though she felt neglected and complained bitterly of his thoughtlessness in booking her into one of Edinburgh's most expensive hotels, The Caledonian, he had accorded her exactly the same treatment as he had Graves, that is, fitted her round his games of golf. And one of his reasons for trying to put her off was that he had wanted to find her suitably grand accommodation with her friend Lady de la Warr. (Ottoline was too impatient to wait until the de la Warrs returned from holiday.) He simply could not imagine her in a humble bed and breakfast and was certainly not as conscious as she was of her failing finances.

Ottoline's real reason for being unhappy during her stay was probably because it became clear during the course of it that he could never care for her in the way she was still hoping he would. It may have been during the long walk they took together the next day that he told her quite specifically that he could 'only like men, that women were antipathetic to him'.[112] It was certainly during this walk that he said how impossible it was to talk seriously to anyone who was so artificial. Clive Bell, who had witnessed Ottoline's nervous departure from Garsington, also remarked on her conspicuous appearance on this visit. Perhaps, as he suggested, she had put on even more make-up, higher heels and grander clothes than usual in the hope of attracting a younger man whom everyone but herself appears to have known was homosexual. Sassoon's response to her was, nevertheless, a cruel one and shows the measure of his self-absorption at the time.

There is no doubt that Ottoline's departure was a relief, but Sassoon was not at the station to see her off. His farewell to Owen, a week earlier, had been quite different, suggesting where his real interests lay. Their 'luminous ... intimacy', as Sassoon called it in *Siegfried's Journey*, was never more apparent than on their last evening together. Owen had been discharged from Craiglockhart, as fit for light duties, on 30 October, but he remained at Edinburgh until 3 November. Sassoon invited him to spend the last few hours before his train left, at midnight, having dinner with him at the Scottish Conservative Club. After a good dinner and a bottle of 'noble' Burgundy had put them in cheerful spirits, Sassoon tells of producing a volume of excruciatingly bad verse, sent to him by its hapless author, Aylmer Strong.[113] Knowing that Owen shared his pronounced sense of humour, particularly for things verbal, Sassoon began to read the most pompous extracts he could find. His most vivid memory of Owen on that last occasion when they were alone together was:

... of his surrendering to convulsions of mirth in a large leather-covered arm-chair. These convulsions I shared until incapable of continuing my recital.

> What cassock'd misanthrope,
> Hawking peace-canticles for glory-gain,
> Hymns from his rostrum'd height th'epopt of Hate?

It was, I think, the word 'epopt' (the grandiloquent poet's version of epopee – otherwise 'epic song') which caused the climax of our inextinguishable laughter though the following couplet, evidently 'written in dejection', had already scored heavily.

> O is it true I have become
> This gourd, this gothic vacuum?

Their mirth was, if anything, increased by the presence of a single dignified old gentleman, whom Sassoon thought secretly envied, or was at least refreshed by their laughter. The laughter was a much-needed release, but it came to seem incongruous to Sassoon that it should remain his most vivid memory of Owen that evening, since Owen was to be killed in France exactly a year later only a week before the Armistice.

When the time came for Sassoon to return to Craiglockhart that evening, besides presenting Owen with Strong's poems, he also gave him an envelope containing ten pounds and a letter of introduction to Robbie Ross. Characteristically he makes no mention of the money in his later account. But generous as it was, it was not as generous nor as useful as the letter of introduction to Ross.

Much has been made of Sassoon's poetic influence on Owen, but perhaps the most helpful thing he ever did for him was to introduce him to his friend. For, though Owen had already met Harold Monro at the Poetry Bookshop, he was still more or less unknown on the London literary scene. Ross, with a generosity and enthusiasm that matched Sassoon's, was now to introduce him to some of the most influential members of the literary establishment. Within hours of responding to Ross's immediate invitation, Owen had met both Arnold Bennett and H.G. Wells. Ross was also to introduce him to Scott Moncrieff, Osbert Sitwell and William Heinemann. Had Owen taken up Sassoon's other offer, of an introduction to Lady Ottoline Morrell, he would have met an even wider circle of literary heavy-weights.

Sassoon probably hoped to see Owen again when he paid his own visit to London ten days after their farewell dinner. (Certainly Owen was disappointed when he discovered that they had missed each other.) His ostensible reason for this brief trip in mid-November was to meet one of his pre-war friends, a Conservative M.P. who had promised to use his influence at the War Office to get him posted abroad after his Medical. There were other incentives, however. Ross had invited him to dine at the Reform with a poet he had wanted to know for some time, Robert Nichols.[114] Not only was Nichols the most popular soldier-poet of the year, his *Ardours and Endurances* far outselling *The Old Huntsman*,[115] but Graves had been enthusing about him to Sassoon since his own meeting with him in January.

Graves, who admired Nichols's earlier poetry and was probably flattered by his request to dedicate part of *Ardours and Endurances* to him, had visited Nichols in London at a private hospital on 21 January 1917. Though officially invalided out of the Royal Artillery with shell shock after only three weeks in action, Nichols was, in fact, suffering from syphilis and had been deprived of his commission on that account, as he confided to Graves. In spite of Graves's shocked reaction, Nichols was immediately drawn to Graves, a feeling the latter somewhat condescendingly reciprocated, as he told Sassoon:

> ... I liked him in a way: quite enthusiastic about the right things – very well-read – so I gave him a hell of a lecture on his ways and, finding he took it well, made friends with him – It was the usual story – shell-shock, friends all killed, too much champagne, sex desperate fornication, syphilis.[116]

Once Graves had rationalized Nichols's sexual relations with women, still an unattractive thought to him personally, he became Nichols's staunchest supporter and by April 1917 he was writing again to Sassoon, 'Robert's an awfully good chap – you'd like him awfully after you'd read his new stuff'.[117] He was evidently still worried by Nichols's heterosexuality, since he euphemistically continued: 'I admit his temperament is not ours but the circumstances I met him in last January were more the exception than the rule and it seems to have been largely bad luck'. By June Sassoon had succumbed and was himself reading Nichols's verse.[118]

Meantime Nichols, almost certainly at Graves's suggestion, had sent his poetry to Edward Marsh with a letter which Marsh's biographer, Christopher Hassall, characterized as 'boyish, desperately earnest, self-dramatizing – a little humourless – eager in the pursuit of art'.[119] Marsh was sufficiently impressed with Nichols's *Invocations* (1915) to help him prepare *Ardours and Endurances* for the press in July 1917. Its extraordinary success was probably due in part to Marsh's involvement. As Hassall noted: 'Quite suddenly Nichols leaps into the small circle of Marsh's close friends with a fervent, occasionally tiresome, but obviously quite irresistible charm!'

The month *Ardours* was published Graves was further enticing Sassoon by quoting a letter from Nichols in which Nichols himself quotes Marsh quoting Masefield: 'Nichols, Graves and Sassoon are singing together like the morning stars'.[120] It was a triangle Graves would try to develop until his attention and energies were diverted to married life: 'There are three inevitables', he was to write to Sassoon, 'two Roberts and a Siegfried rising side by side on the roll of fame all still young and more or less undamaged ...'[121]

How could Sassoon help being intrigued at the thought of meeting someone so warmly recommended and so manifestly successful? And in spite of his high expectations he was not disappointed by Nichols. He enjoyed his exuberant talk about poetry, particularly when it included praise of his own. Though he had not made up his mind about Nichols's work – 'He's *not* as good as Sorley', he wrote to Graves, '– but one can't expect that'[122] – he liked the man unequivocally. Born in the same year as Owen, 1893, Nichols could not have been a greater contrast to him. The son of a solidly middle-class family, whose pedigree Sassoon was personally to trace back to the minor man of letters, John Nichols (1745-1826),

Robert Malise Bowyer Nichols was a product of Winchester and Oxford. At times over-confident both of his poetic and social powers and exuberant to an alarming degree – Sassoon was to receive at least one letter of forty-five pages from him – he was also very moody and needed constant reassurance from his friends. Sassoon came to regard his role with Nichols as quite different from the equally encouraging one he had adopted with the diffident Owen, however: 'You *do* think too much of your works in terms of publicity and *réclame*, Bob. So do I, but I am fighting it down, and struggling to think only of a select and supercritical audience'.[123] He quickly began to see himself as Nichols's 'psychological antithesis', his own 'dangers' being 'verbal constipation and imaginative and constructive timidity', in contrast to Nichols's uninhibited outpourings. If with Owen he had found himself the more confident and authoritative of the two, with Nichols he was to envy and admire the younger man's 'heroic ambitions and attempts'. But it was also true that his admiration for Nichols's poetry, which increased on meeting him,[124] was to diminish almost as quickly, whereas his initially slower appreciation of the less confident Owen's work was to grow steadily.[125] What seems curious is that he ever admired Nichols's verse at all, since it was the kind of poetry he himself had rejected, its bombastic and rhetorical tone glorifying War in a way he could no longer approve:

> ... Heads forget heaviness,
> Hearts forget spleen,
> For by that mighty winnowing
> Being is blown clean.
>
> Light in the eyes again,
> Strength in the hand,
> A spirit dares, dies, forgives,
> And can understand!
>
> And, best! Love comes back again
> After grief and shame,
> And along the wind of death
> Throws a clean flame ...[126]

He was to continue to encourage Nichols in the twenties, but with decreasing conviction.

Sassoon's doubts lay in the future, however. At their first meeting in mid-November he was genuinely impressed by Nichols. His admiration increased when, after rather an alcoholic dinner at the Reform Club, he found himself trapped into sharing a poetry reading with him at the house of the society hostess, Sybil Colefax. Apart from the pleasure of being able to tell the American writer Logan Pearsall Smith how much he enjoyed his *Trivia*, Sassoon loathed his first experience as a literary lion. He had always been shy and the prospect of reading his poems to a room full of mainly female socialites lived up to his worst fears:

> I responded by choosing some of my least ingratiating performances [he read 'They' and 'The Rear-Guard', among others], though so nervous and self-conscious that my muttered undertones must have been inferred rather than audible. I had never read to an audience before, and felt that I was merely the unwilling object of intelligent curiosity. Robbie was furthering his purpose of getting my poems talked about, but his zealousness had outrun discretion. I didn't want to be paraded before these cultivated and agreeable strangers, and for once I was quite huffy with Robbie.[127]

Nichols, on the other hand, revelled in it all:

> ... Nichols – an old hand at the game – proceeded to give an emotional rendering of the war poems which had won him reputation. Sometimes his voice was bold and resonant; sometimes it sank to a plaintive pianissimo. He also indulged in gesticulation, and when reading a stanza, the last line of which was 'I look up and smile', he looked up and smiled. In spite of my friendly interest in him and his writings, all this caused me acute discomfort ...[128]

The difference between the two men could not have been more clearly demonstrated. Yet each admired in the other what they themselves did not possess. Nichols admired Sassoon's restraint and thought his 'staccato tones' at the public reading suited his poems 'splendidly'. He also loved Sassoon's idealism – 'Sassoon's a noble fellow', he wrote to Ross on 18 November 1917 – and Sassoon envied Nichols his utter conviction and complete lack of inhibitions, even if he did also believe that Nichols was 'the poet for people emotionally wallowing in the blues'.[129] Different as they were, however, they were united in their dislike of having Ivor Novello play rag-time, at their hostess's request, between their readings. And they liked each other sufficiently to arrange another meeting for Sassoon's next London visit.

Robert Graves, whose confidence equalled Nichols's, was quite convinced that he had been responsible for introducing Sassoon to Nichols. 'Nice for me to have introduced two such great men', he wrote to Marsh in January 1918. 'I'm beginning to understand more clearly what Georgian poetry means and what it's going to mean by God's Grace'.[130] He was referring to the fact that Marsh had by this time included all three poets in his latest anthology of *Georgian Poetry* (1916-1917), published in December 1917. He had chosen eight poems by Sassoon, eight by Graves and seven longer ones by Nichols, and placed them prominently towards the front of the collection. And he was anxious to draw attention to the newcomers:

> The representation of the older inhabitants has in most cases been restricted

in order to allow full space for the newcomers; and the alphabetical order of the names has been reversed, so as to bring more of these into prominence than would otherwise have been done.[131]

This, the third volume of *Georgian Poetry*, edited by one of Sassoon's first two mentors, Marsh, was dedicated to the second, Edmund Gosse. Both of them, having reacted strongly to Sassoon's realistic War poetry, had clearly come to accept it, since Marsh's selection includes two forceful examples, 'They' and 'In the Pink'.[132] But Marsh's choice also suggests that he still hankered after the earlier, more heroic variety and Sassoon's Romantic vein: he included 'To Victory' and 'The Kiss', as well as the poem Owen so much admired, 'The Death-Bed'.

Marsh opens his selection tactfully with a neutral poem, Sassoon's charming verse 'Letter Home (to Robert Graves)'. His most puzzling choice is 'Haunted', a somewhat indifferent poem which first appeared in *The Old Huntsman*. It certainly fitted in more comfortably with the older generation of Georgians represented in this third anthology, W.W. Gibson, Harold Monro, John Drinkwater, John Masefield, W.H. Davies, Gordon Bottomley, James Stephens and Walter de la Mare, whose work it most nearly resembled. Though Sassoon was to become critical of *Georgian Poetry* later on, to the extent of declining publication in the fifth and final volume, in 1917 he was proud to consider himself a 'humble Georgian'.[133] His prominent place in the third *Georgian Poetry* anthology would, as he anticipated, consolidate the success of *The Old Huntsman* earlier in the year and keep him firmly at the centre of the London literary scene. He had rightly prophesied to Ross in August that 'Georgian Poetry w[ould] keep the pot boiling next year'.[134]

Life at Craiglockhart on Sassoon's return from London in mid-November must have seemed dull by comparison with his brief but flattering literary whirl and this may have helped him to feel more positive about the second Medical Board arranged for him on 26 November. A further incentive was the fact that, just before his first, abortive Medical Board, most of the staff at Craiglockhart had resigned in support of the head doctor. Major Bryce, who was respected and admired by staff and patients alike, had refused to titivate his hospital for inspection. He felt that the visiting General should, for once, see a war hospital as it really was. As Sassoon reported gleefully: 'He went into the kitchen and found that he couldn't see his face reflected in a single frying-pan. Worst of all, most of the medical staff were occupied with their patients, instead of standing about and wasting their time for an hour or two while awaiting the arrival of their supreme therapeutic war-lord.'[135]

The result was the dismissal of the Commandant, Bryce, followed by the resignation of most of his loyal staff. Sassoon learnt of Rivers's resignation only after missing his first Medical, but it made it easier to attend his second. Writing to Dent two days before this second Medical,

Sassoon's tone is both resigned and defensive: 'I have now received an assurance from the W.O. that no obstacles will be put in the way of my resuming my place in the sausage-machine.'[136]

As Sassoon had written to Graves three days earlier, he could not see beyond the War and no longer cared whether he was alive or dead – 'except to look after the two Roberts, and they can do quite well without me'.[137] In an interesting postscript describing Owen's successful visit to Ross, he advises Graves to 'make him the third in your triangle. I am sure he will be a very good poet some day, and he is a very loveable creature'.

It is an ambiguous statement which could mean either that Sassoon himself wanted to opt out of a three-cornered relationship with Nichols and Graves, or that he was anxious to replace the heterosexual Nichols with the homosexual Owen. Either way, Sassoon's response was probably prompted by Graves's change of sexual direction. Graves had announced his engagement to Nancy Nicholson, daughter of the painter William Nicholson, in his letter of 20 November and had written to Robert Nichols at about the same time:

> It's only fair to tell you that since the cataclysm of my friend Peter, my affections are running in the more normal channels and I correspond regularly and warmly with Nancy Nicholson, who is great fun. I only tell you this so that you should get out of your head any misconceptions about my temperament. I should hate you to think I was a confirmed homosexual even if it were only in my thought and went no further.[138]

This marked a distinct change of attitude from that of his April letter to Sassoon, in which he had noted that Nichols's 'temperament [i.e. sexual orientation] is not ours'. A triangle consisting of two heterosexuals, Graves and Nichols, would leave Sassoon in a minority. Graves's defection to the heterosexual camp might also help explain the extremely depressed tone of Sassoon's letter to Graves of 21 November.

It was in a mood of almost complete despair, then, that Sassoon finally went before a Medical Board on 26 November. Not caring much whether he lived or died, he could hardly wait to be passed fit for General Service as Rivers had promised he would be. Rivers, as good as his word, averted the one danger which threatened the interview – that the new commandant might examine Sassoon's irregular dossier – by whisking his chief off for tea before he could do so, leaving Sassoon passed for Service Abroad.

The inconvenient protester had now been silenced and, as a reward, been restored to his former status as 'an officer and a gentleman', a position he had reluctantly sacrificed in pursuit of his principles. But it is unlikely that this played any part in his recantation. Nor is his joky explanation to 'Theo' Bartholomew – that it was 'the only thing I could do to maintain my well known dignity and limelight business!!' – completely convincing,[139] though there is probably some truth in it. His main motive throughout seems to have been returning to his men who, according to Graves, had said 'We'd follow him anywhere'.[140]

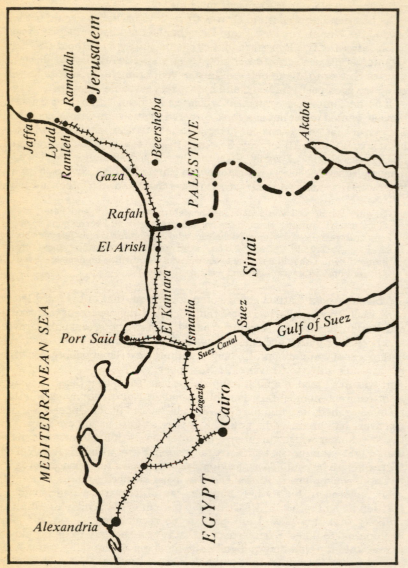

Sassoon's journey from Alexandria to the 25th RWF.

15

'Love Drives Me Back'
(November 1917-May 1918)

Sassoon insisted during his final Medical Board at Craiglockhart that he had not changed his mind about the War and in one sense that was true. Nevertheless his mind was being changed for him. Each new experience took him further away from the patriotic young man who had unthinkingly joined up even before War was declared. Craiglockhart itself, in particular his friendship with Rivers and Owen, had changed him and the five months that followed, uneventful though they seemed, were also to leave their mark. On the surface these five months, spent first at the RWF Depot in Litherland, then Limerick and finally in Palestine, were indulgent ones. While the 1st and 2nd RWF were enduring harsh winters in Italy and France, Sassoon was playing golf at Formby, eating large dinners at the Liverpool Adelphi, hunting gloriously in Ireland or exploring the wildlife of Palestine. Yet the effect of this apparently attractive lifestyle was only to harden his views on the War and to deepen his already strong sympathy for the troops, who seemed to him to suffer most by it.

One of the reasons he had gone back to active service had been the return of his nightmares about the Front – which even Robert Graves was forced to acknowledge were worse than his own.[1] His feeling that he had abandoned his men prevented him from enjoying anything fully until he returned to them. When he did so, albeit in the relatively unthreatening surroundings of Palestine, his absence had given him a sense of detachment which, paradoxically, deepened his compassion:

When I compare my agony of last year with the present [he was to write on 23 April 1918], I am glad to find a wider view of things. I am slowly getting outside it all. Getting nearer the secret places of the heart also, and recognising its piteous limitations. I recognise the futility of war more than ever, and, dimly, I see the human weakness that makes it possible. For I spend all my days with people who, with a very few exceptions, are too indolent-minded to think for themselves. Sometimes I feel as if this slow and steady growth of comprehension will be too much to bear. But, if I am not mad, I shall one day be great. And if I am killed this year, I shall be free. Selfishness longs for escape, and dreads the burden that is so infinitely harder to carry than three years, two years, one year ago. The simplicity that I see in some of the men is the one candle in my darkness. The one flower, in all this arid sunshine. Half-baked aspirations and reasonings are no good. *I will not go mad.*[2]

In practical terms the next five months were, with one exception, to keep him out of danger and, in doing so, to increase his sense of guilt. Only when he was risking his own life, it seems, could he feel guilt-free. Had he rejoined either the 1st RWF in Italy, or the 2nd, who were still at Ypres, he may well not have survived the War at all. Casualties in both battalions were very high indeed.[3]

As it was, the only thing Sassoon had to fear on his return to Litherland Depot at the end of November 1917 was embarrassment. Though unrepentant about both his protest and his apparent abandonment of it, he realized that most of his brother officers would think that he had made 'a proper fool' of himself.[4] Instead of taking the easy home job of cadet instructor he had made a very public stand which, in their eyes, had threatened the honour of the Regiment. Now he was returning sheepishly after four months of safety at Craiglockhart, while they had continued to risk their lives on active service. He did not anticipate rejection – they were too kind and genuine for that – but he did fear their puzzled misunderstanding of his apparent *volte-face*. How could he possibly explain to those trained largely to repress their emotions that it was love of his men which had driven him back?

In the event there was little explanation needed, since the camp was virtually empty. The RWF Depot had been transferred to Ireland only a few days earlier on account of the troubles there. Though the Easter Rising of 1916 had been long since quelled, the situation in Ireland, particularly in the South, remained volatile and a fresh wave of unrest in autumn 1917 called for more British troops there. Most of Sassoon's friends had, therefore, been posted to Limerick, leaving only the Assistant Adjutant and two other officers, out of approximately thirty, known to him. Together with about twenty 'details' and a few hundred recruits and returned hospital cases, they rattled around in a camp designed for thousands.

During his first three days there, from 26 to 29 November Sassoon led what seemed to him a 'python life',[5] eating and sleeping on the floor in the neglected huts, waiting only for his next posting. It came as a relief to be given ten days leave (twelve, unofficially) to take another last farewell of his family and friends. Though still feeling angry and defiant and still wanting to sacrifice himself – 'martyred because he could not save mankind'[6] – he was nevertheless resolved to have as good a time as possible on leave.

For the most part, this seems to have meant being as 'brainless' as possible.[7] It also involved spending as little time at home as he decently could. It was clear to him that his mother would never understand his attitude towards the War; while she wanted him to be as safe as possible, she was still violently anti-German and had found his protest incomprehensible. So there were very few 'safe' subjects left for them to discuss and they spent their time chatting uneasily about such trivialities as food and gardening.

It may have been in an effort to improve the situation, as well as out of liking for him, that Sassoon invited Bob Nichols to share three of his four days at Weirleigh. Writing to Nichols from Litherland on 28 November to confirm an arrangement to lunch together at the Café Royal on Friday the 30th, Sassoon continues:

> I am going down to my mother's house at Matfield in Kent on Friday afternoon for a few days – Please arrange to come down and stay next Saty to Monday there, if you possibly can, as I particularly want you to come. It's no good saying you won't come, because I shall not take any notice!
>
> There'll be no one there but my mother and my dog, and I shall make a beastly row on the piano and talk about poetry, and there won't be much to eat.
>
> But you will like it and we'll get to know each other; which isn't so easy at Colefax's and Café Royals.[8]

To Sassoon's relief Nichols, while just as charming as he had been in London, seemed 'much nicer' in Kent than the rather superficial, over-confident young man he had appeared in more cosmopolitan surroundings.[9] The visit, brief as it was, cemented their friendship, which was to continue for at least another decade. Though not the closest of Sassoon's relationships it is important from the biographical viewpoint, since Sassoon's letters to Nichols in the remaining months of the War help show his state of mind during that period.

His statutory stay at Weirleigh over, Sassoon felt that he had done his duty, except for a lunch with his great-aunt Mozelle, which he arranged for the following Saturday. The rest of his leave was to be pure pleasure. For the most part this meant hunting. While he was in the saddle, galloping through lovely countryside and preferably taking some risky jumps, he could escape. As he noted in his diary for 7 December, after hunting with the Southdown for the second time that week: 'I forgot the war today for fifty minutes when the hounds were running and I was taking the fences on a jolly old grey horse'.[10] He spent his last day of leave similarly occupied, hunting with his friend Loder's pack, the Atherstone. 'Scent poor all day, but good fun', he recorded, 'and lots of Atherstone hedges to jump'.[11]

To satisfy a very different side to his nature he stayed two separate nights in London, both of them at Half Moon Street. On the 5 December he spent the evening with Ross. Heinemann was also invited, ostensibly to see Barrie's *Dear Brutus* with them, but almost certainly as a pretext to discuss Sassoon's next volume, *Counter-Attack*. Sassoon believed that he had sufficient poems for it, though in the event he was to add at least seven more, but Heinemann was doubtful of the timing. To produce a new volume while *The Old Huntsman* was still selling might, he feared, spoil its sales. Nevertheless, it was established in principle that there would *be* another volume and that Heinemann would be its publisher. The War, it seemed, had some compensations.

Sassoon also showed Eddie Marsh his poems, during his second stay in London on 8 and 9 December. Marsh had invited him to breakfast at Raymond Buildings with Robert Nichols to present his two newest contributors – Graves was in Wales – with a copy of *Georgian Poetry 1916-17*. This had already sold over 2,000 copies in its first fortnight, which went some way towards consoling Sassoon for Heinemann's reluctance to rush out another volume of his poems. At least he could be sure that his work was being seen and reviewed. Indeed many of the reviewers were to select his contributions to *Georgian Poetry* for special praise.[12]

Sassoon's whirlwind fortnight of indulgence left him determined to lead a life of 'light-hearted stupidity' whilst he remained at Litherland.[13] At Craiglockhart there had been too much time to think about his problems, but once back in the 'brain-fuddling' army routine, with his time no longer his own, he was mercifully prevented from worrying and he felt at least ten years younger. He had always found it something of a relief to hand himself over to the system and did so now. 'I have done all I can to protest against the war and the way it is prolonged', he wrote in his diary shortly after his return from leave. 'At least I will try and be peaceful-minded for a few months – after the strain and unhappiness of the last seven months. It is the only way I can hope to face the horrors of the front without breaking down completely. I must try to think as little as possible'.[14]

To Bob Nichols he wrote: 'I have given up thinking altogether. I eat jam-roly and roast sirloin by the barrowload, and sleep like a log on the floor of a hut, and am thoroughly hearty and say "ha ha" among the Captains'.[15] When his duties, light ones, were finished for the day, he spent his spare time playing golf at Formby or eating expensive dinners at the Adelphi. The C.O. of what remained of the 3rd RWF, Lt.-Col. Jones Williams, had either forgotten or forgiven his past sins and invited him out to meals with his family in Crosby, a few miles from the Camp. And on 23 December Sassoon took a train to Manchester to meet Dent's friend, Lawrence Haward, curator of Manchester Corporation Art Galleries, a visit which illustrates in a number of ways what Paul Fussell has called the 'polarities', or 'dichotomies', in Sassoon's life.[16]

Not only was Sassoon crossing from the unthinking, animal-like existence of camp life and golf to the cultural and intellectual milieu of the Manchester art world, but he was also moving from the stiff, socially correct sphere of the Officers' Mess to an underworld into which most committed homosexuals of the period had been forced. The final contrast, made even stronger by an invitation to tea with a German family the same day, was between the official army attitude to the War and the pacifists' condemnation of it. For Dent, who was staying with Haward, introduced Sassoon during his visit to another pacifist and homosexual, Goldsworthy Lowes Dickinson.[17] A close friend of E.M. Forster's at King's College, Dickinson was a philosophical writer and essayist who also contributed numerous pacifist articles to the *Cambridge Magazine* during the War. Sassoon knew of his connection with the magazine and may even have seen him briefly in Cambridge before the December 1917 meeting. He would probably already have read Dickinson's *A Greek View of Life* (1896) and welcomed his sections on 'The Greek View of Women' and 'Friendship' in the chapter entitled 'The Greek View of the Individual'. This book, which was seen by some as a veiled justification for homosexuality, had become a bible for many homosexuals by the beginning of the twentieth century. (It had gone into ten editions by the time Dickinson and Sassoon met in Manchester.) Sassoon had certainly read a 'dialogue' by Dickinson along the same lines, since he wrote to tell him of his reaction some time after January 1907: 'Why didn't someone tell me all that when I was eating my heart out at Cambridge in 1906? Also I felt firmly convinced that you have handled the thing with amazing discretion, delicacy and completeness. And there is nothing else to say about it, – except to pray that it may be read by many more who feel as we do'.[18] His meeting with Dickinson would have been exciting under any circumstances, but must have been particularly stimulating in contrast to the conventional existence he was leading. It helped to keep alive his other, secret life.

That other life had received a severe shock only two days earlier, when Sassoon had been forced finally to come to terms with Graves's defection from the homosexual camp. Having already told Sassoon of his intention to marry Nancy Nicholson, Graves felt it necessary to discuss it with him in person. (Sassoon wrote to his homosexual friend, Bartholomew, either in mockery or sheer disbelief, 'Robert Graves is *engaged* to marry Nancy Nicholson'.[19]) And when Sassoon arrived at the 3rd Battalion Garrison at Kinmel Camp near Rhyl, Graves could only 'apologise' for his act of desertion. (He had become officially engaged on 18 December.)

While Graves was extremely happy at the thought of marriage, he understood Sassoon and his position well enough to feel that an apology was necessary. He also felt sufficiently fond of him to want to keep his friendship. Sassoon had made curiously little effort to see Graves while on leave and had subsequently turned down an invitation to participate in a second poetry-reading at the Colefaxes with him on 12 December. His dislike of such events and the long journey down from Liverpool were his excuse, but it is clear that he was already beginning to distance himself emotionally from Graves. On 21 November he had written to Lady Ottoline Morrell that Robert Graves was 'very happy' but that he did not think that he felt as deeply as some people, not even as much as Bob Nichols 'with all his egotism'.[20] It was Graves who was anxious to keep the friendship alive, trying to persuade Sassoon that he would like Nancy, even to the rather comic extent of characterizing her as a 'capable farmer's *boy*' [my italics][21] Sassoon, however, was to resist Graves's efforts to introduce him to Nancy for almost a year and would be conspicuously absent from their wedding in January 1918.

It may have been his sense that he was losing a close friend and ally which made Sassoon feel depressed at the beginning of 1918. On the other hand, Christmas at Litherland had not been a very cheerful affair. A solitary game of golf at Formby, an afternoon alone in the deserted camp and dinner with his C.O. on Christmas Day, followed by 'parlour games', left him viewing his fellow creatures as 'guzzling gabbing grotesques'.[22] The festival itself may have reminded him of the previous year when, though Graves was on leave, he was still Sassoon's closest friend. Christmas was also a time when he habitually remembered absent army friends, asking himself in 1916, for example, 'how many of them are alive and hale on Christmas Day?'[23] That particular year the answer was: 'About half, I expect; perhaps less'. But each year the death toll rose. His nightmares were worse and his expectations for the future even lower. This mood of hopelessness and fear is reflected in a poem written at this time, but not included in his *Collected Poems*:

> ### A Moment of Waking
> I awoke; evilly tired, and startled from sleep;
> Came home to seeing and thinking; shuddered; and shook
> An ugly dream from my shoulders: death with a look
> Of malice, retreated and vanished. I cowered, a horrible heap,
>
> And knew that my body must die; that my spirit must wait
> The utmost blinding of pain, and doom's perilous drop,
> To learn at last the procedure and ruling of fate.
> ... I awoke; clutching at life; afraid lest my heart should stop.[24]

Written at Limerick, the day after his arrival there, 'A Moment of Waking' marks a turning-point in Sassoon's mood. His relief at leaving the desolate depot, his interminable rounds of golf and heavy dinners, is marked by a more positive return to poetry, even though this first piece *is* pessimistic. Crossing from Liverpool to Limerick by the night ferry on Sunday, 6 January 1918, with two other officers, Attwater and the Quartermaster, Hickman, he felt he was making a fresh start.

Though Sassoon had never visited Ireland, his expectations were high, perhaps because he had already enjoyed Somerville and Ross's descriptions of it in *Some Experiences of an Irish R.M.* He certainly thought the people he met there were exactly like characters from the *R.M.* books. Limerick, situated in the south, close to the west coast, was pleasantly rural after the dinginess of industrialized Litherland and the bells of

Limerick Cathedral were certainly more melodious than the sirens of Bryant and May's Liverpool factory.[25] In addition the weather was crisp and seasonal, softening everything under a layer of frost and snow.

Best of all, Sassoon was back with old friends. For of the 120 officers, five of them had been out in France with him in the 1st RWF from 1915 to 1916: Colin Dobell, C.D. Morgan, J.V. Higginson, A.F. Freeman and H.F. Garnons-Williams. 'There are lots of cheery souls here from the 1st and 2nd B[attalio]n,' he reported to Graves on 14 January. 'I share a room with little Billy Morgan – the Albert Medal lad from the 15th Batt[alion]. He is very good company'.[26] Writing to Meiklejohn the day before, he had described Morgan as 'a splendid little lad', an admiration which sprang partly from the fact that he had been wounded four times. Morgan seems to have helped put Sassoon into a more cheerful frame of mind: telling Bob Nichols about him Sassoon confessed 'We don't give a damn for anything, and so the world goes on, and I never read the papers, and to hell with all politicians and capitalists'.[27] With Morgan he could envisage a future where a man might stand 'Saved by unnumbered miracles of chance / ... with war's unholiness behind', lines taken from 'Journey's End', a poem dedicated 'To W.M.M.', that is, William ('Billy') M. Morgan.[28] Morgan was to be one of a few friends to see him off when he was finally posted abroad.

Sassoon also knew at least two of the men in F Company, to which he had been assigned under Jim Ormrod, a further boost to morale. The 'New Barracks' themselves, though hardly 'new' anymore, were much more cheerful than the huts at Litherland and made him feel less like a temporary soldier. He spent hours on the parade-ground there watching young fusiliers drill, or lectured 'roseate' Lance-Corporals on such subjects as 'patrolling', pleasant duties which made it easier for him to avoid thinking.

Apart from enjoying the sight of so many healthy young men, a vivid contrast to the physical and mental wrecks he had encountered at Craiglockhart, Sassoon felt extraordinarily fit himself. There was seldom time or opportunity for brooding. On 9 January he wrote a cautiously optimistic poem, 'In Barracks' the second in two days, which suggests that, though he had long since stopped romanticizing War, he was still inclined to romanticize the troops; it is no coincidence that its last line echoes Housman:

> The barrack-square, washed clean with rain,
> Shines wet and wintry-grey and cold.
> Young Fusiliers, strong-legged and bold,
> March and wheel and march again.
> The sun looks over the barrack gate,
> Warm and white with glaring shine,
> To watch the soldiers of the Line
> That life has hired to fight with fate.

433

Fall out: the long parades are done.
Up comes the dark; down goes the sun.
The square is walled with windowed light.
Sleep well, you lusty Fusiliers;
Shut your brave eyes on sense and sight,
And banish from your dreamless ears
The bugle's dying notes that say,
'Another night; another day.'

(CP, p. 95)

By 12 January Sassoon could write in his diary: 'Peace of mind; freedom from all care; the jollity of health and good companions. What more can one ask for?'[29] But to Nichols on the same day, after claiming that he was 'not worrying much' and was 'very happy working with our company of eighteen-year-olds – a very smart crowd', he admitted 'I'd give a lot to take them into a show, but they'd only get killed, and then I dunno what I'd do'.[30] For he knew at bottom that it was 'a drugged peace, that *will* not think, dares not think': the 'ranks of youth' had become 'the company of death'.[31]

Sassoon's main concern at Limerick, as at Litherland, was to think as little as possible about the future. Knowing that he would shortly be posted abroad and expecting it to be France, where the situation was at its worst, he deliberately distracted himself with escapist activities. Towards the end of the second week, when the frost and snow had turned to more characteristically warm and rainy weather, he began to explore the surrounding countryside. It was on one such exploration that he wrote 'The Dream', a poem inspired by the similarity he glimpsed between rural Ireland and wartime France. So vivid were the recollections this inspired, that he felt himself once more in a 'disconsolate, straggling village street', watching the exhausted troops stumbling into 'some crazy hovel'. But it was their blistered feet, which he had already written about in 'Foot Inspection' (see p. 340-1), that moved him most in memory:

I'm looking at their blistered feet; young Jones
Stares up at me, mud-splashed and white and jaded;
Out of his eyes the morning light has faded.
Old soldiers with three winters in their bones
Puff their damp Woodbines, whistle, stretch their toes:
They can still grin at me, for each of 'em knows
That I'm as tired as they are ... Can they guess
The secret burden that is always mine?
Pride in their courage; pity for their distress;
And burning bitterness
That I must take them to the accursèd Line.

(CP, p. 94)

But Sassoon was still a long way from France and he was determined to make as much of that fact as he could. On Saturday, 19 January, for instance, he walked out to Adare, a small town ten miles south-west of Limerick, and saw the Ireland which he had already imagined before his posting there: 'the wide, shallow, washing, hastening, grey river; the ivy-clad stones of a castle-ruin planted on the banks amid trees. Very romantic scene, on a grey evening'.[32]

After a hurried tea at the Dunraven Arms he had had to rush to catch a train back to Limerick, but he had seen enough to whet his appetite and could think of no better way to enjoy such country than on horseback. So, while his superiors were talking in apprehensive undertones about the growing 'troubles' in the area and the possibility that mobile columns of soldiers might have to be sent out to suppress them, Sassoon started making enquiries about the Limerick Hunt. Nobody in the barracks could help him, since the majors permanently stationed there were more interested in fishing and shooting, but he did discover a talkative horsedealer at Croome, about twelve miles south of Limerick, who was able to introduce him to the local hunt. Somerville and Ross, or Surtees himself, could hardly have invented a more colourful set of people for Sassoon's delight and they were to provide him with rich material for *Sherston's Progress*.[33] There was Dorothea Conyers, a prolific author as well as expert horsewoman,[34] though not quite as impressive as the intrepid Mrs Marshall, the 'finest lady-rider' Sassoon had ever met.[35] Then there was Mike Sheeby ('Mike Shehan' in *Sherston's Progress*), who hired Sassoon horses, and Nigel Baring 'Esq', who looked after him in other ways, sometimes driving him home after a hard day's hunting. There were others, too, but by far the most memorable was an elderly man called Harnett. Sassoon was clearly fascinated by Harnett, whom he describes as 'Blarnett', or more familiarly, 'The Mister' in *Sherston's Progress*, perhaps because the Irishman represented a carefree way of life he envied. Together with his hospitable landlady, Mrs MacDonnell ('O'Donnell' in *Sherston's Progress*), he provides the most vivid scenes in Sassoon's account of his Irish hunting experiences. A short, stout man with light blue eyes, pink face and small white moustache, he appeared just what he was, 'an extraordinarily kind old chap'.[36] Having made his fortune in America, he had returned home to spend it, and was doing so in style. Always ready to buy rounds of drinks for his numerous friends, he was hardly ever sober but seldom so drunk that he was out of control. Sassoon treasured one of his rare utterances, which revealed his philosophy as well as the proverbial Irish gift with words: 'In politics and religion, be pleasant to both sides. Sure, we'll all be dead drunk on the Day of Judgement'.[37] If he had a motto, Sassoon felt it should be: 'We may all of us be dead next week so let's make the best of this one'.[38] Once he took Sassoon under his wing life became even more enjoyable. Before going on an Anti-Gas course at Cork on 22 January, Sassoon had been out once with the Limerick Hunt. After his introduction to 'the Mister', however, he hunted almost daily.

Thus he passed the last week and a half of his stay in a round of pleasure which seemed to him like 'a slice out of 1913', when he had spent six months with Loder's Atherstone Hunt.[39] Generally the Limerick met a few miles from the city, in the hilly country south and south-west of the town, where the names were as romantic as the soulful Irish landscape – Kilfinny Cross, Fedamore, Ballingrane and Ballingarry were only a few of the places Sassoon noted in his diary. Once they strayed as far as the Mullagharierk Mountains and, though the weather was too wild for hunting, Sassoon enjoyed an early luncheon in a spacious and remote old Irish mansion at Glenwilliam and 'rich-flavoured Irish talk' with its aristocratic owner, Tom Atkinson.[40] On one occasion, hilariously recalled and almost certainly embroidered in *Sherston's Progress*, he took young Colin Dobell, who had been with him at Mametz Wood, out for his first real day's hunting. It left 'cheery little Colin', as Sassoon described him, wanting more. But usually his companions were members of the Hunt, who had welcomed him like an old friend. Mrs Marshall invited him to tea, Mrs MacDonnell to lunch and 'the Mister' bought him drinks at every possible opportunity.

'Happy days', Sassoon noted in his diary on 4 February 1918, but they were days always under the shadow of imminent departure. For he had learnt on 21 January that he was on a list of officers going to Egypt and even hunting could not prevent him from thinking of the future, though it undoubtedly helped. The day that the news of his posting came through Sassoon wrote in his diary 'Points in favour of going' and 'Points against going'.[41] The biggest advantage, he felt, was that Egypt was an unknown country to him, where conditions – he rightly anticipated Palestine – would not be so trying as in France and there would be less chance of being killed. But his 'Points against going' show that he still yearned to be where the action was, however dangerous: 'I want to go back to one of the regular battalions. The other place is only a side-show, and I'd be with an inferior battalion'. Quite understandably, he also wanted to be in a unit where he knew people and was known. Though he concluded by saying that he could not make up his mind, he immediately started trying to have himself transferred to either the 1st Battalion in Italy or the 2nd near Ypres. Private Frank Richards in his account of his time with the Royal Welch Fusiliers, *Old Soldiers Never Die* (1933), recorded that Major Kearsley of the 2nd Battalion received a message at this time: AM ORDERED TO EGYPT CAN YOU DO SOMETHING TO GET ME BACK TO FRANCE SASSOON.

Sassoon also wrote at once to Marsh about his posting, asking him if he could do anything about it at the War Office, which Marsh clearly could not. His most impassioned plea, however, appears to have been to Rivers, who wrote a long letter of explanation back. Not only did the doctor doubt that his influence would be effective but, more importantly, he urged that Palestine would be the best place for Sassoon; he probably felt responsible for persuading Sassoon to return to active service and preferred to see him in a relatively safe spot. Appealing skilfully to both his idealism and his romanticism, Rivers argued: 'it is a question whether you would not have more chance of being useful there than in France'. And, though conscious that he himself might be biased by 'the glamour the east' had for him, he reminded Sassoon of 'features of the fighting out there – chiefly in connection with our Arab allies – which still show all the old romance'.[42] While pronouncing himself ready to do anything he could if Sassoon really wanted him to, he clearly thought he should go to Palestine.

Rivers was not alone in this. Graves, who was arranging to take a safe job with the No. 17 Cadet Battalion and settle down with his new wife, wrote to Sassoon on 6 February: 'The contrast between you and me makes me so ashamed: that's why I find it difficult to write. But Sassoon, though I know you wanted to return to a line battalion I know it's much better as it is; the strain in Palestine [won't be] nearly so great on you and you aren't likely, or so likely, to get killed. I'm most awfully keen on you living on'.[43]

Perhaps Sassoon was relieved to be dissuaded from trying for France. At any rate he resigned himself to Palestine and enjoyed his hunting all the more. The kind-hearted members of the Limerick Hunt had restored his faith in his capacity to be 'heedlessly happy'[44] and, knowing that each time out might be his last, he threw himself into it wholeheartedly. On his very last day, with the 4.25 p.m. train to catch to Dublin, he rode out even further than usual to Ballingarry, about eighteen miles from Limerick. Staying with the hounds for longer than was wise he waited till 2.30 p.m. to take the ramshackle local taxi back to 'the Mister's' lodgings, Balinacurra, where Mrs MacDonnell gave him a magnificent, if hasty, lunch of salmon, woodcock and champagne. Arriving at the station with less than a minute to spare, he was seen off to London by three friends, Billy Morgan, Jim Ormrod and Kit Owen – and, of course, the old 'Mister'. Sadly, it would be the last time he would see that endearing character, though a friend was to tell him of the 'Mister's' fate in the 1930s, when, his old house crumbling around him, he wandered the lanes fuddled and poor.

Sassoon had not just hunted at Limerick, however. As usual he had balanced his need for strenuous physical exertion with more intellectual pursuits. In the evenings, and on the rare days when he was not supervizing parades or hunting, he read and wrote poetry. After feeling poems 'piling themselves up inside [his] head' at Litherland, he had been able to get a few down on paper there, but the majority of them were written at Limerick. Perhaps Heinemann's delaying tactics over his next volume convinced him that it was worthwhile trying to add to his collection, or perhaps it was simply that he felt determined to be more positive. (He had resolved at the end of 1917 to 'write happy poems'.[45]) Not surprisingly, none of the verses he produced after Craiglockhart but before returning to France are as fierce as those produced during and just after time spent at the Front, though a number are anti-war. Some of them are positively escapist, emerging with what he whimsically called 'bright faces' rather than 'haggard exasperated eyes'.[46]

Having successfully escaped from the reality of the War for a few months, Sassoon was able to imagine a world, admittedly after death, which resembled the innocent and romantic landscapes of his childhood: an 'Invocation', written to his muse, suggests that his aims in poetry had not really changed and that it was still 'Beauty' he pursued. He was to tell Professor Lewis Chase after the War that this piece, together with 'Thrushes', was the only 'pure poetry' in *Counter-Attack*:

> Come down from heaven to meet me when my breath
> Chokes, and through drumming shafts of stifling death
> I stumble toward escape, to find the door
> Opening on morn where I may breathe once more
> Clear cock-crow airs across some valley dim
> With whispering trees. While dawn along the rim
> Of night's horizon flows in lakes of fire,
> Come down from heaven's bright hill, my song's desire ...
>
> (*CP*, p. 88)

Appropriately, since 'Invocation' is more like the piece which led to Sassoon's introduction to Ottoline ('To Victory') than most of his intervening verse, he sent this poem to her, either in December 1917 when he wrote it, or in early January 1918 and was delighted that she enjoyed something of which he declared himself proud.[47] Sassoon also sent it to the person who had introduced them to each other, someone who shared Ottoline's romantic tastes, Edmund Gosse. 'Your "Invocation" is very beautiful indeed', Gosse wrote on 9 January 1918. 'I think you were never writing better than you are at present'.[48] Though Gosse had finally managed to accept Sassoon's violent trench-satires, he was evidently relieved to be back on more familiar and (to him) more attractive ground. Sassoon, in his pleasure at being on warm terms with Gosse again, was delighted to accept his 'typographical hint'.[49] Gosse pleased him even more by reporting from Marsh that the new Georgian volume was still selling like hot cakes:

> I observe with satisfaction [Gosse continued] that the reviewers seem to accept the hint that you, Graves and Nichols are the clan of the new situation.[50]

Proud of the continuing success of *Georgian Poetry 1916-17*, Sassoon had already sent a copy to Hardy who, in thanking him on 28 December 1917 said he liked half of Sassoon's eight contributions to it. When Sassoon replied immediately, recommending other poems from the volume, Hardy again thanked him, this time for a photographic portrait he had enclosed;

it had been given a place of honour in his writing-room, where it 'calmly overlooked a hopeless chaos of scribbler's litter'.[51] Even more excitingly, from the younger poet's point of view, he ended his letter: 'I shall be so glad to see you walk in some day'. It would be another eleven months before Sassoon could realize his dream and do so.

Meantime, as his departure for Egypt approached, he retreated further into golden memories of childhood and the Weald of Kent. Revising his third tribute to Gordon Harbord, 'Together', his mind lingered on their youthful hunting days on the borders of the Weald. And his final poem about Gordon, 'Idyll', creates yet another vision of his childhood garden:

> In the grey summer garden I shall find you
> With day-break and the morning hills behind you.
> There will be rain-wet roses; stir of wings;
> And down the wood a thrush that wakes and sings ...[52]
>
> (*CP*, p. 113)

On the same day that Sassoon wrote 'Idyll', 1 February, he made yet another attempt to conjure up the happiness of youth in 'Memory':

> Out in the fields, with morning in the may,
> Wind on the grass, wings in the orchard bloom ...

But the poem ends with a strong sense of present unhappiness, in which joy and beauty are only memories:

> But now my heart is heavy-laden. I sit
> Burning my dreams away beside the fire:
> For death has made me wise and bitter and strong;
> And I am rich in all that I have lost.
>   O starshine on the fields of long-ago,
>   Bring me the darkness and the nightingale;
>   Dim wealds of vanished summer, peace of home,
>   And silence; and the faces of my friends.[53]
>
> (*CP*, p. 105)

Sassoon himself felt that this uneasy mixture of romanticism and realism was not 'characteristic' and 'by no means the strongest' of the poems he had written since 1917,[54] whereas the unashamedly romantic 'Idyll' continued to be one of his favourites. This may explain his decision not to attempt to mix the two sides of his nature in a poem he wrote three days later, 'Remorse'. Crammed as this is with realistic details of trench-life, however, it fails to achieve the forcefulness of works like 'Base Details', 'The General' or 'They', lacking their swift narrative action and punchy last line.

Closer in feel to his bitter trench-satires is a poem which may also have been written at Limerick, 'Suicide in the Trenches', describing 'a simple soldier boy' who 'put a bullet through his brain'. Its publication in the *Cambridge Magazine* for 23 February 1918 suggests that it dates from this time, though its harsh realism points to an earlier composition. Its subject matter is similar to Owen's 'S.I.W.' but its ballad-like technique is much closer to that of Housman, whom he was still reading.

When Sassoon was not writing poems in his spare time at Limerick, he was reading, there being little in the way of other cultural activities to interest him. Apart from Barbusse, whom he continued to admire, he was reading Hardy's latest collection of poems, *Moments of Vision*. He was also enjoying Sidney Colvin's biography of Keats, which made him want to re-read his poetry. Fortunately, Ottoline, who kept up her generous stream of presents, had sent him Keats's poems for Christmas, together with *War and Peace*. And though Tolstoi did not appeal to Sassoon at Limerick, he was to find it a great consolation later on. All these books were on a list of those he intended taking to Egypt, though some were abandoned at the last moment, probably because of their weight.[55]

Judging from the other titles on his list he also planned to study Wordsworth's poetry and Shakespeare's sonnets there. As usual he included Housman's *Shropshire Lad* and his two Surtees' favourites, *Mr Sponge's Sporting Tour* and *Mr Facey Romford's Hounds*. Other quintessentially English works, added almost certainly as an antidote to the foreignness of his destination, were Crabbe's *The Borough*, Hardy's *The Woodlanders* and Trollope's *Barchester Towers*. Perhaps as a result of his recent meeting with the Greek scholar Lowes Dickinson, he also included Plato's *Republic*. Pater's *Renaissance*, Bunyan's *Holy War*, Browning's *The Ring and the Book*, together with *The Oxford English Dictionary* and *The Oxford Book of English Verse*, completed this formidable list.

Back in London, which he reached at 7 a.m. on 9 February after a night crossing from Dublin, Sassoon tried to pack as much into his last two days as possible. Scorning sleep, he lunched with Ross and Marsh, who no doubt gave him more good news about the sales of *Georgian Poetry*. And in the afternoon he attempted to catch up on the classical music he missed so much in the largely Philistine army camps. To sit in the Queen's Hall, listening to Beethoven's *Fifth Symphony*, Lalo's *Concerto*, César Franck's *Symphonic Variations* and a new Schmitt *Tone Poem* would be a pleasure by most standards but to one whose ears had been jarred by the constant rag-time and popular tunes of army huts, it must have been bliss. Yet the popular music he had disliked so much at the start was beginning to have a certain power over him by early 1918.

The dichotomy between Sassoon's old life and his new is nowhere so clearly illustrated as in his attitude towards music, as a poem written at Limerick shows. Echoing the syncopated rhythms of the jazz and rag-time which had so irritated him, and incidentally anticipating the modernist experiments of T.S. Eliot and Edith Sitwell, among others, he explores his ambivalent feelings on the subject. After paying tribute to his early favourites, Beethoven, Bach and Mozart, he continues in 'Dead Musicians':

II

Great names, I cannot find you now
    In these loud years of youth that strives
Through doom toward peace; upon my brow
    I wear a wreath of banished lives.
You have no part with lads who fought
    And laughed and suffered at my side.
Your fugues and symphonies have brought
    No memory of my friends who died.

III

For when my brain is on their track,
In slangy speech I call them back.
With fox-trot tunes their ghosts I charm.
'Another little drink won't do us any harm.'
    I think of rag-time; a bit of rag-time;
    And see their faces crowding round
    To the sound of the syncopated beat.
    They've got such jolly things to tell,
    Home from hell with a Blighty wound so neat ...

And so the song breaks off; and I'm alone.
They're dead ... For God's Sake stop that gramophone.
(CP, pp. 92-3)

Just as the War had forced Sassoon into a less precious, less rarefied approach to poetry, so it was forcing him to change his attitude towards music. While the role of country gentleman at Weirleigh had not prepared him for such eventualities, his anger and pity for his friends and, above all, his men had.

Music apart, Sassoon's leave was spent mainly catching up on friends.[56] He shared another meal with Ross on the evening of his first day and afterwards saw Rivers, who must have been relieved that he was not seeing him off to the Western Front. Sassoon's family, whom he visited the next day at his aunt's house in Melbury Road, certainly were. His mother had come up to meet him there and it was almost certainly a tense occasion. 'Mother brave as usual', Sassoon reported in his diary, but it was Ross and Meiklejohn who saw him off at Waterloo the next day, not his mother. Like her sister, who also had sons at the Front, she probably found such farewells very difficult.

Leaving London at 12 noon on Monday, 12 February, Sassoon was in Southampton in time to have dinner at the Dolphin Hotel, before boarding the *Antrim*. Thinking himself bound for Le Havre, the usual crossing, it must have been a surprise to come up on deck early the next day and find

441

that he was in Cherbourg. After a disappointing dinner at the Hôtel des Etoiles, he spent the night in a Rest Camp three miles outside the town. As he wandered idly about the grounds of a nearby château the next morning, he experienced, as on each of his previous trips to France 'that rather pleasant feeling of isolation from all worldly business, which comes when one is "at the war". Nothing much to worry or distract one except the ordinary irritations and boredom of "being messed about" by the Army'.[57]

It was the third time in three years that Sassoon had been in France in February, only this time it was not to be his final destination. Instead he was about to board a train which would take him 1,446 miles to Taranto, where he would then be taken by troopship to Alexandria *en route* for Palestine. His main concern for the next few weeks would be how to deal with the inevitable boredom of army journeys. He had already adopted one of his defence mechanisms by exploring the countryside near the Rest Camp. He had also started to make his diary-entries fuller, noting, for example, with slight snobbishness the speech of the Camp Commandant, Major Flux, who had been promoted from Sergeant-Major – 'anythink else you may wish to partake of'.[58]

Sassoon's greatest resource in the face of boredom, however, was reading. Even before the nine-day train journey started, he had planned which of his books were to help him to pass it. Wisely he chose not too demanding texts – Trollope's *Barchester Towers*, Hardy's *Woodlanders* and Pater's *Renaissance*.[59] It was a choice which suggests a compromise between nostalgia for the rural England he was leaving and an attempt to understand the Italy he was visiting for the first time, that country where, as Pater points out, 'the interest of the Renaissance mainly lies'. A second aspect of Pater which must have seemed particularly pertinent to Sassoon, as he travelled towards yet another war-zone, was Pater's awareness, expressed in Victor Hugo's words in the 'Conclusion' to the *Renaissance*, that 'we are all *condamnés* ... we are all under sentence of death but with a sort of indefinite reprieve'. And it was this conviction which made Sassoon desperate to do what Pater himself saw as the sole antidote to what he called 'the awful brevity of life'; that is, 'to burn always with this hard, gemlike flame'. Sassoon echoes both phrases in his own response to his present journey into the unknown:

> The beginning of a new adventure. I am already half-way into my campaigning dream-life. Funny mixture of reality and crude circumstance with inner 'flame-like' spiritual experience. But this time I know myself, and am quite free to study the others – equipped to interpret this strangest of all my adventures – ready to create brilliant pictures of sunlight and shadow. In the 'awful brevity' of human life I seek truth.[60]

Under Pater's direct influence the 'truth' Sassoon seeks on this journey is truth to sensations, what Pater names 'the special unique impression of pleasure', which calls for the kind of impressionistic criticism he pioneered in the *Renaissance*. Sassoon's descriptions of the scenery he passed on his way from Cherbourg, through Bourges, Lyons, Genoa, Novi, Voghera, Parma, Bologna, Faenza, Foggia and Brindisi, to Taranto glow as never before with impressionistic fervour. On 14 February, after twenty-seven hours on the train and approaching Lyons, he notes with a painter's eye:

6.30 p.m. after reading Pater's 'Leonardo'. Train stops. Black smoke drifting. Get out for a minute. Trees against pale sky – clouds higher, with three stars. The others playing cards by candlelight. Scraps of talk – 'Twist – Stick etc' 'Any more for any more' (men drawing rations). Jock officer going back to Seventh Division. Halt at Bourges – French and English soldiers on platform. American camps on the way. Black men in khaki at Cherbourg. Brown landscapes.[61]

As the journey progresses and the Mediterranean draws nearer, his diary grows more poetical. After stopping at Lyons on the night of the 15th and passing through Avignon, Cannes and Nice – which seem to him to have 'the general atmosphere of a Cook's tour' – he starts to respond to the power of the sea 'softly washing on the brimming shore in the dusk'. And once past Genoa, his impressions become even sharper:

February 18
Through Novi and Vochera [*sic*], where we halt for lunch 12-1. Glaring sunlight and cold wind – dried-up land. All afternoon we crawl through vinelands, with the low, blue, delicate-edged hills on the right – a few miles away, till the sun goes down and leaves an amethyst glow on that horizon, and at 7.30 we reach Bologna.[62]

More vivid still is his description of the journey down the Adriatic coast, which they reach after a night of 'freezing gloom' terminating at Faenza. He notes the snow 'lying thin and half-melting' on the 'low, drab hills' to their right and the 'flat, lavender sea, flecked and broken with foam' against the 'pink slate-coloured horizon'.[63] Sharpest of all is his account of the final stage of the journey from Foggia to Taranto when, far from being dulled as one might expect after such a long journey, his appreciation and his descriptive powers reach their peak:

February 21
Awoke to find the train going through a region of olive-orchards, hoar and ancient, bent and twisted, with rough stone walls, and Primavera spreading her arms in a dazzle of almond-blossom, sunlit and joyous, with the Adriatic, in delicate glimpses of level blue, a mile or two away beyond the bleached-grey boles and branches ... Reached Taranto about 9 in moonlight.[64]

With lyrical passages like these, especially a set-piece on 'Grottiglie at Sunset', Sassoon was preparing himself, consciously or not, for the prose-writing which would follow his War poetry. More particularly he was

providing himself with the raw material for the last work in his fictionalized trilogy, *Sherston's Progress*. Time and again he would turn back to his
diaries to remind himself of what his impressionistic jottings vividly
brought back, that sense of leaving the known and journeying into the
unknown, an experience he found both exciting and disturbing.

However, helpful as they were to be in the future, Sassoon was not
satisfied with his exploration of the picturesque, either in prose or poetry.
(He wrote and destroyed some 'landscape poems' on the journey.[65]) They
seemed to him merely exercises. '*Must* concentrate on the tragic, emotional, human episodes in the drama', he reminded himself: '... I *must* have
the heroic. So goodbye to amiable efforts at nature-poems. If I write I'll
write tense and bitter and proud and pitiful'.[66] He was not being entirely
fair to himself; though there was nothing 'tragic' or 'heroic' for him to
describe on the journey, he had not neglected the 'human' and 'emotional'
aspects of it. In fact, one of the first things he noted about it was the human
element: 'My companions S.W. Harper, M. Robinson and H.G. Howell-
Jones, all decent chaps – Harper of course charming', he wrote in his diary
on the first day of his journey. 'It was he who went to Edinburgh with
Robert Graves, as my "supposed" escort, last July.'[67]

There is nothing like a long journey for testing relationships, however,
and Harper (the 'Hooper' of *Sherston's Progress*), is described five days
later as 'rather hipped and fussy – bad campaigner, I fear'.[68] On the other
hand, Howell-Jones ('Howell' in *Sherston's Progress*), introduced without
comment in his diary, is later praised as 'sensible and philosophical'.[69] But
it was the third member of the group, Robinson, who won his heart 'with
his dear impetuous ways, kind and willing and cheery'. It was undoubtedly
Robinson to whom Sassoon was referring when he wrote to Dent on 19
February 1918:

> Only four in a compartment so there is a fair amount of room. The other
> three are quite pleasant – (one of them rather *more* than that.)[70]

Dent, who kept a London flat especially for his liaisons with young men,
would have known exactly what Sassoon meant. Not surprisingly Robinson, as 'Marshall', figures far more prominently than the others in
Sherston's Progress, where, in the guise of fiction, Sassoon's attraction to
him is underlined:

> M[arshall] is the best of the three. About 21: big and capable; pockets usually
> bulging; hopes to be a doctor. Sort of chap who never grumbles – always
> willing to be helpful.[71]

More like the untidy Graves than the impeccable David Thomas or
Bobbie Hanmer, Robinson nevertheless shared their same youthful enthusiasm, which so appealed to Sassoon. And, if we are to believe *Sherston's*

Progress, he much preferred Robinson's 'jolly face and simple jokes' to Harper's 'youthful charm and good looks but absence of guts'.[72]

Physical attraction was not, in itself, enough, though it was an important ingredient in his sexual relationships. The fact that he shared a seat, which at night became a bed, with Robinson seemed to him significant. There was also an element of protectiveness in this, as in most of his other passions. The young man's 'grown-up babyish face' inspired emotions very similar to those he had felt for Thomas and Hanmer. His relations with men appear to have been divided between those where he adopted a fatherly position and those where he was fathered. Rarely were they with men of his own age.

Robinson, for his part, was probably unaware of Sassoon's sexual attraction to him. A far more practical person than Sassoon, his main concern seems to have been to look after him in a down-to-earth way. Where Sassoon thought of what books to bring, Robinson had thought of a Primus stove, for example, and was able to supply the poet with *café au lait*, a taste not catered for by the army.

Sassoon needed all the comforts he could get. Not only was the journey long and tedious but for most of it he felt ill. The weather, though bright, was frosty and the train bitterly cold. By the fourth day he had a 'touch of fever and chill on his insides', which continued on and off throughout the journey. In order to pass the time as effortlessly as possible, he turned to an 'easy-flowing' book which was not on his list, George Moore's *Lewis Seymour and Some Women* (1917). But he found the book as unappealing as he had the author, when he had met that 'peculiarly unpleasant old gentleman' at Gosse's,[73] and turned back with relief to Pater and Hardy. There were other things to irritate him. Arriving at Taranto late on 21 February, he had been obliged to spend a further night on the stationary train and had had his watch stolen, a serious loss for an officer. But he was grateful that it was not his lucky fire-opal, a present from Ottoline which he wore always round his neck.

Even the greater comfort of a Rest Camp on 22 February could not restore Sassoon's good-humour. Most of the officers there seemed to him lacking in sensitivity and intelligence, except for the doctors who struck him as uniformly wise and kind. (His friendships with Dunn and Rivers had possibly made him less than objective in this respect.) It was the beginning of a hostility towards most commissioned officers, whom he would increasingly compare unfavourably with the 'other ranks'. He detected 'the usual riff-raff' in the Officers' Mess,[74] for example, and, when brought into even closer contact with his kind on board ship, he felt no sympathy for them: 'they seem so self-satisfied, with their card-playing, and singing *Chu-Chin-Chow*'.[75] He complained to Meiklejohn that they appeared to have 'absolutely no *inner* life',[76] an observation almost certainly prompted by his reading of Conrad at the time.[77] The contrast with the frantic socializing of the Officers' Mess could not have been greater.

However superficial the officers seemed, the men struck Sassoon as 'simple and childlike' in the face of danger.[78] Their instinct on ship was to draw physically closer together, in attitudes which delighted Sassoon, partly because they roused a 'sexual emotion' in him.[79] Instead of discussing world-politics and drinking cocktails, they read popular magazines and drank ginger-beer. With no smart uniforms, expensive hair-oils, secret information or media recognition to bolster their sense of self-importance, they were forced into a directness which Sassoon, under the influence of Barbusse and strong homoerotic feelings, romanticized:

> They are part of the huge dun-coloured mass of victims that passes across the shambles of war into the gloom of death where all ranks revert to private. But in their vast patience, in the simplicity of their anger and their mirth, they are as one soul. They are the traditions of human suffering, stripped of all its foolish decorations and ignoble sufferings for individual success and social advancement.[80]

This exaggerated recognition of their virtues, while perfectly genuine, may have sprung partly from his sense of guilt at having deserted them for a time. Sometimes, watching them at a concert party, for example, he could hardly bear the pathos of their situation: 'These men, sitting – standing – tier beyond tier – row beyond row – excluded from life – the show is what they long for – LIFE with its song and dance – life with its brief gaiety'.[81]

Concert parties were mainly for the men rather than the officers, but Sassoon found himself particularly interested in one of them, or at least the preparations for it. Shortly before boarding the liner *Kashgar* on 25 February he had come across members of a Jewish battalion rehearsing behind the camp's tent-lines. What he took to be two well-known London comedians were being admired by other members of the battalion. He particularly noted the 'curved Hebrew beak' of one comedian and the fact that 'another little Jew' whispered something to him.[82] Setting out as he was on the final stages of a journey which would terminate in the Holy Land, he was becoming more aware of Jewishness and his own Jewish roots.

It was a connexion he had started to make on the train down. Writing to Dent from Faenza of Heinemann's promise to publish his latest poems in the coming year, he had joked in Kiplingesque fashion:

> But he must be hoping that my Oriental adventures will
> renew the past in me – and who knows but a second 'Garden
> of Kama' may be forthcoming some day! And
> The magic arabesques of a male and moonlight mould,
> And vivid flaunting symphonies from dug-outs and bazaars, –

> With a camouflage of captains with whiskies and cigars, –
> Thus shall my cock-tail carpet, romantically unrolled,
> Reveal the wars of Jewry, the sherbert of the Stars.
> Awake, harp and lute! my Hebrew heart awake!
> And Amy Woodford-Finden* her melodies shall make.
> I'll sell ten million copies, and Heinemann will say,
> Forsake the fight, and write, and write, for ever and for aye![83]

Allowing for the facetious tone Sassoon generally adopted with Dent, it is clear that his 'Hebrew heart' was finally 'awaking' on this journey to Palestine.

After three days in Rest Camp Sassoon found it a relief to board ship for Alexandria. The *Kashgar*, anchored in the gulf of Taranto in readiness, set sail on 25 February and once adjusted to sea-travel, he began to feel better. The Mediterranean was calm, the night-skies beautiful, and Conrad's *Chance*, his choice for this part of the journey, absorbing. The vastness of the sky at sea made his search for Pater-like sensations seem futile. Yet he was, still struggling to catch the moment, the 'steel-blue' plain of the bay 'glimmering in deepening twilight', the Apennines, blue as the water, appearing 'like a soft rain-cloud on the sea' and other last impressions of Italy. Fortunately, his sense of humour was never far away and this particular diary-entry concludes: 'NB. Don't be too bloody serious'.[84]

Arriving at Alexandria on 28 February, exactly three days after leaving Taranto, Sassoon is still trying to nail down impressions:

> A clear, soft-coloured afternoon, blue sea, creamy, brick-red terra-cotta and grey city, wharves and docks and so on, with smoke drifting and sunshine (no glare) and thickets of masts and funnels. Everything breezy, cheerful and busy.[85]

But he is increasingly dissatisfied with such passages and his diary references to Pater cease. The *Renaissance* had been ideal for his journey through Italy and was to comfort him for another few days in Egypt,[86] 'a good antidote' as he told Meiklejohn, 'to the rather suffocating materialism and lack of imagination' of his surroundings.[87] As he approached the war-zone, however, something on a larger scale was needed. After trying Scott's *The Antiquary*, which he bought at Port Said, he was to settle on another book purchased there, *War and Peace* (he had left the copy Ottoline had sent him in England, presumably because of its weight. By the end of March he would write of Tolstoi's great epic: 'I read *War and Peace* of an evening, a grand and consoling book – a huge vista of life and suffering humankind which makes the present troubles easier to endure, and the loneliness of death a little thing'.[88]

---

* Amy Woodford-Finden was a writer of popular songs, known particularly for her music to Laurence Hope's *Indian Love Lyrics* She died in 1919.

At the beginning of March, on his arrival in Egypt, Sassoon's 'present troubles' appeared relatively minor. Though his overnight train journey to No. 1 Base Depot, Kantara, on the first day of the month was probably uncomfortable, it was not dangerous and gave him pleasant views of the Suez Canal and an unexpectedly fertile garden at Ismailia. Even the depot, situated though it was in 'sandy wastes', had cool ante-rooms and onions, which he liked, for lunch. His eight days' stay there may have been boring, but it was not wholly without incident or enjoyment. On the fourth day, for example, he was transferred, a matter of only a few yards, to his new unit, the 25th (Montgomery and Welsh Horse Yeomanry) Battalion, together with his favourite, Robinson. On the sixth day he got leave to visit Port Said, also with Robinson, and in addition to books managed to stock up on another essential part of his equipment, pipe-cleaners. He even found himself serving on a District Court Martial on 9 March, a detail he omitted from his fictionized life, almost certainly because it was an experience he preferred to forget. Nevertheless, it must have helped break up the monotony of camp life.

In spite of his easy circumstances Sassoon was unhappier in Egypt than he had been on the far more demanding Western Front. After a brief respite on board ship, he was still feeling ill, with severe headaches and a constant cough. The majority of his fellow-officers continued to irritate him, making the camp seem an 'arid waste of officer mentality'.[89] Kantara Base Depot quickly became for him

> the absolute visible expression of time wasted at the war. The sand and the huts and the tents and the faces, all are meaningless. Just a crowd of people killing time. Time wasted in waste places.[90]

After his decision to abandon his protest and return to the War, it must have been an enormous anti-climax to find himself in such an aimless situation. And he was not alone. 'People go "up the line" almost gladly', he noted 'for it means there's some purpose in life'.[91]

Those words were written on 4 March, the day Sassoon was posted to his new unit, a further cause for discontent. Instead of returning to either the 1st or 2nd RWF, both highly respected 'line' battalions, he found himself with the 25th RWF, a battalion formed at Helmia in Egypt only a year earlier from dismounted Montgomery and Welsh Horse Yeomanry. It became part of the Egyptian Expeditionary Force which the British had set up to deal with an attempted Turkish invasion in early 1915.[92] Their main purpose was to protect the Suez Canal from the Turks, who occupied Palestine, the Canal being the main sea-route to the East.

British attempts to break out of the Allied Line, east of the Sinai Desert, had failed until the arrival of General Sir Edmund Allenby in July 1917. Allenby, who had come straight from the fiasco of Arras, devoted his first three months to intensive preparations for an autumn offensive. He cleverly misled the enemy into believing that he would be attacking Gaza for the third time, when he was really preparing to take Beersheba. This was successfully achieved on 31 October 1917, though the 25th RWF alone suffered 250 casualties that day. Gaza followed and the way to the British main objective, Jerusalem, was clear. By 9 December the Holy City had surrendered to Allenby and by 11 December he had entered and occupied it. At the end of the month, having beaten off a counter-attack by the Germans and Turks, he had also strengthened the city's perimeters.

Spasmodic fighting in Palestine followed throughout January and February 1918. By 21 February, Allenby's troops had driven the Turks from Jericho and reached the northern end of the Dead Sea. A further British offensive was already under way by the time Sassoon was transferred to the 25th RWF at the beginning of March. Even as he waited at Kantara Base Depot, the 25th Battalion, attached to the 74th (Yeomanry) Division and part of the 231st Brigade, was seeing active service. On 8 March the 74th Division advanced along the Jerusalem-Nablus road, with the 53rd and 10th Divisions on their right and left respectively.

On 9 March the 231st Brigade rushed enemy defences at Selwad and on 10 March they helped storm the precipitous ridge of Burj el Lisaneh and successfully defend it against three counter-attacks. Finally, on 11 March, the 231st Brigade captured Selim.[93] This was to be the 25th Battalion's final operation in Palestine, however, and, by the time Sassoon joined it near Ramalleh on 14 March, it was engaged in nothing more exciting than holding the recently captured line in quiet conditions. Had there been dangerous action awaiting him, or even a reasonable number of familiar faces, he might have become reconciled to his new unit as quickly as he had accepted the 2nd RWF in 1917. As it was, instead of rejoicing at his relatively safe position, he longed for France and his old battalion.

It had taken Sassoon four days to reach his new battalion, which was stationed near the Jerusalem-Nablus road nine miles north of Ramalleh. Starting with an overnight train journey along the Mediterranean coast to Gaza, he continued north to the railhead at Ludd on 11 March, a ride of nineteen hours altogether, in a cattle truck. His night's sleep in a rest camp near Ludd was almost equally uncomfortable. Continuing his journey by lorry with eleven other officers, one of whom was Robinson, he travelled from Ludd to Divisional Headquarters at Ramalleh on the 12th.

Sassoon had already begun to note details of wildlife in his diary, even at the arid Base Depot, but on this stage of the journey they come to the fore. During his first stop, Latrun, at the foot of the Judean Hills, he is particularly conscious of the sounds in his exotic new surroundings. With a poet's ear he hears a running stream, the wind in the trees, frogs croaking and the strange notes of unknown birds, all sounds he would use in his verse to describe this new land, very different from the Weald of

Kent. Wild and desolate, the Judean Hills were scattered with rocks and stones which looked like thousands of sheep to Sassoon. But there were less bucolic sights to remind him of the purpose of his journey, tractors pulling six-inch howitzers up the slopes and ambulances descending from their heights.

Sassoon was less stimulated by the next stop on the journey, Jerusalem, perhaps because he had expected it to be a 'holy-looking' place, which it was not. Ramalleh itself, eight miles north of Jerusalem and captured by the Allies only two months earlier, impressed him more. Situated on a hill-top, with a line of cypresses surrounding Divisional Headquarters, it seemed mysterious and faintly sinister. More prosaically, it was also very wet and he spent the morning of the next day, 13 March, sheltering in a tent. He had already talked to someone he recognized from the Sussex Yeomanry, a Sergeant Stone, and now spent nearly an hour chatting to a private from the Middlesex Regiment, an indication that he was becoming more reconciled to his situation perhaps. Another sign of this was his growing appreciation of the countryside. Helped by a change in the weather at midday, the landscape, which had struck him as cruel, desolate and unhappy on arrival, now seemed to him 'full of a shy and lovely austerity'.[94] For four hours he escaped the War completely as he studied the innumerable wildflowers and strange birds the colour of the rocks. It was a scene which took him back to his childhood favourite, *Arabia Deserta*, and his own semitic origins. In this 'Old Testament environment' he felt like 'a budding prophet'.[95] It was a striking contrast to Ramalleh with its lorries, camel-columns, limbers and lines of donkeys carrying supplies, all signs of modern warfare, which sat so oddly in this ancient civilization: the very old *versus* the very new.

The heavy transport together with the rain had turned the roads to liquid mud and this may have been the reason why Sassoon carried out the final stage of his journey the next day on foot. Leaving Ramalleh at 8.30 a.m. with Robinson, he walked nine miles through wild hills, which had until a few days previously, been in enemy hands. They found the 25th Battalion bivouacked on a hillside, along rocky terraces, resting after their recent engagement. With two officers killed, three wounded and several more on leave, the battalion was urgently in need of replacements and Sassoon found himself for the first time in charge of a Company. He was promoted to acting Captain, but found himself commanding only one other officer, Harrison, and the hundred 'ragged' soldiers who constituted C Company.

Though they struck him as a 'very slack lot',[96] Sassoon inevitably became fond of them. Two in particular attracted him. One of them, Jim Linthwaite, he had known in the 1st Battalion a few years earlier. (Linthwaite appears as 'Stonethwaite' in *Sherston's Progress*.) Young, handsome, muscular and 'the embodiment of youthful enterprise',[97] he exercised a powerful physical attraction for Sassoon, as did the other young private, Roberts, described by his officer as 'a sort of Apollo', as he played football 'with nothing on but a pair of tight shorts'.[98] But it was a forbidden attraction and one he kept well under control, allowing only the most obviously paternal of interests to manifest itself. (His concern for Linthwaite's 'rotten' boots was, he admitted, a pretext for conversation.) When Linthwaite was waiting to be Court-Martialled for drunkenness later on, for example, he could show his involvement only by giving him fatherly advice, rather than comforting him physically. It seemed so tame by comparison with his wild dreams of saving his life. It was Linthwaite who prompted the remark, 'There was a great deal of sex floating about in this particular effort'.[99] He would also inspire Sassoon's first sustained effort at prose-writing in 1921, a 13,500-word story, 'Beloved Republic', which would prove 'too full of the heart's music' for publication.[100]

Sassoon's fondness for his men was matched by his growing suspicion of the officer class and he made very few exceptions in the 25th Battalion. Though his C.O., had welcomed him genially and shown faith in his efficiency by placing him in command of C Company, Sassoon was highly critical of him. An aristocrat by birth, Colonel Lord Kensington, late of the 15th Hussars, seemed to him 'odiously vulgar and snobbish; a very bad type of British nobleman'.[101] While Sassoon could not prove that he was as 'windy' and incompetent as rumour made out, it was clear to him from the start that his C.O. was the type of coarse, sporting nobleman he disliked, the kind who would look 'exactly right in a grey top-hat yelling the odds in Tattersalls ring at race-meetings'.[102] His CO's preoccupation with the material aspect of things, particularly a good wine or brandy, sometimes made life very pleasant for his junior officers and Sassoon did eventually wonder if he was perhaps less of a fool than he had first thought him, but he never grew genuinely fond of him. And though he acknowledged that the Second-in-Command, Major Rees, was a quietly efficient soldier and a 'thoroughly decent man', he found fault with his 'British reticence' and 'stereotyped manner'.[103] The adjutant, with whom he might have been expected to identify as 'something of an outsider', he dismissed as 'tactless, stupid and diligent'[104] and was scarcely less critical of the four other captains, whom he mostly found snobbish, pretentious and lazy. Of the remaining thirty officers, none seemed in any way remarkable to Sassoon, though he tolerated the two from B Company with whom he shared a tent; Barker, a garrulous thirty-five-year-old ex-commercial traveller from Welshpool and Charlesworth, a gentle, somewhat diffident twenty-four-year-old from Magdalen College, Oxford, who admired Kipling.

On the whole, however, Sassoon was struck by the 'coarse stupidity' of his fellow-officers, whose minds seemed to him clogged with mental deadness'.[105] Only the Medical Officer, Captain W.K. Bigger stood out. Like Doctors Dunn and Rivers, he was very well-informed, and cultivated his own interests. While the others sat drinking cocktails or talking war-shop, he was out in the hills, grubbing at roots or watching birds, the sort of man,

Sassoon thought, who before the War would cruise about on rivers and canals and remote streams, looking at the by-ways of English counties and studying wild-life. A product of Emmanuel College, Cambridge, his knowledge of birds was immense. 'Lean, grimy and brown' with eyes 'like brown pools in a Scotch burn', he looked rather like an untidy bird himself.[106] Sassoon seems to have found his very roughness – scrubby moustache, foul pipe, muddy voice – a welcome contrast to the polished artificiality of the majority of the other officers. He also admired Bigger's 'tenderness for dumb and piping creatures' and his unwillingness to kill them, which suggested a sensitive and caring man uncoarsened by War. His attitude towards his fellow-officers was certainly far kinder and more tolerant than Sassoon's own.

Sassoon had already begun to appreciate the beauty of the Palestinian landscape and its wild-life. Under Bigger's influence he started to study it in earnest, particularly its birds of which he made long lists in his diary. On Easter Sunday, for example, just over a fortnight after his arrival, he spent all afternoon with Bigger in the hills. When rain blotted out the landscape, they squatted in a vineyard over a fire of dry olive-branches and smoked their pipes together till the weather cleared, to reveal clean-cut, delicate skylines.[107] In spite of Sassoon's occasional longing for the English countryside, partly as a result of reading Hardy's *Woodlanders*, he had to admit that the Judean hills were 'much finer really'.[108] He learnt to appreciate them in all weathers and at all times of day, but particularly liked the late afternoon and early evening, when frogs croaked in the wet ground up the wadi and wheatears, pipits and whitethroats flitted and chirped among the small thorn-trees, shrubs and rocks. Under such soothing influences, as well as that of a writer who acknowledged the power of Nature above all else, Wordsworth, his poetic instinct gradually revived. After only a fortnight in his new surroundings, in verse clearly affected by Wordsworth's simplifying impulse and more reminiscent of Sassoon's own early pastoral poems than later satires, he tried to describe his surroundings 'In Palestine':

> On the thyme-scented hills
> In the morning and freshness of day
> I heard the voices of rills
> Quickly going their way.
> Warm from the west was the breeze;
> There were wandering bees in the clover;
> Grey were the olive trees;
> And a flight of finches went over.
>
> On the rock-strewn hills I heard
> The anger of guns that shook
> Echoes along the glen.
> In my heart was the song of a bird,
> And the sorrowless tale of the brook,
> And scorn for the deeds of men.[109]

While it is interesting to see Sassoon experimenting with the sonnet form, using a three-beat rather than the usual five-beat line, 'In Palestine' is an otherwise unremarkable poem and Sassoon wisely excluded it from his next volume of verse as well as from his *Collected Poems*.

It was in prose not poetry that Sassoon managed to bring his new surroundings alive. Writing to Edmund Gosse on 25 March his account gives not only a vivid physical picture of the Palestinian landscape but also hints at other reasons for its special appeal:

We are on the rugged hills looking towards Samaria. These hill-landscapes are magnificent. Our present camp is pitched among fig-trees. The narrow terraces are natural rock-gardens, rich with all kinds of flowers; the wild iris has appeared in great profusion lately – also scarlet tulips. – The red and purple anemones are disappearing after making a great demonstration among the rocks – Cyclamen is still going strong. Now I've given you all the local colour I can muster for the present. The villages on hill-tops rise out of the grey and faint green like heaps of stones. One scarcely sees them at first. They are full of growing Arabs and Bedouins – not over friendly. Long trains of camels and pack-mules move deliberately along the glens through which the road winds, led by dark skinned ruffians in faded blue-green robes; carrying tins of water and other necessaries of life for the army.

Guns boom and echo among the hills; but it is a silent haunted, ancient sort of country, – I was on a high hill one evening, where one could see a great deal of Palestine. The sea on the left, a long way off – with faint yellow line of arid-hills;– ridge beyond ridge rising in front, – the colour of lichen on trees, grey and dim green and brown;– and on the left of the Jordan valley, and a barrier of arid hills, (Arab I believe.)[110]

It is clear from a later part of this letter that Sassoon's sense of his Semitic origins was reinforced still further by the appeal of this historic landscape: 'Personally I should like to do something in the prophetic line', he tells Gosse. 'The Lamentations of Sâshun; I wonder if Heinemann would publish'.

Sassoon also added to his description of the Palestinian landscape, seemingly as an afterthought, 'No sign of *war* in all this country'. Although this was not quite true, it was a significant comment, for he felt almost as far from what he regarded as the 'real' War in Palestine as he had in Ireland, and a similar sense of peace. The Judean Hills even reminded him of Ireland at times, especially after rain, when they looked green and the rocks were not so visible as usual. He had also been reminded of Ireland by a letter from Dorothea Conyers, 'the good soul, full of Limerick hunting, hounds flying over the big green banks and grey walls'.[111]

By the time Sassoon wrote to Gosse about the beauty and peace of Palestine on 25 March, his battalion had moved three miles down the Jerusalem-Nablus road to continue its main task of road-mending. He quickly established a routine suited to his new surroundings:

I get out of bed into a cold bath at 6.15 a.m. [he told Graves on 4 April] and just as I get out of it – the sun looks over the eastern hill and warms me nicely as he shine into my tent.

He took his men out from nine in the morning to four in the afternoon, civilized hours compared with those of trench-warfare. And, though the work was strenuous, it was relatively safe. Supervision was easy and left Sassoon ample time for bird-watching, reading and writing. At 8.30 p.m. he put away either *War and Peace* or the *Oxford Book of English Verse* – and went to sleep. Though he was sad to see Robinson leave for another battalion at the end of the month, he began to feel more positive about his situation. His sense of freedom was increased on 4 April when the officer commanding C Company, Capt. Freeman, returned from leave, releasing him from the full responsibility he had shouldered as Company Commander. As second-in-command of A Company, to which he was transferred, his life became even pleasanter, as his diary entries indicate:

It is a heavenly morning, and a heavenly place; [he wrote on 3 April] and the war is quite subsidiary to the landscape – not a sprawling monster, as in France. As the shadows of huge clouds on the ancient hills – spreading from slope to glen, and moving on – so do our battles pass, leaving no trace of the evil that has been.[112]

The 'sprawling monster' in France was never very far from Sassoon's mind. The bulletins from the Western Front were getting steadily worse and names which meant little to officers who had served only in the Middle East made him aware that the Germans had recaptured all the ground gained in the Somme battles by the end of March. While most of his colleagues remained unconcerned, he grew increasingly apprehensive. In January he had tried to get himself posted to France; now, ironically, he feared such a move. Quite apart from his unwillingness to leave the Judean Hills, he was worried that he might not be able to stand another 'dose' of France.[113]

Even when the news of the 25th Battalion's imminent departure came through in early April, less than a month after Sassoon had arrived in Palestine, he still hoped that they were not destined for France. On 5 April, in what he saw as a 'raffish effort to turn the thing into a joke; for everyone knows we *are* going to France',[114] the Colonel organized a 'selling sweep' on their destination. Sassoon initially refused to join in this 'puerile and ill-bred' show, but finally, in sheer annoyance at the snobbishness of it all, bid £10 for the 'Submarined' ticket, a very real threat which no one else dared to acknowledge. Even he did not realize until later how close he had come to being right.

By this time all local maps had been handed in and hot weather kit cancelled and by 7 April the 25th RWF, together with their neighbours, the 24th Welsh, were on the move. Not only was it the start of their march down to the railhead at Ludd but also, as Sassoon apprehensively noted, 'the first day of our journey to France'.[115] He had nerved himself to face it so many times before that he now felt emotionally exhausted.

Someone of less intense imagination would no doubt have suffered less. France was still a long way off and there was no need to fear that the battalion would reach it quickly. Like all previous army moves, this one was painfully slow and, at times, extremely boring. The march from their camp to Ludd, for example, a distance of only forty-five miles, took four days and even then the men suffered. As Sassoon watched his men staggering along under the weight of their full equipment, all his latent pity for them was aroused:

> Left; left; left, right, left. 110 paces to the minute. The monotonous rhythm of the marching troops goes on in his brain. His eyes blink at the glaring sky; the column move[s] heavily on in front; dusk hangs over them; dust and the pale blue, quivering sky. As they go up a hill their round steel helmets swing from side to side with the lurch of their heavy-laden shoulders. Vans and lorries drone and blunder and grind along the road; the cactus-hedges are caked with dust ... He sees and hears these things through the sweat-soaked weariness that weighs him down; his shoulders a dull ache; his feet burning hot and clumsy with fatigue; his eyes tormented by the white glare of the dusty road. Men before and behind him – no escape. 'Fall out on the right of the road.'
>
> He collapses in the dry ditch.[116]

Though Sassoon did not undergo the same physical hardships as his men – he would certainly not have been carrying his full kit with him and was probably far fitter and better nourished – he did suffer on this march. For he felt, as he had once before at Montagne in December 1915, that he had been in Arcadia: 'It is positive agony to leave these Palestine hills in all their beauty and glory', he noted at the end of the journey.[117] Perhaps it was too beautiful for words, or, it may have seemed to him inappropriate to write pastoral poetry at such a time. Whatever the explanation, he seems to have written only two poems in Palestine and the second of these, 'Shadows', written on the last day of the march, concentrates more on the soldiers than the landscape.[118]

Two days later Sassoon found inspiration for another poem where he least expected it, Kantara. He had been sent ahead from Ludd with the Advance Party on 11 April and, after an uncomfortable overnight train journey in a cattle-truck, arrived back at No. 1 Base Depot. Not expecting to see the 'beastly place' again so soon after leaving it, he cheered himself up by escaping to a salt-lake about a mile from the camp. Hardly less dreary, the lake at least offered him the chance to bathe and the sight of flamingoes:

> ... wheeling by,
> Crowd[ing] the air with white,

Warm-flushed in rosy light
That *flowered* across the sky ...[119]

Such an unexpected sight reminded him of what War had already taught, that beauty could be found in the most desolate of places. It is no coincidence that, when he came to write a poem on the subject ten days later, he should do so in conscious imitation of someone who shared this view, Thomas Hardy. It was probably also Hardy who inspired the yearning for the lush English countryside to be found in the middle verse of 'Flamingoes':

I plodded slow, with vacant gaze
That pictured in my brain
Green fields and quiet rain
Hushing the woodside ways.
And still the place was dead:
No arch leaved overhead
Of leafy-glinting maze.

While both 'Flamingoes' and 'Shadows' are of biographical interest, Sassoon felt that neither showed him at his best and he published neither in his lifetime. But there was another poem written at Kantara of which he was justly proud, 'Concert Party'. In order to divert the men, condemned to remain at the Base Depot for over a fortnight with nothing more than light training to occupy them, an entertainment was arranged for 17 April. It was given by Lena Ashwell, an actress-impresario who had been organizing concert-parties for soldiers since 1914.[120] She and her group struck Sassoon as particularly good and he was deeply moved by their effect on the men. Watching them as they drank in every movement and sound made by the five entertainers, he felt as though he really was by nature 'a seer and dreamer of dreams', as he had sometimes claimed:[121]

Suddenly I recognize that this is indeed the true spectacle of war – that these puppets are the fantastic delight of life played to an audience of ghosts and shadows – crowding in like moths to a lamp – to see and hear what they must lose – have lost. In front there are half-lit ruddy faces and glittering eyes, and behind they grow more dusky and indistinct – ghosts, souls of the dead – the doomed – till on the edge high above the rest one sees silhouetted forms motionless, intent – those who were killed three years ago – and beyond them, across the glimmering levels of sand, legions of others come stealing in – till the crowd is limitless; all the dead have come to hear the concert party in this half-lit oasis of Time.

It is too much; I cannot bear it; I must get up and go away. For I too am a ghost, one of the doomed.[122]

Puppets, shadows, moths and ghosts, all testify to Sassoon's haunted state of mind at this stage in the War. Vivid as these images are, only the shadows and moths remain in the poem which follows. Yet it still manages to convey the shifting, uncertain, even haunted nature of the desert scene, partly by its varied metre, partly by its repetitions, and partly through new metaphors of drifting 'shoals', 'shuffling' sand, a 'wall' of faces and the men's 'hunger' for home:

> ### Concert Party (Egyptian Base Camp)
> They are gathering round ...
> Out of the twilight; over the grey-blue sand,
> Shoals of low-jargoning men drift inward to the sound –
> The jangle and throb of a piano ... tum-ti-tum ...
> Drawn by a lamp, they come
> Out of the glimmering lines of their tents, over the shuffling sand.
>
> O Sing us the Songs, the songs of our own land,
> You warbling ladies in white.
> Dimness conceals the hunger in our faces,
> This wall of faces risen out of the night,
> These eyes that keep their memories of the places
> So long beyond their sight.
>
> Jaded and gay, the ladies sing; and the chap in brown
> Tilts his grey hat; jaunty and lean and pale,
> He rattles the keys ... some actor-bloke from town ...
> *God send you home*; and then *A long, long trail*;
> *I hear you calling me*; and *Dixieland* ...
> Sing slowly ... now the chorus ... one by one
> We hear them, drink them; till the concert's done.
> Silent, I watch the shadowy mass of soldiers stand.
> Silent, they drift away, over the glimmering sand.[123]

(CP, p. 100)

Apart from this concert party, there was little else to relieve the monotony of life at Kantara. Company training occupied the morning from 6.30 to 10 a.m. and some of the afternoon, but to Sassoon the days seemed wasted by petty details to be worried through. He ended each of them exasperated, exhausted and unable to think clearly. His main impression of the camp was of too much sand and sunlight and he welcomed the smallest distractions. Even taking a party of men to get their clothes and blankets boiled seemed worthy of comment, particularly the sight of a hundred 'stark-naked' soldiers waiting at the boilers. And he welcomed a football match between his old Company, C., and his new one, A., on 19 April, enjoying the excuse to admire the scantily clad players who included his favourites, Linthwaite and Roberts.

A week later, just two days before his departure, he spent an evening with Charles Wiggin, who had shared Norman Loder's cottage when Loder had invited them both to hunt in the winter of 1913-14. The 'same nice creature' as he had been four years earlier, he felt as Sassoon did about the War and, while his old Etonian friends discussed the 'Yankee' army and 'our big offensive next year', he and Sassoon reminisced about hunting days over vintage brandy supplied by their hosts, the Norfolk Yeomanry.[124] Another distraction, though not one Sassoon welcomed, was the departure on 20 April of 'the little doc', Captain Bigger, who was to remain in Palestine with the 10th Division.

The one ray of hope for Sassoon in this gloomy situation was the simplicity he continued to find in his men.[125] Unlike the officers, who continued to hide their fears under a sophisticated veneer of boastful talk and too many cocktails, the men seemed genuinely pleased to be going at least in the direction of home. The fact that the Western Front was over two thousand miles nearer to Leicester Square seemed to console them. Most had been in the Middle East without leave since 1915 – a situation Sassoon would try to rectify later – and had very little idea how horrific conditions on the Western Front really were. Though Sassoon admired their serenity, he could not emulate it:

> ... here I am [he wrote the day before leaving Kantara] after nearly four years of this business, faced with the same old haggard aspect of soldier-life – a very small chance of complete escape unblemished – a big chance of being killed outright – ditto of being intolerably injured – a certainty of mental agony and physical discomfort – prolonged and exasperating – a possibility of going mad or breaking down badly: in fact, the whole landscape of the near future bristling with unimaginable perils and horrors, and overshadowed by the gloom of death.[126]

To Sassoon's strained nerves the fear of breaking down was very real. Even his faith in his men might not be sufficient to prevent that, though if he did he believed that Rivers would help restore his sanity. His other great consolation at this time was Tolstoi, whose battle scenes in *War and Peace* reminded him of his own past experiences. In anticipating the wounds and failure he had momentarily forgotten what Tolstoi made so real – the excitement and reckless enthusiasm he felt before the fight, th need to play the hero and, as he puts it in his diary, the 'angry joy of bein ʒ "up against it" ', which would carry him through.

As Sassoon faced his fears in this way, he mentally prepared himself for France and when the 25th RWF left Kantara on the last lap of their Middle Eastern journey on 28 April, he was more or less ready. He still felt confused, intolerant and superficial in his attitude towards the War, but he now believed that the whole business was a pilgrimage towards his death. In this exalted, slightly unreal state, the nearer he got to the War the more he wanted to share its terrors. He was no longer going there to kill people, as he had once wanted to after David Thomas's death; his main purpose now was to look after his men, an escape from his own concerns which he found 'a blessed state'.

Before entirely committing himself to this saintly frame of mind, however, Sassoon indulged in one last selfish wish, to visit E.M. Forster in

Alexandria. On his way down to Egypt in February he had written to tell Dent that he would be passing through Alexandria, giving him an address there to which he could write. Dent immediately thought of his Cambridge friend, E.M. Forster ('Morgan'), who had been in Alexandria since 1915 as a 'searcher' for the Red Cross, and forwarded Sassoon's address to him. By 24 March Forster, delighted by the chance to meet someone with whom he felt he would have a great deal in common, had written to Sassoon. Though he had missed him on his way down to Palestine, they agreed to meet on his way back.

Sassoon, who admired Forster's work 'immensely' and 'entirely sympathized' with his attitude to life, looked forward to the event and, as soon as he knew the details, informed Forster of his imminent arrival.[127] But as he explained in response to Dent's enquiry: 'No I didn't meet Forster and much regret the fact. He wrote me such a nice letter. I was at Alex'er two days on a troopship but no one was allowed ashore. It was exasperating'.[128] There were consolations, however, and appropriately literary ones. 'We failed to meet', Forster was to write to Dent on 2 October 1918, 'but have become, through letters, more intimate perhaps than if we had met. I feel much affection for him. He must be a most delightful creature'.[129] Sassoon was equally admiring. But it was not until after Forster returned from Egypt in January 1919 that the two writers would meet and consolidate a friendship that was to last well into the 1950s.

Sassoon had hoped to meet Forster in Alexandria on 29 April, after an overnight train journey from Kantara. Instead he spent his two days there on board the troopship S.S. *Malwa* with the rest of the 25th RWF. It was one of three battalions on the 10,833-ton P. & O. liner, part of a seven-ship convoy whose voyage across the Mediterranean would be protected by ten destroyers. Though the Divisional General, four Brigadiers and numerous staff officers who accompanied them were almost certainly aware, as the ship's Captain was, of the dangers ahead, Sassoon and his fellow-officers were largely ignorant of them. They were unlikely to know that more than a hundred merchant ships had been sunk by German submarines the previous month. (A transport ship in the convoy behind them was to strike a mine just outside Alexandria.[130]) With provision for only 1,000 men in the lifeboats on a ship carrying 3,300 troops alone, it probably seemed wiser not to inform them of the shoals of U-boats through which they had to pass. Sassoon, whose purchase of the 'submarined' ticket in the sweepstake had been done more from annoyance than informed opinion, reported sympathetically that, such was the Captain's relief after their hazardous six-day voyage, that he burst into tears on the bridge.

Sassoon himself was more aware of a different kind of danger as the ship ploughed through the Mediterranean. Especially at night, when the sleeping bodies of soldiers on deck put him in mind of corpses and the noise of heavy waves recalled the sound of guns, he was reminded of France, that country which he was slowly but inexorably approaching. While continuing with *War and Peace*, he had also been re-reading Conrad's *Lord Jim* in preparation for the sea-journey and had started on Forster's most recent novel, *Howard's End*. All three brought home what the War had taught him, that life was a very serious business indeed. It had been possible for a short time in Palestine to forget the War, but once on board ship for Marseilles he was already mentally back on the Western Front:

> Lights and drinking card-players and wireless operators and navigators within [he wrote halfway through his voyage on 4 May]; chart-rooms, and kitchens and engine-rooms; all that is life, struggling to keep above water. And outside the mystery and unpitying hugeness of death and sleep, the terror that walks by night, and the impossibility of escape.[131]

Yet in spite of his fears and a natural wish to survive, he also felt that it was right to return to the fighting:

> We are going home. The troop-ship, in a thrill
> Of fiery-chamber'd anguish, throbs and rolls.
> We are going home ... victims ... three thousand souls.
>
> (*CP*, p. 101)

These lines conclude 'Night on the Convoy', a poem written almost certainly in Marseilles as Sassoon waited for the next stage in his pilgrimage to begin.

The Good Soldier (May-July 1918)

The last six months of the War are in some ways the most eventful, in others the least so of all for Sassoon. On a personal level it is a stimulating time which includes meetings with important public figures like Winston Churchill, T.E. Lawrence and Robert Bridges, as well as the beginning of warm friendships with Thomas Hardy, Edith Sitwell and a minor but equally interesting character, Frank Prewett. It also sees the consolidation of relationships with Osbert Sitwell and Maynard Keynes, who in turn introduces Sassoon to other members of the Bloomsbury Group. Most decisively of all, it sets the scene for Sassoon's first physical relationship, a passionate affair with Gabriel Atkin which marks his final acceptance of his homosexuality.

In terms of the War, however, it is Sassoon's least dramatic time. Since he is returning to France, a country he already knows, there is none of the thrill he experienced in discovering Ireland, Italy and Palestine. Even the promise of action, to which he almost looks forward, is withheld while his battalion, trained for the Middle East, is retrained for trench-warfare. When he is invalided home for the third time in July, he has spent no more than a week in the Front Line and completely misses the dramatic engagements which follow in August.

Sassoon's own army experience may not have been very eventful in mid-1918, but the War itself had entered its most crucial phase by the time he arrived back in France in May. The Brest-Litovsk Peace Treaty between Russia and Germany signed on 3 March, combined with Germany's efficient railway system, had enabled the Central Powers to transfer large numbers of troops and weapons swiftly from the Eastern to the Western Front and by mid-March they were poised for the offensive. Up to this point the main military initiatives had been taken by the Allies and only the Germans' superior fortifications had prevented a decisive breakthrough. It was now Germany's turn to try to penetrate the Allies' defences and to do so before the mass of fresh, unscarred American troops promised for the summer reached the war-zone. General Ludendorff opened his campaign with a surprise attack on a forty-three-mile front, Arras-St Quentin-La Fère, his aim being to drive the British back from the Somme, the French from the Aisne and to threaten Paris once more. He was only partially successful, however; in spite of forcing the Allies back forty miles in some areas south of the Somme, the northern part of the line held firm, particularly round Arras. He then launched a second great offensive on 9 April in Flanders which opened up a gap thirty miles wide in the Allied line and, by the time Sassoon arrived in France on 7 May, was preparing a third attack on the Marne.

Though Sassoon had reconciled himself to a return to France which he had initially dreaded, Graves was still rejoicing at what he mistakenly believed to be Sassoon's absence from that country. 'You can't think what a relief it is to me that you're not out in France', he wrote to him on 5 May 1918: 'for if you were I would almost have to follow'.[1] Yet even as these words were being written, Sassoon was sailing towards Marseilles.

Besides giving his friend news of the 1st RWF, still in Italy, Graves introduced another topic to his letter which was to worry them both throughout the summer of 1918, the Pemberton Billing affair. On 26 January 1918, Noel Pemberton Billing, an independent Member of Parliament for mid-Hertfordshire, had published a fierce attack on the Government's handling of the War in his magazine, the *Imperialist*. In it he claimed that the German Secret Service had a *Black Book* which contained the names of 47,000 English citizens who were vulnerable to blackmail because of their homosexuality. In a further article in his magazine (by now aptly renamed *The Vigilante*) Robbie Ross was clearly implicated. As Ross's biographer, Maureen Borland, maintains there can be little doubt that Lord Alfred Douglas, still anxious to get his revenge on Ross for his support of Oscar Wilde, was behind the attack.[2] 'Poor old Robby has been very ill and worried lately', Graves reported to Sassoon on 5 May, 'that brute Pemberton Billing has been libelling him again with Alfred Douglas and giving him a rotten time'.[3] Ross would eventually be cleared, but his friends were to claim that it was the strain of the lawsuit, started on 29 May and rumbling on through the summer, which killed him later in the year.

Another source of concern to Sassoon, referred to by Graves in the same letter, was the publication of Sassoon's second volume of War poems, *Counter-Attack*. Heinemann had stalled for some months, ostensibly to give *The Old Huntsman* a chance to sell more copies but partly because he wanted some 'amiable' poems 'to mitigate the horrors' and thought the book too short. He now finally agreed to go ahead. Problems of paper shortage created further delays, but by 5 May Graves was able to assure Sassoon that he had read through the proofs of *Counter-Attack* the previous Saturday; so too had Robert Nichols. Marsh, at Sassoon's request, had already read the collection in manuscript and had used his influence with Heinemann. For, although he had 'grave doubts whether it [was] right from the national point of view to publish the book at all', he admired it as poetry and believed that it would sell well.[4]

By the time Sassoon received Graves's letter, which had gone first to Palestine, he had almost certainly left Marseilles. His three-day stay there had proved a gentle re-introduction to France. After a three-and-a-half hour march to a Rest Camp at Musso just outside the city on the afternoon of 7 May, he had spent his first evening dining lavishly with his C.O., Lord Kensington, in Marseilles. Afterwards they visited a music hall. Apart from the unpleasantness of hearing drunken officers 'jabbering about their exploits (with harlots)',[5] he had enjoyed the occasion, especially the Pommery 1900 and '58 Brandy. The next day, with nothing better to do, he had gone to the Zoo, with the commander of B Company, Capt. W.N. Stables, a fairly close friend with whom he would keep in touch after his return to England.[6] They took the opportunity to explore Marseilles, which seemed to Sassoon a pleasant place, with its climbing streets, bright green plane trees and circle of grey hills. His third and final day, 9 May, was his most enjoyable, partly because the cold drizzle gave way to warmth – 'a proper May-day, with glory in the air'[7] – and partly because a batch of letters arrived for him, including a cheque for royalties on his first 1,000 copies of *The Old Huntsman*. Symbolically, this was also the day he started a new diary. Five months had elapsed since he had left Craiglockhart and now, at last, he was going back into action, as he had then wished. Ironically, after reading the *Daily Mail*'s description of enemy-occupied Morlancourt, which his own battalion had inhabited two years earlier, he was not so sure that he still wanted to.

Using a metaphor taken from his recent visit to the music hall, he wrote on 9 May:

> And all my future is 'tomorrow', or at the most two or three weeks of training for battle. Beyond that the fire-proof curtain comes down ... And it is covered with placards advertising my new volume of remarkable and arresting poems. I cannot believe that the curtain will go up this year and disclose the painted scene of Peace and Plenty. But I am quite prepared to leave my seat in the stalls and go away with Mr Mors [i.e. death], in case he calls for me at the theatre. But all this is silliness – the facts are what we want in our notebooks, and events. So here's to the *next* five months, and the harvest.[8]

Sassoon was wrong on a number of counts. His future readers would not want only 'facts' and 'events' in his diaries, though fortunately that was a rule he rarely managed to keep. And, in spite of his gloomy predictions 'Peace' was to come not long after the '*next* five months' he had allowed himself. But it was his third false prediction – that only two or three weeks' training separated him from battle – that was of most immediate significance. It would be nearly nine weeks before the 25th RWF, trained for desert warfare, were considered ready for the Western Front, weeks which took Sassoon ever nearer to safety.

The truth is that for the first time Sassoon was returning to France without wanting to be a hero. In 'Testament', a poem completed by 9 May, he declares:

For the last time I say – War is not glorious,
Though lads march out superb and fall victorious, –
Scrapping like demons, suffering like slaves,
And crowned by peace, the sunlight on their graves.

You swear we crush The Beast: I say we fight
Because men lost their landmarks in the night,
And met in gloom to grapple, stab, and kill,
Yelling the fetish-names of Good and Ill
That have been shamed in history.
                                        O my heart,
Be still; you have cried your cry; you have played
                                        your part.[9]

As the last line of this poem suggests, Sassoon was still troubled about his own responsibilities in the War but felt that he had done all he could to prevent its continuance and must now resign himself to the situation. His increasing concern for his men made it easier for him to stop thinking so much about himself, perhaps the greatest change the War had brought. As an aspiring poet his main interest had been to explore his own feelings and to concentrate on himself. As an officer his duty was to think of his men and that involved so many mundane details that he no longer had time to brood on his own problems. He was gradually discovering that it was more or less impossible to combine the functions of poet and officer, especially as second-in-command of a Company.

> When I was out here as a platoon-commander I spent half my time in day-dreams [he was to write on 15 June 1918]. I avoided responsibilities. But since I've been with this battalion responsibility has been pushed on to me and I've taken soldiering very seriously ... One cannot be a good soldier and a good poet at the same time.[10]

Sassoon's aim was to be a good soldier and poetry, for the time being, became subservient. But before he took up his full responsibilities as second-in-command of A Company, there was a brief respite while the 25th Battalion travelled to their next destination. Nine hundred miles away, in the Noyelles area of northern France, this involved another long train journey during which Sassoon's duties would be minimal.

Though he was not able to plan books appropriate to the journey, as he had in February, it was almost certainly the thought of three days on a train which prompted him to ask Ottoline the day he set out for a copy of Georges Duhamel's novel, *Vie des Martyrs*. This moving account of an army doctor's compassion for the wounded soldiers in his care had just been published in England as *The New Book of Martyrs* and clearly tied in with Sassoon's own feelings for his men.

Apart from books, Sassoon's second long train journey in three months differed from the first in other ways. This time he was travelling towards the familiar, not away from it, though with none of the safety that familiarity often implies. And it was towards known danger, as opposed to relative safety he went. The bitterly cold nights of his February journey, which had made him ill, were replaced by idyllic May days and nights in which the nightingales sang from every bush and thicket. He had a particular fondness for May and, as the train rumbled along through the Rhone valley, 'green and lovely with early summer',[11] he had what he suspected was an illusory sense of youth and prosperity, a feeling that happiness lay ahead. When he passed the outskirts of Paris on 11 May and gazed down on the city, glowing mysteriously in the evening light, he even allowed himself to wonder if he would ever visit it as a civilian.

Sassoon was in a romantic mood and it is hard not to suspect that he was falling in love again, a suspicion his diary reinforces. Following through his references to the three officers who shared his compartment it becomes clear that he found one of them more attractive than the others. Just as he had been drawn to Robinson on his long trek to Taranto, so on this slightly shorter journey he began to take a close interest in Lieutenant Jowett. While he found the eldest platoon officer, Harry Morgan, a thirty-nine-year-old who had 'knocked about the world' in East Africa and Wales, both sensible and amusing and was even more positive about the nineteen-year-old 'Stiffy' Phillips, a small, shrewd, self-possessed youth with a good sense of fun, it was Jowett he lingered over.[12] The 'Howitt' of *Sherston's Progress*, Sassoon was to dub him 'handsome boy' Jowett and to write a poem about him. His diary references to Jowett's 'smooth, sensual face and large limbs', his 'dark-eyed and lover-like and wistful air' suggest that his admiration was not simply for his qualities as an officer.[13] He could see that Jowett, like Phillips, was inclined to indolence and that he was also rather uncouth, but he found his shyness and gentleness irresistible and believed correctly that, when it came to the test, Jowett would be both reliable and brave.

Jowett is first mentioned during the journey north, which he clearly helped to make enjoyable in spite of its sinister purpose. The weather, too, co-operated and continued fine as they detrained at Noyelles-sur-Mer, seven miles north of Abbeville, on the morning of 12 May. Sassoon found it a pleasure rather than a penance to march the last eleven miles to their billets at Domvast. The village itself, situated eight miles north-east of Abbeville among the orchards of Picardy and only a mile from the forest of Crécy, tempted him to believe that there was hope after all. Yet he knew that the reprieve was temporary and that as soon as training was over he would be leading his men the thirty or forty miles to the Front. Resignation and a determination to enjoy each moment as it came seemed the only sensible responses.

Four days after reaching Domvast, Sassoon wrote to tell Ottoline that arriving there was 'like taking up the thread where it was broken the previous year'.[14] For, although he had never been in this particular village before, it reminded him strongly of earlier French billets, especially those of Morlancourt at the beginning of 1916. 'The floor of Apollo in Picardy' he had written then: 'it was here that he ground the kern and plied the flail, and lived at the farm'.[15] He felt 'rather ghostlike' himself returning to such familiar country; buying eggs and butter from 'Madame' at the farm and hearing army servants in the kitchen stammering 'Blighty French' to the girls gave him a strong sense of *déja-vu*.

To the troops, most of whom had spent their service in Palestine, it was more novel but no less agreeable. Lying so far behind the Front Line, the village had not been spoilt by continuous billeting and the men were in a comfortable barn, while Sassoon was in an actual house. For the third time in his army career he resorted to images of Arcadia – flowering hawthorns, lush orchards, grazing cattle and the sound of church bells. It was perhaps his ability to appreciate the beauty of his surroundings under almost all circumstances which enabled him to remain positive. On his first morning in Domvast, for example, and in spite of rain, he visited the forest of Crécy, where the great battle had been fought 572 years before, and in the 'endless avenues of branching green' was comforted by 'the wind in the beech-wood', a sound which had inspired him to poetry at Flixécourt in 1916.[16]

But it was impossible to escape the War for long. The constant booming of the heavy guns at Amiens and Albert was only one reminder of what lay ahead. Two days after his arrival at Domvast Sassoon was again in the forest of Crécy, this time for training. Though the surroundings appeared to even greater advantage in the sunshine and the men felt that it was 'like being at home again, sir',[17] the significance of the gas drill and bayonet exercises he supervised could not be ignored. The gas drill itself was an ominous reminder that conditions in the trenches had grown even worse since he was last there in April 1917 and he had always found bayonet training 'loathsome'.[18]

So that when, the following day, Sassoon heard Colonel Campbell delivering his famous lecture on 'the spirit of the bayonet' for the second time, he was completely disgusted at this expression of 'Militarism incarnate'.[19] It was a situation full of contradictions; soldiers marching home beneath a peaceful, spacious landscape, with columns of infantry in tin hats suddenly appearing on the Abbeville road among the hornbeam bushes and young wheat. Even at night when the sound of nightingales dominated the air, there was a menacing rumbling in the background and the sky winked and glowed with flashes of distant bombardment. On his third day in Domvast he felt so depressed that he wrote his will, leaving a generous legacy to Robert Graves, who responded by urging him to 'cheer up'; 'they can't kill you' he went on, 'and I infinitely prefer your present friendship to future grateful reflections'.[20]

In spite of Sassoon's increased awareness of death, he carried on as normal, settling in to a routine which continued until 23 May. One of his duties was that of Company catering officer. In an army notebook now at the National Army Museum, in London, there are detailed accounts of the train rations he bought – eggs, potatoes, butter, milk and vegetables – then, canteen stores, in which he included such luxuries as wine, cider and champagne. He was also in charge of provisions for the Company officers, noting at one point that his Company Commander, Capt. Bardwell, was slow to repay him and that it cost '50 centimes a day per officer for mess', with or without champagne he does not say. His chief responsibility was training his men, a mainly outdoor activity which both he and they enjoyed. He tried to make their lectures pleasurable too, spending most evenings studying training manuals in an attempt to present his material in an entertaining form. He was determined to become an efficient company officer, as unlike Capt. Bardwell as possible. Due to take over command of A Company when Bardwell went on leave on 26 May, he wanted to make a better job of it than his superior, whom he despised.

One of the few changes for the better since Sassoon's last tour of duty had been the issue of a manual for *The Training and Employment of Platoons*, a masterpiece of common sense, clarity and condensation by comparison with the heavily academic *Infantry Training, 1914*, which was in any case based on outdated principles. Sassoon made notes in his personal copy of the new manual, the most substantial being his list of '6 C's for Companies':

  (i) Care (of Men)
 (ii) Concentration – (in training begets coolness in action).
(iii) Confidence (in weapons and leaders).
(iv) Common-sense.
 (v) Co-operation = constructive.
(vi) Consolidation (both in Attack and Defence).

'The Big C' he could not resist adding, was 'Campbell (and the offensive Spirit)'.[21] Carried away by his alliteration, he went on to invent a mnemonic of which he was particularly proud: 'clear commands create complete control'.

Sassoon filled another exercise book with notes on 'the Assault', 'Trench reliefs', 'Principles of Defence', 'Platoon Organization', 'Gas Lectures' and 'Tactical Scheme for Platoon', then carefully cross-referenced it. In his anxiety to get his message across he sometimes sounds a little condescending, especially when reminding himself to 'Avoid ... using words which they don't understand. Use very simple, and, when possible, slang words'.[22] But his intentions were completely genuine. Time had brought him even closer to his originally 'ragged' company, whom he now found 'such a decent well-behaved lot that it is a pleasure to work with them and do what one can for their comfort'.[23] Never before had he worked so hard for his men. The reward was an escape from his own individuality which he found a 'very blessed state'.[24]

Another of Sassoon's duties, which he found both amusing and painful, was censoring the men's letters. Those who did not simply fill in the printed Field Service postcards, had comments to make which were sometimes so revealing that he recorded them in his diary. (He also enjoyed their colourful spelling which he lovingly preserved.) One issue which concerned them was leave, particularly when it failed to materialize: 'Well dear I dont sea any sighn of my leave [one man wrote] but if we dont get it soon it will be a grate disappointment to us all ...'[25] A recurring complaint was about sore feet, though Sassoon had done his best on that score. And in spite of more positive remarks, particularly on the weather and fresh farm eggs, it was the men's sufferings which tended to fill their letters: 'And this is the war [Sassoon concluded]. "Everywhere we go here seems such a long way" ... "hope to get leave soon" ... "our officers are fairly putting us through it" ... "expect we'll be going to the line soon" ...'[26]

Everyone expected the worst, but tried to appear cheerful. Sassoon was grateful to Ottoline, who kept up a constant flow of books, perhaps in the hope of distracting him. On 16 May, thanking her for yet another parcel, he says he looks forward to reading the Tolstoi and Peacock and knows he will enjoy Lamb's letters, Apuleius and *Letters from John Chinaman*,[27] but is not sure how he will get on with Carlyle's *Canvas Waves*, a worthy but no doubt heavy work.[28] It was escape not instruction he needed and Ottoline's choice of books mainly offered him that.

There were discordant notes in the Arcadia he was trying once again to build around himself. Three days after Ottoline's books arrived A Company's fourth platoon officer, Badcoe, returned to duty. Caught drunk on parade at Marseilles, he had been lucky to escape with a severe reprimand from the Corps Commander, but he seemed unaffected by the incident. 'Noisy and vulgar as ever', was Sassoon's response.[29] Promoted from lance-corporal and something of a swaggerer, Badcoe was definitely not Sassoon's type, though had he been less unreliable he would probably have overlooked the class differences. As it was he carefully noted Badcoe's dropped aitches in his diary.

Another discordant note which Sassoon found harder to bear, because it affected his men, was the apparent mindlessness of Army orders. On 17 May, for example, he was instructed to take 180 men eight miles in full marching order to the Brigade Baths at Nouvions. Only when he insisted was the 'full marching order' dropped, turning the two-and-a-half-hour march into an almost enjoyable experience. The Brigadier's justification for the original order was that he wanted the men to do plenty of route-marching, an explanation which provoked the ironic rejoinder from Sassoon: 'Quite a useful way of sending them to get a clean shirt!'[30]

Sometimes, when the orders did not affect his own men, he relished their absurdity; 'General Routine Order 2901', for example, read: 'It has been ruled by the Army Council that the act of voluntarily supplying blood for transfusion to a comrade, although exemplifying self-sacrifice and devotion, does not fall within the qualification "Acts of gallantry or distinguished conduct" in paragraph 1919 (xiv) of King's Regulations. (Blood must be *spilt*, not *transfused*. S.S.)' He could not help contrasting this order with an occasion on 20 May, when the 25th RWF joined other units of the 231st Brigade to 'do honour' to Corporal Harold Whitfield (the 'Whiteway' of *Sherston's Progress*) who had captured an enemy machine-gun post and shot and bayonetted the whole team singlehandedly:

> The man who 'voluntarily supplies his blood for transfusion to a comrade' does not – technically – perform an act of gallantry. But one who, in a spirit of animal excitement and over-strain, kills a certain number of Turks is acclaimed by his comrades, and made a fool of by the Mayor and Corporation when he goes on leave, shakes hands with George V and sees his face on the front pages of the gutter-press illustrated papers. The whole thing is childish – not manly – although the man and the deed are intrinsically fine things. The Army is kept going by 'stunts' like these.[31]

However strong his sense of the absurd, Sassoon's bitterness towards those who prolonged the War was greater, particularly when he thought of his men. Reminded by signs of seasonal change that autumn was inexorably approaching, he could not ignore the fact that it would 'bring many of them to oblivion and decay'.[32] Perhaps it was also the news that the battalion was about to leave for its training area which made him so conscious of death. Certainly Duhamel, whom he began reading on 21 May, would have brought to mind the physical devastations of War.

Yet the French doctor was also a comfort, of sorts, as Sassoon noted: 'It was written that you should suffer without purpose and without hope [Duhamel wrote]. But I will not let all your sufferings be lost in the abyss.'[33] The next sentence, which Sassoon marked in his copy of Duhamel but did not reproduce in his diary, reads: 'And so I record them at length'. It was almost certainly his own reason for recording so much about the War himself. All he could do for his men, apart from small things like buying them fresh vegetables with his own money and looking after them generally, was to document their sufferings.

Sassoon turned to Duhamel again when instructions came to start the journey to the Front. The order had reminded him of the previous year's move towards Arras, where 80 per cent of his fellow-officers and a large proportion of other ranks were killed, and he found expression for his feelings in Duhamel's poignant question: 'What became of you, precious lives, poor wonderful souls, for whom I fought so many obscure great battles, and who went off again in the realm of adventure?'[34] Yet another passage Sassoon quotes, concerning the difference between civilian and military graveyards, concludes with words which echo his own growing conviction: 'There must be something more precious than life, more necessary than life ... since we are here'.[35] If War had finally destroyed Sassoon's conventional childhood beliefs, it had also uncovered a deep spiritual need in him.

There are at least six other passages marked by Sassoon in his copy of Duhamel but not included in his diary, most of them describing the extraordinary courage of the common soldier. In one of these he has underlined for extra emphasis the words which seem to have meant most to him in the whole book: '... life here is reduced entirely to terms of suffering'. And it was almost certain suffering to which Sassoon and his men were travelling when they set out from Domvast on 23 May.

Their destination was Habarcq, only seven and a half miles from Arras and even less from Basseux, where Sassoon had stayed for three days in April 1917 on his way to Arras. The first stage of the journey, a sixteen-mile march to Rue, followed by a five-mile march to Magnicourt, was an exhausting business. It began at 2.30 a.m. and ended at 11 p.m. and the 25th were allowed a day's rest after it. Sassoon, who was still thinking of his journey the previous year, when he had passed within six miles of Magnicourt, felt extremely pessimistic about his future and spent part of the day composing a note on his servant, John Law,[36] in case of his death. His evident appreciation of Law's simple goodness shows how far he had come from the young subaltern whose main concern had been the correct shade of khaki shirt. He now clearly aspires to the almost saintlike unselfishness he found in Law:

> ... He is the perfect servant. Nothing could be better than the way he does things, quiet and untiring. I can imagine him figuring as an ideal 'patient' in one of Duhamel's hospital interiors. Of him it might have been written: 'He waged his own war with the divine patience of a man who had waged the great world war, and who knows that victory will not come right away'. He is simple, humble, brave, patient and loving: he is reticent yet humorous. How many of us can claim to possess these things, and ask no reward but a smile?[37]

It is difficult to express such matters without sounding a little sentimental, but Sassoon's appreciation was entirely sincere. So, too, was his desire to emulate Law's virtues. When he tried to analyze his sense of satisfaction over the recent journey, for example, it was not his efficiency as an officer which pleased him, but the fact that single-handedly he had managed to get some tea on the train for five of his exhausted men who had arrived too late to be served. 'It is these little things, done for nameless soldiers', he concluded, 'that make the war bearable'.[38] At the same time, he could not help wondering if he really was 'a good chap, or only rather a humbug'.

The second and final day's journey to the 25th RWF's training area was less demanding, though Sassoon found the ten miles in warm weather 'beastly', partly because of the congestion on the way. It was a sign of how much nearer they were to the Front. Having left Magnicourt at 9 a.m., the battalion arrived about 2 p.m. at Habarcq, a much larger village than Domvast and already overcrowded with troops. The men's quarters were, therefore, not as good as those at Domvast; one of A Company's platoons, for example, was billeted near a burial-ground, which the men referred to as 'the rest camp'. 'No reveilles and route-marches there!' Sassoon heard one exhausted soldier remark.[39]

The officers' accommodation was, as usual, a great deal better than the men's and Sassoon found himself billeted with Bardwell on the third floor of a château with a view of tree tops and a huge cedar. A large, empty building, which seemed to him even more 'barrack-like' after Bardwell left for England the next day, it was to be Sassoon's home for a month, though he did not know it at the time. For he was still expecting to be sent to the Front at any moment and was mentally preparing himself. 'Getting nearer the Line is working me up to a climax', he wrote on his arrival at Habarcq. 'Same old feeling of confidence and freedom from worry'.[40]

Bardwell's departure had a number of important effects on Sassoon. First and foremost, it made him wholly responsible for A Company, the second time in less than three months that he had been put in complete command. There is no doubt that his role as Company Commander drew him even closer to his men and increased his pride in them. 'I have seen a lot of soldiers at the war', he wrote, three weeks after taking over, 'but I have never seen a more well-behaved crowd than my present Company'.[41] He worried about their welfare far more than his own and was to write to Ross on 18 June enclosing a letter for Ottoline's brother, Lord Henry Bentinck, asking if anything could be done about the men's lack of leave: '70% of them haven't been home for nearly two and a half years', he told Ross, 'and many of them, (like Law) left England in Sept. 1915'.[42] Equally, he regretted the absence of any proper form of entertainment for the men in the evenings. This meant that the majority of them went to the local bars and spent most of their money there, 50 per cent of the battalion going to bed drunk every night: 'Because they all know that they will be in hell within a month; ... They are having what is called a good time. Drink and death'.[43] His chief concern was to make their remaining days as enjoyable as possible. A poem Sassoon wrote nearly a fortnight after Bardwell's departure, expresses his very real love for his men:

Reward

Months and weeks and days go past,
And my soldiers fall at last.
Months and weeks and days
Their ways must be my ways.
And evermore
Love guards the door.

From their eyes the gift I gain
Of grace that can subdue my pain.
From their eyes I hoard
My reward ...
O brothers in my striving, it were best
That I should share your rest.[44]

Another important result of Bardwell's absence was that it left Sassoon with a room of his own, where he could retreat from the pettiness and worry of army life. Though he had little energy for versifying after the day's work was over, his privacy enabled him to read books, write letters, keep his diary up to date and even think, activities which kept him sane in a very tense situation. (By 2 June the 25th RWF was on GHQ Reserve and liable to move at twenty-four hours' notice.) Apart from Duhamel, whom he was beginning to find superior to Barbusse, he was reading things which helped him to escape from the War, books like Lamb's *Letters*, Logan Pearsall Smith's *Trivia* and Lytton Strachey's recently-published *Eminent Victorians*. Ottoline was not the only friend to supply him with reading material, though she was his main source; Meiklejohn, for instance, sent him Walter de la Mare's latest poems, on request, and it was Ross who provided *Trivia*. Sassoon also managed to get hold of *The Times Literary Supplement*, the *Nation* and other serious periodicals.

At the same time, Sassoon kept up correspondences with an impressive number of friends, most of which have survived and help to flesh out this period. To Ottoline and Meiklejohn he wrote mainly of books, but to Graves, Dent, Marsh and particularly Robert Nichols, he wrote more frankly of his views on the War. His diary entries at Habarcq, which are reflective as well as factual, also testify to the benefits of having his own room. And, in spite of repeated protests about not being able to write poetry, he produced at least three poems there.

As at Craiglockhart Sassoon tried to keep a few hours after dinner free for such occupations, though he was frequently interrupted by people wanting either to air their grievances or simply chat. The earlier part of the day also resolved itself into a fairly regular routine. As a Company Commander he was kept busy from the time he got up at 6.30 a.m., or earlier, until dinner was over at about 8 p.m. Drawing on his initial week's training programme (from 14 to 22 May), he devised a detailed plan for his first week as Company Commander. Dividing the day into two parts, from 8.15-11.30 a.m. and 2-4 p.m., he then broke down the morning into smaller units, with very few minutes unaccounted for:

8.15-8.45	Inspection and Ginger-up (as Co[mpan]y)
8.45-9.05	B[attle] F[ormation] Assault
9.05-9.15	Break
9.15-9.35	Platoon work; arms drill, etc.
9.35-9.55	Section training

9.55-10.15	Break (with short lecture)
10.20-11	– Gas – Musketry
11.05-11.30	Ginger-up and go home.[45]

His readiness to learn from his mistakes is apparent in a note made after week one: 'Must practise L[ewis]-G[unners]. B[attle] F[ormation] wants improving. Think out schemes. Get to know more about junior N.C.O.s' And in another note he acknowledged what he recognized as possible weak points in his character as a leader: 'tact and care needed – never show signs of excitement'. He even made time to write out a 'Roll of N.C.O.s of A Coy, 25 RWF' and another of 'Duplicates', of which there were many (11 'Evans' and 11 'Jones', for instance). This was probably in order to learn the whole company by name, though it may have been done for his own interest, like the list he made of all the officers in the Battalion. His keenness, conscientiousness and determination to succeed distinguish him sharply from the rather naive and diffident platoon officer of 1915.

Sassoon's commitment to his men went far beyond what his position demanded. Often, after his duties were over, he watched inter-company football matches with them, for example. He also tried to keep in touch with the platoon officers, generally over dinner in the Company mess. His interest in Jowett and Phillips had continued and he noted after the first week's training that one result of his 'personal efforts' was that 'P. & J. [were] getting keen: *both all right.*' Sometimes he had to attend Commanding Officers' Conferences and listen to speeches from the Brigadier, or yet more lectures on Trench Warfare. Occasionally his routine was varied with an inspection by the Divisional General (who made 'a very pleasant impression'[46]), a march to the firing-range eight miles away (his private opinion was that he never hit the target at all), or Brigade Field Days, but essentially it remained stable. It was a healthy and, for officers, far from austere existence, including as it did good food and wine for dinner. (To the eggs, butter, milk, potatoes and other vegetables of the first week, he had managed as catering officer to add coffee, lettuce and sardines, and had augmented the wine, champagne and cider with beer.)

For the most part Sassoon entered into this existence willingly and was totally absorbed by it. Receiving a letter from Graves on 29 May which talked of leave, for instance, he declared in his diary: 'Damn leave; I don't want it. And I don't want to be wounded and wangle a job at home. I want the next six weeks, and success; do I want death? I don't know yet; but the war is outside of life; and I'm in it'.[47] The same day he wrote to Graves himself:

I came in, and read your letter, and began to think – 'damn Robert! damn everybody, except my company' – which was the smartest turn-out you ever saw – (and they *did it all for me* and no one else) – Then I thought – damn Wales – damn leave – and being wounded; damn everything except staying with my company till they're all melted away', (limping and crawling across the shell-holes; lying very still in the afternoon sunshine in dignified, desecrated attitudes – ...) I wish you could see them – They are the best I ever served with – (I don't mean the officers, though some of ours are all right.) And you won't believe it, but I'm training them bloody well. The General made a speech to the officers and N.C.Os but he only said what a certain poet had been rubbing into them every day for six weeks. I can't imagine whence this flame-like ardour came to me; but it has come; and it will last till the end ... There never was such a Battalion since 1916.[48]

On 30 May he was writing to Marsh: 'I am very happy and hard at work training a glorious company'.[49] Yet, as he confessed in the same letter, with direct reference to one of his anti-war poems, 'I try not to think of the result of the training, which will be mostly "poor young chap. I knew his father well" '. And his panegyric to Graves had concluded: 'And in six months they'll have ceased to exist'.

Sassoon's moods fluctuated as wildly as they had once before, after Thomas's death. On 26 May he felt tired and exasperated and on 28 May was too tired even to read. Yet on 30 May he could claim: 'I am still happy, and healthy, and proud of my Company'[50] and on 2 June, in spite of a week of 'unremitting toil over small details', he felt 'stronger and more confident than before'.[51] Then again his mood shifted and on 4 June he was 'jumpy ... nerve-ridden and exasperated', one moment accusing himself of being 'nothing but what the Brigadier calls "a potential killer of Germans (Huns)" ', the next denying it vehemently: 'I am only here to *look after* some men'.[52] Sassoon's overriding mood, however, was an almost mystical state of sacrificial love for his men, whose 'rotten boots' he longed, biblically, to kneel down and kiss.[53] The Furies had not gone away, but they were flying very high during these weeks of training and early summer 'like large lazy griffon vultures in Palestine, – resting on the air, – waiting to swoop down after the battle'.[54] He was '*not* cheerful', he told Bob Nichols emphatically in reply to a long letter from him at the end of May: 'Just filled with health, and gesturing heroically on the brink of the abyss'.[55] Privately he rejoiced that he was not 'alone and sex-ridden' like Nichols, 'the daemon of poesy leading him from gloom to gloom': 'Could he but share my present happiness! Could I but breathe into his haunted mind something of the golden-skinned serenity of my own St Martin's Summer of happy warrior youth!'[56]

Sassoon's 'happy warrior' instincts were to be satisfied sooner than he had expected. By 2 June he knew from the newspapers that, with the Germans on the Marne claiming 4,500 prisoners, the situation was critical for the Allies, but he was totally unprepared to be ordered to the Front at an emergency meeting of Company officers on 6 June. With his C.O. and one other Company commander, Ellis,[57] he was to visit the Neuville-Vitasse sector of the Front Line, approximately three and a half miles south-east of Arras. The 74th Division were to take over there from the 2nd Canadian Division and the C.O. wanted to inspect his part of the Line in advance. Sassoon had heard conflicting reports of the sector. On the one hand, it was said to be the quietest part of the Front, on the other conditions were rumoured to be atrocious, with heavy casualties, a great deal of gas and poor discipline among the conscripts. Nevertheless, he looked forward to visiting it himself, particularly without any command responsibilities. He was still 'Mad Jack' at heart.

Setting out on the morning of 7 June in fine weather, Sassoon, Ellis and their Colonel rode a few miles to Avesnes, where they were given a lift by lorry south to Basseux, the headquarters of the 2nd Canadian Division and Sassoon's final billet with the 2nd RWF the year before. From Basseux they turned north-east to Agny, where they lunched at Brigade headquarters before proceeding another two miles on foot to the headquarters of the 24th Victoria Rifles, the battalion they were due to relieve.

As Sassoon was guided the last stage of the journey to B Company in the Front Line, the area – which he identified as the place where his friends Orme and Conning had died and Ormrod been fatally wounded – looked to him as devastated as ever. Low green-grey ridges fringed with a few half-demolished trees were interspersed with lines of broken walls, the only remaining signs of destroyed French villages. In this Armageddon landscape ruined tangles of wire, disused trenches and the dismal remains of old rest camps reminded him how many times the ground had been fought over. The grass still waved in the breeze, poppies still flamed and larks still sang, but he could not ignore the fact that, after fourteen months of fighting, the Front Line was further back than when he had last seen it.

As Sassoon made his way to the steel hut which constituted B Company headquarters at 7.30 p.m. on a June evening, along the crumbling, dry communication trenches, he noticed how narrow they were and suspected that they would be very muddy when it rained, as it inevitably would. He felt confidence, however, in B Company's commander, Capt. Duclos, who seemed to him 'a fine chap'.[58] Curiously, in spite of his name and the fact that many of his men were French Canadians from Quebec, Duclos spoke no French. But he seemed to Sassoon, who was no doubt measuring himself against him, an inspiring company officer. Though not allowed, as he would have liked, to join in the considerable patrolling activity that went on, he was able to observe the captain's methods with his men. During a raid on his second evening there, when the Germans put over a box-barrage including a lot of aerial torpedoes, Duclos' demeanour seemed to Sassoon worthy of a set prose piece. It is a vivid picture of Front Line conditions:

Captain D– of the – th Canadians has got the right manner, whether it be studied imitation or spontaneous gallantry. He knows just how to walk along a trench when there's a 'trench-mortar strafe' on, and the half-darkness is full of booms and flashes. He never hurries; quietly, with a wise, half-humorous expression masking his solid determination and mastery of the situation, he moves from sentry to sentry; now getting up on the fire-step to lean over beside a flinching youngster who stares fearfully into the drifting smoke that hides the wire where the Bosche may be lying ready to rush forward; now he cracks a joke with some old 'tough'. 'Everything Jake here?' he says, as he passes from one to another – always making for the place where he expects trouble – or where the din is loudest. He leaves a feeling of security in his wake. Men finger their bayonets and pull themselves together. The end of his cigarette glows in the dusk – a little planet of unquenchable devotion.[59]

This is unquestionably how Sassoon himself wished to be with his men.

Whilst appreciating that his visit to the Front after more than a year's absence was a good test of his nerves, Sassoon felt 'a bit of a fool'[60] being there with no responsibilities. He passed some of his time during the long night watches gossiping with Duclos about old battles or cursing the politicians and profiteers. And when Duclos was busy he escaped into his copy of Lamb's letters, the one book he had brought with him. After 'Stand-To' at 2.30 a.m., he would go to sleep and wake up with the usual trench-mouth. Except for the increased danger of gas, it all seemed very familiar and any fears he might have had about his nerves were quickly dispelled.

Expecting to see it again very soon, Sassoon and his brother officers left the Front Line at 3 p.m. on the third day, 9 June. After various delays he was back in his quiet, empty room at Habarcq by 11 p.m., with the trees rustling outside and a very distinctive series of war pictures in his head. His reconnaissance had made him particularly conscious of the 'business-like futility' of trench-warfare, while at the same time giving him a 'fine object lesson in trench organization' from the Colonial troops.[61]

The next morning, reminded by the arrival of the Southdown Hunt annual balance sheet of Gordon Harbord's death and not as thrilled as he might have been by the news that he had been gazetted Acting Captain again, Sassoon suffered a recurrence of what he called his 'war misery'. A friendly letter from E.M. Forster and an article on Sir Walter Scott in the *TLS* may have exacerbated his desire to be elsewhere. Yet when he tried to think of the Pentland Hills and the charm of the Scottish landscape, his thoughts inevitably reverted to Canadians and Lewis-guns.

But as Sassoon pointed out in letters to both Marsh and Gosse the same day, the continual sunshine of the past four weeks made it 'a positive effort to be gloomy' and even mock tank attacks seemed fun in the afternoon sun.[62] As these letters show, he was far more concerned about the Ross-Billing affair than his own safety. In fact, there was no immediate need to worry about himself, since a 'flu epidemic struck the 231st Brigade, putting almost half its men out of action and effectively preventing it from being sent to the Neuville-Vitasse sector as planned.[63] With his usual luck

Sassoon had gained another month's grace. Far from being grateful, however, he grew increasingly frustrated by the waiting. Four days after his return from the Front, inflamed no doubt by his visit there and a glass or two of wine at dinner, he declared 'Damn it, I'm fed up with all this training! I want to go up to the line and *fight!*' Only after his two young protégés, Phillips and Jowett, had fervently agreed with him, did he come to his senses, noting in his diary:

> I shivered, and walked quickly up to the Château – to the quiet room where I spend my evenings with one candle, scribbling notes on the monstrous cruelty of war and the horrors of the front line. 'I want to go and fight!' Thus had I boasted in a moment of folly, catching my mood from the lads who look to me as their leader.[64]

It was not as though Sassoon had been allowed to forget the 'monstrous cruelty' of War. Only two days earlier, on 12 June, he had read with great sadness of the death of a friend, Lt Colin Dobell, 'Little Colin', who had been with him at Mametz Wood and hunted with him in Limerick. Reflecting on his friend's harmless wish for a life of fox-hunting, marriage and peace-time soldiering, he resisted the idealized picture and, instead of writing 'fool-poems' like those he read in *The Spectator* about 'our unforgotten dead', produced a heartfelt protest about the waste of young life:

Colin

One by one they've passed across the scene;
One by one; the lads I've known and met;
Laughing, swearing, shivering in the wet.
On their graves the grass is green;
Lads whose words and eyes I can't forget.

Colin's dead today; he's gone away;
Cheery little Colin, keen to hunt;
Firm and cool and quiet in a stunt.
    Is there any more to say?
Colin's name's been printed in *The Times*,
'Killed in Action'. *He* can't read my rhymes.[65]

Only a pale echo of his earlier protests ('And still the war goes on – *he* don't know why'), 'Colin' nevertheless signals a revival in poetic impulse. His love of 'lads' like Colin, which had prevented him from writing for some time, had now led him back to it again.

It was partly because of a letter from one such 'lad', thanking him for his help in Egypt, that Sassoon turned to another exponent of 'ladslove' for inspiration, Walt Whitman. Reading Whitman's *Sea-Drift* he experienced an emotion he had not felt for many months – 'the *passion* of poetry'. 'Of late I've been moody and nerve-ridden' he told Nichols on 19 June.

'Reading Whitman put me right. He is a glorious old lad'.[66] Whitman's stirring words were made even more resonant for him by the memory of Delius's musical setting of them. Starved as he had been of both poetry and music,[67] the effect was electrical and everything else was forgotten as he tried to express his own turbulent emotions in verse. Three days later he had completed another poem about his 'lads' under the almost hypnotic influence of Whitman:

> *I Stood With the Dead*
> I stood with the Dead, so forsaken and still:
> When dawn was grey I stood with the Dead.
> And my slow heart said, 'You must kill, you must kill:
> 'Soldier, soldier, morning is red.'
>
> On the shapes of the slain in their crumpled disgrace
> I stared for a while through the thin cold rain …
> 'O lad that I loved, there is rain on your face,
> And your eyes are blurred and sick like the plain.'
>
> I stood with the Dead … They were dead; they were dead;
> My heart and my head beat a march of dismay:
> And gusts of the wind came dulled by the guns.
> 'Fall in!' I shouted; 'Fall in for your pay!'
>
> (*CP*, p. 103)

This is an important piece which highlights the new direction Sassoon's war poetry was taking. Compassion rather than anger now dominates. In this, as in its semi-colloquial language, lyrical repetitions and freely expressed 'lad's love', it shows clear signs of Whitman's influence, though its resolutely regular stanza form and rhyme-scheme are very different from the American's fluid free-verse. It is also possible that Whitman's *Drum-taps*, a collection centring round the poet's experience as a nurse in the Civil War, inspired Sassoon's striking metaphor of his heart and head 'beat[ing] a march of dismay'. Likewise the words 'They were dead; they were dead' may be a conscious or unconscious response to another admired poet, Charles Sorley's instructions: 'Say only this: they are dead'.[68]

It was while Sassoon was completing 'I Stood With the Dead' that he finally realized just how difficult it was to combine the roles of soldier and poet, particularly when the poet was also a pacifist. Even on a practical level it was virtually impossible to remember the multitude of small details which filled a company officer's day with a head full of poetry. After a curt reprimand from the Adjutant for failing to return certain books and pamphlets, forgotten in his excitement over Whitman, he reluctantly abandoned poetry, though not before completing his poem and not for long. Only three days after 'I Stood with the Dead' was finished, he was relieved of many of the petty tasks which filled his day and actively encouraged to return to poetry. For on 21 June a second-in-command for A Company finally materialized who proved to be both efficient and an enthusiastic admirer of his work, Vivian de Sola Pinto.[69]

Pinto, who himself wrote poetry, had first encountered Sassoon's work the previous summer at a convalescent home in France, where he had chanced on 'an attractive piece of verse, expressing something felt by many sensitive spirits amid the drabness of trench warfare', 'To Victory'.[70] Shortly afterwards at Rouen Base Camp he had read a review of *The Old Huntsman* which quoted a very different but equally striking poem, 'Blighters'. So that, when Pinto had again been wounded and was convalescing, one of the first things he did was to buy *The Old Huntsman*. It seemed to him, therefore, an extraordinary stroke of luck when he reported to the 25th RWF at Habarcq to find himself assigned to A Company as Sassoon's second-in-command. The guide detailed to take him to A Company's headquarters in the grounds of the partly ruined château led him down a muddy path to a hut, he remembered:

> A tall figure came out of the hut to greet me. Ignoring my smart salute, he shook me by the hand:
> 'I suppose you're my new second-in-command. I've never had one before.'
> 'Yes, Sir ... er, are you the poet Siegfried Sassoon?'
> As I blurted out these words, I knew what the answer was. That splendid, erect figure with the noble head, mane of dark hair, piercing black eyes and strongly sculptured features could only belong to a poet.[71]

Sassoon's response to Pinto was equally positive. Under the guise of 'Velmore' in *Sherston's Progress*, he described a tall, dark, bespectacled young man of scholarly appearance. (Pinto had been at Oxford a year when the War interrupted his studies and was to return there to complete them when it was over.) His previous experience at the Front, Sassoon found, 'gave him a solid basis of usefulness and to this was added a temperament in which kindliness, humour and intelligence divided the honours equally, with gentleness and modesty in readiness to assert themselves by the power of non-assertion'.[72]

While Pinto, like all the men in A Company, was to fall under the spell of Sassoon's 'charismatic personality', which seemed to him to radiate 'heroic energy and generosity',[73] Sassoon more prosaically admired Pinto's ability to deal with the piles of paperwork accumulating daily on his desk. Their real meeting-point, and one which was to prolong their friendship well beyond the end of the War, was their shared passion for poetry, though Sassoon privately thought Pinto's verse 'not original in any way'.[74] When Pinto, on his first evening in the Company mess, produced Flecker's *The Golden Journey to Samarkand* from his pocket and offered to read some of it aloud, Sassoon was the only one who stayed to listen to Flecker's striking lines:

> Across the vast shadow-sweeping plain
> The gathered armies darken through the grain
> Swinging curved swords and dragon-sculptured spears,
> Footmen, and tiger-hearted cavaliers.

Pinto's paraphrase of the last two lines became his stock joke when reporting that the Company was on parade and it was a great consolation to Sassoon to hear the men of whom he was so proud described in such glowing terms. But, as he also made clear to Pinto, Flecker's ornate phrases, however seductive, were no longer an option for him; poetry, he told his second-in-command, 'must grow out of the realities of the human condition. Plain, direct language must be used and all inversions and archaisms must be avoided'.[75]

Only four days after Pinto joined A Company the 25th RWF made their final move toward the Front. The Germans, as a result of their fierce Spring offensives, had advanced in two large bulges (towards Amiens and Paris) in the south and a smaller one in the north on the Belgian border. It was to the northern, not the southern area, that the 25th RWF, recovered from its 'flu epidemic, were now ordered. So that, instead of repeating his short journey to the Neuville-Vitasse sector as expected, Sassoon found himself on a much longer one to the area north of Béthune, near Lillers. (The 74th Division was to replace the 61st in the St Venant-St Floris sector.) On 25 June, therefore, his battalion marched twelve miles for a four-hour ride north by train to St Hilaire, near Norrent-Fontes. After a long and exhausting journey, he was disappointed to find that his new billets were rather cramped and that he was not much nearer to the Front than at Habarcq, that is, approximately nine miles. For he was beginning to feel that it was 'about time to be up and doing'.[76] During the first few weeks of intensive training, he told Dent, 'I was full of energy and worked so hard that I am now dead stale and feeling that it would be a positive relief to go and do some fighting'.[77]

This letter helps fill the gap created by the absence of diary entries from 14 June onwards.[78] So too does a long letter to Marsh on 27 June, describing his situation:

> Think of a frowsty bed in a dingy, fly-buzzing room with a brick floor; and a midden-smelling yard full of whistling soldiers outside the window. A mule brays uncouthly – Afternoon sunshine, and busy noises of boots walking to-and-fro; the clatter of a pail; voices raucous or shrill, – male – British, or female – French; rustle of wind in leaves; drone of aeroplanes over the whole lot.
>
> On the bed someone dozing resentfully, wondering whether its influenza or war-weariness; – head full of jumbled snatches of daily worries, – fitful dreams where everything connected with 'The Company' goes hideously awry, – body full of aches, – falling, falling through the bed with heavy tiredness ...[79]

It is hard to imagine a greater contrast to Sassoon's large, empty room in the Château at Habarcq, but he tried to accept the change cheerfully. At least the wearisome training programme had come to an end as the battalion, together with the rest of the 74th Division, worked on rear defences for the next fortnight. There was also consolation in the fact that his second book of war poems was finally published on 27 June, after endless delays.

Writing to Graves on 28 June about how depressed he feels, Sassoon has clearly not yet received his own copy. When it does arrive on 29 June, his mood changes dramatically. 'I have received an advance copy of the book today', he tells Gosse, in response to Gosse's praise of the 'power and originality' of the new collection, 'and am gloating over it, as only young authors can do; when I had read it through I just sat and looked at it from a distance'.[80]

The title of Sassoon's new book, *Counter-Attack*, taken from the opening poem, suggests that he was still determined to fight the complacency and self-righteousness of the jingoists. Even the colours of the cover, yellow and 'blood-red', as he pointed out, convey defiance. And its dedication to Ross, his greatest encouragement to anti-war satire, seems highly appropriate, both in terms of his deep sympathy for all his friend was suffering in the Pemberton Billing trial and also in terms of the book's content. For almost all of its thirty-nine poems were fiercely critical of the War, unlike *The Old Huntsman*. Sassoon had to a large extent resisted Heinemann's desire for 'some amiable stuff to mitigate the horrors', though he had yielded to pressure from friends to omit two of the fiercer poems, 'Atrocities' and 'The Dressing Station'.[81]

Sassoon called it his 'undertaker' book and informed Osbert Sitwell, whom he knew would appreciate the point: 'The word death, die, dead, recurs more than 40 times in the 39 poems – Dark and darkness – 16 – War: 15. Night: 13. Gloom: 9. Doom: 7. Killed: 5. Corpses – only 3, I am afraid'.[82] Written between May 1917 and February 1918, *Counter-Attack* summed up for both Sassoon and the public his most consistent attitude to the War, which was no longer as shocking to them as it once had been. It seemed highly paradoxical to Pinto, who received a signed copy from Sassoon, that the author of poems such as 'Base Details', 'The General', 'Lamentations', 'Does It Matter' and 'Fight to a Finish' should also be 'a first-rate soldier and most aggressive Company Commander'.[83] But, as Pinto himself admitted, Sassoon's attitude was not really very different from a large part of the British army by 1918: 'He was convinced that modern warfare was an unspeakable horror and he deeply distrusted those for whom it had become a vested interest, but, as he put it once to me, we were ruddy well going to beat the Germans'.[84] Sassoon himself no longer attempted to resolve the contradiction, if there was one, and the reviews, when they came, would confirm that his attitude was no longer considered outrageous. The public had finally caught up with him.

After the excitement of receiving *Counter-Attack* Sassoon had to wait another week before anything of note happened. When it did, he fortunately jotted it down in a separate notebook which was not, like his diary, lost. The fact that he found the Deputy-Chaplain General's sermon to the 74th Division on Sunday, 7 July, worthy of a lengthy note – 'What the Bishop Said' – suggests that he had not lost his satiric edge.[85]

In a masterly introduction Sassoon compares the Bishop to a 'well-nourished Anglican Gramophone' which plays 'well-worn Records: Patriotism, Insular Imperialism, Hun-Hatred', and in the main body of the piece sums up the argument by which the Establishment hoped to bolster the morale of the troops. Apart from the 'fact' that 'the Germans have got the initiative and are hammering us very hard', there was a great deal of wishful thinking in the Bishop's sermon. Were the troops, for example, really 'more enthusiastic about winning the war than they were last year'? Was it truly 'religion that keeps [the troops'] morale so high'? And were the Americans coming across in large enough numbers to tip the balance, as the Bishop claimed? It may have been true that the Allies held the seas, but were the Germans actually 'getting weaker every week'?

Sassoon had his doubts, but he gained sardonic enjoyment from being compared to the Early Christians, who were burnt alive and thrown to the lions, as well as having 'J. Christ' presented as the 'warrior Son of God who moves among the troops and urges them to yet further efforts of sacrifice'. ('And slaughter?' Sassoon queried.) He noted with some relish the Bishop's concluding recitation of 'God goes marching on', delivered 'with lifted hand'. It seemed to him the spiritual equivalent of Campbell's Bayonet Fighting lecture, and he was probably not surprised to find that 'the troops rather liked it'. So confidential, pink and well-nourished was the Bishop that he could imagine him in the role of discreet butler to the Holy Family. He could not resist turning his observations about the Bishop into a satirical poem, 'Vicarious Christ' which, though not his best, is interesting because it anticipates one direction his poetry would take in the 'twenties.[86]

The day after the Bishop's sermon, 8 July, riding towards the Front on a battalion reconnaissance, Sassoon had strong reason to doubt that the Germans *were* getting weaker. As at Neuville-Vitasse, they had driven the Allies back many miles earlier in the year and were holding the line strongly near Merville. The 25th RWF were to relieve the 1st East Lancashires the next day in the right sub-sector, covering St Venant. Primed with map-references and urgent instructions from the Orderly Room, Sassoon was going up to obtain all possible information from the retiring battalion.

Jogging along the Pavé road from Lillers to St Venant on the Company charger, he felt both excited and anxious, convinced that if he made one mistake everything would go wrong with the relief. After five or six miles he crossed the La Bassée canal and rode on another two miles to Battalion

Headquarters. There he was given food and drink, then guided on foot to the Front Line. In the absence of communication-trenches he was led along a path which ran through damaged crops and willows, past the support unit's dug-outs, to the large shell-hole which served as Company Headquarters.

Though the British had been driven back beyond Merville they were still in the flat plain of the Lys Valley, in what had been a quiet back area where peasants still worked their land. Driving across the plain today it is still possible to see the problems which faced both armies in such low, open country. They had been forced to build breastworks rather than trenches for the greater part of their defences, since it was impracticable to dig trenches in such marshy ground. One of the 25th RWF's first duties on taking over the Line would be to cut the crops and clear two wide swathes on either side of the barbed wire. It seems ironic that, after training so vigorously in trench warfare, it would be their earlier Middle Eastern experience of patrolling in open country that would help them most.

So that when Sassoon was allowed to witness a small raid by the 1st East Lancashires, which enabled him to see what the sector was really like, it was not a reassuring sight. Instead of the solid defences of the Canadian trenches at Neuville-Vitasse, there were merely a series of breast-high sentry-posts stretching about three-quarters of a mile and connected by a shallow ditch. No Man's Land was a cornfield, containing more corn than barbed wire and varying in length from a hundred to two hundred yards.

After an hour or two at the Front Sassoon set off home in the early morning, hoping that his five pages of hastily scribbled notes would be useful. But, in spite of his anxiety, as he rode past the shuttered houses of a sleeping village he experienced a moment of extraordinary exhilaration which he never forgot:

What I felt was a sort of personal manifesto of being intensely alive – a sense of physical adventure and improvident jubilation; and also, as I looked at the signs of military occupation around me, a feeling that I was in the middle of some interesting historical tale. I was glad to be there, it seemed; and perhaps my thoughts for a moment revisited [Craiglockhart] and were reminded of its unescapable atmosphere of humiliation. That was how active service used to hoodwink us. Wonderful moments in the War, we called them, and told people at home that after all we wouldn't have missed it for worlds. But it was only one's youngness, really, and the fact of being in a foreign country with a fresh mind. Not because of the War, but in spite of it, we felt such zest and fulfillment, and remembered it later on with nostalgic regret, forgetting the miseries and grumblings, and how we longed for it to come to an end. Nevertheless, there I was, a living antithesis to the gloomier entries in my diary, and a physical retraction of my last year's protest against the 'political errors and insincerities for which the fighting men were being sacrificed'.[87]

Instead of sympathizing with the fighting men involved in the unsuccessful raid he had just witnessed, he found himself resolving to make a better job of it with his own soldiers. Such were the self-contradictions he experienced daily.

Looking back on his reconnaissance trip to the 1st East Lancashires, Sassoon doubted its usefulness. But at least one valuable purpose was served by it; when A Company was ordered to lead the 25th RWF up to the Front later the same day, at least he knew the way. Pinto had insisted that he have a good sleep on his return and he set off on the evening of 9 July very much 'on his toes'.[88] The unpleasantness of the journey comes through forcefully in 'Battalion Relief', one of his less well known War poems, in which the irony of the title and the reference to 'Harvest soon, / Up in the line' also show which way his thoughts were tending:

> *'Fall in! Now get a move on.'* (Curse the rain.)
> We splash away along the straggling village,
> Out to the flat rich country, green with June ...
> And sunset flares across wet crops and tillage,
> Blazing with splendour-patches. (Harvest soon,
> Up in the Line.) *'Perhaps the War'll be done*
> *'By Christmas-Day – Keep smiling then, old son.'*
>
> Here's the Canal: It's dusk; we cross the bridge.
> 'Lead on there, by platoons.' (The Line's a-glare
> With shell-fire through the poplars; distant rattle
> Of rifles and machine-guns.) *'Fritz is there!'*
> *'Christ, ain't it lively, Sergeant? Is't a battle?'*
> More rain: the lightning blinks, and thunder rumbles.
> *'There's overhead artillery!'* some chap grumbles.
>
> What's all this mob at the cross-roads? Where are the guides? ...
> 'Lead on with Number One.' And off they go.
> 'Three-minute intervals.' (Poor blundering files,
> Sweating and blindly burdened; who's to know
> If death will catch them in those two dark miles?)
> More rain. 'Lead on, Headquarters.' (That's the lot.)
> *'Who's that? ... Oh, Sergeant-Major, don't get shot!*
> *'And tell me, have we won this war or not?'*

(CP, p. 102)

Apart from the ominous storm the nine-mile march was uneventful and by 1 a.m. on 10 July Sassoon was back in the same Company shell-hole he had left the previous morning, the only difference being that he was now in charge. As he signed the list of trench-stores taken over – 30,000 rounds of small arms ammunition, 12 gas gongs, 572 grenades, 120 shovels, 270 Very lights, 9 reaping hooks and various other items – he anticipated a busy four days ahead. For A Company was left with only one platoon officer, his favourite, Jowett. Phillips had been made Lewis-gun officer for the Battalion, while Morgan and Badcoe had been sent away on courses.

Pinto describes how he and Sassoon personally settled the four platoons at their rather exposed posts before retreating along a shallow ditch to their shell-hole-cum-Company-Headquarters. It was impossible in such conditions to organize regular watches at night as in a connected trench-system. But Sassoon, who was longing for action, decided that he and his second-in-command should divide the night into two halves, during which one of them would 'hold the fort' in Company Headquarters while the other patrolled the posts. Determined that A Company should demonstrate its superiority to the Germans as soon as possible, he spent most of his turn on duty crawling through the cornfields in No Man's Land with a knob-kerry and some hand-grenades in his pockets. Pinto remembers him actually reaching a German post and bringing back a stick bomb, though Sassoon places the incident in broad daylight on the following day in *Sherston's Progress*, probably to accentuate both his foolhardiness and courage. For him the first evening's experience was marked by a less dramatic but equally significant event.

Sassoon had been out patrolling with Jowett and a number of N.C.O.s for practice and, after sending the others back, had made a second round of the sentry posts alone. On returning to his shell-hole, where a large shallow dug-out served as both dining- and bed-room, he saw that Jowett 'lay dead beat and asleep in an ungainly attitude, with that queer half-sullen look on his face', a 'visible representation' of all 'the dead and sleeping multitudes of the War'.[89] (Sassoon had noted in his diary two months earlier: 'Handsome Jowett asleep on the floor, with his smooth, sensual face and large limbs (as usual, he looks as if dead).')[90] This simple experience became the basis for one of his most moving war poems, a disturbing mixture of passion and compassion expressed in deceptively artless language:

> ### The Dug-Out
> Why do you lie with your legs ungainly huddled,
> And one arm bent across your sullen, cold,
> Exhausted face? It hurts my heart to watch you,
> Deep-shadow'd from the candle's guttering gold;
> And you wonder why I shake you by the shoulder;
> Drowsy, you mumble and sigh and turn your head ...
> *You are too young to fall asleep for ever;*
> *And when you sleep you remind me of the dead.*
>
> (*CP*, p. 102)

Sassoon thought these 'eight vigil-haunted lines' 'memorable' and was wise to cut the four lines which had followed on their first publication.[91] It was to be his last war poem based directly on trench experience.

The narrator's apparent unkindness in shaking his sleeping subaltern awake in 'The Dug-Out' is a particularly effective way of underlining his irrational fear that the young man is dead, since lack of sleep was a serious problem at the Front, particularly for company commanders. It did not, however, prevent Sassoon from energetically pursuing plans for an offensive. After his daring raid on the German line, during which he claims to have encountered four enemy soldiers face to face, he continued to lead patrols into No Man's Land. A bad strafe on the evening of the second day frightened even him and nearly ended his life, when a 5.9 shell scored a direct hit on his dug-out. But the shell was, miraculously, a dud and his ardour only temporarily dampened. By the next day, 12 July, he was in fighting mood again and what he called his 'rather feckless 1916 self'.[92]

The day had been quiet but the weather stormy and the shelling of the pack animals bringing rations to the Front had left A Company short of food. It seems to have been the final straw. The 25th were to be relieved the following night and Sassoon was determined to have one last 'really good patrol'.[93] Pinto, who was far more cautious, argued that it would serve no purpose and begged him not to risk it, but Sassoon insisted that they must maintain their supremacy in No Man's Land. Another excuse was that he needed to locate a machine-gun which seemed to be firing from outside the German lines. His real reason for going out, he later felt, was his need to escape from the worry and responsibility of his position, and annoyance at the thought of being blown to bits while he sat in the dug-out: 'I was tired and over-strained and my old foolhardiness was taking control of me'.[94] As on the hunting-field, he could only keep going by doing something spectacular.

Resigned to the inevitable but still fearing the worst, Pinto instructed their Company Sergeant-Major to send an urgent message to neighbouring B Company not to fire on Sassoon as he returned. Meanwhile, Sassoon set out with a young corporal from the last post on A Company's right flank.[95] The plan was to get as near to the rogue machine-gun as possible and then frighten its crew with their Mills bombs. It was 1 a.m. when they set out and pitch-black. But it took them over two hours to crawl across No Man's Land and by the time they were within striking distance dawn was breaking.

Pinto, supervising 'Stand-To' back in their sector, was becoming increasingly anxious, with just cause. Sassoon and his efficient companion, having managed to throw their bombs, had rapidly retreated like 'a pair of scared badgers',[96] but were still in No Man's Land. As they rested in a sunken road the corporal's fresh young face, lit by the rising sun, seemed to Sassoon to assert not only their supremacy over No Man's Land, but also the supreme satisfaction of being alive on a perfect summer's morning. Throwing caution to the wind in characteristic fashion, he removed his steel helmet and stood up to survey the German Line.

Though well hidden from the enemy, however, Sassoon was clearly visible to his own men, one of whom took careful aim. Moments later

Sassoon felt a terrific blow to the head and assumed that his last moment had come. Pinto, meantime, had set off in search of him and was just in time to witness the incident. He afterwards maintained that the gun was fired by a zealous sergeant from A Company, who had forgotten to check whether his Company Commander was back and had mistaken him for a German. Sassoon supported this view publicly in *Sherston's Progress*, but Robert Nichols, who talked to him shortly after the incident, offered a far more dramatic explanation. On a letter received from Sassoon in hospital he noted:

> He had been grazed by a bullet fired by one of his own sentries coming in. Somebody said the sergeant knocked up the recruit's rifle just as he pulled the trigger. There was not wanting talk to the effect that the High Command had decided he should die. I think it was wild talk. But the fact remains that he was a very inconvenient figure.[97]

It certainly is far more plausible that the shot was 'friendly fire' from a raw recruit rather than an experienced sergeant, but perhaps Sassoon preferred the inherent irony of being shot by one of his keenest men. There is nothing to support the conspiracy rumours that 'the High Command had decided he should die', though Sassoon would probably have enjoyed those as well. He was only too ready to acknowledge that he had been 'a very inconvenient figure'.

Another friend, Wintringham Stables, who was with the 25th RWF at the time, implies that Sassoon was something of a problem to his superiors in his version of events. Sassoon made his nightly forays, he maintained, in order to get an accurate sketch of the German front line immediately opposite the battalion. But when their Brigadier learnt of his activities he was angry: 'You know my Brigade Order', he told Stables. 'No Company Commander to go outside his wire except on an order issuing from brigade'. Knowing Sassoon as he did, Stables passed this order on in writing, 'so that there could be no possible reason for misunderstanding'. Stables interpreted Sassoon's final sortie, therefore, as a deliberate flouting of the rules in order to complete his sketch of the German front. If this version is correct, then Sassoon's superiors must have been relieved to see him leave.[98]

Pinto's main concern when he reached Sassoon in No Man's Land was, not who had fired the shot, but how much damage it had done. Sassoon's face was covered in blood and he assumed the worst. The corporal, however, had already discovered that it was only a flesh wound, though hardly the 'graze on the temple' with which Sassoon reassured Pinto. Medically it was described as a 'glancing wound over the right parietal of the skull' and was more serious than he suggested; had the sentry aimed an inch or two to the right he would certainly have died. As it was, he staggered back to his Company unaided.

Once Sassoon realized that his wound was not fatal, his thoughts turned to his men. It seemed 'an unspeakable thing to leave [them] in the lurch, to go away into safety'.[99] 'I won't say goodbye; I'm coming back', he told his Sergeant-Major as he set off for Battalion Headquarters, to have his wound dressed. But as he blundered into the Aid Post there, he had already travelled a mile and a half from the Front. He was equally insistent as he said long farewells to the C.O., the Adjutant and other H.Q. officers: 'You'll see me back in three weeks', he shouted. But as various ambulances ferried him still further away to the Casualty Clearing Station, near St Omer, his words began to sound rather hollow.

Whereas on the first day Sassoon had genuinely tried to persuade an R.A.M.C. Colonel to keep him at the Main Dressing Station till his wound healed, after a restless night in Casualty Clearing he offered only token resistance to being sent down to the Base. He still wanted to stand out against all the profiteers and hypocrites at home, but his physical weakness was sapping his will. And even if he had had the strength to refuse, he suspected that everyone would think him mad, especially with a head-wound. 'Who ever heard of anyone refusing to go down the line with an honourable wound?' he asked.[100]

So, on 15 July, Sassoon found himself at No. 8 Red Cross Hospital in Boulogne, being fussed over by sympathetic nurses. Still haunted by the memory of his Company, which had become as precious to him as his family, he tried to appear hearty and well, though he felt neither: 'All that was decent in me disliked leaving them to endure what I was escaping from. And somehow the idea of death had beckoned to me – ghastly though it had been when I believed that I had been killed'.[101]

It was clearly time for a long rest and when a nurse informed him of his imminent departure for England he could no longer resist. His 'proud, angry resolve', his 'tenderness' for his men had faded into what he guiltily construed as 'a selfish longing for safety'.[102] A month earlier he had urged Robert Nichols to pay a visit to Weirleigh mainly out of concern for his mother. Now he longed to be there himself. He could already see in his mind's eye 'the door into the garden at home, and Mother coming in with a basket of roses. And my terrier ... and the piano ...'[103]

'A Loathsome Ending'
(July-November 1918)

When Sassoon left France for England on 18 July 1918 it was for the last time, though he did not know it. Determined not to desert his men, as he saw it, he was already planning to return to them even before he left. But as the weeks passed his resolution weakened. Exhausted in both body and mind, he could not no longer struggle against the odds. He had genuinely steeled himself to resist what he called a 'Blighty wangle',[1] but once in England he lacked the energy to argue his way back to the Front for the fourth time. As everyone but himself agreed, he had gone well beyond the call of duty in caring for his men, but his guilt at not returning to them would persist to the end of the War and beyond. It was as if he could only justify his tortured physical attraction towards particular men by showing an altruistic, asexual love for all his men: 'I know that it is the only way I can keep my soul clean', he wrote desperately in his diary on 15 July, as he struggled to resist the lure of home.

Fortunately the matter was not in his hands. His wound was slow to heal and there was a danger of infection, so the doctors at Boulogne decided to send him back to England. Arriving at the American Red Cross Hospital No. 22 at Lancaster Gate, in London, on 18 July, he was put into a large ward which overlooked Hyde Park. As he lay listening to the civilian hum of London traffic, it seemed to him specially subdued for the benefit of patients, but he may have been comparing it with the din of the Front Line. Except for the loss of Ottoline's lucky opal, which had been stolen in Boulogne, it was an outwardly perfect solution. Occasional visits by Royalty and more frequent ones by Winston Churchill's American mother, Lady Randolph, soothed his ego as well as his brow. And there were numerous visitors to welcome the wounded hero home.

They swarmed in on his very first afternoon – his mother, Marsh, Ross, Meiklejohn, Nichols and Osbert Sitwell – and began to merge in his bewildered brain, 'MarshMoonStreetMeiklejohnArdoursandendurancSitwellitis'.[2] As he wrote to Graves, one of the few friends absent on the occasion, their 'Jabber – Gesture – Jabber – Gesture' proved too much for his frayed nerves and complications set in. He was moved to a smaller room and, as he battled against fever and sleepless, guilt-ridden nights, all visitors were banned. One of the banned was Dent, to whom he wrote to explain, with uncharacteristically confused syntax and sprawling hand, on 20 July:

> Those people kept coming and saying someone else had arrived, and I wanted to see everyone separate, and now you've got lost in the crush – and I don't suppose you'll ever speak to me again.[3]

'Such a crowd' it had seemed to him in his weakened, feverish state and, since he had agreed to see his relatives on the Sunday, he suggested that Dent put his visit off until Monday, 22 July. But on 21 July he had to write again to defer Dent's visit: 'Now they say I mustn't see anyone till Tuesday! as I got a headache and couldn't sleep'. Similar letters were sent to other friends and by 24 July he was still in a disturbed state.

In his irritability, restlessness and depression – what he wittily called his 'sleeplessexasperuicide'[4] – Sassoon wrote to the one person he hoped might fully understand his state, Graves. While still in France he had sent Graves, whom he knew to be in financial difficulties, a generous £23 for his twenty-third birthday and Graves had replied with a long, appreciative letter. If he had only himself to consider, he wrote, he would gladly change places with his friend, in spite of his fear of the La Bassée country and poison gas.[5] As for Sassoon's accusation of his 'not writing deeply', Graves protested:

> ... blast you, you old croaking corbie [i.e. raven] aren't I allowed for the honour of the regiment to balance your abysmal groanings with my feather-top rhymes and songs. And I have written croakingly too lately but I haven't sent you specimens because I think its bad taste – most ungrateful when God's so nice to me.[6]

Sassoon had replied from his French hospital and in his next letter Graves jokingly congratulated him on getting a bullet through his 'napper' and for writing to him more sanely, perhaps seeing a connection between the two. Continuing their tradition of verse letters, he also included ten lines of a poem which started:

> Poor Fusilier, vexed with the Fate
> That keeps you there in France so late ...[7]

It was this poem which prompted Sassoon to reply on 24 July in a verse letter, which probably pleased them both at the time, but which was to become the cause of much trouble later on.[8] Its jumpy, changing staccato rhythms and jumbled contents are convincing proof of Sassoon's extreme nervous tension at this time, the occasional breakdown of the verse reflecting his own unstable condition:

17. 'A Loathsome Ending' (July-November 1918)

Dear Roberto,
I'd timed my death in action to the minute –
(The Nation with my deathly verses in it) –
The day told off – 13 – (the month July) –*
The picture planned – O Threshold of the dark!
And then, the quivering Songster failed to die
Because the bloody Bullet missed its mark.

Here I am: They *would* send me back –
Kind M.O. at Base; Sassoon's morale grown slack;
Swallowed all his proud high thoughts & acquiesced ...
O Gate of Lancaster, O Blightyland the Blessed ...

After another erratic twenty-two lines Sassoon's ironic exploration of his sense of guilt and humiliation continues:

O yes, he's doing very well and sleeps from two till four.
And there was Jolly Otterleen† a-knocking at the Door –
But Matron says she mustn't, not however hard she knocks,
(Though she's bags of golden Daisies & some Raspberries in a Box,)

Be admitted to the wonderful & wild & wobbly-witted
Sarcastic soldier-poet with a Plaster on his crown,
Who pretends he doesn't know it – (he's the Topic of the Town).

He then reverts to his pride in his Company, whom his (and Graves's) friend, Captain Stable has written to say are doing 'better and better'. His final outburst, full of defiant references to popular songs, must have made Graves realize how shaken his friend was:

But I don't care; I made them love me although
they didn't want to do it, and I've sent them a
glorious Gramophone and God send you back to me‡
Over the green eviscerating sea – And I'm
ill and afraid to go back to them because those
five-nines are so damned awful
When you think of them all bursting and you're
lying on your bed, with the books you loved and
Longed for on the table; and your head All
Crammed with village verses about Daffodils and
Geese ... O Jesu make it cease – ...

'Does this break your heart ... What do I care?' Sassoon concluded, though softening his apparent defiance by signing himself with the name Graves

---

* 'I Stood with the Dead' was printed in *The Nation*, 13 July 1918, the day Sassoon was wounded.
† i.e. Lady Ottoline Morrell.
‡ 'You Made Me Love You', 'I Didn't Want to do It' and 'God Send You Back to Me' were all lines from well-known songs of the day.

had given him, 'Sassons'. He had also responded cynically in the same poem to Graves's request for some of his 'Persian gold' (to guarantee a loan):

> Yes, you can touch my Banker when you need him.
> Why keep a Jewish friend unless you bleed him?

To which Graves responded three days later, with a reference to his own ancestry: 'Why keep a German friend unless you grieve him?'

Graves had opened this letter of 27 July with another painful joke based on his conviction that Sassoon had been misled by Ottoline and her Pacifist circle: 'God preserve you from your friends the Rottalines and the Bolshevists and the syphilitic young poets!'[10] He believed that the only person who could help Sassoon in his distracted state was the same one who had persuaded him to return to the fighting, Dr Rivers. Graves had admired Rivers greatly when they met at Craiglockhart and knew that he had already visited his ex-patient at Lancaster Gate from two passages in Sassoon's verse letter. Though jokey and playful, with their extended pun on Rivers's name, these passages suggest that Sassoon himself felt that Rivers was his only hope and that he still believed he ought to go back to the Front:

> ... O Rivers please take me And make me
> Go back to the War till it break me.
> Some day my brain will go BANG,
> And they'll say what lovely faces were
> The soldier-lads he sang ...

Rivers, now based in London, had visited Sassoon on 23 July, in spite of the efforts of the stern matron, Mrs Fisher, to prevent him. Judging from the description in *Sherston's Progress*, which is placed significantly at the end as the climax to the protagonist's war-experience, he was already having the effect Graves hoped for. 'My futile demons fled him', Sassoon's narrator records, '– for his presence was a refutation of wrong-headedness ... I knew that I had a lot to learn, and that he was the only man who could help me'.[11] Rivers, the one character to appear as himself in this version of Sassoon's life, is typically reticent during their meeting but his presence brings the comfort and reassurance a loving parent gives to an unhappy child:

> He did not tell me that I had done my best to justify his belief in me. He merely made me feel that he took all that for granted, and now we must go on to something better still. And this was the beginning of the new life toward which he had shown me the way ...[12]

Rivers's positive influence was recognized by the hospital staff, who allowed him to visit Sassoon while other friends, like Ottoline, were being turned away.

Even when Sassoon began to feel better at the beginning of August, he was still seeing very few people. 'It is very upsetting', he explained to Cockerell in one of his rare letters of the period, '– coming back to life after saying goodbye to it!'[13] Though letter-writing was still something of an effort, and in any case discouraged by his doctor, reading offered its usual comforts. Apart from the large box of books he had brought back from France, he had managed to get hold of Forster's *A Room with a View*. Swamped as he felt by gushing females – Rivers, he noted, was the only male around – he particularly appreciated Forster's 'conversations of foolish women'.[14] He was also reading Keats's letters and asking friends for other books, preferably light and amusing. Meiklejohn obliged with a collection of *A Hundred and Seventy Chinese Poems* published by Methuen that year, though it could hardly have struck the patient as 'light'.

As Sassoon's health gradually improved he started to think about his own writing again and by mid-August was in 'full blast', as he put it to Nichols on the 15th: 'making the most gorgeous poetry. I simply can't stop ... it pops out so quick that I can't believe it's any good. And then I read it again and gurgle with bliss'.[15] If Sassoon was as prolific as he suggests at Lancaster Gate, he must have destroyed a number of poems, since, of the four included in his letter to Nichols, at least two had originated elsewhere,[16] leaving only two or three new poems. The first of these, 'Dedication', may help to explain why so few have survived from this period:

> To your blithe limbs, your steadfast-gazing eyes
> And your young trust in life, I gave my song.
> All that was yours I claimed to make me wise;
> All that was kind and clean and scornful of wrong
> I snatch'd from your proud hands to keep me strong.
>
> O body's loveliness that leap't for joy!
> O Spirit that burned within, a rose of fire! ...
> > voice
> They have murdered the ~~face~~ that was you; and the dreams of a boy
> Pass to the gloom of death with a cry of desire:
> And I alone remain; dumb with my pain,
> Watching the stain of blood on your brow; and the deep
> Calm that you wear, like a lover slain in sleep.

Ostensibly a lament for a dead soldier-friend, this reads more as a 'cry of desire' for a 'lover slain in sleep' to quote its own ninth and twelfth lines. The lingering physical detail – 'blithe limbs', 'steadfast-gazing eyes', 'proud hands', 'body's loveliness', 'face' and 'brow' – the tender reference to 'the dreams of a boy' and the narrator's passionate involvement in the young soldier's 'death' (a popular Jacobean metaphor for sexual consummation) probably struck Sassoon as revealing too much of his homoerotic feelings and it was never published. It may also explain why Nichols suggested that it needed rewriting.

Another poem written at this time suffered the same fate as 'Dedication' and probably for the same reason, that it was too explicit an outpouring of his sexual longings. Entitled 'The Vigil', Sassoon describes it in a letter to Marsh as 'forty lines of blank verse written round Whitman's "Vigil of silence, love and death, vigil for you my son and my soldier" '.[17] Wishing to escape from his 'bitter little epigrammatic poems', which threatened to become a habit of mind, he felt drawn towards 'larger canvasses, sort of Whitmanesque effects of masses of soldiers'.[18] The 'big poem' which emerged attempts to express 'the biggest thing I feel', a reference no doubt to his overwhelming love and pity for all the young men he had seen die in the War. This, too, appears to have been destroyed.[19]

One of the two War-poems Sassoon did allow to survive from his Lancaster Gate phase, 'Can I Forget?', expresses a similar sense of loss but in less explicit, at times highly derivative terms. Echoing Kipling's 'Lest We Forget'[20], Binyon's 'We will Remember Them'[21] and Whitman's 'O Captain! my Captain!', Sassoon's poem is yet another attempt to come to terms with his guilt in the comfort and security of his hospital bed:

> Can I forget the voice of one who cried
> For me to save him, save him, as he died? ...
>
> Can I forget the face of one whose eyes
> Could trust me in his utmost agonies? ...
>
> I will remember you; and from your wrongs
> Shall rise the power and poignance of my songs:
> And this shall comfort me until the end,
> That I have been your captain and your friend.[22]

Sassoon's other War-poem of the period, 'Great Men', was inspired by the visit of the Duke of Connaught to Lancaster Gate. Sassoon's two 'bad-tempered verses'[23] deal scathingly with the 'monstrous tyranny ... brought to birth' by such 'Great Men':

> ... You Marshals, gilt and red,
> You Ministers and Princes, and Great Men,
> Why can't you keep your mouthings for the dead?
> Go round the simple cemeteries; and then
> Talk of our noble sacrifice and losses
> To the wooden crosses.[24]

Writing about his conflicts in this way seems to have helped Sassoon resolve them and by mid-August he was able to report to Marsh that 'the furies [had] flapped out of the window'.[25]

Whether it was this image which inspired the fourth poem Sassoon sent to Nichols on 15 August, or whether 'Butterflies' is simply an expression of his recovering sense of beauty and significance in life, it does at any rate show a distinct change of mood. Like its subject, it is a slight poem which looks both backward to his youthful descriptions of summer dawns and forward to one type of work to come, a short pastoral piece where observation of nature leads to reflection on the significance of the poet's own life. In this particular case the butterflies become emblems of a new start, however shaky:

> … And they are as my soul that wings its way
> Out of the starlit dimness into morn:
> And they are as my tremulous being – born
> To know but this, the phantom glare of the day
>
> (*CP*, pp. 111-12)

'Butterflies' was one of the few poems to please Sassoon at Lancaster Gate – it was 'real good' he told Nichols, who was about to leave for America.[26] He was happy to help with Graves's poetry, in spite of his recent criticisms, and suggested a number of revisions to his latest manuscript.[27] Another poet to whom he wrote at this time, Vivian de Sola Pinto, was also about to publish his work.[28] Sassoon, however, seems more concerned to tell his ex-second-in-command how he feels about leaving the Front:

Letters from the Battalion are rather agonizing – they just give one a heart-pain, that's all. My servant Law puts the most poignant simple things in (apparently quite unconsciously). You know what I feel about Blighty. The callous vulgarity of the majority here is beyond anything. I have been in this place since July 18 and haven't yet 'put my uniform on' to dazzle the V.A.D.S. [i.e. the nurses known as Voluntary Aid Detachments] . One can't have a 'good time' without peace of mind, and I got more of that commodity with A Company than anywhere else. I lie and sweat in bed at night and wonder what you're all up to, my dears. I wish to God I could lend you some of the empty luscious comfort that is heaped around me.[29]

Not until the second half of the letter does Sassoon refer to Pinto's forthcoming book, begging him not to worry what reviewers say of it.[30] This allows him to mention reviews of his own book. For one of the most consoling aspects of life at Lancaster Gate was the praise that began to pour in for *Counter-Attack*.

By the time Sassoon wrote to Pinto on 4 August there had been at least sixteen reviews and many more were to come.[31] He could not resist drawing his friend's attention to three of the best, J.C. Squire's in *The New Statesman* (3 August), Winifred Blatchford's in *The Clarion* (19 July) and Max Plowman's in *The Labour Leader* (25 July). As with *The Old Hunts-*

man he saved all the reviews for his press-cutting book, with the noticeable exception of a hostile one in *The Nation* by John Middleton Murry. He had regarded both the magazine and the reviewer as allies, so was particularly shocked by it.

Ross, who brought him many of the press-cuttings in hospital, had become expert at fielding hostile criticism, however, and assured him that bad reviews often did more good than adulatory ones. Murry's article had appeared on 13 July, the day he was wounded, and had angered Sassoon's friends. Philip Morrell, urged by an outraged Ottoline (who had pressed Murry to write the review in the first place) wrote at once to *The Nation* defending Sassoon's work and Sassoon, in turn, wrote to thank him for doing so.

On the whole, though, the critics were positive and showed far more understanding of Sassoon's viewpoint than they had the previous year in reviewing *The Old Huntsman*. The *TLS*'s anonymous critic, for example, represents a number of reviewers who, while questioning whether such harshly realistic satires could be called poetry, are nevertheless full of admiration:

> There is a stage of suffering, so these poems seem to show us, where any expression save the barest is intolerable; where beauty and art have something too universal about them to meet our particular case ... but [Sassoon's] contempt for palliative or subterfuge gives us the raw stuff of poetry.[32]

For the critic of *Common Sense* (20 July 1918) 'nothing so drives home to the imagination the sheer, breaking horror' of the War as the fact that, 'though an artist, [Sassoon] has been unable so to see through his experiences as to make poetry of them' – something of a back-handed compliment. Even the *Morning Post*, a bastion of the jingoistic, allows that, having 'served gallantly in the war', he has 'a right to enter a minority report' and praises him as a poet of 'power and precision'.[33] A number of the more learned reviewers hail him as the English verse equivalent of the French writer he had chosen to preface *Counter-Attack*, Henri Barbusse. Winifred Blatchford, in an enlightened rejection of Keats's over-simplification that 'Beauty is Truth: Truth Beauty' claims:

> As Barbusse saw [War], so [Sassoon] sees it. But his vision is no less true than was the beauty-cleansed vision of his brothers in arms and art. It is a matter purely temperamental; and because Barbusse gave us in *Le Feu* the cruellest and most harrowing of all war chronicles – without a glint of sunshine, a blossom scent, or a ray of comfort – it does not necessarily follow that Barbusse's account of war is less true than accounts more tolerant and tolerable.[34]

Predictably, praise came from the pacifists, notably from Max Plowman, who had himself faced Court Martial and imprisonment when, like

Sassoon, he refused to go on serving in the army.[35] 'What recognition', Plowman asked in the *Labour Leader* for 25 July, 'is the country going to give to Mr Sassoon for writing this book?' By publishing *Counter-Attack*, he argued, Sassoon had 'rendered about the best public service it is at present possible to offer. He has delivered the finest counter-attack in the war by making a breach in the sinister ranks of official reticence and unofficial ignorance and self-complacency. *He has told the truth about the war*'. *The Tribunal* was equally fulsome.

Some critics were so admiring of this outspoken book, which fitted in so well with the disillusionment of the time, that they chose not only to praise Sassoon but to attack his (admittedly few) critics. A reviewer in the *Teacher's World* for 11 September 1918, for instance, opens a lengthy piece with a quotation from Murry's 'very-much-talked-of review':

'Mr Sassoon's verses', says this very capable critic, 'touch not our imagination, but our sense. We feel not as we do with true poetry or true art that something is, after all, right, but that something is intolerably and irremediably wrong. And God knows (he continues) something is wrong – wrong with Mr Sassoon, wrong with the world that has made him the instrument of discord so jangling why should one of the creatures of the earth be made to suffer a pain so brutal that he can give it no expression, that even this most human and mighty relief is denied him?'

The rest of the *Teacher's World* review is then devoted to defending Sassoon against such attacks, concluding that, even if his verse is *not* poetry, it is the 'raw stuff' of it and 'posterity will be glad of him'.

Grateful as Sassoon must have been for such loyal defenders, the critics who pleased him most would have been those who saw a development in his poetry since *The Old Huntsman*. And of these the literary pundit, John Squire, in the highly respected *New Statesman*, probably had first place:

Mr Sassoon's verse has improved; his vocabulary is at once more restrained, more ample, and more accurately used; and, with his honesty, his passion and his skill, he will, I think, live to write very fine poetry when the foulness of the war has been left behind and he can turn to write of the things he loves instead of the things he hates.

But even Squire's praise was qualified by the notion that first-rate poetry cannot spring from negative emotions; it would be some time before most critics would dare to believe that it could. And when, finally, they did Sassoon, ironically, would be on the other side, fiercely opposed to such modernists as T.S. Eliot who had helped bring about a change in aesthetic theory. Meantime, Sassoon had to wait for unqualified praise of his War poetry from the critics and rely for it instead on his friends.

One friend who had admired the poems in *Counter-Attack* from the start was Wilfred Owen. Though he and Sassoon had not met since their prolonged contact at Craiglockhart, where they had discussed many of the pieces in the book, they had remained in close touch. Thanks to Sassoon's introductory letter to Ross, Owen had also met many of Sassoon's friends. It was he, not Sassoon, who had attended Graves's marriage to Nancy Nicholson in January 1918 and, during his friend's unavoidable absence in Ireland, Palestine and France, had dined with faithful Meiklejohn at the Reform Club. One Ross connection of which Sassoon would not have approved was Charles Scott Moncrieff, who took Owen under his wing. But Sassoon would have been pleased at Owen's increasing intimacy with the Sitwells, whom he also hoped to know better. After leaving Edinburgh Owen had spent some time in the Sitwells' home town, Scarborough, to which he returned at the beginning of June 1918. (He had enjoyed being mistaken for Osbert Sitwell when ordering a copy of Edith Sitwell's *avant-garde* anthology, *Wheels 1917*, in a local bookshop.)

Meantime Owen had written faithfully to his 'greatest friend', Sassoon, who replied not quite so faithfully.[36] From the moment he heard that Sassoon was wounded and back in London, he had been determined to see him again, but it was not until the third week of August that he was able to do so. In spite of Scott Moncrieff's efforts at the War Office, Owen had failed to get the instructorship which would have kept him safely in England and by 9 August was on a list for France. When, at the last moment, he failed to pass his Medical Board, he was nevertheless still entitled to furlough and left for Shrewsbury and London. After a brief stay with his family, he was in London by Wednesday, 14 August and on Thursday was dining with Sassoon and Meiklejohn at the Reform.

It is possible that this Reform Club dinner was Sassoon's first venture out of hospital, since on 8 August he had written to tell Owen that he was still 'no good' and was seeing no one but Ross, who was about to leave for Sussex. But his moods still fluctuated wildly and the same day he had also told Gosse that he was 'feeling much better'.[37] Certainly he was well enough by 17 August to spend a long afternoon with Owen at Osbert Sitwell's. This was to be the sole occasion when they were all three together, though none of them knew it at the time. Owen's failure to pass his Medical had encouraged him to hope that Scott Moncrieff might still succeed in getting him an instructorship in England. So that it was a relatively light-hearted occasion, with none of the elegiac overtones it would afterwards acquire.

Both Sassoon and Owen had met Sitwell separately at Ross's the previous winter and liked him very much. Army postings had prevented both of them from seeing him again the same winter or following spring. But Sassoon's interest in Osbert, and his brother Sacheverell ('Sachie'), had been kept alive by Dent, who had himself met them for the first time early in 1918 and wrote to enthuse. On the same day that Sassoon was sending his 'love' to the brothers *via* Dent (26 June), Osbert was writing to beg him to take care of himself: 'We *cannot* afford to lose a *poet* – and especially you'.[38] It was a flattering start and Sassoon replied at once. Towards the end of his letter he asks:

> Have you met Wilfred Owen, my little friend, whose verses were in the Nation recently?
> He is so nice, and shy, and fervent about poetry, which he is quite good at, and will do *very well* some day.[39]

Scott Moncrieff had already shown the Sitwells Owen's work, which had prompted them to ask for a contribution to *Wheels 1918*, and Osbert had been one of Sassoon's first visitors at Lancaster Gate. It was, therefore, quite natural that, when Owen finally managed to get to London, they should both wish to see Osbert. His invitation to tea was, accordingly, very welcome.

Sassoon's War years had been marked by chance meetings which would fascinate posterity more, but this one was no less intriguing. On the surface there were a number of things the three men had in common. They were all serving army officers, all artistically inclined and all poets. Having met Ross, it is also more than likely that they all acknowledged themselves as homosexuals at that time. There were, however, profound differences between them. Their physical distinctiveness – Sitwell the tallest, Owen the smallest – neatly reflected a very marked difference of social class. Sitwell, the eldest son of a baronet, a product of Eton and the Grenadier Guards, was at the top of the social scale, Sassoon, with Marlborough and Cambridge behind him, in the middle and Owen, whose father still occupied a fairly humble job on the railways and was entirely innocent of either public school or university education, on the lower slopes.

Perhaps even more importantly, they also differed greatly in temperament. As Sassoon was to discover, Sitwell was quick and capricious where he was slow, and stimulating and provocative where he longed for restfulness. Owen, too, whose 'unassumingness', 'selflessness', 'lack of egotism' or self-advancement he had already recognized at Craiglockhart, could not have been more different from the other two. (The Sitwells' ability for self-advertisement was to increase with the years.) Part of Owen's unassertiveness may have stemmed from the fact that, unlike Sassoon, he was not yet established as a poet, though his stock was rising. Osbert, on the other hand, seems to have suffered none of Owen's diffidence, in spite of the fact that his only significant publications were in his sister's anthology. One of the few differences that might have worked in Owen's favour was that, despite Moncrieff's efforts, he was still expecting to be sent back to the Front, while Osbert, invalided back to England, tamely did duty in Chelsea Barracks and Sassoon was finally accepting that he would be staying in England for the rest of the War. It was a situation which probably gave Owen a slight moral edge.

The greatest difference between the three poets, however, was in their work, a difference which would emerge more distinctly and matter more to Sassoon later on. It is significant that at Dent's first meeting with Sitwell, when their host had asked Sitwell how his 'revolution' was progressing and Dent had suggested that he 'ought to go into partnership with Siegfried Sassoon', Sitwell had replied, rather critically:

Oh, do you think so? I think Siegfried Sassoon's a man of sound common-sense who speaks his mind, but I couldn't call him a revolutionary.[40]

Sassoon, while finding Sitwell's satiric verse 'a great joy',[41] quickly recognized that his desire to shock went far deeper than his own wish to disturb civilian complacency. 'The stormy petrels of modern literature' seemed to him an entirely appropriate way of describing Osbert and his siblings. Owen, with his readiness to experiment, was slightly nearer to the highly experimental trio, as they had recognized when they invited him to contribute to their *avant-garde* magazine. But he was still a long way from their deliberate outrageousness. And Sassoon had already acknowledged the differences between himself and Owen when they worked together at Craiglockhart, though by the time of this meeting he felt he was moving more in Owen's direction. Altogether, it was a meeting of 'true', but very different minds.

One of Sitwell's greatest assets was his social skill and he made quite sure that the afternoon went well. Knowing the passion both his guests felt for music and how deprived of it they were in wartime, he had arranged to start with a harpsichord recital given by his friend, Violet Gordon-Woodhouse.[42] For two hours she enchanted them with her virtuosity and elegance, during which Owen sat 'dazed with happiness at the fire and audacity of the player'.[43] The afternoon was hot and cloudless and, following a sumptuous tea at Sitwell's house in Swan Walk, Chelsea – Sassoon particularly remembered 'ices of incredibly creamy quality'[44] – they crossed the road to the ancient Chelsea Physic Garden. Here they wandered happily about among its herbs and flowering shrubs. It was indeed, as Sassoon records a 'sybaritic' afternoon, a 'delectable negation of war-time conditions'.[45]

Wartime conditions were never far away, however, and eventually Sassoon had to report back to Lancaster Gate. Owen, who had already been too 'listlessly happy' to catch his intended train back to Scarborough,[46] further delayed his return by accompanying Sassoon to his hospital. It was their one opportunity for private talk that day and they almost certainly spent part of the time discussing the likelihood of Owen returning to the Front. Sassoon has often been cited as encouraging him to do so, but the opposite is in fact the case. He had already told Marsh that it was a 'great relief' to him that Owen had been prevented from going to France,[47] and it was probably during their talk after leaving Sitwell's that he threatened to 'stab him in the leg' if he tried to return to the Front.[48] When it became a *fait accompli*, however. he would do his best to be objective, by telling him that it would be 'good for his poetry'.[49]

Owen was too upset at parting to say a coherent goodbye on the steps of the hospital and was quite resolved not to upset Sassoon when his draft came through by telling him so. It would, therefore, be nearly a fortnight before he was to contact his 'dearest of all friends' again – from France. In a brave attempt to face the future unafraid he would write, with not a little truth: 'Battle is easier here; and therefore you will stay and endure old men and women to the End, and wage the bitterer war and more hopeless'.[50] In just over another two months he would be dead, killed by a cruel stroke of Fate a week before the Armistice. But it was to be several more months before Sassoon learnt of his death, a loss he would never be able to accept philosophically.

Meantime in August, while Owen faced the possibility of another spell at the Front, Sassoon suffered the opposite problem: what was he to do now that it looked almost certain that he would remain in England? He had already written to Marsh at the end of July, suggesting that he might use his influence to get him a job 'as a sort of official artist in words', the only 'cushy' job he could contemplate.[51] But when Marsh responded by offering him a 'green-tabs and arm-chair soldiering' post, he turned it down: 'I simply *couldn't* do it under any circumstances'.[52] As he had written to Edward Carpenter two days before his visit with Owen to Sitwell:

> ... Of course it is unthinkable.
> I told them that I want to go as an ordinary worker in some works in a large town. (I have Sheffield in my mind's eye.)*
> I don't know whether I am strong enough to stand the effort, but it is worth trying, isn't it?
> I know nothing about Labour, except that the whole world depends on it. And I'm one of those people who can only learn things by coming in the closest possible contact with them. Books tell me nothing. Voices and faces awake 'the fire, the sweet hell within; / The unknown want, the destiny of me'. – O that old man, how grand he is.[53]

It is clear from his closing reference to Whitman that Sassoon had been profoundly influenced by his attitudes, as well as his poetic technique. The ground had been prepared by his first meaningful contact with working-class men in the army, a contact which had become ever closer and more admiring as the War passed. It was one influence which would lead him, to his family's and some friends' dismay, to contemplate standing as a Labour party candidate in September 1918, to help that party in the 'Coupon' election towards the end of the year and to accept a post on a left-wing newspaper a few months after that.

---

* Carpenter, who extolled the benefits of manual labour, lived near Sheffield.

Sassoon's next letter to Carpenter came from Scotland and was in the nature of a holding operation, though he repeated his determination 'not to be bluffed into an arm-chair job'.[54] He had known from early August that he was due for convalescence in Berwickshire, though not exactly when. On Saturday, 10 August he had written to tell Ottoline that he planned to leave London by the middle of the following week, but did not do so until after Owen's visit, the probable reason for the delay. It was not until Sunday, 18 August that he set out for Scotland and even then he did not go straight to his convalescent home, Lennel, at Coldstream. Instead he took the opportunity to revisit Craiglockhart, where he spent three nights. So that it was 21 August before he reached his final destination.[55]

Sassoon's first impression of Lennel was that it seemed entirely unlike a convalescent home, but simply a country house run by its owners. To his evident relief there was not a doctor or uniformed nurse in sight. It was rather like Chapelwood Manor on a larger scale, offering recuperation to about a dozen officers. Situated on a hillside in a sheltered, south-facing position, it offered magnificent views of the River Tweed, the rolling Cheviots and the brooding Lammermuir Hills. Flodden Fields, site of the famous battle, lay only a few miles away and Berwick-on-Tweed and Edinburgh were relatively near at hand.[56]

The house itself was built on an ancient site forming part of the mediaeval Earldom of Dunbar, the nineteenth-century building replacing earlier ones dating from the twelfth century onwards. After passing first to the Cistercian Abbey of Coldstream in the fifteenth century, Lennel became the property of the first Earl of Haddington in 1634 and remained in his family until 1903. Robert Burns had visited it in 1787 and Beatrix Potter rented it as her holiday home in 1894. But Sassoon's most exciting discovery was that it had a Surtees connexion: Lord Elcho, to whom *Mr Sponge's Sporting Tour* was dedicated, had used it as his hunting lodge. Sassoon nearly 'swooned with emotion', he told Ottoline, when he learnt this and even managed to identify part of the rambling, oddly-shaped house in Leech's illustrations to *Mr Sponge*, the scene where Lord Scamperdale is seeing Jack Spraggon into the dog-cart at his front door. (He was delighted to discover the name John Spraggon on a local tombstone.) One of his greatest pleasures to begin with was an attempt to identify other details of the district described by his favourite pre-War author.

Sassoon spent many hours on a bicycle in this pre-eminently escapist pursuit. Riding through the mysterious countryside, or just sitting in the lovely grounds of Lennel listening to the Tweed murmuring below the garden did more for his gloomy state of mind than all his friends' pep talks and he soon found himself in a 'comparatively cheerful and unspeculative frame of mind'.[57] Unable, for the moment, to fight his situation, he allowed himself to enjoy it and reverted quickly to his pre-War self. Cycling many miles during the day and writing a little lyrical poetry in the evenings, he felt he could have been back in Kent in 1913 before his life had so drastically changed. As he let his mind relax from the strains of the past four years, he could now safely admit that army life had 'persistently interfered' with his 'ruminative and quiet-loving mentality'.[58] His stay at Lennel was to be a very important stage in the winding-down process ahead of him.

Another unexpectedly enjoyable feature of life at Lennel was the company – unexpected because Sassoon had been largely antagonized by the inmates of his previous convalescent home. He says little of his host, Major Walter Waring, except to tell Cockerell on 6 September that the major is in Fez. But he is full of praise for his hostess, Lady Clementine Waring, a small, businesslike woman, known as 'Clemmie' to her friends.[59] Aware that most of her guests had mental as well as physical needs, she not only produced a succession of delicious meals but managed her 'supposedly nerve-disordered guests', Sassoon found, 'with undeviating adroitness and good-humour'.[60] Clemmie also provided for her guests' needs in other ways. Like Ottoline at Garsington, she had created a beautiful Italian garden in the grounds and, together with her husband, built up a fine library. Their taste in pictures, unfortunately, seemed 'too awful' to Sassoon,[61] but he spent many hours in their library on rainy days.

Sassoon was horrified to discover that one handsome octavo edition of Hardy had been badly mauled by a previous officer, who appeared to have opened its uncut pages with his finger. Having spent almost a day trimming the jagged edges with his nail-scissors Sassoon went on to read Hardy himself, *Two on a Tower* and *A Pair of Blue Eyes* among others. 'Glorious Hardy' he wrote to John Drinkwater on 30 August, 'I will go and pour ointment on his feet some day, when they let me out of this charming hospital'.[62] He also read some Flecker, perhaps with Pinto still in mind, and D.H. Lawrence's *Sons and Lovers* for the first time. He found Lawrence 'tremendously alive', on occasions 'a great genius', but also thought that he wrote 'very carelessly',[63] a comment which underlines his own meticulous working methods. Interestingly, he found a biography of Whitman in the library, as well as a more predictable collection of books on 'picturesque Berwickshire'.[64] It may have been another nature book, W.H. Hudson's *Birds and Man* which enabled him to identify the gold-crested wren that alighted on his pillow one morning, an event which prompted Owen to write from France: 'While you are apparently given over to wrens, I have found brave companionship in a poppy, behind whose stalk I took cover from five machine-guns and several howitzers'.[65]

Lady Waring clearly enjoyed having such a literary guest in her house and immediately ordered thirty copies of his latest book. She also gave him Richard Burton's *The Kasidaha of Haji Abdu El Yezdi: A Lay of the Higher Law* (1914), perhaps as a recognition of his eastern ancestry. Her inscription – 'A souvenir of days and talks by the Tweed – S.S. from C.W. 1918' – suggests that they got on well together. She was a broad-minded woman, rumoured to be a collector of Oscar Wilde at a time when that was considered very daring, and probably made Sassoon feel even more relaxed at Lennel.

One book Sassoon had failed to finish at Lennel was Winston Churchill's life of his father, Lord Randolph, which he found 'too political'.[66] He had probably been prompted to attempt Churchill's book, after receiving a note from the great man himself to the effect that he hoped to find Sassoon a sufficiently 'unsavoury, dangerous and exhausting job'. The note was almost certainly a result of Marsh's efforts and Sassoon's somewhat ungracious response to them. It probably never occurred to Sassoon that he might soon meet Churchill face to face.

Ottoline, meantime, did her best to keep Sassoon up to scratch politically. In response to his first letter from Lennel she sent a swift reply, enclosing in it a statement by Bertrand Russell, whose pacifist stance had lost him his lectureship at Trinity College, Cambridge, and whose friends were trying to find him the fellowship they felt he deserved elsewhere. Russell had been sentenced to six months imprisonment for his anti-War writings early in 1918 and had only recently been released. Sassoon, grateful for Russell's help in composing his own protest, not only offered to donate money for Russell's support, but also suggested other possible supporters wealthier than himself.[67] He duly sent his own contribution to the Russell fund, but by the time he did so it is clear that he was already far more involved with another of Ottoline's potential lovers. Indeed, it may have been a letter from Sassoon on 4 September that first aroused her interest in the man concerned.

While Sassoon describes most of the people at Lennel as 'amiable', special praise is reserved for Lady Waring and a fellow-guest of whom he has become very 'fond', Frank Prewett. Born in Canada in 1893 and known simply by the name of his home-town, Toronto, Prewett attracted Sassoon both physically and intellectually. He claimed Iroquois ancestry, which might have been responsible for his striking high-cheek-boned face, and possibly for his keen insight into human nature. Sassoon certainly thought so. He found Prewett a remarkable as well as a romantic character, delightful when in a cheerful frame of mind, but liable to fits of moodiness and aloofness, which could have been explained by his two years' service in the Ypres salient and other nightmarish spots. (He had been 'delivered' from the Front, Sassoon noted ironically, by a huge shell bursting near him.) His mood-swings from black depression to spiritual animation suggested to Sassoon a streak of genius and he was particularly excited when he discovered that Prewett was an aspiring poet. The poems themselves seemed to him 'blurred and embryonic', but there was something in them which interested him and raised his expectations.[68] Though Prewett was never to succeed publicly as a poet, Sassoon would help him for the next five years as he struggled to establish himself; and would find his second volume 'thoughtful and sensitive' in its observations of nature and of a 'distinctive strangeness' in tone and expression.[69]

Sassoon was to be of great help to Prewett in the publication of his book, *The Rural Scene* in 1924, by which time the younger man was becoming something of a liability, but at Lennel in 1918 their friendship was mutually advantageous. While Sassoon encouraged and advised him in both his reading and writing, the handsome 'Canadian-French-Red Indian', as Sassoon described him to Marsh, provided pleasant company for his bicycling expeditions. Prewett, the son of a farmer, shared Sassoon's countryman's eye for detail, so richly rewarded in the Border country. Unfortunately he did not have Sassoon's physical stamina and often returned tired and taciturn from their long rides. There was one ride he did enjoy, however, partly I suspect because it was taken by car. Late in September he and Sassoon drove about twenty miles to Lindisfarne Castle, where Heinemann had been staying with the owner, Edward Hudson, the proprietor of *Country Life* magazine. Heinemann had visited Sassoon at Lennel earlier in the month, but by the time the author had managed to respond to Heinemann and Hudson's invitation to visit Lindisfarne, both had been called back to London on business.

So, after driving across the wet sands to Holy Island at low tide, Sassoon and Prewett spent the afternoon with the sole occupant of the castle, the celebrated cellist, Madame Suggia.[70] Hearing her play a Bach suite in 'the reverberant chamber of a lonely and historic castle – her 'cello's eloquence accompanied only by the beat and wash and murmur of waves breaking against the rocks below the windows' remained one of Sassoon's most precious memories of his convalescence.[71] It was the first time that he had felt completely remote and absolved from the deadly constraints of the War.

There is little doubt that part of Sassoon's sense of freedom and romance at Lindisfarne sprang from Prewett's presence with him. He had probably already composed the lyrical poem prompted by seeing the young Canadian in Indian dress:

> *Fancy Dress*
> Some Brave, awake in you tonight,
> Knocked at your heart; an eagle's flight
> Stirred in the feather on your head.
> Your wide-set Indian eyes, alight
> Above high cheek-bones smeared with red,
> Unveiled cragg'd centuries, and led
> You, the snared wraith of bygone things –
> Wild ancestries of trackless Kings –
> Out of the past ... So men have felt
> Strange anger move them as they knelt
> Praying to gods serenely starred
> In heavens where tomahawks are barred.
>
> (*CP*, p. 110)[72]

Though this stops short of a declaration of love, it suggests strong physical and romantic feelings towards its subject. There is something dangerous, predatory and fascinating in the picture. Sassoon would admit four years later that his 'intimacy with Toronto Prewett began with a strong sexual attraction' which 'horrified' Toronto when he became aware of it.[73] It may be that Prewett first realized how Sassoon felt on their trip to Lindisfarne, though it is unlikely that anything explicit was said. While Sassoon had gradually come to admit his homosexual preferences to himself and a few trusted friends, he was still not ready to give these inclinations physical expression, even if Prewett had been ready to respond.

So the relationship remained outwardly platonic, though inwardly it coloured Sassoon's existence at Lennel. Life had rarely seemed so good. He was quickly regaining his physical strength, his surroundings were idyllic and he was in love. Furthermore, he was writing poetry with pleasure again and knew himself firmly established in the literary world. Before he left London, Gosse had written to him, with his usual magisterial authority:

> Your last little volume of poems has attracted, I think, a great deal of attention. You must be careful how you write now, for the Eye of the Lettered Public is upon you. You have the chance of making a great reputation.[74]

When Sassoon replied that he was writing 'with extreme caution', Gosse wrote again, even more positively: 'You have been making a stride onwards lately, it seems to me'. Written on 8 August, a month before Sassoon's thirty-second birthday, it was a good portent for the future.

Whether Sassoon was encouraged by Gosse's praise, or simply happier and more relaxed at Lennel, he produced at least ten poems there.[75] Apart from his piece on Prewett, their inspiration came mainly from his surroundings, as the title of one of them, 'Sunset at the Borders', suggests. So that when, for example, he returns to one of his favourite themes, 'Beauty', he explores it in terms of the natural wonder that surrounds him:

> O Never hast thou shone before my gaze
> A pure unswerving statue, cold and bright.
> But as a tree, aspiring toward the light
> And changing with the conflict of my days,
> I set thee on some hill against the sky,
> Where thou art flush'd with bloom in early morn;
> Thy voice the bird that sang when joy was born;
> Thy leaves the gold that showers when song must die

The rest of this unpublished sonnet, sent to Robert Nichols from Lennel in late August, deals predictably with the poet's belief that beauty will 'absolve' and 'free' him, even in the 'pit of Death'. In defining beauty

Sassoon was constantly aware of Keats's phrase 'Beauty that must pass' and in 'Vision', also written in late August, he continues to explore 'all things that pass':

> ... They fling delight across the world; they call
> To rhythmic-flashing limbs that rove and race ...
> A moment in the dawn for Youth's lit face;
> A moment's passion, closing on the cry –
> 'O Beauty, born of lovely things that die!'
>
> (*CP*, p. 117)

The War had forced on Sassoon an awareness of life's transience and he was resolved to seize the 'moment's passion'. In 'Falling Asleep', a slightly later, more discursive exploration of beauty, both of Nature and Art, he seems to be coming to terms with separation from his men through the soothing effects of that beauty:

> ... but now the beauty swings
> Across my brain, ghost of remembered chords
> Which still can make such radiance in my dream
> That I can watch the marching of my soldiers,
> And count their faces; faces; sunlit faces.
>
> (*CP*, p. 123)

This calmer note, so different from the tortured, bitter tone of the previous three years, marks Sassoon's final acceptance that, for him at least, the War was coming to an end. When the 'Wraiths' do return to haunt him, in the poem of that name, they do so gently:

> ... Peering from face to face,
> Until some heart shall call
> And keep them, for a breath,
> Half-mortal ...
>
> (*CP*, p. 112)

And when he does write two more War poems, one is based on the ancient battle of 'Flodden Fields', now inhabited by 'simple harvest-folk', the other a generalized account of men's need of 'God in Battle'. Neither seemed to him worthy of publication.

Sassoon was far prouder of another poem written at Lennel, 'Ancient History', which Graves also thought 'wonderful'.[76] This is a poem based on the familiar story of Cain and Abel and, I believe, on Sassoon's trips with Captain Bigger in the Judean hills. By looking at Abel's murder from their father, Adam's viewpoint and reversing the usual interpretation, Sassoon achieves a powerful effect. His chosen sonnet form naturally lends itself to a consideration of Cain in the octet:

> ... 'He was the grandest of them all – was Cain!
> 'A lion laired in the hills, that none could tire;
> Swift as a stag; a stallion of the plain,
> Hungry and fierce with deeds of huge desire.'
>
> *(CP*, p. 109)

This is followed by Adam's reflections on Abel, an opportunity to describe another kind of male beauty and one which Sassoon himself undoubtedly found attractive:

> Grimly he thought of Abel, soft and fair –
> A lover with disaster in his face,
> And scarlet blossom twisted in bright hair.
> 'Afraid to fight; was murder more disgrace? ...'

'Ancient History' manages to suggest that it is about far more than the individuals concerned. It can be read as an allegory on War *versus* Art, the masculine *versus* the feminine, or even as an insight into Sassoon's own struggle to define his masculinity in the light not only of his homosexuality, but also the conflicting demands of War and Art. T.E. Lawrence, involved in a similar conflict, admired the poem very much indeed.

Another poem Lawrence admired greatly, 'Limitations', also refers to Adam and was almost certainly written at Lennel. Part of Sassoon's attempt to find 'a more flexible form of expression', it opens with a description of his own creative processes and probably refers back to his attempt to write a Whitmanesque poem called 'The Vigil':

> Yes; you can do it, once you get a start;
> All that you want is waiting in your head,
> For long-ago you've learnt it off by heart.
>   ...
> Begin: your mind's the room where you have slept,
> (Don't pause for rhymes), till twilight woke you early.
> The window stands wide-open, as it stood
> When tree-tops loomed enchanted for a child
> Hearing the dawn's first thrushes through the wood
> Warbling (you know the words) serene and wild.
>
> *(CP*, p. 121)

Once again the poet, facing his 'limitations', urges himself to be himself, to allow himself the emotional release he has resisted for so long:

> You've got your limitations: let them sing,
> And all your life will waken with a cry:
> Why should you halt when rapture's on the wing
> And you've no limit but the cloud-flocked sky? ...

'And all you need', he tells himself in conclusion, 'Is just that flash of joy

508

above your dream'. Again the tone is calm, the mood positive, both very different from that of the War poems.

The last but one piece Sassoon wrote at Lennel came about in a rather unexpected way. He knew that Winston Churchill, through Marsh's intervention, wanted to talk to him and he also felt, by the end of September that he needed a change. Occasional trips to Edinburgh were pleasant, though no substitute for London. It had been a relief to leave Lancaster Gate, but after six weeks his appreciation of Lennel was beginning to wane. Already by 20 September he had told Gosse: 'All the fire is dying out of me, here with my porridge and five glasses of milk a day ...'[77] Graves had written to him on 25 September asking him to contribute to a miscellany, *The Owl*, which he and his father-in-law, the artist William Nicholson, planned to launch.[78] And only two days later he had received a letter from the Hampstead Labour Party, inviting him to stand as an M.P. for the constituency. All in all, London seemed a great deal more stimulating than the uneventful life he was leading in the Scottish Border country, however beautiful. So on 30 September he set out for five days in the metropolis, which were to prove as hectic if not more so than any of his frantic Wartime socializings.

During his stay at Marsh's flat in Raymond Buildings Sassoon came into contact with almost all the important social and cultural groups of the day, some of which overlapped. There was the Ross set, which met mainly at the Reform and his apartment in Half Moon Street, the Marsh set, which was busy welcoming the Russian Ballet back to London, together with Ottoline Morrell's circle, the Bloomsbury group and the Sitwells' clique. In addition Marsh organized an interview with Winston Churchill, the ostensible purpose of the visit, and Sassoon himself took the opportunity to see Heinemann about the sales of *Counter-Attack*, which he was delighted to find was in the third impression, completing 3,500 copies.

From 1 October till his exhausted departure on 5 October Sassoon found no respite from the relentless social round. And during the course of it he made a bewildering number of new friends, most importantly Lytton Strachey and Desmond MacCarthy of the Bloomsbury group, Maurice Baring at the Reform and Noel Coward at Half Moon Street. Ross also introduced him to the only member of the Sitwell trio he had not met, Edith, with whom he was to have a long if sometimes difficult relationship. In the midst of this frenzied activity Sassoon also found time to see Rivers and his old army friend, Ralph Greaves.

The first day was typical of what was to follow. During lunch with Ross and Arnold Bennet at the Reform, he was introduced to Maurice Baring, a poet, novelist and diplomat, whose work he already knew. A trip with Ross to see *Papillons* performed by the Russian Ballet in the evening was followed by a visit to Gordon Square, where he was entertained by members of the Bloomsbury group – the economist Maynard Keynes, whom he knew, and the writer Lytton Strachey, whom he did not. The painter Duncan Grant was also there. Sassoon then returned to Marsh's flat for what was left of the night. The next day was even more crowded, with lunch at the Royal Automobile Club, where Ross introduced him to Edith Sitwell and another member of Bloomsbury, Clive Bell. (The third guest, Massingham, he already knew.) Ross had then invited Ottoline Morrell, rarely a relaxing companion, to tea at Half Moon Street and Marsh had insisted Sassoon have dinner and accompany him to the Russian Ballet's *Prince Igor* afterwards.

The third day started differently, the long-awaited interview with Churchill taking place at the Hotel Metropole in the morning. Winston had told Marsh that he might be able to find his protégé a post in the Ministry of Munitions, a job which Sassoon realized in advance would be ludicrously at odds with his various protests against the War. Though Churchill claimed to know several of the poems in *Counter-Attack* by heart, this had apparently not occurred to him, but Sassoon expected very little in the way of a job. He was, however, looking forward to meeting a man who had already established a great reputation for himself.

Both in his manner, which went far beyond official graciousness, and in the time he was prepared to give, Churchill surprised Sassoon. Having established a common interest in hunting and an admiration for his poems, Churchill proceeded to question him at length on his attitude to the War and, though this quickly turned into a monologue on the virtues of warfare, Sassoon was both flattered and impressed. It was only when Marsh appeared for the second time to inform Churchill that the First Lord of the Admiralty, Lord Fisher, was waiting for his appointment, that Churchill brought the meeting to an end, but not before offering Sassoon a job. Even though Sassoon knew that he would never agree with Churchill's views and could not, therefore, accept his offer, he left feeling that Churchill was extremely likeable.

It was probably Churchill's influence, as well as a good bottle of champagne, which caused Sassoon to contradict himself almost immediately. He was having lunch at the Waldorf the same day with Ralph Greaves and found himself agreeing with his 'smooth-haired whimsical philosopher' friend that, however bad the War, it had been an 'improvement on a lot of the aimless things one did in peace-time'.[79] Greaves, in spite of his own loss of an arm, thought Churchill absolutely right in claiming that the War had brought out the best in some people. His own advice to Sassoon was not to think too much about the problem, advice which the poet found easier to follow, ironically, when he was actually at the Front.

By the end of this lunch Sassoon had already had enough excitement for one day, but he went on with Greaves to yet another performance by the Russian Ballet, *Carnaval*. After taking Greaves to tea at Ross's and ignoring his mounting exhaustion, Sassoon then dined as Maynard Keynes's guest at the United Universities Club. It was almost certainly at

Keynes's insistence that he visited the Russian Ballet yet again, in *Cleopatra*. Keynes was becoming emotionally involved with the Russian ballerina, Lydia Lopokova, whom he would eventually marry, and Sassoon was introduced to her and to her co-star, Leonide Massine, after the performance.

In spite of his extreme fatigue he had been thrilled by Massine's virtuoso dancing, which merged in his mind with his talks to Churchill and Greaves about the War. The result, a poem he was to complete the following month, shows that his thoughts were still with his men, as he contrasts the stage death of Massine with the many real deaths he had witnessed:

> *To Leonide Massine in 'Cleopatra'*
> O beauty doomed and perfect for an hour,
> Leaping along the verge of death and night,
> You show me dauntless Youth that went to fight
> Four long years past, discovering pride and power.
>
> You die but in our dreams, who watch you fall
> Knowing that tomorrow you will dance again.
> But not to ebbing music were they slain
> Who sleep in ruined graves, beyond recall;
> Who, following phantom-glory, friend and foe,
> Into the darkness that was War must go;
> Blind; banished from desire. O mortal heart
> Be still; you have drained the cup; you have played your part.
>
> (*CP*, pp. 104-5)

The last two lines of this piece, an echo of his earlier, unpublished poem 'Testament', suggest that Sassoon's struggle was not yet over. He himself described his state after seeing Massine as 'overwrought'. The sensible thing would have been to go straight back to bed at Raymond Buildings, but he knew that it was his last chance to see Ross before returning to Scotland. Ross was about to leave England for several months in the role of consultant to the Melbourne Art Gallery and Sassoon's own future plans were uncertain. Of all his London friends, he had come to value Robbie the most. So, in spite of a severe headache and an overdose of socializing, he set off for Half Moon Street, hoping for a last, quiet talk with Ross.

Sassoon found Ross alone, as he had said he would be, but looking worried and exhausted. The strains of the Billing trial, together with the preparations for his Australian trip, had taxed his already poor health. He had also exerted himself more than was wise to make Sassoon's London visit a success. They both needed a restful evening, but were not to get it. Shortly after Sassoon's arrival Scott Moncrieff came in with a young, and to Sassoon unknown, friend, Noel Coward. Both men irritated him and not just because they were depriving him of a quiet farewell talk with Ross. He had not forgotten Scott Moncrieff's hostile review of *The Old Hunts-*

man and, in spite of his efforts to get with one of Robbie's closest friends, he was antagonized by him personally. There may also have been an element of jealousy over Moncrieff's growing intimacy with Owen. Nor did he respond to Coward, still a very young and unknown 'boy actor', as he rather whimsically announced himself to be. Normally delighted by praise of his work and by requests to sign his books, Sassoon found Coward 'gushing' and suspected that even the tolerant Ross thought him too effusive.

After an hour, with his headache worse than ever, Sassoon left abruptly. Ross, fortunately, followed him down the stairs and they were at least able to say goodbye in peace. Though neither knew it, it was to be their last meeting. Sassoon later read into the long look that Ross gave him as he held his hand on the doorstep a 'presentiment of final farewell',[80] but at the time he merely noted Ross's exhaustion, too busy wondering whether they would be able to meet before he left for Australia.

There was certainly no time to see Ross on Sassoon's last day in London, which was the busiest of all. The morning was spent talking to Heinemann, then Rivers and lunch, at the Eiffel Tower in Soho, was with Ottoline. Her ostensible reason for arranging the lunch was to introduce Sassoon to Desmond MacCarthy, yet another member of the Bloomsbury group, but she was also desperate to see him before he returned to Lennel. Though she had been very hurt by another of his tactless remarks – that her artificial manner made it impossible for him to talk to her – and in spite of the fact that he had turned down her generous offer of some farm work and a cottage at Garsington, she was still too fond of him for her own peace of mind. For his part Sassoon was far more interested in Toronto Prewett, who had arrived in London with Lady Waring and who dined with him, Marsh and 'Clemmie' at the Carlton that evening. Appropriately, they went on to see *The Man from Toronto* and their meeting with the actress Iris Hoey afterwards was the last social occasion in another exhausting day. Ironically, it was the only day of Sassoon's visit not to include Ross in it, yet it was to be his last day alive.

By the time Sassoon arrived back at Lennel on the evening of 5 October, Ross was dead. But he was not to hear of his death for another two days and on 6 October, assuming him to be still alive, he wrote him a letter which ended: 'You are the dearest thing ever invented, Robbie'.[81] It may have been the arrival of this letter at Half Moon Street which prompted the distraught Nellie Burton to telegram Sassoon the sad news. She had discovered him dead when she went to wake him from an afternoon nap on the 5th, but had probably been too preoccupied with funeral arrangements to telegram earlier. Ross had suffered from chronic bronchitis and gastritis, as well as severe asthma, and the doctor's diagnosis had been heart failure, a diagnosis Sassoon found ironic: 'this was the only occasion on which his heart failed him', he was to write, 'either in personal courage or in generosity towards his friends'.[82] To Marsh, who had also telegrammed him the news on the 7th, he confessed: 'It is a terrible knock. I shall never forgive you if you die without my permission'.[83]

Graves, who reported in his letter of 12 October that his soldier brother-in-law, Tony Nicholson, had died the same day, felt equally shocked and deprived: '... there'll never be another Robbie, cynical, kind-hearted, witty champion of lost causes, feeder of the fatherless and widowed and oppressed – I feel his loss more than people could suppose'.[84] Like most of Ross's friends he had been worried about his precarious health, but his sudden death at forty-nine was a great shock. Gosse, who had been like a father to Ross, believed that to a large extent he had brought about his early death by his tireless efforts for the underdog, which had exposed him to so much persecution over the years.

Ross's defiant stand for homosexuality had made him many grateful friends, however, particularly among the young and it was not only Sassoon and Graves who missed him. Wilfred Owen, for instance, whom Ross had generously introduced to his wide and influential circle the previous year, told his mother that he found Ross's death 'more affecting ... almost' than many of the deaths he had witnessed at first hand in France.[85] Yet when Sassoon came to pay public tribute to Ross he felt constrained by the punitive laws governing homosexual practices at that time and was unable to mention what many considered Ross's greatest achievement, his championship of homosexuals, Oscar Wilde in particular. (Sassoon was to tell Sidney Cockerell in 1944 that in his chapters on Ross in *Siegfried's Journey* he had had to be 'extremely careful; but as he very seldom spoke about Wilde to me I have been able to avoid all that without any loss of veracity'.[86]) This may explain the curious woodenness of his 'Elegy (to Robbie Ross)', the last poem he wrote at Lennel. This was probably commissioned by the *Nation*, where it appeared on 18 October, and it reads as such. Its stilted, rather formal phrases were no doubt literally true of Ross but they fail to convey the spontaneous delight Sassoon had felt in his company:

> Your dextrous wit will haunt us long
> Wounding our grief with yesterday.
> Your laughter is a broken song;
> And death has found you, kind and gay.
>
> We may forget those transient things
> That made your charm and our delight:
> But loyal love has deathless wings
> That rise and triumph out of night.
>
> So, in the days to come, your name
> Shall be as music that ascends
> When honour turns a heart from shame ...
> O heart of hearts! ... O friend of friends.
>
> (*CP*, p. 107)

Besides being asked to commemorate Ross in verse, Sassoon was also approached about editing his literary remains. But as Gosse pointed out, Ross's talent lay not so much in his writing as in his brilliant conversation and the task was never completed. The only writing of his to appear after his death was a collection of his letters, subtitled *Friend of Friends* from the final line of Sassoon's elegy.[87]

Ross had probably been more prepared for his death than his friends were. When Sassoon had visited him two days earlier, he had found Ross reading the Bible, though he denied that he was getting ready to meet his Maker. He also carried in his pocket a prose meditation on death by the Scottish poet William Drummond, *A Cypress Grove* (1630). It was this book – altered almost certainly by Ross, who loved puns, to *A Cypress Grove* – which Nellie Burton gave Sassoon as a memento, perhaps at his request. She also gave him Ross's miniature edition of Virgil, which he treasured. Ross's death had upset him greatly and undoubtedly blighted his last ten days at Lennel. He told Carpenter on 8 October that he was 'quite numbed' by it. His only consolation was Prewett, who helped him through the days following Burton's telegram. He was becoming increasingly fond of the young Canadian and had already arranged to see him at Oxford in November. (Prewett was to start at Christ Church in October.)

Apart from Prewett and Lady Waring, however, there was no one he would really miss at Lennel. When a Medical Board at Edinburgh cleared him on 17 October, therefore, he was not very sorry to leave. Stopping only to visit a friend at Portobello, on the outskirts of Edinburgh, he travelled directly south to spend his four weeks' leave among family and older friends. In his final letter to Ross he had said that he was accepting Arnold Bennett's 'offer', almost certainly a job at the Ministry of Information, but that he wanted to discuss it with Ross first. In Ross's absence he seems to have determined against the job after all. He also decided against spending a night in London as originally planned, but carried straight on to Weirleigh.

One of Sassoon's strongest temptations to give in to a 'Blighty' had been the thought of home, of his mother coming in with roses from the garden, of his dog Topper, his booklined study and his piano. Once back there he seems to have sunk into a state of recuperative vegetation which lasted two and a half weeks. By mid-October the Peace negotiations were coming to a head and it is more than likely that he was reflecting on his own future as he idled through his time there. 'I've been here the last ten days', he wrote to Dent on 28 October, 'the quietest place on earth' and confessed to having 'as much brain as my dog Topper, which isn't much'.[88]

Sassoon wrote little or no poetry, though 'Memorial Tablet', with its references to 'sermon-time' and 'Squire in his pew' is more likely to have been inspired by a visit to the local church with his mother than by the other place its October date suggests, Lennel. His mother's militarism, which he compared to that of Churchill, made it very difficult for him to get on with her, he told Marsh, but she was still the most unselfish person he knew and he still needed her. His reference to Ottoline as a 'jolly good sort' in his Dent letter suggests that he needed her too and that he was keeping up with his correspondence, but there is no evidence of any other activity. He was simply recharging his batteries, knowing that his strenuous social life was about to begin again. For Marsh, not content with introducing him to Winston Churchill, was now arranging for him to meet someone who was to become almost equally famous, T.E. Lawrence.

So, in spite of his statement to Dent on 28 October that he 'could not bear the idea of London', Sassoon was there again a week later for dinner with the distinguished Hejaz campaigner, who had specifically asked to meet him. One of the results of *Counter-Attack*'s success was that Sassoon himself was considered worth knowing. Whereas previously his friends had introduced him to well-known people almost as a favour, they now began to think it a favour to be allowed to introduce him. Fortunately, his natural modesty had prevented him from becoming blasé about his fame and he was flattered to be asked to meet Marsh's friend. He would have been even more excited had he realized what a remarkable person Lawrence was and how famous he was soon to become.

The young Colonel, who had only just arrived back in London from the Middle East, had not yet become a legend there, though he had already caused a stir the previous week by refusing to be invested with the C.B. and D.S.O. at Buckingham Palace. Partly for security reasons, the fighting in the Middle East had received far less attention than that in France and it was not until the War was over that Lawrence's exploits there would be publicized and attract massive media attention. His own articles in *The Times* at the end of November 1918 were to start a process which would be accelerated by the American journalist, Lowell Thomas's film about him in 1919 and continue until and beyond his early death in 1935.

As it was, Sassoon knew very little of Lawrence's extraordinary story, though he was better informed than most about the situation in the Middle East and must have heard something of his daring raids on the Turks. When Marsh introduced them over dinner at the Savoy, his first impression of the 'Hejaz Colonel' was of a reticent, rather scholarly man, quite different from the conventional military type he had expected. Lawrence was also smaller and more youthful than his rank had suggested. Unwilling to be drawn out about his military exploits, he was very ready to discuss Arabia in another context, that of Charles Doughty. Sassoon, whose youthful worship of Doughty had led him to read some of his more obscure work, was impressed by Lawrence's own knowledge of Doughty's epic poems, as well as the fact that Lawrence had not only corresponded with Doughty, like Sasson, but also knew him personally. From Doughty they proceeded to another elaborate stylist, Henry James, whom Marsh imitated with great success. (It was one of his party tricks.)

Sassoon pleased Lawrence at this first meeting by exclaiming rather naively that he could not understand how Lawrence came to be a Colonel, but it became quite clear from his discussion of the Peace settlement which followed that he was very experienced and able. Sassoon could only listen with 'respectful curiosity', which turned to astonishment when Marsh began to criticize President Wilson for, like many people, Sassoon regarded the American statesman as 'the heaven-sent leader of the Allied Nations'.[89] Lawrence, enigmatic as always, reserved his opinion.

The impression Lawrence left on Sassoon at this first meeting was of a pleasant, unassuming person. 'Had I been told that I was meeting one of the most extraordinary beings I should ever know and idolize', he was to write, 'I should have refused to believe it. He was, I briefly informed my diary, "the Hejaz general, a little Oxford archeologist, who admires Doughty and called him 'a Viking' " '.[90] Yet only a few months later society would be agog about Lawrence and his romantic military exploits and Sassoon would find himself buttonholed by eager hostesses, who hoped he might bring 'his friend, Colonel Lawrence' to lunch with them.

Sassoon and Lawrence had a number of things in common and the relationship was to develop in the 1920s, continuing until Lawrence's death. They not only shared a love of Doughty and the Middle East, but also a deep nostalgia for the past which had led both of them to devote their first year at university mainly to William Morris's medieval romances. Like Morris they both loved fine printing and both collected rare books. In each the aesthete was combined rather unusually with the man of action. Both had entered the War at its outset and had gained a reputation for great physical courage, resulting in an M.C. for Sassoon and a D.S.O. for Lawrence. Though Sassoon was thirty-two and Lawrence thirty when they met, neither was married nor seemed likely to be. They were to have a number of friends in common in the 1920s, most notably E.M. Forster, who shared their schoolboyish humour as well as their sexual tastes. More importantly, Forster regarded literature as his *raison d'être*, as Sassoon had always done, and by 1918 Lawrence was beginning to feel the same. Though archaeology and his championing of the Arab cause had occupied most of his life up to that point, his desire to write was gradually becoming even more vital to him. And when he finally completed his first version of *The Seven Pillars of Wisdom*, Sassoon would be one of the privileged few asked to read it. His resulting admiration for Lawrence's prose was more than matched by Lawrence's appreciation of his poetry. Unable to write poetry himself, Lawrence had an enormous respect for those who could, which explained his wish to meet Sassoon in the first place.

It is therefore odd, as Sassoon noted in retrospect, that at their initial meeting they did not discuss Thomas Hardy, whom they both admired, especially since Sassoon was about to pay his first visit to the great poet and novelist. Sassoon's decision to visit Hardy was one result of his final acceptance that his active part in the War was at an end. Even if fighting continued beyond the expiry of his leave, which seemed unlikely, he was now convinced that he would never be sent back to France. His delay in paying a visit which Hardy himself had suggested, and which his disciple longed for, had stemmed mainly from an uncertainty about his future. The War had made him admire Hardy more than any other living writer and now that it was coming to an end, he wanted to worship in person.

As if the excitement of visiting Hardy on 6 November was not enough, Marsh had also arranged for Sassoon to pay a second visit to Churchill before catching his train to Dorset. Added to the thrill of meeting Lawrence the previous evening, it was all too much and Sassoon slept badly. His 'queer dream' (no pun intended) with 'a bit of Toronto in it'[91] suggests that he was also disturbed by the thought of seeing Prewett, whom he had arranged to visit after Hardy. He seems to have found Prewett physically more disturbing than previous loves, perhaps because the tight hold he had kept on his sexual urges during his time with attractive young soldiers was beginning to relax as the War at last appeared to be ending.

Churchill certainly believed it was; he was full of 'victory talk' when Sassoon met him for a few minutes on the morning of 6 November. Though still impressed Sassoon could not help thinking that he sounded slightly 'inhuman ... like a leading article'.[92] He rightly suspected that England intended to increase its power enormously in the coming Peace and was proposing to 'skin Germany alive'.[93] It was, therefore, something of a relief to leave Churchill and make his way to Waterloo for the 12.30 train to Dorchester. He carried with him a message from Marsh, with whom he had stayed the night, – the offer of the next dedication of *Georgian Poetry* and a request for a poem by Hardy in his Little Book.[94]

The day was bright and frosty and Sassoon was in good spirits as the train made its way westwards. These were slightly dashed at Bournemouth when he discovered that, distracted by thoughts of how the Hardy of his imagination would compare with the real person, he had got into the wrong part of the train at Waterloo and been left behind. After sending an apologetic telegram to the waiting Hardys, he took a slow train to Dorchester and eventually arrived at Max Gate at 6.45 p.m. It was, therefore, dark when the horse cab lumbered up to the porch and he had only a vague impression of a small house set among trees. Thomas and Florence Hardy seemed equally diminutive – a 'little old gentleman' and his 'small wife'[95] – and Sassoon felt horribly large and hearty.

Naturally shy himself, Sassoon realized that the Hardys were equally so to begin with, making Thomas's voice sound worn and slightly discordant. As he became more confident, so it became firmer and less strained, even vibrant at times. His appearance underwent a similar transformation in Sassoon's eyes, from that of extreme frailty (he was seventy-eight at this time and had never seemed physically robust) to unusual agility for a man of his age. His movements gradually became 'brisk, purposeful and compact' and he carried himself with 'almost military erectness'.[96] In strong light he looked all of his years, 'a dear and delightful old country gentleman', with his bald head, beaky nose and drooping grey moustache, but in shadow he seemed to Sassoon quite ageless:

> .. the wisdom of the ages in human form. For that time-trenched face ... was genius made visible, superhuman in its mystery and magnificence. This was the face of the life-seer who had transmuted the Wessex country into a cosmogony of his imagination, who had humanized it and revealed its unrecorded meanings and showings with patient power and mastery of half-tones and subdued colours ...[97]

The legend, it seemed, could co-exist with everyday reality. Hardy was both human being and wizard, though he took care to conceal the latter from most people's eyes:

> *At Max Gate*
> Old Mr Hardy, upright in his chair,
> Courteous to visiting acquaintance chatted
> With unaloof alertness while he patted
> The sheep dog whose society he preferred.
> He wore an air of never having heard
> That there was much that needed putting right.
> Hardy, the Wessex wizard wasn't there.
> Good care was taken to keep him out of sight.
>
> Head propped on hand, he sat with me alone,
> Silent, the log fire flickering on his face.
> Here was the seer whose words the world had known.
> Someone had taken Mr Hardy's place.
>
> (*CP*, p. 263)

Once Hardy had shown him up the narrow stairs to his bedroom, Sassoon had already begun to feel more at ease with him. And after Hardy had realized that Sassoon was not the 'huge swell' his Philpot portrait had suggested, he too began to relax. During Sassoon's stay they talked mainly of poets and poetry, of Shakespeare, Shelley, Keats and Browning, but not in a self-consciously intellectual way. 'What I was offered at Max Gate', Sassoon wrote, 'was homeliness'; they discussed their favourites with 'uncritical gratitude for their glories'.[98] When Sassoon asked Hardy why 'Ah, did you once see Shelley plain?' was such a memorable poem, he gave the kind of answer with which Sassoon could identify: 'Because Browning wrote it from his heart'.[99]

Sassoon gained Hardy's confidence by not trying to seem clever and by his genuine interest in everyday humanity. And Hardy taught him 'the simplicity of true greatness'.[100] Sassoon later claimed that this was a much-needed lesson when they first met, but it is hard to believe that he was anything but extremely modest and unpretentious in Hardy's presence. Hardy certainly enjoyed his company and was to welcome him back to Max Gate many times in the next nine years. He had no children of his own and found him 'a wonderful pleasure and delight', telling Masefield that he 'loved [him] like a son'.[101] His signed photograph to the younger man was the first of a number of gifts.

Though Sassoon does not mention it in his diary, he and Hardy went for walks together during his two days, both of which continued bright and frosty. He had been grateful for Hardy's vivid evocation of the English countryside while he was in France and must have found it an unforgettable experience seeing some of it with him. As he commented afterwards, Hardy was 'the nearest thing to Shakespeare' he would 'ever go for a walk with'.[102] On the other hand, he told Dame Felicitas Corrigan that Hardy's philosophy of life depressed him; but that was said after he had become a Roman Catholic and there is no sign of it in his account of their first meeting. On the contrary, he found Hardy's outlook on that occasion both humorous and charmingly gay. The pessimism and bitterness, if it existed, was in his writing.

One of the most pessimistic of Hardy's novels is *Jude the Obscure*, set partly in a thinly-disguised Oxford, and Sassoon may well have had it in mind as he left Dorset on 8 November to visit Prewett there. Prewett had started his studies at Christ Church almost certainly with financial help from Sassoon and it was natural that the two should want to meet. Sassoon had decided to combine seeing him with a stay at nearby Garsington. He knew that Ottoline, who had been pressing in her invitation, was extremely hospitable and would not mind him bringing a friend, especially one who was young, handsome and literary. In fact, he may deliberately have introduced her to Prewett in the hope of diverting her too-ardent attentions from himself.

This visit certainly marked the end of her romantic feelings for Sassoon. As she told Virginia Woolf a week after he left, she had found him 'terribly, terribly *spoilt*. I *never* want to see him again – so coarse, so ordinary, so just like any other conceited young guardsman – I felt he had been seeing *odious* people, who had changed him *completely*'.[103] Even allowing for both Ottoline's and Virginia's tendency to exaggerate, Sassoon must have said or done something to provoke such a bitter response.

All he really wanted at Garsington was to be left free to digest the events of the previous few days. As it was, he was plunged into yet more excitement. Ottoline, partly to please him and partly to show him off, no doubt, had arranged for him to have lunch with John Masefield, who in turn planned to introduce him to the Poet Laureate, Robert Bridges. Everything, as Sassoon said, seemed to be happening at once. He had never met Masefield and was eager to do so, and he had admired Bridges' work since he was twenty.

So on 9 November he set off on a borrowed bicycle for Masefield's house at Boar's Hill, to the south-west of Oxford. It was a longer journey than he had anticipated from Garsington and, by the time he arrived breathless and apologetic at the top of Boar's Hill, the Masefields had finished lunch. Masefield handled the potentially embarrassing situation well, personally bringing Sassoon the food which had been kept hot for him and chatting to him while he ate it. His warm welcome, together with his calm and unassuming manner put his guest quickly at his ease.

It was a relief to find that he showed no resentment at all of Sassoon's parody of him in *The Daffodil Murderer*. Sassoon had always insisted that he genuinely admired Masefield's work in spite of parodying it and he still did so. ('I've been reading Masefield's new book of poems', he had written to Graves in April 1917. 'He uses the word "beauty" 76 times in 90 pages – but some of the things are lovely'.) Masefield's feelings about Sassoon's work were expressed in the presentation inscription he wrote in a book he gave him that day: 'For Siegfried, with deepest admiration from John Masefield. Nov 9 1918'.[104] But they had their differences and not only in poetic technique. Masefield was convinced, probably correctly, that Sassoon did not approve of his less critical attitude towards the War.

Nevertheless they got on well together and Sassoon was to revisit the 'great, kind and simple' man on a number of occasions. At this first meeting, Masefield was far more established as a poet and much more assured as a person. Only eight years older than Sassoon he seemed to him more mature in every way. 'He is a kindly, manly figure', Sassoon recorded in his diary, 'deep rich voice and young-looking face, grey hair. Face made on a small scale, but a lot of nobility and tenderness in it'.[105] The photograph he signed for Sassoon shows a grave man of approaching middle-age. By comparison Sassoon felt even more immature than usual. He had already shown his impetuosity by pouring out details of his visit to Hardy over lunch. He was to feel even sillier when they visited the Poet Laureate in the afternoon.

Sassoon had looked forward to this visit very much. Bridges' *Spirit of Man* anthology had been of great comfort to him at the Front and he thought the poet himself an 'exquisite writer of verse', who had never been surpassed 'in perfection of form and language'.[106] Together with Hardy, he believed Bridges to be one of the two great poets alive. He was probably also aware that Bridges shared his own interest in music and had written at least four poems for musical settings by the time they met. He was certainly aware of the flattering fact that Bridges had told Gosse in June 1917 that Sassoon had 'more of the real stuff' in him than almost any other poet of his generation, since Gosse had instantly passed this on to his young friend.[107] So when he was introduced to the venerable septuagenarian with his magnificent bard-like head and fine patrician features, he quite understandably assumed that Bridges had agreed to the meeting and would be welcoming, if not warm. It was, therefore, a shock when Bridges, in response to Masefield's introduction, simply glared at him. Only after asking Masefield whether it was true that the German Emperor had resigned did he register Sassoon's existence, with one of the most surprising remarks Sassoon had ever experienced: 'What did you say his name was – Siegfried Digweed?' Sassoon was so taken aback at the time that he could not even bring himself to mention it in his diary. Retrospectively, however, he could see both the humour of the situation and the probable explanation for it.

Bridges was a staunch Conservative who hated Socialism and his first topic of conversation had been, not literature, as might have been expected, but 'those Socialists'. It seemed to Sassoon more than likely that his remarks were aimed at himself as a 'reprehensible supporter of Socialist opinion' and that Bridges had awaited his arrival with the deliberate intention of 'taking me down a few pegs'.[108] Viewed in the light of subsequent, far pleasanter experiences of him, Sassoon could also see that it was entirely characteristic of Bridges to hector him in the way he did. The older poet had admired the technique of his War poetry, but could hardly be expected to approve its content. Proud and self-conscious, he was not known for his tolerance. There was often, Sassoon noted, 'something of the self-contradictory schoolboy about him'.[109] When presenting himself at Buckingham Palace to receive his Laureateship, for example, he had remarked to the Lords-in-waiting that he 'didn't want any of their Stars and Garters'. Sassoon generously concluded that it was his 'unrestrained naturalness which caused these somewhat petulant exhibitions of rudeness'. And, as he was to discover, it was that same naturalness which made him such good company at times. He came to understand one friend's description of Bridges as 'gloriously grumpy' and to believe that his 'nobility of mind atoned for his inurbanities of behaviour'.[110] In fact, the 'Digweed' episode was to be the only occasion when he would see Bridges in a bad humour. He later blamed his younger self for not understanding that it came about partly because Bridges had been depressed by the four long years of War and the fact that his lovely house, Chilswell, had recently been burnt down. (They met in the gardener's cramped and rather gloomy cottage where he was temporarily living.)

There may have been other reasons why Bridges reacted as he did. Sassoon makes very little reference to the problems of having a German Christian name during the First World War, but it is not impossible that the jingoistic Bridges reacted hostilely to it. His absurd rhyme 'Digweed' ('Siegfried' is still pronounced by people who knew the poet with a short first syllable and long second one) would have come naturally to a poet intent on registering covert criticism. The only retaliation Sassoon allowed himself was in his diary, where he wrote that the Poet Laureate was 'shaggy and self-conscious and rather hectoring' and that he 'did not like him'.[111] As he cycled back through the dark streets of Oxford he probably regretted the meeting, which he could not help comparing with his visit to that other illustrious writer at Max Gate:

> The more I think of Hardy the greater his simplicity seems ... What a contrast to arrogant old Bridges with his reactionary War-talk. The one supreme tragic artist, the other a splendid craftsman with a commonplace mind.[112]

It had been an emotionally draining day but there was more to come. With her insatiable appetite for company Ottoline had invited Francis Meynell and his wife, the pianist Hilda Saxe, to dinner, together with Aldous Huxley, then an assistant-master at Eton. Sassoon noted that Francis Meynell, the son of Wilfred and Alice Meynell and himself a poet, publisher and book designer, talked Labour politics, his wife played Beethoven, Brahms and Moussorgsky, but says nothing of Huxley's contribution. It is likely that, while he enjoyed discussing politics with Meynell and listening to some of his favourite music played by his wife, he did not respond to the young Oxford graduate. Strikingly tall and thin, with a slight stoop, everything about Huxley seemed aloof, even his near-blindness giving him a remote, withdrawn air. To someone as insecure as Sassoon Huxley's famous family connections and his socially impeccable education at Eton and Balliol were probably most off-putting. And Huxley seems to have felt equally unresponsive. Ottoline was rather 'put out ... that Aldous treated [Sassoon] with great coolness and reserve, almost unfriendliness'.[113] When she asked him why, his answer was 'undergraduate insolence'. It was probably more than that. As an aspiring poet, who had yet to establish himself in spite of three published volumes of verse, Huxley was perhaps jealous of Sassoon's recently-acquired fame. But he did admit to Ottoline that he wished he could have 'got on more easily with Sassoon'. He felt with him 'something of the same difficulty as with Graves – the sense of being out of contact and not knowing how to get into it', a situation he found 'baffling'.[114] It may have been that Huxley, whose poor eyesight had prevented him from enlisting as so many of his Oxford friends had done, felt rather out of things with the heroic soldier-poet, possibly even antagonized. For his part, Sassoon often reacted adversely to those he considered 'intellectuals', as Huxley undoubtedly was. He was later to refer unkindly and disparagingly to Huxley's 'blind-alley brilliance'.[115] Nevertheless, they must have reached some kind of accord eventually, since Sassoon was to ask Huxley to write for him when he became a literary editor in 1919.

For the time being relations between the two were noticeably cool. There was one subject, however, which would have united even Sassoon and Huxley that evening, the abdication of the Kaiser, which Meynell announced. 'Dear Toronto', Sassoon noted, 'sat very quiet and listened',[116] but he must have been the exception, for it was a sensational piece of information. The peace process had been going on in earnest since the end of September, when the German General Ludendorff had urged Field-Marshal Hindenburg on the 28th (the day Passchendale was recaptured by the British) to seek an immediate armistice, and Bulgaria had been forced to accept defeat by the Allies on the 30th. When Allenby finally took Damascus and the British prepared to break through the Hindenburg Line on 1 October, Ludendorff begged the Kaiser in person to issue a German peace offer immediately. Political unrest in Germany was adding to her problems and by 4 October her Chancellor, Prince Max, finally telegraphed Washington requesting an armistice. He made it clear, however, that this was not a surrender, only an attempt to end the War without pre-conditions, and President Wilson rejected his advance. A first condition of any armistice, he insisted, must be the evacuation of all occupied territories. The start of the second Battle of Cambrai on 8 October and the final breakthrough of the Hindenburg Line on the 9th forced Germany to accept Wilson's terms and on the 11th they began to withdraw from France and Belgium, though the fighting continued.

In England Lloyd George was still afraid that, if the Allies made peace too soon, Germany would have time to recover, and an even more militant faction wanted complete defeat. Nevertheless, another important move towards peace occurred on 19 October when all German U-boats were ordered to return to their bases, bringing a virtual end to submarine warfare. By 22 October, however, the German Chancellor was not yet ready to accept what he called 'a peace of violence', but the following day was ordered to prepare realistic armistice terms by Wilson. And on the 24th Ludendorff and Hindenburg were still unwilling to acquiesce in what was now clearly a *fait accompli*. Their 'fight to the finish' telegram to all Army Group commanders alarmed the German Government, which threatened to resign, and Ludendorff was forced to do so instead. By 25 October the Turks had been routed from their northernmost stronghold, Aleppo, and the following day began their own armistice talks with the Allies.

A day later Germany's last great ally, Austria, resolved to seek a separate peace and German sailors mutinied. It was quite clear that Germany was now on her own. But fighting on the Western Front continued, even after War on the Middle Eastern and Italian Fronts had ceased and even after the Allies had agreed on 3 November to a formal German request for an armistice. Ironically, Wilfred Owen, who believed that the Allies had deliberately 'thwarted' earlier peace efforts,[117] died the day after this formal request was made and many more were to die needlessly in the week of negotiations that followed. For in spite of General Groener's warning to the Kaiser that the armistice must be signed by 9 November at the latest, delegates did not arrive at the armistice meeting in the Forest of Compiègne until the 7th. The Kaiser himself was still refusing to abdicate and it was not until the 9th that he finally accepted the inevitable. News of his abdication that evening at Ottoline's would have made it quite clear to Sassoon that the Armistice was imminent. The next day the German Government formally accepted the Allies' stringent terms, though the legal documents were not signed until 5.10 a.m. on the morning of the 11 November. The Armistice itself was set for 11 a.m. that day, the eleventh day of the eleventh month.

Sassoon was in no mood for rejoicing. His close contact with Marsh during October and early November and his two meetings with Churchill had made him aware that this time the peace talks were in earnest and his most likely response would have been that of Owen, resentment that Germany's earlier tentative offers had not been taken seriously at the time. This had been the main reason for his public protest in 1917 and he had not changed his position. Though still ignorant of Owen's death, he could not forget how many people, some very dear friends, had died in the War and was sickened by the thought that it had been carried on a moment longer than seemed to him necessary. Safe himself, he had anxiously followed his surviving friends in the 1st, 2nd and 25th Battalions of the RWF through the last months of the fighting, as they took part in some of the fiercest battles on the Western and Italian Fronts.[118]

So instead of going up to London to join in the euphoric Armistice Day celebrations on 11 November, or even going into Oxford to mark the occasion, Sassoon stayed quietly in the country. When a peal of church bells from Garsington village signalled that the actual moment of peace had arrived, he was walking alone in the water-meadows of the river Thame below Cuddesdon. For him the War had ended not with a bang but a whimper. There had been no easy, jingoistic assurances to keep him going and even now, when he found himself on the winning side, he experienced no sense of patriotic triumph, only a desire for 'Reconciliation':

> When you are standing at your hero's grave,
> Or near some homeless village where he died,
> Remember, through your heart's rekindling pride,
> The German soldiers who were loyal and brave.
>
> Men fought like brutes; and hideous things were done;
> And you have nourished hatred, harsh and blind.
> But in that Golgotha perhaps you'll find
> The mothers of the men who killed your son.
>
> *(CP*, p. 99)

Later in the day, unable to resist the temptation to see exactly how the capital was celebrating, Sassoon caught a train to London. There, in the congested streets and undergrounds, he found masses of people, many of them drunk, waving flags and generally, as he thought, making fools of themselves. A display of mob patriotism which disgusted him far more than the foulest of trenches, it seemed to him 'a loathsome ending to the loathsome tragedy of the last four years'.[119]

Afterword

The War had really ended for Sassoon when he left France in July 1918, though technically he remained in the army on indefinite sick-leave till 11 March 1919, when the *London Gazette* announced:

> Lt. (acting Captain) S.L. SASSOON MC relinquishes his acting rank, is placed on the retired list on account of ill-health caused by wounds 12 March 1919 and is granted the rank of Captain.

Yet in a sense the War never ended for Sassoon, a situation he anticipates in a poem written the month he left the army:

Aftermath

Have you forgotten yet?...
For the world's events have rumbled on since those gagged days,
Like traffic checked while at the crossing of city-ways:
And the haunted gap in your mind has filled with thoughts that flow
Like clouds in the lit heaven of life; and you're a man reprieved to go,
Taking your peaceful share of Time, with joy to spare.
But the past is just the same – and War's a bloody game ...
Have you forgotten yet? ...
Look down, and swear by the slain of the War that you'll never forget ...
Do you remember the rats; and the stench
Of corpses rotting in front of the front-line trench –
And dawn coming, dirty-white, and chill with a hopeless rain?
Do you ever stop and ask, 'Is it all going to happen again?' ...

(CP, pp. 118-19)

Sassoon later objected to being known mainly as a war-poet, but he was endlessly to recycle the material which had initially made his name. Less than a decade after the publication of *Counter-Attack* he would return to the War for a prose trilogy which was to consolidate his fame, *Memoirs of a Fox-Hunting Man* (1928), *Memoirs of an Infantry Officer* (1930) and *Sherston's Progress* (1936). And when that was completed he returned to the same material for the third time in his three-volume autobiography, *The Old Century* (1938), *The Weald of Youth* (1942) and *Siegfried's Journey* (1945). Significantly, a fourth volume, not based on his War experiences, was left unfinished. As though caught in a time warp, Sassoon seemed to have a

525

compulsive need to re-live that particular part of his life in his work. In notes he made towards another book in 1935, he observed:

> It is significant that I have always – and increasingly – seen and felt the present as material for memories – I am as it were *living in the past already*, and the mechanism of my mind frames and diminishes experience into a delicate, narrated reminiscence, nicely illustrated with visualisations.
> This is my 'attitude to life' – the *ruminant onlooker* – forced to play a speaking part ...[1]

It might be argued that the War both made and unmade Sassoon. As a young man determined to be a poet but with no clear sense of direction, it had given him a subject as well as the experience and passion to turn that subject into memorable verse. And as a mature writer who seemed again to have lost a sense of direction, the War provided the way forward in his fictional and autobiographical prose trilogies. When that material was finally exhausted, however, so too was Sassoon's creative impulse until, with his turning to religion and eventual conversion to Roman Catholicism in the 1950s he found a new subject for his work.

It was not only as a writer that Sassoon was changed by the War. As a person, too, he benefited from the experiences of 1914 to 1918, however unbearable. A charmingly self-absorbed and immature young man at the outbreak of War, he gradually learnt to think more of others, particularly his men, who opened up a whole area of society previously closed to him. Conservative with a big and a small 'c' in 1914, by 1918 he was seriously considering a life spent in the service of the working-classes, though that plan was never to materialize.

The obverse side of the coin, however, was the sense of instability the War created in Sassoon, as in many of his contemporaries. After 1918 his life seemed to him 'distracted and experimental and confused'. Many of his old connexions were abandoned but those which came to fill their place were not entirely easy. One of the positive effects of the War would be to enable him to explore areas he had avoided before, in particular his sexuality. It was the War which had brought him into contact with first Dent, then Ross and their predominantly homosexual circles. In 1911 he had assured Carpenter that he was still 'unspotted', but one of his first decisive acts after the Armistice would be to embark on a passionate physical affair with a soldier eleven years younger than himself. Though the relationship was to continue for at least six years, after the first excitement it was not very satisfactory and Sassoon explored a number of others during the 1920s. Not until 1933, when to many people's surprise he married, was he to find any stability. When that, too, proved illusory he finally turned to religion and the last decade of his life was to be his most serene. 'Siegfried's Journey', far from being finished with the War, was only just beginning.

THORNICROFT or THORNYCROFT

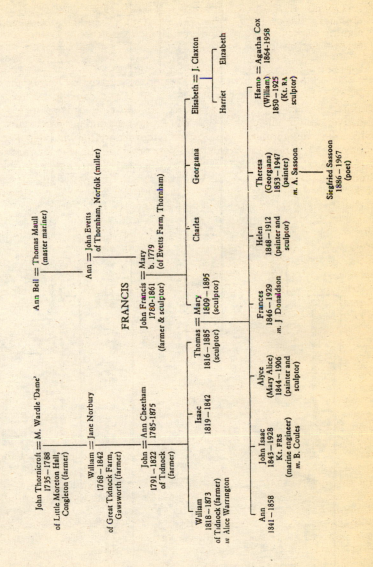

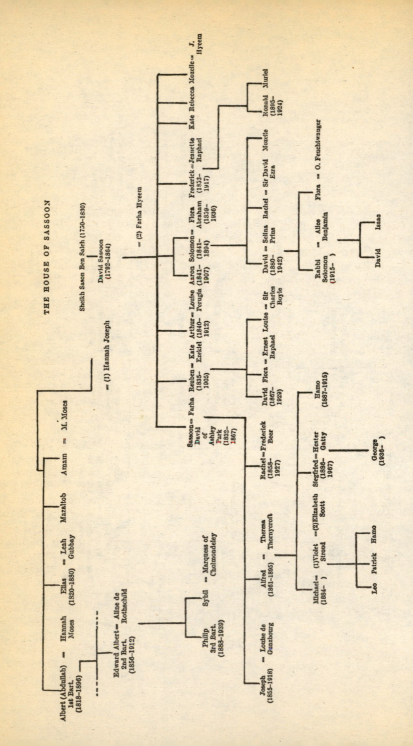

THE HOUSE OF SASSOON

Acknowledgements

My first acknowledgement must go to George Sassoon, who encouraged me to write this life of his father and allowed me to quote from his work. Other members of the family have also been extremely helpful, in particular, Hamo Sassoon, Lady Lettice Strickland-Constable, Timothy Thornycroft, Jacques Sassoon and the late Mrs Leo Sassoon. Sassoon's godson, George Byam Shaw, and his wife Maggie, have likewise contributed a great deal.

I have been fortunate in having the advice of experts at every stage in this book, especially Philip Guest, Dominic Hibberd, Tony Laughton, Patrick Quinn, David West, Charles Wheeler and Patrick Campbell, who all helped to check my typescript.

In addition, I should like to thank the following librarians and archivists at libraries and archives throughout Britain and America: especially Kathleen Cann at Cambridge University Library, Stephen Crook, Philip Milito and Rodney Phillips at the Berg Collection, New York Public Library, Kenneth Lohf at Columbia University Library, Vincent Giroud at the Beinecke Rare Book Library, Yale, Saundra Taylor and William Cagle at the Lilly Library, Indiana University, David Koch and Shelley Cox at Special Collections, Southern Illinois University, Cathy Henderson at the Harry Ransom Humanities Research Center at the University of Texas at Austin, Leila Ludeking and Laila Miletic-Vejzovic at the University of Washington at Pullman, Christopher Sheppard at the Brotherton Library, Leeds University, Terry Friedman, Ben Dhaliwal and Helen Upton at the Henry Moore Centre for the Study of Sculpture at Leeds, the late Martin Taylor of the Imperial War Museum Library, Bryan Frinchett Maddock and Norman Holme of the Royal Welch Fusiliers Archives at Carnaervon, J.R. Maddicott of Exeter College Library, Oxford, Margaret Clarke of the Fitzwilliam Museum, Cambridge, Colin Harris of the Bodleian Library, Oxford, Mrs S. Johnson of Clare College Library, Cambridge, and the staffs of the British Library, Rutgers University Library, State University of New York at Buffalo Library, McMaster University Library, Hamilton, Ontario, University of Marquette Library, Milwaukee, the Library of Congress, University of Delaware Library, University of Arkansas Library, the Public Record Office, Kew, and the National Army Museum.

Acknowledgements

I am also very grateful to William Reese, Roy Davids, Harry and Bridget Spiro and Colin Franklin for giving me access to their collections.

In the course of writing this book I have received help, advice and encouragement from many individuals, so many that I have been forced simply to list them alphabetically: Lady Helen Asquith, Rolf Barber, Jenny Barty-King, Claire Blunden, Maureen Borland, Laurel Brake, Keith Budge, Charles Cholmondeley, Mrs Vivien Clarke, Roland Constantine, Gabrielle Cross, Susan Crump, Jonathan Cutbill, Sister Clemente Davlin, Sue Edwards, Geraldine Elwes, James Fergusson, Robert Fessenden, Byron and Hilary Gangnes, Jonathan Gathorne-Hardy, 'Pom' Gibbons, Terry Halladay, Angela Harding, Lady Anne Hill, Philip Hoare, Haro Hodson and Elizabeth Mavor, Marian Kamlish, Grizel Kennedy, Louise Lambe, Pat Laurence, the late Jim Lewton-Brain, Leonard MacDermid, Sister Margaret Mary McFarlin, Noel Morgan, Eric Norris, Michael O'Regan, Michael Pierson, Jeremy and Anne Powell, the late John Richardson, Karen Robertson, Pat Robertson, Peggy Rust, Siobhain Santry, the late James Byam Shaw, Timothy d'Arch Smith, Fred, Michelle and Betsy Schwarzbach, Elizabeth Tagert, Una West, Lisbet Wheeler, Ann Williamson and Marjorie Wynne.

I should like to thank Faber & Faber for permission to quote from Siegfried Sassoon's fictional and autobiographical prose trilogies and George Byam Shaw and Roy Davids for allowing me to reproduce so many of their wonderful photographs. Unless otherwise stated, all photographs are from their collections.

I also wish to acknowledge quotations from *Ottoline at Garsington: Memoirs of Lady Ottoline Morrell* 1915-1918, edited by Rober Gathorne-Hardy (Faber & Faber, 1974); *Siegfried Sassoon: Poet's Pilgrimage* by Dame Felicitas Corrigan (Victor Gollancz, 1973); *Marble and Bronze* by Elfrida Manning (Trefoil Books, 1982); *Siegfried Sassoon: A Critical Study* by Michael Thorpe (Leiden University Press, 1966); *Edmund Gosse* by Ann Thwaite (OUP, 1984); *Edward Marsh* by Christopher Hasall (Longmans, 1959); *Goodbye to All That* by Robert Graves (Penguin Books, 1960); *Taking it Like a Man* by Adrian Ceasar (Manchester University Press, 1993); *The Great War and Modern Memory* by Paul Fussell (OUP, 1975); *Ackerley: A Life* by Peter Parker (Constable, 1989); *Wilde's Devoted Friend* by Maureen Borland (Lennard Publishing, 1990); *Men Who March Away* edited by I.M. Parsons (Chatto & Windus, 1966); *Robert Graves* by R.P. Graves (Weidenfield Nicolson, 1986); *Wilfred Owen: Collected Letters* (OUP, 1967); *Wilfred Owen: War Poems and Others* edited by Dominic Hibberd (Chatto & Windus, 1975); *Meredith* by Siegfried Sassoon (Constable, 1948).

The warmest thanks of all should go to my family for their patience, forbearance and practical help over the last seven years: my children, Kate, Philip, Emma, Alice, Trim, and, above all, my husband, Cecil Woolf.

J.M.W.

Endnotes

Abbreviations

(a) Sources

AM: National Army Museum, London
Berg: Berg Collection, New York Public Library
BL: Department of Manuscripts, British Library, London
BLL: Brotherton Library, University of Leeds
Bodley: Bodleian Library, Oxford
Buffalo: University of New York at Buffalo
Columbia: Columbia University Library, New York
CUL: Cambridge University Library, Cambridge
HMC: Henry Moore Centre for Study of Sculpture, Leeds
HRHRC: Harry Ransom Humanities Research Center, University of Texas at Austin
IWM: Imperial War Museum, London
Lilly: Lilly Library, Indiana University
Rutgers: Rutgers University Library
USI: Special Collections, University of Southern Illinois at Carbondale

(b) Main works and editions used

CP: Siegfried Sassoon. *Collected Poems* (London, Faber paperback, 1961)
D1:   *Siegfried Sassoon Diaries 1915-1918* (London, Faber, 1983)
D2:   *Siegfried Sassoon Diaries 1920-1922* (London, Faber, 1981)
D3:   *Siegfried Sassoon Diaries 1923-1925* (London, Faber, 1985)
GTAT: Robert Graves. *Goodbye to All That* (Penguin Books, 1960)
Hassall: Christopher Hassall. *Edward Marsh* (London, Longmans, 1959)
Keynes: *Bibliography of Siegfried Sassoon* by Geoffrey Keynes (London, Hart-Davis, 1962)
MFM: Siegfried Sassoon. *Memoirs of a Fox-Hunting Man* (London, Faber, 1928; Faber Library edition, 1943, used)
MIO: *Memoirs of an Infantry Officer* (London, Faber, 1930; Faber paperback, 1973, used)
OAG: *Ottoline at Garsington: Memoirs of Lady Ottoline Morrell, 1915-1918*, edited by Robert Gathorne-Hardy (London, Faber, 1974)
OC: Siegfried Sassoon. *The Old Century and Seven Years More* (London, Faber, 1938; Faber paperback, 1968, used)
RR:RWF: *Regimental Records of the Royal Welch Fusiliers*, compiled by C.H. Dudley Ward (London, Forster Groom, 1928), vol. 3.
SJ: *Siegfried's Journey* (London, Faber, 1945)

SP: *Sherston's Progress* (London, Faber, 1936; Penguin Books edition, 1948, used)

SS:PP: Dame Felicitas Corrigan. *Siegfried Sassoon: Poet's Pilgrimage* (London, Victor Gollancz, 1973)

WIK: *The War the Infantry Knew 1914-1919: a Chronicle of Service in France and Belgium with the Second Battalion, His Majesty's Twenty-Third Foot, the Royal Welch Fusiliers* [compiled and edited] by One of their Medical Officers [Capt. J.S. Dunn] (London, P.S. King, 1938)

WP: Siegfried Sassoon. *The War Poems* (Faber, 1983)

WY: Siegfried Sassoon. *The Weald of Youth* (London, Faber, 1942)

(c) Correspondents

AB: Arnold Bennett
DFC: Dame Felicitas Corrigan
EG: Edmund Gosse
ED: Edward Dent
EM: Edward Marsh
HGW: H.G. Wells
HT: Hamo Thornycroft
JC: Joe Cottrell
JD: Julian Dadd
LOM: Lady Ottoline Morrell
RG: Robert Graves
RM: Roderick Meiklejohn
RR: Robert Ross
SCC: Sydney Carlyle Cockerell
SS: Siegfried Sassoon
WO: Wilfred Owen

Introduction

1. Dame Felicitas Corrigan wrote a 'spiritual biography' of SS during his life-time and with his co-operation, *Siegfried Sassoon: Poet's Pilgrimage* (Gollancz, 1973), but its parameters were deliberately limited.

2. D2, p. 53.

3. SJ, p. 105.

4. ibid.

5. SS quotes Church in a letter to Herbert Palmer, 18 Aug. 1940, HRHRC.

6. SS:PP, p. 16. She may have had in mind John Henry Newman's 'Definition of a Gentleman' in his *The Idea of a University*.

7. OAG, p. 152.

8. Letter from Geoffrey Keynes to DFC on the publication of SS:PP in 1973, 'Siegfried Loraine Sassoon: a Centenary Essay' by DFC.

9. From SS's fourth, unpublished, unfinished volume of autobiography, now in the hands of a private collector.

10. Letter from Stephen Tennant to G.A. David (of the Sorbonne), 12 Nov. 1971, collection of Hugo Vickers.

11. SS:PP, p. 15.

12. Siegfried Sassoon, *Meredith* (London, Constable, 1948), pp. 98-9.

13. Bernard Bergonzi, *Heroes' Twilight: a Study of the Literature of the Great War* (London, Constable, 1965); Paul Fussell, *The Great War and Modern Memory* (OUP, 1975); John H. Johnston, *English Poetry of the First World War* (Princeton University Press, 1964); Jon Silkin, *Out of Battle: the Poetry of the Great War* (OUP, 1972).

14. Michael Thorpe, *Siegfried*

Sassoon: a Critical Study (Leiden University Press, 1966).

15. Adrian Caesar, *Taking It Like a Man* (Manchester University Press, 1993); Patrick Quinn, *The Great War and the Missing Muse* (Susquehanna University Press, 1994); Paul Moeyes, *Siegfried Sassoon: Scorched Glory* (Macmillan, 1997).

16. Patrick Campbell, *Siegfried Sassoon: a Study of the War Poetry* (Jefferson, N. Carolina, T. McFarland, not yet published).

Chapter 1

1. MIO, pp. 230-1.

2. For information about the Sassoon family my main sources have been Cecil Roth's *The Sassoon Dynasty* (Robert Hale, 1941), Stanley Jackson's *The Sassoons* (Heinemann, 1968) and Jacques Sassoon, whose father shared a grandfather with SS.

3. SS:PP, p. 47.

4. See, for example, Stanley Jackson's description of Albert Sassoon's London début at Queen's Gate, attended by the Prince of Wales. See p. 72.

5. See p. 39.

6. See p. 77.

7. For many of the following details I am indebted to Elfrida Manning's two books on the Thornycroft family history: *Bronze and Steel: the Life of Thomas Thornycroft, Sculptor and Engineer* (King's Stone Press, 1932) and *Marble and Bronze: the Art and Life of Hamo Thornycroft* (London, Trefoil Books, 1982). I have also consulted Chloë Baynes's completion of her mother, Rosalind Thornycroft's autobiography, *Time Which Spaces Us Apart* (Privately Printed, 1991).

8. Family legend claims that John Francis's wife, Mary Evetts, was Nelson's cousin, through their respective mothers, who were both daughters of a Mrs Anne Suckling.

9. John Francis had gained the patronage of the Duke of Sussex in an unusual way. Francis had saved the life of a woman who had jumped into the Serpentine, in Hyde Park, and the Duke, as President of the Royal Humane Society, had presented him with the Society's medal for it.

10. Interview with Lady Lettice Strickland-Constable on 1 May 1991. I am grateful to Lady Lettice, whose mother, Mary Thornycroft, was Siegfried's first cousin, for giving me a number of fascinating insights. She also allowed me to see her own collection of letters from Siegfried.

11. For example, Mrs Arthur Sassoon (née Louise Perugia), Mrs Edward Sassoon (née Aline de Rothschild), Mrs Solomon Sassoon (née Flora Abraham) and Sybil Sassoon, who became the Marchioness of Cholmondeley.

12. When I talked to Siegfried Sassoon's nephew, Hamo Sassoon, in April 1991, in answer to my question about the two sides of the family, he said, 'I'm a Thornycroft', adding that Siegfried had made the same remark to him when they got to know each other in the 1930s. Cf. SS to Mr Carter, 27 Sept. 1948, HRHRC.

13. OC, p. 45.

14. ibid., p. 67.

15. WY, p. 113.

16. SJ, p. 74.

17. WY, pp. 22-3.

18. Siegfried gives an account of this and subsequent meetings with his great-aunt Mozelle in WY, pp. 249-51. He had met her occasionally as a child in his father's sister's house. Mozelle, born in 1855, had married a Mr J.M. Hyeem in 1873 and had at least one daughter, Louise. She was widowed in 1891. When SS met her again in 1914 he kept up the friendship till well into the 1920s.

19. WY, p. 251.

20. SS to RG, undated, USI.

21. This appears as a manuscript fragment, entitled 'Jewish Gold', in SS's handwriting at USI.

22. SJ, p. 32 and a letter from SS's

wife, Hester Gatty to her sister-in-law, Pamela Gatty, *c.* 1960 in the Gatty Papers at CUL.

23. SS:PP, p. 36.

24. Letter from Stephen Tennant to G.A. David, 12 Nov. 1971, collection of Hugo Vickers.

25. SS to DFC, 25 June 1965, SS:PP, p. 47 and SJ, p. 202.

26. Michael Thorpe, *Siegfried Sassoon: a Critical Study* (Leiden University Press, 1966), p. 60.

27. D1, p. 123.

28. ibid., p. 197.

29. WY, p. 251.

30. SS to DFC, 25 June 1965, SS:PP, p. 47.

31. SS to Haro Hodson, 4 Nov. 1948, in the possession of the recipient.

32. SS to SCC, 31 Oct. 1942, HRHRC.

33. SS's 1927 diary, now in the hands of a private collector.

34. SS to DFC, 25 June 1965, SS:PP, p. 47.

35. OC, p. 39.

36. ibid., p. 41.

37. When Mary Thornycroft grew seriously ill at the end of January 1895, all her children gathered in the neighbourhood.

38. Mrs Emilie Barrington, the friend and biographer of G.F. Watts, wrote that Mary's statuette, 'The Skipping Girl', was characteristic of its author (*Marble and Bronze*, p. 37).

39. *Marble and Bronze*, p. 37.

40. When Thomas Thornycroft died in 1885, Mary made up her mind to devote the remainder of her life to finishing his life-long work, 'Boadicea', which was finally erected at Westminster Bridge (*Marble and Bronze*, p. 100).

41. *Marble and Bronze*, pp. 81 and 127.

42. ibid., p. 99.

43. HT to Agatha Cox, 17 Nov. 1883, HMC.

44. *Marble and Bronze*, p. 127.

45. ibid.

46. ibid., p. 30, from a letter to Thomas Thornycroft's first patron, Mr Dickinson.

47. ibid., p. 32.

48. *Bronze and Steel*, p. 34.

49. 'The Waterlily' is now in the National Maritime Museum at Greenwich.

50. Another reason for Thomas's move from Wilton Place may be that he had bought it on a short lease, which would explain how he was able to afford it in the first place. When the Thornycrofts moved into Moreton House, Melbury Road, in May 1877, Thomas, Mary, their sculptor son, Hamo, and painter daughters found themselves at the centre of an artists' colony, which included the painters G.F. Watts and Frederick Leighton. Thomas, who bought the land jointly with Hamo, was shrewd enough to build a large semi-detached house, half of which was subsequently sold off.

51. See OC, pp. 141-6 for a detailed account of this holiday.

52. *Marble and Bronze*, p. 49.

53. *Time Which Spaces Us Apart*, p. 11.

54. OC, p. 298.

55. John Donaldson had come home from India, where he was embanking the River Hooghly, to help John Thornycroft start the Thornycroft works, which most people believed had been set going as much by his ability as John's inventive genius. In fact, Lady Lettice Strickland-Constable said that it seemed to the rest of the Thornycroft family 'a scandal' that Uncle Don had not been made a partner. She also maintained that the Donaldsons thought the Thornycrofts 'frightful flibbertigibbets – always painting pictures'.

56. 'Pop' concerts in the nineteenth century had a very different meaning from late twentieth-century usage. They appear to have been the equivalent of our modern-day 'Proms'.

57. Mary Thornycroft exhibited busts of Flora Sassoon and S.D. Sassoon in the 1864 Royal Academy Exhibition. Rachel was said by the family to be romantically interested in Hamo, but he was unresponsive (*Marble and Bronze*, p. 83).

58. Cecil Roth gives an interesting account of Ashley Park in *The Sassoon Dynasty*, pp. 192-3.

59. *The Sassoons*, p. 75.

60. 'Mangnall's Questions' refers to a book by the schoolmistress Richmal Mangnall (1769-1820) called *Historical and Miscellaneous Questions for the Use of Young People* (1800), which was composed in question and answer format. Numerous editions were issued by Longmans and other publishers throughout the nineteenth century, revised and augmented by other authors. Mrs Gaskell refers to it in her novel, *Wives and Daughters* (1866).

61. Alfred Sassoon is recorded in Exeter College's Entrance Book as having matriculated on 15 October 1879 and then appears in a Residence Book as residing up to and including Michaelmas term 1881, when he is marked down as 'suspended'. (This does not mean that he was in academic disgrace, merely that he had removed his name from the books.) He took no degree, nor did his younger brother (S.D.'s third son), Frederick Meyer Sassoon, who matriculated at the same time, aged 17 to Alfred's 18. Frederick resided at Exeter College until spring 1884. I am indebted to Exeter College's Librarian and Archivist, J.R. Maddicott, for this information.

62. See *The Sassoon Dynasty*, p. 200 and *The Sassoons*, p. 75. Sarah Bernhardt, in *In My Double Life* (Heinemann, 1907) reports losing, at Alfred's house in 1877, a bracelet from which hung a single diamond drop presented to her by Victor Hugo after her opening night in *Hernani*. Alfred had wanted to give her a replacement bracelet, but she refused, preferring,

it seems, to record dramatically that 'he could not give me back the tear of Victor Hugo'. In fact, she had only mislaid the bracelet and continued to wear it for many years. If this story is true, it suggests that Alfred was extremely precocious, since he could only have been sixteen at the time.

63. OC, p. 293.

64. The following account of Alfred and Theresa's engagement and marriage is based mainly on Hamo Thornycroft's letters to his fiancée, Agatha Cox, from November 1883 to February 1884 at HMC.

65. HT to Agatha Cox, 1 Feb. 1884, HMC.

Chapter 2

1. I am grateful to Michael Sassoon's daughter-in-law, Mrs Leo Sassoon, for information about him. Michael told her that he was a twin, but that the other twin did not live.

2. Lady Lettice Strickland-Constable made this suggestion. Another possibility is that Michael was named after Hamo Thornycroft's sculptor friend, Michael Lawlor, with whom he had worked closely in 1882.

3. Hamo Thornycroft wrote to his fiancée, Agatha Cox, on 13 Jan. 1884: 'The note I enclose made me feel sure that I could talk to [Mr Loraine] about Theresa's secret wedding' (HMC). Loraine, who subsequently became a canon, had almost certainly prepared Theresa for confirmation in about 1870.

4. I am grateful to Pom Gibbons for this information. St Stephen's, where SS was christened on 10 Oct. 1886, was at Stanley Road, Tunbridge Wells. The church was demolished shortly afterwards and replaced by a tin hut, in which Hamo was christened on 15 September 1887. When a new church was built on the site it was called St Barnabas.

5. Birth control has been practised

since ancient times, but by the late nineteenth century it was becoming both more scientific and more generally acceptable, though the Church of England did not give even limited approval to it until 1930. The legal battle was won in Britain in 1878 when Charles Bradlaugh and Annie Besant were acquitted in 1878 of publishing an 'obscene' book on the subject, though a doctor was still struck off the Medical Register in 1886 for publishing a handbook on contraception. Marie Stopes did not open her clinic in London until 1921.

6. Alfred's father, Sassoon David Sassoon, must have made his will before his next to youngest son was born – perhaps before setting out on his journey from India to England in 1858 – since Alfred is not mentioned in it. He may have intended to revise it, but was prevented by his unexpected death in 1867 at the age of thirty-five. Whilst his eldest son, Joseph, is left almost everything and his daughter Rachel is given £10,000 (per annum) in trust, Alfred (who comes under the heading of any other son living at his death) is left only £5,000 (per annum). Alfred's mother is given control of his money until he is twenty-one, hence his readiness to ignore her threats of withholding his money in November 1883, when he would already have been twenty-two. Hamo wrote to Agatha Cox on 19 November 1883: 'I saw Sassoon's father's will (or rather an epitome of it) this morning and all seems right, and the youth is free. He will be very well off.' (HMC).

7. HT to Agatha Cox, 6 April 1884, HMC.

8. OC, p. 107. Weirleigh is still referred to by some locals as 'the ugly house'.

9. The 'tower' or spire was demolished as unsafe in the 1950s. Sassoon owned a book illustrated by Harrison Weir (*The Poultry Book* by W.B. Teget-Meier), which he inscribed

'bought at Newbury – these drawings were made at Weirleigh 20 years before I was born there'. (Phillips' Bath Sale Catalogue, 31 Oct. 1994). Weir also invented cat shows in 1871.

10. SS to SCC, 20 July 1947, HRHRC.

11. MFM, p. 23. Weirleigh garden is still beautiful but very different from its late nineteenth-century state. The lower, northern part of it has been taken over by Kent Water Board for a reservoir, many of the labour-intensive herbaceous borders have disappeared and most of the garden sheds and greenhouses. Theresa's studio and the old cottage remain, now converted to separate dwellings, and a small open garage has been added on what was the upper lawn. The three separate lawns have been made into one, which slopes considerably. Weirleigh itself, having been divided into two houses in the 1920s, was again divided after Theresa's death into numerous flats. It has since been turned back into two houses. Many of the features in the northern, larger half remain and its present owners, Mr and Mrs Charles Wheeler, who have been extremely helpful to me in my researches, have restored much of it to its original state.

12. OC, p. 124.

13. WY, pp. 35-6.

14. *The London Mercury*, June 1929.

15. MFM, pp. 78-9.

16. ibid., p. 20.

17. OC, p. 147.

18. ibid., p. 73.

19. ibid., pp. 28, 34-5, 53-4.

20. A dog-cart is a two-wheeled driving-cart with cross seats back to back. The Sassoons kept a horse specially for this purpose and the dog-cart was very much part of Siegfried's memories of Weirleigh. In a letter to H.M. Tomlinson of 4 March 1955, he tells him 'I still dream that I am driving a dog-cart'. (See Christie's Sale Catalogue, South Kensington, 3 April 1992, p. 14).

21. OC, p. 35.

22. ibid., p. 29.

23. Hamo Thornycroft's engagement diary for 1887, HMC.

24. This information was given to me by Mary's daughter, Lady Strickland-Constable. See also OC, p. 294. SS still had his father's old musical instruments in his possession at the time of his death.

25. See Hamo Thornycroft's diary for 30 December 1893, HMC and WY, p. 73.

26. OC, pp. 24-5.

27. ibid., pp. 292-3.

28. HMC.

29. ibid.

30. SS to SCC, 26 Oct. 1942, HRHRC. By a curious coincidence Theresa's niece's daughter, Lady Lettice Strickland-Constable, went to live in the next-door studio – no. 9 Pembroke Studios – after her children were grown up and, without knowing that Alfred Sassoon had lived at no. 8. She described it as a 'fairly well-heeled place, with its central garden and studios round it'. Off the road and with its own porter, it was 'safe, quiet and very cosy'. Alfred was not prepared to suffer too much for his art, it would seem.

31. HMC.

32. OC, p. 77.

33. SS to DFC, 25 June 1965, SS:PP, p. 48.

34. SS to Lady Lettice Strickland-Constable, 6 Nov. 1947; letter in possession of the recipient.

35. OC, pp. 13-14.

36. 'Celebrated Storeys', Brenchley [c. 1894-5], a manuscript collection of stories in Sassoon's hand, is at Columbia.

37. OC, p. 149.

38. ibid., p. 55.

39. ibid., pp. 26 and 162.

40. Called 'Some of my favourites' and written about 1894, this 20-page manuscript notebook is now at Columbia. It contains a series of little essays on various butterflies. While the watercolour and coloured ink illustrations, though unfinished, are lively and imaginative, the written work is obviously dictated in parts, containing such technical terms as 'mode of flight' and 'forewing'. It also has a table of contents, listing the different butterflies.

41. OC, p. 60.

42. ibid., p. 31.

43. D2, p. 236. Sassoon interpreted this dream as somehow connected with his fear of water, but it is difficult to resist making a Freudian connexion between water and sex here.

44. OC, pp. 31-2.

45. Maskelyne was a famous conjurer of the period who performed at the Egyptian Hall, London.

46. Sassoon claims, in OC (p. 39), that the HMS *Speedy* was launched by Princess May, but I have found nothing to support this.

47. By 1906, destroyers had become so large that, because of the difficulty of getting them under Thames bridges, it was decided to move the Thornycroft works to Woolston, near Southampton. The First World War gave Sir John's shipbuilding works a tremendous fillip. Coinciding as it did with the invention of the internal combustion engine and the improvements in the steam engine, it gave rise to even more sophisticated torpedo boats, vital in the defence of Britain. In view of Siegfried's own war-protest, it is ironic that his uncle should have been so heavily involved in what might loosely be called the 'arms industry'. Apart from ship-building Thornycrofts also developed a vehicle-building side to the works at Basingstoke in 1898. This was eventually absorbed into AEC, who in turn became part of Leyland. The ship-building side still continues. Bought by Vosper in 1965/66, it was nationalized soon afterwards, but in 1980 privatized again. Sir John's great-grandson, Timothy Thornycroft, to whom I am indebted for most of this information, says that the firm is much happier as a result of denationalization.

48. OC, p. 69.

49. ibid., p. 40.

50. ibid., p. 69 and interview with Lady Lettice Strickland-Constable.

51. OC, p. 69.

52. Another of Siegfried's cousins, Hamo Thornycroft's daughter, Rosalind, felt similarly overwhelmed by her Isle of Wight cousins, though also a little critical of their hearty, physical approach to life: 'They were altogether "county" and led very grand, pleasant lives with horses, yachts, dogs and Jersey cattle. We bathed a lot and the red-haired girls dived from the top of a pair of steps which had been taken out into the water for that purpose. Cousin Ada wore a green bathing-dress. The red hair with the green bathing-dress and the side-dive she did were considered very beautiful by father. Such were the things we admired in our family … Cousin Mary, like Siegfried, had a collection of butterflies and moths. Oliver also collected, but our collection was certainly smaller and less admirable than theirs …' (*Time Which Spaces Us Apart* by Rosalind Thornycroft, completed by Chloe Baynes (Balcombe, Somerset, 1991, pp. 9-10)).

53. See OC, pp. 47-8 and letters from Hamo to Agatha Thornycroft, HMC.

54. Information on Alfred Sassoon's illness has been taken from his will and Siegfried's account in OC, pp. 30-1.

55. See pp. 12-13.

56. OC, pp. 45-6.

57. SS gives the time of Alfred's death as mid-March in OC, but Alfred's will clearly states that he died on 18 April.

58. OC, p. 50.

59. Nothing could have been more English than Brenchley church, built in 1233, and more of a contrast to a Jewish cemetery in the Mile End

Road, East London. Alfred was buried in a different row from his father Sassoon David Sassoon, but in one of the family graves. Flora, who was buried on 10 March 1919, was interred in a reserved grave, adjacent to her husband.

60. OC, pp. 51-2.

61. ibid., p. 56.

62. ibid., p. 65.

Chapter 3

1. OC, p. 55.

2. ibid., p. 59.

3. ibid.

4. ibid., p. 63.

5. ibid., p. 70.

6. MFM, p. 10.

7. OC, p. 150. Sassoon is clearly remembering Fräulein Stoy when he writes in MIF: 'I thought of an old German governess I had known, and how she used to talk about "dear old Moltke and Bismarck" and her quiet home in Westphalia where her father had been a Protestant pastor' (MIF, p. 33).

8. OC, p. 153.

9. For this and other information about Tom Richardson and Siegfried's early life, I am deeply indebted to Tom's son, the late John Richardson. In two long interviews, one of them held at Weirleigh itself, and four written pieces, he gave me an invaluable insight into the period and many illuminating details.

10. WY, p. 73.

11. MFM, p. 21.

12. 'The Painting of Cockbird', an unpublished article by the late John Richardson, written November 1986, p. 5.

13. MFM, p. 17.

14. 'The Green of the Spring', an unpublished article by the late John Richardson, written in 1990, p. 2.

15. SJ, p. 216.

16. OC, p. 85.

17. *Cricket Country*, 1944, 'Among the Moderns', p. 44ff.

18. *The Best of Friends: Further Letters to Sir Sydney Carlyle Cockerell*, edited by Viola Meynell (London, Hart-Davis, 1956), p. 67: SS to SCC, 18 June 1939.

19. SS:PP, p. 31.

20. WY, p. 60.

21. This and the three previous quotations are taken from OC, pp. 104-5.

22. This story is found in a manuscript notebook in the Sassoon collection at the Rare Book and Manuscripts Room at Columbia.

23. HRHRC.

24. Michael's car repair workshop used to fit wooden running-boards to Model-T Fords, since the standard metal ones bent and became slippery. It was an improvement not approved by the manufacturers.

25. See 'A Short History of the Sassoon Family' by Sue Edwards, *Siegfried Sassoon Centenary* brochure, 1986, p. 3. I am indebted for much of my information about Michael Sassoon and other family matters to his youngest son, Hamo Sassoon, who kindly allowed me to talk to him in Jimena, Spain, from 17 to 21 April 1991. He also gave me an introduction to his sister-in-law, Joan Sassoon, who added further insights. (Joan Sassoon died 12 July 1995.)

26. Michael married Violet Mildred Stroud, one of twins like himself, in 1907. They had three sons: Alfred Lionel Thornycroft (b. 1909), Norman Basil Arundel (b. 1910) and Hamo (b. 1920). Violet died in 1954 and Michael remarried in 1957. His second wife, Elizabeth Florence Scott, survived him.

27. Michael referred to Cecil Roth's book, *The Sassoon Dynasty*, as 'the Sassoon Dysentry' but his son thinks that he was probably disguising some pride in his family with this remark.

28. See D3, p. 89 (entry for 21 November 1921): 'Since January I've "given away" £530 (apart from £130 lent to Michael, which he won't repay …)'.

29. SS to SCC. 20 July 1947, HRHRC.

30. Letters from SS to Edward Carpenter of 27 July 1911 and 2 August 1911 (Sheffield City Libraries). See also OAG, p. 230.

31. See D1, p. 46.

32. OC, p. 155.

33. ibid., p. 243.

34. ibid., pp. 41-2.

35. i) 'The poems, Brenchley, 1896-97' ('For Mamsy'); ii) Volume of poems for Theresa Sassoon's birthday, March 1897; iii) More Poems by S.L. Sassoon, Oct 20-Dec 25, 1897; iv) The Poems by Siegfried Sassoon, 1898; v) The Blue Poetry Book 1898 ('For Wirgie'); vi) The Poems, 1898 ('For Aunty Lula'); vii) The Red Poetry Book, Christmas 1898 ('For Uncle Hamo'); viii) A Book of verses. Jan 1899; ix) The Poems. 1899.

36. OC, p. 157.

37. Columbia. Many of the poems in Siegfried's first 1896-7 volume are repeated in the second volume, which he prepared for his mother's birthday in March 1897. At least five of the nine childhood volumes were prepared specifically as presents for family or friends and contain a great deal of repetition, thus giving a clear indication of the poems Siegfried himself liked. In quoting the early poems I have given them as they appear, except for the use of the full-stop. Perhaps because he was reminded, as most children have to be, not to forget a full-stop at the end of a sentence, Siegfried tends to put a full-stop at the end of every line of his poetry. Since this makes it rather difficult to read, I have sometimes silently omitted them for the sake of sense. His spelling I have faithfully followed.

38. D3, p. 174.

39. OC, p. 86.

40. Quoted from *More Poems 1897* by Dame Felicitas Corrigan in SS:PP, p. 54.

41. OC, pp. 75-6.

42. *The Green of the Spring*, pp.
10-11.

43. MFM, p. 10.

44. Major Edgeworth Horrocks,
J.P., lived at nearby Mascalls House
until he died in 1908. He was the
grandfather of Lt.-Gen. Sir Frederick
Morgan, K.C.B., who planned the
D-Day landings. In 1901 Major
Horrocks built a Parochial Hall in
memory of his wife, Elizabeth.

45. OC, p. 75.

46. Sassoon noted in the MS of
MFM, now at Columbia, that Jack
Barchard was 'a composite character –
1/2 R[ichard] E[llis] M[archant] and
1/2 "Ronnie" Mitchell, a gentleman
farmer at Yalding, who bowled
successfully for Eton and was a
nephew of R.A.H. Mitchell
(1843-1903), a famous cricketer and
Eton master. R[onnie] M[itchell] was
killed at Gallipoli'. Richard Marchant
died in 1939.

47. Forty years later, following the
publication of OC, SS was to write to a
Mr Hardcastle: 'Only yesterday I had
a charming letter from Bessie
Marchant (Mrs Hugh Wormald) who
has lived at East Dereham in Norfolk
for many years. She tells me that she
had forgotten many of the things I
describe, but remembered her essay
on Shelley' (letter of 2 Oct. 1938,
HRHRC).

48. OC, p. 79.

49. Ellen Gosse (1850-1929; née
Epps) was the niece of a homeopathic
doctor who had treated EG's mother,
unsuccessfully, for cancer. Ellen had
left home by the time EG met her at
Ford Madox Brown's studio and had
her own studio in Devonshire Street
by the time he proposed to her in
October 1874. A 'new' woman,
feminist and something of an
intellectual, she initially refused, in
order to pursue her own promising
career. Three months later, however,
she suddenly capitulated and they
were married in 1875. Both Theresa

and her painter-sister Helen were at
the wedding.

50. WY, p. 90.

51. OC, p. 115. EG continued to
present books to Siegfried, who
remembered reading his *Critical
Kit-Kats* and *On Viol and Flute* in the
garden at Weirleigh at the age of
twelve. He had also been given
another of EG's books by Ellen Batty.

52. D2, p. 237. A number of letters
from Helen Wirgman to SS have
survived from 1908 and 1909 and are
now at CUL. Quotes attributed to her
are taken from this collection.

53. OC, p. 119.

54. ibid., p. 115.

55. ibid., p. 123.

56. SS to DFC, 14 Feb. 1961,
SS:PP, pp. 69-70.

57. Letter of 21 July 1940 from Dr
John Shaw Dunn to SS, Columbia.

58. MS notebook version of OC,
Columbia.

59. Cecil Roth, in *The Sassoon
Dynasty* (p. 199) sees Rachel's
editorship of both *The Observer* and
The Sunday Times as a 'tour de force',
but not a brilliant success. He points
out that, when Rachel came to sell
The Observer in the early 1900s, it
was sold to Lord Northcliffe for only
£4,000. When Northcliffe had 'put it
on its feet', however, he sold it to
Waldorf Astor for £60,000.

60. Clarence Hamilton, who had
attended Matfield Grange School
before going to Rugby and Cambridge,
eventually became Vicar of Windsor.

Chapter 4

1. Edward VII became friends with
a number of David Sassoon's sons,
Reuben and Arthur in particular. His
own relatively modest income of
£100,000 was insufficient for his
lavish life-style and the Sassoons
were happy to supplement it in
various ways. Edward's relations with
wealthy Jewish families, which
included the Rothschilds as well as

the Sassoons, did something to overcome the anti-Semitism of much of English Society at the time.

2. Alice Mary Norman was, according to her grand-daughters, Pat Robertson and Jenny Barty-King who kindly talked to me and lent me material, 'the power behind the throne'. Brought up in an enlightened way, she was considered extremely modern when she arrived in Sevenoaks, where she was the first woman to ride a bicycle in public.

3. Cecil Norman produced a series of articles describing the New Beacon's history in the school magazine, *The Beacon*, in the 1960s. I have drawn heavily on Cecil Norman's articles, as well as on my interview with his daughters.

4. OC, p. 199.

5. ibid., p. 201.

6. Rupert Croft-Cooke, *The Glittering Pastures* (London, Putnam, 1962), p. 102.

7. SS inscribed one copy of his privately-printed *Sonnets* (1909): 'My Dear Mr Norman – These are some things of mine. I hope that you will like them. About half of them have appeared recently in "The Academy". Yours sincerely Siegfried Sassoon'.

8. Siegfried's failure to mention the name of his teacher in these, his least favourite subjects, presumably resulted from their failure to give him the inspiration he needed to persevere in academic work of any kind. However, he did keep a photograph of someone who probably taught music at the school, a Miss Frances Perkins, who played first violin to Hamo's second violin in the New Beacon's 1901 end-of-term concert.

9. Apart from playing cricket with at least two of his ex-schoolmasters at Weirleigh after he left the New Beacon, Siegfried continued to play both games with E.M. Jackson and Cecil Norman, who became a member of a large number of teams, their colourful names including the Cryptics, the Sevenoaks Vine, Band of Brothers, Free Foresters and Blue Mantles. He remembered Siegfried's habit of raising his elbows from his sides before bringing over his arm for bowling and his accurate and 'stylish' batting. The two were to remain in touch for more than thirty years.

10. While waiting for a rugby pitch to be built, Mr Norman organized soccer in the winter terms and hockey in the spring. Neither of these sports elicited any comment from Siegfried, though he did win a prize for hockey in 1901. Nor does he say anything about the boxing and other rigorous exercises which were carried out in the temporary tin gymnasium under the supervision of a Sgt Moss. He is unlikely to have enjoyed anything quite so organized and he positively disliked the club-swinging. Swimming he continued to fear and he must have been relieved that the school had not yet acquired its own pool. He makes no mention of athletics, which in any case occupied no very important place in the school's programme, though there was an annual Sports Day.

11. *Summoned by Bells* (London, John Murray, 1960), p. 66.

12. Frank Fletcher, *After Many Days* (London, Robert Hale, 1937), p. 115.

13. ibid., p. 131.

14. Jean Moorcroft Wilson, *Charles Hamilton Sorley, a Biography* (London, Cecil Woolf, 1985), p. 51.

15. OC, p. 208.

16. Sassoon is probably alluding to Walter Pater's philosophical romance, *Marius the Epicurean* (1885), in which Marius seeks spiritual truths rather than worldly satisfaction, though Gould himself was too old to have been named after Pater's protagonist.

17. WY, p. 252.

18. Letter to Sassoon from Christopher H. Teesdale, 3 July 1930, CUL.

19. Gould had been a boy at Marlborough himself from 1867 to 1870 under the third Master of the

College, the Reverend G.G. Bradley. He had come back to teach there in 1875, for the first year under the Reverend F.W. Farrar and then for the whole of Bell's mastership.

20. The Reverend George Cotton left Marlborough in 1858 to become Bishop of Calcutta. He was drowned in the Hooghly River in 1866, so was not alive to appreciate the honour of having Cotton House named after him in 1872. Cotton is said to have been the model for Hughes's 'the young master' in *Tom Brown's Schooldays*.

21. The Marlburian Assistant Master, John O'Regan, when he became Housemaster of B3 House in 1907 tried to do away with hot baths in the spring and summer terms, because he thought they made the boys soft. His prefects rebelled, however.

22. OC, p. 209. Sassoon gives the matron's name as Miss Boult in his autobiography, but a letter from her to him on 7 April 1930, is signed 'Mrs H.C. Bolt'. Beside reminiscing about Cotton House and his illness there, she also offers him cheap, clean accommodation in her boarding-house at Bude, where she has retired, CUL.

23. Letter from Christopher H. Teesdale, 3 July 1930, CUL.

24. ibid.

25. John and Michael O'Regan, *John O'Regan and his Family Background*, a privately printed memoir by O'Regan's sons, p. 196.

26. OAG, p. 230.

27. Letter from SS to Edward Carpenter, 2 August 1911, Sheffield City Libraries.

28. OC, p. 212.

29. ibid., p. 218.

30. See *Hymns Ancient and Modern*, p. 457. This hymn would indeed have been relatively easy for SS to play.

31. OC, p. 221.

32. A.R. Pelly, an Old Marlburian, writes in his unpublished memoirs: 'I remember Meyrick ("Murke"), who was in charge of the Museum and the Natural History Society, once coming down the Museum stairs carrying a pile of books which slipped through his hand and cascaded to the bottom. "Damn!" he said with great vigour and warmth. It so happened that the Master passed at the bottom of the stairs at that moment and we giggled. "Damn!" said Murke. "Why shouldn't I say Damn? Damn! Damn! Damn!" getting louder and louder. The Master completely ignored it.' (A copy of Pelly's memoirs is at Marlborough College.) Sassoon kept a cutting on Edward Meyrick, F.R.S., in the manuscript of OC, which pointed out that he was at Marlborough until 1914 and that he was a lepidopterist, who had a collection of over 100,000 specimens of the micro-lepidoptera, which include clothes-moths.

33. Lupton was known as 'Jimmy Luppers' to his friends, but Beverley Nichols, who found Lupton's pronounced sniff extremely irritating, referred to him disparagingly as 'Mr Upton'. Joseph MacDougal Lupton had been at Eton, where he won a scholarship to King's College, Cambridge. At Marlborough (1891-1927), he was Master of A House, School Librarian, Chaplain and a Captain and Adjutant in the Officers Training Corps. He taught German. After his retirement from Marlborough in 1927, he became Vicar of Christchurch, Savernake from 1927 to 1934 and died in 1947.

34. OC, p. 228.

35. *After Many Days*, p. 134.

36. Michael O'Regan kindly sent me a photocopy of the original poem. When Sassoon quoted it in OC (p. 229), he either silently corrected the third from last line (to 'And blows *are not* so hard') or misquoted slightly.

37. Cotton House library has recently been restored. Two portraits of SS now hang there, one of them a photo silkscreen of him by Vincent Stokes and David Allen, commemorating his poetic awakening on the site.

38. OC, p. 230.

39. This poem appears in SS's 1903 notebook, which was sold by Roy Davids to Colin Franklin in 1996.

40. See pp. 123-7 for an account of SS's attempt to win the Chancellor's Medal at Cambridge in 1905-6.

41. This book was sold at Sotheby's saleroom, Bond Street, in July 1992 and catalogued by James Fergusson, who bought it at that sale.

42. OC, p. 227.

43. When Pat O'Regan became housemaster of B3 in 1907, he must have been aware of the dangers of allowing boys out early on winter mornings without any kind of sustenance, since he made it a rule that they could not leave the House before cocoa was ready for them.

44. Frank Fletcher, who arrived to replace Canon Bell as Master of Marlborough in September 1903, writes in his autobiography: 'On one occasion, to avoid a widespread epidemic of mumps, I sent the School home ten days early for their Christmas holidays' (*After Many Days*, p. 137).

45. The three boys who died at Marlborough during the Lent term of 1902 were almost certainly victims of the same complications of measles which nearly killed SS. They were very close to him in age and died within a week of each other, probably the week that he was most seriously ill with pneumonia. Pearson Bailey Magrett, aged 16, died on 25 Feb. 1902; Douglas Scott Oram, aged 15, died on 28 Feb. 1902, and William Gill Spear, aged 14, died on 4 March 1902.

46. SS wrote in his diary for 27 April 1904: 'Had lunch at Beacon and biked to Tonbridge. Had 1/2 an hrs batting with Humphreys and Seymour'. (This diary is now in the possession of Tony Laughton, who kindly allowed me to study it.)

47. The Corps, part of the Cadet Movement, was started at Marlborough College in 1860 and attached to the 2nd Volunteer Battalion of the 2nd Wiltshire Regiment in 1870. See also WY, p. 275.

48. OC, p. 241.

49. ibid., p. 234.

50. ibid.

51. Mr Colin Franklin bought Sassoon's diary for 1903, in which these details were preserved, and kindly allowed me to study it.

52. OC, p. 225. See also the Cotton House records.

53. According to SS, in 1903 the question of altering the height of the wicket was being widely discussed. See OC, p. 239.

54. OC, pp. 240-1. 'The Extra Inch' appeared in *Cricket*, xxii, no. 623, 9 April 1903, signed 'Siegfried Loraine Sassoon'. It was reprinted in *The Book of Cricket Verse*, edited by G. Broadrib, 1953.

55. 1903: 'Spring (With all due deference to Lord Tennyson's opinions)', *Cricket*, xxii, no. 625, 23 April, p. 91, signed 'S.L.S.'; 'To Wilfred – Bowling (A reminiscence of the Second Test Match) (When Wilfred Rhodes a'bowling goes)' *Cricket*, xxiii, no. 650, 28 Jan [probably 1904], p. 13, signed 'S.L.S.' 1904: 'Yuletide Thoughts (At Yuletide all my thoughts are far remote)' *Cricket*, xxiii, no. 679, 2 Dec., p. 476, signed 'S.L.S.' 1905: 'Dies Irae (What of the days to be?)' *Cricket*, xxiv, no. 700, 10 Aug., p. 332, signed 'S.L.S.'

56. This edition is now in the possession of Mr William Reese of New Haven, Connecticut.

57. D2, p. 267.

58. OC, p. 243. I have failed to find any of SS's school reports and have had to rely on his memory of their contents.

Chapter 5

1. OC, p. 244.

2. ibid., p. 251.

3. In the 'List of Successes' for 1887 to 1932, Henley House records an overall rate of 1025 (out of 1112) for Oxford, Cambridge and the Armed Forces. Of these, 755 places were for Oxford and Cambridge entrance.

4. Both the house and lake have survived and now belong to the National Union of Railwaymen.

5. Much of this information was given to me by Eustace Malden's daughter, Angela Harding, who kindly allowed me to interview her at some length.

6. William Paley, *Evidences of Christianity* (1794), a work which became a textbook for Oxford and Cambridge entrance examinations.

7. Eustace Malden's son, Jack, was also a good cricketer and played for Sussex. SS, commenting on Eustace's death in 1947, to a friend Rolf Barber, remembers his wicket-keeping for Kent above all else.

8. While SS was writing OC, in which he describes his time at Henley House, he sent his printer's proofs to Henry Malden's daughter, Jane, and also to Eustace Malden, who was still alive in 1938 and still interested in games. (He took part in local putting competitions.) Eustace was 'touchingly pleased' with the Henley House chapter, which he thought very good. (SS to Mr Hardcastle, 2 Oct. 1938, HRHRC.)

9. OC, p. 260.

10. SS to ED, 18 Dec. 1915, CUL.

11. E.B. Rawsthorne carried on at Henley House until about 1937, when the establishment was beginning to fail. In a letter to Mr Hardcastle, who had clearly attended Henley House himself, SS says that he was 'specially pleased by your tribute to the Teacher, as I'd half feared that I'd sentimentalised him in memory' (Letter of 2 Oct. 1938, HRHRC).

12. OC, p. 256.

13. As late as November 1918 Sassoon spent a week playing golf with George Wilson at Rye (see SJ, pp. 109-111). And he was still in touch with George when the latter died, unexpectedly young, in 1929.

14. WY, p. 159.

15. ibid.

16. SS to Arthur E. Risdale (who appears in SS's fiction as 'Arthur Brandwick), 4 Aug. 1940, CUL.

17. i.e. *c*. 1906-1911 – Master of the Galway Blazers, Ireland; 1911-1913 – Master of the Southdown Hunt, Sussex; 1913-1914 – Master of the Atherstone Hunt, Warwickshire; 1914-1919 – Joint Master of the Fitzwilliam Hunt, Cambridgeshire (post filled by his wife, Phyllis Loder while he serves in the First World War); 1920 onwards – Master of the Atherstone Hunt again.

18. WY, pp. 57-8.

19. OC, p. 259.

20. Henry F. Thompson to SS, 1 Nov. 1916, CUL.

21. OC, p. 249.

22. ibid., p. 262.

23. See note 61 of Chapter 1.

24. OC, p. 266.

25. SS told Michael Thorpe that his brother, Hamo, 'knew the Olivier girls and Rupert Brooke' (*Letters to a Critic*, Kent Editions, 1976, p. 22). He gives no indication that he himself met them, perhaps because he had left Cambridge by then.

26. Stanley Jackson, *The Sassoons* (London, Heinemann, 1968), p. 134.

27. OC, p. 268.

28. William Loudon Mollison (1851-1929) had come to Clare from Aberdeen University as a scholar in 1872, became a Tutor in 1880, a Senior Tutor in 1894 and Master in 1915. He was a distinguished mathematician (lecturing in Mathematics from 1877 to 1882), as well as a sound classical scholar, known for his mental alertness, energy and perseverance. Sassoon admired him greatly, but remembered him as 'a fussy, over-anxious man with a nervous stammer' (OC, p. 269).

29. SS:PP, p. 55.

30. Sassoon went on adding to his anthology until at least 1910, cramming poems into every available space at every conceivable angle. There are a number of extracts from William Morris, more pieces by William Watson and Robert Louis Stevenson, and some from Robert Bridges, Francis Thompson, Andrew Lang, James Elroy Flecker, Arthur O'Shaughnessy, Richard Le Gallienne, Edgar Allan Poe, Yeats, Walter de la Mare and Joachim du Bellay. A poem by Stephen Phillips written in 1905 is subsequently crossed through as though in disapproval.

31. SS:PP, p. 55.

32. ibid.

33. Sassoon bought the *Poems* of William Watson (London, John Lane, 2 vols, 1905) in 1906.

34. 1906: 'To a Blood' (In a Modern Manner)('Is it a man? – but nay') *The Cambridge Review*, xxviii, no. 678, p. 317, signed 'SS'; 'Prospice' (Through Blue Spectacles) [After Browning] *The Granta*, xix, no. 424, 19 May, pp. 335-6, signed 'SS'. 'Darak and Daimla – an Inanity' (by Stephen Philips [*sic*], Junr.) ('A dramatic piece') *The Granta*, xix, no. 425, May, pp. 340, 342, signed 'SS'; 'Par-les-Eaux-du-Perrier' (with acknowledgements to the shade of the Psalmist) ('By the waters of Perrier') *The Granta*, xix, no. 426, 2 June, p. 369, signed 'SS'; 'The Bomb' (After the manner of R.B[rowning]) ('Give me the bomb; I poise it lightly – so –') *The Granta*, xix, May Week no., 9 June, pp. 24-5.

35. Oliver Thornycroft (1885-1956) was a friend of Michael Sassoon in particular. After schooling at Bedales, he went up to Cambridge in 1903 and left in 1906 with a B.A. He had no further connexions with Clare after that and did not, as was usual, remain on the College board. One of the 'engineering' Thornycrofts, Oliver eventually went to work for his uncle John at the Thornycroft's Southampton works which had opened in 1904. Hamo Sassoon, when 'ploughed' in his 'General' planned to join him there, but decided to return to Cambridge instead and eventually gained his B.A. there in June 1909.

36. Guilford's medieval interests emerge most clearly in his two books of 'Select Extracts' for *Texts for Students*, published by S.P.C.K. – *Sports and Pastimes in the Middle Ages* (1920) and *Travellers and Travelling in the Middle Ages* (1924).

37. Letter from SS to Guilford, 12 July [1906]. This and other letters from SS to Guilford, ending with a postcard in 1929, are now at BL. There is also a letter from Guilford at CUL.

38. SS:PP, pp. 55-6.

39. SS to Louis Untermeyer, 11 Oct. [1920], at Lilly.

40. SS:PP, p. 56.

41. One copy of *Poems* (1906), at CUL, suggests that he sent it to almost everyone he knew, since 'Ethel Leeds', to whom it is inscribed, was by no means a close friend.

42. OC, p. 277.

43. ibid., p. 282.

44. SS inscribed a picture of his aunt Agatha: 'This photograph has great interest in connexion with *Tess of the D'Urbervilles*. T.H. after meeting Mrs Hamo Thornycroft at the Gosse's [*sic*] on July 23, 1889, wrote in his diary "of the people I have met this summer, the lady whose mouth recalls more fully than any other beauty's the Elizabethan metaphor 'Her lips are roses full of snow' is Mrs H.T.'s."

'T.H. himself told me that while writing of Tess he had her face in mind more than any other. This photograph (taken some time in the late '80s) seems to me a suitable picture of Tess. [SS's monogram]' – Sotheby's Catalogue, 18 July 1991, p. 63.

45. D2, pp. 130-1 for more details of Hamo.

46. OC, pp. 273-4.

47. *Marble and Bronze*, p. 159.

48. HT to SS, 20 March 1907, CUL.

49. Sassoon's response to Hamo's letter was, infuriatingly, to ask his advice. Hamo gave it in a letter of 9 April 1907 and it remained the same: 'it is *most* important for a literary career that you should take a University degree, and my advice is that you should do so' (CUL). He was still urging SS to try for the Bar in December 1907.

50. See SS's brief *curriculum vitae* for Ernest Benn's sixpenny 'Augustan Books of English Poetry' series, edited by Edward Thompson, and now at Bodley.

Chapter 6

1. OC, p. 289. SS also refers to 'my childhood which lasted so long (until I was twenty-three, anyhow)'. D1, p. 26.

2. WY, p. 214.

3. The Royal Societies Club was at 63 St James's Street.

4. WY, p. 208.

5. Sassoon and Thompson continued to write to each other after Thompson went out to Ceylon with a rubber-planting firm. Thompson's ill-health prevented him from serving in the First World War, to his great regret, but he kept in touch with SS during and after it. He married in the late 1920s but his wife died unexpectedly a few years later and by 1930 he was alone again in Ceylon and, as he told SS, very miserable. There are a number of letters from Henry Thompson to SS at CUL.

6. WY, p. 50.

7. ibid.

8. ibid., p. 55. SS had five books on golf in his extensive library, two of them by Bernard Darwin, containing autograph letters by him.

9. From an unpublished article, 'Sport and Literature' in the possession of William Reese Company, New Haven. SS had bought Nyren's *The Young Cricketer's Tutor* from a Brighton bookseller, A.J. Gaston, in 1900 for the modest sum of half a guinea. He would later present it to another keen cricketer with strong literary connexions, Edmund Blunden, but would replace it in his collection in 1934, when an enthusiastic bookseller wrote to offer him a replacement copy signed by the editor himself, Keats's mentor, Charles Cowden-Clarke. This new copy he presented to Blunden in exchange for the original Gaston copy, and between its pages he inserted a skit 'in the style of William Shakespeare'. Published 'privately' in 1955 by the Golden Head Press as 'An Adjustment', it was wittily introduced and explained by SS's friend Philip Gosse.

10. We know from his autobiography, *Basingstoke Boy*, that John Arlott read SS's works. (He ran a series of literary programmes on BBC radio during and after the Second World War.) We also know that SS and Neville Cardus corresponded, admiringly. Since Arlott and Cardus were friends, it would be surprising if Arlott had not met SS.

11. These scorebooks are in the possession of the cricket collector, Tony Laughton, to whom I am indebted for most of what I know about SS's cricket library, which Mr Laughton acquired.

12. WY, p. 63.

13. ibid., pp. 63-7.

14. Dennis Silk, *Siegfried Sassoon* (Tisbury, Compton Russell, 1975).

15. David Foot, *Beyond Bat and Ball* (Melksham, Good Books, 1993), p. 51.

16. Letters from HT to Theresa Sassoon, 2 Oct. 1908 and 10 May 1909, CUL.

17. SS's collection of hunting books included Trollope's *Hunting Sketches*, works by Somerville and Ross, Surtees, C.J. Apperley's *The Life of*

John Mytton, Otho Paget's *Hunting and the Duke of Portland's Memories of Racing and Hunting*. He also kept detailed hunting diaries between 1909 and 1914, which became a major source of reference for MFM.

18. SS:PP, p. 31.

19. As Sir Alan Lascelles, a friend of SS's in later years, writes in his introduction to the Folio Society's edition of MFM: 'All through the century between Waterloo and Mons, fox-hunting was – to the constant bewilderment of foreigners – an essential thread in the tapestry of English life'.

20. 'Rambling Thoughts on Horses and Hunting', MS at HRHRC.

21. WY, p. 70.

22. SS to Delphine Turner, no date, Berg.

23. D2, p. 19. There is no mention of a third brother, Henry's, attitude towards horses.

24. MFM, p. 122.

25. Capt. A. Gordon Taylor to SS, no date, CUL.

26. Gordon Harbord to SS, 2 Feb. 1917, IWM.

27. Robert Smith Surtees (1805-64) was a journalist and novelist who wrote mainly about fox-hunting. His principal works were *Jorrocks's Jaunts and Jollities* (1838); *Handley Cross* (1843), *Hillingdon Hall* (1845) and *Mr Sponge's Sporting Tour* (1853).

28. Capt. A. Gordon Taylor to SS, no date, CUL.

29. D2, p. 141.

30. WY, pp. 41-2.

31. D2, p. 63 and WY, pp. 41-7.

32. ibid., p. 135.

33. WY, pp. 29-33.

34. D2, p. 192.

35. ibid., p. 253.

36. ibid., pp. 280-1.

37. SS to SCC, 26 Aug. 1952, HRHRC.

38. WY, p. 111.

39. There are bars of music given as a guide to metre in *Rough Drafts* (1906) at Columbia.

40. WY, p. 107.

41. ibid., p. 110.

42. SS:PP, pp. 95-6. From this and other references in letters and diaries, it is clear that SS was particularly fond of the following pieces, among much else: two Elizabethan songs, 'Fain would I change that note' and 'When to her Lute Corinna Sings' and most of Dowland's songs; the chaconne from Bach's *Partita* no 2 for solo violin; 'None but the weary heart'; Fauré's *Après une Rêve*; Brahms's *Intermezzo* in B flat; Mendelssohn's *Octet*; Schumann's music for the ballet *Papillons*; Borodin's *Prince Igor* and Moussorgsky's *Boris Godounov*; Elgar's *Violin Concerto* and *Oratorio*; Chopin's *Études*; Debussy's *Preludes*; Wagner's *Tristan and Isolde* and *The Mastersingers*; the operas of Vaughan Williams, but *not* those of Charles Stanford or Ethel Smythe; Warlock's 'glorious' *Corpus Christi Carol*, and Schubert's *trios*.

43. See *Rough Drafts* (1906) at Columbia.

44. ibid.

45. Sassoon wrote to the Irish novelist, Forrest Reid (1875– 1947), probably in 1908: 'I am sending you a sort of masque which I have written. It is supposed to contrast *natural* and *forced* art – of any sort. Anyhow I hope you will be amused'.

46. *Orpheus in Diloeryum* started life, according to its author, as 'an unactable one-act play which had never quite made up its mind whether to be satirical or serious ...' He had become increasingly interested in the drama, particularly Shakespeare's plays. On 2 Oct. 1906, he told Guilford that he had been thinking of writing a play of his own, on Tristan and Isolde, but had eventually rejected it as 'too stagey'. His interest in Orpheus, that other love-stricken musician, went even further back; he had included two extracts about the legend in his 1905 poetry anthology, one from Shakespeare's *Henry VIII*, the other from Alfred Noyes's 'Orpheus and Eurydice'. Though printed in the form of a play, with a list of 'The Persons' involved, SS's *Orpheus* was clearly not intended to be acted. Nevertheless, he decided, having discovered how relatively cheap printing could be, to have it produced as a booklet at his own expense.

47. Sir Arthur Bliss (1891-1975) did not marry until 1925 and was not knighted until 1950, so that Sassoon must have presented his copy years later.

48. WY, p. 15.

49. ibid.

50. ibid.

51. Helen Wirgman to SS, 26 Aug. 1908, CUL.

52. EG to SS, 28 March 1908, Rutgers.

53. OC, p. 300.

54. SS was not at all strict in his handling of the sonnet form. Roughly speaking he adhered to the Petrachan model with its break between octet and sestet, sometimes leaving a line space to indicate it, sometimes not. His rhyme scheme rarely followed the strict Italian pattern. In a letter from T.W.H. Crosland to SS quoted in Sotheby's Catalogue, London, 14 Dec. 1992, p. 62: 'As to the "Melodies" [1912] why in the name of the Devil have you gone and spoilt all your sonnets by putting a Shakespearean octet with the Italian sestet. You might as well breed parrots with peacocks tails. It is lucky I am not reviewing you or you would have heard about this'.

55. SS wrote to his friend Guilford in 1906 that he had been trying to get some of his sonnets published in the *Temple Bar* magazine, but had been rejected. He felt *The Academy* might be more suitable.

56. WY, p. 9.

57. SS to Ralph Hodgson, 14 June 1932, Beinecke.

58. SS to SCC, 26 Feb. 1942, HRHRC.

59. ibid.

60. Until 1909 SS's only publications had been in *Cricket, a Weekly Record of the Game*, *Granta* and an obscure poetry magazine called *The Thrush*, which had printed a roundel called 'Dawn-Dimness'. Though the last contribution had been paid for – 3s. 6d. SS meticulously records – it could hardly be counted as acceptance by the literary world to which he aspired.

61. Geoffrey Keynes points out that, though SS tells us that he had ordered 35 copies of the standard edition, his inscription in the one surviving copy refers to only 25 having been produced. See Keynes, p. 25.

62. WY, p. 18.

63. SS had admired C.M. Doughty (1843-1926) since 1907 when he had read his epic poem, *The Dawn in Britain* (1906); like many people at the time he was unaware of Doughty's classic, *Travels in Arabia Deserta* (1888), though he was to enjoy it greatly in later years. He was very surprised to receive a gracious reply to his letter praising *The Dawn in Britain*. In it Doughty not only claimed, in characteristically archaic language, to have met 'some kindly there resident members of the Sassoon family at Poona' in India, but also to be a friend of Theresa Sassoon's close acquaintance and neighbour, Major Horrocks. (See WY, pp. 19-21.)

64. EG to SS, 5 Dec. 1909, Rutgers.

65. This copy is in the possession of William Reese, New Haven.

66. WY, p. 28.

67. EG to SS, 6 Dec. 1911, Rutgers.

68. ibid., 30 June 1912, Rutgers.

69. SS wrote in a proof copy of *Amyntas*, 'This proof copy is the only one in existence, as no copies were printed. SS'. And R.J. Roberts, reviewing Geoffrey Keynes's Sassoon bibliography, notes that the ledgers of the Chiswick Press record the abandoned printing of a play,

Amyntas, a Mystery (*Book Collecter*, 11, 4, Winter 1962, p. 521). *Amyntas* did appear, however, in the periodical, *The Antidote*, for 8 March 1913, and parts of it were later included in *Discoveries* (1915), under the title 'Romance'.

70. There is another interesting possible connexion between the use of the name 'Amyntas' and homosexuality, of which SS himself may have been aware through EG. *Amyntas*, published by the *Mercure de France* in 1906, was the title chosen by André Gide for a volume of his African reminiscences. The Gide critic, Linette F. Brugmans claims: 'The title Amyntas is from Vergil: "Quid tunc si fuscus Amyntas?" (What matter if Amyntas be dark?) Gide's imagination construed Amyntas as no human being, but "an imaginary idol" – the "Saharan Apollo" (*Journal*, 9 April 1930)'. As Brugmans points out, the critics received the book with concerted silence, but on 28 July 1909, Edmund Gosse wrote to ask Gide: 'What is "Amyntas" ' and had, perhaps, discussed the matter with his protégé, SS.

71. SS to EM, 6 July 1914, Berg. SS asks Marsh his opinion of the abandoned play.

72. Nevill Forbes (1883-1929), who got a First in Modern Languages at Oxford in 1906, after studying for his doctorate at Leipzig, returned to Oxford to become Reader in Russian in 1910, the year SS went to stay with him there. He became a full Professor in 1923. He had fifteen publications to his credit, all in the field of Slavonic studies. SS told Carpenter 'he is a delightful person (in spite of that queer, ungainly exterior of his)'.

73. SS also had in his library at his death, *Ioläus: an Anthology of Friendship* (1906) and Carpenter's *Sonnets* (1912).

74. *Coming Out* (London, Quartet, 1977), p. 80.

75. ibid.

76. SS to Edward Carpenter in the Carpenter collection at Sheffield City Libraries.

77. ibid., 2 Aug. 1911, Sheffield.

78. This handwritten sonnet was included in the copy of *Twelve Sonnets* sent to Edward Carpenter, now in the possession of William Reese, New Haven. Carpenter praised two of the pieces in it, 'A Melody' and 'Perilous Music' and concluded, rather patronizingly, 'You have evidently some skill as *well* as feeling'. (Letter of 31 July 1911 described in Sotheby's Bond Street Sale Catalogue for 13 Dec. 1993 as part of SS's library.

79. D1, p. 166.

80. Carpenter to SS of 17 Aug. 1918.

81. Carpenter included with his first reply a book in German, which SS, rather hopefully, promised to read. This was probably an offprint of Carpenter's *Uber die Beziehungen Zwischen Homosexualitat und Prophetentum* (On the Connexion Between Homosexuality and Divination), printed in a German journal in April and July 1911.

82. SS to Carpenter, 2 Aug. 1911, Sheffield.

83. WY, p. 121.

84. ibid., p. 122.

85. 'An Ode for Music' was published, with emendations tactfully suggested by Crosland, in *The Antidote* for February 1913.

86. WY, p. 127.

87. ibid., p. 124.

88. ibid., pp. 125-6.

89. Crosland also offered to publish, for ten pounds, SS's *Orpheus in Diloeryum* in 1913, but when he saw how heavily SS had revised his 1908 version of this 'unactable one-act play', he demanded another ten pounds. When the money was not forthcoming and his letter unanswered, production was halted and the work remained unpublished. All that remains is a set of proof sheets bound up for the author and later given to Dr W.H.R. Rivers, who bequeathed it to St John's College, Cambridge. Another set of proof sheets was destroyed. See Keynes, pp. 21-2.

90. WY, p. 129.

91. SS to DFC, 14 Feb. 1961 and SS:PP, p. 68.

92. Edward Carpenter to SS, 13 March [1912/13?] included in Sotheby's New Bond Street Sale of 'English Literature … Books', 13 Dec. 1993, p. 63.

93. EG to SS, 13 Feb. 1913, Rutgers.

94. EG to HT, 2 July 1883, HMC.

95. Anecdote related by Sassoon himself to Rupert Hart-Davis in September 1958. (See *The Lyttleton Hart-Davis Letters*, vol. 3, 1981, p. 141.)

96. Hamo was proposed by Frederick Leighton, G.D. Leslie and Sir Lawrence Alma-Tadema and admitted as an A.R.A. in 1881.

97. WY, p. 91.

98. SS dates this visit as 1911 in WY, but the 'Book of Gosse' (which is now at CUL) gives it as 6 May 1909.

99. WY, p. 100.

100. Aldous Huxley to Julian Huxley, 13 Dec. 1917, *Letters*, ed. by Grover Smith (London, 1969).

101. WY, p. 145.

Chapter 7

1. Christopher Hassall, *Edward Marsh* (London, Longmans, 1959), p. 501.

2. Some of the Imagists early members included Ezra Pound, Amy Lowell, Richard Aldington, Hilda Doolittle, John Gould Fletcher and F.S. Flint.

3. WY, p. 139.

4. ibid., p. 138.

5. ibid.

6. i.e. Robert Ross.

7. WY, p. 142.

8. Berg.

9. WY, p. 195.

10. ibid., p. 196.

11. Berg.

12. SS seems to have forgotten that EG's old friend, Mrs Jeyes, was also at this dinner.

13. WY, p. 188.

14. In sending the American writer, Louis Untermeyer, a manuscript book of poems, SS was scathing in his self-criticism. (Letter of 11 Oct. 1920, Lilly.) At least sixteen of these poems were written after *The Daffodil Murderer*, but none was ever published.

15. WY, p. 175.

16. SS to EM, 1 May 1914, Berg.

17. WY, p. 206.

18. Whereas SS claims in WY that he was 'unable to write a line of poetry' (p. 209) at Raymond Buildings in May 1914, in SJ he states that 'the South Wind poem had been written one May day morning in 1914, in my room in Raymond Buildings' (pp. 103-4).

19. TLS, 31 May 1917.

20. WY, p. 216.

21. SS claimed that 'They', for example, 'just wrote itself' (WP, p. 57).

22. WY, p. 203.

23. W.W. Gibson, one of the most popular of the Georgian poets, had quarrelled with Monro early on and this may have prejudiced other Georgians against Monro.

24. RR to SS, 13 June 1914, Lilly.

25. This is probably how SS saw it in retrospect. In fact, he fails to mention an invitation to the Gosses on 14 July with his Uncle Hamo, Aunt Agatha, some of his Donaldson relatives and EM. He was also invited to tea with EG at the House of Lords on 18 July, though there is no record of whether he went or not.

26. WY, p. 221.

27. It is interesting to note SS's conscious echo of Brooke in 'A Footnote on the War' (WP, p. 149).

28. SS owned at least nine of W.H. Davies's works, which he had discovered through Helen Wirgman in about 1907.

29. SS to EM, 6 July 1914, Berg.

30. SS to DFC, 28 July 1965; SS:PP, p. 66.

31. WY, p. 254.

32. ibid., p. 255.

33. ibid., p. 265.

34. ibid., p. 264.

35. ibid., p. 217.

36. ibid., p. 218.

Chapter 8

1. SS wrote, 'It seemed almost as if I had been waiting for this thing to happen, although my own part in it was so obscure and submissive' (MFM, p. 220).

2. WY, p. 274.

3. ibid., p. 272.

4. See Jean Moorcroft Wilson, *Charles Hamilton Sorley, a Biography* (London, Cecil Woolf, 1985), pp. 157-60.

5. MIO, p. 128.

6. H.I. Powell-Edwards, *The Sussex Yeomanry and 16th (Sussex Yeomanry) Battalion, Royal Sussex Regiment, 1914-1919* (London, Andrew Melrose, 1921), p. 14.

7. MFM, p. 225.

8. ibid., p. 219.

9. This booklet, together with two copies of the *Cavalry Training* manual, were among a large number of army publications owned and preserved by SS until his death. The majority are now at the Royal Welch Fusiliers Archives at Caernarvon. There are also some of his military booklets, including *Notes for Territorial Yeomen*, at AM.

10. MFM, p. 219.

11. ibid.

12. Soon after their arrival at Canterbury, the Sussex Yeomanry were asked by the War Office for Volunteers to serve abroad. It was intimated that if 80% of any unit volunteered, that unit would go abroad as a unit when sufficiently trained.

The Territorial Force could not realistically expect more than 20% to volunteer. Government figures were afterwards lowered from 80% to 60% and the Sussex Yeomanry had no difficulty in qualifying and subsequently went abroad as a unit.

13. SS to EM, 17 Aug. 1914, Berg.

14. SS was staying at Roper House, Canterbury by 10 Nov. 1914, as a letter to EM in the Berg Collection shows.

15. During the autumn and winter of 1914, according to the 1st/1st Sussex Yeomanry's regimental diary, 'the steady flow of men from the Regiment to take commissions in the New Army had already assumed considerable proportions ... It had become apparent that the War was likely to be a long one and that the active role of Cavalry in the Western theatre of war was suspended, until one side or the other broke the line ...' So the regiment settled down to a new programme of training in 1915. By August 1915 the regiment was asked to volunteer for dismounted service in the Mediterranean and did so. They then had to do a crash course in Infantry training. They left England on 21 Sept. 1915 and sailed in to Mudros Bay on 4 Oct. 1915.

16. MFM, p. 228.

17. SJ, p. 17.

18. Keynes (*Bibliography*) gives the number of copies printed as fifty, but a letter from Charles Whittington & Griggs (printers, of Chancery Lane) of 26 June 1922, telling SS how many copies of his books were printed by the press between 1911 and 1915, gives the number as sixty-five.

19. 'Romance' is a song taken from his unpublished play, *Amyntas*.

20. The poems were almost certainly sent to the printers at the end of February, since a poem written in March 1915 – 'What the Captain Said at the Point-to-Point' – was not included in *Discoveries*, but was printed in a later collection. We know that 'South Wind' was written at

Gray's Inn in May 1914, and from internal evidence, that 'Tree and Sky' and 'Alone' date from the same time. Apart from 'Romance' the rest were almost certainly written in his burst of poetic energy in the early spring of 1915. SS dated 'Wonderment' 1915 and, as I have shown, sent two previous poems from the collection – 'Storm and Rhapsody' and 'Wisdom' – to EM on 27 Feb. 1915. 'Storm and Rhapsody' (re-titled 'Storm and Sunlight' at EM's suggestion) clearly refers to the period SS spent with the Sussex Yeomanry and gives some idea of the primitive conditions he suffered there: 'In barns we crouch, and under stacks of straw ... Drip, drip; the rain steals in through soaking thatch. / By cob-webbed rafters to the dusty floor.' (*CP*, p. 62)

21. *Cambridge Magazine*, 2 June 1917.

22. SS states in MFM that Capt. Ruxton had served in the Royal Welch Fusiliers, but there is no record of a Capt. Ruxton in the Regiment at the time SS suggests. Nor do any of the other ex-soldiers he mentions fit the facts. He may deliberately have concealed the true identity of the man who used his influence to smooth SS's way to a commission, perhaps because the person concerned was still alive.

23. MFM, p. 229.

24. ibid., p. 230.

25. In the general re-organization of the Army between 1900 and 1914 the Militia, which could not previously be sent abroad, was turned into the Special Reserve, to feed the Regulars with drafts in time of war.

26. MFM, p. 233.

27. In 1881 the idiosyncratic spelling of 'Welch' was changed to the more usual 'Welsh', but after the First World War the Regiment was given permission to revert officially to the older spelling, which some Welsh maintain is the only correct one.

28. Robert Graves, *Goodbye to All That* (Penguin Books, 1960), p. 73.

29. The RWF permanent headquarters was at Wrexham, but a temporary training depot had been set up in Litherland, Liverpool, at the outbreak of War.

30. D1, p. 130. The Litherland Camp was situated between Church Road and Moss Lane on what is now the site of Amos, Hythe, Kent, Mead and Springfield Avenues, and also to the north of Moss Lane on what are now the Osborne and Daley Road estates. There were two large fields, one known as Camp Field, the other as French (possibly Trench) Field. See articles in *The Crosby Herald* of 28 March, 4 April and 11 April 1996.

31. MFM, p. 235.

32. ibid., p. 236 and MIO, p. 224.

33. SJ, p. 17.

34. ibid.

35. *Taking It Like a Man: Suffering, Sexuality and the War Poets Brooke, Sassoon, Owen, Graves* (Manchester University Press, 1993), pp. 67-8.

36. SS:PP, p. 75.

37. *The Collected Letters of Charles Hamilton Sorley*, edited by Jean Moorcroft Wilson (London, Cecil Woolf, 1990), pp. 218-19.

38. SS wrote in his diary on Christmas Day 1916, concerning a probable food shortage in 1917: 'The sideboard in this Formby golf-club doesn't look like it yet; enormous cold joints and geese and turkeys and a sucking pig' (D1, p. 106).

39. Royal Welch Fusiliers' Archives, Caernarvon. See reproduction of the '6 Cs' on p. 43 of Sotheby's Bond Street 'English Literature and History' catalogue, 18 July 1991.

40. SS had at least thirty-five First World War army manuals and maps in his library at his death, several of them in multiple copies. His markings reveal his anxiety that the men he commanded should understand why they were being asked to do certain things. In *The Training and*

Employment of Platoons, for example, SS has picked out passages stating 'true discipline should aim at the development and not the repression of the intelligence of the individual'; 'The method is to drill regularly for short periods every day, and to make the drill intelligible by having its purpose understood'; 'practices must be made intelligible and interesting, and monotony avoided; men should be encouraged and not driven'; and many more such.

41. D1, p. 104.

42. MFM, pp. 240-3 and D1, pp. 44-5.

43. GTAT, p. 149.

44. In the one letter I have seen from David Thomas to SS, on 26 Aug. 1915, now at CUL, he gives his address as, Llanedy Rectory, Pontardulais, South Wales.

45. D1, p. 45.

46. Sydney Carlyle Cockerell, who lived in Cambridge, wrote in his diary that by the end of 1915, 10,000 members of the University had enlisted. There were less than 450 male undergraduates, though there was still a full complement of female students at Newnham and Girton Colleges and many cadets being trained at other colleges. (Sydney Carlyle Cockerell's diaries are in the Department of Manuscripts, British Library.)

47. EG wrote to SCC on 28 July 1915, presumably recommending SS. On 18 March 1915 he had introduced himself to SCC by letter, invoking their mutual friend Sir Sidney Colvin, and asking if he might see a copy of a Swinburne letter in SCC's possession for his projected biography of the poet. Letters followed thick and fast and the two men met for the first time just over a month later to discuss Swinburne, since EG felt the subject was too delicate to trust to a letter. See letters of EG to SCC, at BL.

48. SCC's diary entry for 1 Aug. 1915, loc. cit.

49. SJ, p. 148.

50. ibid.

51. SS:PP, pp. 225-6.

52. *The Best of Friends: Further Letters to Sydney Carlyle Cockerell*, edited by Viola Meynell (London, Hart-Davis, 1956), p. 166.

53. ibid., p. 167.

54. SS presented SCC with a book of manuscript poems and his Philpot portrait for the Fitzwilliam Museum and SCC presented SS with, among other things, a copy of Thomas Hardy's signed Suetonius and a William Morris silver cup for his son, George. Together they helped raise money for the widow of Charles Doughty and organized a fund for the poet Charlotte Mew.

55. SJ, p. 149.

56. SS to T.H. White, 1 Dec. 1938, HRHRC.

57. Edward Joseph Dent (1876-1957), musicologist, opera translator, professor of music at Cambridge, was a fellow of King's from 1902 to 1908 and again from 1926 till his death in 1957.

58. SS to ED, Aug. 1915, CUL.

59. ibid., 18 May 1916, CUL.

60. D1, p. 106.

61. RG to RR, 24 Nov. 1916, Lilly.

62. SS to RG, 9 April 1917, USI.

63. Dorothy wrote to SS in the 1940s and reminisced about meeting him at 'Appleby Blobbs', almost certainly a reference to Appleby Magna, or Appleby Parva, both of which are only a few miles from Atherstone, where Loder lived. CUL.

64. D1, p. 94. Dorothy Hanmer married the Master of the Grafton Hunt and settled down in Everdon Hall at Daventry in Northamptonshire.

65. Robert Baldwin Ross, 1869-1918.

66. Maureen Borland, Ross's biographer, wrote to me on 26 Oct. 1993: 'On page 190 of *Wilde's Devoted Friend* I quoted the date of the Gosse party at which both Ross and Sassoon were guests. I wrote that paragraph after extensive conversations with the late Professor Giles Robertson and J-P. B. Ross. They told me that from their parents and from their Uncle Alex [Ross] they all remembered Robbie saying he wished he had been able to offer Sassoon the hand of friendship before he did, but he felt constrained by his litigation battles with Bosie Douglas and Crosland.'

67. SJ, p. 6.

68. D1, p. 131.

69. RR to Cecil Sprigge, 25 May 1918, quoted in *Robert Ross, Friend of Friends*, edited by Margery Ross (London, Cape, 1952), p. 328.

70. Michael Thorpe, *Siegfried Sassoon: a Critical Study* (Leiden, 1966), p. 45, n.6.

71. SJ, p. 31.

72. SS to SCC, 20 Nov. 1944, HRHRC.

73. SS to John Bain, 12 May [1917], IWM.

74. ibid.

75. *The Marlburian*, 21 June 1917, pp. 89-90. John Bain, who taught the Army class at Marlborough, knew more intimately than most of the staff, the majority of those killed in the War. Between 1914 and 1919 he wrote a series of 'In Memoriam' poems, including one to another war-poet, Charles Hamilton Sorley, though Sorley was not in his form.

76. Written on 18 Dec. 1915 and originally titled 'Brothers', 'To My Brother' was first published in the *Saturday Review* for 26 Feb. 1916. In line 5, SS first wrote 'But I am *with the fighters in the field*' and in line 8, 'And through your victory mine shall be revealed'.

77. MFM, p. 242.

78. SS to ED, n.d., Nov. 1915, CUL.

79. D1, p. 126.

80. ibid., pp. 26-7.

81. SS to ED, n.d., Nov. 1915, CUL.

82. This story was told to me by Peter Haworth, whose family knew Michael Sassoon in Canada and who visited Mrs Sassoon at Weirleigh.

83. MFM, p. 244.

Chapter 9

1. D1, p. 275.

2. MFM, p. 244.

3. See William Allison and John Fairley, *The Monocled Mutineer* (London, Quartet Books, 1979), p. 53.

4. D1, p. 20.

5. GTAT, p. 149. Minshull Ford was a regular soldier with the rank of Captain in August 1914. It seems more likely that he began to 'scatter his cash' when he became C.O. of the Battalion, with a substantial increase in pay and allowance. RG is not always accurate.

6. Edward John Greaves embarked for France on 8 June 1915, was wounded on 4 July 1916 and returned to England permanently on 17 July 1916.

7. There was another officer in the 1st RWF by the name of Guy Stanley Barton.

8. JD embarked for France 1 Nov. 1914, was wounded 14 May 1916, rejoined his unit on 5 July 1916, was wounded again 3 Sept. 1916 and returned to England permanently on 10 Sept. 1916. Edward Leslie Orme embarked for France 30 Sept. 1915, was wounded 4 June 1916 but remained in France and was killed in action 27 May 1917.

9. JD's sister. Elfreda, wrote to SS on 15 Jan. 1937 after her brother's death: 'I've always felt since I read "A Whispered Tale" that you understood him well and greatly cared for him', CUL.

10. Letter from JD to SS, 10 Nov. 1929, CUL.

11. SS wrote about Edmund Dadd as 'Edmunds' in his fiction, concealing the brotherhood of Julian and Edmund, just as he concealed that of Edward and Ralph Greaves, perhaps because he felt it would give too strong a clue as to their real identity.

12. JD to SS, 20 Jan. 1929, IWM.

13. MFM, p. 253.

14. Charles Hamilton Sorley to Dr Wynne Willson, 4 Aug. 1915, *The Collected Letters of Charles Hamilton Sorley*, edited by Jean Moorcroft Wilson (London, Cecil Woolf, 1990), p. 243.

15. MIO, pp. 76-80 and 94 and GTAT, p. 146.

16. WIK, p. 166.

17. RG's contention did not, in fact, apply to the Royal Welch Fusiliers, which had an unusually high proportion of writers in it; besides RG and SS, there were Bernard Adams (*Nothing of Importance*), Frank Richards (*Old Soldiers Never Die*), David Jones (*In Parenthesis*), Llewelyn Wyn Griffith (*Up to Mametz*) and the poets Vivian de Sola Pinto and Ellis Humphrey Evans (known as 'Hedd Wyn').

18. D1, p. 21.

19. SS to RG, 2 March 1930, Buffalo.

20. D2, p. 162.

21. Hassle, p. 79.

22. SS to EM, 14 July 1916, Berg.

23. SS to RR, 18 March [1917], Lilly.

24. Brig.-Gen. C.I. Stockwell to SS, copied in SS's hand and included in a letter to JD, 3 March 1931, IWM.

25. MIO, p. 108.

26. ibid.

27. ibid.

28. SS. to Nellie Gosse, 6 Jan. 1916, BLL.

29. D1, p. 21.

30. *In Broken Images: Selected Letters of Robert Graves, 1914-1946*, edited by Paul O'Prey (London, Hutchinson, 1982), p. 37.

31. SS to DFC, 1 June 1962, SS:PP, p. 63.

32. See Martin Taylor, 'Two Fusiliers: the First World War Friendship of Robert Graves and Siegfried Sassoon', *Imperial War Museum Review*, no.7, and Dominic Hibberd, ' "The Patchwork Flag": an Unrecorded Book by Robert Graves', *Review of English Studies*, no. 41, vol. 164, Nov. 1990, pp. 521-32.

33. SS to RG, undated but *c*. 1923, USI.

34. See *Fairies and Fusiliers* (London, Heinemann, 1917).

35. MFM, p. 247.

36. D1, p. 20.

37. ibid., p. 21.

38. *The Great War and Modern Memory* (London, OUP, 1975), p. 282.

39. Fragment dated 7 Aug. 1916, HRHRC.

40. D1, p. 236.

41. ibid., p. 262.

42. See *Ackerley: a Life* (London, Constable, 1989), pp. 92-3.

43. Undated letter from V. King to SS, CUL.

44. 'Memories of Siegfried Sassoon', *Journal of the Royal Welch Fusiliers*, March 1968, vol. 17, no. 1, pp. 12ff.

45. D1, p. 79.

46. These and the distances which follow are approximate, many of them having been converted from kilometres.

47. D1, p. 24.

48. ibid., p. 22.

49. ibid., pp. 22-3.

50. ibid., p. 28.

51. GTAT, p. 149.

52. MFM, p. 257.

53. ibid., p. 250.

54. D1, p. 25.

55. ibid.

56. ibid., p. 31.

57. SS to Nellie Gosse, 6 Jan [1916], BLL.

58. SS's copy of *A Shropshire Lad* was the Grant Richards, 1912 edition, which was small enough to slip into his pocket. It was inscribed 'Siegfried Sassoon / 1st R.W. Fus. Nov. 1915 / 2nd R.W. Fus. March 1917 / 25th R.W. Fus. March 1918'.

59. SS admires Housman's lecture 'The Name and Nature of Poetry', which he quotes in an article ('A Poet on Poetry') written, by request, for *The Listener*, 1935, but never published, though set up and proofed. This was seen as 'a veiled attack on the modernists' (SS's words). Housman's words were: 'I think that to transfuse emotion – not to transmit thought, but to set up in the reader's sense a vibration corresponding to what was felt by the writer – is the peculiar function of poetry'.

60. D1, p. 26.

61. SS told DFC that he wrote another poem, 'A Child's Faith', at 'about the same time' as 'The Redeemer', but it was almost certainly written later, after he had arrived in Montagne. (Cf. SS:PP, p. 77).

62. D1, p. 28.

63. WIK, p. 287.

64. BL.

65. WP, p. 20.

66. D1, p. 32. SS had undoubtedly read Pater's essay 'Apollo in Picardy', an outstandingly frank homosexual essay, published posthumously in *Miscellaneous Studies* (1895).

67. The penultimate line of 'To Victory' was included only after the first version appeared and other slight changes in punctuation made. SS left the details of spelling and punctuation to Dent.

68. SJ, p. 8.

69. EG was very close to Lord Haldane, who was in charge of the War Office till Lord Kitchener took over. He was also a friend of the Prime Minister, Herbert Asquith.

70. Apart from SS's initials, the poem had the words 'By a Private Soldier At the Front' added misleadingly under its title in *The Times*.

71. D1, pp. 36-7.

72. MFM, p. 257.

73. National Army Museum, Sassoon collection, Army Book 152 – Correspondence Book, signed 'Siegfried Sassoon, 1st RWF January 1916'.

74. 'The Quartermaster' was first published in D1, pp. 43-4. In the version SS sent to ED, for consideration by *The Cambridge Magazine*, the third line of stanza three read 'weak' for 'tired', and the fifth line of the same stanza read 'smoky' for 'swarming'.

75. Letter from JD to SS, 29 Jan. 1929, IWM.

76. CUL.

77. Cottrell's letters to SS are at IWM. Cottrell died 13 Jan. 1925.

78. Letter from SS to ED, 17 Feb. 1916, CUL.

79. WP, p. 22. SS also included a poem in a letter to EM on 10 Feb. 1916, 'Winter in Picardy', probably written during the same rest period.

80. SJ, p. 29.

81. See D1, p. 42. The Virgin leant over, which made her look as though she were offering the baby Jesus in her arms to the people below. It was said that, if she fell, the War would end.

82. CUL.

83. SJ, p. 28.

84. ibid., p. 29.

85. SS to ED, 11 March 1916, CUL.

86. *To Keep the Ball Rolling: the Memoirs of Anthony Powell* (London, Penguin, 1983), p. 348.

87. S.N. Behrman, *Tribulations and Laughter: a Memoir* (London, Hamilton, 1972), p. 28.

88. ibid.

89. *Wilde's Devoted Friend*, p. 272.

90. *Manchester Guardian*, 11 Oct. 1935.

91. op. cit., p. 42.

92. *To Keep the Ball Rolling*, p. 349.

93. *Tribulations and Laughter*, p. 181.

94. ibid., p. 16.

95. This was almost certainly Moffat-Smith, to whom SS refers in his diary (D1, p. 80). Gordon Harbord, also a member of the Southdown, refers to 'Moffat' in his letter to SS, at IWM.

96. D1, p. 40.

97. SS to ED, 11 March 1916, CUL.

98. Clifford Inglis Stockwell D.S.O., embarked for France on 1 Sept. 1914. There is a vivid description of him in Frank Richards's *Old Soldiers Never Die* (p. 35). RG agreed entirely with Richards's picture. Stockwell was coming from the 59th Brigade of the 7th Division, while Minshull Ford had been promoted to command the 91st Brigade.

99. D1, p. 39.

100. JD to SS, 1 Dec. 1929, IWM.

101. Though Stockwell and SS did not remain in touch after SS left the 1st Royal Welch Fusiliers, they re-established contact after SS's description of the 1st RWF in MFM (1928). Stockwell also wrote to comment disparagingly on RG's GTAT (1929). IWM. He invited SS to stay with him at Green Park House, Hampton Court, Leominster: 'Rather a Liberty Hall here I'm afraid but unless you've changed a lot it might suit you'. CUL. In the same letter, he also reassured SS: 'I'm not as snotty as I was 16 years ago and my "sense of humour" is "still extant" '.

102. SS must have bought Bridges' *The Spirit of Man* back from his stay in England, since it was not published until January 1916. (2nd and 3rd impressions followed in Feb. and March 1916.) SS is almost certainly referring to Bridges' selection of fragment 3 from Shelley's *Prince Athenase*, which opens: ' 'Twas at the season when the Earth upsprings / From slumber' and Shelley's 'The Question'.

103. WP, p. 25.

104. RR:RWF, p. 186.

105. D1, p. 44.

106. MFM, p. 274. In his grief, SS copied out in French on the back of the title-page of a Greek text which had belonged to Thomas: 'Vous qui pleurez, venez à ce Dieu, car Il pleure / Vous qui souffrez, venez à Lui, car Il guérit. / Vous qui tremblez, venez a Lui, venez à Lui, car Il soutient / Vous qui passez, venez à Lui, venez à Lui, car Il demeure.'

107. D1, p. 45.

108. ibid.

109. ibid.

110. Contained in a letter from SS to ED, 5 April 1916, CUL.

111. See the typewritten copy of the poem made from SS's manuscript original by ED in his collection of letters from SS at CUL. This also shows that SS omitted six lines from the end of section two in his final version.

112. SS himself was not of this opinion. By 18 May 1918 he thought all his poems 'tosh', he told ED 'except the "Last Meeting" and "The Working Party" ' (CUL).

Chapter 10

1. RG is the main source for the 'Mad Jack' legend. Another friend from the 1st RWF, Julian Dadd, denies that SS was known by such a nickname. Since this denial is to be found in a letter sympathizing with SS over RG's many inaccuracies in GTAT, it is in itself suspect, however.

2. SS to ED, 5 April 1916, CUL.

3. D1, p. 52.

4. ibid. This poem is dated 2 April [1916].

5. ibid., p. 53.

6. *The Diary of Virginia Woolf*, vol. IV, 28 April 1935, p. 307.

7. SS to ED, 5 April 1916, CUL.

8. Corporal 'Mick' R. O'Brien, was born in Cardiff, joined the RWF in Nov. 1914, fought at Neuve Chapelle, Festubert and Loos and was killed in action on 26 May 1916.

9. CUL.

10. D1, pp. 47-8.

11. ibid., p. 48.

12. SS adopted this more shocking version for publication. 'The Redeemer' went through numerous revisions, even after the second version was completed in March 1916. For SS's detailed alterations and instructions to ED on the subject, see the Dent papers at CUL.

13. In the original version which SS sent to ED the poem opens 'Curves up the dark a spume of falling flares', and 'mirthless laughter' less threateningly 'shakes' (rather than 'rakes') 'the whistling night'. The phrase 'no one stirs' starts out as the more impersonal 'nothing stirs' and the rats are originally 'stealthy' not 'nimble' scavengers.

14. D1, p. 48.

15. ibid.

16. This still exists in a typed copy in ED's collection at CUL: 'That's how a lad goes west when at the front, / Snapped in a moment's merciful escape, / While the ~~dun~~ dark year goes lagging on its course / With widows grieving down the streets in black, / And faded mothers dreaming of bright sons / That grew to men, and 'listed for the war, / And left a photograph to keep their place'.

17. SS to Nellie Gosse, 22 March 1916, BLL. It is interesting to note that one of RG's many mistakes in GTAT is the statement that he went on leave in April 1916.

18. Berg.

19. Letter from Gordon Harbord to 'Ken/Sig/Geoff', 8 April 1916, from the Royal Artillery Headquarters, 36th Division, now at IWM.

20. One of his rejected poems from this period, 'The Giant-Killer', is reproduced in D1, p. 56.

21. SJ, p. 17.

22. *Siegfried Sassoon*, p. 24.

23. Keynes, p. 41.

24. See MIO, p. 7, SS told ED in a letter of 5 April 1916: 'Do you know what I am called out here? "The Kangaroo" – heaven knows why! but I suppose it is a term of endearment'. It was perhaps also because he had once owned a horse of that name, or simply because of his occasionally jerky movements.

25. D1, pp. 57-8.

26. MIO, p. 9.

27. D1, p. 60.

28. See GTAT, p. 226.

29. See *Taking It Like a Man*, p. 78.

30. *Letters to a Critic* (Kent Editions, 1976), pp. 18-19. Ian Parsons has written in his Introduction to *Men who March Away* (London, Chatto & Windus, 1966), 'in spirit ["The Kiss"] is so completely alien to the author's whole attitude to war. For that reason, Mr Sassoon was understandably reluctant to let me reprint it, fearing that it might be taken as meant seriously – as a "fire-eating" poem. "As a matter of fact", so he told me in subsequent correspondence, "I originally wrote it as a sort of exercise – in Anglo-Saxon words, as far as I could manage it – after being disgusted by the barbarities of the famous bayonet-fighting lecture. To this day I don't know what made me write it, for I never felt that I could have stuck a bayonet into anyone, even in self-defence. The difficulty is that it doesn't show any sign of satire" '.

31. C.K. Ogden (1889-1957) was proprietor and editor of *The Cambridge Magazine* from 1912 to 1923, also editor of *Psyche* from 1920 to 1952 and of *The International Library of Psychology, Philosophy and Scientific Literature* from 1921 to 1957.

32. SS to ED, 30 April 1916, CUL.

33. ibid., 17 April 1916 and 30 April 1916.

34. 'The Last Meeting', CP, p. 35.

35. 'A Letter Home' was written from Flixécourt in May 1916 and received a versified reply, 'Letter to S.S. from Mametz Wood' from RG in July 1916. The latter poem was subsequently published in RG's *Fairies and Fusiliers* (1917).

36. D1, p. 61.

37. MIO, p. 116.

38. D1, p. 61.

39. ibid., p. 63.

40. SS to ED, 5 June 1915, CUL.

41. D1, p. 66.

42. ibid.

43. RR:RWF, p. 186.

44. See JD's notes to RG's GTAT in the SS papers at IWM.

45. D1, p. 67.

46. F.M. Earl Kitchener of Khartoum, the Secretary of State for War, was drowned on 5 June 1916 when H.M.S. *Hampshire* struck a mine and sank.

47. D1, pp. 74-5. RG's reference to 'Limbo' comes in a poem of that name in *Over the Brazier* (1916) which he presented to SS.

48. D1, p. 75.

49. SS to ED, 5 June 1916, CUL.

50. ibid., 17 April 1916, CUL.

51. SS to EM, 19 April 1916, Berg.

52. This, and the following quotation, are from D1, pp. 78-9.

53. D1, p. 79.

54. MIO, p. 47.

55. D1, p. 83.

56. MIO, p. 56.

57. ibid.

58. MIO, p. 58. SS also attempts to describe this nightmare scene in 'The Road' (CP, p. 32).

59. D1, p. 88.

60. Hassall, p. 398. SS's estimates of the fleeing Germans varies from forty to sixty, depending on the version read.

61. MIO, p. 67.

62. RR:RWF, p. 202.

63. WP, pp. 42-3.

64. Now at HRHRC.

65. MIO, p. 69.

66. Of these eight had died at Mametz Wood and fifty-seven were wounded there, approximately half their overall losses.

67. D1, p. 92.

68. MIO, p. 70.

69. ibid., p. 77.

70. D1, p. 92.

71. ibid., p. 93.

72. ibid., p. 92.

73. ibid., p. 94.

74. ibid.

75. The manuscript of this poem (at HRHRC) is dated 18 July, and was clearly written with RG in mind. A second note, 'RG July 19th' is crossed out and replaced with 'M.H.G. July 25th', a reference to Marcus Goodall who was killed at Puchvillers on 14 July 1916. A second poem, 'The Traveller', was also dedicated 'To M.H.G.' in August 1916.

76. From 'Letter to S.S. from Mametz Wood', *Poems 1914-1926* (London, Heinemann, 1927), pp. 54-7.

77. JD to SS, 19 Aug. 1930, CUL.

78. D1, p. 98. 'Oh my songs never sung' is from RG's 'The Shadow of Death', *Over the Brazier*. 'The great, greasy Caucasus' is a quotation from the first version of RG's 'Letter to S.S. from Mametz Wood'.

79. D1, p. 97.

80. 'With trench fever a fellow had a very high temperature, you could see he had. It wasn't dysentry but he had constant diarrhoea, it left him weak and listless'. Capt. Burke of the Devonshire Regiment, quoted in *The Great War and Modern Memory*, p. 19.

81. CUL.

82. See D1, p. 99. All the manuscripts referred to here are at HRHRC.

83. WP, p. 44.

84. MIO, p. 88.

85. SS to ED, 23 Feb. 1917: ' "The Nation" evidently scorns my poetry, so you [i.e. *The Cambridge Magazine*] can print "Died of Wounds" if you still want it. Substitute "Christ" for "God" in the 2nd verse' (CUL). SS suspected that the young soldier had been at High Wood at its worst.

86. *The Westminster Gazette*, which had rejected a number of SS's anti-war poems, published 'Stretcher Case' on 28 Sept. 1916.

87. From Virginia Woolf's review of *The Old Huntsman and Other Poems* in the TLS, 31 May 1917.

Chapter 11

1. USI.

2. Capt. Dunn, or one of his

contributors, reported RG's characteristically quirky return to life in the following fashion: 'Now Graves writes to the C.O. that the shock of learning how much he is esteemed has recalled him from the grave, and that he has decided to live for the sake of those whose warm feelings he has misunderstood' (WIK, p. 246, diary entry for 31 July 1916).

3. SS to ED, 4 Aug. 1916, CUL.

4. RG to SS, 7 Aug. 1916, Berg.

5. Sotheby's English Literature and History Catalogue, London, Thursday, 18 July 1991, p. 50.

6. *The Spoon River Anthology*, a collection of 245 verse epitaphs, or voices from the dead, by Edgar Lee Masters, was extremely popular and seemed somewhat scandalous when it was first published in the U.S. in 1915. Perhaps SS is referring to the stark realism of Masters' verse.

7. SJ, p. 41.

8. WP, p. 46.

9. SS:PP, pp. 80-82.

10. 'The One-Legged Man' and 'The Hero' were dated August 1916 in Rupert Hart-Davis's edition of *WP* and placed in such a position as to suggest that they were written at Somerville College, presumably on internal evidence. SS himself, however, clearly implies in SJ that both poems were written at Weirleigh in Sept. 1916, though he was not always entirely accurate in his recall.

11. SJ, p. 19.

12. ibid.

13. When 'The One-Legged Man' was reprinted in CP, SS joined stanzas two and three into a single stanza. Only one verbal change ('corn-stalked' for the original 'corn-stooked') was made to the version he first sent to ED. The poem was first published in its original form in *The Cambridge Magazine* of 11 Nov. 1916.

14. RG, in a letter to SS of 23 Aug. 1916, now in Berg, refers to this poem as 'The Pensioner' and comments on 'the awful grimace at the end of it'. The date of this letter is further evidence that SS had written at least a first draft before Sept. 1916. He includes the following, probably first, version in an undated letter to RG written from Weirleigh, where he was staying by 18 Aug. 1916: 'This was that thriving county which had seemed / Lost for all time when he was dodging shells:-/ Doing his bit; how frequently he'd dreamed / Of the gray steeple and the distant bells. / – And now he'd tumbled back; he found it more / Desirable than ever it was before. / How right it seemed that he should reach the span / Of comfortable years allowed to man! / – Splendid to eat and sleep and choose a wife, / Saved by red wounds from further risk to life! / "Thank God", he thought, "they had to amputate / My leg!" Then hobbled through the garden-gate'. ('Oh please laugh', SS added, 'I did try so hard to be mildly funny' (USI).)

15. Adrian Caesar argues that the content of 'The Hero' presented SS with a problem central to all writing about the War. The brother officer must choose between having to tell the suffering mother 'gallant lies' or the brutal truth. Though he chooses the former SS himself is attempting to convey the 'truth' by contrasting the officer's indifference to Jack with his attitude towards the bereaved mother. 'But the poem implicitly demonstrates that the bereaved need consolation', Caesar concludes, 'and militates against the truths of war being told'. Told to whom? SS is surely making a distinction between telling the hurtful truth to the suffering mother and conveying it to the public at large, who might take note and protest against the continuation of war. It is not, as Caesar seems to imply, a simple choice between telling the truth or perpetuating lies.

16. SJ, p. 19.

17. 'The One-Legged Man' was published in *The Cambridge*

Magazine on 11 Nov. 1916, 'The Hero' on 18 Nov. 1916.

18. Rupert Hart-Davis dates 'Died of Wounds' July 1916 and a preliminary draft of the poem, titled 'In Hospital', at HRHRC, is dated 27 July 1916, but it is highly likely that SS revised and completed the poem in the tranquillity of Oxford.

19. SJ, p. 7.

20. Garsington is only a few miles south-east of Oxford, off the B480.

21. The Hon. Dorothy Brett (1883-1977) was the daughter of the second Viscount Esher. She enrolled at the Slade in 1910 and became a friend of Dora Carrington, Mark Gertler, D.H. Lawrence and many other writers and painters of the time.

22. OAG, 1974, p. 121.

23. ibid., p. 122.

24. Emslie John Horniman (1863-1932), a connoisseur of art and travel.

25. SJ, pp. 14-15.

26. D1, p. 101.

27. ibid., p. 102.

28. ibid.

29. SS to ED, 23 Feb. 1916, CUL.

30. Richard Perceval Graves, *Robert Graves: the Assault Heroic (1895-1926)* (London, 1986), p. 160.

31. ibid.

32. GTAT, p. 288.

33. RG to SS, 23 Aug. 1916, Berg.

34. See note 32 of Chapter 9.

35. These were eventually to become RG's *Goliath and David* and SS's *The Old Huntsman and Other Poems*.

36. GTAT, p. 191.

37. SJ, pp. 20-24.

38. ibid., p. 21.

39. SS to RR, 18 March 1917, Lilly.

40. Messalina was the third wife of the Roman emperor Claudius. She was notorious for her profligacy, avarice and ambition.

41. SJ, p. 23.

42. SS to ED, 28 Oct. [1918?], CUL.

43. SJ, p. 23.

44. RR himself felt that the earlier

work was, for the most part, best forgotten. As SS notes in SJ: 'He had worked through my pre-war pamphlets, but had advised against including more than a few of the poems in a published collection. "They rather remind me of the delicious teas of 30 years ago", he had remarked, quoting the well-known "Mazawattee" advertisement'.

45. Letters from Blunden to SS indicate that GTAT so infuriated both of them with its errors, misconceptions, faulty versions of their shared experiences and RG's attitude in general, that Blunden suggested to SS that they prepare a definitive, annotated copy which they would present to the BL. This was the copy, but it was never presented and remained in SS's library. There are approximately 5,631 words of annotation on 250 of the book's 448 pages.

46. GTAT, p. 191.

47. D1, p. 125.

48. GTAT, p. 192.

49. RG to RR, 16 Sept. 1916, Lilly.

50. B.H. Liddell Hart, *History of the First World War* (London, Papermac edition, 1992), p. 249.

51. JD to SS, 22 June 1930, CUL.

52. ibid., 19 Aug. 1930.

53. I am grateful to Philip Guest for identifying 'Fernby' as V.F. Newton.

54. Letters from Cottrell to Stansfield of 3 Sept. 1916 and 4 Sept. 1916, IWM.

55. Letter and notes from JD to SS, 19 March 1929, IWM.

56. Jacques Sassoon's father, David, was SS's cousin.

57. SS must have received Heinemann's letter on 2 Oct. at Weirleigh and almost immediately have written 'The Tombstone-Maker', since there is an allusion to it in his letter of 5 Oct. to ED: 'And here's a sweet thing for you to put in the Cambridge Magazine; ... And "Theo" [i.e. A.T. Bartholomew] can reprint it with a heavy black border and "not lost but gone before" on the opposite page' (CUL).

58. Lilly.

59. D1, p. 71.

60. WP, p. 57.

61. D1, p. 95.

62. ibid., p. 106.

63. ibid., p. 107.

64. ibid., p. 142.

65. SS's notes for his talk of 12 April 1920, now in the hands of a private collector.

66. Though Mozelle went to stay with her daughter Louise, at Beckenham, after her husband's death in 1891, she kept a place of her own at 12 Wilbury Road, Hove. SS asked for a copy of his first volume of war-poetry to be sent to her at that address.

67. D3, p. 140.

68. RG to SS, 26 March 1917, Berg.

69. Letter from SS to RM, 9 Sept. 1917, HRHRC.

70. MIO, pp. 101-2.

71. SS to ED, 3 Dec. 1916, CUL.

72. Adrian Caesar, op. cit., pp. 82-3.

73. D1, p. 121.

74. WP, p. 61.

75. 'This is a cruel and unworthy libel. No section of the whole community has shown more courage or devotion than the class you have so gratuitously sneered at. The House of Lords has sacrificed, in proportion, more of its members and connections than any other in the country' (EG to SS, 17 Feb. 1917, Rutgers).

76. SS to EG, 27 Feb. 1917, BLL.

77. See RG to RR on 22 Oct. 1916 (Lilly).

78. RG to SS, 30 Nov. 1916, Berg.

79. As SS was to point out to RR in a letter of 3 Oct. 1917 (Lilly). Bernard ('Bill') Adams (?1890-1917) had been with SS for eight months in the 1st Battalion RWF. Adams wrote an account of this time, published as *Nothing of Importance* (London, Methuen, 1917) which mentions SS once under the name of Scott. Adams

showed SS a typescript of his book before he died of wounds in Feb. 1917 and SS found it 'by no means bad'. When the book was published, he annotated his copy which he eventually gave to WO. He told RG that, if he and RG had re-written and added to it, it would have been a classic. Later, when Adams's sister was thinking of reprinting the book, SS offered to write an introduction to it.

80. RG to SS, 30 Nov. 1916, Berg.

81. RG told EM that he and SS had great difficulty in talking about poetry, since the other officers were terribly curious and suspicious. If SS wanted to show him some verses in the mess, therefore, he would pretend it was his latest recipe for rum punch.

82. SS usually played golf with RG, who sometimes 'annoyed' his 'serious golfing temperament' by 'play[ing] the fool' on the links. (D1, p. 111).

83. Since RG scorned hunting, SS turned to another officer, R. Brocklebank, for company. A local man, Brocklebank took SS home to Spittal for 'a cheery evening' after a day's hunting near Tiverton Smithy. SS was sorry to see him leave for France before him on 9 Jan. 1917 and even sadder to learn of his death there five months later.

84. D1, pp. 118-9.

85. When Heinemann had rejected RG's poems in favour of SS's in October 1917, RG had been chagrined and decided to print nine of the poems from his collection privately. SS suggested his own printers, the Chiswick Press, and on 18 January 1917 posted RG's poems to the press on his friend's behalf. The next day RG was told that he had 72 hours leave before going to France, so that it was SS who corrected the proofs when they arrived at Litherland Camp on 27 January. He made extensive corrections, going so far as to reject two poems ('To My Unborn Son' and 'The Last Post') and replace them with two others ('Careers' and 'Lady Visitor in the Pauper Ward'). He also called for revised proofs, concluding: 'The wrapper is too *shiny*, and must be *red*; not magenta-pink'. *Goliath and David* was dedicated to their mutual friend, David Thomas.

86. D1, p. 124.

87. D1, p. 124. Though SS did not attempt to have 'The Elgar Violin Concerto' published immediately, he did think it sufficiently interesting to include a slightly revised version in SJ (p. 44).

88. WP, p. 64.

89. D1, pp. 107-8.

90. ibid., p. 107.

91. There are at least three versions of this poem, one of which is published in D1 (p. 116), the second in WP (p. 66) and the third in CP. A comparison of all three suggests that SS recognized the force of his original version, which I take to be the one given in his diary. It also reveals a great deal about SS's working methods. Having quickly jotted down two verses in one of his favourite stanza forms, in which a quatrain is followed by a couplet, he subsequently rewrote it, strengthening phrases such as 'where the dead soldiers go' to the more condensed and evocative 'where Armageddon ends'; likewise, 'When my mad anger for his death was hot', becomes 'When for his death my brooding rage was hot'.

92. Blunden's note on the MS of 'Enemies' at HRHRC.

93. D1, p. 120.

94. D1, p. 126.

95. As Michael Thorpe, echoing Vivian de Sola Pinto, has pointed out, SS's most effective satires obey 'the simplest prescriptions of Georgian rhyming verse in everything but the diction, so that the satiric effect is accentuated by clothing a disreputable body in formal dress. The diction makes all the difference' (*Siegfried Sassoon*, p. 23).

96. SS himself thought well of 'The Choral Union', which he included in his CP. 'I've got a really good one about a drunk man going to hear the "Messiah" and thinking he's got to heaven', he wrote to ED, 5 Jan. 1917 (CUL).

97. RG claimed in a letter to SS of 26 March 1917 (Berg), that they had been on 'excellent terms' throughout.

98. SJ, p. 40.

99. D1, p. 115.

100. SJ, p. 43.

101. ibid., p. 40.

102. D1, p. 109.

103. *Mr Britling Sees It Through* (1916), Bk II, chapter 4.

104. D1, p. 127.

Chapter 12

1. See OAG, pp. 168-9, SJ, pp. 46-7 and Miranda Seymour, *Ottoline Morrell: Life on the Grand Scale* (Sceptre, 1993), pp. 372-3. Ottoline suggests that this meeting occurred on Wednesday, 14 February, but is not always very accurate.

2. D1, p. 132.

3. SS to RM, 25 March 1917, HRHRC. SS also told his uncle Hamo, who knew Hardy personally, that after some gruelling experience in the trenches he would sit down calmly to read Hardy's *Selected Poems*, which he carried in his pocket.

4. See D1, pp. 133 and 134.

5. MIO, p. 118.

6. ibid., p. 119.

7. SS to RM, 28 Feb. 1917, HRHRC.

8. SS to RR, 22 Feb. 1917, Lilly.

9. ibid.

10. D1, p. 133.

11. SS to RR, 22 Feb. 1917, Lilly.

12. SS to ED, 23 Feb. 1917, CUL.

13. SS to RR, 8 March 1917, Lilly.

14. SS gives conflicting accounts of his visits to Rouen. He seems to have spent 4 March there and also the following Saturday and Sunday, 10-11 March.

15. D1, pp. 139-40.

16. See SJ, p. 29.

17. 'In the Church of St Ouen', WP, p. 72.

18. 'The Optimist' (WP, p. 74) was sparked off by SS's visit to the barber's in Rouen, where he heard a fellow-customer complaining that the Allies had 'got the Germans absolutely beat'. The verse rendering of the incident ends rather lamely.

19. RG claimed in GTAT (p. 201) that SS deliberately tried to follow him to the 2nd Battalion, then, when he found RG gone, attempted to get transferred back to the 1st. This is not borne out by SS's own account of the situation.

20. WP, p. 73.

21. D1, p. 143n.

22. Cf. 'The Dragon and the Undying', 'Two Hundred Years After' and 'Sick Leave', among others.

23. SS to RR, 1 April 1917, Lilly.

24. WIK, p. 307.

25. ibid., p. 308.

26. ibid.

27. GTAT, p. 196.

28. JC to SS, 29 March 1917, IWM, and letter from Capt. John Dunn to SS, 31 Jan. 1927, CUL.

29. MIO, p. 134.

30. WIK, p. 552.

31. ibid., p. 308.

32. MIO, p. 137.

33. Greaves was born 17 Sept. 1889 at Lymington, Hants, not so far from SS and they probably met out hunting. Greaves served with the Royal Army Service Corps as a despatch rider from 1914 to 1915 and was then attached to the 2nd RWF from Sept. 1916 until he was injured by a grenade in April 1917. He died a year before SS in Jan. 1966 at Sevenoaks, Kent, and, though SS did not attend the funeral, he did write to Greaves's widow, Laura, with his condolences, which suggests that they had remained in touch over the years. I am grateful to Siobhain Santry for many of the above details.

34. It seems odd that SS should not have maintained the relationship

between the Greaves brothers in MIO; on the contrary, he deliberately disguised the brothers' family link by giving the older the surname 'Barton' and calling the younger 'Wilmot'. There is at least one letter to the older brother about the younger at IWM.

35. WIK, p. 308.

36. There is a copy of this photograph in the archives of the Royal Welch Fusiliers at Caernarvon.

37. MIO, p. 163.

38. ibid., p. 311.

39. RG recalled in GTAT that Orme, who had joined the RWF straight from Sandhurst, at the first battle of Ypres, found himself commanding a battalion reduced to only about forty rifles. With these, and another small force, the remnants of the 2nd Bn the Queen's Regiment, reduced to two officers and 30 other ranks, he helped to recapture three lines of trenches and was himself killed.

40. SS names Orme as his companion on a trip into Amiens on 21 March 1917 (D1, p. 144), but not for his trip to Heilly sur l'Ancre. He does, however, refer to 'Ormand' (his pseudonym for Orme) in his account of the Heilly trip in MIO (pp. 132-3).

41. Yates, who was a Regular, had been Q.M. with the 2nd RWF since 1912.

42. MIO, p. 136.

43. RG to SS, 26 March 1917, Berg.

44. WIK, p. 286.

45. ibid., p. 504.

46. Dunn's initials are 'J.C.' not 'J.S.' as sometimes given in SS studies.

47. Letter from Col. Crawshay to SS., n.d., CUL.

48. GTAT, p. 173.

49. ibid.

50. SS to RG, 14 March 1917, USI.

51. MIO, p. 135.

52. WIK, p. 468.

53. ibid.

54. ibid., p. 400.

55. Dunn to SS, 18 Feb. 1926, CUL.

56. WIK, p. 401.

57. WP, pp. 147-8. The following quotation is from a letter from SS to John Graves, 20 Aug. 1947, William Reese of New Haven.

58. MIO, p. 141.

59. WIK, p. 298.

60. ibid., p. 310.

61. ibid., p. 369.

62. SS to RR, 1 April 1917, Lilly.

63. RG to SS, 26 March 1917, Berg.

64. ibid.

65. WIK, p. 326.

66. ibid., p. 306.

67. CP, p. 67.

68. D1, p. 149.

69. WIK, p. 309.

70. MIO, p. 142.

71. D1, p. 151.

72. MIO, p. 143.

73. WIK, p. 311.

74. SJ, pp. 46-7.

75. WIK, p. 311.

76. MIO, p. 145.

77. WIK, p. 311.

78. LOM claimed that she had given the opal to SS at their last meeting in London.

79. *First World War* (London, 1994), p. 322.

80. See WIK, p. 317.

81. ibid., pp. 315-16.

82. WP, p. 77.

83. WIK, p. 318.

84. Heinemann to RR, 21 Jan. 1918, Lilly.

85. SS describes this incident in IO and the poem 'The Rear-Guard', but it does not appear either in his diary or WIK. It is possible that he based it on something he did record in his diary (under 'Things to Remember'): 'Kirkby shaking dead German by the shoulder to ask him the way' (D1, p. 157).

86. WIK, p. 320.

87. ibid., pp. 320-1.

88. D1, p. 156. These are the last words of RG's poem 'Escape'.

Chapter 13

1. The 2nd Royal Welch Fusiliers continued in the same sector, mainly in support. Tunnel Trench, though part of it was gained, was lost again and the Germans finally gave up the 'block' voluntarily. (See WIK, pp. 329-35.) On 23 April Ralph Greaves lost his arm in what Dr Dunn described as a 'bull-at-a-gate attack', the third in nine days, which left behind it 'the dead of five battalions'. Dunn blamed the Brigade, which he found 'remote in action, and ineffectual' (WIK, p. 339).

2. *The New Witness*, 18 Oct. 1918.

3. Note to 'The Rear-Guard' in WP, p. 76.

4. On the other hand, 'Wounded', written on 24 April and published only in his diary, makes no direct reference to Arras.

5. D1, p. 161.

6. ibid., pp. 161-2.

7. SS to LOM, 26 April 1917, HRHRC. SS told RG in a letter of 23 March 1917 that Russell had just sent him his book, presumably *Justice in War-Time*.

8. SS to LOM, 9 May 1917, HRHRC; SS to John Bain, 12 May 1917, IWM; SS to ED, 24 May 1917, CUL.

9. MIO, p. 176.

10. ibid. In his letter of 9 May 1917 to LOM, however, SS also suggests that, if he were awarded another medal, it would strengthen his position when he started 'playing hell with the British smuggery'.

11. Harold Williams was a remarkable man who spoke 35 languages, including dialects from remote parts of Russia.

12. *Beginning Again* (London, Hogarth Press, 1964), p. 123.

13. SJ, p. 50.

14. OC, p. 141.

15. Typescript in the possession of a private collector.

16. D2, p. 127.

17. ibid., p. 128.

18. Sotheby's English Literature and History Catalogue, London, 18 July 1991, p. 111.

19. Quoted in an article written by H.M. Tomlinson for the Society of Authors, 1946.

20. D1, p. 245.

21. ibid., p. 163.

22. SS to Edmund Blunden, 21 Jan. [1928?], HRHRC.

23. See *Tribulations and Laughter*, p. 110.

24. SJ, p. 50.

25. Bennett placed SS's photograph in his bedroom.

26. Bennett to SS, 26 June 1923, Columbia.. The volume he referred to was *Recreations* (1923).

27. Bennett to SS, 3 Sept. 1923. Murry was the editor of *The Adelphi*, which he used to some extent to promote the work of his wife, Katherine Mansfield, whose writing was presumably not to Bennett's taste.

28. SS gives the date erroneously as 10 May.

29. *Marble and Bronze*, p. 173.

30. SS to RG, 23 May 1917, USI.

31. D1, p. 168.

32. RR to SS, 23 May 1917, Lilly.

33. WO to his father, 26 Aug. 1917, *Collected Letters*, edited by H. Owen and J. Bell (London, OUP, 1967), p. 488.

34. SS to LOM, 4 Feb. 1917, HRHRC.

35. See Lytton Strachey wrote to Virginia Woolf, 21 Feb. 1917: 'That wretched woman, the Lady O. Morrell writes to me as follows – "Do you think you could write to Virginia, and ask her if she could get Sassoon's book of Poems, and if she would review it kindly … I think if he heard that his work had 'Promise' it might make him want to Live – to do things in the Future. But it is all ghastly and he can hardly bear it. Shall I shoot Lloyd George?"'

36. TLS, 31 May 1917.

37. SS to RG, 24 June 1917, USI.

38. *The Nation*, 16 June 1917.

39. 'The Bayreuth-Baghdad Line', *New Witness*, 28 June 1917.

40. Letter from Charles Scott-Moncrieff to SS, 8 July [1917], from SS's own press-cutting book now in the possession of William Reese of New Haven.

41. RR to SS, 2 June 1917, Lilly.

42. D1, p. 168.

43. EG to SS, 29 May 1917, Rutgers.

44. ibid., 29 May 1917, Rutgers.

45. RR to SS, 18 May 1917, Lilly.

46. See *Robert Ross: Friend of Friends*, edited by Margery Ross (London, Cape, 1952), p. 313.

47. Verse letter from A.P. Graves to SS, 22 May 1917, CUL.

48. RR to SS, 20 May 1917, Lilly.

49. SS to RG, 23 May 1917, USI.

50. D1, p. 163.

51. *Beginning Again*, p. 129.

52. SS to EM, [December 1917?], Berg.

53. D2, p. 109.

54. Squire's *Selected Poems from Modern Authors* (1933), for example, included five pieces by SS.

55. D3, p. 138.

56. SS to ED, 14 May 1917, CUL.

57. D1, p. 165.

58. ibid., pp. 165-6.

59. RG had written to SS on 21 April 1917 from his job as Cadet Training Officer at Wadham College, Oxford, telling him to 'Get a cushy quick, old thing, and I'll work this sort of job for you here' (Berg). He had followed this up on 12 May by offering to get him such a job at either Oxford or Cambridge: 'You'd be stupid not to take it; you're no further use in France' (Berg). On 23 May RR had begged him 'for God's sake write to Cambridge at once and get that fixed up' (Lilly) and by 24 May SS was contemplating what had previously seemed unthinkable: 'Can't make up my mind whether to do anything about "getting a job" [he wrote to ED in Cambridge]. I fear my D.S.O. is fading into the realms of vision' (CUL).

60. D1, p. 166.

61. SS was almost certainly thinking, not of 'The Mower to the Glow-worms' but the first stanza of 'Damon the Mower'.

62. Morley of Blackburn, John Morley, 1st Viscount (1838-1923) was a statesman and a biographer, just the kind of writer to appeal to the Brasseys. SS is probably referring either to his life of *Voltaire* (1872) or *Rousseau* (1873), possibly *Diderot and the Encyclopaedists* (1879).

63. D1, p. 165.

64. ibid., p. 167.

65. D1, pp. 173.

66. ibid., p. 172.

67. See MIO, p. 191, where Dottrell, alias Cottrell, refers to 'Young Brock', killed with the 1st RWF in May 1917. SS wrote to RG on 23 May 1917, two days before composing this poem: 'But poor Brocklebank got killed after performing prodigies as bombing officer' (USI). The only problem with this theory is that Brocklebank was shot in the arm, side and leg, not the head, but SS might have altered this detail for dramatic effect.

68. D1, p. 172.

69. SJ, p. 48.

70. JC to JD, 17 May 1917 and JC to SS, 30 May 1917, IWM.

71. 'The Supreme Sacrifice', WP, p. 81, first published in *The Cambridge Magazine*, 9 June 1917.

72. SS to RG, 23 May 1917, USI.

73. D1, p. 157.

74. SS to ED, 2 June 1917, CUL.

75. WP, p. 80. His original version opened rather flatly: 'They set him quietly down' and involved a passive narrator and somewhat melodramatic repetition of the final word, 'dying'.

76. Both were published in *The Cambridge Magazine*, but 'In an Underground Dressing-Station' came first on 9 June 1917. 'Editorial Impressions' is wrongly attributed to the Craiglockhart period in WP, but is clearly referred to as already

completed in a letter to ED of 24 May 1917 (CUL). It was published in *The Cambridge Magazine* of 22 Sept. 1917. In the same letter to ED SS encloses another piece of what he calls 'restrained irony', a sonnet called 'News from the Front'. He never managed to get the first two lines of this to his satisfaction and the poem was published only in *The Cambridge Magazine* (2 June 1917). Its main interest lies in the fact that the protagonist, who is just back from the Front, has a wife who is more realistic than he is, an unusually positive view of women for SS at this time.

77. *Siegfried Sassoon*, p. 32 and 'The Literature of the First World War', *The Modern Age*, edited by Boris Ford ('Pelican Guide to English Literature' series, vol. 7, Penguin, 1961), p. 162.

78. D1, p. 167.

79. See two letters from SS to ED, undated but probably written on 6 and 8 June 1917 (CUL).

80. See *Glyn Philpot, 1884-1937: Edwardian Aesthete to Thirties Modernist* by Robin Gibson, Catalogue published by the National Portrait Gallery, London, 1984. I am also indebted to Philpot's niece, Gabrielle Cross, for much of the information which follows.

81. op. cit., p. 17.

82. SJ, p. 50.

83. ibid., p. 49.

84. D2, p. 158.

85. Notes taken during an interview with Gabrielle Cross on 20 Nov. 1992.

86. Philpot started studying at Lambeth Art School at the age of fifteen.

87. *The Tatler*, 27 Feb. 1918.

88. SJ, p. 51. SS contemplated selling the portrait a number of times, but finally gave it to the Fitzwilliam Museum, where he knew SCC would appreciate it. It now hangs in his old college, Clare, at Cambridge.

89. See RN's Introduction to the

first American edition of
Counter-Attack (New York, 1918).

90. SJ, p. 50.

91. ibid., p. 49.

92. H.W. Massingham (1860-1924) was a liberal journalist who edited the *Daily Chronicle* from 1895 to 1899 and *The Nation* from 1907 to 1923, the year before he died.

93. The secret treaties between Russia and Europe were finally made public on 27 Nov. 1917. Massingham was turning more and more to the Left and the Labour Party itself, after an uneasy truce with the Liberals, was beginning to question the Government's handling of the War.

94. Bertrand Russell (1872-1970) had also lost his teaching job at Cambridge in July 1916 as a result of his pacifism. While sticking closely to the facts in other respects, SS makes two interesting changes in MIO when describing his meeting with Russell. He has Markington (i.e. Massingham) introduce Sherston (his fictional self) to Thornton Tyrrell (i.e. Russell), probably in order to play down the influence of Ottoline, which he was openly to deny later. More curiously, he makes Sherston deny ever having heard of the already well-known philosopher, whom he is convinced he will not be able to understand. His intention was no doubt to emphasize his protagonist's naivete and lack of intellectual grasp, but it probably also reflects SS's own lack of confidence in that direction. In fact, he had not only heard of Russell before they met, but had actually been reading Russell's *Principles of Social Reconstruction* the previous month. And since the book was inscribed to him by the author, they must have been well aware of each other's existence by June 1917.

95. See Christie, Manson & Wood's sale catalogue, 4 June 1975, of 'The Library of the late Siegfried Sassoon', p. 93, and SJ, pp. 48 and 52.

96. Lees-Smith later achieved

Cabinet rank as Postmaster-General in a Labour Government.

97. SS acknowledged this later, in talking to Dr W.H.R. Rivers at Craiglockhart, but provided no explanation for it. He may simply have wished to spare his superiors further embarrassment and annoyance.

98. The original statement at IWM differs very slightly from the version SS included in MIO and other places, its one significant difference being the omission of 'military' before 'conduct' in the penultimate paragraph.

99. RG to SS, 19 May 1917, Berg: 'As you say, we're losing the War heavily'.

100. D1, p. 176.

101. MIO, p. 203.

102. Cottrell wrote to SS on 30 May 1917, concerning Orme's death: 'It is doubly hard lines as an exchange was ordered between Moody, who was with this Bn [i.e. the 1st] and who rejoined the 2nd Bn a week ago – and Orme. But the C/O 2nd Bn refused to allow Orme to leave till after this show. I saw young Orme a couple of days ago at our Sports and he was very much upset at not being allowed to join us – Especially as Moody had gone to the 2nd Bn'.

103. SS to LOM, 3 July 1917, HRHRC.

104. SS to A.T. Bartholomew, 4 July 1917, quoted in Keynes, p. 37.

105. See the case-notes of Dr W.H.R. Rivers, 23 July 1917, on SS, reproduced in P. Fussell's *Sassoon's Long Journey* (1983), pp. 134-5: 'He had never previously approved of pacifism and does not think that he was influenced by this communication' [i.e. with the pacifists in the Summer of 1916].

106. SS owned both the French and English editions of *Le Feu* (*Under Fire*, translated by Fitzwater Wray, London, Dent, 1917) and was to preface his second collection of war poems, *Counter-Attack*, with a passage from the book.

107. D1, p. 176.

108. ibid., p. 175.

109. Attitudes towards public protests about War have, of course, changed profoundly since the First World War. Nowadays a serving Brigadier's protest about aspects of the Gulf War, for example, arouses no such harsh measures.

110. SJ, p. 56.

111. ibid., p. 54.

112. SS to DFC, 17 May 1965, SS:PP, p. 65.

113. MIO, pp. 210-14.

114. The interview had been with Col. Edwards, whom SS described as a 'military don'. SS gives a fictionized account of his journey and a city air-raid in MIO, pp. 207-10.

115. RG to SS, 30 June 1917, Berg.

116. This is also the title of a lecture given by Dr W.H.R. Rivers in 1917 and reprinted in his book, *Instinct and the Unconscious* (1920). SS had not met Rivers, a doctor at Craiglockhart Hospital, when he wrote the poem, but is unlikely to have alighted on this title by coincidence. He almost certainly gave it the title after he heard of Rivers's lecture.

117. When Edward Thompson brought out a selection of SS's poems in Ernest Benn's Augustan Books of English Poetry series, SS did not want many of his War poems included, but the only one he absolutely prohibited Thompson to include was 'Repressions of War Experience'. See correspondence between Thompson and SS at Bodley.

118. D1, p. 177.

119. ibid., p. 178.

120. ibid., p. 180.

121. SJ, p. 56.

122. See RG to RR, 9 July 1917 (Lilly), and D1, p. 178.

123. D1, p. 179.

124. ibid., pp. 180-1. Bennett also wrote to RR, confidentially, on 17 July

1917: 'The fact is, my dear Robert, I am much concerned about Sassoon. He wrote & told me, & I replied with what I thought to be a judicious letter. You see I do not know him well enough to write very intimately without seeming impertinent. I agree with you that he must be a little deranged. If I knew who his C.O. was, and you thought it proper, I would send a line to his C.O. But if he has not already gone & made a fool of himself the best thing would be for you & any other of his more intimate friends solemnly to see him' (*The Letters of Arnold Bennett*, edited by James Hepburn, London, O.U.P., 1968, p. 36).

125. *Marble and Bronze*, p. 174.

126. See Maureen Borland, *Wilde's Devoted Friend*, p. 259.

127. D1, p. 179.

128. *Wilde's Devoted Friend*, p. 271.

129. SS to RR, no date July 1917, Lilly.

130. *Marble and Bronze*, p. 175.

131. ibid.

132. JC to SS, 11 July 1917, IWM.

133. Lilly.

134. SS was later to point out the inaccuracies of this account but RG failed to correct it in subsequent editions.

135. GTAT, p. 214.

136. D1, p. 192.

137. Hassall, p. 416.

138. SS probably completed 'Lamentations' and 'The Effect' at the Exchange Hotel.

139. SS to Edward Carpenter, 9 Oct. 1917 from Craiglockhart: 'I was forced to appear at [a Medical Board] (by a threat of incarceration in a lunatic asylum)', Sheffield City Libraries.

140. MIO, p. 235.

141. GTAT, p. 216.

142. SS to Edward Carpenter, 9 Oct. 1917, commenting on a ballad about him by Carpenter, Sheffield City Libraries.

143. Letter from HGW to SS, July

[1917], McMaster University, Hamilton, Ontario, Canada.

144. JD to SS, 1 Jan. 1929, IWM.

145. One such objector, Max Plowman, was known personally to SS. In his Preface to Plowman's book, *War and the Creative Impulse* (Headley Bros, 1919), Henry Nevinson tells us that Plowman enlisted in the Territorial Field Ambulance and later took a commission in an infantry regiment and went to France in 1916. 'He fought through the battles of the Somme in that year, was blown up ... and sent home with concussion in July 1917'. Back in England he found attitudes changed, 'ideals gone' and asked to be relieved of his commission on the grounds of conscientious objection. Following his publication of a statement, or explanation, of his attitude to the War in January 1918, Plowman was Court Martialled and dismissed from the army. He was later 'called up', but eventually ordered to 'find work of national importance', which he refused to do. Fortunately, he was saved from further trouble by the Armistice. His objection to the War was based mainly on religious grounds. Plowman sent SS a copy of his book in 1919.

146. *The Times*, 31 July 1917.

147. SJ, p. 56.

148. ibid., p. 57.

Chapter 14

1. SS wrote this in 1954. See 'An Appendix to Chapter 5 of *Siegfried's Journey*', an autograph account of SS's protest, quoted in Sotheby's English Literature and History Catalogue, London, 18 July 1991, p. 95.

2. B.H. Liddell Hart, *History of the First World War* (London, Papermac, 1992), p. 327.

3. Russia declared a formal ceasefire with Germany on 1 Dec. 1917, which was signed on 15 Dec., allowing the Germans to transfer

approximately 900,000 men to the Western Front.

4. SP, p. 30.

5. ibid., p. 31.

6. WIK, p. 372.

7. SP, p. 7.

8. SS describes Harper as 'Hooper' in SP.

9. The building still stands though its name has been changed to Napier College.

10. SS to LOM, 19 Aug. 1917. D1, p. 184.

11. ibid., 30 July. D1, p. 183.

12. SS to ED, 25 July 1917, CUL, and SP, p. 7.

13. SP, p. 52.

14. ibid., p. 53.

15. SS to RG, 4 Oct. 1917, USI.

16. William Halse Rivers Rivers (1864-1922). The duplication of 'Rivers' is puzzling but accounts for the initial 'R' in his name.

17. SP, p. 7.

18. ibid., p. 27.

19. SS acquired a copy of Rivers's new book, *Kinship and Social Organization* (P.S. King, 1914) in Aug. 1917.

20. One of Rivers's close friends and colleagues, the eminent neurologist, Sir Henry Head, whom SS was also to know, had asked Rivers to co-operate on an experiment to trace the progress of the regeneration of damaged nerves. Head had proposed to have his own radial nerve severed and sutured and Rivers had agreed to assist at such an operation. He had also helped Head chart the regeneration process of the nerve during the five years that followed.

21. Quoted in an article in *St Bartholomew's Hospital Journal* (Nov. 1936) by Walter Langdon-Brown.

22. Rivers was subsequently transferred to the Royal Flying Corps as a consultant psychiatrist at the end of 1917.

23. *Conflict and Dream* (London, Kegan Paul, Trench, Trubner & Co., 1923), p. 167.

24. ibid., p. 171.

25. ibid.

26. P. Fussell, *The Great War and Modern Memory* (OUP, 1975), p. 101.

27. SP, p. 7.

28. SS to EM, Aug. 1918, Berg.

29. See 'Revisitation', CP, p. 221.

30. SS to EM, Aug. 1918, Berg. See also S.N. Behrman, *Tribulations and Laughter*, p. 9.

31. SP, p. 8.

32. Quoted in *Sassoon's Long Journey*, edited by P. Fussell, p. 135.

33. *Behind the Lines* (Yale University Press, 1987), pp. 65ff.

34. *Taking It Like a Man*, p. 88.

35. op. cit., p. 65.

36. SS to LOM, 30 July 1917; D1, pp. 183-4.

37. D1, p. 184.

38. Gordon and Geoffrey Harbord's letters to SS are at IWM.

39. Gordon Harbord to SS, 5 Oct. 1916, IWM.

40. ibid., 13 March 1915, IWM.

41. ibid., 13 May 1915, IWM.

42. Geoffrey Harbord to SS, 13 Sept. 1917, IWM.

43. SS to Carpenter, 29 Aug. 1918, Sheffield City Libraries.

44. Gordon's death was announced in *The Times* on 21 Aug. 1917: 'Lt. (Temp. Capt.) Stephen Gordon Harbord, M.C., R.F.A., third son of Rev. H. & Mrs Harbord, Colwood Park, Bolney. Aged 27'.

45. SP, p. 11.

46. SS refers only briefly to 'one of my best friends' being killed in Aug. 1917 in SP, but does not name him for obvious reasons.

47. Though not included in SS's CP, this has been preserved in his published diary (D1, pp. 185-6).

48. WP, p. 98.

49. Rupert Hart-Davis dates the finished version of 'Together', 'Limerick, 30 January 1918', but it is clear from a letter SS wrote to RM on 29 Dec. 1917, in which he quotes a slightly different version of the second stanza of the poem, that it was almost completed by then. (The letter to RM is in HRHRC.) SS himself dated the poem 'August 1917' in a MS book he made up of the *Counter-Attack* poems.

50. SJ, p. 58.

51. WO to Susan Owen, 11 Sept. 1917, and from WO to Leslie Gunston, 22 Aug. 1917 (*Collected Letters of Wilfred Owen*, edited by Harold Owen and John Bell (London, OUP, 1967), pp. 494 and 485).

52. SJ, p. 58.

53. Related by Peter Parker in *The Old Lie, the Great War and the Public School Ethos* (London, Constable, 1987), p. 193.

54. In a letter of 2 March 1930 to RG (at Buffalo) in which he criticizes GTAT, SS regrets RG's treatment of WO and the 'cowardice' story. He thinks that RG only met WO twice, once in Oct. 1917 at Craiglockhart and once at RG's wedding in Jan. 1918, whereas he saw him every day for about three months. He believed that WO was 'not in a very shaky condition', though he did note his 'slight stammer' in SJ.

55. WO to Susan Owen, 27 Sept. 1917, *Collected Letters*, p. 496.

56. ibid., 8 Aug. 1917, *Collected Letters*, p. 482.

57. *Collected Letters*, pp. 484-5.

58. WO to Susan Owen, [12] Sept. 1917, *Collected Letters*, p. 494.

59. WO To Mary Owen, 29 Aug. 1917, *Collected Letters*, p. 489.

60. *War Poems and Others*, edited by Dominic Hibberd (London, Chatto & Windus, 1975), p. 73.

61. WO to Leslie Gunston, 22 August 1917, *Collected Letters*, p. 486.

62. SJ, p. 59. When SS sent LOM a copy of the hospital magazine, *The Hydra*, in early Sept. 1917, with WO's 'Song of Songs' in it, he commented: 'The man who wrote this brings me quantities and I have to say kind things. He will improve, I think!' (Quoted by Dominic Hibberd in *Wilfred Owen: The Last Year*, p. 43.)

63. I am indebted for this

information and some of what follows to Dominic Hibberd's invaluable edition of WO's *War Poems* (London, Chatto & Windus, 1976).

64. SJ, p. 60.

65. ibid., p. 59.

66. I am grateful to D.J. Enright for bringing this letter to my attention.

67. See Chapter 9, pp. 213-17.

68. SJ, p. 71.

69. As well as being a pun on 'Hydro', 'Hydra' was probably a reference to the many-headed monster of Greek myth, with the implied parallel of the Craiglockhart patients struggling with the 'hydra' of shell-shock.

70. 'Wirers', WP, p. 90.

71. WP, p. 92.

72. ibid., p. 93.

73. SS to RR, 3 Oct. 1917, D1, p. 187.

74. D1, p. 194.

75. SS to LOM, 28 Oct. 1917, HRHRC.

76. SS to RR, 3 Oct. 1917, D1, p. 188.

77. WO to SS, 5 Nov. 1917, *Collected Letters*, p. 505.

78. WO to Susan Owen, [12] Sept. 1917, *Collected Letters*, p. 494.

79. ibid., 7 Sept. 1917, *Collected Letters*, p. 492.

80. WO to SS, *Collected Letters*, p. 512. WO means 'August', not September, of course.

81. WO to Susan Owen, Sat. [29 Oct. 1917], *Collected Letters*, p. 503.

82. Glyn Philpot's niece, Gabrielle Cross, a close friend of Harold Owen's, told me that when Harold was editing his brother Wilfred's letters, SS agreed to let him see all Wilfred's letters to him. When he arrived for that purpose, SS went upstairs to get them, but then decided against it and subsequently burned some of them. Harold believed that there was something too personal in some of them, though he did not necessarily believe that Wilfred and SS had been lovers.

83. WO to Susan Owen, [12] Sept. 1917, *Collected Letters*, p. 494.

84. WO to SS, 5 Nov. 1917, *Collected Letters*, p. 506.

85. SJ, p. 63.

86. ibid.

87. ibid.

88. Jonathan Cutbill made this claim during a long telephone conversation with me about SS and WO's relationship.

89. Extract from SS's diary for 7 Feb. 1954, quoted in SS:PP, p. 87.

90. 'Sick Leave' was sent to LOM on 17 Oct. 1917 and published as 'Death's Brotherhood' in *The English Review* in Jan. 1918; 'Attack' was published in *The Cambridge Magazine* of 20 Oct. 1917.

91. D1, p. 157.

92. SS to EM, 16 July 1919, Berg.

93. SS told Professor Lewis Chase, in a letter of 25 Jan. 1922, that 'Thrushes', together with 'Invocation', was 'the only pure poetry' he wrote at this time, an interesting insight in to how little the War had really changed his notion of poetry. RG seems to have shared his view, writing to ask him in Nov. 1917, not to send 'any more corpse poems' but to 'stick to your splendid Thrushes'.

94. R.A. Sampson was still writing to SS in 1933. See SS Collection at CUL.

95. Margaret Sackville (d. 1963) published her own War poems, *Pageant of War* (London, Simpkin, Marshall, Hamilton, Kent & Co., 1914).

96. See SS wrote to RR on 26 Sept. 1917 (D1, p. 187). Strong's own verse would be adjudged 'fairly rotten', not only by SS and WO when they had great fun at its expense at their farewell dinner, but also by posterity.

97. SS to RR, 3 Oct. 1917 (D1, p. 188).

98. WO to Susan Owen, 14 Oct. 1917, *Collected Letters*, p. 499.

99. 'The Rear-Guard' appeared in the issue of 15 Sept. 1917.

100. SS's MS book of poems at HRHRC dates the first draught of 'Prelude' 1 Sept. 1917, whereas WO refers to SS having written his 'exquisitely painful war poem' on 6 Sept. 1917. It may simply have been revised a few days later.

101. *The London Mercury*, June 1929.

102. *Taking It Like a Man*, p. 92.

103. ibid.

104. See SS's diary entries for 2 July 1916 (D1, p. 85) and 6 July 1916 (D1, pp. 88-9).

105. When Rivers's sister Bertha wrote to thank SS for his picture of 'Will', or 'Doc Willie', as even his family sometimes referred to him, she recalled that he had spent the greater part of this fortnight's leave at their poultry farm, Mount House, Downs Road, near Gravesend.

106. SS to LOM, 11 Oct. 1917, HRHRC.

107. SP, p. 36.

108. ibid.

109. SS to LOM, [17 Oct. 1917], (D1, pp. 190-1).

110. SP, pp. 34-5.

111. SS to LOM, 28 Oct. 1917 and 29 Oct. 1917 (D1, p. 193).

112. OAG, p. 230.

113. There is a slight mystery about this occasion since, as Dominic Hibberd notes in his *Wilfred Owen: the Last Year*, when SS gave the book, *A Human Voice*, to WO, he dated it 26 Oct., yet he clearly implies in SJ that the date of their last dinner together was 3 Nov. 1917 (SJ, pp. 64-5). It may be that he conflated his account of a previous dinner with WO on about 26 Oct. with their last one, for artistic purposes, and that the 'poetry-reading' from Strong he describes took place on the earlier occasion.

114. SS says in SP that the venue for this meeting was the Café Royal, perhaps to make the occasion sound more special, or perhaps out of genuine confusion, since he lunched with Nichols a few weeks later at the Café Royal.

115. *The Old Huntsman* had sold 700 copies by 17 Aug., which SS considered 'quite good' (SS to RR, 17 Aug. 1917, Lilly).

116. RG to SS, 25 Jan. 1917, Berg.

117. ibid., 21 April 1917, Berg.

118. SS had copies of RN's *A Faun's Holiday* (London, Chatto & Windus, 1917) and *Poems and Phantasies* (London, Chatto, 1917) in his library, in which he had signed his name and the date, 'Siegfried Sassoon, June 1917'.

119. Hassall, p. 413.

120. RG to SS, 3 July 1917, Berg.

121. ibid., [late Dec. 1917/early Jan. 1918?], Berg.

122. ibid., 5[?] June 1917, USI.

123. This and the two following quotations come from a letter from SS to RN of 5 Nov. [1925?], Berg.

124. By 15 May 1918 SS was writing to RG that 'Bob Nichols' was 'the best poet of the three', USI.

125. SS explained his slowness to recognize WO's genius in a letter to RN of 28 Oct. 1930 '– but then I hadn't seen his last magnificent war poems'. This, and other letters written to RN from SS between 1917 and 1930 were deposited at Bodley by RN in 1930, on condition that the letters would not be shown during his or SS's lifetime, that there should be no publication of the letters during his lifetime, except with SS's permission. In giving his permission for the letters to go to Bodley, SS wrote to RN on 28 Oct. 1930: 'They may help – if anyone cares to investigate – to explode any idea that I was a well-controlled individual in 1918'.

126. 'The Day's March', *Men Who March Away*, edited by I.M. Parsons (London, Chatto & Windus, 1966), pp. 42-3.

127. SJ, p. 68.

128. ibid.

129. SS to LOM, 21 Nov. 1917 (D1, p. 195).

130. Hassall, p. 437.

131. From the 'Prefatory Note' to *Georgian Poetry, 1916-17*.

132. SS wrote to RR, in an undated letter of Summer 1917: 'I had a long letter from Eddie Marsh yesterday in which he says "I've been most awfully pleased at the success of [*The Old Huntsman*]; it's had a noble reception. *You think* I don't like your war poetry, but I do now. (*Not*, as you may think, because it has been received well!)" ...' (*Friend of Friends*, p. 313). EM may also have been influenced by RG's flattering letter: 'I Hear you've been converted to Siegfried Sassoon's new poetry: the later stuff is very curious and vigorous. I don't know if you realize that you are responsible for giving me advice which I passed on to him' (n.d., [Summer 1917] Berg).

133. SS to EM, 31 Oct. 1917, Berg.

134. SS to RR, 17 Aug. 1917, Lilly.

135. SP, pp. 45-6.

136. SS to ED, 24 Nov. 1917, CUL.

137. SS to RG, 21 Nov. 1917, Berg.

138. *In Broken Images: Robert Graves: Selected Correspondence* (London, Hutchinson, 1982), p. 89. RG's Charterhouse friend 'Peter' (G.H. Johnstone) had been arrested for homosexual offences earlier in the year. RG had described his affection for him as 'pseudo-homosexual'.

139. SS to A.T. Bartholomew, 15 Dec. [1917], CUL.

140. RG to SS [Dec?] 1917, Berg.

Chapter 15

1. See undated letter from RG to SS, [February 1918?]: 'My nerves have been bad recently, and attacks of the horrors ... But you have them worse than me' (Berg).

2. D1, p. 238.

3. See WIK, p. 419, re the 2nd Bn RWF.

4. SP, p. 55.

5. SS to LOM, 22 Dec. 1917, HRHRC.

6. SP, p. 57.

7. ibid.

8. SS to RN, 'Wednesday' [28 Nov. 1917], Bodley.

9. SS to LOM, 4 Dec. 1917, HRHRC.

10. D1, pp. 196-7.

11. ibid., p. 197.

12. See 'Current Literature' by J.C. Squire, *New Statesman*, 24 Nov. 1917; *TLS*, 27 Dec. 1917; *The Nation*, 19 Jan. 1918; *The Welsh Outlook*, July 1918; *The Dial*, 15 Aug. 1918. The review in *The Nation*, which may have been written by its editor, H.W. Massingham, was particularly enthusiastic.

13. SP, p. 60.

14. D1, entry for 19 Dec. 1917, pp. 197-8.

15. SS to RN, 22 Dec. [1917], Bodley.

16. See Fussell, *The Great War and Modern Memory*.

17. Goldsworthy Lowes Dickinson (1862-1932), educated at Charterhouse and King's College, Cambridge, where he lived as a Fellow from 1887 till his death. Studied medicine but never practised. Lecturer in political science from 1896 to 1920. Most successful works include *The Greek View of Life* (1896), *Letters from John Chinaman* (1901), *Justice and Liberty* (1908), *Religion and Immortality* (1911), *East and West* (1914) and *International Anarchy 1904-14* (1926). Is credited with inventing the name 'League of Nations'. SS had a copy of Lowes Dickinson's *The Choice Before Us* (London, Allen & Unwin, 1917), signed 'Siegfried Sassoon, Sept. 10, 1917', that is, the period when he was at Craiglockhart. The absence of a personal inscription by the author suggests that SS did not really know Dickinson by the time they met in Manchester in December 1917.

18. SS to Goldsworthy Lowes Dickinson, 19 Dec. [post 1906], G.L. Dickinson papers, King's College, Cambridge.

19. SS to A.T. Bartholomew, 15 Dec. 1917, CUL.

20. SS to LOM, 21 Nov. 1917, HRHRC.

21. RG to SS, undated letter of late Dec. 1917, or early Jan. 1918, Berg.

22. SS to RM, 29 Dec. 1917, HRHRC.

23. D1, p. 108.

24. ibid., pp. 201-2.

25. The bells of Limerick Cathedral were almost certainly the inspiration of SS's poem, 'Joy-Bells' (CP, p. 91) written at this time.

26. SS to RG, 14 Jan. 1918, USI.

27. SS to RN, 12 Jan. 1918, Bodley.

28. Not included in CP, 'Journey's End' was first published in D1 (p. 202). SS described it as 'a rather feeble sonnet', the rest of which 'fail[ed] to evolve' (SJ, p. 75).

29. D1, p. 203.

30. SS to RN, 12 Jan. 1918, Bodley.

31. D1, p. 203.

32. ibid.

33. SS wrote to A.T. Bartholomew on 2 February [1918], in reference to his hunting activities: 'The people I meet are exactly like in the Irish R.M. books' (CUL).

34. Dorothea Conyers (1873-1949) was the daughter of Col. J. Blood Smyth, but took her writing name from her first marriage (in 1892) to Col. Charles Conyers, by whom she had a son and a daughter. A year after his death in 1916, she married Capt. J. White and it was at their house, Nantinan, at Rathteale that she entertained SS during his stay in Ireland. Her interest in poetry is evident from the fact that, as SS reported to RG, she had bought 20 copies of the latter's *Over the Brazier* and was keen to have an autographed copy of his *Fairies and Fusiliers*. She herself was to write more than thirty books, most of them fiction, though she also wrote *Recollections of Sport in Ireland* and *Sporting Reminiscences*.

35. D1, p. 209.

36. SP, p. 66.

37. ibid., p. 81.

38. ibid., p. 74.

39. SS to LOM, 4 Feb. 1918, HRHRC.

40. SP, p. 77.

41. D1, pp. 205-6.

42. Rivers to SS, 1 Feb. 1918, McMaster University, Hamilton, Ont., Canada.

43. Berg.

44. SP, p. 85.

45. D1, p. 198.

46. SS to LOM, 26 Dec. [1917], HRHRC.

47. 'Invocation' was published in *The Nation* in Dec. 1917.

48. Rutgers.

49. EG had suggested that 'Beloved' in the first line of the second stanza should be changed to 'Belov'd', to facilitate reading.

50. Rutgers.

51. Thomas Hardy to SS, 8 Jan. 1918, Manuscript Collection, Eton College.

52. 'Idyll' was first published in the *New Statesman* for 29 June 1918, then in SS's privately printed *Picture-Show* (1919).

53. 'Memory' was first published in the magazine *To-Day* in March 1918, then in *Picture-Show* (1919).

54. SS to EM, 16 July 1919, Berg.

55. Tolstoi's *War and Peace* was included in SS's list of 'Books to Take to Egypt' (D1, p. 210), but, like Scott's *The Antiquary* and Meredith's poems, also included in the list, SS records buying it at Port Said. He may have wanted to take them, but left them in England because of their weight (Tolstoi was in 3 vols), then bought them in Egypt.

56. Apart from RR, EM, RM and Rivers, SS also saw his publisher, William Heinemann, his solicitor, J.G. Lousada, and Philpot's friend, J.J. Shannon (1862-1923), an American-born portrait-painter who lived near Holland Park.

57. D1, p. 212.

58. ibid.

59. *Studies in the History of the Renaissance*, a collection of essays published in 1873, was the first of several volumes which established Walter Pater (1839-1894).

60. D1, pp. 212-13.

61. ibid., p. 212.

62. ibid., p. 214.

63. ibid.

64. ibid., p. 215.

65. ibid., p. 218.

66. ibid.

67. ibid., p. 212.

68. ibid., p. 214.

69. ibid.

70. CUL.

71. SP, p. 88.

72. ibid., p. 90.

73. SS had met Moore several times at EG's house, as he relates in WY (p. 212). See also a letter from SS to ED, 31 Oct. 1915, CUL.

74. D1, p. 216.

75. ibid., p. 217. *Chu-Chin-Chow* was a popular musical by Oscar Asche and Frederic Norton.

76. SS to RM, 25 Feb. 1918, HRHRC.

77. For the Polish writer, the 'clear, starry nights' of a sea-journey were 'brilliant evidence of the awful loneliness, of the hopeless obscure insignificance of our globe lost in the splendid revelation of a glittering, soulless universe, which should oppress our spirit and crush our pride' (*Chance*, pt. 1, chap. 2).

78. D1, p. 242.

79. ibid.

80. ibid., p. 243.

81. ibid., p. 235.

82. ibid., p. 216.

83. SS to ED, 19 Feb. 1918, CUL.

84. D1, p. 218.

85. ibid.

86. SS to LOM, 6 March 1918, HRHRC.

87. SS to RM, 25 Feb. [1918], HRHRC.

88. D1, p. 227.

89. ibid., p. 219.

90. ibid.

91. ibid.

92. The British continued to keep a fairly large garrison in Egypt, even at the expense of sending much-needed reinforcements to the Dardanelles.

93. See *A Brief Record of the Advance of the Egyptian Expeditionary Force, July 1915 to October 1918*, compiled from Official Sources (Cairo, The Palestine News, 1919).

94. D1, p. 222.

95. ibid., p. 223.

96. SS to LOM,, 20 March [1918], HRHRC.

97. SP, p. 130.

98. D1, p. 236.

99. ibid., p. 262.

100. D2, p. 67. This story has not yet come to light.

101. D1, p. 229.

102. ibid.

103. ibid., p. 240.

104. ibid.

105. ibid., p. 225.

106. ibid.

107. SS must have had Bigger in mind when he described Adam in 'Ancient History': 'Adam, a brown old vulture in the rain, / Shivered below his wind-whipped olive-trees; / Huddling sharp chin on scarred and craggy knees' (CP, p. 109).

108. D1, p. 224.

109. ibid., pp. 226-7.

110. SS to EG, 25 March [1918], Rutgers.

111. D1, p. 227.

112. ibid., p. 228.

113. ibid., p. 229.

114. ibid.

115. ibid.

116. ibid., p. 232.

117. ibid., p. 234.

118. See ibid., pp. 232-3.

119. ibid., p. 237.

120. Lena Ashwell (1872-1957).

121. D1, p. 236.

122. ibid., p. 235.

123. 'Concert Party' was first published in the *New Statesman*, 17

Aug. 1918, then in *Picture-Show*. It was also included in CP.

124. D1, p. 239.

125. ibid., p. 238.

126. ibid., pp. 239-40.

127. SS to ED, 26 June 1918, CUL.

128. ibid.

129. CUL.

130. The transport ship *Leasowe Castle* sank on 27 May 1918 with the loss of most of her passengers, including soldiers from the Warwickshire Yeomanry.

131. D1, p. 244.

Chapter 16

1. RG to SS, 5 May 1918, Berg.

2. Maureen Borland, *Wilde's Devoted Friend* (Oxford, Lennard Pbg, 1990), p. 277.

3. RG to SS, 5 May 1918, Berg. There is a letter at Columbia University from the editor of *The Observer*, dated 15 Oct. 1949, asking SS to write a review of Methuen's complete text of Wilde's *De Profundis* for their issue of 30 Oct. 1949: 'Your name was suggested to me by Mrs Lucas, who is a niece of Robbie Ross, and I feel very strongly that the work should be reviewed by someone who knew Ross and who can assess the case against Alfred Douglas. It seems to me that although older people do realise the harm that Douglas did to Wilde, the younger generation of whom many came under Wilde's spell, are not at all aware of the facts'.

4. Hassall, p. 348.

5. D1, p. 247.

6. SS describes Stable (as 'S.'), D1, p. 241. There are two letters from Wintringham Stable to SS at IWM and one by him about SS to the newspaper after SS's death. These make it clear that he appreciated SS's poetry and that he also enjoyed the brandy SS sent out to him in France. Another link between them was RG, in writing to whom on 24 July 1918, SS mentions Stable.

7. D1, p. 246.

8. ibid., pp. 246-7.

9. 'Testament' was first published from a manuscript in SS's letter of 9 May 1918 to LOM (HRHRC) in *Poetry of the Great War: an Anthology*, edited by Dominic Hibberd and John Onions (London, Macmillan, 1986). WO said, probably on SS's authority, that it was written 'on the boat', that is, the troopship returning from Alexandria, but I believe that it was completed in the rest camp near Marseilles, since the theatrical metaphor of the last two lines was almost certainly suggested by the same visit to the music-hall which flavoured his diary entry for 9 May. Though the poem remained unpublished in SS's lifetime, the last two lines are adapted for a poem which was published, 'To Léonide Massine in "Cleopatra" ': '... O mortal heart / Be still; you have drained the cup; you have played your part' (CP, p. 105).

10. D1, pp. 270-1.

11. ibid., p. 247.

12. Harry Morgan serves as the model for 'Harry Jones' in SP and 'Stiffy' Philipps for 'Stiffy Roberts' in the same book.

13. D1, pp. 252 and 269.

14. SS to LOM, 16 May 1918, HRHRC.

15. D1, p. 32.

16. ibid., p. 248.

17. ibid.

18. ibid.

19. ibid., p. 249.

20. RG to SS, [n.d.] May 1918, following SS's letter of 15 May to RG, Berg.

21. Archives of the Royal Welch Fusiliers, at Caernarvon, Wales.

22. This notebook, now at AM, is signed with SS's CC's initials – 'T.B.B.' – but it is clearly written by SS.

23. SP, p. 118.

24. D1, p. 251.

25. ibid., p. 250.

26. ibid.

27. *Letters from John Chinaman* (1901) was a series of letters written by Goldsworthy Lowes Dickinson on his visit to China.

28. Duhamel's *Vie des Martyrs* is not mentioned in this letter of 16 May 1918, but was almost certainly included in the parcel, since he started to read it shortly afterwards.

29. D1, p. 251.

30. SP, p. 120.

31. D1, p. 254.

32. ibid., p. 255.

33. *The New Book of Martyrs*, translated into English by Florence Simmonds (London, Heinemann, 1918), p. 32. SS's copy of this book is now in the possession of William Reese.

34. *The New Book of English Martyrs*, p. 53.

35. ibid., p. 87.

36. The 'Bond' of SP. SS was to help him in a number of ways after the War.

37. D1, pp. 256-7.

38. ibid., p. 257.

39. ibid., p. 258.

40. ibid.

41. ibid., p. 267.

42. SS to RR, 18 June 1918, HRHRC. This letter also refers to the Pemberton Billing case and SS was grateful to get it back from a Col. Blackshear in 1954, to whom he wrote on 22 Jan. 1954: 'Many thanks for your courtesy and consideration in returning my letter to Robbie Ross, (which really is too intimate for public circulation …)' (HRHRC).

43. D1, p. 268.

44. D1, p. 263.

45. This document is at AM.

46. D1, p. 258.

47. ibid., p. 259.

48. SS to RG, 29 May [1918], USI.

49. SS to EM, 30 May 1918, Berg.

50. D1, p. 259.

51. ibid.

52. ibid., p. 261.

53. SS to RN, 2 June 1918, Bodley.

54. ibid.

55. ibid.

56. D1, p. 261.

57. Capt. R.A. Ellis commanded D Company. He was to die of wounds on 22 Sept. 1918. SS had written elsewhere in his dairy of Ellis: 'E. a suburban snob, who used to "go to the city" '.

58. D1, p. 264.

59. ibid., p. 266.

60. SP, p. 132.

61. ibid., p. 135.

62. SS to EG, 10 June 1918, Rutgers.

63. The influenza epidemic of 1918 killed more people worldwide than the War itself. 150,000 people in England alone died, 1,700 of them in one day.

64. D1, p. 269.

65. ibid., p. 267. Lt. Colin MacPherson Dobell, 1st RWF (attached 9th Bn) died of wounds 30 May 1918 at the Battle of the Marne.

66. SS to RN, 19 June 1918, Bodley.

67. 'O Music! I am starving for it Robert', SS wrote to RN in the same letter of 19 June 1918. Clearly Arnold Bennett shared SS's love of music. Writing to him on 7 July 1918, the novelist says 'I always maintain that we ought to have a private band even in the Ministry of Information, to keep our souls from shrivelling up' (Columbia).

68. See Sorley's 'When You See Millions of the Mouthless Dead', *Collected Poems*, edited by Jean Moorcroft Wilson (London, Cecil Woolf, 1985), p. 91.

69. Vivian de Sola Pinto (1895-1969) was a poet who also became a critic (best known for his *Crisis in English Literature*, London, Hutchinson, 1939) and Professor of English Literature at Nottingham University. He remained in touch with SS after the War, until at least 1945, when he inscribed *The Road to the West* (a collection of sixty Soviet war poems) to him.

70. *Y Ddraig Goch*, the Journal of

the Royal Welch Fusiliers, March
1968, vol. 17, no. 1, p. 12.

71. ibid., p. 13.

72. SP, p. 140.

73. op. cit., p. 13.

74. SS to RM, 7 July 1918, HRHRC.

75. Pinto's account of this occasion
is quoted by Paul Fussell, *Siegfried
Sassoon's Long Journey* (London,
1983), p. 159.

76. SP, p. 141.

77. SS to ED, 26 June 1918, CUL.

78. SS claimed to have lost this
section of his diary, but see SS to RR
of 18 June (HRHRC) It is possible
that SS never recovered his diary
from RR, who died a few months later.
It is also possible, given the fact that
he thought it might 'amuse' RR, that
it contained explicit references to his
feelings for his men which he did not
wish to share with anyone else.

79. SS to EM, 27 June 1918, Berg.

80. SS to EG, 29 June 1918,
Rutgers.

81. 'Atrocities' was subsequently
published in *War Poems* (Heinemann,
1919) and also appeared in the
American edition of *Picture-Show*
(1920).

82. SS to Osbert Sitwell, 3 July
1918, HRHRC.

83. op. cit., p. 14.

84. ibid.

85. D1, pp. 272-3.

86. See WP, p. 141.

87. SP, p. 147.

88. ibid., p. 149.

89. ibid., pp. 151-2.

90. D1, p. 252.

91. See SJ, p. 71. SS claims to have
written this poem in hospital at
Lancaster Gate and all twelve lines
were published in *The Nation* in
August 1918. He had included these
in a letter to RN on [29?] July 1918
(Bodley) and RN agreed with his
suggestion that he cut the last four
lines, which read: 'Go out into the
glimmering peace of daybreak; / You
should be wild with gladness like the
lark, / Above this dim brown rustling

corn, above / These haunted willows
looming through the dark.' As SS
noted, in a letter to LOM, these lines
'weaken the effort, though they are
part of the picture – the glimmering
country outside the door' (letter of 27
Aug. 1918, HRHRC). He did not
include them when 'The Dug-Out' was
published in *Picture-Show* (1919).

92. SP, p. 154.

93. ibid., p. 157.

94. ibid., p. 158.

95. SS names this corporal 'Davies'
in SP. Since there were *eight* Daviess
in A Company – there would have
been no need to disguise the name –
so this was probably his real name.

96. SP, p. 161.

97. Bodley.

98. Information contained in a
letter by Sir Wintringham Stable in
the *Daily Telegraph* (13.9.67) in
Sassoon's nephew, Leo's, personal
possession, which ends: 'He was a
most *delightful* companion: No "Mad
Jack" but his dedicated courage was
unique. It was not foolhardiness but
dedicated courage of the highest
order'. Stable goes on to say that SP
'contains a number if inaccuracies in
relation to events of that particular
time from which I infer that his head
wound in some measure have have
impaired his memory'.

99. D1, pp. 273-4.

100. ibid., p. 274.

101. ibid., p. 275.

102. SS to RN, 2 June [1918,
misdated 1917 by RN], Bodley.

103. D1, p. 275.

Chapter 17

1. SS to EM, 15 July [1918], Berg.

2. SS uses this term in the verse
letter he sent to RG on 24 July 1918.
'Moon Street' was a reference to
Ross, who lived there, and
'Ardoursandendurans' referred to RN,
who had published *Ardours and
Endurances* in 1917.

3. SS to ED, 20 July 1918, CUL.

4. Verse letter from SS to RG, 24 July 1918, USI.

5. Following RG's marriage in January 1918 his wife, Nancy, was expecting their first child.

6. RG to SS, 9 July [1918], Berg. In his newly married happiness RG had begun to write nursery rhymes, songs and ballads, many of which were to appear in *The Treasure-Box* (1919) and *Country Sentiment* (London, Martin Secker, 1920).

7. Included in a letter from RG to SS, 16 July [1918]. RG thought that SS was still in France.

8. When RG included an inaccurate and incomplete version of this poem, without asking SS's permission, in GTAT in 1929, SS immediately insisted that all copies sold must be recalled and the poem cancelled. Fortunately, from the bibliographical point of view, a number of copies survived containing the poem, including one annotated by SS and Edmund Blunden, which is now at Berg. I have preserved the original layout of this verse letter, wherever possible. It was reprinted in full in WP, pp. 130ff.

9. RG to SS, 27 July [1918], Berg.

10. RN had been invalided out of the army with syphilis, but RG is unlikely to be referring so disparagingly to someone he still considered a close friend. He is probably using the term metaphorically

11. SP, p. 170.

12. ibid.

13. SS to SCC, 4 Aug. 1918, Berg.

14. SS to ED, n.d. July 1918, CUL.

15. SS to RN, 15 Aug. [1918], Bodley.

16. 'Via Crucis', based on a picture by Kennington, was a revision of a poem written two years earlier, on 12 Aug. 1916, and 'The Dug-Out', annotated 'St Venant, July 1918', was probably started there but completed at Lancaster Gate.

17. SS to EM, [August 1918], Berg.

18. ibid., [July 1918], Berg.

19. There is a possibility that SS's 'big' poem is 'Limitations' (CP, p. 121), which he told Desmond MacCarthy was an attempt to find 'a more flexible form of expression'.

20. From 'Recessional'.

21. From 'For the Fallen'.

22. D1, p. 278.

23. SS to C.K. Ogden, 10 Aug. 1918, McMaster University, Hamilton, Ontario.

24. WP, p. 134.

25. SS to EM, [Aug. 1918], Berg.

26. SS to ED, 22 Aug. [1918], Bodley.

27. RG's poems were privately printed by the Chiswick Press in 1919, as *The Treasure Box*.

28. Vivian de Sola Pinto, *Spindrift* (London, Chapman & Hall, 1918).

29. D1, p. 277.

30. ibid.

31. *Counter-Attack* received at least thirty reviews between 5 July and 14 December 1918 in England alone.

32. *TLS*, 11 July 1918.

33. *The Morning Post*, 2 Aug. 1918.

34. *The Clarion*, 19 July 1918.

35. See note 145, Chapter 13.

36. All but two of SS's replies have been lost.

37. SS to EG, 8 Aug. 1918, Rutgers.

38. Osbert Sitwell to SS, 26 June 1918, University of Washington Libraries at Pullman.

39. SS to Osbert Sitwell, 3 July 1918, HRHRC.

40. ED to SS, 20 Feb. 1918, CUL.

41. SS to ED, 26 June 1918, CUL.

42. Violet Kate Eglinton Gordon-Woodhouse (née Gwynne; 1872-1948), was an amateur but highly gifted harpsichordist and clavichordist, a pioneer of the revival of early music.

43. Osbert Sitwell, *Noble Essences* (London, 1950), pp. 108-9.

44. SJ, pp. 71-2.

45. ibid., p. 72.

46. *Noble Essences*, p. 109.

47. SS to EM, undated but sent from the Red Cross Hospital, [1918], Berg.

48. *Wilfred Owen: Collected Letters*, p. 571.

49. SJ, p. 72.

50. WO to SS, 31 Aug. 1918, *Collected Letters*, p. 571.

51. SS to EM, undated but sent from the Red Cross Hospital, Berg.

52. ibid.

53. SS to Edward Carpenter, 15 Aug. 1918, Sheffield City Libraries.

54. ibid., 3 Sept. [1918], Sheffield City Libraries.

55. SS says that his diary for this period was lost but he afterwards noted that he left London on 17 Aug. and arrived at Coldstream on 20 Aug. However, it is unlikely that he left his Lancaster Gate hospital on the same evening that WO delivered him back there. It is far more likely that he left London on 18 Aug. and got to Coldstream on 21 Aug., the day he wrote to tell LOM of his arrival there.

56. Berwick-on-Tweed is approximately fifteen miles, Edinburgh approximately forty-nine miles.

57. SJ, p. 73.

58. ibid., p. 74.

59. I am indebted for these and many other details about Lennel to Miss Grizel Kennedy from whose mother's family, the Warings bought the house in 1903. Lennel survives today, relatively unchanged from the time when SS knew it, as a nursing-home.

60. SJ, p. 75.

61. SS to EM, 26 [Aug. 1918], Berg.

62. SS to John Drinkwater, 30 Aug. 1918, University of Marquette, Milwaukee.

63. SS to Professor Lewis Chase, 25 Jan. 1922, Library of Congress.

64. Ernest de Selincourt's biography of Walt Whitman. SS also read A.C. Bradley's *Romance of Northumberland*, George Moore's *Story Teller*, A.C. Bradley's *Oxford Lectures on Poetry* and A.P.

Primrose's *Rosebery's Chatham*. He failed to finish Carlyle's *Sartor Resartus*.

65. SJ, p. 73. The phrase 'brave companionship' echoes SS's 'brave brown companions', in 'Prelude: the Troops', perhaps intentionally.

66. SS to RM, 18 Sept. 1918, HRHRC.

67. See SS's letter to LOM of late Aug. 1918 at HRHRC, where he suggests that she should mention the affair to E.P. Warren of Corpus Christi College, Oxford, and hopes that Lowes Dickinson will do the same thing independently.

68. SJ, p. 75.

69. ibid.

70. Guilhermina Suggia (1888-1950) was an Italo-Portuguese cellist of international fame.

71. SJ, p. 76.

72. This was first published in the New York *Bookman* in Jan. 1919, then in *Picture-Show* the same year. SS notes, in an annotated copy of *Picture-Show* at HRHRC, that 'Fancy-Dress' was written at Lennel in Sept. 1918.

73. D2, p. 162.

74. EG to SS, 8 Aug. 1918, Rutgers.

75. Three of these – 'Flodden Field', 'God in Battle' and 'Beauty' – were included in a letter of 28 Aug. 1918 to RN (Bodley) and one – 'Tariff Reform' – included in a list of poems he intended to put into *Picture-Show* (1919), but not finally included. 'Sunset on Border' was also written at Lennel. The remaining five – 'Fancy-Dress', 'Vision', 'Falling Asleep', 'Wraiths' and 'Ancient History' – were published in *Picture-Show*.

76. RG had written on 11 Sept. 1918: ' "Ancient History" is wonderful …' and suggested three minor emendations. SS sent it, with two of RG's suggested changes, to *The Nation*, where it was published on 28 Sept. 1918.

77. SS to EG, 20 Sept. 1918, Rutgers.

78. *The Owl* was to be a bi-annual miscellany of poems, stories and pictures. It ran for only two numbers.

79. SJ, p. 81.

80. ibid., p. 84.

81. SS to RR, 6 Oct. 1918, Lilly.

82. SJ, p. 84.

83. SS to EM, 7 Oct. 1918, Berg.

84. RG to SS, 12 Oct. 1918, Berg.

85. WO to Susan Owen, 15 Oct. 1918, *Collected Letters*, p. 585.

86. SS to SCC, 20 Jan. 1944, HRHRC.

87. *Robert Ross: Friend of Friends*, edited by Margery Ross (London, Cape, 1952). SS allowed some but not all of the passages chosen from his letters to RR to appear. A collection of RR's articles, *Masques and Phases*, was published by Arthur L. Humphreys in 1909, dedicated to Harold Child.

88. SS to ED, 28 Oct. 1918, CUL.

89. SJ, p. 87.

90. ibid.

91. D1, p. 280.

92. ibid.

93. ibid.

94. Since 1912 EM had asked poets to copy their verses into his rather coyly named Little Book but all had avoided the first page. SS persuaded Hardy, without too much difficulty, to fill this place of honour.

95. SJ, p. 89.

96. ibid., p. 92.

97. ibid.

98. ibid., p. 90.

99. ibid.

100. ibid., p. 91.

101. LOM to SS, 10 Jan. 1923, Columbia.

102. SJ, p. 91.

103. Letter from Virginia Woolf to Vanessa Bell [19 Nov. 1918], *Letters*, v. II, p. 297.

104. The book Masefield gave SS was *J.M. Synge: a Few Personal Recollections* (1916).

105. D1, pp. 281-2.

106. SS to Professor Lewis Chase, 25 Jan. 1922, Library of Congress.

107. See SJ, p. 50 and a letter from SS to RG, 24 June 1917, USI.

108. SJ, p. 95.

109. ibid.

110. ibid.

111. D1, p. 282.

112. ibid.

113. OAG, p. 200.

114. ibid.

115. Quoted in Stephen Tennant's unpublished diary for 12 Oct. 1928, Berg.

116. D1, p. 282.

117. WO to Susan Owen, 29 Oct. 1918, *Collected Letters*, p. 590.

118. The 1st RWF remained in Italy with the 7th Division until the end of the War and, with the Honourable Artillery Company, had the distinction of being the first troops to cross the River Piave and thus opened the battle named Vittorio Veneto, which began the final offensive against the Austrians. The 2nd RWF remained in France with the 38th Division. After a relatively peaceful summer on the Ancre, it fought the Battles of Albert, the Hindenburg Line, Havrincourt, Epéhy, St Quentin Canal, Cambrai, Selle and Sambre. The 25th RWF was with the 2nd Bn at the Hindenburg Line and Epéhy.

119. D1, p. 282.

Afterword

1. Unpublished papers in the hands of a private collector.

A Select Bibliography

(Dates given are of first publication)

A. Works by Siegfried Sassoon

Collected Poems: 1908-1956 (London, Faber & Faber, 1961).
Counter-Attack and Other Poems (London, Heinemann, 1918).
The Daffodil Murderer (London, John Richmond, 1913).
Diaries 1915-1918, ed. Rupert Hart-Davis (London, Faber & Faber, 1983).
Diaries 1920-1922, ed. Rupert Hart-Davis (London, Faber & Faber, 1981).
Diaries 1923-1925, ed. Rupert Hart-Davis (London, Faber & Faber, 1985).
Letters to a Critic, Introduction & notes by Michael Thorpe (Nettlestead, Kent: Bridge, Conachar, 1976).
Memoirs of a Fox-Hunting Man (London, Faber & Faber, 1928).
Memoirs of an Infantry Officer (London, Faber & Faber, 1930).
Meredith (London, Constable, 1948).
The Old Century and Seven More Years (London, Faber & Faber, 1938).
The Old Huntsman and Other Poems (London, William Heinemann, 1917).
Picture-Show (London, William Heinemann, 1919).
Siegfried's Journey: 1916-1920 (London, Faber & Faber, 1946).
Sherston's Progress (London, Faber & Faber, 1936).
The War Poems, ed. Rupert Hart-Davis (London, Faber & Faber, 1983).
The Weald of Youth (London, Faber & Faber, 1942).
Sassoon's early, privately printed volumes have also been consulted: *Poems* (1906), *Orpheus in Diloeryum* (1908), *Sonnets and Verses* (1909), *Sonnets* (1909), *Twelve Sonnets* (1911), *Poems* (1911), *Melodies* (1912), *Hyacinth* (1912), *Amyntas* (proof copy, production abandoned, 1912) and *Ode for Music* (1912).

B. Secondary Sources

Adams, B. *Nothing of Importance* (London, Methuen, 1917).
Barbusse, H. *Under Fire (Le Feu)* trans. Fitzwater Wray (London, Dent, 1917).
Barker, Pat, *Regeneration* (Viking, 1991)
Behrman, S.N. *Tribulations and Laughter: a Memoir* (London, Hamilton, 1972).
Bennett, A. *Letters of Arnold Bennett*, ed. James Hepburn (London, OUP, 1968-).
Bergonzi, B. *Heroes' Twilight: a Study of the Literature of the Great War* (London, Constable, 1965).
Caesar, A. *Taking It Like a Man: Suffering Sexuality and the War Poets* (Manchester, Manchester University Press, 1993).

Cockerell, S.C. *The Best of Friends: Further Letters to Sir Sydney Carlyle Cockerell*, ed. Viola Meynell (London, Hart-Davis, 1956).

Corrigan, Dame Felicitas. *Siegfried Sassoon: Poet's Pilgrimage* (London, Gollancz, 1973).

Darton, J. Harvey. *From Surtees to Sassoon* (London, Morley & Kennerley, 1931).

Dickinson, G. Lowes. *The Autobiography of ...*, ed. D. Proctor (London, Duckworth, 1973).

Duhamel, G. *The New Book of Martyrs* (*Vie des Martyrs*), trans. Florence Simmonds (London, Heinemann, 1918).

Dunn, J. [Editor] *The War the Infantry Knew* (London, P.S. King, 1938).

Edwards, H.I. Powell. *The Sussex Yeomanry and 16th (Sussex Yeomanry) Battalion, Royal Sussex Regiment, 1914-1919* (London, Andrew Melrose, 1921).

Fletcher, Frank. *After Many Days* (London, Robert Hale, 1937).

Fussell, P. *The Great War and Modern Memory* (London, OUP, 1975).

Gilbert, M. *The First World War* (London, Weidenfeld & Nicolson, 1994).

Graves, R. *Goodbye to All That* (London, Cape, 1929).

Graves, R. *In Broken Images: Robert Graves: Selected Correspondence*, ed. P. O'Prey (London, Hutchinson, 1982).

Graves, R.P. *Robert Graves: the Assault Heroic (1895-1926)* (London, 1986).

Hassall, C. *Edward Marsh* (London, Longmans, 1959).

Hibberd, D. *Wilfred Owen: the Last Year, 1917-1918* (London, Constable, 1992).

Hynes, S. *A War Imagined* (London, Bodley Head, 1990).

Jackson, S. *The Sassoons* (New York, Dutton, 1968).

Johnston, J.H. *English Poetry of the First World War* (Princeton, Princeton University Press, 1964).

Keynes, G. *A Bibliography of Siegfried Sassoon* (London, Hart-Davis, 1962).

Lane, A. *An Adequate Response: the War Poetry of Wilfred Owen and Siegfried Sassoon* (Detroit, Wayne State University Press, 1972).

Liddell Hart, B.H. *History of the First World War* (London, Macmillan, 1992).

Manning, E. *Bronze and Steel: Life of Thomas Thornycroft, Sculptor and Engineer* (Kingstone Press, 1932).

Manning, E. *Marble and Bronze* (London, Trefoil Books, 1982).

Moeyes, P. *Siegfried Sassoon: Scorched Glory: A Critical Study* (London, Macmillan, 1996).

Morrell, Lady Ottoline. *Ottoline at Garsington: Memoirs of Lady Ottoline Morrell: 1915-1918*, ed. R. Gathorne-Hardy (London, Faber & Faber, 1974).

Owen, Wilfred. *Collected Letters*, ed. H. Owen and J. Bell (London, OUP, 1967).

Owen, Wilfred. *War Poems and Others*, ed. D. Hibberd (London, Chatto & Windus, 1973).

Parfitt, G. *English Poetry of the First World War* (London, Harvester, 1990).

Parker, P. *The Old Lie: the Great War and the Public School Ethos* (London, Constable, 1987)

Pinto, V. de Sola. *The City that Shone: an Autobiography (1895-1922)* (London, Hutchinson, 1969).

Pinto, V. de S. *Crises in English Poetry* (London, Hutchinson, 1939).

Quinn, P. *The Great War and the Missing Muse* (Selingsgrove, Susquehanna University Press, 1994).

Richards, F. *Old Soldiers Never Die* (London, Faber & Faber, 1933).

Ross, R. *Friend of Friends (1869-1918)*, ed. M. Ross (London, Cape, 1952).

Roth, C. *The Sassoon Dynasty* (London, Robert Hale, 1941).

Seymour, M. *Ottoline Morrell: Life on the Grand Scale* (London, Hodder & Stoughton, 1992).

Silk, D. *Siegfried Sassoon* (Tisbury, Wilts: Compton Russell, 1975).

Silkin, J. *Out of Battle: the Poetry of the Great War* (London, OUP, 1972).

Sitwell, O. *Noble Essences* (London, Macmillan, 1950).

Skaife, Major E. *A Short History of the Royal Welch Fusiliers* (London, 1926).

Stallworthy, J. *Wilfred Owen* (London, Chatto & Windus and OUP, 1974).

Taylor, M. *Lads* (London, Constable, 1988).

Thorpe, M. *Siegfried Sassoon: a Critical Study* (Leiden, Leiden University Press, 1966).

Thwaite, A. *Edmund Gosse: a Literary Landscape, 1849-1928* (London, OUP, 1984).

Weeks, J. *Coming Out* (London, Quartet, 1977).

Index